Family Therapy

An Introduction to Theory and Technique

Family Therapy

An Introduction to Theory and Technique

Second Edition

Edited by

Gerald D. Erickson
York University

Terrence P. Hogan
University of Manitoba

Brooks/Cole Publishing Company
Monterey, California

Brooks/Cole Publishing Company
A Division of Wadsworth, Inc.

Printed in the United States of America
10   9   8   7   6   5   4   3   2   1

Library of Congress Cataloging in Publication Data

Erickson, Gerald D   comp.
　　Family therapy.

　　Bibliography: p.
　　Includes index.
　　1. Family psychotherapy.   I. Hogan, Terrence P.
II. Title.
RC488.5.E74   1981   616.89'156   80-28686
ISBN 0-8185-0437-4

Acquisition Editor: *Claire Verduin*
Production Editors: *Sally Schuman and Patricia E. Cain*
Cover Design: *Katherine Minerva*
Typesetting: *Thompson Type, San Diego, California*

To Our Wives,
Rosemarie Anich-Erickson
and
Elizabeth Anne Hogan

Preface

The better part of a decade has passed since the publication of the first edition of *Family Therapy: An Introduction to Theory and Technique.* During the 1970s, a number of new and exciting developments have changed the field of family therapy. These recent developments are reflected in the fact that approximately three-fourths of the articles contained in this edition either have appeared since the publication of the first edition or are appearing here for the first time.

Although we thought it necessary to update the contents of the book, a guiding purpose was to include a selection of the "classic" papers from the field that have endured and demonstrated their continuing importance for the family therapy movement. For example, the theoretical material developed by Jay Haley in "The Family of the Schizophrenic: A Model System" (see Part I) and "Marriage Therapy" (see Part II) is of fundamental importance in understanding the practice of many current family therapists and has probably never been stated more clearly elsewhere. At the same time, we have dropped several contributions from the first edition that could have with all justification been included in this volume. For these omissions, we can only plead pressures of space.

We noted in the preface to the first edition that, "when we review the expanding literature of family therapy, it quickly becomes clear that no theoretical focus is acceptable to all or even to most practitioners." Our view on this matter has not changed. Indeed, the term *family therapy* used out of context conveys little usable information. Ten years ago the diversity characterizing this field was perceived as something of a liability, and many family therapists looked forward to the appearance of a "grand synthesis" that would resolve theoretical and therapeutic differences and transform family therapy into something resembling a unitary phenomenon. It now seems clear that such a synthesis is neither possible nor desirable and that family therapy as an orientation to practice is still entirely open to new developments from many directions. Above all, we are convinced that students and beginning practitioners need to be acquainted with a wide range of models of practice, methods, and techniques in family therapy. To learn and practice any single method of therapy, no matter what its source, is perhaps best seen as a learned handicap.

Our purpose, then, is to present a selection of the major papers that have appeared in the literature of family therapy theory and technique. This book is intended primarily as a textbook or an ancillary book of readings for students of psychotherapy in the fields of social work, clinical psychology, psychiatry, and counseling. It can also serve as a representative survey of the family therapy literature and, as such, can be used by practicing psychotherapists in any of the mental health professions.

Family Therapy: An Introduction to Theory and Technique includes papers that are representative of several broad areas within the general topic of a family therapy orientation to practice. The book is organized into five sections. Part I, "Historical and Theoretical Background," includes several classic papers and provides an early exposure to some of the major past and current issues in family therapy. For example, is the family a system? Is family therapy effective? Part II, "Models of Practice," introduces the reader to the thoughts and ideas of several key figures in the field of family therapy. Many practitioners now focus their work on specific target populations, such as families dealing with alcohol problems, the divorcing, and the poor, and several articles in Part III, "Specific Areas of Practice," discuss how family therapists deal with such populations. Part IV, "A Variety of Techniques," focuses on the various technical methodologies currently utilized by a wide number of family therapists. Part V, "Extending the Scope of Family Therapy," includes papers that, in our view, point out the directions in which family therapy is moving in the 1980s. Each part begins with an introduction in which we discuss the papers included in that part from the viewpoint of a family orientation to practice.

We thank Dr. John E. Bell for his consistent encouragement of our work, as well as Claire Verduin and Loraine Brownlee of the Brooks/Cole staff for their editorial assistance. We are indebted to our secretaries, Jeannine Watson, of the University of Manitoba, and Marilyn Salerno, of York University, for their invaluable aid. Thanks also are due to those who reviewed the manuscript: Joseph D. Anderson, Shippensburg State College; Margaret Blake, University of Northern Colorado; Craig C. Gilbert, University of Nevada; Sandra L. Guest, University of Central Florida; and Barry L. Levin, University of Missouri-Columbia. Lastly, our thanks to our wives and families for their support during the preparation of the book.

Gerald D. Erickson
Terrence P. Hogan

Contents

Family Therapy

An Introduction to Theory and Technique

1

Historical and Theoretical Background

Approximately 30 years ago, a major shift occurred within the helping professions from an individual-practice orientation to intervention on a broader level. Interpersonal, environmental, and situational factors gradually emerged as important elements in the treatment process. These factors ranged from current stresses in an individual's life to social class and cultural influences, to the influence of the immediate family, and finally, to the functioning of the family as a system, which theorists were making the first, tentative efforts to describe. Currently, the broad umbrella of family treatment covers descriptions and therapeutic efforts directed both at the immediate social environment of whole families and at their social networks. This wide range of social territory lies at the base of the myriad treatment approaches possible within a family practice orientation. Indeed, the family therapy field is unified by the assumption that both explanation and change for an individual problem must be sought in and through the social context. To understand any particular form of family therapy, one must understand which unit of social reality is the focus of treatment. Is it an individual, a dyad, a triad, a nuclear family, a family and all its helpers, a family and kinship members, a family and everyone it knows, or still another unit? Although this book is addressed primarily to the intact nuclear family or the partial nuclear family as the focus of practice, there are several articles that represent major exceptions to this focus, with the entire final section documenting current changes in the scope of family therapy.

Family therapy can best be defined as " . . . the psychotherapeutic treatment of a natural social system, the family, using, as its basic medium, conjoint interpersonal interviews" (Walrond-Skinner, 1976). The variety of theories, methods, styles of practice, and techniques that have been developed over three decades in dealing with this natural

1

social system have defied a classification acceptable to everyone in the field. Attempts have been made, for example, to categorize therapists, one such categorization being the "conductors" or "reactors" of Beels and Ferber (1969). A second categorization places therapists on a continuum from A to Z, A representing the position taken by individual therapists who occasionally see families in conjunction with their individual practice, Z the position occupied by practitioners with a total family orientation (Group for the Advancement of Psychiatry, 1970).

We continue to believe that a three-fold classification based on the therapist's theoretical orientation provides the most useful and pragmatic approach. Hence, in our view, most family treatment approaches can be thought of as either systems based, psychodynamically based, or behaviorally based. Clearly articulated descriptions of psychodynamically based family practice are increasingly rare in the literature (even though the psychodynamic model is part of the intellectual inheritance of many family therapists), while behavioral contributions are rapidly increasing. Over the past decade, several systems approaches have gained popularity in the field. These include structural family therapy (Minuchin, 1974), problem-solving therapy (Haley, 1976), and "Bowen-theory" (Bowen, 1976). A perusal of the literature reveals that some classification schema seems indicated and useful. Yet the practice of many therapists may not fall totally within any category. Indeed, one of the editors of this book classifies his own practice as a "network-based, problem-solving, task-centered, experiential family therapy."

The movement over three decades from an individual orientation to a family orientation has been uneven and halting. How this movement took place or whether the development of family therapy is continuous or discontinuous with that of individual therapy is still not a settled matter. Twenty years ago, Spiegel and Bell (1959) could say that " . . . the study of the family as a significant system in its own right has no history, no body of commonly accepted concepts, no established findings." Although few would agree with that conclusion today, neither would they agree with Jackson and Satir who, in their 1961 review of the development of family diagnosis and therapy, commented that "the direction towards our present concepts about treating illness as an integral part of the total family interaction can be seen as slowly evolving and inevitable." A more complete discussion of the evolutionary aspects of family therapy can be found in the writings of Zuk and Rubenstein (1965), Guerin (1976), and Walrond-Skinner (1976). The argument that family therapy represents a discontinuous change from all that had gone before in individual therapy is perhaps best put by Haley (1971).

We can find no evidence in the literature that family therapy "grew out of" any previously existing theoretical base or sets of concepts. Although theory and techniques generally can be seen in an evolutionary perspective, the development of a knowledge base around the family as a unit of conceptualization in the development of treatment methodologies appears to be something new. For instance, Burgum's paper (1942) "The Father Gets Worse: A Child Guidance Problem" describes a series of cases in which the treatment of a mother/child conflict was followed by the father adopting the problematic behaviors of the mother that had initially brought the mother and child into treatment. These observed behaviors could not be adequately explained by either the theories or the available language of the day. Some 15 years later, Jackson (1957) observed the same type of behavior in clinical practice and, in "The Question of Family Homeostasis," was able to account for the shifting nature of apparent individual symptomatology in terms of a family system. Jackson found that viewing the family as a system aided in understanding why, when one family member's problems (or symptoms) seem to improve, another family member develops a new problem.

It thus appears likely that, in addition to "normal" evolutionary changes affecting psychotherapy as a whole, a direct outside influence occasioned and greatly stimulated the growth of family therapy. This influence was the adaptation of the systems approach. Systems theory, which was initiated in the biophysical sciences, allows the family to be viewed as a functioning unit. An individual is able to receive information and stimulation from the environment, to process this information internally, and to act upon it. From the systems viewpoint, the family is an operative system that functions in an analogous manner. Family therapists are then able to involve themselves in various parts of the family system in order to affect its total behavior.

A shift in practice orientation from the individual to wider units of practice has had important consequences for students in the mental health professions. These consequences may be summarized in part by saying that therapists in training are required to shift their orientation in at least three related areas (Erickson, 1973):

1. From perceiving individual behavior to perceiving a larger context of behavior.
2. From bringing about change through an individual professional relationship to bringing about a systemic change through the participation of a professional in an ongoing social system.
3. From passivity to activity within the social situation of the interview.

These changes represent major shifts in orientation, and we hope that the articles in Part I, as well as those later in the text, will assist the reader in understanding and undergoing this demanding process.

Common to all forms of family therapy that have survived over the past 30 years is an acknowledgment of the therapist's difficult struggle to shift his or her orientation as a practitioner from the individual to the larger group. John Bell's statement perhaps best typifies the matter when, after ten years of experience as a family therapist, he said:

> I had to wipe clean the blackboard of my mind and find a fresh piece of chalk to write large: the *family* is the problem . . . here was the crux of the matter. Here was the transition in thought that I must make. This is the new idea, seemingly so small, but actually so major [Bell, 1963, p. 3].

In the following articles, we attempt to provide a representative sample of the earliest papers that combine both a systems orientation and a focus on major theoretical issues. John Bell's paper was originally read at the Eastern Psychological Association meetings in 1953. It is the first complete representation of a method of family treatment, and, because of the paper's originality and incisiveness, it remains of considerable value today. The paper by Don Jackson and that of Jay Haley were landmark papers and illustrate the adaptation of systems terminology and concepts to the illumination of clinical material. The paper by David Olson and colleagues presents a "state-of-the-art" critique of marital and family therapy as of 1980. He presents an overview of schools of thought and an innovative approach to classify family therapy and demonstrates a rigorous approach to detailing basic theoretical concepts and isolating promising trends.

It can be said fairly that none of the family therapy approaches discussed or described in this book has been adequately tested empirically. A number of trenchant criticisms have been made of the effectiveness of family therapy (Fischer, 1979; Wells, Dilkes, & Trivelli, 1972), and it seems clear, if for no other than political reasons, that a research component will increasingly find its way into the efforts of mental health practitioners. In this respect, however, we should recall that an important influence running throughout the 30-year history of family therapy has been an emphasis on providing a new world view rather than scientific description. Some years ago, in concluding a review of theories and research related to family interactional processes and schizophrenia, Mishler and Waxler (1965) commented that "they are less like scientific theories than artful constructs arrived at independently through different perspectives and methods of conceptualization. Their value for other investigators, like that of art, lies in giving us a new way to look at the world" (p. 315). The resulting view of the individual as embedded in an organization of relationships that amplify and maintain a "problem" has enriched both the practice of professionals and the organization of mental health services. Yet, careful documentation and validation have lagged far behind practice innovations. David Olson's paper takes up the important question of evaluation in family therapy.

Gerald Zuk's paper is in the vanguard of recent literature concerned with values and family intervention. On the horizon is a growing interest in examining family practice in terms of ethics or proper human conduct. In Henry Lennard's apt phrase, the issue is *"Who can do what to whom in the name of what!"* (Lennard & Lennard, 1979). We believe that students in the field (along with seasoned practitioners) may benefit from examining the fit between that particular formulation and the range of techniques and models of practice found in this text and elsewhere. For example, to what extent is a practitioner "justified" in imposing a "double-bind" or a paradoxical directive (see Part IV)? With whom should the therapist stand in a child custody fight? And does the therapist want the families' goals in therapy, or does the therapist have a set of goals perhaps never shared with the family? Such questions and many of a similar nature deserve careful consideration, and, to a greater extent than in the past, they will require the new generation of therapists to develop sensitivity and discrimination in examining their own values, means, and ends.

REFERENCES

Beels, C., & Ferber, A. Family therapy: A view. *Family Process*, 1969, 8, 280–318.

Bell, J. E. A theoretical position for family group therapy. *Family Process*, 1963, 2, 1–14.

Bowen, M. Theory in the practice of psychotherapy. In Philip Guerin (Ed.), *Family Therapy: Theory and Practice*. New York: Gardner Press, 1976, 42–90.

Burgum, M. The father gets worse: A child guidance problem. *American Journal of Orthopsychiatry*, 1942, 12, 474–485.

Erickson, G. D. Teaching family therapy. *Journal of Education for Social Work*, 1973, 3, 9–16.

Fischer, J. *Effective casework practice*. New York: McGraw-Hill, 1979.

Group for the Advancement of Psychiatry. *Treatment of Families in Conflict*. American Psychiatric Association: Washington, D. C., 1970.

Guerin, P. *Family therapy: Theory and practice*. New York: Gardner Press, 1976.

Haley, J. *Changing families*. New York: Grune & Stratton, 1971.

Haley, J. *Problem solving therapy*. San Francisco: Jossey-Bass, 1976.

Jackson, D. D. The question of family homeostasis. *Psychiatric Quarterly Supplement*, 1957, 31, 79–90.

Jackson, D. D., & Satir, V. A review of psychiatric developments in family diagnosis and family therapy. In N. W. Ackerman, F. L. Beatman, & S. N. Sherman (Eds.), *Exploring the base for family therapy*. New York: Family Service Association of America, 1961.

Lennard, H. L., & Lennard, S. C. *Ethics of health care*. Woodstock, N. Y.: Gondolier Press, 1979.

Minuchin, S. *Families and family therapy.* Cambridge: Harvard University Press, 1974.

Mishler, E., & Waxler, N. Family interaction processes and schizophrenia: A review of current theories. *Merrill-Palmer Quarterly of Behavior and Development,* Vol. XI, 1965, 269–315.

Parloff, M. B. The family in psychotherapy. *Archives of General Psychiatry,* 1961, 4, 445–451.

Walrond-Skinner, S. *Family therapy: The treatment of natural systems.* London: Routledge and Kegan Paul, 1976.

Spiegel, J. P., & Bell, N. W. The family of the psychiatric patient. In S. Arieti (Ed.), *American handbook of psychiatry.* New York: Basic Books, 1959.

Wells, R. A., Dilkes, T., & Trivelli, N. The results of family therapy: A critical review of the literature. *Family Process,* 1972, 11, 189–207.

Zuk, G. H., & Rubenstein, D. A review of the concepts on the study and treatment of families of schizophrenics. In I. Boszormenyi-Nagy & J. Framo (Eds.), *Intensive Family Therapy.* New York: Harper & Row, 1965.

Family Group Therapy—A New Treatment Method for Children

John E. Bell

When I was in London in 1951, a casual remark of Dr. John Sutherland to the effect that Dr. Bowlby of the Tavistock Clinic was experimenting with group therapy with families, stimulated my interest in studying some of the potentialities of this method for the treatment of behavior problems in children. To my knowledge there were no other precedents to fall on in applying the method than an article which Dr. Bowlby wrote in 1949 (1) where he discussed the occasional use of a group meeting with the whole family as an adjunct to individual therapy.[1] My intent was, however, to use family group therapy as the sole method of treatment.[2]

The results with seven initial groups seen over the past one and one-half years have been sufficiently promising that I feel the technique has wide applicability. It is able to bring dramatic, and often speedy, improvements in family living and direct changes in the maladapted behavior of children. My time has been limited, so that I have never been able to carry more than three groups at one time, holding weekly conferences with each. It takes long years to accumulate experience at this rate. I feel that I have now learned enough of the course that treatment takes, and the errors one is likely to make that I am ready to share my preliminary findings with others.

In beginning this treatment I had in mind that it would need to be based on talking and, thus, that it would not be adapted to very young children. From theoretical knowledge, developmental studies, and prior experience in indi-

Reprinted from *Family Process*, Vol. 6, 1967, pp. 254-263. Reproduced by permission.

[1]Since preparing this paper, I have become acquainted with the work of Dr. R. Dreikurs, of the Community Child Guidance Center of Chicago. In close study of his articles (2-6), I have not discovered that he was using the technique described here, although he has emphasized the need of simultaneous treatment, partly in groups, of all members of the family and of others in the community, such as teachers, who are linked to the family.

[2]Actually, I had misunderstood the reference to Dr. Bowlby's work and had made the assumption that, with him, group therapy was being used in an experimental way as the only method. In conversation with him in Boston in March, 1953, I confirmed that he had not been using family groups other than as an occasional supplement to individual therapy.

vidual therapy with children, I assumed that a lower age limit might be about nine years of age, perhaps higher in the cases of children with limited ability or severe emotional blocking.

Three of my family groups have included eight-year-old children. In one instance the group consisted of a stepfather, mother, and eight-year-old girl. It is still too early to assess whether the outcome was satisfactory. At the moment I have reservations about it, but more on the basis of limitations of the parents than because of the inability of the child to participate effectively. The other family with an eight-year-old consists of four children, two girls, fourteen and nine, the eight-year-old, a boy, a five-year-old boy, Peter, and their parents. Initially I excluded Peter, the five-year-old. The other three children kept constantly referring to him, making such comments as "How can we solve the family problems if Peter is not here?" "He's one of the family and if we decide anything he won't know what it is." I invited Peter to the third session, and he remained with us for three months of conferences. I put out play material for him. It became increasingly obvious that the eight-year-old felt that Peter's presence was justification for his isolating himself from the group seated around the table. So finally it was decided that Peter should stay home. Since that time the eight-year-old has engaged actively in the group discussions, seemingly identifying himself with the older members of the group and attempting to hold his own on a verbal level. Therapeutic progress has been rapid since Peter left. In the third family, the eight-year-old is functioning mentally on a high level and no communication problems have arisen.

Since this technique is a verbal one, its use is probably contraindicated with the most withdrawn children. This has not yet been tested. I am not prepared to rule out cases with major personality difficulties. Certainly some of those cases with which I have dealt have had serious problems, and the changes that have been wrought do not appear to be superficial. For example, in the case of an adopted girl of thirteen years of age, the referring symptoms were inability to play with the other children in the neighborhood, uncontrollable behavior at home with much lying, outbursts of temper, and sullen withdrawal from family activities and a school maladjustment so severe that she was being faced with expulsion. It became evident that the girl was strongly identifying herself with a rather rigid and hostile father and with her older brother, a son of the parents. Over the year and a half of treatment, we saw her identification shift toward the mother, with a consequent adoption of feminine patterns of behavior and the disappearance of the symptomatic masculine traits. Central to this change was the releasing of the girl from clinging dependence on the mother and from inhibition of expression of hostility to her father. It was not long after the girl was openly telling her father how angry he made her and how she had to lie to protect herself from his irritability that her total adjustment showed the dramatic changes, not only at home but also at school where she is doing acceptable work and no longer is a behavior problem.

My method has evolved into the following program.

I. THE INITIAL INTERVIEWS

A beginning is made by a joint conference with the father and mother. This is for the purposes of securing the parents' story of the problems the child is facing, the history of the development of the child, and for interpreting to them the method that will be used. In this initial interview I tell the parents that I will serve as a kind of referee, whose job is to see that everyone gets a chance to take part in the discussion, and that I will especially support the child because it is necessary to win his confidence that it is safe and desirable for him to express himself freely. I warn the parents that the child will probably be demanding of changes in his routine at home, that I will not make decisions for them about how the family is to be run, but that I would feel it helpful for them to go along with making feasible changes, especially at the beginning, even though these may be somewhat inconvenient for them. I prepare the parents also for the child's hostility, since the earliest expressions of the child are usually hostile. I reassure them that the more the hostility is expressed the more we may expect expressions of affection and willingness to adapt on the part of the child. I also assure the parents that they will have a chance to express their real feelings, problems, and wishes for the family in the conferences, since the goal of the treatment is the development of new and better communication between all members of the family, but that at the beginning it is more helpful to set the stage for the children to speak freely by their keeping somewhat in the background.

Up to now the parents' response to the first interview has been enthusiastic. This may be partly because of a feeling of relief that something is to be done to help them with their problems, but I feel that it relates to the method of treatment, also. For one thing, I have heard several express a conviction that this method seems to them a natural approach to treatment. I believe various attitudes underlie this spontaneous expression of enthusiasm for the approach.

First, a deep longing for a closer family bond. That this grows out of primary biological relationships, reinforced by the fundamental tradition of the family as a basic unit in our culture is not a sufficient explanation for this longing. Psychology has emphasized enough in recent years the responsibility of parents for children's problems that they nearly always feel considerable personal guilt when the family does not function well. Treating the whole family as the problem has the effect of recognizing the responsibility of everyone in the family for the problem. Blame is no longer directed against one individual, but the difficulties are recognized as a misfortune of the whole group.

Second, suspicion about treatment is reduced. In the more common approach to treatment, where mother is seen separately from the child, and father is seldom a part of the therapeutic relationship, it is inevitable that there will be curiosity, suspicion, and jealousy of the relationships that are established. This will show itself in various forms of resistance that must be dealt with for the effective progress of the therapy. Within family group therapy there is an immediate reassurance that whatever happens will be common knowledge. This has some negative aspects as far as the treatment is concerned, but has been verbalized by parents who have previously been working in individual therapy as a desirable aspect of this approach.

Third, the immediate advantages of the father's participation in therapy. This should be self-evident. In my experience with this approach, I have not found fathers reluctant to take part—not nearly as reluctant as when they are approached for individual therapy. I have been somewhat surprised that they are even willing to go to considerable lengths to rearrange business schedules, to postpone getting home for dinner after the day's work, to make somewhat complicated transportation plans so that the members of the family can be picked up from home, school, dental appointments, dancing classes, and so on, and brought to the therapy hour. I may have been dealing with a selected group of fathers, but my experience is that they get into the spirit of the therapy often more rapidly than the mother. This may be because mothers feel that they have been carrying the major share of the burdens of the child's disturbance and are relieved of this heavy responsibility by the father's active participation in the treatment. At least mothers have made comments to this effect within the family conferences.

After the practical details of the treatment hours have been worked out with the parents, the first session with the family as a whole is scheduled. At this first session I tell the children that I have talked with their mother and father and that we are getting together because they feel the family is not as happy as it should be. I aim to structure the situation by including the following in my comments during the first session. I recognize, first, that grownups are big, strong, sometimes bossy, and often fail to understand children. As a result they sometimes so run the family that the children are afraid to talk about their real feelings and real wishes. Second, that this therapy is a unique situation in that I am a grownup who is here to make sure that each child gets a chance to talk about the things that seem to him to make the family unhappy. Third, that I am on the children's side, as indeed the parents really are, but that parents sometimes don't know how to take the children's side best, and that we can help them here to understand what the children feel and want. Fourth, that their mother and father really want to change things so that the children will be happier and be able to have more say in how the family is to be run. Fifth, that I am to see that everyone gets a chance to talk about important things and to work out together the plans for the family, but that I am only an umpire or a referee. I will not make decisions for the family.

The rationale behind this orientation is manifold. I want the child to feel that he has support for expressing his own point of view and encouragement for his own efforts to grow, to take responsibility and to experience freedom for self-direction. I want the child to sense that the feelings he harbors toward the parents are worth talking about and desirable to talk about, even if they are negative feelings. I want the parents to recognize that I am not assuming control of the family, that it remains within the family, and that I am not an advice giver but an interpreter of the family relationship. This has special relevance for the fathers, who may be easily threatened, experience has shown, if the therapist is active in directing family affairs. I want the family, and especially the children, to know that it is by talking that we hope to work. That the child usually grasps this quickly was illustrated by Michael, a ten-year-old, who moved his chair right over next to mine as I was speaking and said "Good. Now we can have a war! (bang, bang, bang)."

II. THE CHILD-CENTERED PHASE

After the orientation statement has concluded, I encourage the child to tell us what he thinks makes the family unhappy. By my attitude I discourage the parents from too much speaking at the beginning. If they talk at this time they usually are full of complaints about the behavior of the child, and I do not wish to set up the therapy as a reinforcement of their authority. It frequently takes considerable time during the first hour to help the child to speak. I keep reassuring him that he does not need to speak until he feels ready, that he will not be punished if he does not speak, and that his parents have promised to rearrange things to make the family better for him.

All the children have begun by pointing out annoyances connected with the rules and routine of living—perhaps they can't stay up to see a favorite T.V. program, or Dad won't play games, or Mother nags about their getting out for school in time, or the allowance is not sufficient. I try to deal with these concrete issues as they come up, by asking how the child would propose to solve the problem. Sometimes he demands complete acceptance of his solution by the parents, sometimes he is ready to work out a compromise, but at the beginning I hope the parents will go as far as the child wishes. I usually leave the way open for future consideration of the issue by saying we can see how it works and, if anyone needs to talk about it later, we can bring it up again. The speed of movement in therapy at this point depends on the willingness or ability of the parents to readjust the family to fit in with the child's wishes. If they go along readily, the child exhausts his demands in a few weeks and the therapy enters the next stage.

III. THE PARENT-CENTERED PHASE

The next major period of the therapy begins when the child gets to the point of saying "Everything is going good." Then the parents enter the picture actively. They begin to complain about ways in which the child irritates them, worries them, and so on. Often this is initiated by talking about difficulties at school or in the community rather than in the home. I bring the center into the home by interpretation that we can do little in the conferences about those things that take place outside the home and that often these difficulties are signs of disturbances in the home. Considerable hostility in the parents builds up in the first therapy stage. The explosion of this hostility creates a delicate situation, for it is important to permit the parents to express this feeling and yet to protect the relationship of the therapist with the child. Three methods of handling this are used:

a. stating that the child will and must have his say too;
b. interpreting to the parents the normalcy of child's behavior when it is appropriate for his age. Gesell's and other developmental studies are handbooks for this therapy;
c. helping the child to express his point of view regarding the complaints by interpreting that he must have his reasons for acting this way.

The consequence of this parental explosion is defense on the part of the child—defense that usually takes the form of counter-attack and frequently the expression of hostile feelings that have been repressed, the recall of incidents that have never been spoken of with the parents, the expression of fears that account for the behavior, and the telling of episodes at school and elsewhere that contribute to the difficulties in the home. For example, when Michael's parents complained about his seemingly irrational difficulties in leaving home, driving in the car, and being separated from the mother, Michael recalled an incident that took place when he was three and that he had never before mentioned to his parents. He was driving toward home with his mother and was misbehaving in the car. About three blocks away from home the mother's patience could not contain itself and she stopped the car, put Michael out, and told him to walk home, which he did. On one other occasion, when the family was driving to New York City, the parents threatened to put him out of the car. For six or seven years after these episodes, Michael was car-sick and thoroughly disagreeable whenever the family went driving. But after telling this he travelled happily and without car-sickness for six weeks throughout the country with his family. He carried everywhere a signed affidavit from his parents that they would not throw him out of the car; and his demand for the affidavit was accepted without question by the parents.

Through the weeks of this parental complaint and child's defense emerges deepening understanding on the part of all regarding the nature of the emotional bonds between the various members of the family and the nature of the forces that determine behavior. In spite of the attack, recrimination, bitterness, and not infrequent tearfulness, during the conferences at this stage, life goes more smoothly at home. The intense catharsis of negative feeling in the conferences does not carry over, for the most part, to the home. It appears that in the home there is increased tolerance and mutual planning and carrying out of the joint living of the family—punctuated by the occasional explosion. Often when the hostility gets most intense, we have the bonds between the members of the family strengthened as for instance when Mickey, an 11-year-old who had threatened to run away from home three weeks earlier, said during a particularly tense conference: "But I don't want to run away any more. I love you too much." But it is not only the children who provide these positive feelings. Parents at this stage often say to the child "Now I realize how wrong I have been." Or "I guess the real problem is not with you but with us."

The parent-centered stage of the therapy develops into concern with the parent's problems. This takes various forms. In one instance the therapy was concluded at this point, I believe with excellent therapeutic results, although I would have been more content if there had not been a sudden break. I attribute the termination to my error in management. The week before, I had seen the mother and the two children without the father, who was tied up in a business deal from which he could not get free. In this session I had permitted all three to bring out floods of resentment against the father. Next conference, when it could not help but be apparent to the father what the content of the previous session had been, he reacted with intense fury, and this was the last time I met the family. I learned from that not to see a part of a family group. If one member cannot come, we postpone the session. The only exception to this rule is when it is preplanned in a conference of the whole family for me to see alone one or more members, as for instance the parents, which I find is sometimes necessary. After such a conference I make a brief report to the whole family on the content of what we have talked about. In the case of the family that broke off the contact, I have happened to meet informally each of the members of the family since that time. Each one reports striking improvement in the family. Even the father has greeted me warmly but with some underlying tension that I attribute to continuing hostility to me. I am sure this is in part hostility toward the wife and two children displaced on to me.

Therapeutically it appears good for the father to have me as a scapegoat, although I would have preferred to see this treatment go into the final stage that has been characteristic of the other groups that have terminated.

IV. THE FAMILY-CENTERED PHASE

Normally the final stage has been marked by the following:

a. disappearance of many of the referral symptoms. Not all disappear since some of them are now reinterpreted by the parents and lose their disturbing effect;
b. the appearance of laughter in the conferences, frequently growing out of the parents laughing at themselves;
c. the reporting of incidents during the week when the whole family worked together to resolve a problem that had arisen; or,
d. incidents in which the family engaged pleasurably in some mutual activity;
e. the volunteering of the child to take on necessary chores for the family;
f. the spontaneous expression of the feeling that the family life is going so well that the conferences are no longer necessary. "I guess we can manage ourselves now without you."

In this brief account I have not perhaps made clear enough the role that interpretation plays. I am more active than being simply a listening referee. At each of the four stages interpretation is necessary. At the beginning I must interpret and reinterpret my role in the group. Before the therapy can proceed I have often to interpret to the family the resistance of the child to participation. As therapy centers more and more on the child occasionally it is necessary to interpret to the parents what appears to be the basis of the child's resentment about routines and rules. At this level I have also to reinterpret my own relationship to the family, for the parents often persist in trying to make me an ally against the children. At the third level when the parents begin to become vocal, I have to verbalize the feelings and reactions that are being engendered in the group and something of their historical and current basis. When the parents are facing their own problems, I find myself pointing out parallels between their own childhoods and the experiences of their children, the ways in which their childhood experiences have contributed to their present difficulties, and the effects of their communications on the children. I have often to point up that the child's increasing knowledge of the parents is not to be feared. In the final stages I play a role in pointing out what is now the mode of communication in the family and its consequences. At this time usually comes also a recapitulation of what has happened through the various stages of the treatment.

It is only appropriate that I should also mention some of the limitations to this method that I have encountered or that are potentially present.

1. Limits on age. The families I have worked with have included children from 8 to 16 years of age. I am relatively certain I could not use this method with younger children. I believe the age level could be extended upwards, as long as the family is living together as a unit. This might mean that it would be effective with younger hospitalized patients, but I do not know.

2. Time is a crucial and sometimes a limiting factor. I have found it helpful to have a somewhat flexible schedule. Since all members of the family group apparently need to be present, some allowances have to be made for demands on members of the family as well as for sickness. Since I have only seen families on a weekly basis, and a conference missed produces a long interval, I have set up a basic conference time and made temporary adjustments as necessary, keeping in mind the goal of as much continuity as possible. As with any therapy, the overall duration of treatment varies. My longest series has been one and one half years, my shortest two months.

3. Limits of economic and cultural background. These are unexplored questions. My families, with one exception, have been from the middle class. The parents have had above average education and ability. The one exception was that of a house painter and his family. For them the technique needed considerable modification. I do not know whether this was personal to the family or a general condition of work with groups where lower intelligence, education, and different mores apply.

4. Limits on level of parental adjustment. I would say that in two of my families the parents were badly adjusted to one another but that in neither case were the difficulties such that separation was imminent. If we had a more serious disturbance between the parents I do not know how the therapy would work. With one family it was necessary to discontinue work with the whole family group for a period in order to work with the parents alone. I believe the family conferences brought home to them, in a way that would not have been otherwise possible, their own need of help. I am not sure, however, that this could have been accomplished without a basic desire on the part of the parents to hold their marriage together.

5. Technical limits. I have been conscious during my work of complexities in family adjustment beyond those revealed by individual therapy. This makes this method singularly appropriate as a research tool. As an example of an insight that has been made plain to me through work with two of the families, I have observed how rejection by one parent is in many ways equivalent to rejection by both parents. Joan, an 11-year-old adopted girl put it this way: "Daddy doesn't love me like he does Margaret (her older sister) and even when mummy does nice things for me I am always afraid that she won't love me either." It is quite evident that the mother really prefers Joan but even her warm affection occasions anxiety and not security in Joan. This has been evident as a pattern in one other case, and I was not previously sensitized to this as a familial pattern. Maybe all the observations that I make have been recorded in the literature, but I keep running into relationships that I would not have anticipated. These I find new to evaluate, to interpret, to understand, and sometimes I am not prepared to deal with them. Maybe with more experiences I shall not be as surprised as I sometimes find myself—and I hope my technical proficiency will improve.

In many issues the best method of handling them is not plain. I sense that detailed normative data on family adjustments, similar to those available about child development, would be of great practical value. Many normative issues regarding family life and adolescence emerge, which need to be dealt with specifically rather than by the generalities that characterize much of our present knowledge. Through such a therapeutic technique as this we may be able to deepen our understanding of adolescent behavior in relation to the family. In recent years child psychology has so stressed the young child, the pre-school period, that we have not progressed far beyond the insights of G. Stanley Hall and the workers of his era into development during the pre- and post-pubertal years. Family group therapy offers a tool for analysis of one of the most crucial segments of life during this period.

REFERENCES

1. Bowlby, J., The study and reduction of group tensions in the family, *Human Relat.*, 2, 123–128, 1949.
2. Dreikurs, R., *The Challenge of Parenthood*, New York: Duell, Sloan & Pearce, 1948, xvi, 334p.
3. Dreikurs, R., "Counseling for family adjustment," *Indiv. Psychol. Bull.*, 7, 119–137, 1949.
4. Dreikurs, R., "Psychotherapy through Child Guidance," *Nerv. Child.*, 8, 311–328, 1949.
5. Dreikurs, R., "Technique and dynamics of multiple psychotherapy," *Psychiat. Quart.*, 24, 788–799, 1950.
6. Dreikurs, R., "Family group therapy in the Chicago Community Child Guidance Center," *Ment. Hyg.*, 35, 291–301, 1951.

Family Rules: Marital Quid Pro Quo

Don D. Jackson

Because they are so obviously and invariably composed of only one man and one woman each, marriages in our society are usually described in terms of sexual differences, which are of course considered innate or at least fixed characteristics of the individuals involved. All manner of behaviors quite removed from primary sexual differences can be brought into the framework of male-female differences, which framework then becomes an explanatory model of marriage. This view pervades our popular mythology of sexual stereotypes, it influences marriage manuals and similar advisory accouterments, and it certainly guides our scientific study of the marital relationship, no matter how inconsistent or unspecific this theory proves to be. The rich variety of forms which anthropologists have shown us "masculinity" and "femininity" take in marriage across the world should indicate something is amiss with the assumption that absolute, specific sexual differences in marriage are of heuristic value. The function of such differences in organizing a special relationship is seldom considered; it may be that a shared belief in any difference at all would serve the same purpose. It is proposed here that the individual differences which are so evident in marital relationships may just as reasonably be a result of the nature of that relationship as of the nature of the individuals who compose the relationship.

Heterosexuality is not the only unique feature of marriage; there is another characteristic which, strangely enough, often goes unnoticed, but may be the most important aspect of marriage: it is the only well-known, *long-term collaborative relationship*. Thus there are several nonsexual aspects which must be considered in any analysis of marriage and marriage problems.

1. It is a *voluntary* relationship, even though undertaken in a culture which views marriage as almost compulsory.
2. It is a *permanent* relationship; that is, it is supposed to be a lifetime contract. ("Till death do us part.")
3. Marriage in the western world is an *exclusive* relationship, in which the parties are supposed to be virtually sufficient each unto the other, with a marked exclusion of third parties and outside relationships.

Reprinted from *Archives of General Psychiatry*, Vol. 12, 1965, pp. 589–594. Reproduced by permission.

4. It is a broadly *goal-oriented* relationship with many vital mutual tasks to be carried out on a long-term basis and marked by time-bound eras—each with its special problems.

To describe these premises of marriage is not to imply that they are necessarily realized nor that the parties enter into marriage with such concepts in mind. These are shared beliefs about the nature of marriage as an institutionalized relationship, and the assets and liabilities of marriage as a legal arrangement stem, in large part, from the workability of these norms.

Unused as we are to thinking in terms of different kinds of relationships (rather than different kinds of individuals), still we can see that there are probably no other dyadic relationships which, *regardless of the sex of the partners*, can be similarly characterized. For instance, the assumption (not to say the reality) of permanency excludes most other volitional relationships which are not troubled by the curious paradox of "having to want to stay together." The *homosexual "marriage"* comes to mind immediately as a possible example of a relationship in which primary sexual differences are absent but the relationship problems as outlined above are more or less relevant. We might question whether being against the social grain—two against the world—has something to do with the durability of some such relationships. Yet, even in homosexual "marriages" there is the evolution of sex-role differences. Homosexuals may choose for their relatively permanent partners their opposites in terms of "masculinity" and "femininity" (and they often use a sex-role language for their relationship even when parent-child or sibling terms would seem more appropriate). While it can always be asserted that sex-role identification preceded the relationship (i.e., one partner is "really" female), this cannot be proven; so, just as in heterosexual marriage, the differentiation of the individuals along sex lines can be seen as primary *or* as a means of working out the problems posed by the rules of the marital relationship—that is, as effect, not cause.

Other instances in which the same relationship problems seem to be posed are fairly easily distinguished. In the *roommate* arrangement, for instance, volition, relative permanence, and mutual tasks do frequently apply; but there is no expectation that the two will not engage in highly important, independent, third-party relationships. In fact, it would be unusual for each roommate *not* to maintain independence or external coalitions with regard to financial, sexual, intellectual, and even companionship needs. Lacking a premise of virtual self-sufficiency of the dyad, the roommate arrangement also avoids many of the problems which arise in marriage. *Business relationships* are oriented to an explicit and specific central goal, as opposed to marriage which cannot be said to have any single goal. In fact, for marriages we have to make up goals such as "the rearing of children" or "companionship" even when such functions can successfully be carried on without legal or secular blessings. Business relationships are also necessarily diluted by a wide variety of intrinsic factors, not the least of which are the time-defined working day and, again, the vital role of third parties such as customers, staff, even the stock market. There must be enduring, nonhomosexual relationships between, perhaps, unmarried possibly related women; here one thinks of the maiden aunts or old maid school teachers of our American mythology, and one begins to wonder how such relationships are worked out. Unfortunately for our research interests, these relationships seldom come to the attention of professionals. So it seems we are unable by means of counter-example to prove immediately whether marriage is the way it is because a man and a woman are involved, or because it is a unique kind of a relationship for any two people at all. *Thus, it is possible that one could outline marriage as a totally nonsexual affair, nearly excluding all sexual differences, or at least minimizing the causal role usually assigned such differences.*

The sex-role view of marriage is so widely accepted that the position just taken seems nearly impudent. It nevertheless seems important to reconsider some of our beliefs about marriage since our present knowledge of individual theory is quite exhaustive when contrasted with the paucity of systematic knowledge of relationships per se. In our traditional conceptual framework, the individual is held by the boundaries of his skin, and whatever transpires between two such captives—that which is neither clearly "I" nor clearly "thou"—is a mystery for which we have no language or understanding. Our thoughts, research efforts, and even what Benjamin Whorf called "our view of the cosmos" are limited or facilitated by the language which we use. Therefore, we must first have a language which enables, even forces, us to think interactionally. The necessity for a language with which to study interaction may lead to the abandonment of terms which belong to the study of the individual in favor of terms which focus on the relationship. The concept of "family rules" (1) represents one such tool. The observation of family interaction makes obvious certain *redundancies*, typical and repetitive patterns of interaction which characterize the family as a supraindividual entity. One of the simplest such rules is proposed in this paper, the marital quid pro quo, an alternative to the theory of individual differences in marriage.

To suggest that the individual, sex-aligned differences which we witness in marriages may not be due to individual sexual differences, or indeed have anything to do with biological sexual requirements, is not to say these differences do not exist. To the contrary, just such differences can be the basis of working out a relationship. The stresses and successes of marriage still need not be attributed to sexual or even individual personality differences, but could conceivably be expected to be true of any hypothetical relationship which is also voluntary, permanent, exclusive, and task-oriented. The actual differences between marriage partners are probably not nearly so important as the difficulty in collaborating; furthermore, any two people in these conditions have to work out rules based on differences or similarities. Sexual differences are readily available, but if there were no real differences to help define the relationship, differences would probably be made up. In this light, our present language of marriage imposes many encumbering myths about maleness and femaleness. For it seems that differences are inevitable in a relationship, especially in an ongoing, goal-oriented relationship such as marriage. Imagine two perfectly identical persons—not real-life identical twins who have long since become distinguishable to themselves and others—but a carbon-copy pair who are in fact the same person in two bodies. If such a pair were to live together, it is obvious they would have to evolve differences which did not before exist. The first time they approached a door that must be entered in single file, the die would be cast. Who is to go first? On what basis is this decision to be made? After it is made and effected, can things ever be the same again? If they fight, someone must win. If one precedes and the other forbears, it cannot then be said they are identical, since one would be aggressive, thoughtless, or "the one who takes the initiative," while the other would be passive, patient, or sluggish. In short, a relationship problem which has nothing to do with individual differences—for there were none in our hypothetical pair—has been solved by evolving differences which may be considered shorthand expressions of the definition of the relationship which was achieved. Later, these differences are available to handle other, similar circumstances wherein identical simultaneous actions are neither possible nor desirable. There is an old European tale of a detective posing as a lodger in a boarding house where a number of mysterious suicides have occurred. He notices across the courtyard from his window an old woman who is weaving. As he becomes entranced by her elaborate movements he begins to mimic them. Then with slow horror it becomes apparent to him that it is she who is following *his* movements, not he who is following hers. As the cause and effect become inextricably tangled, he throws himself out the window at the spinner.

When we consider the work to be done by marital partners—moneymaking, housekeeping, social life, love-making, and parenting—the tasks which must be attempted and to greater or lesser degree accomplished, then we are overwhelmed by the impossibility of sameness and the efficiency of differences. In the marital relationship, at least, two individuals are faced with the challenge of collaboration on a wide variety of tasks over an indefinite, but presumably long, period of time. In most of these areas—sexual, financial, occupational—no simple or nonpersonal division of labor is obvious. Cultural stereotypes are of some help, but even these appear to be fluid in middle-class America.

From research done on the parents of white, middle-class families observed at the Mental Research Institute, it seems that the way couples handle this crucial relationship problem is by a marital quid pro quo. When two people get together, they immediately exchange clues as to how they are defining the nature of the relationship; this set of behavioral tactics is modified by the other person by the manner in which he responds. The definition which is agreed to (and if the marriage is to work some sort of agreement must be reached), this definition of who each is in relation to the other can best be expressed as a *quid pro quo.* Quid pro quo (literally "something for something") is an expression of the legal nature of a bargain or contract, in which each party must receive something for what he gives and which, consequently, defines the rights and duties of the parties in the bargain. Marriage, too, can be likened to a bargain which defines the different rights and duties of the spouses, each of which can be said to do X if and because the other does Y. Quid pro quo, then, is a descriptive metaphor for a relationship based on differences, and expression of the redundancies which one observes in marital interaction. One of the most common quid pro quos observed in white, middle-class, suburban families is the following arrangement: the husband is, broadly, an instrumental type who deals with matters logically and intellectually and is considered the practical, realistic one; his wife is the more sensitive, affecting, or "feeling" sort of person who understands people better than things. This sort of quid pro quo is extremely utilitarian for the sort of life such a couple is likely to lead, since the exchange implies a fairly clear division of labor which defines the contribution made by each. Carried to the extreme, this quid pro quo could result in rigidity and misunderstanding, though it is probably not as prone to pathology as some other relationship agreements. That this arrangement has little to do with fixed "sex roles" as we ordinarily think of them has been confirmed by Robert Leik (2) who recently measured this mode of differentiation in actual families as well as "mock family" stranger groups (i.e., stranger groups with the same sex and age composition as the real families tested). He found that:

> The traditional male role (instrumental, non-emotional behavior) as well as the traditional female role (emotional, non-task behavior) appear when interaction takes place among strangers. *These emphases tend to disappear when subjects interact with their own families* (italics mine).

And he concluded that:

> In general, the relevance of instrumentality and emotionality is quite different for family interaction than for interaction among strangers. This major finding poses new problems for the theoretical integration of family research with that based on ad hoc experimental groups. Such integration is possible only through recognition of the fact that *the context of the interaction with strangers places a meaning on particular acts which is different from the meaning of those acts within the family group* (italics mine).

Thus, though this quid pro quo is a common and culturally convenient arrangement, it is not intrinsic to sex roles in marriage. Quite the opposite— the ongoing family relationship apparently custom-tailors the marital bargain to its own particular situation.

Another type of quid pro quo is a "time-bound" relationship—that is, one in which the marital agreement is seriate. If A says to B, let us do X, spouse B assents because they have established a time-bound relationship in which the next move would be B's. The husband may suggest to his wife that they go to a movie; she says yes, and then she has the right to say, we can have a beer afterwards. Similarly, the wife may take certain rights which the husband will grant because he knows he will have a turn in the near future. This time-binding is finite, and while it may not always be a matter of minutes (as it is in sexual intercourse) or of days, it is probably not months or years. Flexibility in time-binding is probably another word for "trust" in a relationship, and this may be the most workable of quid pro quos.[1]

The phenomenon of time in relationships—especially marriage—needs study. Relationships that are not rigidly time-bound have great flexibility, while some of the crises of various periods of family life may relate to time. That is, the unspoken promise never kept may, with the passing of time, become more obviously unlikely to be kept, e.g., that the husband will spend more time with the family as soon as his business gets on its feet becomes less believable as time goes by and the children grow up; at some point the "promise is broken" simply by the passage of time.[2]

There is then a peculiar relationship which can be observed in both marital

[1]Trust is obviously a key concept in marital and even national relationships. It is a belief that the other will do for you what you just did for him, and since you do not know when this will occur, trust appears not to be time-bound. But there are probably intervening signals which declare A's intent to repay B, even though no specific date is ever set. I hope not to have my life insurance cashed, but that ad of the great Rock of Gibraltar constantly refurbishes my trust.

[2]So-called menopausal depression is often related by clinicians to the onset of woman's inability to have children. My own observations led me to seriously question this. Among other considerations is the fact that the wish for a child may help deny an unsatisfactory marriage.

and exploitative political situations, when the quid pro quo is not in fact time-bound but is treated as if it was. If A says to B, let us do X, B says yes because A indicates that eventually B will get his reward. B's day is allegedly coming, and though it never does, A keeps acting as if it is going to and B keeps acting as if he accepts this. These are often pathological relationships which in marriage are frequently characterized by depression and even suicide. The vicious cycle aspect of this relationship is apparent—the more B lets himself be conned, the more he has coming eventually and the less free he is to try another game, since he has so much already invested.

If the gist of these examples has been clear it should not be necessary to point out that the quid pro quo is not overt, conscious, or the tangible result of real bargaining. Rather, this formulation is the pattern imposed by the observer on the significant redundancies of marital interaction, and should always be understood metaphorically, with the tacit preface, "It seems as if . . . ." The specifics of marital bargaining are not of interest to us. It is at the level of exchange of definitions of the relationship (and, therefore, of self-definition within the relationship) that we can usefully analyze in terms of quid pro quo. If we were to focus only on the content level of marital interaction, we might miss the probability that the so-called masochist does not like or need to suffer—he gets something out of the relationship by using the one-down position as a tactic.

Note, for instance, the following example.[3]

H: I wish you would fix yourself up. Take $50 and get a permanent, a facial— the works!
W: I'm sorry, dear, but I don't think we ought to spend the money on me.
H: *!!#*! I want to spend it on you!
W: I know, dear, but there's all the bills and things. . . .

Here the apparently one-down behavior of the wife is actually quite controlling. If we look beyond the particular $50 about which they are disputing, we can see the relationship they have worked out: the husband is allowed to complain about the wife and act in charge, but the wife indicates she does not intend to follow his orders, that in fact his orders are stupid and, since she sets no time conditions, we do not know if she will ever get a permanent or not. This is one clue to the quid pro quo. Rather than executing a piece of action, this couple is going through a repetitive exchange which defines and redefines the nature of their relationship. Thus on another occasion:

H: Hey, I can't find any white shirts!
W: I'm sorry, dear, they're not ironed yet.
H: Send them to the laundry! I don't care what it costs!
W: We spend so much on groceries and liquor. I felt I should try to save a few pennies here and there.
H: Listen for *!!#*, I need shirts!
W: Yes, dear, we'll see about it.

Note that just as the wife does not specify *when*, nor whether she is really saying yes or no, the husband does not insist on clear, definite information. It would be misleading to ascribe motivation to this couple. To say he likes to bluster or she likes to frustrate him is senseless and yet irrefutable. What is

[3]These are not transcribed couples but were reported in couple therapy.

important is their interactional system: once having established such a pattern of interaction, they are victim of blindness and reinforcement.[4] Further, their roles are defined not by "male agressiveness" and "female passivity," but by the simple fact that wives are supposed to be pretty and to take charge of the laundry and husbands are affected by whether or not wives fulfill these expectations.

This is so obvious, yet we as researchers are victims of the sex-role propaganda, too. Most psychiatrists would probably doubt that a family in which the husband runs the house and the wife brings home the money could rear apparently healthy children. Yet in two such examples brought to our attention this appears to be the case. To understand why these couples function well, we would do much better to analyze their present relationship and seek to identify their particular quid pro quo than to seek the answer in their individual backgrounds and calculate the probabilities that such individuals would meet and marry.

It is becoming more accepted among clinicians that there are no marital relationships which are unbalanced or impoverished for *one* spouse. Observation of the interaction reveals the "bargain" struck between alcoholic and spouse, between wife-beater and wife. The quid pro quo reasoning, then, is still tautological and, within its own sphere of proof, just as irrefutable as notions of human instincts and sex roles. If one believes that marriage is a relationship bargain and is the judge of the terms of this bargain in any particular case, then he can prove his own hypothesis. Again it is important to restate that the concept of family rules in general and of the quid pro quo in particular is only a descriptive metaphor imposed by the observer on the redundancies he observes in interaction. This is not only *true* in the many important areas of the social sciences where the researcher must be both judge and jury, but it is also highly desirable as long as we avoid the pitfall of reification and acknowledge the fictitious nature of all our constructs. This is a necessary first step if we are to devise a language which will elucidate and convey the process, not the property. Our goal is to do verbal justice to the phenomena in which we are avowedly interested. In our early attempts at interpersonal research, we are constantly limited by the only terminology we have—an ill-fitting bequest from theories of the individual. The notions of family rules and marital quid pro quo are levers to force us away from the characteristics of individuals onto the nature of their interaction, and are at least somewhat more appropriate to describe the phenomena we will observe in interaction.

It is possible that the formulation of "rules" such as the quid pro quo has enormous predictive potential. If we are reasonably accurate in our formulation of a metaphor for a couple's relationship, we can forecast the likelihood of success or failure and even the fate of children in the family system. For instance:

> The "Big Daddy-Baby Doll" arrangement is not likely to be a workable quid pro quo. While Baby Doll may be able to continue her half of the bargain for some time, the material offerings with which Big Daddy must be constantly forthcoming are,

---

[4]B. F. Skinner has stated that aperiodic negative reinforcement is the most potent conditioner. Because couples are apart a good deal and engage in a variety of contingencies some of their negative interactions take on an aperiodic aspect. This may make it difficult for A to label B in black and white and yet enhance B's vulnerability.

after all, finite in number. There are only so many countries to tour and so many jewels which can be bought and worn. No matter what his wealth, her satiation will probably eventually endanger the quid pro quo so that the marriage must terminate or find a new level of operation.

Other arrangements may survive the early period of marriage but cannot be expected to accommodate children. For instance:

A couple had a quid pro quo of total independence: each pursued his own career and was succeeding. They scorned the usual financial and housekeeping arrangements, basing all decisions on the maximization of the independence of both. Though one might wonder how it happened in an atmosphere of total independence, the wife became pregnant; her career and way of life were drastically limited. The marriage foundered because the original quid pro quo could not possibly be made to include maternity and motherhood. A new relationship had to be established.

Some parental relationships can survive the onslaught of a little stranger, but cannot accommodate his emotional health:

The family maxim seemed to be "People who live in glass houses shouldn't throw stones." Husband and wife scrupulously avoided even the mildest and—to us—vital criticism of each other, and in turn was not criticized by the spouse. This ban on information, however, provides a poor teaching context for children and is not likely to encourage healthy, spontaneous curiosity. The marriage lasts, but the brighter-than-average son was referred to therapy for marked academic under-achievement.

These examples are, of course, retrospective. But our success in postdiction of psychopathology in children from the blind analysis of examples of marital interaction in terms of the quid pro quo leads us to hope that, with refinement, prediction and prophylaxis of pathological systems are possible.

SUMMARY

A theory of marriage is proposed which is based on the relationship rather than the individuals. Specifically, the quid pro quo formulation holds that the similarities and differences between spouses comprise the metaphorical "bargain" on which the marital relationship is based. The advantages of this scheme are that (1) we have a language which aids our observation of truly interactional phenomena, and (2) there is the promise of improved predictive power when the "rules" of the relationship are grasped.

REFERENCES

1. Jackson, D. D.: Study of Family. Family Process 4: 1–20 (March) 1964.
2. Leik, R. K.: Instrumentality and Emotionality in Family Interaction. Sociometry 26:131–145, 1963.

The Family of the Schizophrenic: A Model System

Jay Haley

This paper will attempt to show that schizophrenic behavior serves a function within a particular kind of family organization. The emphasis in this description will be on the interactive behavior of the schizophrenic and his parents rather than on their ideas, beliefs, attitudes, or psychodynamic conflicts. This work is largely based on an examination of a small sample of families participating in therapeutic sessions where parents and schizophrenic child, as well as siblings, are seen together and recorded. An excerpt from a recording of a family session will be presented and analyzed in terms of the observable behavior of family members, to illustrate the hypothesis that the family of the schizophrenic is a special kind of system which can be differentiated from other family systems.

The hypothesis that schizophrenia is of family origin has led to a number of investigations of schizophrenic patients and their parents. These studies include both impressions of family members and attempts at statistical measurement of individual traits of parents or the conflict between them. Typically the mother of the schizophrenic is described as dominating, over-protective, manipulative of the child and father, and also overtly rejecting (18). The father is usually described as weak and passive, holding aloof from the patient (15, 17), and occasionally overtly rejecting and cruel (8). Many investigators mention a certain percentage of fathers or mothers who appear "normal."

Besides reporting descriptions of the individuals in the family, investigators report on the relationship between the parents on the assumption that conflict between father and mother could be related to disturbance in the child. Lidz and Lidz (13) reported in 1949 that 20 of 35 schizophrenic patients had parents who were clearly incompatible. Tietze (20) reported in the same year that 13 of 25 mothers of schizophrenic patients reported unhappy marriages and nine marriages which were described as "perfect" were found by the investigator to be otherwise. In 1950 Gerard and Siegal (7) found strife between 87 percent of the parents of 71 male schizophrenic patients in contrast to 13 percent found in the controls. In the same year Reichard and Tillman (17) noted the unhappy marriages of parents of schizophrenics. Frazee (8) in 1953 reported that 14 of 23 parents were in severe conflict with each other and none had only moderate conflict in contrast to 13 control parents who had only moderate conflict. Lidz (16) reported in 1957 that all of 14 families of schizophrenic patients contained marital relationships which were seriously disturbed. Bowen (6) describes the parents in this type of family as experiencing "emotional divorce." Wynne used the term "pseudo mutuality" to describe the difficulties family members have with each other (23).

These studies provide strong evidence for conflict between the parents of schizophrenics, but do not clarify what strife between parents has to do with schizophrenia in a child. After all, there is conflict between parents who do not have schizophrenic children. Similarly, to show that the mothers of schizophrenic patients are dominating and overprotective and the fathers weak and passive does not clarify how schizophrenia is appropriate in families with such parents. Psychiatric terminology seems particularly unsuited to this problem. The language of psychiatry either describes the processes within an individual, such as his needs, fantasies, anxieties, and so on, or provides static descriptions of two individuals in dominant-submissive or rejecting or dependent relationships. When schizophrenia is described in the traditional psychiatric way, and when other family members are seen with the biased emphasis upon the processes in the individual, it is difficult to relate schizophrenia to a family.

Currently most groups investigating schizophrenia and the family are recognizing that the total family unit is pathogenic, and there are attempts to develop a language which will describe the interaction of three or more people. A transition would seem to have taken place in the study of schizophrenia; from the early idea that the difficulty in these families was caused by the schizophrenic member, to the idea that they contained a pathogenic mother, to the discovery that the father was inadequate, to the current emphasis upon all three family members involved in a pathological system of interaction. Although it would seem impossible at this time to provide a satisfactory language for describing the complex interaction of three or more people, this paper will suggest a rudimentary approach to such a descriptive system. An essential requirement of any such description is that it show the adaptive function of schizophrenic behavior within the family system.

The present paper is a product of the current research conducted by the Bateson project. Historically this project began as a general investigation of the nature of communication and began to focus on the communication of the schizophrenics in 1953. The observation that the schizophrenic consistently mislabels his communication led Bateson to deduce that he must have been raised in a learning situation where he was faced with conflicting levels of message. From this came the "double bind" hypothesis (5) which was put together with Jackson's emphasis on schizophrenia serving a homeostatic function in the family (12). The research project then brought together the families of schizophrenics to observe the actual behavior in the family. Basically the double bind hypothesis was a statement about two-person interaction, and it has been extended to areas outside of schizophrenia (9, 11). When the family was seen as an interactive unit, there was an attempt to extend the double bind concept to a three person system (21). Currently the project is attempting to devise a theoretical system for describing the family as a unit, and this attempt has led to several papers (2, 3, 4), including this one.

The importance of describing a total system rather than elements within it may explain some of the inconsistencies in the description of individuals in the family and conflict between them. For example, it is possible that a mother could show rejecting traits when her child is ill and dependent upon her, and overprotective traits when he begins to recover and attempt to achieve independence from her. Similarly, parents may not show discord when their child is psychotic and they are drawn together by this burden, but conflict could appear should the child behave more assertively and so threaten to leave them. Alanen (1) studied mothers of schizophrenic patients and found many of them within the limits of the "normal" on the basis of Rorschach tests and individual interview. He mentions, almost in passing, "Some of the cases in which the mother of a schizophrenic patient had been relatively healthy belong to those in which the father was seriously disturbed. The wives of all fathers who had developed chronic psychosis belong, for example, to this category." If the "normality" or the pathology of a family member depends upon the influence of the behavior of other family members at that time, only a study of the total family system will show consistent findings.

The focus of a family study should be on the total family and on the interaction of parents and children *with each other* rather than on the interaction of family members with interviewers or testers. What a family member reports to an investigator about his relationship with another family member is only hearsay evidence of what actually takes place. To study the system of interaction in the family of the schizophrenic it is necessary to bring family members together over a period of time and directly observe them relating to one another. Inevitably the fact of observing the family introduces a bias into the data, for they may behave differently when observed than when not observed. It would seem to be impossible to leave the observer out of this sort of study, and the problem is to include him in the situation in such a way as to maximize the information he can gain. The most appropriate type of observation would seem to be in a therapeutic context. There is serious doubt as to whether this type of family can be brought together without therapeutic support. If the parents are merely asked to be observed interacting with their schizophrenic child, the question is automatically raised whether they have something to do with the illness of the child; accordingly guilts and defenses are aroused and must be dealt with in the situation. Long-term observation of the family is also necessary since they may give one impression in a single interview and quite another when they have talked together many times and pretenses are dropping. The presence of a therapist is necessary as sensitive areas in the relationships are touched upon when family members get more intensively involved with one another. Long-term observation also provides an opportunity to verify hypotheses and make predictions as family patterns are observed occuring again and again. Finally, the introduction of a therapist makes possible the observation of a family responding to planned intervention. As ideas are presented to the family, or as therapeutic change is threatened, the family can be observed maintaining their system under stress.

Although the expense of regular filming of therapy is prohibitive, the occasional use of film and the constant use of tape recordings provide data which may be studied at leisure.

AN ILLUSTRATION OF FAMILY BEHAVIOR

Since few investigators have the opportunity to observe a schizophrenic and his parents interacting with one another, an illustration is offered here. The following excerpt is transcribed verbatim from a recording of an interview where a patient and his parents were seen weekly as an adjunct to his individual therapy, because of his previous inability to see his parents for even a few minutes without an anxiety attack. The patient, a 39-year-old man, suffered a breakdown in the army and was diagnosed as a schizophrenic. After discharge he returned home and remained with his parents for the following ten years. There were several abortive attempts to leave home and go to work. He was employed for little more than a year during those ten years and was supported by his parents during his temporary absences from home. When he entered the hospital, at the insistence of his parents, he was hallucinating, behaving in a compulsive way, exhibiting bizarre mannerisms, and complaining of anxiety and helplessness.

Earlier in the interview the patient had been saying he felt he was afraid of his mother, and finally she brought out a Mother's Day Card she had just received from him. It was a commercial card with the printed inscription, "For someone who has been like a mother to me." The patient said he could see nothing wrong with the card nor understand why his mother was disturbed about receiving it.

> *Patient:* Uh, read the outside again.
>
> *Mother:* All right, the outside says, "On Mother's Day, with best wishes"—everything is very fine, it's wonderful, but it's for someone else, not for your mother, you see? "For someone who's *been* like a mother to me."
>
> *Father:* In other words, this card made mother think. So mother asked me ...
>
> *Mother:* (interrupting) When you ...
>
> *Father:* (continuing) what I think about it. So I said, "Well, I don't think Simon—meant that way, maybe he ...
>
> *Patient:* (interrupting) Well, I mean you can interpret it, uh—uh, you've been like a mother is, uh, supposed to be.
>
> *Father:* No, no.
>
> *Patient:* (continuing) a good—a real good mother.
>
> *Therapist:* Why don't you like the idea that he might have deliberately sent that?
>
> *Father:* Deliberately? Well ...
>
> *Mother:* (overlapping and interrupting) Well, that's what I ...
>
> *Father:* (continuing) well, he says he didn't, he agrees ...
>
> *Mother:* (continuing) Well, I mean I believe our son would have ...
>
> *Father:* (overlapping and continuing) that he couldn't get another card.
>
> *Patient:* (interrupting) Well, I meant to sting you just a tiny bit by that outside phrase.
>
> *Mother:* (overlapping) You see I'm a little bit of a psychiatrist too, Simon, I happen to—(laughing) So I felt so—when you talked to (the therapist) I brought along that card—I wanted to know what's behind your head. And I wanted to know—or you made it on purposely to hurt me—Well, if you did, I—I ...
>
> *Patient:* (interrupting) Not entirely, not entire ...

Mother: (interrupting and overlapping) I'll take all—Simon, believe me, I'll take all the hurt in the world if it will help you—you see what I mean?

Therapist: How can you . . .

Mother: (continuing) Because I never meant to hurt you—Huh?

Therapist: How can you hurt anybody who is perfectly willing to be hurt? (short pause)

Father: What's that?

Mother: I uh—a mother sacrifices—if you would be—maybe a mother you would know too. Because a mother is just a martyr, she's sacrificing—like even with Jesus with his mother—she sacrificed too. So that's the way it goes on, a mother takes over anything that she can help . . .

Therapist: (interrupting) What mother?

Mother: (continuing) her children.

Patient: (interrupting and overlapping) Well, uh, I'll tell you Ma—listen. Ma, I didn't mean to—to sting you exactly that outside part there.

Therapist: Well, you said so.

Patient: Oh, all right, but it—it wasn't that exactly. No, I'm not giving ground—uh—it's hard to explain this thing. Uh—uh—What was I going to say. Now I forgot what I was going to say. (short pause) I mean I felt that this—this is what I mean, uh—that I felt that you could have been a better mother to me than you were. See there were things.

Mother: Uh . . .

Father: Well you said . . .

Patient: (interrupting) You could have been better than you were. So that's why—that's that—I felt—it was, uh—uh, was all right to send it that way.

Mother: Well, if you meant it that way that's perf—that's what I wanted to know—and that's all I care—you see. But I still say, Simon, that if you would take your father and mother just like they're plain people—you just came here and you went through life like anybody else went through—and—and don't keep on picking on them and picking them to pieces—but just leave them alone—and go along with them the way they are—and don't change them—you'll be able to get along with everybody, I assure you.

Patient: (interrupting) I mean after all a card is a card—why I d—it seems to me kind of silly (anguish in his voice and near weeping) to bring that thing in here—they have sold them at the canteen, Ma . . .

Therapist: Are you anxious now . . .

Patient: Why . . .

Therapist: Are you anxious now because she said . . .

Patient: I shouldn't be blamed for a thing like that, it's so small . . .

Mother: (overlapping) I'm not blaming you.

Patient: (continuing) I don't even remember exactly what the thing was.

Mother: (overlapping) Well, that's all I wanted to know (laughs).

Patient: (continuing) I didn't want to—to—to—to blame you or nothing.

Therapist: Will you slow down a minute. Are you anxious now because she said she didn't like to be picked on? And you've sort of been picking on her today. Is that what's making you so—upset?

Patient: No, it's now what's making me upset. That they s—after all, mother's got to realize that those people—the people that sell the cards—they sell them and people buy them—the wording isn't exactly right—I've stood for half an hour in a store sometimes picking—picking out a card to send mother or to send to one of the family where I wanted to get the wordings just so—and the picture on the thing just so. I was just too particular, that was before I took sick . . .

Therapist: I think you did that this time too—

Patient: (continuing) And came back to the hospital. No I wasn't—I bought that thing in five minutes. There was only a choice of four cards—but of course that helped. But I—I—I—uh, I—I do have—I've changed now with those cards, I'm not as particular as I used to be. I mean uh—peop—they sell those cards and, uh—I don't think that they—they got—they don't mean anything by the words. Uh,—they're sold for people to buy, they're sold for people to buy.

Therapist: (overlapping) The person who sends them ought to mean something by the words.

Patient: No, but I . . .

Therapist: And you seem to be denying that you sent . . .

Patient: No, I think that can be interpreted in different ways.

Therapist: Sure, it's pretty safe, but not quite safe enough apparently.

Patient: Is that the way you feel too?

Therapist: I feel you tried to say something indirectly so you'd be protected.

Patient: (interrupting) No, I wasn't, I just felt that—that—that thing . . .

Therapist: Now you're . . .

Patient: (continuing) was—was—all right I'm changing a little bit. Uh,—that that mother was a good enough mother. It says "For someone that's been like a mother to me."

Father: A *real* mother.

Patient: Yeah, a *real* mother—so that's all.[1]

Despite its brevity, this excerpt illustrates a typical kind of interaction in this type of family. From the point of view of psychiatric diagnosis, the patient manifests such symptoms as: 1) blocking and forgetting what he was going to say; 2) showing concretistic thinking when he says "a card is a card"; 3) implying that someone else caused the difficulty ("They sell them in the canteen" and later in the interview implying in a rather paranoid way that it was the fault of a post office clerk for mailing it); and 4) claiming amnesia ("I don't even remember what the thing was"). Although less dramatic than symptoms manifested by the full-blown psychotic patient, his behavior could be said to be schizophrenic.

Another family could have responded in this situation rather differently. Should a child in another family send his mother such a card, she might respond to it in any of a variety of ways. And whatever way chosen, her husband and child would also have a range of possible ways to respond to her. This particular family selects these ways, and a description of this family must 1) describe the formal patterns in this type of interaction in such a way as to 2) differentiate the patterns from other possible ones, or those in other families.

POSSIBILITIES OF A THREE-PERSON SYSTEM

One way to describe a particular family is to present its type of interaction against the background of the potential ways a mother, father, and child might interact with one another. If any set of parents and child are brought together in a room, what sort of communicative behavior is potentially possible between them?

1. Whatever they do together can be seen as communication between them; each will do something and each will respond. Although it seems obvious, it is

---

[1]This excerpt is not offered as an example of family therapy but rather as an example of family behavior. The parents in this case were not considered to be patients and the family as a unit was not officially undergoing treatment.

particularly important to emphasize that family members cannot avoid communicating, or responding, to one another when they are in the same room. If one speaks to another and he does not answer, his not-answering is a response in a real and meaningful sense.

2. Not only must parents and child communicate with each other, but each must communicate on at least two levels. Whatever one says and does will inevitably be qualified by the other things he says and does, and when any piece of communication is *about*, or qualifies, another piece of communication they can be said to be of different levels. Whenever anyone speaks to another person he must qualify what he says because he must speak in a tone of voice, with a body movement, with other verbal statements, and in a particular context. What he says will be qualified with an indication of what sort of statement it is, *i.e.*, a joking statement, a sincere one, an unimportant one, a command, a suggestion, and so on. A man can smile and murder as he smiles, and if his behavior is to be described both levels of communication must be included.

If a man says, "I won't stand for that any more!" in a tone of voice which indicates anger and with a gesture of putting a stop to it in a situation where what he says is appropriate, then his statement and qualifications can be said to be congruent, or to "affirm," each other. Messages and their qualifiers can also be incongruent. If a mother makes a punishing statement while labeling what she does as benevolent, she is disqualifying what she says, or manifesting an incongruence between her levels of message. It is important to note that she is not contradicting herself. Contradictory statements are of the same level, such as, "I will do it," and "I won't do it." Incongruent statements are of different levels: "I will do it," said in a tone of voice which indicates, "Don't take what I say seriously." Whether family members qualify their own statements incongruently or congruently, and under what circumstances they do so, can be described as they interact with one another.

3. The three people in the room must also qualify each other's statements. As they respond to one another, they are inevitably commenting upon, or classifying, each other's statements. They may affirm what each other says, or they may disqualify the other's statements by indicating that isn't the sort of thing that should be said. If mother says, "I brought you some candy," and her son says, "You treat me like a child," the son is disqualifying his mother's communication. If he accepts it with a statement of thanks, he is affirming her statement. A description of parents and child must include whether, and under what circumstances, they affirm or disqualify each other's behavior.

4. When three people are in a room, some sort of leadership will take form, even if only in terms of who will speak before the others do. Any one of the three may initiate something, and the other two may go along with him or attempt to take leadership themselves. In some families, father and child may consistently turn to mother for a decision, other families may label father as the final arbiter, while other parents may lean on their child for the initiation of what is to happen.

5. The three people may also form any or all of various possible alliances. It is possible for the three of them to ally against the outside world, or for one to ally with someone in the outside world against the other two, or two may ally against the third. In some families father and mother may form a coalition

against the child, in others the child may ally with one of his parents against the other, and so on.

6. Finally, when something goes "wrong," there are a variety of possible arrangements for the three people to handle blame. All three may each acknowledge blame, one may never accept blame for anything, two may consistently blame the third, and so on.

This list of some of the possibilities in a three-person system is made more complex by the fact that a family member may form an alliance but indicate he isn't forming one, or may take blame but qualify his statement with an indication that he really isn't to blame. The possible range of maneuvers is considerably increased when people are seen to communicate at multiple levels.

THE RULES IN THE FAMILY OF THE SCHIZOPHRENIC

Given a potential range of behavior between three people in a family system, it becomes possible to look at any one type of family as restricted to a certain range of that potential. No one family will interact in all possible ways: limited patterns of interaction will develop. The patterns described here are those in a particular sample and are those which occur when parents and schizophrenic child interact *with each other.* They may behave differently with other people, including psychiatric investigators or siblings of the schizophrenic child. Although siblings are included in our observation of this type of family, the description offered here is of the three person system, partly for simplification in this presentation and partly because parents and schizophrenic child form a special triadic system in the larger family unit.

The ways family members qualify their own statements

Consistently in this type of family the individual members manifest an incongruence between what they say and how they qualify what they say. Many people do this under certain circumstances, but when these family members interact they confine themselves almost entirely to disqualifying their own statements.

In this excerpt, the mother confronts her son with the Mother's Day card because she didn't like it, but she emphasizes what a wonderful card it is. Then she says she wants to know what was behind his head and if he sent it to hurt her, and she laughs. In a context of accusing him of hurting her, she says she wants to be hurt and is willing to take all the hurt in the world to help him. Her description of herself as a special person who will sacrifice all is qualified a few moments later by the statement that she and her husband are just plain people and her son should treat them like anybody else. This "benevolent advice" is offered in a punishing tone of voice and context. When her son says she shouldn't blame him, she qualifies in an incongruent way.

The father is only briefly in this excerpt, but while there he indicates that the son didn't mean to say what the card said, and, besides, the card said she was a real mother.

The son also manifests incongruent behavior. He sends a card to his mother on Mother's Day which indicates she is not really his mother. He further qualifies this message by indicating there was nothing wrong with it and then suggests that it says she is like a mother is supposed to be. Following this, he indicates that it means she could have been a better mother than she was. He then protests that it was silly of her to bring the card in and qualifies this with the statement that they sell them in the canteen. Besides he doesn't remember what the thing was. After indicating that he bought the card hurriedly, he qualifies this by saying it took him five minutes to choose among four cards. He adds that one should be careful in choosing cards with exact wording, but people sell those cards and they don't mean anything by the words. Finally, he qualifies his greetings by saying that it meant she was not only a good enough mother but a real mother.

The more extreme incongruence between the son's levels of message differs from that of his mother, and this difference will be discussed later. Yet basically a similar pattern of communication is apparent. The mother does not say, "You shouldn't have sent me this card—what do you mean by it?" which is implied by her bringing the card to the session. The son doesn't say, "I sent it to you to sting you, but I'm sorry I did now." The mother is condemning him for sending her the card, but she qualifies her messages in such a way that she indicates she isn't condemning him. The son apologizes for sending the card, but he qualifies his apology in such a way that he isn't apologizing. Father indicates the son didn't mean what he said, and the card didn't say what he didn't mean anyhow. Although these incongruencies between what is said and how it is qualified are apparent in the verbal transcript, they are even more apparent when the vocal inflections on the recording are heard. Mother's tone of voice and laughter are inappropriate and thereby disqualify what she is saying, and father and son similarly do not make a flat statement which is affirmed by the ways they say it.

One can listen to many hours of recordings of conversations between parents and schizophrenic child without hearing one of them make a statement which is affirmed. Usually if one finds an exception, it proves on closer examination to fit the rules. For example, during a filmed session a family was asked to plan to do something together and the father said in a positive way that they were going to do this and do that. He fully affirmed his statements by the ways he said them. However, a few minutes later he said he was only saying these things because they should say something in front of the camera, thus disqualifying his previous statements.

How family members qualify each other's statements

Although it is possible for family members to affirm or disqualify each other's statements, in this type of family the members consistently disqualify what each other says. In this excerpt it is difficult to find any statement by one person affirmed by another. The son has actually disqualified his mother's whole past maternal behavior at one stroke by sending her such a card. When she protests, he indicates her protests are not valid. Similarly, the mother disqualifies the greeting she received from her son and also his defenses of it. When he indicates there is nothing wrong with it, she labels this as in error. When he indicates he knew what he was doing and meant to "sting" her a bit, she indicates this was in error. Father joins them to disqualify both the son's message, since he didn't mean it, and his defense of the message. No one affirms what anyone says except 1) when the son says he doesn't remember what the card was, and his mother says that is all she wanted to know; 2) when the father says the card means she is a real mother, and the son agrees. Both of these affirmations involve symptomatic behavior by the son: amnesia and distortion of reality. From this excerpt one might hypothesize that the family members will disqualify what each other says except when the child is behaving in a symptomatic way. Such a hypothesis requires more careful investigation. Apparently even symptomatic behavior by the child is usually disqualified except in certain contexts. When the mother is under attack, the parents may affirm psychotic behavior but not necessarily at other times.

It might be argued that the behavior in this excerpt is exceptional since it deals with a moment of crisis. However, analysis of other interviews suggests that the pattern is typical. In a previous paper (5) the relationship between mother and schizophrenic child was described as a "double bind" situation in that the mother imposed incongruent levels of message upon the child in a situation where the child must respond to conflicting requests, could not comment on the contradictions, and could not leave the field. Further investigation indicates that this kind of communication sequence is a repetitive pattern between all three family members. Not only is each constantly faced with conflicting levels of message, but each finds his response labeled as a wrong one. (Family therapy with this type of family has its unrewarding aspects since almost any comment by the therapist is similarly disqualified.)

Typically if one family member says something, another indicates it shouldn't have been said or wasn't said properly. If one criticizes the other, he is told that he misunderstands and should behave differently. If one compliments the other, he is told he doesn't do this often enough, or he has some ulterior purpose. Should a family member try to avoid communicating, the others will indicate this "passivity" is demanding and indicate he should initiate more. All family members may report they always feel they are in the wrong. However, they do not necessarily directly oppose each other or openly reject one another's statements. If one suggests going to a particular place, the other may not say "no," but rather he is likely to indicate, "Why must we always go where you suggest?" Or the response may be the sigh of a brave martyr who must put up with this sort of thing. Typically the family members may not object to what one another says, but to their right to say it. Often open disagreements are prevented by an atmosphere of benevolent concern and distress that the other person misunderstands. Family members may also respond in an affirmative way when their response would be appropriate only if the person had made some other statement.

It is important to emphasize that a formal pattern is being described here which may manifest itself in various ways. A mother may be overprotective and thereby disqualify what the child does as insufficient or inadequate. She may also be rejecting and similarly disqualify what he does as unacceptable. She may also withdraw when the child initiates something as a way of disqualifying his offer. Similarly, father may viciously condemn mother or child or merely be passive when they seek a positive response from him, and in both cases he is disqualifying their communication.

Although it is not uncommon for people to disqualify each other's statements, ordinarily one would expect affirmation also to occur. However, when observing these families one does not hear even affectionate or giving behavior appreciated or affirmed. If one person indicates a desire for closeness, another indicates this is done in the wrong way or at the wrong time. (However, if one suggests separation the other will also indicate this is the wrong thing to do. Typically in these families the mother regularly threatens separation but does not leave, and the father does not often threaten separation but spends a good deal of his time away from home or "leaves" by drinking heavily while staying home.) Typically family members behave as if they are involved in what might be called a *compulsory relationship*. For example, a mother in one family indicated with some contempt that her husband was afraid to leave her because he could not stand being alone. She suggested he was cruel to her because he was angry at being tied to her. She also rejected his affectionate overtures because she considered them only a kind of bribery to insure staying with her. She herself was unable to leave him even for a night, though he was drunk several nights a week and beat her regularly. Both felt the association was not voluntary, and so neither could accept as valid any indication from the other about wanting to be together. A compulsory relationship is also typical of the parent and schizophrenic child. Since the child is considered incapable of leaving home and associating with others, his staying at home is taken as involuntary. Therefore should he indicate a desire to be with his parents, they tend to disqualify his overtures as merely a request that they not turn him out, and he finds his affectionate gestures disqualified.

Leadership in the family

Since family members tend to negate their own and each other's communication, any clear leadership in the family is impossible. Typically in these families the mother tends to initiate what happens, while indicating either that she isn't, or that someone else should. The father will invite her to initiate what happens while condemning her when she does. Often they suggest the child take the lead, and then disqualify his attempts. These families tend to become incapacitated by necessary decisions because each member will avoid affirming what he does and therefore is unable to acknowledge responsibility for his actions, and each will disqualify the attempts of any other to announce a decision. Both the act of taking leadership and the refusal to take leadership by any one family member is condemned by the others. The family "just happens" to take actions in particular directions with no individual accepting the label as the one responsible for any action.

Alliances

Similarly, no labeled alliances are permitted in the family. A family coalition against the outside world (represented, say, by an observer) breaks down rather rapidly. Such individuals are also unable to form an alliance of two against one. Often they may appear to have such an alliance, as they tend to speak "through" one another. For example, the mother may ask for something for her child as a way of indicating that her husband deprives her, and so appear in alliance with the child. Or when the parents begin to express anger at each other, they may turn on the child for causing their difficulties and so appear in a coalition against him. Yet should the coalition be labeled, it will break down. If the child says, "You're both against me," one or the other parent will disqualify this remark and so deny the coalition. If father should say to mother, "Let's stick together on this," she is likely to say, "I'm afraid you'll back down at the last minute," or "It isn't my fault when we don't stick together." The mother and child may appear to form a coalition against the father, but should the child say, "Father treats us badly," mother is likely to say, "He has his troubles too," even though a moment before she may have been complaining to the child about how badly they were both treated by the father. Family members behave as if an alliance between two of them is inevitably a betrayal of the third person. They seem to have difficulty functioning in a two-person relationship, and as a result the separation of any one of the three from the others is a particular threat.

What confines the members so rigidly within their system is the prohibition on intimate alliances of one member with someone outside the family. As a result, the family members are inhibited from learning to relate to people with different behavior and so are confined to their own system of interaction.

Defense against blame

Characteristically the mothers in these families defend themselves by "transfer of blame." Such a defense follows from the mother's consistent manifestation of incongruent levels: what she does, she qualifies as not having been done or not done in that way. If the child becomes disturbed, it happens "out of the blue." If anything goes wrong, mother indicates it is the fault of someone else. In those rare instances where she does admit she did something wrong, she indicates she did it only because she was told to, or out of duty, so that it wasn't her fault. She may also indicate that something must be wrong with the other person, since he ought not to have been affected by what she did, particularly when she didn't really do it. Even when her behavior affects someone pleasantly, she must deny that it was her fault. Typically she presents herself as helplessly pushed by forces outside her control.

The fathers also follow the family rule of incongruently qualifying their messages, yet they cannot use the same denial of blame and remain with their wives. They tend to use types of defense which complement her defense, and these are of three kinds: 1) Fathers who are withdrawn and passive, accept the blame their wives put upon them, but indicate by their unresponsiveness that they are blamed falsely and do not agree with her. 2) Fathers who have temper tantrums and blame their wives, put the blame on false or exaggerated grounds so the wife can easily point out her innocence. This type of father is easily blamed since he is dominating and tyrannical, yet by going too far he indicates he is an innocent victim driven by forces outside his control. 3) Some fathers do not blame their wives but also do not blame themselves or anyone else. Such fathers make an issue of semantic difference. If asked if they or their wives are at fault, a typical reply is, "Just what do you mean by 'fault'?" By accepting no implicit definition and not defining anything themselves, they obscure everything. Any particular father may manifest these three types of defenses, all of which involve both disqualification of one's own statements and a disqualification of the other person's statements.

The child tends to use two types of defense. When "sane" he may blame himself and indicate that everything wrong with the family centers in him, an attitude the parents encourage, while at the same time he gives an impression of being blamed unjustly. When "insane" he negates his own statements and those of others by denying that anything happened. Or, if it did, he wasn't there—besides it wasn't him and it happened in another place at a time when he had no control over himself. The "withdrawal from reality" maneuvers of the schizophrenic make it impossible for him to blame himself or his parents since he defines himself as not of this world.

THE "DIFFERENT" BEHAVIOR OF THE SCHIZOPHRENIC

The inability of the schizophrenic to relate to people and his general withdrawal behavior seem understandable if he was raised in a learning situation where whatever he did was disqualified and if he was not allowed to relate to other people where he could learn to behave differently. Should he be reared in a situation where each attempt he made to gain a response from someone was met with an indication that he should behave in some other way, it would be possible for an individual to learn to avoid trying to relate to people by indicating that whatever he does is not done in relationship to anyone. He would then appear "autistic." However, the peculiar distortions of communication by the schizophrenic are not sufficiently explained by this description of his learning situation. If schizophrenic behavior is adaptive to a particular type of family, it is necessary to suggest the adaptive function involved when a person behaves in a clearly psychotic way.

The recovering schizophrenic patient, and perhaps the pre-psychotic schizophrenic, will qualify what he says in a way similar to that used by his parents. His behavior could be said to be "normal" for that family. However, during a psychotic episode the schizophrenic behaves in a rather unique manner. To suggest how such behavior might serve a function in the family, it is necessary both to describe schizophrenia in terms of behavior and to suggest the conditions under which such behavior might occur. To describe schizophrenic behavior, it is necessary to translate into behavioral terms such diagnostic concepts as delusions, hallucinations, concretistic thinking, and so on.

What appears unique about schizophrenic behavior is the incongruence of all levels of communication. The patient's parents may say something and disqualify it, but they will affirm that disqualification. The schizophrenic will say something, deny saying it, but qualify his denial in an incongruent way. Schizophrenic behavior described in this way has been presented elsewhere (10), but it may be summarized briefly here.

Not only can a person manifest an incongruence between levels of total message, but also between elements of his messages. A message from one person to another can be formalized into the following statement: *I (source) am communicating (message) to you (receiver) in this context.*

By his body movement, vocal inflections, and verbal statements a person must affirm or disqualify each of the elements of this message. The symptoms of a schizophrenic can be summarized in terms of this schema.

1) *Source.* A person may indicate that *he* isn't really the source of a message by indicating that he is only transmitting the idea of someone else. Therefore he says something but qualifies it with a denial that *he* is saying it. The schizophrenic may also qualify the source of the message in this way, but he will qualify his qualifications in an incongruent way. For example, a male schizophrenic patient reported that his name was Margaret Stalin. Thus he indicated that *he* wasn't really speaking, but by making his denial clearly

fantastic he disqualified his denial that he was speaking. Similarly a patient may say the "voices" are making the statement. In the excerpt presented, the patient denies that *he* is responsible for the greeting card message by saying "they sell them in the canteen," and yet this denial is by its nature self-disqualifying and so his messages become incongruent at all levels.

2) *Message.* A person may indicate in various ways that his words or action are not really a message. He may indicate, for example, that what he did was accidental if he blurts something out or if he steps on someone's foot. The schizophrenic may indicate that his statement isn't a message but merely a group of words, or he may speak in a random, or word salad, way, thus indicating that he isn't really communicating. Yet at the same time he manages to indicate some pertinent points in his word salad, thus disqualifying his denial that his message is a message. In the excerpt given above, the patient says, "a card is a card," as a way of denying the message communicated. He also says that he doesn't remember what the thing was, thus denying the message existed for him. However, both these qualifications of the message are also disqualified: the card obviously isn't merely a card, and he can hardly not remember what the thing was when he is looking at it.

3) *Receiver.* A person may deny this element in a message in various ways, for example by indicating he isn't really talking to the particular person he is addressing, but rather to that person's status. The schizophrenic patient is likely to indicate that the doctor he is talking to isn't really a doctor, but, say, an FBI agent. Thereby he not only denies talking to the physician, but by labeling the receiver in a clearly fantastic way he disqualifies his denial. Paranoid delusionary statements of this sort become "obvious" by their self-negating quality.

4) *Context.* A person may disqualify his statement by indicating that it applies to some other context than the one in which it is made. *Context* is defined broadly here as the situation in which people are communicating, including both the physical situation and the stated premises about what sort of situation it is. For example, a woman may be aggressively sexual in a public place where the context disqualifies her overtures. The typical statement that the schizophrenic is "withdrawn from reality" seems to be based to a great extent on the ways he qualifies what he says by mislabeling the context. He may say his hospital conversation is taking place in a palace, or in prison, and thereby disqualify his statements. Since his labels are clearly impossible, his disqualification is disqualified.

These multiple incongruent levels of communication differentiate the schizophrenic from his parents and from other people. If a person says something and then negates his statement we judge him by his other levels of message. When these too are incongruent so that he says something, indicates he didn't, then affirms one or the other, and then disqualifies his affirmation, there is a tendency to call such a person insane.

From the point of view offered here, schizophrenia is an intermittent type of behavior. The patient may be behaving in a schizophrenic way at one moment and in a way that is "normal" for this type of family at another moment. The important question is this: under what circumstances does he behave in a psychotic way, defined here as qualifying incongruently all his levels of message?

In this excerpt of a family interaction, the patient shows psychotic behavior when he is caught between a therapist pressuring him to affirm his statements and his parents pressuring him to disqualify them. From this point of view, the patient is faced with a situation where he must infringe the rules of his relationship with the therapist or infringe his family rules. His psychotic behavior can be seen as an attempt to adapt to both.[2] By behaving in a psychotic way he could 1) affirm his statement about his mother, thus following the rule in the therapeutic relationship for affirmative statements, 2) disqualify his critical statement of the mother, thus following the family rules that mother is not to be blamed in a way so that she can accept blame and all statements are to be disqualified, and 3) synthesize these two incompatible theses by indicating that the message wasn't his (it wasn't really a message, he couldn't remember it, and he didn't really send it). It can be argued that psychotic behavior is a sequence of messages which infringe a set of prohibitions but which are qualified as not infringing them. The only way an individual can achieve this is by qualifying incongruently all levels of his communication.

The need to behave in a psychotic way would seem to occur when the patient infringes a family prohibition and thereby activates himself and his parents to behave in such a way that he either returns within the previous system of rules or indicates somehow that he is not infringing them. Should he successfully infringe the system of family rules and thereby set new rules, his parents may become "disturbed." This seems to occur rather often when the patient living at home "improves" with therapy. When improving in therapy he is not only infringing the family prohibitions against outside alliances but he may blame the mother in a reasonable way and affirm his statements or those of others. Such behavior on his part would shatter the family system unless the parents are also undergoing therapy. The omnipotent feelings of the schizophrenic patient may have some basis, since his family system is so rigid that he can create considerable repercussions by behaving differently.

A patient is faced with infringing family prohibitions when 1) two family prohibitions conflict with each other and he must respond to both, 2) when forces outside the family, or maturational forces within himself, require him to infringe them, or 3) when prohibitions special to him conflict with prohibitions applying to all family members. If he must infringe such prohibitions and at the same time not infringe them, he can only do so through psychotic behavior.

Conflicting sets of prohibitions may occur when the individual is involved with both mother and therapist, involved with a therapist and administrator in a hospital setting (19), or when some shift within his own family brings prohibitions into conflict. This latter would seem the most likely bind the patient would find himself in when living at home, and an incident is offered here to describe psychotic behavior serving a function in the family.

A twenty-one-year-old schizophrenic daughter arrived home from the hospital for a trial visit and her parents promptly separated. The mother asked the girl to go with her, and when she arrived at their destination, the grand-

---

[2]An attempt to synthesize two incompatible situations by a perceptual change is suggested in Weakland and Jackson (22). Describing an incident during a psychotic breakdown, they say, "Psychotic delusions allowed him to free himself of decision making. For example, the cab driver is a hospital attendant in disguise. There is no problem in Home vs. Hospital; it has been resolved."

mother's home, the patient telephoned her father. Her mother asked her why she turned against her by calling the father, and the daughter said she called him to say goodbye and because she had looked at him with an "odd" look when they left. A typical symptom of this patient when overtly psychotic is her perception of "odd" looks, and the problem is how such a message is adaptive to the family pattern of interaction.

The incident could be described in this way. The mother separated from father but qualified her leaving incongruently by saying it was only temporary and telling him where she was going. The father objected to the mother's leaving, but made no attempt to restrain her or to persuade her to stay. The daughter had to respond to this situation in accord with the prohibitions set by this family system: she had to disqualify whatever she did, she had to disqualify what her mother and father did, she could not ally with either mother or father and acknowledge it, and she could not blame the mother in such a way that the mother would accept the blame.

The girl could not merely do nothing because this would mean remaining with father. However, by going with the mother she in effect formed an alliance and so infringed one of the prohibitions in the family system. The girl solved the problem by going with mother but telephoning her father, thus disqualifying her alliance with mother. However, her mother objected to the call, and the daughter said she only called him to say goodbye, thus disqualifying her alliance with father. Yet to leave it this way would mean allying with mother. She qualified her statement further by saying she called father because she gave him an "odd look" when she left him. By having an odd look, she could succeed in not siding with either parent or blaming mother. She also manifested schizophrenic behavior by qualifying incongruently all levels of message and thereby adapting to incongruent family prohibitions. Previously the girl could withdraw to her room to avoid the alliance problem, but when mother stopped staying home while saying she was going to leave, and left while saying she was not really leaving, the girl was threatened by a possible alliance whether she went with her mother or stayed at home. Her incongruent, schizophrenic behavior would seem necessary to remain within the prohibitions of the family at those times. If one is required to behave in a certain way and simultaneously required not to, he can only solve the problem by indicating that *he* is not behaving at all, or not with this particular person in this situation. The girl might also have solved the problem by disqualifying her identity, indicating the context was really a secret plot, indicating that what she did was what voices told her to do, or speaking in a random or word salad way. In other words, she could both meet the prohibitions in the family and infringe them only by disqualifying the source of her messages, the nature of them, the recipient, or the context, and so behave in a psychotic fashion.

It is important to emphasize that schizophrenic behavior in the family is adaptive to an intricate and complicated family organization which is presented here in crude simplicity. The network of family prohibitions confronts the individual members with almost insoluble problems. This particular incident was later discussed with the parents of this girl, and the mother said her daughter could have solved the problem easily. She could have stayed with father and told him he was wrong in the quarrel which provoked the separation. This would seem to be the mother's usual way of dealing with this kind of situation—she stays with father while telling him he is wrong. However, the mother leaves herself out of this solution by ignoring the fact that she asked her daughter to go with her. This request was even more complicated—the mother asked the daughter to go with her during a period when the mother was saying the daughter must return to the hospital because she could not tolerate associating with her. When the parents reunited later that week, the girl was returned to the hospital because mother said she could not stand daughter in the room watching her, and she could not stand daughter out of the room thinking about her.

The approach offered here differs from the usual psychodynamic explanations. It would be possible to say that the mother's concern about leaving the daughter with the father, even when she could not tolerate the girl's company, might center in the family's concern about incestuous desires between father and daughter. Such a psychodynamic hypothesis could be supported. Later in therapy the father and daughter planned a picnic alone together when they decided they should see more of each other without the mother being present. The evening of the day this was arranged, the therapist received a telephone call from the disturbed mother. She reported that she and her husband had been drinking and arguing all evening and she reported that her husband had told her it was natural for a father to have sexual relations with his daughter. The husband's report was that he had not said this. (He had said it was natural for a father to have sexual *feelings* for his daughter, but this did not mean he would do anything about it.) This crisis over suggested possible incest could be explained by saying that the threat of closeness between father and daughter aroused forbidden incestuous desires in them. However, it was the mother who made an issue over the possible incest. From the psychodynamic point of view, hints and discussions of incest would represent unconscious conflicts. From the point of view offered here, this type of discussion is an aspect of family strategy. To label a relationship as possibly incestuous would be one further way of enforcing a prohibition on alliances between father and daughter. Such a maneuver is similar to one where the mother inhibits a relationship between father and daughter by insisting that the father should associate more with the daughter, thus arousing his negative behavior as well as the issue of whether he neglected the daughter. The approach offered here does not deal with supposed motivating forces within the individuals concerned, but with the formal characteristics of their behavior with each other.[3]

THE FUNCTION OF FAMILY BEHAVIOR

The difficulty for this type of family would seem to lie in the inflexibility of their family system. They often maintain the system despite the sturdy attempts of a family therapist to help them deal with each other more amicably. Apparently family members gain only discord, dissension, and a constant

[3]Although statements in the form of family rules deal with observable behavior and are therefore verifiable, the verification depends to some extent upon the skill of the observer. Such statements are more reliably documented by placing the family in a structured experimental situation where the results depend upon whether or not the family functions under certain prohibitions. The Bateson project is now beginning a program of experiments with families similar to the small group experiments of Alex Bavelas.

struggle with one another, or periods of withdrawal in a kind of truce, yet they continue so to behave. It would be possible to postulate psychodynamic causes for this type of behavior, or self-destructive drives could be sought, but an attempt is made here to develop an alternative descriptive language centering on the peculiar sensitivity of people to the fact that their behavior is governed by others.

When people respond to one another they inevitably influence how the other person is to respond to them. Whatever one says, or doesn't say, in response to another person is a determinant of the other person's behavior. For example, if one criticizes another, he is indicating that critical statements from him are permissible in the relationship. The other person cannot not respond, and whatever response he makes will govern the critical person's behavior. Whether the criticized one gets angry, or weeps helplessly, or passively accepts the criticism, he must either be accepting the rules or countering with other rules. These rules for relationships which people establish with each other are never permanently set but are in a constant process of reinforcement as the two people interact and govern each other's behavior.

Every human being depends upon other people not only for his survival but for his pleasure and pain. It is of primary importance that he learn to govern the responses of other people so they will provide him satisfaction. Yet a person can only gain satisfaction in a relationship if he permits others to cooperate in setting the rules for the relationship and so influence and govern him. The person who dare not risk such control over him would seem to provoke his own misery by attempting to avoid it. If someone has suffered a series of hurts and frustrations with people he trusted, he tends to try to become independent of people—by not getting involved with them in such a way that they can gain control over his feelings or his behavior. He may literally avoid people; he may interact with them only on his own terms, constantly making an issue of who is going to circumscribe whose behavior; or he may choose the schizophrenic way and indicate that nothing he does is done in relationship to other people. In this fashion he is not governing anyone and no one is governing him.

The family of the schizophrenic would seem to be not only establishing and following a system of rules, as other families do, but also following a prohibition on any acknowledgement that a family member is setting rules. Each refuses to concede that he is circumscribing the behavior of others, and each refuses to concede that any other family member is governing him. Since communication inevitably occurs if people live together, and since whatever one communicates inevitably governs the behavior of others, the family members must each constantly disqualify the communications of one another. Should one affirm what he does or what another does, he risks conceding that he is governed by the other with all the consequences that follow being disappointed again by an untrustworthy person. Schizophrenic behavior can be seen as both a product and a parody of this kind of family system. By labeling everything he communicates as not communicated by him to this person in this place, the schizophrenic indicates that he is not governing anyone's behavior because he is not in a relationship with anyone. This would seem to be a necessary style of behavior at times in this type of family system, and it may become habitual behavior. Yet even psychotic behavior does not free the individual from being governed or from governing others. The person who insists that he does not need anyone at all and is completely independent of them requires people to put him in a hospital and to force feed him. To live at all one must be involved with other people and so deal with the universal problem of who is going to circumscribe whose behavior. The more a person tries to avoid being governed or governing others, the more helpless he becomes and so governs others by forcing them to take care of him.

A MODEL FOR DIFFERENTIATING TYPES OF FAMILIES

What is lacking in the study of interpersonal relations is a method of describing, by way of some analogy, the process which takes place when two or more people interact with one another. Although there are models for inner activity, e.g., the id-ego-superego metaphor, there is not yet a model for human interaction. Implicit in the approach to the schizophrenic family offered here there is such a model. The essential elements of it are: 1) the proposition that human communication can be classified into levels of message, 2) the cybernetic idea of the self-corrective, governed system. If a family confines itself to repetitive patterns within a certain range of possible behavior, then they are confined to that range by some sort of governing process. No outside governor requires the family members to behave in their habitual patterns, so this governing process must exist within the family. A third essential point is that when people respond to one another they govern, or establish rules, for each other's behavior.

To describe families, the most appropriate analogy would seem to be the self-corrective system governed by family members influencing each other's behavior and thereby establishing rules and prohibitions for that particular family system. Such a system tends to be error-activated. Should one family member break a family rule, the others become activated until he either conforms to the rule again or successfully establishes a new one.

A system of three organisms each governing the range of behavior of the other two, and each communicating at multiple levels, is both a simple idea and a complex model. Yet such an approach offers a general theoretical framework within which the specific rules of any one type of family system can be classified. The rudiments of such a system are suggested here at the most general level. The family of the schizophrenic is a particularly good model for this approach because of the narrow limits of their system. Our few preliminary observations of families containing children without symptoms, children who are delinquent, and children with asthma lead us to believe that the interaction in the family of the schizophrenic is unique. Members of other types of family sometimes disqualify each other's statements but only under certain circumstances. Mutual affirmation will also occur. We have observed, for example, parents of an asthmatic child finishing each other's sentences and having this approved. Should the father of a schizophrenic finish the mother's sentence, it seems inevitable that she would indicate he provided the wrong ending. In other families leadership will stabilize into a pattern accepted by family members. Certain alliances will be allowed in some types of families, notably the delinquent where the child is capable of forming labeled alliances in gangs outside the family. In the family of the schizophrenic the range of behavior is as limited and inflexible as is the behavior of the schizo-phrenic in contrast to other people.

The observation of this type of family system inevitably takes place after the child has manifested a schizophrenic episode. Whether the family behaved in a similar way prior to his diagnosis is unknowable. In this sense it is difficult to assert that the interaction in his family "caused" schizophrenia. There are two possibilities. 1) If the family is a self-corrective system and the child behaves intermittently in a schizophrenic way, then schizophrenic behavior is a neces-sary part of this family system. 2) Alternatively, schizophrenic behavior is a result of a particular family system which has been disrupted by forces outside the system, such as maturation of the child or environmental influence. The family then reorganizes a new system which includes the schizophrenic behavior as an element, and this is what we are presently examining. The evidence leads us to believe that schizophrenic behavior in the child is rein-forced by the present family system.

Although psychotic behavior may serve a function in a family system, a risk is also involved. The patient may need to be separated from the family by hospitalization and so break up the system, or he may enter therapy and change and so leave the system. Typically the parents seem to welcome hospitalization only if the patient is still accessible to them, and they welcome therapy for the patient up to the point when he begins to change and infringe the rules of the family system while acknowledging that he is doing so.

REFERENCES

1. Alanen, Y. The mothers of schizophrenic patients. Acta psychiat. et neurol. scandinav., **33**: Suppl. 124, 1958.
2. Bateson, G. Cultural problems posed by a study of schizophrenic process. Presented at the American Psychiatric Association, Conference on Schizophrenia. Honolulu, 1958. In press.
3. Bateson, G. The group dynamics of schizophrenia. Presented at the Institute on Chronic Schizophrenia and Hospital Treatment Programs, Osawatomie State Hospital, Osawatomie, 1958. In press.
4. Bateson, G. The new conceptual frames for behavioral research. Presented at the Sixth Annual Psychiatric Institute Conference at the New Jersey Neuro-Psychiatric Institute, Princeton, New Jersey, 1958. In press.
5. Bateson, G., Jackson, D. D., Haley, J., and Weakland, J. Toward a theory of schizophrenia. Behavioral Sc., **1**: 251–264, 1956.
6. Bowen, M., Dysinger, R. H., and Basaminia, B. The role of the father in families with a schizophrenic patient. Paper presented at the annual meeting of the American Psychiatric Association, May, 1958.
7. Gerard, D. L., and Siegel, J. The family background of schizophrenia. Psychiat. Quart., **24**: 47–73, 1950.
8. Frazee, H. E. Children who later became schizophrenic. Smith. Coll. Stud. Social Work, **123**: 125–149, 1953.
9. Haley, J. Control in psychoanalytic psychotherapy. Progr. Psychotherapy, **4**: 48–65, 1959.
10. Haley, J. An interactional description of schizophrenia. Psychiatry, to be published.
11. Haley, J. An interactional explanation of hypnosis. Am. J. Clin. Hypnosis, **1**: 41–57, 1958.
12. Jackson, D. D. The question of family homeostasis. Psychoanalyt. Quart., **31**: Suppl; 79–90, 1957.
13. Lidz, R. W., and Lidz, T. The family environment of schizophrenic patients. Am. J. Psychiat., **106**: 332–345, 1949.
14. Lidz, T., Parker, B., and Cornelison, A. R. The role of the father in the family environment of the schizophrenic patient. Am. J. Psychiat., **113**: 126–132, 1956.

15. Lidz, T., Cornelison, A. R., Fleck, S., and Terry, D. The intrafamilial environment of schizophrenic patients. I. The Father. Psychiatry, **20**: 329–342, 1957.
16. Lidz, T., Cornelison, A. R., Fleck, S., and Terry, D. The intrafamilial environment of schizophrenic patients. II. Marital schism and marital skew. Am. J. Psychiat., **114**: 241–248, 1957.
17. Reichard, S., and Tillman, G. Patterns of parent-child relationships in schizophrenia. Psychiatry, **13**: 247–257, 1950.
18. Rosen, J. N. *Direct Analysis.* Grune & Stratton, New York, 1951.
19. Stanton, A. H., and Schwartz, M. S. *The Mental Hospital.* Basic Books, New York, 1954.
20. Tietze, T. A study of the mothers of schizophrenic patients. Psychiatry, **12**: 55–56, 1949.
21. Weakland, J. The double bind hypothesis of schizophrenia and three-party interaction. In *The Study of Schizophrenia.* Basic Books, New York. In press.
22. Weakland, J. H., and Jackson, D. D. Patient and therapist observations on the circumstances of a schizophrenic episode. A. M. A. Arch. Neurol. & Psychiat., **79**: 554–574, 1958.
23. Wynne, I. D., Ryckoff, I. M., Day, J., and Hirsch, S. E. Pseudomutuality in the family relations of schizophrenics. Psychiatry, **21**: 205–220, 1958.

Values and Family Therapy

Gerald H. Zuk

Two value systems commonly emerge in family conflict, one which may be labeled the "continuity" system, the other the "discontinuity" system. Symptoms in members tend to erupt after an impasse between competing values which tends to produce pathogenic relating. The therapist addresses both symptoms and underlying value conflict.

Therapist interventions take three forms: as a go-between who facilitates communication; as a side-taker who takes positions pro or con on family issues; and as a celebrant who is a societal representative of continuity in the face of crisis and transition. In each form the therapist exerts special leverage by expressing "continuity" or "discontinuity" values, depending on the current condition of the family, in particular an assessment of pathogenic relating among members.

Most family therapy is short-term because, despite the interest of the therapist in an extended relationship needed for new learning, that is the way most families want it. Therefore, the best method will be that which most effectively accommodates itself to the relatively brief time-frame allowed by the majority of families. The paper describes aspects of a method which is especially suited to the brief time-frame, although not limited by it, and which is believed to produce consistently good results in either short- or long-term cases.

In the early days of family therapy—meaning in the early 1950s—when its major thrust was to investigate family dynamics associated with schizophrenia, and to test its efficacy as a therapy of schizophrenia, the problem of values in family therapy and dynamics was considered of subsidiary importance and given little consideration. The two major factions in family therapy in the fifties, the analytically-oriented therapists and the communicationists, hardly addressed the problem.

MAJOR ACHIEVEMENTS IN FAMILY THERAPY

From 1950 through the early 1960s

Of advances in this period, there are four that seem most significant: (1) A confirmation of Harry Stack Sullivan's view that it took longer to "learn"

"Values and Family Therapy," by Gerald Zuk. In *Psychotherapy: Theory, Research, and Practice*, Vol. 15, No. 1, Spring 1978, pp. 48–55. Copyright 1978 by American Psychological Association, Division of Psychotherapy. Reprinted by permission.

schizophrenia than infancy and early childhood, but that adolescence and young adulthood were also important stages in causation, and that the family was a key source of systematic reinforcement for the kind of learning necessary to produce the illness. (2) The double-bind hypothesis, conceived by the Palo Alto Group (Bateson et al., 1956), although not the complete explanation of schizophrenia they had hoped, nor effective as a treatment method, was the most original, creative concept of the period in that it showed how families systematically reinforced irrational modes of thinking in members prone to schizophrenia. (3) While family therapy proved neither more nor less effective as a treatment method than other psychotherapies, it did produce some remarkable instances of symptom reduction in schizophrenics—sometimes in a remarkably brief period. (4) Family therapy experience confirmed the notion that schizophrenia was an illness of diverse origins which clearly ran different courses in individuals.

The intense focus of the 1950s on schizophrenia may itself have contributed to a disinterest in the problem of values in family therapy, for it is such a dramatic phenomenon that it tends to mute others. In their work with families, the analytically-oriented therapists maintained the traditional neutral stance toward values, and the communicationists practically duplicated their attitude. When values were mentioned, they seemed to basically reflect the white, middle class family value system. Only one of the early workers in the field (Midelfort, 1957) suggested it was helpful if the therapist was familiar with the ethnic and religious origins of the psychiatric patient and his family; or even that he be a member of the same ethnic-religious group.

From the mid-1960s through mid-1970s

With the advent of the community mental health movement in the mid-1960s family therapy underwent a radical change. For the first time therapists began to see a wide range of families presenting diverse problems. Many referrals were made as "behavior problems" bearing little if any relation to accepted psychiatric nosology. In my opinion the five major advances of the period have been as follows: (1) A commitment to crisis-oriented, short-term or brief family therapy as opposed to other models, due mainly to the fact that this was the model that *families* would accept. (2) A commitment to the problem of how to engage families in therapy, due to the fact that so many were lost during attempts to engage them. Once engagement "took," it appeared that various short- and long-term therapy models could be successful. (3) A commitment to exploring the value systems by which families operated, due to the growing conviction that the family value system was among the most important determinants of whether a family would become engaged in therapy. (4) A focus on values expressed by the *therapist* and on values attributed by the *family to the therapist*, such as might be related to their expectations about the therapy or its outcome. Analytically-oriented therapists in the 1960s were suggesting that beginners should undergo a personal experience in family therapy or a study of their own families. Although this never did gain much acceptance, in the 1970s it became obvious that therapists had to be more sensitive to the values they were communicating to families, and also more sensitive to the family values which might restrict or limit their readiness for therapy. (5) A focus on the *nuclear* family rather than three or more generations, particularly on the marital couple, due to the difficulty of involving more than two generations in therapy and the large increase in referrals presenting a discordant marriage. I think it is also true that even in cases where children had been identified as symptomatic, therapists increasingly came to focus on the marital couple as the "source" of the symptoms.

FAMILY VALUE SYSTEMS

Goal and definition

The aim of this section is to present a system of values used by families. In the next section "Technique in Family Therapy," there will be an attempt to relate values to family therapy technique.

There are many definitions of the word value, but here it will mean *an attitude, belief or way of evaluating events that typifies a person or group*. The focus on values reflects my belief that it is a central issue in any broadly-based theory of family therapy.

Conflict in families

Elicitation of conflict often consumes a major portion of family interviews, and rightly so because conflict provides rich material for the therapist. The issues over which family members quarrel probably number in the hundreds. Therapists listen to arguments over family finances, childrearing practices, relations with extended family and friends, job commitment of the husband versus his expected duties at home, and so on. These are the "contents" of some of the manifold quarrels, but conflict can also be viewed from the perspective of the "parties" involved. In family therapy, because the nuclear family is present in most instances, there are three main "parties": (1) males versus females, especially husbands versus wives; (2) the older versus younger generation, especially parents versus children; and (3) the nuclear family versus other, usually larger social units, such as the extended family, the neighborhood or institutions.

In family interviews husbands and wives can and do accuse each other of all sorts of misdeeds, bad intentions, or lies. Sometimes this is done in an open manner, sometimes not. Another male versus female conflict is that between brother and sister. Conflict between parents and children is also common in family interviews. It may be over the disarray of the child's bedroom. Or it may be about the selection of the first "date" of the adolescent, or the hour he or she is expected home from dates. Still later it may be about the choice of careers. Generational conflict may also exist between parents and *their* parents. It may, for example, arise when parents' parents remind them of supposed duties or obligations to other family members. Conflict between the nuclear family and other social units is commonly observed in family interviews. In some instances there is squabbling with neighbors because children have trespassed property. A family receiving welfare payments may be challenged to show why payments should be continued. Parents may be upset with the school which sends home a poor report card on a child. Or a child may be brought home by police after being picked up on suspicion of delinquency.

Two value systems in families

Observation in family interviews suggests that, with respect to values expressed toward each other, the "parties" do not enter into conflict in a completely random manner. For example, in conflict between husbands and wives, wives are more likely to express certain values than their husbands. These I have referred to elsewhere (Zuk, 1975) as "continuity" values. The values expressed by husbands were designated "discontinuity" values. Furthermore, I suggested that the "continuity-discontinuity" polarity held with respect to values expressed in conflict between parents and their children, with children commonly expressing the "continuity" values, parents the "discontinuity" values. And in conflict between the nuclear family and other social units, the nuclear family expressed "continuity" values while charging other social units, such as the neighborhood, with holding "discontinuity" values. When a wife had conflict with her husband, she took the "continuity" position; but when there was conflict between parents and children, she then joined her husband in maintaining "discontinuity" values. So it was possible for a family member, depending on which "parties" were in conflict, to switch sides from the "continuity" to "discontinuity" position. To know specifically what the "continuity" and "discontinuity" value systems are composed of, Table 1 is reproduced (from Zuk, 1975, p. 29).

TABLE 1. Categories of Contrasting Values Expressed in Family Interviews

	Values	
Categories	"Continuity"	"Discontinuity"
1. Affective/Attitudinal	Empathic, Sympathetic, "Warm"	Distant, Reserved, "Cool"
2. Moral/Ethical	Anticonformist, Idealistic, Egalitarian	Disciple of Law and Codes, Pragmatic, Elitist
3. Cognitive/Conceptual	Intuitive, Holistic	Analytic, Systematic
4. Tasks/Goals	Nurturing, Caretaking	Achieving, Structuring

There are four categories listed within the two value systems: (1) the affective/attitudinal; (2) the moral/ethical; (3) the cognitive/perceptual; and (4) tasks/goals. The affective/attitudinal category distinguishes those affects, emotions or attitudes that may be labeled empathic, sympathetic or "warm" from those that may be labeled distant, reserved or "cool." The former are "continuity," the latter "discontinuity." The moral/ethical category distinguishes anticonformist, idealistic and egalitarian values ("continuity") from values expressed by the disciple of law, order and codes, and pragmatic and elitist values ("discontinuity"). The cognitive/perceptual category distinguishes intuitive and holistic values ("continuity") from the values of system and analysis ("discontinuity"). The tasks/goals category distinguishes the values of nurturing and caretaking ("continuity") from those expressed by the desire for achievement and structure ("discontinuity").

As an example of how the table applies to family life, let us consider the very common conflict over childrearing practices. When we hear arguments between husband and wife over the raising of children, typically it is the wife who accuses her husband of misunderstanding the situation due to his distance, reserve and acting too "cool." She may simply accuse him of not caring, of being uninvolved. The husband, on the other hand, typically responds (retaliates may be the more appropriate word) that his wife is the victim of her emotions when it comes to the children: she is too sympathetic, too "warm." He says she lacks proper perspective. This is an example of the "continuity-discontinuity" division of values expressed along the affective/attitudinal axis. Of course, there are exceptions to the rule (as in clinical work there are always exceptions), but the pattern exists.

In a childrearing conflict in which the parents and children are at odds, more commonly the children accuse the parents of holding "discontinuity" values, and the parents accuse the children of holding "continuity" values. The argument, for example, may be over the time the children are expected home for dinner. The parents have set the time and the children persistently are tardy and give weak excuses. When the issue is confronted, the children typically charge the parents as too rule-and-regulation oriented. The parents maintain that the children are disobedient or rebellious and anticonformist. The conflict is typically waged along the moral/ethical dimension of the "continuity-discontinuity" value system structure.

In a childrearing conflict in which the nuclear family and other social units such as the neighborhood are engaged, more commonly the nuclear family takes the "continuity" position, the neighborhood the "discontinuity" position. An example is the neighbor who complains to parents that their children are making too much noise, or have damaged property. The parents are inclined to defend their children by insisting that all children are noisy or break things and that the neighbors should make allowances. The neighbors reply that good parents discipline their children for misbehavior, and that the attractiveness of the neighborhood must be maintained. Here again is the "continuity-discontinuity" dispersion mainly expressed along the ethical/moral dimension.

The nuclear family versus other social unit conflict can itself be further broken down into conflict over race, ethnic origin, religion, social class level, and even political association. For example, in family interviews with blacks, it is not uncommon to hear whites described as too achievement oriented, too impersonal, too rational. On the other hand, with whites blacks are described as impulsive, lacking in orderliness. The whites are usually assigned the "discontinuity" values, the blacks the "continuity" values.

In interviews with families of Southern European origin, persons of Northern European origin will be labeled too reserved, too controlled, too orderly. Southerners will be described by Northerners as impulsive, overemotional. In interviews with middle class families, lower class will be described as impulsive, unorganized, overemotional. Lower class families will refer to the middle class as too rigid, overcontrolled, too orderly and systematic. Gentiles will refer to Jews as too achievement oriented, too conscious of material well-being; while Jews will criticize Gentiles for being wishy-washy, hypocritical in their ideals and methods. Families whose politics are conservative will describe those with liberal politics as wishy-washy, prone to idealize; whereas liberal families will criticize conservatives as too rational, too rigid. In these comparisons also there is a nonrandom assignment of values according to the "continuity-discontinuity" system.

The power concept in relation to values

In an interesting paper, Distler (1970) contends that there is a revolution among youth due to a culture shift from what he terms a patristic-instrumental culture to a more matristic-expressive culture. He refers to hippies as a prime example of a youth group which has adopted values of their mothers. He cites Adler to the effect that in the history of Western society there have been shifts between the patristic-instrumental and matristic-expressive. He also cites Keniston and Gutmann's formulation that alienated, uncommitted young men were in effect "living out" their mother's unresolved identity crisis.

In a brilliant paper written originally in German in 1932, Fromm (1970) indicates the likelihood of the change from the patriarchal to a matriarchal structure of society. Fromm cites the theory of J. J. Bachofen, the German sociologist-philosopher, who in 1861 first published "Mother Right." According to Bachofen, the matriarchal principle is that of life, unity and peace. Through caring for her infant, the mother extends her love beyond herself to others with the aim of preserving and beautifying the existence of others. While the matriarchal principle is that of universality, the patriarchal principle is that of restrictions. Along with Distler, Fromm notes that certain matriarchal tendencies can be observed in radical youth, and he cites other evidence of an increasing matriarchal trend in Western society today. Referring to the fact that in history matriarchy and patriarchy have frequently clashed, Fromm says that in other instances they have formed a creative synthesis, as in the case of the Catholic Church and Marx's concept of socialism. But when they are opposed to each other, dire consequences for the individual can result:

> ... the matriarchal principle manifests itself in motherly overindulgence and infantilization of the child, preventing its full maturity; fatherly authority becomes harsh denomination (sic) and control, based on the child's fear and feelings of guilt. ... The purely matriarchal society stands in the way of the full development of the individual, thus preventing technical, rational, artistic progress. The purely patriarchal society cares nothing for love and equality; it is only concerned with man-made laws, the state, abstract principles, obedience. (p. 83)

I would refer the reader to Table 1 at this point, because there is more than a passing resemblance between the "continuity" value system and what Fromm and Bachofen described for the matriarchal system, and between the "discontinuity" value system and what they described for the patriarchal system.

Has there been a shift from the patriarchal to the matriarchal in recent decades, as Fromm suggested? Parsons (1955) and his colleagues suggest and provide evidence that the nuclear family has emerged as the dominant family form in recent decades. I have suggested (Zuk, 1971) that under the pressures of American society, the nuclear family is inevitably one in which the mother assumes an increasingly central role with her children, the father an increasingly peripheral role. The tendency of children is to overlearn or over-identify with the values expressed by their mothers, with the result that they are poorly adapted to the values dominant in society which are primarily male values. I prefer the terms "continuity" and "discontinuity" rather than matriarchal and patriarchal (or expressive and instrumental, following Parsons), because I believe they are more inclusive, but my conclusion regarding the fate of children in present-day society is the same as that of Fromm and the others. Because they are so identified with the values of their mothers ("continuity" values) and because these values differ from those held by their fathers ("discontinuity" values), children, particularly males, are bound to have a difficult transition as they make their way into a society still dominated by male ("discontinuity") values.

Thus I agree with Fromm and the others when they suggest that Western society has shifted in the direction of the matriarchal principle, but do not think this should be taken to mean that Western, specifically American, society *is* matriarchal. On the contrary, it is still overwhelmingly patriarchal (although I would prefer to say that it overwhelmingly reflects "discontinuity" values). Yet in that essential unit of society which is the nuclear family, "continuity" values *have* become dominant. Children and their mothers are allied against and antagonistic toward fathers and society, and the result for the individual in society reflects this condition of stress. The peculiar dilemma of fathers is that they have been caught between what Alvin Toffler has referred to as "future shock" and a further gradual weakening of their position in the nuclear family as a result of declining ties with the extended family. I think these factors are interrelated: rapid technological advance has required greater mobility on the part of the nuclear family, which has weakened ties with extended family (which validated and confirmed the importance of the father's role in the nuclear family), and the result is a decline in the father's role.

Generally speaking, those who take the "continuity" position in conflict situations tend to think of themselves and be thought of as less powerful than those who take the "discontinuity" position. Less powerful can refer to physical or numerical strength, or to material wealth. For instance, women as wives tend to think of themselves as less powerful than men as husbands. Children tend to think of themselves as less powerful than parents. And the nuclear family believes itself to be less powerful than other social units. Historically women, children and the nuclear family have been less powerful when compared to men, parents and other social units. In times past, the power differential was significantly greater than it is today, and I would surmise that the evolution of value systems in society has played a prominent role in reducing the power differential. As men and women, parents and children, and the nuclear family and other social units have related to each other over the centuries, have struggled with one another and sought to resolve those struggles, and as a result of powerful pressures brought to bear by technological and other cultural innovations, new values have evolved to characterize the relationships. The trend of these new values, in my opinion, has been to reduce the power differential between the groups, although not totally erasing it.

TECHNIQUE IN FAMILY THERAPY

I have previously laid out (Zuk, 1971, 1975) what seemed to me the basic functions of the family therapist which, taken together, constitute the whole of his role: (1) when he acts as go-between; (2) when he acts as side-taker; and (3) when he acts as celebrant. But I have not pointed to an interrelation of these role functions with the "continuity-discontinuity" value system structure, and will do so here. I hope to show that within each of the role functions the therapist responds basically in either of two ways: either in accord with the "continuity" position, or the "discontinuity" position. In carrying out his role, the therapist is always expressing values of one sort or another, and I think it is helpful if he recognizes that these values are essentially of the two types considered at some length in this paper.

As go-between the therapist mediates or facilitates discussion with and within the family, or he sets limits and imposes rules which are intended to regulate discussion. As indicated in Table 2, when the therapist mediates or facilitates discussion, he is espousing "continuity" values. When he sets limits and imposes rules, he is espousing "discontinuity" values.

TABLE 2. Values in Relation to the Therapist's Role

Role Functions of Therapist	Values	
	"Continuity"	"Discontinuity"
1. Go-Between	Mediator, facilitator of communication	Sets limits, imposes rules or regulation on communication
2. Side-Taker	Sides with wife against husband, children against parents, nuclear family against community	Sides with husband against wife, parents against children, community against nuclear family
3. Celebrant	Espouses mercy, compassion, forgiveness	Espouses justice, upholds law, codes, regulations

As side-taker, the therapist aligns himself with one party or another in the family; he is, so to speak, for or against certain family members in disputes that arise in interviews. If, for example, he sides with a wife against her husband, or a child against parents, or the nuclear family against another social unit, he is espousing "continuity" values. If he sides in the opposite direction in the combinations mentioned above, then he is espousing "discontinuity" values.

As celebrant, the therapist certifies family events or happenings as either important or unimportant, relevant or irrelevant, and may comment on the nature or meaning of the event or happening for the family presently and in the future. When as celebrant the therapist expresses compassion, or speaks on behalf of mercy or forgiveness in the face of the event or happening, and asks family members to do likewise, then he is espousing "continuity" values. When, on the contrary, he expresses moral indignation, is stern and insists that justice be done in the face of the event or happening, then he is espousing "discontinuity" values.

Short-term therapy; The engagement process

In the past several years the trend in the field of family therapy toward short-term technique has been one of the notable events. The positive results of short-term work (Leventhal et al., 1975) are reasonably persuasive. Among the reasons given for the good results, one of the most significant is that the majority of families allow the therapist access for a limited amount of time. *Good results flow from the fact that the therapist does not abuse the brief time limit established by the majority of families.* It is odd that many therapists who are proponents of short-term methods appear quite oblivious to this. Rather they seem entrapped in the old argument with the advocates (usually psycho-analytically-oriented therapists) of the long-term approach in psychotherapy, based on the view that personality change was the major goal and that such change obviously required an extensive period of time. Many short-term advocates are preoccupied with proving, for example, how useless insight is in producing change, and thus fail to see that the majority of families will simply not tolerate long-term contact with a therapist.

In my view short-term methods work well, perhaps best, in family therapy because they are consistent with the expectations of the majority of families. The majority do not want a long-term contact, for such a prospect frightens most and is a major precipitant of premature termination. In the past few years I have concentrated on an aspect of therapy technique that seemed to me critical—the technique of engaging families who are poorly motivated for therapy or whose motivation is mixed. Quantitative reports by Sager et al. (1968), Shapiro and Budman (1973), Solomon (1969), and Slipp et al. (1974) highlight the need to find means to engage families of diverse origins.

Family values play a significant role in the effectiveness of short-term methods because values affect the expectations of families about therapy. Generally speaking, if therapy is expected to work—whether it be short-term or long-term—it works. But values play an especially significant role in whether or not families will become *engaged* in therapy. My experience actually leads me to the following statement: once families are engaged, the outcome is likely to be successful regardless of whether the succeeding method used is short-term or long-term. I have come to the conclusion that establishing the engagement is about half the battle. I am not a strict proponent of the short-term method in family therapy, even though it is the most appropriate method for the majority of cases. Therapists should encourage families to continue so long as they are willing to deal with issues affecting their lives, and so long as they are responsive to the therapist's direction. In numerous cases, particularly with lower class families, poor minority groups and families seen at the point of crisis, symptomatic relief may be obtained during the engagement itself. (Symptomatic relief during the engagement also is not uncommon in well-motivated, white, middle class families). But with the lower class, poor minority and crisis-type families, once symptomatic relief has been obtained, there is a tendency to quit therapy even when its continuation is encouraged by the therapist. From the point of view of the therapist, the therapy may be judged a failure, but from the family's point of view it was successful in that it produced the desired result in the desired time.

Studies are showing that change in brief therapy is frequently of a relatively permanent nature. Not only does the patient feel that help has been obtained, but relief and improvement are maintained over a significant period of time. Of course, certain psychoanalytic workers have objected that even though short-term methods appear effective, they are superficial; and that in order to produce so-called dynamic change, the long-term method is required. But a recent [study] by Malan et al. (1975) . . . reported on a group of eleven neurotic individuals who appeared improved "psychodynamically" after only one or two psychiatric interviews. These individuals, followed up over periods of from two or more years, seemed substantially improved in overall functioning, to have insight into factors responsible for their improvement, and to have a sense that they were more in control of their lives than they had been when they sought help. Following an initial evaluation interview or two with a psychiatrist (some of these were patients judged not acceptable for or likely to be amenable to psychotherapy), the individuals felt relieved and were able to make use of friends for aid and advice in a way they were unable to previously. At follow-up they cited the initial interview or two as critical for producing an immediate change upon which they were able to build over time.

I have found that even a single interview or two with a family can have a therapeutic effect that persists and develops with time, despite the fact that the family leaves treatment for one reason or another. The therapist may be disappointed with what he considers a premature termination, but the family may be grateful beyond words for the experience.

REFERENCES

Bateson, G., Jackson, D., Haley, J. & Weakland, J. Toward a theory of schizophrenia. *Behavioral Science*, 1956, **1,** 251–265.

Distler, L. The adolescent "hippie" and the emergence of a matristic culture. *Psychiatry*, 1970, **33,** 362–371.

Fromm, E. *The crisis of psychoanalysis*. New York: Holt, Rinehart, & Winston, 1970.

Leventhal, T., & Weinberger, G. Evaluation of a large-scale brief therapy program for children. *American Journal of Orthopsychiatry*, 1975, **45,** 119–133.

Malan, D., Heath, E., Bascal, H. & Balfour, H. Psychodynamic changes in untreated neurotic patients: II. Apparently genuine improvements. *Archives of General Psychiatry*, 1975, **32,** 110–126.

Midelfort, C. *The family in psychotherapy*. New York: McGraw-Hill, 1957.

Parsons, T. The American family: Its relation to personality and social structure. In T. Parsons & R. Bales (Eds.), *Family, socialization and interaction process*. Glencoe, Ill.: Free Press, 1955, 3–33.

Sager, C., Masters, Y., Bonall, R., & Normand, W. Selection and engagement of patients in family therapy. *American Journal of Orthopsychiatry*, 1968, **38,** 715–723.

Shapiro, R. & Budman, S. Defection, termination and continuation in family and individual therapy. *Family Process*, 1973, **12,** 55–67.

Slipp, S., Ellis, S. & Kressel, K. Factors associated with engagement in family therapy. *Family Process*, 1974, **13,** 413–427.

Solomon, M. Family therapy dropouts: Resistance to change. *Canadian Psychiatric Association Journal*, 1969, **14,** 21–29.

Zuk, G. *Family Therapy: A triadic-based approach*. New York: Behavioral Publications, 1971.

Zuk, G. *Process and practice in family therapy*. Haverford, Pa.: Psychiatry and Behavior Science Books, 1975.

Marital and Family Therapy: A Decade Review

David H. Olson
Candyce S. Russell
Douglas H. Sprenkle

This paper reviews and highlights the mushrooming growth of marital and family therapy during the 1970s. Like an awkward youth, the field struggled for conceptual clarity and empirical support for its clinical practices. The field gained credibility and emerged as a viable treatment approach for most mental health problems. Entering the 1980s, the field is beginning to develop integrative conceptual models, utilize clinically relevant assessment techniques, conduct systematic outcome research and develop preventative and enrichment programs.

In the last decade, marital and family therapy has emerged as a significant and separate mental health field. Treating relationships is no longer a practice carried out in secret by a small number of practitioners as it was in the 1950s but is now a service provided by most mental health agencies. It is becoming the treatment method of choice for problems ranging from sexual impotency to child abuse, and from cases of adolescent delinquency to problems with alcoholism. Increasingly, the public has become aware of these services and they are requesting, even demanding, relationship-oriented treatment. Truly, the field of marital and family therapy reflects the *Zeitgeist*.

The mushrooming interest in marital and family therapy is reflected by a variety of indicators. First, there have been over 1,500 articles and 200 books on marital and family therapy published between 1970–1979. The number of journals on this topic has increased from two in the early 1970s to more than 10 in 1979. The American Association for Marriage and Family Therapy (AAMFT) increased its membership from about 1,000 in 1970 to almost 8,000 in 1980. Also, a second organization was formed called the American Family Therapy Association.

"Marital and Family Therapy: A Decade Review," by D. H. Olson, C. S. Russell, and D. H. Sprenkle. In *Journal of Marriage and the Family*, 1980, *42*. Copyright 1980 by the National Council on Family Relations. Reprinted by permission.

The rapid emergence and acceptance of marital and family therapy has had a dramatic impact on the entire mental health profession. *First,* the traditional distinctions between marriage counseling and family therapy from the 1960s has faded so that it is now more accurate to describe marital and family therapy as a unitary, but not fully unified and integrated, field. It is, therefore, appropriate to talk about *the field* of marital and family therapy. *Second,* the emergence of this field has attracted professionals interested in working with persons within a relationship context and has become a "melting pot" of therapists. It has, thereby, broken down, but not destroyed, the identity of traditional professional groups, *i.e.,* psychologists, psychiatrists, social workers. *Third,* many types of emotional and physical problems are treated within a relationship context. Increasingly, professionals are finding that treatment of most problems can be more effectively accomplished and maintained if the client's significant others are involved in the treatment process. *Fourth,* the field is increasingly focusing on all types of relationships ranging from gay and cohabiting couples to single-parent and reconstituted families. However, the majority of services are still offered to individuals in a marriage and family relationship. *Fifth,* the field is beginning to deal with individuals at all stages of a relationship ranging from those beginning their relationship (premarital counseling), to those terminating their relationship (divorce counseling), and to those forming new family structures (custody resolution counseling). *Sixth,* the type and variety of agencies and settings that offer family-oriented services has mushroomed. This trend has become so prominent that it is difficult to identify professional agencies that do not offer such services. Even medical clinics are beginning to offer family-oriented treatment, and medical schools are developing a new field called family practice.

The *hallmark* and unifying characteristic of the field of marital and family therapy is the emphasis on treating problems within a *relationship context.* This practice was reinforced theoretically in the last decade by the emergence and acceptance of family systems theory. As a result, family systems theory has seen further development and has provided a general theoretical orientation for many marital and family therapists.

Viewed from a developmental perspective, the field of marital and family therapy has emerged from its infancy in the 1950s, achieved childhood in the early 1960s, adolescence in the late 1960s and has reached young adulthood in the 1970s.

In the decade review of the 1960s (Olson, 1970), marriage counseling and family therapy were described as young "fraternal twins" developing along parallel but surprisingly separate lines. While the benefits of interchange seemed obvious and necessary, the relative autonomy of the two fields was seen in their separate training centers, their divergent literatures, sources of theory, type of clientele served, and professional organizations.

During the 1960s, these two youthful professions were developing with a great amount of vigor but without a sufficient amount of rigor. Not unlike youth, both fields experienced enormous growth spurts which resulted in limited conceptual or empirical grounding. Specifically, the main feature of clinical practice could best be described as therapists "doing their own thing."

However, in the decade of the 1970s, the two professions began to converge and they clearly established their presence and identity as a separate mental health field. Reaching young adulthood was achieved by developments therapeutically, conceptually and empirically. *Therapeutically*, schools of therapy and specific therapeutic techniques were developed for working with couples and families. *Conceptually*, therapists generated a wealth of concepts, often redundant, that related to marital and family dynamics. Increasingly, family therapy and family dynamics were understood within a family systems orientation. *Empirically*, both the quality and quantity of outcome research on the effectiveness of marital and family therapy improved.

The remainder of this paper will review the major theoretical developments and the outcome research on the effectiveness of marital and family therapy in the 1970s. Because of the great amount of literature published in the last decade, this review will be selective and will only highlight the major trends and studies. Lastly, this review will indicate promising trends and future directions that will, we hope, facilitate the development and identity of marital and family therapy as a separate and competent mental health field.

THEORETICAL DEVELOPMENTS IN MARITAL AND FAMILY THERAPY

In his previous Decade Review article, Olson (1970:516) reported that "the search for *the* theory of marital (and family) therapy is slowly changing to a realization that there needs to be considerably more exploration of various theoretical approaches before a more integrated and comprehensive approach can be developed." This exploration is perhaps the benchmark of theory development in the decade of the seventies.

The exploration and refinement of existing ideas has characterized the decade rather than the introduction of dramatically new theoretical approaches. Most recent family therapy literature has been either: (1) the integration and refinement of previous models (*i.e.*, Minuchin's (1974) synthesis of family development, family systems, and structural-functionalism); (2) simplified descriptions of previous theoretical work (i.e., cookbooks or working-guides of family therapy and text books of family therapy); or (3) extension of existent theoretical models to specific problems like chemical addiction (Stanton, 1979; Steinglass, 1976) and aging (Herr and Weakland, 1979).

The charge that marriage and family therapy is a technique in search of *a* theory (Manus, 1966) is probably no longer applicable. In addition to refining particular theoretical approaches, steps have been taken to examine the presuppositions of the various theories (Paolino and McCrady, 1978; Ritterman, 1977; Levant, 1980) and therapists (Foley, 1974).

Classification: A first step

The exploration of various theoretical approaches has been enhanced by several deliberate attempts at classification. In the previous decade, the only scheme cited in the literature was Beels and Ferber's (1969) classification based on the role of the therapist. In the current decade, the Group for the Advancement of Psychiatry (1970) gave attention to the goals of treatment. Foley (1974) compared the similarities and differences among therapists on the eight dimensions of history, diagnosis, affect, learning, values, conscious versus unconscious, transference, and the therapist as model or teacher. Relying more on the theoretical orientation of the family therapists, Guerin (1976) identified two basic groups, those with a psychodynamic and those with a systems orientation. The psychodynamic group included individual, group, experiential and Ackerman-type approaches while the system group was composed of strategic, structural and Bowenian family therapy.

Ritterman (1977) utilized the "mechanistic" versus "organismic" views of systems to compare family therapy approaches. Structural family therapy was represented as organismic, and the Mental Research Institute communications theory was described as mechanistic. Although this analysis was criticized (Weakland, 1977b), it does point to the value of examining the epistemological assumptions on which the various family theories are based. After extending and critiquing Ritterman's schema, Levant (1980) inductively developed a paradigm which described three schools of family therapy: historical approaches, structure/process approaches and experiential approaches.

The most sophisticated critique and comparative analysis of the psychoanalytic, behavioral, and systems theory (Bowenite and communications) approaches to marital therapy was conducted by Gurman (1978). He systematically compared these theoretical orientations on the following characteristics: (1) the role of the past and the unconscious; (2) the nature and meaning of presenting problems and the role of assessment; (3) the importance of mediating goals; (4) and the importance of ultimate goals and various therapist roles.

Integration and model building

Although it is useful to classify and describe various approaches to family therapy, a critical step is to begin integrating concepts and principles and develop theoretical models. One recent attempt to develop an integrative model of the family was done by Olson, Russell and Sprenkle in their Circumplex Model (Olson *et al.*, 1979; Olsen *et al.*, 1980). The Circumplex Model of Marital and Family Systems will be used to organize and summarize the conceptual development in the field of family therapy and to demonstrate the conceptual similarity across the various approaches.

In developing the Circumplex Model, three dimensions emerged from the conceptual clustering of concepts from six social science fields, including family therapy. The three dimensions were: *cohesion, adaptability,* and *communication.* Evidence for the salience of these three dimensions is the fact that numerous theorists and therapists have independently selected concepts related to these dimensions as critical to their work (Table 1).

Empirical evidence for the significance of the three dimensions is found in a survey conducted by two family therapists at Purdue University (Fisher and Sprenkle, 1978; Sprenkle and Fisher, 1980). A sample of 310 members of the American Association for Marriage and Family Therapy (AAMFT) rated and ranked 10 family cohesion concepts, seven family adaptability concepts, and 17 family communication concepts in terms of their importance as: (1) aspects of healthy family functioning; and (2) goals for guiding the therapists' interventions with couples and families.

Considering aspects of healthy family functioning, the mean rating for the cohesion and adaptability variables was 3.9 and the mean rating for communication was 4.0. These results suggested that all three dimensions were seen as "very important" (5 = crucial; 4 = very important; 3 = important; 2 = somewhat important; 1 = not important) by this group of therapists.

Examining the *goals of therapy,* the mean ratings were 3.6 for cohesion, 4.1 for adaptability and 4.0 for communication. These ratings suggest that these dimensions were "usually" considered a goal of therapy (5 = always; 4 = usually; 3 = often; 2 = seldom; 1 = never). Within the limits of these self-report data, it seems clear that a large and representative group of family therapists is willing to attribute considerable importance to these concepts. It is also important to note that the theoretical allegiances of these therapists were extremely diverse.

Family cohesion is defined as the emotional bonding that family members have toward one another (Olson *et al.,* 1979). At the extreme high end of the cohesion dimension (enmeshed systems) there is an over-identification with the family which results in an emotional, intellectual and/or physical closeness. The low extreme of cohesion (disengaged systems) results in emotional, intellectual and/or physical isolation from the family. It is hypothesized that the central area of this continuum is most viable for family functioning because individuals are able to *experience* and *balance* being independent from, as well as connected to, their families.

TABLE 1. Theoretical Models of Family Systems Utilizing Concepts Related to Cohesion and Adaptability and Communication Dimensions

	Cohesion	Adaptability	Communication	Others
Benjamin (1974 and 1977)	Affiliation	Interdependence		
Epstein, Bishop and Levin (1978)	Affective involvement	Behavior control, Problem solving, Roles	Communication, Affective responsiveness	
French and Guidera (1974)		Capacity to change power		Anxiety; role as symptom carrier
Kantor and Lehr (1975)	Affect dimension	Power dimension		Meaning dimension
Leary (1957) and Constantine (1977)	Affection-hostility	Dominance-submission		
Lewis *et al.* (1976) and Beavers (1977)	Closeness, Autonomy, Coalitions	Power negotiation	Affect	Mythology
Parsons and Bales (1955)	Expressive role	Instrumental role		

Family adaptability is the second major dimension and is defined as the ability of a marital or family system to change its power structure, role relationships, and relationship rules in response to situational and developmental stress (Olson *et al.,* 1979). As with cohesion, adaptability is a continuum when the central levels of adaptability are hypothesized as more conducive to marital and family functioning than the extremes. In family theory, adaptability was originally presented as homeostasis or the ability of a system to maintain equilibrium (Haley, 1964). More recently, writers have stressed the dual concepts of morphogenesis (system altering or change) and morphostasis (system maintaining or stability) and the family's need for a dynamic balance between these two (Speer, 1970; Wertheim, 1973, 1975).

Families very low on adaptability (rigid systems) are unable to change even when it appears necessary. On the other hand, families with too much adaptability (chaotic systems) also have problems dealing with stress and problems. Thus, a balance of stability and change appears most functional to individual and family development (Olson *et al.*, 1979).

By placing these two dimensions of cohesion and adaptability at right angles, Olson *et al.* (1979) have developed a Circumplex Model which delineates 16 *family types.* These authors have also developed a series of hypotheses with direct clinical utility derived from the Model, several of which have already been tested empirically (Olson *et al.*, 1980).

The integrative nature of these dimensions will be shown through a brief description of the work of two of the most prominent family therapists of the past decade: Salvador Minuchin and Carl Whitaker. Because of their clear stylistic differences as well as varying theoretical emphases, these two therapists might appear to be working toward very different goals. Yet, fundamentally, both stress what has been described as a balanced position on the dimensions of family cohesion and adaptability.

The theme of cohesion is highly developed in Minuchin's work (1974; Minuchin *et al.*, 1975; Minuchin *et al.*, 1978). He writes that the human experience of identity has two elements: a sense of belonging and a sense of separateness. A family's structure may range from the one extreme of the "enmeshed" family to the other extreme of the "disengaged" family. In the former, the quality of connectedness among members is characterized by "tight interlocking" and extraordinary resonance among members. The enmeshed family responds to any variation from the accustomed with excessive speed and intensity. In sharp contrast, individuals in disengaged families seem oblivious to the effects of their actions on each other. "Actions of its members do not lead to vivid repercussions ... the overall impression is one of an atomistic field; family members have long moments in which they move as in isolated orbits, unrelated to each other" (Minuchin *et al.*, 1967:354).

Minuchin also devoted considerable attention to family adaptation. He stresses the importance of the family's capacity to change in the face of external or internal pressures, *i.e.*, those related to developmental changes such as the addition or loss of members or changes in life-cycle stages. Minuchin notes that many families in treatment are simply going through transitions and need help in adapting to them. "The label of pathology would be reserved for families who, in the face of stress, increase the rigidity of their transactional patterns and boundaries, and avoid or resist any exploration of alternatives" (Minuchin, 1974:60).

Carl Whitaker (1975a, 1975b, 1977; Napier and Whitaker, 1978) is probably the most influential experiential family therapist of the decade. His emphasis on therapy as a "here and now" experience, on unconscious process, "psychotherapy of the absurd," and "the therapist as artist rather than technician" ostensibly suggests that he has little in common with Minuchin. Yet, the need for balanced cohesion in families is also crucial to Whitaker's understanding of healthy family functioning and the goals of family therapy. Whitaker (1977:4) writes that a healthy family is "one that maintains a high degree of inner unity and a high degree of individuation. This includes the freedom to leave and return without family dissension and a comfort in belonging to intimate sub-groups outside the family and on occasion, including outside intimates in the family." Also, like Minuchin, Whitaker believes there should be clear boundaries surrounding the parental sub-system. Whitaker calls this the need for a "generation gap."

Whitaker also stresses several themes highly relevant to family adaptability. One of these is his emphasis on role flexibility. He thinks it important that the father can feel free to play the spoiled brat at the dinner table, the mother can be a little girl, the daughter can play mother to the father and the father can have a make-believe affair with his daughter without provoking his spouse's jealousy. The point is that no one individual gets "stuck" playing one rigid role all of the time. In addition to encouraging flexible roles, Whitaker also emphasizes the positive value of shifting alliances. For example, he thinks it is exciting and dynamic when, *temporarily,* mother and daughter team up against father, or father and daughter against mother. The formation of triangles is not inherently evil as long as they don't become rigid triangles. On the other hand, Whitaker also emphasizes that the family needs to provide its members enough of a sense of stability to afford a sense of security amidst life's inherent untidiness. Another way of stating this is that the family should fall somewhere between extreme morphogenesis and extreme morphostasis.

Family communication has been stressed by most family theorists from Ackerman to the present. It is emphasized especially by those associated with the "Palo Alto" communications group (Watzlawick *et al.,* 1967; Watzlawick *et al.,* 1974; Satir, 1972). Also, many practitioners have begun to isolate the specific components of effective marital and family communication (Miller *et al.,* 1975) and have created skill development workshops to facilitate family communication (Miller *et al.,* 1976; Guerney, 1977).

In conclusion, there appears to be considerable consensus across family therapists about the salience of the cohesion, adaptability and communication dimension. How these dimensions are operationalized, hypothesized to relate to each other and utilized in therapy are still areas requiring considerable investigation.

SCHOOLS OF FAMILY THERAPY

Although a few of the pioneers of family therapy continue to influence the field, several schools of family therapy have emerged to the forefront in the decade of the 1970s.

Structural family therapy

This highly influential school centers around Salvador Minuchin and the Child Guidance Center in Philadelphia. Some of Minuchin's key ideas have been described previously. The structural approach to family therapy focuses on how the myriad of sub-systems which encompass and comprise families are connected. Minuchin's key notion of "boundary" refers to the degree of permeability which characterizes such systemic interfaces. By interacting with a family's various subsystems, a structural family therapist assesses its structural viability. Therapeutic interventions follow on the basis of rearranging the family's structure in a way which attempts to: (1) establish a clear generational hierarchy; and (2) promote semipermeable boundaries (*i.e.*, neither enmeshed nor disengaged).

Strategic family therapy

1. *Haley's Approach:* Haley (1976) blends Minuchin's structural work with formal ideas of communication theory. Although he strives for a clear generational hierarchy, he describes his diagnostic and intervention work in terms of communication rather than "structural engineering." Haley focuses on the presenting problem (*e.g.*, symptomatic behavior) and tries to see what communicative function the problem has in the sequence of family events which embody it. His task is then to change the sequence, which, if effectively done, will change the outcome (*e.g.*, alleviation of symptomatic behavior).

2. *Mental Research Institute Communicational Approach:* (Watzlawick *et al.*, 1967; Watzlawick *et al.*, 1974; Watzlawick and Weakland, 1977; Sluzki, 1978). If one were to drop the parts of Haley's work which connect with structural family therapy, one would come close to having the MRI communication approach. The MRI method is not necessarily a school of family therapy, but since it was derived from a context historically associated with family therapy, it has been treated as such. The MRI group strictly attends to the chess-game-like approach to solving problems. Thus, the context of the problem is first perceived and then altered. A change is metaphorically tagged as a "second-order change" when the target of change is the system and not just the symptom. This group has given particular attention to therapeutic paradox and the use of therapeutic language which addresses the right (nonrational) hemisphere of the brain. The work of Gregory Bateson (1972, 1979) and Milton Erickson (Haley, 1973) has had a significant impact on the MRI orientation.

3. *The Strategic Group Approach:* (Selvini *et al.*, 1978, 1980; Papp, 1977, 1980; Hoffman, 1976). Selvini's strategic group model in the treatment of schizophrenic transaction is based on a blending of the work of Bateson, Haley, and Watzlawick. The group tends to do strategic work in the way in which Pentagon officers plan a battle. At the heart of this approach is a paradoxical relabeling maneuver called "positive connotation," in which the family's homeostatic, yet dysfunctional, organizational pattern is respected. The injunction not to change, paradoxically, gives the family freedom to change. The group also uses a wide variety of other paradoxical maneuvers, including family rituals, to achieve their ends. This strategic approach is also becoming popular in the United States and is utilized by such therapists as Silverstein, Papp, and Hoffman at the Ackerman Family Institute in New York. Another strategic group is located at the Menninger Foundation in Topeka and is headed by Arthur Mandelbaum (1977).

Experiential family therapy

The leading proponents of this school are Whitaker (1977), Napier (Napier and Whitaker, 1978) and Keith (Keith and Whitaker, 1978). A number of Whitaker's key ideas have been presented previously. The term *experiential family therapy* is Whitaker's label for what is essentially an existential orientation. These therapists emphasize personal and family growth through experiencing one's own irrationality and "craziness." Dysfunctional families are depicted as locked into their own rationality which must be blocked by "right brain" strategies such as use of metaphor, absurd overstatement of the clients' problem, or the therapist discussing his own "craziness."

Social learning approach

Another school of therapy has organized itself around the tenets of social learning theory. In an excellent review of this approach and its relationship to family intervention, Vincent (1980) makes it clear that social learning theory does not have a unified set of propositions. Rather the "theory" is an assembly of several models: most importantly, operant learning and social exchange theories, along with smatterings of general systems theories (Alexander and Barton, 1976) and attribution theory (Margolin and Weiss, 1978). Their emphasis on "states" versus "traits" is shared by other theoretical approaches. What distinguishes this group most markedly is its emphasis on observational assessment methods, behavioral specifics and the interplay of data, theory, and clinical application.

Social learning theory has had a significant effect because its basic tenets are readily translatable into treatment modalities and techniques that can be tested empirically. Although social learning conceptualizations of marital and family distress vary somewhat, all of these therapists stress that intervention is most effective if it focuses on increasing positive acts and decreasing negative ones. These behavioral changes are hypothesized to produce positive changes in feelings and cognitions about relationships.

Gerald Patterson and colleagues (Patterson, 1976; Patterson et al., 1975) have developed systematic social learning programs for problem children which actively involve parents and teachers as change agents. They have also completed some of the intensive studies of behavioral change in families.

Weiss and colleagues (Weiss, 1978; Weiss et al., 1972; Birchler et al., 1975; and Vincent, 1980) have done extensive studies on the use of social learning theory for understanding and changing interaction patterns in marital systems. Recently, Weiss (1978) has described how to integrate problem-solving and communication skills into behavioral marital therapy. Stuart's (1976) early work with distressed couples in the early 1970s using an "operant interpersonal approach" was a stimulus to more rigorous theorizing and studies.

James Alexander and his colleagues have worked extensively with families of delinquents (Alexander and Barton, 1976). Alexander's work represents an interesting synthesis of behavioral and family systems approaches. Testing system reciprocity (interdependence), these investigators found that in normal families members tended to reciprocate supportive but not defensive communication; the reverse is true in delinquent families. Social learning techniques were employed to increase the rate and reciprocity of supportiveness in these families.

Concluding comments

This review has suggested that the hallmark of the current decade has been less the development of dramatically new theories and more the expansion and refinement of existing ones. One might well ask whether the existence of these multiple theories of marriage and family therapy is a boon or a bane. As we attempted to demonstrate in our section on "Integration and Model Building," we believe there is considerable conceptual similarity among these divergent views and the fact that the theories were often developed independently of one another provides construct validity for the three dimensions of cohesion, adaptability and communication.

It should also be mentioned that the various *actions* taken in therapy that flow from the divergent theories are often more similar than would be expected (Gurman, 1978). As a result, the various schools of marriage and family therapy seem to have become less dogmatic in their approach and less triumphal in their assessments of their efficacy. Perhaps there is a growing appreciation of the sentiment behind the words of Framo (1973:211) who stated: "I have been impressed with how similarly experienced family therapists function in the actual therapy situation, despite differences in theoretical persuasion."

OUTCOME RESEARCH ON THE EFFECTIVENESS OF MARITAL AND FAMILY THERAPY

During the last decade, the empirical outcome literature has improved in both quantity and quality. This progress is clearly documented by the several comprehensive reviews already available (e.g., Beck, 1976; Gurman, 1973, 1975; Gurman and Kniskern, 1978a, 1978b; Jacobson, 1978b; Jacobson and Margolin, 1979; Jacobson and Martin, 1976; Masten, 1979; Wells and Dezen, 1978; Wells et al., 1976). This review will differ from most others by focusing on the trend toward *specification of treatment by presenting problem*.

The review is selective rather than exhaustive. Analog studies, which include nondistressed populations, will generally not be included. With minor exceptions, the literature reviewed is published and readily available. In a review of this type, space limitations make it difficult to do justice to the increasing complexity and sophistication of each study. We have, therefore, developed a detailed summary table of the outcome studies by presenting symptoms which can be obtained by writing the first author.

We must caution, however, that this summary does *not* allow us to identify the "treatment of choice" for each presenting problem. This is because even though therapists have indicated they primarily used a specific therapeutic approach, their *actual* treatment programs are *not* well specified and there is, therefore, considerable heterogeneity within therapeutic approaches. However, if consistent findings and themes emerge across studies, one can have greater confidence in the value of the therapeutic approach for a given presenting symptom.

The trend in the family therapy field appears to be toward specifying which mode of therapy is most effective for which group of clients presenting which sort of problems. This is a more effective approach to therapeutic outcome studies. As Frank (1979:312) suggested: "Instead of continuing to pursue the therapeutic relatively unrewarding enterprise of statistically comparing the effectiveness of different therapies, we should focus on particular forms of therapy that seem to work exceptionally well with a few patients and seek to define the characteristics of both the therapy and the patients that lead to this happy result."

An alternative to focusing on presenting symptoms is to focus on the type of family system. Olson et al. (1980) have emphasized the importance of *system* diagnosis prior to intervention. A given "symptom" may serve multiple functions in a relationship system. Therefore, the "system diagnosis" and presenting complaint may not uniformly covary. For instance, Killorin and Olson (1980) describe the course of therapy with four alcoholic families, each of whom operated at different (though extreme) levels of family cohesion and adaptability. Also, there are other recent projects where the type of system is diagnosed prior to treatment, specific treatment programs are planned and outcome is assessed for a narrowly defined treatment group (e.g., Alexander and Barton, 1976; Minuchin et al., 1978; Stanton et al., 1979; Steinglass, 1979).

Although we feel it is important to consider both the family system and presenting symptoms in assessing a family, we have decided to organize the studies by presenting symptoms to make the review more useful to therapists. This format also is congruent with the way researchers have organized their studies. For summary purposes, Table 2 arranges treatment strategy by presenting problem.

Alcoholism

The value of diagnosing the "system" rather than the "symptom" is illustrated by the work of Steinglass et al. (1977) at George Washington University. By carefully observing intoxicated and nonintoxicated behavior in a variety of familial dyads (father-son, brother-brother, husband-wife), the Steinglass group noted the development of rigid sets of interactions that permitted the enactment of behavior otherwise avoided (e.g., warmth, caretaking behavior, animated affect).

In a recent study, Steinglass (1979a) studied the problem-solving behavior of "wet" and "dry" family triads using Reiss' card-sort procedure. These laboratory findings are consistent with the group's clinical observations that families frequently appear more willing to deal with problems and conflict when the alcoholic family member is drinking.

The implication of this research is that therapeutic intervention should be aimed at increasing the behavioral repertoire of the interactional system (e.g., increase its flexibility during nonintoxicated periods). Davis et al. (1974) have incorporated learning theory into this perspective and, thereby, emphasize the value of focusing on the factors which maintain alcoholic behavior. The "adaptive consequences" may be different for each system and may operate at several system levels: intraindividual, dyadic, family or beyond. Once the adaptive consequence of the alcoholic behavior in a given system has been determined, the therapeutic goal is to help the family to manifest that adaptive interaction while sober. Homogeneity of symptom function is not assumed.

Six month follow-up data on eight of the 10 couples treated by Steinglass (1979b) reveals mixed results. The eight couples included nine identified as alcoholics. At follow-up, five of the nine demonstrated significant decreases in the pattern and context of their drinking. While the therapy appeared to be successful in altering marital communication on both behavioral and self-report measures, these changes followed no clear pattern and were not necessarily associated with increased satisfaction with the relationship. Steinglass concludes that the six-week treatment program was sufficient to "shake up" a rigid pattern but not sufficient to produce long-term behavioral change.

It is important to point out that most of the outcome literature reported during the 1970s does not report clinical interventions guided by such

TABLE 2. Relationship-Oriented Treatment Strategies Yielding Some Degree of Documented Effectiveness by Presenting Problem**

Presenting Problem	Behavioral Exchange Contracting	Conjoint Couples Group Therapy	Behavioral Family Therapy	Conjoint Interactional Family Therapy	Structural Family Therapy	Strategic Family Therapy	Zuk's Triadic Approach	Multiple Family Therapy	Drug Therapy plus Marital Therapy	Family Crisis Intervention (Langsley et al.)
Alcoholism	X	X								
Drug abuse					X	X		X		
Juvenile status offense			X*	X*	X					
Adolescent psychopathology			X	X			X			
Childhood conduct problems			X							
School and work phobias								X		X
Psychosomatic symptoms						X				
Adult depression									X	
Marital distress	X									

* Though labeled behavioral, the Alexander group at Utah actually used a mix of behavioral and communication approaches in conjoint family sessions.

** Limited primarily to outcome studies reported 1970–1979.

*** Based largely on principles from communication theory.

"system-specific goals." Using less "system-specific" goals, the controlled research studies of Corder *et al.*, (1972), Cadogan (1973), Hedberg and Campbell (1974), and McCrady *et al.*, (1977) each report significant reduction in drinking behavior for spouse-involved groups as compared with individual treatment approaches. Of particular importance may be the apparent ability of spouse-added conditions to increase the length of the clients' involvement in therapy of whatever kind (*e.g.*, Ewing *et al.*, 1961).

Investigators in this area have been helpful in sensitizing professionals to the dangers of stereotyping families based on presenting complaint and the importance of bringing the symptom into the laboratory or therapy room for observation. While the general homeostatic function of alcoholic behavior has been supported by the work of the last decade, Orford (1975), Kennedy (1976), and Steinglass (1979b) have each stressed the importance of acknowledging the specific way a given *system* may be making *use* of that *symptom*.

Drug abuse

Whereas the adult is most often the "identified patient" in studies of alcoholism in the family, adolescents or young adults are most often the "identified patients" in cases in which drug abuse is the presenting complaint. Increasingly, family therapists are interpreting drug abuse as part of the system's attempt to adapt to loss. The loss may be through launching, death, or disengagement from a career (Harbin and Maziar, 1975; Stanton, 1979). The addiction functions to allow dependency and connectedness at the same time that the young adult is allowed to *appear to be independent* through open violation of society's standards regarding the use of drugs. Although the addict appears to be flagrantly independent and distant, he or she is nevertheless loyal to the family, which maintains its stability and homeostasis by defining the addict as dependent and as incompetent (Alexander and Dibb, 1975, 1977; Noone and Reddig, 1976).

The family treatment of drug problems has taken several forms, including: conjoint and group marital therapy, parent groups, concurrent parent and adolescent groups, sibling groups, multiple family therapy, and social network intervention. The most common family treatment has been conjoint family therapy based on a variety of theoretical approaches or "schools."

Some of the most impressive conjoint family treatment has been conducted by Stanton and his colleagues (Stanton *et al.*, 1979) at the Philadelphia Child Guidance Clinic. Their therapy is based on a combination of Minuchin's structural approach (Minuchin *et al.*, 1978) and Haley's strategic approach (Haley, 1976, 1980). They compared the outcome of this therapy with that of two control conditions: (1) family movie viewing at research site; and (2) individual therapy. Addicts in each condition were on methadone. Cases were randomly assigned to treatment modes. A six-month post-treatment follow-up found family treatment to be 1.4 to 2.7 times as effective as other forms of therapy in producing days free from opiate, nonopiate drugs, and alcohol use. Family therapy was also effective in reducing conflict and involving fathers more in family interaction.

A second study comparing brief structural family therapy with group therapy for relatives and a control condition found no difference at 4-6 month follow-up between the number of patients free from substance abuse and those still using drugs (Ziegler-Driscoll, 1977). The inexperience of therapists with the structural approach to therapy, the unfamiliarity of project consultants with the client population, and the hostility of the hospital context to the approach may be significant factors contributing to the unimpressive outcome. Clearly, the generalizability of various family therapy approaches from one treatment setting to another is at issue.

Another approach which reports some degree of success with drug addiction in controlled studies includes multiple family therapy. In a one-year follow-up of narcotics addicts treated in an in-patient setting, Hendricks (1971) reported 41 percent of the experimental group to be free of illegal drugs as assessed by urinalysis as compared with 21 percent of the controls. The experimental group had received an average of five and a half months of multiple family therapy in addition to the "overall in-patient program." Unfortunately, clients were not randomly assigned to experimental or control conditions.

While case descriptions of marital therapy are available in the literature (e.g., Spark and Papp, 1970; Polakow and Doctor, 1973), this treatment does not enjoy a large following or rigorous documentation of success. Stanton et al. (1979) suggest that marital therapy with most addicts will not be successful unless the relationship with the family of origin is dealt with first.

Juvenile offenses

The court system makes a distinction between "status offenses" (e.g., running away from home, promiscuity, curfew violation), which are offenses only because the child is not yet of legal age, and more serious crimes involving injury to persons and property. In the family therapy literature these are sometimes referred to as "soft-" and "hard-core" delinquency. Most of the reports of successful treatment of juvenile offenders in a family context involve status offenses (e.g., Alexander and Barton, 1976; Klein et al., 1977; Beal and Duckro, 1977; Druckman, 1979).

In a series of research projects, Alexander and his colleagues have documented: (a) differences in the content and process of communication in the families of "soft-core delinquents" and controls (Alexander, 1973); (b) the modification of family communication through a short-term behavioral family intervention (Alexander and Parsons, 1973); and (c) a lower rate of client recidivism and sibling referral in a behaviorally treated group as compared with controls (Klein et al., 1977).

The initial diagnosis was that delinquent families demonstrated significantly higher rates of defensiveness and lower rates of supportiveness than adaptive families. Also, delinquent families reciprocated defensive communications whereas adaptive families reciprocated supportiveness. Alexander and colleagues then developed a four-week behavioral program for groups of five families aimed at decreasing defensive communication and increasing reciprocity with regard to supportiveness.

Using relatively inexperienced therapists, the Alexander group has been able to demonstrate the superiority of this program package over both individual client-centered and psychodynamic family approaches to counseling (Alexander and Barton, 1976). Though the program is billed as "behavioral," it clearly contains elements of communication training.

Several other family-oriented approaches have received some degree of support, though generally having less well-designed studies than the Alexander program. These include crisis intervention fashioned after Langsley *et al.* (1968) combined with a communication emphasis (Beal and Duckro, 1977), eclectic conjoint family therapy based on the writings of Milton Erickson, Haley, Minuchin and Whitaker (Johnson, 1977), and using adolescent groups followed by eclectic conjoint family therapy (Druckman, 1979).

In summary, only the Johnson (1977) study included juveniles who had committed crimes against persons or property. The impressive findings of the Alexander group must be tempered by an awareness of their select population: upper-lower- and middle-class religious (70 percent Morman) families whose children were referred for status offenses. The findings may not generalize to highly urbanized populations living in a social context with a different value system. With the possible exception of Minuchin *et al.* (1967), family therapy has yet to be shown to be effective with more serious categories of juvenile offenses.

Adolescent psychopathology

As with the outcome literature in family therapy in the juvenile court setting, the outcome literature on family therapy in the hospital setting would profit from a more precise investigation of the interaction of *system diagnosis* with treatment. Studies by Evans *et al.* (1971), Wellisch *et al.* (1976) and Ro-Trock *et al.* (1977) include hospitalized adolescents with a variety of traditional diagnoses: Schizophrenic reaction, adolescent adjustment reaction, character disorder, depressive reaction, borderline psychosis, psychosomatic disorder and manic-depressive psychosis. Each of these "disorders" may be associated with different family processes and, therefore, may be responsive to different family or non-family intervention.

Evans *et al.* (1971) report on the treatment of hospitalized adolescents who received either individual psychotherapy or individual plus family treatment. While Evans reports a higher rate of return to work or school and greater improvement in presenting symptoms where family therapy had been experienced, these findings must be viewed with caution. The comparison group had been denied family therapy because the family had "excessive pathology," was "incomplete," "resistant," lived in another city, had a language barrier, or was of a low socioeconomic level. Thus, the families who received conjoint treatment started out "healthier" and presented qualities which led therapists to think they would be more successful in therapy.

In a well designed study which compared effectiveness of an eclectic family therapy approach (therapists had training in psychodynamic, behavioral and communication approaches) with individual therapy, Wellisch *et al.* (1976) randomly assigned 28 adolescent subjects to either the experimental or control conditions. The treatment consisted of 10 sessions in both conditions. The target unit of adolescent and his/her mother and father were assessed on several self-report and behavioral instruments. In addition, the mother of each adolescent subject gave a telephone report of the adolescent's community adjustment three months after discharge. Though the self-report and behavioral measures of family process were difficult to interpret, the family treatment condition was clearly superior to individual treatment in terms of days lost before returning to work or school and instances of hospitalization. After three months, 43 percent of the adolescents in the individual therapy group had been rehospitalized compared with none of the adolescents who took part in family therapy.

Using a nonhospitalized population, Garrigan and Bambrick (1977) studied the impact of family therapy on families of adolescents who were attending a school for the emotionally disturbed. Twenty-eight families were randomly assigned either to family therapy or parent discussion groups. The therapy group made significant gains over the control group in the following areas: (1) perceived congruence and empathy in the marital relationship; (2) rate of return to normal classroom setting; and (3) reduction in sadistic, domineering and bizarre behaviors in the classroom. Family therapy did not have an effect on either the parents' or the adolescents' self-concepts or anxiety.

Childhood conduct problems

Patterson (1976) and colleagues at the Oregon Research Institute have taken the lead in developing treatment programs for families of children (specifically boys) referred for a variety of conduct problems, including: hyperactivity, fighting, lying, stealing, bedwetting, non-compliance with authority, whining and yelling. The treatment package is based on social learning theory and is now designed for groups of parents. The treatment program includes: (1) use of a programmed text (*Families* or *Living with Children*); (2) learning to define, track and record target behaviors; (3) modeling of parenting techniques through role play; and (4) learning to write contingency contracts. Patterson (1974) reports on the outcome of 27 such cases, including many lower socio-economic level families and father-absent units.

Two sets of outcome data were collected: (1) rates of 14 noxious behaviors made in the home by trained observers, yielding a "total deviant" score (TD); and (2) parents' daily reports on specific problem behaviors (PDR). At termination, approximately two out of three boys exhibited reductions of 30 percent or more from baseline; six (22 percent) showed increases. At the 12 month follow-up, there was a nonsignificant trend toward increased improvement.

Using subsets of these 27 families, Wiltz and Patterson (1974) found the full four weeks of the treatment package to be superior to the passage of time alone (waiting list controls). Walter and Gilmore (1973) compared four weeks of treatment with four weeks of a placebo group meeting and found nonsignificant increases in targeted deviant child behavior in the placebo group and significant decreases in the experimental group.

Using the Oregon treatment package and waiting list control, Karoly and Rosenthal (1977) report similar treatment effects for families of aggressive boys. Their outcome measures included the Moos Family Environment Scale in addition to home observation of behavior and a child psychiatric problem list.

Work and school phobias

Though school phobias in children have been understood as an expression of separation anxiety since 1941 (Johnson *et al.*, 1941), it is only recently that the dyadic focus on mother and child has been broadened to include the entire family, particularly the father.

Skynner (1974), in his work with 20 school phobic children, suggests that the child's anxiety is partly a response to parental inability to set clear, firm limits. The father in these families was either a peripheral figure or a "dependent child" himself, unable to involve his wife as a spouse, and thus weaken her intense attachment to the child.

Pittman et al. (1968) had earlier discussed the similarities between work phobias and school phobias, noting also the high frequency of school phobias in the histories of work phobias. Pittman and his colleagues have been successful in using insight-oriented crisis family therapy to help the wife or mother allow the man to disengage from her. This approach was found to be successful with all five cases of work phobias assigned to family-oriented crisis therapy, whereas a comparison group of six cases treated in individual psychotherapy resulted in about 50 percent successfully returning to work or school. Skynner (1974) reports an 85 percent success rate with school phobias using a group-analytic approach involving the entire family.

Psychosomatic symptoms

One important demonstration of the effectiveness of family therapy during the last decade comes from those structural (e.g., Minuchin et al., 1975; Minuchin et al., 1978) and strategic (e.g., Palazzoli, 1974) therapists working with anorexia nervosa, brittle diabetes, and asthma. Unfortunately, these were not controlled studies and they did not collect any data on the family system. However, they do report outcome on the patient in terms of objective criteria (e.g., weight gain, blood sugar levels, respiratory functioning and hospitalization rates) on populations presenting life-threatening behavior with typically very poor prognosis (e.g., Bruch, 1974).

Through a series of metabolic studies using nonpsychosomatic diabetic children as controls, Minuchin et al. (1978) described the role of the child in his/her parents' disputes. Five characteristics of psychosomatic family functioning emerged from these observations: (1) enmeshed subsystem boundaries; (2) overprotectiveness; (3) rigidity; (4) lack of conflict resolution; and (5) the child's involvement in parental conflict. The combination of these five family processes are seen as sufficient to involve an already physiologically vulnerable child in a process of somatization. The family context and circular causal model are highlighted by these investigators.

The therapeutic maneuvers used by the Philadelphia group flow logically from the five dysfunctional patterns identified above. Using material unique to each family in treatment, therapists suggest the illness is under voluntary control, challenge enmeshed boundaries and overprotection without devaluing "togetherness," induce conflict while blocking its avoidance and increase the intensity of crisis until the system is able to calibrate at a new level of functioning with less rigidity.

Using these restructuring operations with 53 anorexic families, Minuchin and his colleagues (1978) have reported an 86 percent recovery rate. The median length of treatment was six months, typically conducted at weekly intervals. Sixteen different therapists, including psychiatrists, psychologists and social workers, conducted the therapy. Outcome was evaluated in two areas for the identified patient: remission of anorexic symptoms (weight gain) and psychosocial functioning in relation to home, school, and peers.

The Minuchin group has also reported success with families of brittle diabetics and psychosomatic asthmatics. Structural interventions into the family system resulted in marked improvement in 62 percent of the diabetics and 90 percent of the asthmatics (Minuchin *et al.*, 1975).

Reinhart *et al.* (1972) reported good success with 30 anorexic families using a combination of individual psychotherapy and concurrent family therapy with a different therapist. However, the details of the family therapy process and outcome research are not well documented. Silverman (1977) reported good success with 65 anorexic patients using a combination of hospitalization, individual psychotherapy and separate weekly sessions for the parents. Similar positive results are reported by Goetz *et al.* (1977) using collaborative forms of family therapy.

Adult depression

Regardless of whether disturbed marital relationships precede or follow the depressive reaction, clinicians recognize the involvement of the spouse in maintenance of the depression. "The 'well' partner, along with having angry, guilty and negative feelings, also feels augmented self-esteem and feels important and relevant to the patient" (Janowsky *et al.*, 1970).

Chemotherapy has been a well-accepted intervention with depressed neurotic outpatients regardless of other types of psychotherapy offered. In the first large-scale (N=196) controlled study of the interaction effects of chemotherapy, marital therapy, minimal contact and placebo, Friedman (1973, 1975) reports drug therapy to have a superior early (4 weeks) effect upon symptom relief and enhanced perception of the marital relationship. Marital therapy was superior in perception of the marital relationship and family role task performance by the end of 12 weeks of treatment. Outcome measures included both therapist and patient observations.

The exact interventions practiced in Friedman's marital therapy are not described, which will make replication of his findings difficult. A long-term follow-up would also be desirable, especially in light of the trend for the effects of marital therapy to gain over the effects of chemotherapy after 12 weeks.

In a controlled study of 20 depressed patients, McLean *et al.* (1973) report success with behavioral-exchange marital therapy. Treatment included immediate feedback on spouse's perception of interactions as well as training in social learning principles and reciprocal behavioral contracts.

Marital distress

Marriages have traditionally been treated from a dynamic perspective and only recently from behavioral and systems perspectives (Paolino and McCrady, 1978). The bulk of the outcome literature on marital therapy has appeared since Stuart's 1969 case reports and has represented approaches developed primarily from social learning and exchange principles. Using procedures which are "structured" and clearly described, several research teams have been able to document the effectiveness of behavioral therapy above baseline behavior, waiting list control and placebo groups (*e.g.*, Weiss *et al.*, 1972; Azrin *et al.*, 1973; Jacobson, 1977, 1978a; Jacobson and Margolin, 1979; O'Leary and Turkewitz, 1978). The focus of behavioral marriage therapy is on teaching spouses to learn positive (noncoercive) methods of effecting behavior changes in one another. The primary techniques used to accomplish that include: (1) communication skill training; (2) problem-solving; and (3) contingency contracting. The skills are taught through modeling, structured exercises, and feedback. In the last decade, behavioral marital therapy has shifted from only emphasizing reinforcement to also focus on problem-solving and communication (Weiss, 1978).

Of all the approaches to family intervention, the behavioral approaches to marital therapy have made the most progress in identifying the change-inducing components of their therapy and in specifying type of intervention by client group. An important study with respect to this issue was conducted by Turkewitz and reported in O'Leary and Turkewitz (1978). Thirty couples were matched in groups of three on years married and reported level of marital satisfaction and then were randomly assigned to one of three conditions: (1) communication therapy; (2) behavioral contracting plus communication therapy; or (3) waiting list control. The couples were moderately distressed but not presenting alcoholism, psychotic disorders or sexual dysfunction. Treatment lasted 10 weeks. At four-month follow-up, couples in both treatment groups reported significant improvement in their communication and an increase in marital satisfaction from pretreatment. Although there were no differences between the two treatment groups, further analysis revealed an age by treatment interaction. Couples who were married an average of seven years and were an average of 29 years old responded more favorably to communication training combined with behavioral contracting, whereas couples married an average of 18 years with an average age of 41 responded more favorably to communication therapy alone.

Behavioral marital therapies have been severely criticized for demonstrating their effectiveness on a select population of relatively mildly distressed couples, and for emphasizing technique ("technolatry"), over the therapeutic relationship (e.g., Gurman and Knudson, 1978; Gurman and Kniskern, 1978b; Gurman et al., 1978). Jacobson's (1979) most recent outcome study demonstrates that behavioral therapy can be useful in working with more distressed couples. This study investigated the use of problem-solving training (including communication training but *not* contracting) with six severely disturbed marriages. At least one of the spouses in each couple presented individual distress (primarily depression or schizophrenia) in addition to relationship problems of long duration.

Summary of improvement rates by type of therapy

Reporting gross improvement rates across several studies by type of marital and family therapy masks important interaction effects (Bergin, 1971). However, such rates may offer a useful gross comparison with other types of psychotherapy as we look back upon the decade.

Table 3 summarizes improvement rates for four types of marital therapy and for family therapy specified by "identified patient." Details of these studies can be obtained from Gurman and Kniskern's (1978b) recent review. Overall, it appears that marital and family therapy improvement rates are superior to those reported for individual therapies.

The following implications for practice are supported by the empirical research reviewed above, and overlap with the recommendations Gurman and Kniskern (1978b) make for the training of marriage and family therapists:

1. Conjoint marital therapy appears more useful than individual therapy for improving marital relationships.
2. Family therapy appears as effective as individual therapy for a wide range of presenting problems. However, for most presenting problems, it is not possible to specify the best type of family treatment.
3. No one "school" of marital or family therapy has been demonstrated to be effective with a wide range of presenting problems.
4. Therapist relationship skills are important regardless of the conceptual orientation or "school" of the family therapist.

TABLE 3. Improvement Rates in Marital and Family Therapy

	No. of Studies	No. of Patients	Outcome (%)		
			Improved	No Change	Worse
Marital Therapy					
Conjoint	8	261	70	24	1
Conjoint group	15	397	66	30	4
Concurrent and collaborative	6	464	63	35	2
Individual	7	406	48	45	7
Total	36	1528	61	35	4
Family Therapy					
Child as I.P.	10	370	68	32	0
Adolescent as I.P.	9	217	75	25	0
Adult as I.P.	11	475	65	33	2
Mixed I.P.	8	467	81	17	2
Total	38	1529	73	26	1

Abstracted from "Research on Marital and Family Therapy: Progress, Perspective, and Prospect," by A. S. Gurman and D. P. Kniskern. In S. L. Garfield and A. E. Bergin, *Handbook of Psychotherapy and Behavior Change.* Copyright 1978 by John Wiley & Sons, Inc. Reprinted by permission.

Advances and suggestions for outcome research

The decade of the 1970s has seen the following *advances* in the empirical evaluation of relationship therapy:
1. Use of multi-method assessment aimed at multiple system levels.
2. Increased use of "objective" as well as "subjective" data.
3. Inclusion of comparison and control groups.
4. Use of short-term follow-ups.
5. Acknowledgement of deterioration.
6. Development of sequential research projects which link an understanding of relationship dynamics to intervention.

The following are *recommendations* for future outcome research based upon the progress already documented. There should be:
1. Increased assessment of outcome by practicing therapists, which will require diagnosis and follow-up assessment.
2. Continued use of multiple outcome measures, including combinations of "subjective," "objective," and "system-relevant" measures.

3. Greater specification of treatment procedure applied to a narrowly defined client group.
4. Continued effort to match treatment to relationship dynamics rather than to presenting complaints—e.g., match treatment to "system" rather than to "symptom."
5. Investigation of the generalizability of treatment approaches to different settings.
6. Investigation of the generalization of treatment effects from the marital to parent-child subsystems and vice versa.

PROMISING TRENDS AND FUTURE DIRECTIONS

Bridging research, theory and practice

The bridging of research, theory and practice has generally been lacking in the area of marital and family therapy (Olson, 1976; Sprenkle, 1976). Although some headway has been made in this regard during the past decade, it has primarily been because one individual utilized all three perspectives, not because of any cooperative efforts by several individuals specializing in these areas. Some of these more integrated projects such as those directed by Alexander, Guerney and Patterson have made significant contributions to the field in the last decade and they are described in greater detail elsewhere (Olson, 1976).

The lack of integration of research, theory and practice has retarded the development of each of these domains. There are many ways, however, that family researchers and family therapists can be helpful to each other (Olson, 1980). Hopefully, the next decade will bring more collaboration between these two groups because they have each suffered conceptually and methodologically from their mutual isolation.

Treating family systems versus family symptoms

A potentially revolutionary idea regarding treatment is to change the focus of marital and family therapy from focusing on the *presenting symptom* to the *type* of marital and family *system*. Increasingly, in the last decade, treatment centers have emerged based on the type of presenting symptoms in one or more family member (*i.e.*, alcoholism, drug abuse, child abuse, wife abuse, juvenile runaways, incest and sexual problems).

These symptom-oriented treatment centers have emerged primarily because of state and federal funding which, in turn, was generated because of public and professional concern about these issues. Since specific problems are easy to identify and rally support for, treatment programs and centers have simply taken advantage of these funding opportunities.

Even our review of outcome research has been organized by presenting symptom because this has been the predominant theme of studies in this decade. Researchers have, therefore, also been seduced by the availability of grants for work on certain specific symptoms and by the apparent simplicity of forming symptomatically homogeneous groups.

A major limitation with symptom-focused treatment is that family members often receive treatment from different, and often therapeutically and economically competing, programs and agencies. This is because problem families often encounter multiple symptoms which are dynamically related. For example, a family with an alcoholic parent may frequently also have problems with spouse and/or child abuse, incest and sexual dysfunction.

Another consequence of symptom-oriented treatment is that it focuses too much attention on the presenting complaint and, thereby, suggests more individually-oriented treatment. There is, however, an increasing trend for even symptom-oriented centers to treat problems within a family or relationship context.

A major problem with symptom-oriented treatment is that reducing or eliminating a symptom in one family member doesn't guarantee that new symptoms may not later emerge in the same person or in another member in the same family. In fact, family therapists have anecdotally reported that treating a symptom without changing the family system will only provide temporary symptomatic relief.

However, the *quantum leap conceptually* to treatment programs based on the *type of family system* has only begun to emerge. Whereas most treatment programs continue to be symptom focused, most experienced family therapists tend to focus less on the presenting symptom and focus more on the type of marital and family system.

An example of the application of a family-based treatment program based on the type of family system was conducted at the Family Renewal Center in Minneapolis (Killorin and Olson, 1980). Four consecutive families that came for treatment because of an alcoholic family member were diagnosed using the Circumplex Model of Marital and Family Systems (Olson *et al.*, 1980). One interesting finding was that, even though all four families had the same presenting complaint, *i.e.*, an alcoholic family member, the diagnosis indicated that all four families had very different family systems. One family represented each of the four extreme family types on the Circumplex Model: rigidly enmeshed, rigidly disengaged, chaotically enmeshed and chaotically disengaged.

In most traditional alcohol treatment programs, these four different family systems would have received the same treatment program because they had the same presenting symptom. However, in this project, the goals for treatment and therapeutic strategies were specifically designed for the type of family system. This enabled the therapist to more adequately observe the changes in the family system and assess the impact of treatment.

Pilot and case studies have indicated that family treatment can be more effective and efficient when treating the family system rather than the presenting symptoms. The next decade will, hopefully, demonstrate, clinically and empirically, the utility of more family system-based treatment. If a shift from treating family symptoms to family systems seems a more viable approach to treatment as is already evidenced by experienced family therapists, diagnostic assessment and treatment of families will need to become more system-focused.

Unfortunately, the development of family system-oriented treatment has been retarded because the field has not developed effective and efficient ways of conceptually and/or empirically describing types of marital and family systems. The next section will briefly review the emerging work in the development of typologies, both conceptual and empirical, and their usefulness for bridging research, theory and practice.

Typologies of marital and family systems

The use of typologies of couples and families constitutes a major break-through for the field because they help to bridge the gap between research, theory and practice (Olson, 1980). Typologies, whether developed empirically or intuitively (theoretically and clinically), offer numerous conceptual and methodological advantages over traditional variable analysis.

Conceptually, they bridge research and practice because the focus is on actual couples and families rather than on variables. For example, describing a family system as a "rigidly enmeshed" type provides considerable information about the family since the typology incorporates and summarizes a cluster of variables uniquely related to each type. The result is that typological studies are easier to directly translate and apply to couples and families.

Typologies enable a researcher or therapist to: (1) classify and describe couples and families on a number of variables; (2) summarize numerous characteristics of all the cases within a particular type; (3) establish criteria which determine whether a couple or family fits within a particular type; and (4) distinguish and describe differences between types.

Methodologically, typologies enable an investigator to: (1) pool statistical variance across a number of variables uniquely related to each type; (2) empirically discover more stable and meaningful relationships between variables and types; (3) translate the findings directly to couples and families rather than to variables.

In the last few years, there has been increasing interest among family scholars in identifying types of marital and family systems. The major typologies have been developed intuitively and have suffered from one or more of the following problems: (1) criteria for classifying are not clearly specified; (2) procedures for assigning couples to types are subjective and ambiguous with unknown reliability; and (3) types are not exhaustive or mutually exclusive (Miller and Olson, 1978).

Cuber and Haroff (1955) developed one of the first inductively derived typologies of *marriages* based on interviews with high status couples. Ryder (1970a) developed a topography of husbands and wives regarding personality traits that emerged from condensed interview reports with 200 couples. Kantor and Lehr (1975) developed a typology of *families* based on the concepts of open, closed and random systems. Constantine (1977) has extended their four-player model into a more comprehensive and unified typology. Lewis *et al.* (1976) developed a descriptive analysis of dysfunctional, mid-range and healthy families. Wertheim (1973) developed a typology based on three aspects of the morphogenesis-morphostasis dimension. She described eight types of family systems and these were related to the empirical types of families described by Reiss (1971).

The empirical approach to developing typologies of marital and family systems is becoming more popular because of recent developments in computer programs on cluster analysis and small-space analysis. Some of the first attempts to develop "couples types" empirically was done by Goodrich *et al.* (1968) and Ryder (1970b), in which profile analysis was used to describe newlywed couples. Shostrum and Kavanaugh (1971) used a self-report instrument to develop types of couples based on their scores on the dimensions of anger-love and strength-weakness. Moos and Moos (1976) developed a typology of families based on their Family Environment Scale. Using the Ravich Interpersonal Game-Test, Ravich and Wyden (1974) described eight types of marital interaction patterns.

Olson and his colleagues have been working for the past five years developing two different approaches to couple and family typologies, one empirical and the other theoretical. The empirical approach has focused on typologies of couples and families based on their verbal interaction patterns (Miller and Olson, 1978). The interaction was generated by the Inventory of Marital Conflicts (Olson and Ryder, 1970) and other related Inventories. The theoretical typology is the Circumplex Model of Marital and Family Systems developed by Olson *et al.* (1979).

Advances in clinical assessment

Although a variety of diagnostic tools have been developed which could be used by marital and family therapists (Cromwell *et al.*, 1976; Cromwell &. Fournier, 1980), the statement made by Olson (1970:512) in the last decade review of the field still applies: "Most therapists seem to make their diagnostic evaluations in rather unsystematic and subjective ways using unspecified criterion that they have found helpful in their clinical practice."

However, for the field to advance it is important to learn what types of therapeutic intervention work best with specific presenting symptoms or family systems. As Broderick (1976:XV) stated: "It is a simple-minded but often overlooked concept that couples are different and require differential diagnosis procedures leading to different treatment procedures."

There are a variety of reasons why most marital and family therapists do not currently use standardized diagnostic tools for their clinical assessment. *First,* most therapists have not clearly identified the conceptual dimensions they consider important for diagnostic assessment. *Second,* there is a lack of concern with systematic diagnosis since it often had little relationship to the therapeutic approach used. *Third,* most marital and family assessment tools do not assess clinically relevant concepts, are not designed for use in clinical settings and do not adequately capture the complexity of marital and family systems.

There are, however, some recent attempts to base the treatment program on the diagnostic assessment. These bridging projects are different because they can be accomplished only when the conceptual, clinical and empirical domains are integrated. Three examples of projects where this integrated approach was attempted are the McMaster Model of Therapy by Epstein and colleagues (Epstein *et al.*, 1978; Santa-Barbara *et al.*, 1977), the Circumplex Model by Olson and colleagues (Olson *et al.*, 1979; Olson *et al.*, 1980), and the Timberlawn project by Lewis and colleagues (Lewis *et al.*, 1976; Beavers, 1977). All three projects have developed clinical indicators for diagnosis and research procedures for assessing couples and family systems. These assessment tools enable the investigators to do clinical diagnosis before treatment and post-evaluation at the end of treatment.

There are also attempts to develop more clinically relevant and useful diagnostic tools for couples and families. In this regard, Cromwell and colleagues are continuing to describe the value of "systemic diagnosis" (Cromwell and Keeney, 1979; Cromwell, 1980) which integrates systems theory and a multi-level (individual, interpersonal and total system), multi-trait, and multi-method assessment. This comprehensive approach is very ambitious but reflects the type of systematic assessment that has been lacking in the field to date.

In conclusion, there are few therapeutic models where there is an integration between the clinical assessment and the therapeutic approach. This type of integration could be accelerated if family therapists and family researchers worked together in a more collaborative manner. Also, there are numerous other benefits to both therapists and researchers if they formed a more cooperative relationship (Olson, 1980).

Sex therapy

The publication of Masters and Johnson's *Human Sexual Inadequacy* (1970) did a great deal to establish sex therapy as a legitimate form of intervention in the decade of the seventies. It helped spur the rapid growth of a variety of sex clinics and programs (Hartman & Fithian, 1972; Annon, 1971, 1975; Kaplan, 1974, 1979; Maddock, 1976; Fischer and Gonchos, 1977). The American Association of Sex Educators, Counselors, and Therapists (AASECT) also grew rapidly in size and initiated a certification program for professionals in this discipline.

Although there is considerable diversity across treatment programs, the new sex therapies share the following commonalities in that they: (1) emphasize the mutual responsibility of the couple for the sexual dysfunction; (2) stress information and education in treatment; (3) attend to attitudinal change and performance anxiety; (4) increase communication skills and effectiveness of sexual technique; (5) prescribe changes in behavior; and (6) change destructive life styles and sex roles (LoPiccolo, 1978).

There is also increasing recognition of the pervasive interaction between the sexual dysfunction and the marital relationship (Kaplan, 1974; Messersmith, 1976). There has been a trend away from the intensive and costly residential co-therapy format of Masters and Johnson to outpatient programs in the client's home community with a single therapist (Messersmith, 1976). The result of the latter approach appears as successful as the former (Kaplan, 1974, 1979). Although the emphasis has been on working with couples, groups have been formed with individuals having sexual complaints (Schneidman and McGuire, 1976) as well as different sexual problems (Lieblum *et al.*, 1976).

As noted in several reviews of the efficacy of sex therapy (Hogan, 1978; Gurman and Kniskern, 1978; Sotile and Kilmann, 1977) we do not know which components of the various sex therapy programs contribute to their success. There has, however, been a rather high success rate for some sexual dysfunctions (premature ejaculation, impotence, non-orgasmic response) across various treatment programs. Even though these empirical studies were lacking in scientific rigor (Kockott *et al.*, 1975), "there seems to be general agreement that sex therapy works ... but why and when are questions yet to be answered" (Kinder and Blakeney, 1976:1).

Divorce therapy

The 1970's witnessed the emergence of a new sub-specialty—divorce therapy. It was stimulated in part by the large increase in the number of divorces during the past decade (708,000 in 1970; 1,170,000 in 1979) and the growing awareness that divorcing individuals need help uncoupling and dealing with this process. While marital therapy often has operated on the implicit assumption of "saving marriages," it is perhaps a sign of the times that divorce therapy ". . . does not focus on improving the husband-wife relationship but on decreasing the function of that relationship with the goal of eventual dissolution of that relationship." Even the criteria for successful marital therapy (Brown, 1976:410) has been expanded to include helping individuals through the process of dissolving their relationship.

Although a number of helpful works have appeared on the divorce process (Levinger and Moles, 1979; Salts, 1979), its effect on children (Wallerstein and Kelly, 1980), and the process of divorce therapy (Brown, 1976), there is almost no empirical research on divorce therapy *per se*. Most of the relevant data are from marriage counseling cases where divorce was an unintended outcome. Sprenkle and Storm (1980a) have demonstrated how the misuse of these data has led to the untested assumption that individual rather than conjoint therapy is more effective for divorcing persons. These authors (1980b) have also prepared a critique of the methodology of research related to divorce therapy.

Divorce, like marriage, is a complex process that proceeds in stages and considerable work needs to be done to determine the intervention strategies most appropriate for particular families and circumstances. At this point we know considerably more about therapists' views of divorce therapy (Kressel and Deutsch, 1977) than we have empirical evidence about the process and outcome.

Preventative and enrichment programs

One promising trend in the last five years has been the increasing interest in developing marital and family enrichment programs. Reviews of the historical development of the marital enrichment movement have been completed by Mace and Mace (1976), Otto (1976) and L'Abate (1974). Most marital and family therapists have been so preoccupied with treating problematic relationships that they have failed to develop or use more preventative approaches. Vincent (1967, 1977) has long been an advocate of focusing on marital health and he has identified the barriers to this preventative orientation in the mental health field.

Although a goal of the enrichment programs has been preventative by attempting to improve the quality of the marital and family relationship, there have been two basically different types of enrichment programs. While both types of enrichment approaches have been primarily focused on couples rather than families, one approach focuses on structured communication skill building programs while the other is composed of more loosely focused programs often called "marriage encounter."

Although marriage encounter programs were developed in the last decade, they have gained increasing acceptance as churches have begun sponsoring these programs. The Catholic church developed one of the earliest versions of marriage encounter (Bosco, 1972; Koch and Koch, 1976) and now most church denominations have developed some type of marriage encounter program. David and Vera Mace (1976) have been leading advocates of marriage enrichment. They have developed an Association for Couples for Marital Enrichment (ACME) which offers weekend retreats and other programs for couples.

The second approach to marital enrichment has been the more structured communication skill building programs. These programs have been more systematically developed and researched and represent a significant advance in the field. Miller and associates (1976) have developed a Couples Communication Program (CCP) and recently completed a program for families entitled "Understanding Us." Guerney and colleagues (1977) have developed a Conjugal Relationship Enhancement (CRE) program (Rappaport, 1976) and a program for Parent-Adolescent Relationship Development (PARD). L'Abate and associates (1974, 1977) have developed and evaluated a variety of programs for marital and family enrichment.

In a recent review of marital enrichment programs, Gurman and Kniskern (1977) concluded that one must be cautious about the overly zealous claims about the impact of these programs—especially the marriage encounter programs. They reviewed 29 studies of marital and premarital enrichment programs and found only six had an untreated control group. Although these studies generally demonstrated positive change, the results should be tempered by the serious methodological limitations of these studies.

Another promising preventative approach is the development of premarital programs and tools for preparing couples for marriage. There is growing evidence that traditional lecture programs for premarital couples most often offered by churches are not very effective (Norem et al., 1980; Druckman et al., 1979). A recent Canadian study by Bader and associates (Microys and Bader, 1977) demonstrated that experiential programs are helpful to premarital couples. Another recent study (Druckman et al., 1979) found that a structured premarital instrument called PREPARE was more useful than traditional education programs.

SUMMARY

Marital and family therapy became a significant mental health profession during the 1970s. *Conceptually,* numerous family concepts and ideas were developed, and integrative models began emerging in the late 1970s. *Clinically,* schools of family therapy became identified with specific techniques and training centers. *Empirically,* more effective assessment tools were developed, and systematic outcome research was being conducted.

Promising new directions for the 1980s include the development of integrative models that bridge research, theory and practice. Theoretical and empirical typologies are being developed which facilitate the bridging process. Specialities are emerging like sex and divorce therapy, and there is increasing interest in preventative and enrichment programs for couples and families.

The authors wish to thank Alan Gurman and James Hawkins for their constructive comments on this paper. Also, we appreciated the assistance of Bradford Keeney on the theory section and the work of Raymond Atilano on the summary of outcome studies.

REFERENCES

Alexander, B. K., & Dibb, G. S. Opiate addicts and their parents. *Family Process,* 1975, *14,* 499–514.
Alexander, B. K., & Dibb, G. S. Interpersonal perception and addict families. *Family Process,* 1977, *16* (March), 17–28.

Alexander, J. F. Defensive supportive communication in normal and deviant families. *Journal of Consulting and Clinical Psychology*, 1973, *40* (February), 223–231.

Alexander, J. F., Barton, C., Schiavo, R. S., & Parsons, B. Systems-behavioral intervention with families of delinquents: Therapist characteristics, family behavior and outcome. *Journal of Consulting and Clinical Psychology*, 1976, *44*, 656–664.

Alexander, J. F., & Barton, C. Behavioral systems therapy with delinquent families. In D. H. Olson (Ed.), *Treating relationships*. Lake Mills, Iowa: Graphic, 1976. Pp. 167–188.

Alexander, J., & Parsons, B. Short-term behavioral intervention with delinquent families: Impact on family process and recidivism. *Journal of Abnormal Psychology*, 1973, *81*, 219–225.

Alexander, R., Lucas, M. D., Duncan, J. W., & Piens, V. The treatment of anorexia nervosa. *American Journal of Psychiatry*, 1976, *133*, 1034–1038.

Annon, J. S. *The behavioral treatment of sexual problems. Vol. I: Brief therapy*. Honolulu: Enabling Systems, 1971.

Annon, J. S. *The behavioral treatment of sexual problems. Vol. II: Intensive therapy*. Honolulu: Enabling Systems, 1975.

Azrin, N. H., Naster, B. J., & Jones, R. Reciprocity counseling: A rapid learning-based procedure for marital counseling. *Behavior Research and Therapy*. 1973, *11*, 365–382.

Bandler, R., & Grinder, J. *The Structure of Magic, I*. Palo Alto, Calif.: Science and Behavior Books, 1975. (a)

Bandler, R., & Grinder, J. *Patterns of the hypnotic techniques of Milton H. Erikson, M.D., I*. Cupertino, Calif.: Meta Publications, 1975. (b)

Bandler, R., Grinder, J., & Satir, V. Changing with Families. Palo Alto, Calif.: Science and Behavior Books, 1976.

Bateson, G. Steps to an ecology of mind. New York: Ballantine, 1972.

Bateson, G. Mind and nature: A necessary unity. New York: E. P. Dutton, 1979.

Beal, D., & Duckro, P. Family counseling as an alternative to legal action for the juvenile status offender. *Journal of Marriage and Family Counseling*, 1977, *3* (January), 77–81.

Beavers, W. R. *Psychotherapy and growth: A family systems perspective*. New York: Brunner/ Mazel, 1977.

Beck, D. F. Research findings on the outcomes of marital conseling. In D. H. Olson (Ed.), *Treating relationships*. Lake Mills, Iowa: Graphic, 1976. Pp. 433–473.

Beels, D. C., & Ferber, A. Family therapy: A view. *Family Process*, 1969, *8* (September), 280–318.

Benjamin, L. S. Structural analysis of social behavior. *Psychological Review*, 1974, *81*, 392–425.

Benjamin, L. S. Structural analysis of a family in therapy. *Journal of Counseling and Clinical Psychology*, 1977, *45*, 391–406.

Bergin, A. E. The evaluation of therapeutic outcomes. In A. E. Bergin & S. L. Garfield (Eds.), *Handbook of psychotherapy and behavior change*. New York: John Wiley & Sons, 1971.

Birchler, G. R., Weiss, R. L., & Vincent, J. P. Multi-method analysis of social reinforcement exchange between maritally distressed and non-distressed spouse and stranger dyads. *Journal of Personality and Social Psychology*, 1975, *31*, 349–360.

Bosco, A. *Marriage encounter: The re-discovery of love*. St. Meinard, Indiana: Abbey Press, 1972.

Boszormenyi-Nagy, I., & Spark, J. *Invisible loyalties*. Hagerstown, Maryland: Harper and Row, 1973.

Bowen, M. The family as the unit of study and treatment. *American Journal of Orthopsychiatry*, 1960, *31*, 40–60.

Bowen, M. Theory in the practice of psychotherapy. In P. Guerin, Jr. (Ed.), *Family therapy: Theory and practice*. New York: Gardner Press, 1976. Pp. 42–90.

Bowen, M. Family therapy in clinical practice. New York: Jason Aronson, 1978.

Broderick, C. Foreword. In D. H. Olson (Ed.), *Treating relationships*. Lake Mills, Iowa: Graphic, 1976. Pp. xv–xvii.

Brown, E. M. Divorce Counseling. In D. H. Olson (Ed.), *Treating relationships*. Lake Mills, Iowa: Graphic, 1976.

Bruch, H. Perils of behavior modification in treatment of anorexia nervosa. *Journal of the American Medical Association*, 1974, *230*, 1419–1422.

Budman, S., & Shapiro, R. *Patients' evaluations of successful outcome in family and individual therapy*. Unpublished manuscript, University of Rochester Medical School, 1976.

Cadogan, D. A. Marital group therapy in the treatment of alcoholism. *Quarterly Journal of Studies on Alcoholism*, 1973, *34*, 1187–1194.

Colapinto, J. The relative value of empirical evidence. *Family Process*, 1979, *18* (December), 427–442.

Constantine, L. Designed experience: A multiple, goal-directed training program in family therapy. *Family Process*, 1976, *15* (December), 773–788.

Constantine, L. *A verified system theory of human process.* Paper presented at Dept. of Family Social Science, at University of Minnesota, 1977.

Cookerly, J. R. Evaluating different approaches to marriage counseling. In D. H. Olson (Ed.), Treating relationships. Lake Mills, Iowa: Graphic, 1976. Pp. 475–498.

Corder, B. F., Corder, R. F., & Laidlaw, N. D. An intensive treatment program for alcoholics and their wives. *Quarterly Journal of Studies in Alcohol,* 1972, *33,* 1144–1146.

Cromwell, R. E. A systems approach to marital and family diagnosis. *Journal of Counseling and Psychotherapy* (in press).

Cromwell, R. E., & Fournier, D. G. Diagnosing relationships: Clinical assessment for marriage and family therapists. San Francisco: Jossey-Bass (in press).

Cromwell, R. E., & Keeney, B. P. Diagnosing marital and family systems: A training model. *Family Coordinator,* 1979, *28* (April), 101–108.

Cromwell, R., Olson, D., & Fournier, D. Diagnosis and evaluation in marital and family counseling. In D. H. Olson (Ed.), Treating Relationships. Lake Mills, Iowa: Graphic, 1976. Pp. 499–516.

Cuber, J. F., & Haroff, P. B. The significant Americans: A study of sexual behavior among the affluent. New York: Appleton-Century, 1955.

Davis, D., Berenson, D., Steinglass, P., & Davis, S. The adaptive consequences of drinking. *Psychiatry,* 1974, *37,* 209–215.

Druckman, J. M. A family-oriented policy and treatment program for female juvenile status offenders. *Journal of Marriage and the Family,* 1979, *41* (August), 627–636.

Druckman, J. M., Fournier, D. M., Robinson, B., & Olson, D. H. *Effectiveness of five types of pre-marital preparation programs.* Final Report for Education for Marriage. Grand Rapids, Mich., 1979.

Epstein, N. B., Bishop, D. S., & Levin, S. The McMaster model of family functioning. *Journal of Marriage and Family Counseling,* 1978, *40* (October), 19–31.

Evans, H., Chagoya, L., & Rakoff, V. Decision-making as to the choice of family therapy in an adolescent in-patient setting. *Family Process,* 1971, 10 (March), 97–110.

Ewing, J. A., Long, V., & Wenzel, G. G. Concurrent group psychotherapy of alcoholic patients and their wives. *The International Journal of Group Psychotherapy,* 1961, *11,* 329–338.

Fisher, B. L., & Sprenkle, D. H. Therapists' perceptions of healthy family functions. *The International Journal of Family Counseling,* 1978, *6,* 9–18.

Fischer, J., & Gonchos, H., (Eds.) *A handbook of behavior therapy with sexual problems, Vols. 1 & 2.* Elmsford, N. Y.: Pergamon Press, 1977.

Foley, V. D. An introduction to family therapy. New York: Grune and Stratton, 1974.

Framo, J. Symptoms from a family transactional viewpoint. Pp. 271–308. In C. Sager and H. Kaplan (Eds.), *Progress in group and family therapy.* New York: Brunner/Mazel, 1972.

Framo, J. In Ferber, A., Mendelsohn, M., & Napier, A., *The Book of Family Therapy.* Boston: Houghton Mifflin, 1973.

Framo, J. Personal reflections of a family therapist. *Journal of Marriage and the Family,* 1975, *1* (January), 15–28.

Framo, J. Family of origin as a therapeutic resource for adults in marital and family therapy: You can and should go home again. *Family Process,* 1976, *15* (June), 193–210.

Frank, J. D. The present status of outcome studies. *Journal of Consulting and Clinical Psychology,* 1979, *47,* 310–316.

Friedman, A. S. Drug therapy and marital therapy in outpatient depressives. *Psychopharmacology Bulletin,* 1973, *9,* 55–57.

Friedman, A. S. Interaction of drug therapy with marital therapy in depressive patients. *Archives of General Psychiatry,* 1975, *32,* 619–637.

Garrigan, J., & Bambrick, A. A family therapy for disturbed children: Some experimental results in special education. *Journal of Marriage and Family Counseling,* 1977, *3* (January), 83–93.

Goetz, P. L., Succop, R. A., Reinhart, J. B., & Miller, A. Anorexia nervosa in children: A follow-up study. *American Journal of Orthopsychiatry,* 1977, *47,* 597–603.

Goodrich, D. W., Ryder, R. G., & Rausch, H. L. Patterns of newlywed marriage. *Journal of Marriage and the Family,* 1968, *30* (August), 383–389.

Gould, E., & Glick, I. A. The effects of family presence and brief family intervention on global outcome for hospitalized schizophrenic patients. *Family Process,* 1977, *16* (December), 503–510.

Grinder, J., & Bandler, R. The structure of magic, II. Palo Alto, Calif.: Science and Behavior Books, 1976.

Grinder, J., DeLozier, J., & Bandler, R. Patterns of the hypnotic techniques of Milton H. Erikson, M.D., II. Cupertino, Calif.: Meta Publications, 1977.

Group for the Advancement of Psychiatry Reports. *The field of family therapy.* Report No. 78. New York: Science House, 1970.

Guerin, P. J., Jr. *Family therapy: Theory and practice.* New York: Gardner Press, 1976.

Guerney, B., et al. *Relationship enhancement.* San Francisco: Jossey-Bass, 1977.

Gurman, A. S. The effects and effectiveness of marital therapy: A review of outcome research. *Family Process,* 1973, *12* (June), 145–170.

Gurman, A. S. The effects and effectiveness of marital therapy. In A. S. Gurman and D. G. Rice (Eds.), *Couples in conflict.* New York: Jason-Aronson, 1975. Pp. 383–406.

Gurman, A. S. Contemporary marital therapies: A critique comparative analysis of psychoanalytic, behavioral and systems theory approaches. In J. Paolino, Jr. and B. S. McCrady (Eds.), *Marriage and marital therapy.* New York: Brunner/Mazel, 1978. Pp. 445–566.

Gurman, A. S., & Kniskern, D. P. Enriching research on marital enrichment programs. *Journal of Marriage and Family Counseling,* 1977, *3* (April), 3–11.

Gurman, A. S., & Kniskern, D. P. Deterioration in marital and family therapy: Empirical clinical and conceptual issues. *Family Process,* 1978, *17* (March), 3–20. (a)

Gurman, A. S., & Kniskern, D. P. Research on marital and family therapy: Progress, perspective, and prospect. In S. L. Garfield and A. E. Bergin (Eds.), *Handbook of psychotherapy and behavior change.* New York: John Wiley and Sons, 1978. Pp. 817–901. (b)

Gurman, A. S., & Kniskern, D. P. Technolatry, methodolatry, and the results of family therapy. *Family Process,* 1978, *17* (September), 275–281. (c)

Gurman, A. S., & Kniskern, D. P. *Handbook of family therapy.* New York: Brunner/Mazel, 1981.

Gurman, A. S., & Knudson, R. M. Behavioral marriage therapy: I. A psychodynamic-systems critique and reconsideration. *Family Process,* 1978, *17* (June), 121–138.

Gurman, A. S., Knudson, R. M., & Kniskern, D. P. Behavioral marriage therapy. IV. Take two aspirin and call us in the morning. *Family Process,* 1978, *17* (June), 165–180.

Haley, J. Research on family patterns: An instrument measurement. *Family Process,* 1964, *3* (March), 41–65.

Haley, J. *Changing families.* New York: Grune and Stratton, 1971.

Haley, J. *Uncommon therapy.* New York: W. W. Norton, 1973.

Haley, J. *Problem-solving therapy.* San Francisco, Calif.: Jossey-Bass, 1976.

Haley, J. Ideas which handicap therapists. In M. Berger (Ed.), *Beyond the double bind.* New York: Brunner/Mazel, 1978. Pp. 65–82.

Haley, J. Leaving home: The therapy of disturbed young people. New York: McGraw-Hill, 1980.

Harbin, H. T., & Maziar, H. M. The families of drug abusers: A literature review. *Family Process,* 1975, *14* (September), 411–431.

Hartman, W., & Fithian, M. Treatment of sexual dysfunction. Long Beach, Calif.: Center for Marital and Sexual Studies, 1972.

Hedberg, A. G., & Campbell, L. A comparison of four behavioral treatments of alcoholism. *Journal of Behavior Therapy and Experimental Psychiatry,* 1974, *5,* 251–256.

Hendricks, W. J. Use of multifamily counseling groups in treatment of male narcotic addicts. *International Journal of Group Psychotherapy,* 1971, *21,* 84–90.

Herr, J. J., & Weakland, J. H. Counseling elders and their families. New York: Springer, 1979.

Hoffman, L. Breaking the homeostatic cycle. In P. Guerin (Ed.), *Family therapy: Theory and practice.* New York: Gardner Press, 1976. Pp. 501–519.

Hogan, D. R. The effectiveness of sex therapy: A review of the literature. In J. LoPiccolo and L. LoPiccolo (Eds.), *Handbook of sex therapy.* New York: Plenum Press, 1978. Pp. 57–84.

Jacobson, N. S. Problem-solving and contingency contracting in the treatment of marital discord. *Journal of Consulting and Clinical Psychology,* 1977, *45,* 92–100.

Jacobson, N. S. A review of the research on the effectiveness of marital therapy. Pp. 395–444. In T. J. Paolino and B. S. McCrady (Eds.), *Marriage and marital therapy: Psychoanalytic, behavior and systems theory perspectives.* New York: Brunner/Mazel, 1978. (a)

Jacobson, N. S. Specific and non-specific factors in the effectiveness of a behavioral approach to marital discord. *Journal of Consulting and Clinical Psychology,* 1978, *46,* 442–452. (b)

Jacobson, N. S. Increasing positive behavior in severely distressed marital relationships: The effects of problem-solving training. *Behavior Therapy,* 1979, *10,* 311–326.

Jacobson, N. S., & Margolin, G. Marital therapy: Strategies based on social learning and behavior exchange principles. New York: Brunner/Mazel, 1979.

Jacobson, N. S., & Martin, B. Behavioral marriage therapy: Current status. *Psychological Bulletin*, 1976, *83*, 540–556.

Janowsky, D. W., Leff, M., & Epstein, R. S. Playing the manic game. *Archives of General Psychiatry*, 1970, *22*, 252–261.

Johnson, A. M., Falstein, E. I., Szurek, S. A., & Svendsen, M. School phobia. *American Journal of Orthopsychiatry*, 1941, *11*, 702–711.

Johnson, T. F. The results of family therapy with juvenile offenders. *Juvenile Justice*, 1977, *28*, 29–33.

Kantor, D., & Lehr, W. *Inside the family*. San Francisco: Jossey-Bass, 1975.

Kaplan, H. S. The new sex therapy. New York: Quadrangle, 1974.

Kaplan, H. S. Disorders of sexual desire. New York: Brunner/Mazel, 1979.

Karoly, P., & Rosenthal, M. Training parents in behavior modification: Effects on perceptions of family interactions and deviant child behavior. *Behavior Therapy*, 1977, *8*, 406–410.

Keeney, B. P., & Sprenkle, D. H. *Ecosystemic epistemology: Critical implications for family therapy*. Unpublished manuscript, 1980.

Keith, D., & Whitaker, C. A. Struggling with the impotence impasse: Absurdity and acting-in. *Journal of Marriage and Family Counseling*, 1978, *4* (January), 69–77.

Kennedy, D. L. Behavior of alcoholics and spouses in a simulation game. *Journal of Nervous and Mental Disease*, 1976, *162*, 23–24.

Killorin, E., & Olson, D. H. *Clinical application of the circumplex model to chemically dependent families*. Unpublished manuscript, University of Minnesota, 1980.

Kinder, B. H., & Blakeney, P. *Treatment of sexual dysfunction: a review of outcome studies*. Unpublished manuscript, University of Texas Medical Branch, 1976.

Klein, N. C., Alexander, J. F., & Parsons, B. V. Impact of family systems intervention on recidivism and sibling delinquency: A model of primary prevention and program evaluation. *Journal of Consulting and Clinical Psychology*, 1977, *45*, 469–474.

Koch, J., & Koch, L. The urgent drive to make good marriages better. Psychology Today, 1976, *10*, 33–35.

Kockott, G., Dittmar, F., & Nussett, L. Systematic desensitization of erectile impotence: A controlled study. Archives of Sexual Behavior, 1975, *4*, 493–500.

Kressel, K., & Deutsch, M. Divorce therapy: In-depth survey of therapists' views. *Family Process*, 1977, *16* (December), 413–443.

L'Abate, L. Family enrichment programs. *Journal of Family Counseling*, 1974, *2* (January), 32–44.

L'Abate, L. *Enrichment: Structured intervention with couples, families, and groups*. Washington, D. C.: University Press of America, 1977.

Langsley, D., Pittman, F., Machotka, P., & Flomenhaft, K. Family crisis therapy—results and implications. *Family Process*, 1968, *7*, 145–158.

Leiblum, S. R., Rosen, R. C., & Pierce, D. Group treatment format: Mixed sexual dysfunctions. *Archives of Sexual Behavior*, 1976, *5*, 313–322.

Levant, R. F. A classification of the field of family therapy: A review of prior attempts and a new paradigmatic model. *American Journal of Family Therapy*, 1980, *8*, 3–16.

Levinger, G., & Moles, O. C. Divorce and separation: Context, causes, and consequences. New York: Basic Books, 1979.

Lewis, J. M. *How's your family?* New York: Brunner/Mazel, 1979.

Lewis, J. M., Beavers, W. R., Gossett, J. T., & Phillips, V. A. No single thread: Psychological health in family systems. New York: Brunner/Mazel, 1976.

LoPiccolo, J. Direct treatment of sexual dysfunction. In J. LoPiccolo and L. LoPiccolo (Eds.), *Handbook of sex therapy*. New York: Plenum Press, 1978.

Mace, D., & Mace, V. Marriage enrichment: A preventative group approach in couples. In D. H. Olson (Ed.), *Treating relationships*. Lake Mills, Iowa: Graphic, 1976.

Maddock, J. W. Sexual health: An enrichment and treatment program. In D. H. Olson (Ed.), *Treating relationships*. Lake Mills, Iowa: Graphic, 1976. Pp. 355–382.

Mandelbaum, A. The inhibited child: A family therapy approach. In E. J. Anthony and D. C. Gilpin (Eds.), *Three Clinical Faces of Childhood*. New York: Spectrum, 1977. Pp. 121–130.

Manus, G. I. Marriage counseling: A technique in search of a theory. *Journal of Marriage and the Family*, 1966, *28* (November), 449–453.

Margolin, G., & Weiss, R. L. Comparative evaluation of therapeutic components associated with behavioral marital treatments. *Journal of Consulting and Clinical Psychology*, 1978, *46*, 1476–1486.

Masters, W. H., & Johnson, V. E. Human Sexual Inadequacy. Boston: Little, Brown & Co., 1970.

McCrady, B. S., Paolino, T. J., Longabaugh, R. L., & Rossi, J. Effects on treatment outcome of joint admission and spouse involvement in treatment of hospitalized alcoholics reported. Pp. 120–121. In T. J. Paolino and B. S. McCrady (Eds.), *The alcoholic marriage*. New York: Grune & Stratton, 1977.

McLean, P. D., Ogston, K., & Grauer, L. Behavioral approach to the treatment of depression. *Journal of Behavior Therapy and Experimental Psychiatry*, 1973, 4, 323–330.

Messersmith, C. E. Sex therapy and the marital system. In D. H. Olson (Ed.), *Treating relationships*. Lake Mills, Iowa: Graphic, 1976. Pp. 339–353.

Microys, G., & Bader, E. *Do pre-marriage programs really help?* Unpublished manuscript, University of Toronto, 1977.

Miller, B. C., & Olson, D. H. *Typology of marital interaction and contextual characteristics: Cluster analysis of the IMC*. Unpublished manuscript, Family Social Science, University of Minnesota, 1978.

Miller, S., Corrales, R., & Wackman, D. B. Recent progress in understanding and facilitating marital communication. *The Family Coordinator*, 1975, 24 (April), 143–152.

Miller, S., Nunnally, E. W., & Wackman, D. Minnesota couples communication program (MCCP): premarital and marital groups. In D. H. Olson (Ed.), *Treating relationships*. Lake Mills, Iowa: Graphic, 1976.

Minuchin, S. *Families and family therapy*. Cambridge, Mass.: Harvard University Press, 1974.

Minuchin, S., Baker, L., Rosman, B., Liebman, R., Milman, L., & Todd, T. A conceptual model of psychosomatic illness in children. *Archives of General Psychiatry*, 1975, 32, 1031–1038.

Minuchin, S., Montalvo, B., Guerney, B., Jr., Rosman, B., & Schumer, F. *Families of the slums: An exploration of their structure and treatment*. New York: Basic Books, 1967.

Minuchin, S., Rosman, B. L., & Baker, L. *Psychosomatic families: Anorexia nervosa in context*. Cambridge, Mass.: Harvard University Press, 1978.

Moos, R., & Moos, B. Typology of family social environments. *Family Process*, 1976, 15 (December), 357–371.

Napier, A. Y., & Whitaker, C. A. *The family crucible*. New York: Harper and Row, 1978.

Noone, R. J., & Reddig, R. L. Case studies in the family treatment of drug abuse. *Family Process*, 1976, 15 (September), 325–332.

Norem, R. H., Schaefer, M., Springer, J., & Olson, D. H. *Effective premarital education: Outcome study and follow-up evaluation*. Unpublished manuscript, Family Social Science, University of Minnesota, St. Paul, 1980.

O'Leary, K. D., & Turkewitz, H. Marital therapy from a behavioral perspective. In T. J. Paolino and B. S. McCrady (Eds.), *Marriage and marital therapy*. New York: Brunner/Mazel, 1978. Pp. 240–297.

Olson, D. H. Marital and family therapy: Integrative review and critique. *Journal of Marriage and the Family*, 1970, 32 (November), 501–538.

Olson, D. H. Empirically unbinding the double bind. *Family Process*, 1972, 11 (March), 69–94.

Olson, D. H. *Treating relationships*. Lake Mills, Iowa: Graphic, 1976.

Olson, D. H. Insiders' and outsiders' views of relationships: Research strategies. In G. Levinger and H. Rausch (Eds.), *Close relationships*. Amherst: University of Massachusetts Press, 1977. Pp. 115–135.

Olson, D. H. *Family research and family therapy: Bridging two different worlds*. Paper presented at conference on Family Observation, Behavioral Assessment, and Intervention, Arizona State University, Tempe, Arizona, 1980.

Olson, D. H., Russell, C., & Sprenkle, D. H. Circumplex model of marital and family systems II: Empirical studies and clinical intervention. In J. P. Vincent (Ed.), *Advances in Family Intervention, Assessment and Theory* (Vol. 1). Greenwich, Conn.: JAI Press, 1980. Pp. 129–176.

Olson, D. H., & Ryder, R. G. Inventory of marital conflicts: An experimental interaction procedure. *Journal of Marriage and the Family*, 1970, 32 (August), 443–448.

Olson, D. H., & Sprenkle, D. H. Emerging trends in treating relationships. *Journal of Marriage and Family Counseling*, 1976, 4 (October), 317–330.

Olson, D. H., Sprenkle, D. H., & Russell, C. Circumplex model of marital and family systems: I. Cohesion and adaptability dimensions, family types, and clinical applications. *Family Process*, 1979, 18 (March), 3–28.

Orford, J. Alcoholism and marriage: The argument against specialism. *Journal of Studies of Alcohol*, 1975, 36, 1537–1563.

Otto, H. A. *Marriage and family enrichment: New perspectives and programs*. Nashville: Abingdon, 1976.

Palazzoli, M. S. Self starvation: From the intrapsychic to the transpersonal approach to anorexia nervosa. London: Chaucer Publishing, 1974.

Paolino, T. J., & McCrady, B. S. Marriage and marital therapy: Psychoanalytic, behavioral and systems theory perspectives. New York: Brunner/Mazel, 1978.

Papp, P. (Ed.). Family Therapy: Full Length Case Studies. New York: Gardner Press, 1977.

Papp, P. The Greek chores and other techniques of family therapy. Family Process, 1980, 19 (March), 45–58.

Parsons, T., & Bales, R. F. Family, socialization and interaction process. Glencoe, Ill.: The Free Press, 1955.

Patterson, G. R. Interventions for boys with conduct problems: Multiple settings, treatments, and criteria. Journal of Consulting and Clinical Psychology, 1974, 42, 471–481.

Patterson, G. R. Parents and teachers as change agents: A social learning approach. In D. H. Olson (Ed.), Treating relationships. Lake Mills, Iowa: Graphic, 1976.

Patterson, G. R., Hops, H., & Weiss, R. L. Interpersonal skills training for couples in early stages of conflict. Journal of Marriage and the Family, 1975, 37 (May), 295–303.

Patterson, G. R., Reid, J. B., Jones, R. R., & Conger, R. E. A social learning approach to family intervention. I. Families with aggressive children. Eugene, Ore.: Castalia Publishing, 1975.

Pittman, F., Langsley, D., & DeYoung, C. Work and school phobias: A family approach to treatment. American Journal of Psychiatry, 1968, 124, 1535–1541.

Polakow, R. L., & Doctor, R. M. Treatment of marijuana and barbituate dependency by contingency contracting. Journal of Behavior Therapy and Experimental Psychiatry, 1973, 4, 375–377.

Postner, R., Guttman, H., Sigal, H., Epstein, N., & Rakoff, V. Process and outcome in conjoint family therapy. Family Process, 1971, 10 (December), 451–473.

Rappaport, A. F. Conjugal relationship enhancement program. In D. H. Olson (Ed.), Treating relationships. Lake Mills, Iowa: Graphic, 1976.

Ravich, R., & Wyden, B. Predictable pairing. New York: Wyden Publishing, 1974.

Reid, J. (Ed.) A social learning approach to family intervention. II. Observation in home settings. Eugene, Ore.: Castalia Publishing, 1978.

Reinhart, J. B., Kenna, M. D., & Succop, R. A. Anorexia nervosa in children: Outpatient management. Journal of American Academy of Child Psychiatry, 1972, 11, 114–131.

Reiss, D. Varieties of consensual experience: I. A theory for relating family interaction to individual thinking. Family Process, 1971, 10 (March), 1–27.

Riskin, J. Nonlabeled family interaction: Preliminary report on a prospective study. Family Process, 1976, 15 (December), 433–440.

Riskin, J. Paradigmatic classification of family therapy theories. Family Process, 1977, 16 (March), 29–46.

Ritterman, M. K. Paradigmatic classification of family therapy theories. Family Process, 1977, 16 (March), 29–48.

Rosenblatt, P., & Titus, S. Together and apart in family. Humanitas, 1976, 12 (November), 367–379.

Ro-Trock, G. K., Wellish, D. K., & Schoolar, J. C. A family therapy outcome study in an inpatient setting. American Journal of Orthopsychiatry, 1977, 47, 514–522.

Russell, C. Circumplex model of family systems: III. Empirical evaluation with families. Family Process, 1979, 18 (March), 29–46.

Ryder, R. A topography of early marriage. Family Process, 1970, 9 (December), 385–402. (a)

Ryder, R. Dimensions of early marriage. Family Process, 1970, 9 (March), 51–68. (b)

Salts, C. Divorce process: Integration of theory. Journal of Divorce, 1979, 2, 233–240.

Santa-Barbara, J., Woodward, C. A., Levin, S., Streiner, D., Goodman, J. T., & Epstein, N. B. Interrelationships among outcome measures in the McMaster family therapy outcome study. Goal Attainment Review, 1977, 3, 47–58.

Satir, V. Peoplemaking. Palo Alto, Ca.: Science and Behavior Books, 1972.

Satir, V., Stachowiak, J., & Taschman, H. A. Helping families to change. New York: Jason Aronson, 1975.

Schneidman, B., & McGuire, L. Group therapy for nonorgasmic women: Two age levels. Archives of Sexual Behavior, 1976, 5, 239–248.

Selvini Palazzoli, M., Boscolo, L., Cecchin, G., & Prata, G. Paradox and Counterparadox. New York: Aronson, 1978.

Selvini Palazzoli, M., Boscolo, L., Cecchin, G., & Prata, G., Hypothesizing—Circularity—Neutrality: Three guidelines for the conductor of the session. Family Process, 1980, 19 (March), 3–12.

Shapiro, R., & Budman, S. Defection, termination, and continuation in family and individual therapy. Family Process, 1973, *12* (March), 55–67.

Shostrum, E., & Kavanaugh, J. *Between man and woman.* Los Angeles: Nash Publishing, 1971.

Sigal, J., Barris, C., & Doubilet, A. Problems in measuring the success of family therapy in a common clinical setting: Impasse and solutions. *Family Process,* 1976, 15 (June), 225–233.

Silverman, J. A. Anorexia nervosa: Clinical and metabolic observations in a successful treatment plan. In R. A. Vigersky (Ed.), *Anorexia nervosa.* New York: Raven Press, 1977. Pp. 331–339.

Skynner, A. C. School Phobia: A reappraisal. *British Journal of Medical Psychology,* 1974, *47,* 1–16.

Sluzki, C. E. Marital therapy from a systems theory perspective. In T. J. Paolino, Jr., and B. S. McCrady (Eds.), *Marriage and marital therapy.* New York: Brunner/Mazel, 1978. Pp. 366–394.

Sotile, W. M., & Kilmann, P. R. Treatment of psychogenic female sexual dysfunctions. *Psychological Bulletin,* 1977, *84,* 619–633.

Spark, D., & Papp, P. Critical incidents in the context of family therapy: Critical incident No. 6. In N. W. Ackerman (Ed.), *Family therapy in transition.* Boston: Little, Brown, 1970.

Speck, R., & Attneave, C. *Family networks.* New York: Pantheon, 1973.

Speer, D. C. Family systems: Morphostasis and morphogenesis, or is homeostasis enough? *Family Process,* 1970, *9* (September), 254–278.

Sprenkle, D. H. The need for integration among theory, research and practice in the family field. *The Family Coordinator,* 1976, *24* (July), 261–263.

Sprenkle, D. H., & Fisher, B. L. Goals of family therapy: An empirical assessment. *Journal of Marriage and Family Therapy.* In press.

Sprenkle, D. H., & Storm, C. L. The unit of treatment in divorce therapy. In A. S. Gurman (Ed.), *Practical problems in family therapy.* New York: Brunner/Mazel, 1980. (a)

Sprenkle, D. H., & Storm, C. L. Divorce therapy: The first decade review of research and implications to practice. Paper presented at the Annual Meeting of the National Council on Family Relations, Portland, 1980. (b)

Stanton, M. D. Family treatment approaches to drug abuse problems: A review. *Family Process,* 1979, *18* (September), 251–280.

Stanton, M. D., Todd, T. C., Steier, F., Van Deusen, J. M., Marder, L. R., Rosoff, R. J., Seaman, S. F., & Skibinski, I. *Family characteristics and family therapy of heroin addicts: Final report 1974–1978.* Report prepared for the Psychosocial Branch, Division of Research, National Institute on Drug Abuse, Department of HEW, October, 1979. U.S. Govt. Printing Office: Washington, D.C.

Steinglass, P. Experimenting with family treatment approaches to alcoholism 1950–1975: A review. *Family Process,* 1976, *15* (March), 97–123.

Steinglass, P. The alcoholic family in the interaction laboratory. *The Journal of Nervous and Mental Disease,* 1979, *167,* 428–436. (a)

Steinglass, P. An experimental treatment program for alcoholic couples. *Journal of Studies on Alcohol,* 1979, *40,* 159–182. (b)

Steinglass, P., David, D. I., & Berenson, D. Observations of conjointly hospitalized 'alcoholic couples' during sobriety and intoxication. Family Process, 1977, *16* (March), 1–16.

Stuart, R. B. Operant-interpersonal treatment for marital discord. *Journal of Consulting and Clinical Psychology,* 1969, *33,* 675–682.

Stuart, R. B. An operant interpersonal program for couples. In D. H. Olson (Ed.), Treating Relationships. Lake Mills, Iowa: Graphic, 1976.

Vincent, C. E. Mental health and the family. *Journal of Marriage and the Family,* 1967, *29* (February), 18–38.

Vincent, C. E. Barriers to the development of marital health as a health field. *Journal of Marriage and Family Counseling,* 1977, *4* (July), 3–11.

Vincent, J. P. The empirical-clinical study of families: Social learning theory as a point of departure. In J. Vincent (Ed.), *Advances in Family Intervention, Assessment, and Theory (Vol. I).* Greenwich, Conn.: JAI Press, 1980. Pp. 1–28. (a)

Vincent, J. P. *Advances in Family Intervention, Assessment, and Theory (Vol. I).* Greenwich, Conn.: JAI Press, 1980. (b)

Wallerstein, J. S., & Kelly, J. E. *Surviving the break-up: How children actually cope with divorce.* New York: Basic Books, 1980.

Watzlawick, P. *The language of change.* New York: Basic Books, 1978.

Watzlawick, P., Beavin, J. H., & Jackson, D. D. *Pragmatics of human communication.* New York: Norton, 1967.

Watzlawick, P., & Weakland, J. H. (Eds.) *The Interactional View.* New York: W. W. Norton, 1977.

Watzlawick, P., Weakland, J., & Fisch, R. *Change: Principles of problem formation and problem resolution*. New York: Norton, 1974.

Weakland, J. H. Family somatics: A neglected edge. *Family Process*, 1977, *16* (September), 263–272. (a)

Weakland, J. H. Comments on Ritterman's paper. *Family Process*, 1977, *16* (March), 46–47. (b)

Weakland, J., et al. Brief therapy: Focused problem resolution. *Family Process*, 1974, *13* (June), 141–167.

Weiss, R. L. The conceptualization of marriage from a behavioral perspective. In T. J. Paolino and B. S. McCrady (Eds.), *Marriage and marital therapy*. New York: Brunner/Mazel, 1978. Pp. 165–239.

Weiss, R. L., Hops, J., & Patterson, G. *A framework for conceptualizing marital conflict, a technology for altering it, some data for evaluating it*. Paper presented at the Fourth International Conference on Behavior Modification, Banff, Alberta, Canada, 1972.

Wellisch, D., Vincent, J., & Ro-Trock, G. Family therapy versus individual therapy: A study of adolescents and their parents. In D. H. Olson (Ed.), *Treating relationships*. Lake Mills, Iowa: Graphic, 1976. Pp. 275–302.

Wells, R. A., & Dezen, A. E. The results of family therapy revisited: The non-behavioral methods. *Family Process*, 1978, *17* (September), 251–274.

Wells, R. A., Dilkes, T., & Burckhardt, T. The results of family therapy: A critical review of the literature. In D. H. Olson (Ed.), *Treating relationships*. Lake Mills, Iowa: Graphic, 1976. Pp. 499–516.

Wertheim, E. Family unit therapy and the science and typology of family systems. *Family Process*, 1973, *12* (December), 361–376.

Wertheim, E. The science typology of family systems. II. Further theoretical and practical considerations. *Family Process*, 1975, *14* (September), 285–308.

Whitaker, C. A. Psychotherapy of the absurd: With a special emphasis on the psychotherapy of aggression. *Family Process*, 1975, *14* (March), 1–16. (a)

Whitaker, C. A. A family therapist looks at marital therapy. In A. S. Gurman, Jr., and D. G. Rice (Eds.), *Couples in conflict: New directions in marital therapy*. New York: Aronson, Inc., 1975. (b)

Whitaker, C. A. The hindrance of theory in clinical work. In P. J. Guerin, Jr. (Ed.), *Family therapy: Theory and practice*. New York: Gardner Press, 1976.

Whitaker, C. A. Process techniques of family therapy. *Interaction I (Summer)*, 1977, 4–19.

Wiltz, N. A., & Patterson, G. R. An evaluation of parent training procedures designed to alter inappropriate aggressive behavior of boys. Behavior Therapy, 1974, *5*, 215–221.

Ziegler-Driscoll, G. Family research study at Eagleville hospital and rehabilitation center. *Family Process*, 1977, *16* (June), 175–189.

2

Models of Practice

Although family therapy has, as we have seen, developed from various theoretical positions, a degree of consistency has been maintained—through the influence of a number of models represented by a few key people. These "models of practice" are those practitioners who have made outstanding contributions to the field, have described their work in some detail, and have, in general, provided latecomers to the field with clear standards and individualized methods. Several have also functioned as leaders of "sub-schools" within the family therapy movement. All of these models of practice have had a powerful effect on practitioners of family therapy—through their writings, their appearances at conferences and institutes, and their clear expositions of their principles and methods.

The papers included in Part II demonstrate the broad differences that exist between theories of family therapy and theories of individual psychotherapy. Further, broad differences are also seen when one family therapy theory is compared to another.

David Kantor and William Lehr published their views of the family in their well-known book *Inside the Family* (1975). This book formed the foundation of their *systems model* of family therapy, now referred to as the "Boston" or "Cambridge" model. Stephen L. White's paper "Family Theory According to the Cambridge Model" summarizes Kantor's and Lehr's approach, offering a lucid introduction to their work. The model, avoiding a theory of pathological families, is said to pertain to all families and describes both what may be observed empirically and also the nature of family experience. They offer four interlocking frameworks that form the girding for therapy: *Interfaces, Dimensions, Typal Arrangements,* and *the Four Player System.*

Jay Haley is one of the most prolific writers in the field of family therapy, both documenting his own work and summarizing and commenting on the work of others. One of the early workers at the Mental Research Institute in California, he

later served as Director of Family Research at the Philadelphia
Child Guidance Clinic, was the first editor of the journal *Family Process*, and is a founder of the Family Therapy Institute in
Washington, D. C. His classic paper "Marriage Therapy" is a
clear exposition of his emphasis on describing relationships
and the means to shift relationships. Especially evident is
Haley's concern with the power dynamics of relationships,
formulated in his descriptions of events in which one person
seeks change in a relationship with another.

While associated with Jay Haley for several years at the
Mental Research Institute in Palo Alto, California, Virginia Satir
established a separate path and direction through her work in
a communications-experiential approach to family therapy.
Her book *Conjoint Family Therapy* (1967) is one of the best-
known works concerning family therapy; and her indefatiga-
ble work as a leader of encounter groups, as a consultant to
social agencies, and as a demonstrator of family therapy has
made her perhaps the most widely known family therapist.
Her paper, presented originally to the staff of the Fort Logan
Mental Health Center, explains her view of the development of
family therapy and her general approach to families.

Gerald H. Zuk, of the Eastern Pennsylvania Psychiatric Institute, is best known for his triadic approach to family therapy
and, in particular, his "go-between" process (Zuk, 1971). The
paper included here not only presents Zuk's views on family
therapy but also represents a major contribution to the literature through the inclusion of a concise and complete description of the go-between process.

A recent and major theoretical approach to family therapy is
behavior modification. Traditionally behavior modification
procedures have focused on more limited sequences of behavior than a consideration of the entire family. From Robert
Liberman's paper "Behavioral Approaches to Couples and
Families" as well as from other behavioral contributions in this
text, it can be seen that the language and concepts of theories
based on learning theory are expanding to include wider units
of behavior. Liberman's application of operant learning theory
to couples and families provides a clear explication of the
behavior modification approach.

Nathan Ackerman was long associated with both the early
history of family therapy and its development as an orientation to practice. He first published a paper on "The Unity of
the Family" (1938), and his books *Psychodynamics of Family
Life* (1958) and *Treating the Troubled Family* (1966) contained a
framework found most acceptable to practitioners with a
psychoanalytic orientation. His paper included here presents
his views on the role and functions of a family therapist from a
psychodynamic perspective.

The human growth and potential movement of the 1960s

and early 1970s, although diminished in some respects as a force propelling therapists into an examination of their personal impact as therapists/persons and even dismissed in some quarters as merely an expression of "narcissism," continues to find expression in the writings of practitioners who prefer a humanistic base to their work. One of the leading proponents of this view is Walter Kempler. His paper on "Experiential Psychotherapy with Families," containing the twin maxims of experiential practice ("attend to current interaction" and "engage your full personality"), affords the student a sound set of examples in the "use of self" in practice.

Elsa Leichter and Gerda Schulman have been working and documenting their work with multiple-family groups for some 15 years. Their work combines a family orientation with some of the advantages found in a group approach—especially mutual learning and support. By analogy, the approach is closely related to the constructed network or "similar peer" (Gottlieb, 1980) forms of practice developed in recent years. For example, just as a self-help group of recent widows (similar peers) need both information about their immediate situations and emotional support, so too may a group of families sharing major characteristics or similar problems benefit from mutual aid and mutual learning. The paper included here by Leichter and Schulman details their multi-faceted approach in a model that can be used by experienced as well as beginning practitioners.

REFERENCES

Ackerman, N. W. The unity of the family. *Archives of Pediatrics*, 1938, *55*, 59–62.
Ackerman, N. W. *The psychodynamics of family life: Diagnosis and treatment of family relationships.* New York: Basic Books, 1958.
Ackerman, N. W. *Treating the troubled family.* New York: Basic Books, 1966.
Gottlieb, B. Social networks and social support in the design of preventive interventions. *Helping Networks and the Welfare State.* University of Toronto, Faculty of Social Work, 1980.
Kantor, D., & Lehr, W. *Inside the family.* San Francisco: Jossey-Bass, 1975.
Langsley, D., Kaplan, D., Pittman, F., Machotka, P., Flomenlaft, K., & DeYoung, C. *The treatment of families in crisis.* New York: Grune and Stratton, 1968.
Satir, V. *Conjoint family therapy.* Palo Alto: Science and Behavior Books, 1967.
White, S. L. Family Theory According to the Cambridge Model. *Journal of Marriage and Counseling*, 1978, *4*, 91–100.
Zuk, G. H. *Family therapy: A triadic-based approach.* New York: Behavioral Publications, 1971.

Family Theory According to the Cambridge Model

Stephen L. White

The family systems theory of David Kantor and William Lehr as expressed in their book, Inside the Family, *forms the foundation for the model of family therapy which is taught at the Family Institute of Cambridge. This paper is a summary of an introduction to that theory. Their concepts of family boundaries, dimensions, typal arrangements, and the four player system are presented and discussed.*

The theoretical work of Kantor and Lehr (1975) forms the foundation for the Family Institute of Cambridge, one of the three components of what Constantine (1976) refers to as "the Boston model" of family therapy. Their work, and the institute which teaches and refines it, is distinctive enough to deserve its own identity and its own name. "The Cambridge model" is the obvious choice. This paper is an attempt to present the major ideas of Kantor and Lehr, thereby providing an introduction to the Cambridge model of family theory and therapy.

Those who study the family are fond of speaking of systems and structures and process. What does all of this mean? Indeed, can anyone agree on what these ideas are about? Even more vexing is the question of how these ideas, and others, are related in a way that gives the observer a comprehensive framework upon which to order what he sees, hears, and feels when he spends time with families. The framework developed by Kantor and Lehr is refreshingly different from other theories of the family, among other reasons, simply because it is comprehensive; it attempts to address questions which previous theories have chosen not to examine. Moreover, their theory is not a theory of "dysfunctional" or "pathological" families. Rather, it is a product of the direct observation of many different kinds of families over a period of nearly ten years. This theory gives the researcher, as well as the family therapist, a new language with which to describe ordinary, everyday family life in a whole-family, systematic way.

"Family Theory According to the Cambridge Model," by S. L. White. In *Journal of Marriage and Family Counseling*, Volume IV, Number 2. Copyright 1978 by the American Association for Marriage and Family Therapy. Reprinted by permission.

The work of family observation and therapy begins with identification of structures in a family system and the determination of which structures work and which do not. To observe structures, one needs a vocabulary with which to name and classify elements and functions of structures. The four broad frameworks for understanding structures set forth by Kantor and Lehr describe not only what is observed empirically, but also what is experienced phenomenologically in the family. They are: *Interfaces*, *Dimensions*, *Typal Arrangements*, and the *Four Player System*. Each of these interrelated parts of their theory will be discussed in the following sections.

INTERFACES

Families are open systems by virtue of their dependency upon continual interchanges with the environment for their viability (Buckley, 1967, p. 50). There are, as well, interchanges which occur within the family system itself among its various components. That these interchanges occur can be inferred from the activity, in a metaphorical sense, which takes place at the point or points where components of systems meet or interface. Each of these components of systems must be conceptualized as having metaphorical walls or boundaries which set them apart, one from another. Meetings of systems or subsystems at interface cause each unit to shape and reshape its space and to regulate traffic in and out of this space.

Kantor and Lehr propose that "the family system is composed of three sub-systems that interact with each other as well as with the world outside: these are the *family-unit subsystem*, the *interpersonal subsystem*, and the *personal subsystem*" (p. 23). Each of these three subsystems are set apart by their own boundaries. Since families have an infinite variety of ways in which to organize themselves from subsystem to subsystem, each family should be studied in its entirety rather than in terms of its separate parts.

When we think of subsystem boundaries it is useful to think spatially. Boundaries can be thought of as demarcating certain areas of physical space. Each of the circles in Figure 1. can be thought of as a boundary surrounding its own subsystem. The largest circle is the unit boundary, the next largest the interpersonal boundary, and the smallest the personal boundary.

Families have a number of ways in which they can regulate traffic at interface. At the unit boundary, for example, one family may communicate to those who approach that they must slow down and go through a lengthy period of scrutiny before admission is granted. Conversely, other families may communicate to approaching outsiders that there are no special requirements for admission to the unit boundary other than the mere presence of the outsider who instantly becomes very much an insider.

The interpersonal boundaries of a family are encountered once an outsider has gained entry into the family's outer perimeter. The man from the gas company who enters a home to read the gas meter may gain easy passage through the unit boundary but may not be able to enter any of the space occupied by the family members. He is not invited to participate in the life of the family in any way. The interpersonal subsystems of another kind of family may watch for the mailman on a snowy day and invite him in for a hot drink and intimate conversation. Usually, though, a visitor to the family at the interpersonal interface must experience a period of negotiation during which he must locate the boundaries of the various subsystems and find ways to cross them.

A family member may find himself in a situation in which he must regularly negotiate his entry into the interpersonal space of the family. He may place himself there of his own volition or he may be assigned this place in the family by complex family maneuvers. Such a family member experiences himself and is experienced as "the different one" or "the outsider" and sometimes "the crazy one." Kantor and Lehr believe, following R. D. Laing's (1964) concept of mystification, that this confinement of an individual to this *"intraspace"* can be traumatic and disorienting for the individual and is a "potential source of serious emotional disorder" (Kantor and Lehr, 1975, p. 28).

FIGURE 1.

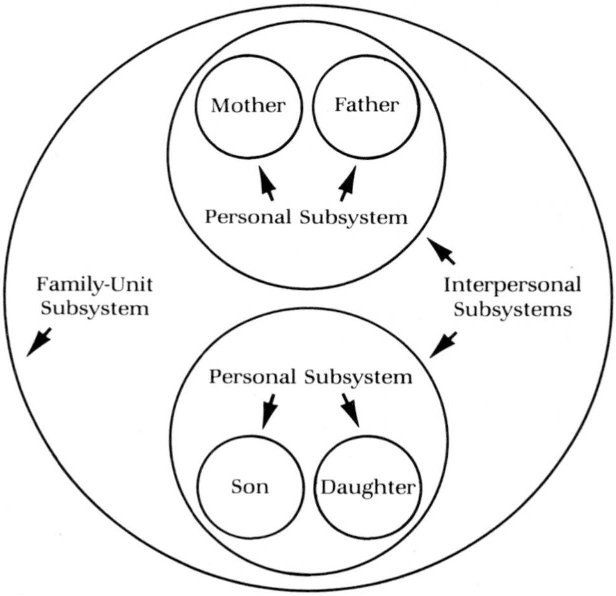

The personal subsystem in the family may be likened to "ego" in psychoanalytic theory and the personal boundary is roughly analagous to the ego boundary. This boundary defines the individual members of the family. Kantor and Lehr point out that a person in a family "leads a kind of double life, one as 'member' and the other as 'self' " (p. 29). These dual lives are experienced objectively and subjectively as occurring simultaneously.

In brief, boundaries define where interfaces occur. In a family, there is a unit boundary, the metaphoric wall between the world and the interior of the family; interpersonal boundaries, the interface among people inside the family; and personal boundaries, which delimit the interior of individuals. There can be a great deal of confusion, for example, if A feels he is encountering B at the interpersonal or personal boundary when B feels that interaction is really taking place at the unit boundary.

DIMENSIONS

The Dimensions of family have to do with what a family's goals are in terms of *power, affect*, and *meaning* (Target Dimensions) and the ways a family uses *time, space*, and *energy* (Access Dimensions) to achieve its goals. A determination of the type of family being observed will inform the observer about a given family's goals or targets. The kind of characteristic strategies a family employs to reach its target will help the observer learn about the ways in which the family uses the Access Dimensions to reach those targets.

No matter how they are achieved, each subsystem described in the section above seeks certain goals which fall within three broad categories: (1) Affect—a sense of intimacy and nurturance; (2) Power—the freedom to try to obtain what is wanted in terms of money, goods, or skills; a sense of efficacy; (3) Meaning—a sense of identity, a philosophical framework. These, then, are the *Target Dimensions*.

These targets or goals are reached via *Access Dimensions*. The first is the dimension of *Space* which deals with the ways a family develops, maintains and defends its system and subsystem territories and the way it regulates distance among its own members (p. 41).

Time is the second Access Dimension. This sphere of family life deals with the ways through which families arrange their lives in time. Entire families and each of their sub-units must make constant decisions about when work and play events will take place. They must see to it that the various subsystems in a family are "in phase" with one another through the maintenance of harmonious rhythms. More abstract concepts are subsumed in this dimension such as what a family will value from the past and what it will envision for the future.

The third Access Dimension is *Energy* and this addresses the question of how families store and expend their resources for action. The daily course of family life requires that energy be used up in some manner. Families may use energy, among other ways, in a steady, measured fashion or in spurts or bursts of energy followed by relative calm. When energy is expended, it must eventually be replenished. Again, different families have different means of fueling. Some families may experience an evening meal with everyone present as a fueling time both in the physical and the emotional sense. On the other hand, some families may use up more energy than they take on during such a gathering of all family members.

To understand the complexity of the Access Dimensions it will be useful to carefully study the Appendix which is an outline of each method of Access with their respective mechanisms and submechanisms. Brief definitions of these components of the Access Dimensions are given. All of these dimensions with several of their submechanisms can be operating at any one time in the life of a family.

TYPAL ARRANGEMENTS

According to Kantor and Lehr there are three basic types of families based on three quite different homeostatic models. This is a radical departure from other theorists who believe there can be only one homeostatic ideal of families: steady or harmonious equilibrium. The three types take into account the authors' observation that different families seem to adopt different equilibrium-disequilibrium ideals. The basic family types are open, closed, and random, each having its own characteristic configurations of Access and Target Dimensions. One or the other of these types are not viewed as healthy or unhealthy; each type can "work" or not according to the strategies by which it lives out its espoused ideals. It is strategy, not type, which is seen as either "enabling" or "disabling". Since there is no right or wrong type, the family therapist must be aware of how his own typal preference or bias interacts with the family's typal ideals. Kantor and Lehr's formulation of a classification system for families is a promising attempt to answer Ackerman's assertion that "The labor of designing a clinically-oriented classification of families, however arduous, is a must" (Ackerman, 1971, p. 153). This attempt is not only a departure from the steady state model of homeostasis, it is also a departure from the even more tiresome and useless practice of classifying families around their major symptom carriers. The idea of "schizophrenic families" or "delinquent families" does not acknowledge that some symptoms may change over time nor that multiple symptoms may be present in the same family (Riskin and Faunce, 1972).

We shall examine each of the three typologies below. However, before proceeding, a warning is in order. The three constructs which follow are definitions of "typal ideals" which, in pure form, probably do not exist in the real world of family life. These typologies are useful for conceptualizing families only because most families tend to have more of the characteristics of one type than of another.

Closed-type

The *Closed-Type* family in some ways resembles Minuchin's (1967) "enmeshed" family and Reiss' "consensus-sensitive family" (1971). The structure is rigid and the subsystems are seemingly "stuck" together. Space in the closed-type family is fixed and carefully guarded by those in authority in the family. Parents see to it that doors are locked, family reading material and T.V. shows are screened, and that children scrupulously report their comings and goings. Strangers encountering the unit boundary are closely scrutinized. Privacy and territoriality sometimes bordering on suspiciousness of outsiders are seen in these families.

In the Time dimension events in closed families take place with little or no variation from rigid regular daily schedules. These families are primarily oriented toward the past or to the future in order to preserve ideals of the past and to strive for better things in the future.

Energy in the closed family is steady energy; the taking in and the expenditure of energy is carefully governed so that resources do not become depleted and so that there are no sudden bursts of energy. "Indeed, investing strategies in the closed family are such that discipline becomes a high art, for members are expected to expend energy directly toward specific targets, without deviating away from them toward others" (p. 122).

The "core purpose" of the closed-type family is stability through tradition. To this end the ideals in the Affect dimension are durability, fidelity, and sincerity. Authority, discipline, and preparation are the prized ideals in the target dimension of Power. In the Meaning dimension the ideals are certainty, unity, and clarity. Stable structures are relied upon as reference points for order and change.

Random-type

The typal arrangements set forth by Kantor and Lehr can be thought of as on a continuum of order and stability, on the one hand, to lack of order and chaos, on the other. Before considering the mid-point of the continuum, the *Open-Type* family, we shall examine what is, in some ways, the polar opposite of the closed-type: The *Random-Type* family. The random family is reminiscent of Minuchin's (1967) "disengaged" family and Reiss' (1971) "interpersonal distance-sensitive" family. Structurally, these families are more fragmented than the closed-type, with each family member having less "connection" with other members.

Contrasted with the boundary patterns of the closed family, random families have quite fuzzy boundaries at the unit interface. Space is dispersed with each person developing his own bounding patterns for defending his own and his family's territory. These individual bounding patterns usually do not correspond with one another. Traffic in and out of the family is loosely regulated even where strangers are concerned.

Time in these families is irregular. In the rare event that schedules are established they are quickly forgotten or ignored. Events occur at the whim of each family member. There is a temporal fluidity which fosters syncopated rhythms. In such families the orientation is primarily toward the present.

The ways in which energy is taken in and dispensed follow logically from this type's use of space and time. Energy is continually fluctuating. Kantor and Lehr suggest that these are high-energy families because of the "institutionalization of behavioral flux in seeking access to potentially unlimited energy sources" (p. 137). Often these random families exert such great forces of energy that they seemingly fly apart in a truly chaotic fashion that crosses the border into crisis. In such situations one family member will attempt to organize the family into some sort of order, thus saving it from dissolution.

In the random family the core-purpose is exploration through intuition. This is mirrored in the Affect targets of rapture, whimsicality, and spontaneity. Power dimension ideals are interchangeability, free choice, and challenge. Finally, the Meaning targets are ambiguity, diversity, and orginality. Unstable structures are experimented with as reference points for order and change.

Open-type

The *Open-Type* family sounds very much like a small democracy and even more like the television version of the "all-American family". It is neither too tightly nor too loosely bounded. There is a degree of order, but it is tempered by negotiation and the ability to change.

The unit boundary of the open family may be thought of as a "semi-permeable membrane" which allows a certain amount of traffic in and out of the system. Interchange with extra-familial space is promoted. Generally, space is moveable in these families.

Similarly, time in the open family is variable. While the orientation of these families emphasizes the present, this orientation is modifiable to include events at the past-present and present-future interfaces. Events generally take place according to specific temporal notations, but are always negotiable and modifiable.

Energy in the open family is flexible. There is a good deal of variety in the ways these families fuel. "Investment strategies ... are such that members are able to capitalize on two divergent trends, the tendency toward dispersion and the tendency toward concentrations" (p. 129).

Adaptation through consensus is the core purpose of the open family. In order to arrive at this, the target ideals in the Affect dimension are responsiveness, authenticity, and latitude. In the power dimension, they are resolution, allowance, and cooperation. Meaning dimension ideals are relevance, affinity, and tolerance. Order and change are expected to be a product of the interaction of *relatively* stable structures.

In order to provide a basis for at least a superficial comparison of the three family types, let us imagine a situation involving a family consisting of a mother, father, adolescent daughter, and her younger brother. We shall examine how each of the three family types would appear to a young man coming to the home to take the adolescent daughter out on a date.

As the boy approaches the front door of a closed-type family, he finds the doorway well lighted and the family name on the door. After ringing the doorbell he hears the voice of a man asking him to identify himself. Once he has done so, Mr. Closed opens the door, greets him formally saying "We were expecting you. Mary will be ready in a moment." The boy is then led into the living room where he is met by Mrs. Closed who invites him to have a seat. At this point Mr. and Mrs. Closed begin a conversation designed to learn more about the boy's family, his after-school part-time job, and where he intends to take their daughter on their date. When Mary enters, Mr. Closed frowns about the young man's bad manners at not standing up. Mary's younger brother enters for a peek at her boyfriend, is introduced, and is promptly sent off to watch T.V. in another room. Mary takes a seat and listens as her parents deftly convey their feelings and ideas about the values of modern young as compared to their own values which are "old fashioned." Finally, Mrs. Closed tells the young people to be on their way. Mr. Closed asks the boy to bring Mary home by 11:00 p.m. After Mary and her friend leave the house, Mr. and Mrs. Closed begin an uneasy vigil which continues until Mary's return home at the stroke of eleven o'clock.

Life at the home of the open-type family is not so ordered and carefully bounded as it is in the closed family. As our hero approaches, he is met by three other boys a bit younger than he. One of them, apparently his girlfriend's younger brother says, "You must be here for Cindy. Come on in." The four boys enter the house just as some relatives and their friends are leaving. There are a few moments of confused "hello's" and "goodbye's" until the relatives are gone and the door is closed behind the boys. Cindy's brother announces her caller and then invites him into the den with his friends saying, "She's never ready on time." Cindy's mother rushes into the den to say hello before going to her Yoga lesson across town. "Kevin, why don't you get Cindy's friend a cold drink?" she asks. "I'll get it," says Mr. Open, who is just coming up from his work bench in the basement for a cold beer. The boy relaxes in the den and joins Mr. Open, Kevin, and his friends in a lively discussion about how birds manage to migrate back and forth from the same place each year. The warm, interesting, and friendly discussion continues until Cindy finally appears, a half hour late, all apologies. The young couple departs for their date, everyone wishing them a good time.

Our young man's next date is with the teenage daughter in the random-type family. Punctual as always, he arrives at the Random home at 8:00 p.m. and knocks the door knocker. As he knocks, the door swings open, not having been tightly closed. Inside, he can hear a strange blend of rock music in one room and a recording of flamenco guitar from another room. A young boy who is coming down the stairs sees the caller at the door and invites him in but does not introduce himself. He is carrying a large book and a notebook which he places on the coffee table at the sofa where he sits. After a few moments of silence, the visitor, still standing, asks, "Is Helen ready to go out?"

"Are you Joe?" asks the young boy.

When the visitor answers yes, the boy begins laughing and runs out of the room yelling "Helen! Joe's here!" A moment later, Helen enters the room, all apologies. "Joe, I thought we were going out tomorrow night. Can you wait while I get ready?" Before Joe can answer, Helen is hit in the back of the head by a pillow thrown by an unidentified person in the next room. Helen spins around and chases her attacker, the two of them screaming and laughing at each other. In another room, Joe can hear the voices of an adult man and woman. The woman, upset, is asking the man when he intends to repair a broken chair. "I keep meaning to fix it, but something else always comes up" is his answer. The scene continues in this chaotic vein until, after a half hour Helen reappears ready to go out. The young couple leaves unnoticed.

THE FOUR PLAYER PARTS

The last major component of Kantor and Lehr's theory of family process deals with the place of the individual in this systems view of the family. Although the decomposition law of General Systems Theory states that the part (read individual) is *more* than a fraction of the whole (read family), some systems therapists have rightly been accused of paying too little attention to the individual members of a family. While Kantor and Lehr have steered clear of the inner workings of personality, they have developed a scheme of four basic types of maneuvers of individuals in families which provide a link between the "black box" of inner dynamics and systems thinking. This model provides a way to consider the individual as actor, interactor, and effector in a family system and provides "a convenient means for describing and analyzing interpersonal processes . . ." (p. 177). The Four Player Parts are *Mover*, *Opposer*, *Follower*, and *Bystander*. In a single interactional sequence, the Mover initiates action, the Opposer resists the action, the Follower moves to support either the Mover or the Opposer, and the Bystander comments upon the entire sequence. An example:

> There has just been a fight between Father and Ted.
> Mother: "Let's play Scrabble!" (Mover)
> Father: "Okay. I'll pass out the pieces." (Follower)
> Ted: "I'm going over to Bobby's house."(Opposer)
> Sue: "Every time Ted and Dad have an argument, you want us to play a game together."(Bystander)

Since this is primarily a theory of the family, the intrapersonal workings of family members are of no concern here. What is of concern is the individuals' behavior as it relates to, and interacts with, the behavior of other individuals in the family. Kantor and Lehr use the term "psychopolitics" to describe this area of study which deals with the interface between a person's inner directedness or self-consciousness (psycho) and his outer directedness or system consciousness (politics). This is an important area of study because just as family process can shape or alter a member's internal feedback system, so can his internal feedback system shape and alter family process.

The importance of the *Bystander* in a systems view of the family must be stressed. Every system, mechanical, biological, or social, must have a mechanism by which the system can determine whether or not it is "on course" toward its goals. This mechanism is called feedback and can be either negative or positive. Negative feedback, in effect, says to the system "We are off course and we need to correct this error in order to reach our goal." Thus, negative feedback has a correcting influence upon the system. On the other hand, positive feedback or "deviation amplifying feedback" is not correcting for, in effect, it says to the system "Everything is fine the way it is so let's just keep going the way we are now going." In this way, deviations from the system's goal are not corrected and are, over time, amplified (Hoffman, 1971).

The effective *Bystander*, that individual who comments upon family transactions, may serve the family system much in the same way that the observing ego serves the individual in psychoanalytic theory. Just as the observing ego can have a "correcting" influence upon the whole ego, the bystander helps a family modify its course toward its espoused goals. Indeed, those who have studied the double bind have observed that the double bind cannot operate if someone in the family comments upon it. Many troubled families do not have effective bystanding. Bystanding, then, is a function of the therapist as, for example, when he says, "I notice that whenever you and your husband begin to discuss your relationship, your two sons begin to argue." As therapy proceeds, the therapist will attempt to increase the ability of the family to observe its *own* strategies and comment upon them. For Kantor, the issue of instituting effective bystanding in a family is an ethical as well as a theoretical problem. He has said, "The client owns the power to change. Any therapy that does not empower a family to make its own changes is not a therapy with which I wish to be affiliated. Therefore, the empowering of the bystander is crucial to me" (Kantor, 1976).

This overview of Kantor and Lehr's complex and multi-faceted theory of family process is in no way intended to be a summary of every subtle point of their theory. Rather, it is intended to be an introduction to that theory through a brief examination of the basic structure or skeleton of their ideas. This telescoped explication of their theory of family will be the foundation for a closer examination of the original work.

APPENDIX: AN OUTLINE OF THE METHODS OF ACCESS WITH THEIR MECHANISMS AND SUBMECHANISMS

I. *Space*
    A. *Bounding*—establishing and maintaining territory.
        1. Mapping—determining the nature of the outside world.
        2. Routing—directing of interior and exterior traffic.

3. Screening—defending borders and filtering incoming and outgoing traffic.
4. Patrolling—maintaining the unit boundary so that Screening is effective.

B. *Linking*—regulating physical and conceptual distance.
  1. Bridging—bringing members into closer contact.
  2. Buffering—separating persons (the obverse of Bridging).
  3. Blocking Out—coercive separating of persons or objects.
  4. Channeling—coercive bringing together of people and objects.
  5. Recognizing—establishing the potential or non-potential for all Linking maneuvers.

C. *Centering*—setting guidelines for organizing and using space.
  1. Locating—scanning the family field to determine what is working or not working for the family.
  2. Gathering—the coming together of family members to maintain or change the system.
  3. Designing—establishing goals and priorities for the family.
  4. Arranging—balancing and ordering a family's design with its resources.

II. *Time*
A. *Orienting*—selecting, directing, and maintaining of attitudes and behaviors toward the past, present, and future.
  1. Past Orienting—remembering, re-experiencing, or re-enacting past events.
  2. Present Orienting—becoming aware of what is happening and being experienced in the here and now.
  3. Future Orienting—anticipating, imagining, and/or planning that which is to come.
  4. Nontemporal Orienting—fantasizing, dreaming, or meditating in "private" time unbounded by "consensual" time.
  5. Integrating—organizing past, present, future, and nontemporal experiences.

B. *Clocking*—regulating experienced events over time.
  1. Sequencing—developing and maintaining order to events.
  2. Frequency Setting—regulating how often events take place.
  3. Duration Setting—establishing how long events will last.
  4. Pacing—determining the speed at which events take place.
  5. Scheduling—planning when events will occur; establishing deadlines.

C. *Synchronizing*—regulating the total use of time.
  1. Monitoring — assessing whether the system's use of time is beneficial.
  2. Priority Setting—determining which events are, and which are not, important to most family members.
  3. Programming—developing guidelines for the use of time in accordance with the family's goals.
  4. Coordinating—adjusting the movements of family members so that they are in some way meshed and overlapped.

     5. Reminding—making family members aware of the goals of the family; maintaining, enforcing, and altering their goals.

III. *Energy*
    A. *Fueling*—acquiring energy.
      1. Surveying—locating the sources of energy.
      2. Tapping—determining which energy sources to use.
      3. Charging—taking in of energy; increasing the amounts of energy available to a system.
      4. Storing—maintaining a reservior of available energy.
      5. Requisitioning—commenting on the family's fueling process by the family.
    B. *Investing*—regulating the use of energy.
      1. Reconnoitering—locating targets for family energies.
      2. Attaching—directing energy toward specific targets.
      3. Committing—devoting energy to targets.
      4. Detaching—removing energy from targets; the reverse of Attaching.
      5. Accounting—regulating the expenditure of energy in terms of quantity and intensity.
    C. *Mobilizing*—implementing guidelines for the flow of energy.
      1. Gauging—determining how much energy is needed.
      2. Budgeting—developing a plan for regulating the flow of available energy.
      3. Mustering—focusing and rousing energy.
      4. Transforming—regulating the level (high, medium, low), form (emotional, muscular, conceptual, imaginative) and charge (positive, neutral, negative) of available energy.
      5. Distributing—assigning energy from where it is stored to where it is needed.

REFERENCES

Ackerman, N. The growing edge of family therapy. *Family Process*, 1971, *10*, 143–156.
Buckley, W. *Sociology and modern systems theory*. Englewood Cliffs, N.J.: Prentice-Hall, 1967.
Constantine, L. L. Designed experience: A multiple, goal-directed training program in family therapy. *Family Process*, 1976, *15*, 373–387.
Hoffman, L. Deviation-amplifying processes in natural groups. In J. Haley (Ed.), *Changing families*. New York: Grune and Stratton, 1971.
Kantor, D. From a lecture given at the Family Institute of Cambridge, Cambridge, Massachusetts, February 4, 1976.
Kantor, D., & Lehr, W. *Inside the family: Toward a theory of family process*. San Francisco: Jossey-Bass, 1975.
Laing, R. D., & Esterson, A. *Sanity, madness, and the family*. New York: Basic Books, 1964.
Minuchin, S. *et al. Families of the slums*. New York: Basic Books, 1967.
Reiss, D. Varieties of consensual experience. *Family Process*, 1971, *10*, 1–35.
Riskin, J., & Faunce, E. E. Interactional family research: A methodological review. *Family Process*, 1972, *11*, 365–456.

Marriage Therapy

Jay Haley

Although it is becoming more common for psychotherapists to interview married partners together, there are no orthodox procedures for the treatment of a marriage. In fact there is no formal description of pathological marriages and therefore no theory of what changes must be brought about. The psychodynamic approach, or role theory emphasis, leads to discussions of the individual problems of husband and wife and not to descriptions of the marital relationship.

The emphasis here will be upon types of relationship in marriage, but no attempt will be made to present a full exposition of the complexities of marriage; the focus will be upon marital distress and symptom formation. After a description of certain types of relationships, there will be a discussion of the kinds of conflicts which arise, and finally a description of ways a marriage therapist intervenes to produce shifts in relationship.

WHEN MARRIAGE THERAPY IS INDICATED

Marriage therapy differs from individual therapy because the focus is upon the marital relationship rather than the intrapsychic forces within the individual. It also differs from family therapy, where the emphasis is upon the total family unit with a child typically chosen to be the problem. Technically the term should be confined to that type of treatment where the therapist interviews the couple together. However, the variations are many: some therapists will see both marital partners separately, others will see one partner while occasionally seeing the spouse for an interview, and others will see one partner while referring the other elsewhere with collaboration between the two therapists. Actually the psychotherapist who does only individual psychotherapy and refuses to see the spouse of a married patient is involved in indirect marriage therapy. Not only is much of the time of individual treatment devoted to discussions of marital affairs, but if the individual changes, the marital relationship will change—or terminate.

Reprinted from *Archives of General Psychiatry*, Vol. 8, 1963, pp. 213–234. Reproduced by permission.

There are certain situations where marriage therapy is specifically indicated:

A. When methods of individual psychotherapy have failed, marriage therapy is appropriate. Often in such cases the patient is involved in a marital relationship which is inhibiting his improvement and perpetuating his distress to the point where individual psychotherapy is too small a lever to make a large change. For example, a woman with constantly recurring anxiety attacks and insomnia failed to improve in individual psychotherapy despite considerable exploration of her childhood. When her husband was brought into the treatment it was discovered that he was continually behaving in an irresponsible and unpredictable way. He was not only failing in business without taking any steps to prevent this failure, but he was surreptitiously writing bad checks time after time, despite his protests to his wife that he would never do so again. The onset of her anxiety attacks occurred with his first failure in business and his cavalier dismissal of this event. The continual conflict between husband and wife over his refusal to take responsibility in his business or in his family was handled by the wife with recurrent attacks of helpless anxiety, and her problem was more marital than individual.

B. Marriage therapy is indicated when methods of individual psychotherapy cannot be used. Since most individual psychotherapy consists of countering what a patient offers, the therapist is incapacitated if the patient offers nothing. Marriage therapy then becomes one of the few possible procedures. For example, a woman developed a fear of heart failure as part of a series of anxiety attacks which forced her to quit her job and remain at home unable to go out anywhere alone. She sought psychotherapy, and the therapist asked her to say whatever came to her mind. She said nothing. She would answer specific questions as briefly as possible, but she would not volunteer statements about her feelings or her life in general. After two sessions in which the woman said nothing, and the therapist said nothing, the woman discontinued treatment and sought another therapist. Clearly the woman would not permit the therapist to wait her out in the hope that the cost of treatment would ultimately force her to say what was on her mind. When she began marriage therapy with her husband present in the interview, the wife became more loquacious, since she found it necessary to correct her husband when he was asked about her problems. She could not let her husband's portrait of her difficulties stand. To revise his version she had to provide her own and demonstrate her feelings about him, providing the leverage to start a change.

C. Marriage therapy would seem indicated when a patient has a sudden onset of symptoms which coincides with a marital conflict. Although most patients with symptoms tend to minimize their marital difficulties—in fact, the symptom is apparently used to deny marital problems—there are times when symptoms erupt in obvious relation to a spouse. For example, a husband developed an anxiety state which confined him to bed and cost him his job. His collapse occurred when his wife went to work over his objections. In another case a woman developed a variety of hysterical symptoms while on vacation with her husband. They quarreled, and her husband gambled away the vacation money, knowing that her greatest fear in life was of gambling, because her father had continually gambled away all the family money. Although the onset of a symptom can always be seen as a product of a change in a family relationship, in some cases the connection is so obvious that treatment of the marriage is indicated.

D. Of course this type of therapy is indicated when it is requested by a couple who are in conflict and distress and unable to resolve it. (However, it is not unusual even in this circumstance for some therapists to advise them to seek individual treatment separately.) Typically one spouse, usually the wife, seeks marriage therapy, while the other comes in reluctantly. Even though one spouse may need a special request, both partners will usually come in, because if one partner in a marriage is miserable the other is too.

Finally, marriage therapy is indicated when it appears that improvement in a patient will result in a divorce or in the eruption of symptoms in the spouse. Therapists have a responsibility to the relatives of a patient if they bring about a change. If a patient with severe symptoms says his marriage is perfect, and if his spouse also indicates this idea, then it is likely that improvement in the patient will lead to divorce or symptoms in the spouse.

THE FORMAL THEMES OF MARRIAGE

A marriage is an extraordinarily complex and continually changing affair. To select a few aspects of the marital relationship and emphasize them is to do some violence to the incredible entanglement of two people who have lived together many years. A few formal themes, those most relevant to marital strife and symptom formation, will be mentioned here.

When a man and woman decide their association should be solemnized and legalized with a marriage ceremony, they pose themselves a problem which will continue through the marriage: now that they are married are they staying together because they wish to or because they must? The inevitable conflicts which arise in a marriage occur within a framework of a more or less voluntary relationship. A marriage seems to function best when there is some balance between the voluntary and compulsory aspects of the relationship. In a successful marriage, the couple define their association as one of choice, and yet they have sufficient compulsion in law and custom to stay together through the conflicts which arise. If divorce is too easy, there is too little compulsion in the marriage to survive the problems. When divorce is too difficult, the couple can begin to suspect that they are together because they must be and not out of choice. At either extreme, a marriage can be in difficulty. It is not so much whether a marriage *is* a compulsory or a voluntary relationship, but how the couple choose to define it. For example, a woman may wish to stay with her husband but be unwilling to concede that her choice is voluntary, and therefore she says that they cannot separate for religious reasons. Another wife might insist that she could leave her husband at any time, defining the relationship as voluntary, although her history would indicate that she had a rather desperate need of him and could not leave him.

An example of a marriage which was so voluntary that the wife did not feel committed to her husband can be used for illustration. A woman in business for herself prior to her marriage agreed to sell the business at her husband's request because he wished to be the provider for the family. However, she took the money obtained in the sale and placed it in the bank in her own name "just in case the marriage did not work out." The marriage foundered on this act. The husband felt the wife was unwilling to commit herself to him: the wife behaved as if the marriage was a voluntary association which she could leave at any time, so she would make no concessions in her relationship with her husband.

At the other extreme is the type of relationship where the couple behave as if they are compelled to stay together. This type of relationship occurs where there are strict religious rules about marriage, when one of the spouses develops incapacitating symptoms, or when one of them puts up with "impossible" behavior from the other.

A compulsory marriage is like that relationship between cell mates in a prison. The two people get along because they must, but they are uncertain whether they would choose to be together if they had a free choice. A wife who suffers incapacitating symptoms will be indicating to her husband that she is unable to survive alone. A husband who turns to drink whenever his wife must go away for a day, or when she threatens to leave him, will persuade her that he cannot live without her. This is not necessarily taken as a compliment if a spouse indicates he cannot do without his mate; implicit in such an arrangement is the idea that they are only together because they must be and perhaps any other person in the house might do, but no one else would have them. When spouses begin to think of their relationship as compulsory, bad feeling is generated.

A marriage may begin as a compulsory relationship. For example, a man attempted to discuss breaking off his engagement with his fiancée, and the girl jumped out of his parked automobile into oncoming traffic and ran wildly down the street. Later she told him she would kill herself if he did not marry her. He married her. From that point on, he was in doubt whether she really wished to marry him or was only desperately trying to escape a dreadful home situation. The girl was in doubt whether he married her because he wanted to or because of fear she would kill herself.

When one spouse continues the marriage even though treated badly by the other, a compulsory type of relationship occurs. If a husband puts up with more than is reasonable from his wife, the wife may begin to assume that he must be staying with her because he has to, not because he wants to, and the marriage is in difficulty. Sometimes a spouse will appear to test whether he or she is really wanted by driving the other to the point of separation. It is as if they say, "If my mate will put up with anything from me, I am really wanted." However, if the spouse passes the test and puts up with impossible behavior, the tester is not reassured about being wanted but becomes convinced the spouse is doing so because of an inability to leave. Once this pattern has begun, it tends to be self-perpetuating. A wife who believes that her husband stays with her because of his own inner desperation rather than because he wants her will dismiss his affectionate approaches as mere bribes to stay with her rather than indications of real affection. When she dismisses her husband's affection, he tries even harder to please her and so increases her belief that he stays with her out of desperation rather than choice. When the husband can no longer tolerate the situation, he may make a move to leave her. The moment he indicates he can do without her, the wife begins to feel she may be a voluntary choice and be attracted to him again. However, such a wife will then test her husband again by extreme behavior. When he responds permissively she again feels he is unable to leave her, and the cycle continues.

The extreme oscillation which can occur in a marriage is typical of those cases where a couple comes to a therapist for help in getting separated from each other. Some spouses will separate and go back together and separate again over the years, unable to get together and unable to get apart. The major problem in helping the separating couple is discovering which direction they seem most to want to go. Sometimes a couple merely wants an excuse from an outsider to go back together so that neither will have to risk being the first to suggest living together again. In more complex repetitive separations there is usually a pattern of one spouse wanting to end the marriage until the other also wants it; then there is temporary reconciliation. For example, a young couple began to have trouble after a few years of marriage and the wife had an extramarital affair. The husband forgave her. She had another affair; they separated. After a while they tried living together again, but the affairs still rankled. The husband continued to blame her for her actions; the wife blamed him for depriving her in such a way that she turned to someone else. They separated but continued to associate. When they entered therapy the husband wanted them to go back together again but was uncertain about it. The wife, having taken up with another man, did not want to live with her husband, yet she wanted to associate with him and consider possible future reconciliation. At one moment the husband insisted on immediate divorce, at the next he asked for a reconciliation. Each time he spoke more firmly about his plans for a divorce, the wife began to discuss the great potential of their marriage and how fond she was of him. When the husband talked about going back together, the wife discussed how miserable their marriage had been. After several sessions attempting to clarify the situation, the issue was forced by a suggestion that if the couple continue treatment they do so in a trial period of living together. Faced with returning to her husband, the wife refused. The husband managed to arrange a divorce, although when he was no longer compulsively involved with her, the wife was finding him attractive again.

The progress of a marriage

Though their information about one another may be minimal, two people have already established ways of relating to each other at the time they marry. The act of marriage, typically an act of conceding they really want each other, requires a different sort of relationship and can provoke rather sudden shifts in behavior. A woman, for example, might be forgiving of all her fiancé's defects until the marriage ceremony, and then she might set about reforming him. A man might be quite tolerant of his fiancée's inability to show affection, but when they are married he might insist she undergo a major change. The man who was pleased to find such a submissive girl may discover after marriage that she is quite insistent about taking charge of him. Usually, however, the patterns which appear in a marriage existed in some form prior to the cere- mony. People have a remarkable skill in choosing mates who will fit their needs, although they may insist later they married the unexpected. The girl who needs to be treated badly usually finds someone who will cooperate. If someone feels he deserves very little from life, he tends to find a wife who feels she deserves very little; both get what they seek.

The process of working out a satisfactory marital relationship can be seen as a process of working out shared agreements, largely undiscussed, between the two people. There are a multitude of areas in living together which a couple must agree about. For example, is a husband to decide what sort of work he will do, or will his wife's concern about prestige dictate his employment? Will the husband be allowed to freely criticize his wife's housekeeping, or is that her domain? Who is to handle the budget? Is the wife to comfort her husband when he is unhappy or become exasperated with him? How much are outsiders to intrude into the marriage, and are in-laws outsiders? Will the wife or the husband be the irresponsible one in the marriage?

Each situation that a newly married couple meets must be dealt with by establishing explicit or implicit rules to follow. When the situation is met again, the rule established is either reinforced or changed. These rules are of three sorts: (a) those rules the couple would announce, such as a rule that the husband can have a night out with his friends each week, (b) those rules the couple would not mention but would agree to if they were pointed out, such as the rule that the husband turns to his wife when faced with major decisions, and (c) those rules an observer would note but the couple would probably deny, such as the rule that the wife is continually to be on the defensive and the husband accusatory and never the reverse. It is important to note that the couple cannot avoid establishing these rules: whenever they complete a transaction, a rule is being established. Even if they should set out to behave entirely spontaneously, they would be establishing the rule that they are to behave in that way.

The couple must not only set rules, but they must also reach agreement on which of them is to be the one to set the rules in each area of their marriage. The process of working out a particular rule always occurs within a context of resolving who is setting the rule. For example, a wife might not object if her husband has an evening out—unless he insists upon it; then she might object, but her objection would be at a different level. Similarly, a husband might not protest if his wife wishes to send her mother money, but if the wife implies that he has no say in the matter he might then announce objections. In the early days of a marriage each spouse might graciously let the other be labeled as the one in charge of the various areas of the relationship, but ultimately a struggle will set in over this problem.

As a part of the struggle to reach agreement on rules for living with each other, a couple is inevitably establishing another set of rules—those rules to be followed to resolve disagreements. The process of working out conflict over rules becomes a set of meta-rules, or rules for making rules. For example, two people might establish the rule that they will only resolve a difference after the husband has made an issue of the matter. When the wife has tested his concern by provoking him until he treats the matter as important, then they will resolve it. Or a couple might establish the meta-rule that they will never fully reach agreement on any rule, and so they maintain a state of indecision. Similarly, the act of avoiding certain areas of discussion is an establishing of meta-rules about how to deal with those areas.

If a marital relationship could be worked out by the application of agreement on rules, who is to make them, and how to make them, a marriage would be quite a rational affair. Obviously it is not. Couples find themselves struggling with great intensity of feeling over minor matters in a most irrational way. This intensity of feelings about who is to set rules in the marriage would seem to have several sources. A major cause is the fact that any marital partner was raised in a family and so given long and thorough training in implicit and explicit rules for how people should deal with each other. When a person gets married, he attempts to deal with a spouse who was given training in a different institution. The couple must reconcile long-term expectations which have all the emotional force of laws of life. The wife raised in a family where an open show of emotion was forbidden will become disturbed when her husband expresses his feelings strongly, even though she might have married him because she wished to move in that direction. The husband whose mother made an issue of being an excellent housekeeper may find it difficult to tolerate a wife who is not, and he may take her inability as a personal comment on him rather than mere inefficiency. It is sometimes difficult to realize how subtle are the patterns we learn in our families, where we are exposed to millions of messages over time. For example, the "proper" distance one should stand from another person while talking to him will vary from family to family. A person may feel uneasy because the other person is too close or too far away without ever realizing that there is a disagreement in how far apart they should stand. The transition to a person's own family from a previous one requires considerable compromise with inevitable conflict.

Describing marriage in terms of working out rules for living together is another way of describing marriage as a process of defining relationships. Any rule established by a couple defines a certain type of relationship, and all relationships can be roughly classified into two types: complementary or symmetrical. A complementary relationship is one where the two people exchange *different* sorts of behavior, such as one giving and the other receiving. A symmetrical relationship is one where they exchange the *same* sorts of behavior, such as both giving. A rule that a husband is to comfort his wife when she is in distress defines a relationship as complementary. Similarly, an agreement that the wife is to have equal say about the budget is a mutual definition of a symmetrical relationship in that area. In a reasonably successful marriage a couple is capable of establishing both complementary and symmetrical relationships in various areas of their marriage. The husband can take care of his wife and she can accept this, the wife can take care of her husband and he can accept it, and they are able to exchange the same sort of behavior. When a couple is unable to form one of these types of relationship, the marriage is restricted. If a marital partner has had unfortunate experiences with certain types of relationship in the past, he or she might be unable to permit this type in a marriage. For example, if a wife has been disappointed in complementary relationships with her parents, she will respond to her husband's attempts to take care of her in a way that indicates she would prefer a symmetrical type of relationship. A wife might be unable to follow any directions given by her husband if following directions in her past cost her too much. Once when a wife was asked why she did not do what her husband told her, she said, "Why, I'd just disappear. I'd have no identity." Similarly, a husband might be unable to take direction from his wife or even let her take care of him when he is ill (and so he only retires to a sick bed when he has collapsed). He may indicate that he wants her to be an equal, but he does not want her to "mother" him. An inability to accept a range of types of relationships creates a marriage which is to some extent a depriving situation for both spouses.

Conflict in marriage

Marital conflict centers in (a) disagreements about the rules for living together, (b) disagreements about who is to set those rules, and (c) attempts to enforce rules which are incompatible with each other.

For a honeymoon period after marriage each spouse is willing to overlook the disagreements which develop. When the husband is treated by his wife in a way he does not like, he avoids mentioning it for fear of hurting her feelings. When the wife discovers some aspect of her husband which irritates her, she does not bring the matter up because she wishes to avoid conflict. After a period of time the couple have a rousing fight in which they express their opinions. After such a quarrel, there are changes made, and each is willing to compromise. Often they overcompensate by going too far as they give in to each other, and this overcompensation provides the need for the next conflict.

If a couple is unable to have a fight and so bring up what is on their minds, they are dealing with each other by withdrawal techniques and avoiding any discussion of certain areas of their relationship. With each avoidance, the area that cannot be discussed grows larger until ultimately they may have nothing they can safely talk about. One of the functions of a marriage therapist might be to provoke a couple to fight and say what is on their minds so they do not continue to punish each other indirectly for crimes which have never been brought up as accusations. When a couple cannot fight, all issues which require defining an area of the relationship are avoided. The couple will then eat together and watch television side by side, but their life has little shared intimacy. At the other extreme a couple may stabilize into a relationship which requires constant fighting. They repeatedly share demonstrations of strong feeling for each other, but they cannot reach amiable agreement on who is to control what in the marriage.

The more easily resolved conflicts in a marriage are those involving which rules the couple will follow. The two people may disagree about an aspect of living together or about how they should deal with each other, but they can reach a compromise which resolves the matter. Sharing the work about the house, agreeing on friends or types of social life, and problems of consideration for each other in various areas of living can lead to disagreement which is reasonably easy to resolve.

Although disagreements tend to be about which rules to follow, emotional fights tend to be about *who* is to make the rules, and this problem is not so easily solved by compromise. For example, a wife may insist that her husband hang up his clothes so that she does not have to pick up after him like a servant. The husband might agree with his wife that she should not be his servant, and so agree to the definition of the relationship, but he still might not agree that *she* should be the one to give him orders on what to do about his clothes. What rule to follow is more easily discussable than who is to make the rules to follow. The process of defining who is to make the rules in the marriage will inevitably consist of a struggle between any couple. The tactics in this struggle are those of any conflict: threats, violent assault, withdrawal, sabotage, passive resistance, and helplessness or physical inability to do what the other wants. The power struggle is not necessarily pathological. However, it can become pathological if the conflict continues in a circular pattern or if one or the other spouse attempts to circumscribe the mate's behavior while indicating that he or she cannot help it. Labeling behavior as "involuntary" requires symptomatic behavior and leads to pathological relationships.

When the issue between two people centers on who is to make the rules, they will behave as if basic rights are being violated. Similarly, the internal burning which goes on within spouses who have withdrawn from each other and are not speaking will center in conflict over who is to define what sort of relationship they will have. Typically the two spouses will be silent but busy rehearsing conversation in their heads; this conversation will include lines such as, "Who does he think he is," and "If she thinks I'll put up with that she has another think coming." The question of rights involves a complicated labeling procedure in any discussion. The wife might not mind being advised by her husband, and so be cooperating in a complementary relationship, if he offers the advice in just the right way or if she has asked for it. However, she may stoutly oppose such a relationship if her husband has initiated it or insisted upon it. Similarly, a husband might be quite willing to treat his wife as an equal in a certain area, but if she demands that he do so he may lose his willingness. The physical violence which can occur over minor matters is generated by a struggle at this control level of marriage. Whether to go to one movie or another may lead to threats of divorce when the conflict centers on who is to tell who what to do in the marriage.

If marital partners communicated only a single level message, conflicts would be more easily resolvable because cycles of conflict would not be generated. For example, if a husband only bids for a complementary relationship and the wife only responds with an acceptance or with a counter-offer for a symmetrical relationship, then the issue can be resolved between them. However, people do not communicate only on a single level, so they offer each other messages which define one type of relationship at one level of communication and an incompatible type of relationship at another level of communication. The conflict produced cannot easily be resolved and in fact usually provokes a response which perpetuates the conflict. For example, if a wife *orders* her husband to *dominate* her, the couple is caught in a network of incompatible definitions of the relationship. If the husband dominates her at her insistence, he is being dominated. To put this another way, if he accepts the secondary end of a complementary relationship by doing what she says, he is faced with a paradox if what she says is that he must tell her what to do. This is like the paradox involved in the statement "disobey me." If the respondent disobeys, he is obeying and if he obeys he is disobeying. A similar situation occurs if a husband orders his wife to supervise or take care of him. Similarly, the paradox occurs if a wife insists that her husband assert himself in relation to his mother and not be a "mama's boy" by letting himself be dominated by a woman. The more he is forced by his wife to assert himself with mother, the more he is accepting being dominated. Two incompatible types of relationship are simultaneously being imposed. Sometimes a wife will quite explicitly say that she wants her husband to dominate her in the way she tells him to— without realizing the incompatibility of her requests.

The communication of bids for two incompatible types of relationship can occur whenever there is an incompatibility between (a) the behavior defining the relationship and (b) the type of relationship implicit at the level of *who* is defining the relationship. For example, if a wife tells her husband to pick up his clothes she is indicating that their relationship should be symmetrical; each person should pick up his own clothes. However, *when she tells him to do this* she is defining the relationship as complementary—she orders and he is to follow the orders. The husband is then faced with two different definitions of the relationship, so that whichever way he responds he cannot satisfy both requests. If he picks up his clothes, accepting the symmetrical definition, he is following her directions and so accepting a complementary definition. He cannot accept one definition without the other unless he comments on the situation in a way that redefines it. More likely he will erupt in indignation while uncertain what he is indignant about, and his wife will similarly be indignant because he erupts over this simple request.

A further area of conflict for a couple occurs if there is an incompatibility between (a) the meta-rules they establish for resolving disagreements about rules and (b) the rules themselves. For example, a couple might reach an agreement that whenever they are in conflict about the rules for dealing with each other, the husband will make the final decision and set the rules. However, the final decision he might make could be that he and his wife are to be equals, or in a symmetrical relationship. If they are equals, he cannot be the rule-setter, yet that is the rule he sets. Similarly, a couple may establish the rule that they will resolve all disagreements in a mutually satisfactory way—by discussion and compromise. However, when the wife attempts to express her opinion on a particular issue, the husband may point out that getting emotional does not solve anything, and since she won't listen to him, he will withdraw from the field. His behavior defining the relationship as complementary on a particular issue is incompatible with their agreement to handle issues symmetrically, and the result is mutual dissatisfaction and indignation.

In summary, conflict between a married couple can arise in several areas: (a) conflict over what sort of rules to follow in dealing with each other and so what sort of relationship to have, (b) conflict over who is to set the rules, with the types of relationship defined by the ways this conflict is worked out, and (c) a conflict over the incompatibility between these two levels; a relationship defined in one way on the first level conflicts with the relationship defined another way on the other level. Besides these conflicts, another may be generated by (d) an incompatibility between the process of working out conflicts and the conflicts themselves, so that what will be resolved at one level is incompatible with what can be resolved at another.

Almost any marital conflict which occurs can be described within this formal scheme, even though the description is confined to two levels instead of the multiple levels of communication which occur in human relations. Presumably, too, this scheme would apply to marriages in different cultures, since it is not a description of which rules a couple follows, which would be culture-bound, but a description at a more formal level. A couple in any culture must deal with what rules to follow, who is to enact them, and what rules to follow to resolve disagreements. In a changing culture there will inevitably be more conflict, as there will be in cross-cultural marriages. The shift in the status of women in America has produced a breakdown in many of the elaborate ways of defining relationships between men and women which were once taken for granted as courtesy procedures. As a result a man is often faced with a wife who insists that she be treated as an equal while simultaneously insisting that he take charge of her in a complementary relationship.

If one describes marital relationships in terms of conflicting levels of communication, the description is complex, but any less complex description is too oversimplified to be useful. For example, to describe a marriage as one where there is "a dominating wife and a dependent husband" does not include the idea that the husband might be provoking his wife to be dominating so that actually he is "dominating" what sort of relationship they have. Similarly, the "submissive" wife can actually be the one who, by helpless maneuvers, is managing whatever happens in the relationship.

When paradoxical communication occurs in a marriage, the conflicts are the most difficult type for a couple to resolve on their own. Such situations occur with any incompatible set of messages. For example, a double bind occurs when a husband indicates his wife should show an interest in sex and initiate the activity, but when she does he behaves unresponsively because she is being demanding and managing. If a husband receives his wife's advances as too demanding and her absence of advances as prudishness, the wife is wrong whatever she does. Similarly, a wife may encourage her husband to initiate sexual relations, but when he does she may indicate that he is imposing on her, and if he does not, that he is disinterested in her.

When these paradoxes occur in the sexual area they represent themes which appear throughout the marriage as incompatible definitions of the relationship. A husband is defining the relationship as symmetrical when he encourages his wife to initiate sexual relations, and if he also indicates she should not do so, he defines the relationship as complementary. The two incompatible definitions in this area place the wife in a double bind: whichever way she responds, agreeing to his definition of the relationship, will be opposed by him as a wrong definition. The wife might find a solution by posing incompatible definitions of the relationship in return. She might do this in "normal" ways or by developing symptoms. As an example of a "normal" way to offer an incompatible definition of the relationship in response, the wife might talk about initiating sex, and so define the relationship as symmetrical, but leave all such initiating up to her husband, and so define the relationship as complementary. Or she might indicate an interest in sexual relations and then appear indifferent so that her husband must pursue her; she has then initiated sexual relations, but she also has not, since the major move resides with him.

Symptoms can be seen as a product of, or a way of handling, a relationship in which there are incompatible definitions of the relationship. It is easy to assume that a wife's symptoms which interfere with sexual relations are only expressions of her guilt and fears about sex, but she might be demanding less of her husband in this involuntary way because he has indicated that she should (in such a way that she cannot accuse him of doing so). If a husband asks his wife to show an interest in sexual relations and opposes her when she does, the wife can become unable to because of symptomatic distress. Similarly, a wife who cannot tolerate "surrendering" to her husband in a complementary relationship but insists that he take charge in the relationship, may produce impotency in the husband as a convenience to them both. If one is asked to do something and not do it at the same time, a possible response is to be unable to do it—which means indicating that one's behavior is involuntary. The physiology of the human being seems to cooperate in this situation even to the point of producing somatic symptoms.

Resistance to change

A married couple in difficulty cannot be rational about the matter. Both husband and wife might know perfectly well how they could treat each other to relieve their distress, despite an appearance of misunderstanding, but they continue to provoke discomfort in themselves and each other. When a therapist tries to bring about a change, he finds two central problems that inhibit a shift in the relationship.

One problem in the way of change is a couple's persistence in protecting each other. Although they could be making wild attacks upon one another, or be appearing to tear each other down constantly, a little probing usually reveals that they are protecting each other in a variety of ways, thus keeping the system stable. For example, a wife who was the manager in a marriage would insult her husband in the therapy session for his drinking, lack of consideration, bad behavior, and general boorishness. Alone with the therapist one day she said the real problem was the fact that her husband was just a baby and she was tired of mothering him. When the therapist asked why she had not brought this up in a session with her husband present, the woman was shocked at the idea of hurting his feelings in that way. Yet she was consistently indicating that he was a baby in her eyes without ever making the accusation explicit so the husband could deal with it.

One of the functions of an angry quarrel in a marriage would seem to be to give the participants permission to stop protecting each other temporarily. Typically a wife and husband will let each other know what areas are too sensitive for discussion. When one of these areas is touched upon, they will respond in an anxious or angry way, so that further discussion will not occur. When a spouse finds one of these undiscussable areas to be a central problem in their relationship, he or she often will not discuss it because of the other person's sensitivity there. Yet often a change can occur only if there is discussion, not necessarily because understanding is brought about, but because a change is being made in the rules for who is to talk about what. That is, if a wife has established the implicit rule that something is not to be discussed and then the husband discusses it, his act of discussing it signifies a change in the relationship quite independent of whatever enlightenment may occur because of the discussion.

Although it might be considered a natural aspect of marriage that the couple protect each other, there are aspects of protectiveness which are not so amiable. If a wife does not discuss something because she feels her husband cannot tolerate it, she will be exhibiting a lack of respect for him which may be unjustified and which he will feel as patronizing. The problem in the marriage can center more in her lack of respect for her husband than it does in the content of the sensitive area. Similarly, if a wife restrains her own abilities and accomplishments so that she will not outshine her husband, she is not necessarily doing him a favor. For example, a wife decided not to continue in school and get a higher degree because she would then have had a higher academic status than her husband. When a wife decides to restrain herself for such a purpose, not only will she be patronizing her husband, but she may be using this protection as an excuse when there are a number of other reasons why she would not seek a higher degree. Usually if one mate is protective of another, there are unexpressed needs being served. For example, there may be a bargain involved. If a man protects his wife on a certain issue, it is often with the implicit agreement that she will therefore protect him on another issue. This may be all right unless the marriage is in distress. Such a state usually indicates that one or the other is getting the poorer part of the bargain. Should one cease such protection, the other does also, and changes can occur. A further aspect of protection is the confusion that occurs over who is protecting whom. Rather typically, if a spouse prefers not to discuss something to protect the other spouse, there is self-deceit involved. For example, a husband might indicate that his wife cannot tolerate a discussion of sex when, in fact, he is the one who becomes uncomfortable in such a discussion, but his wife will accept the label as the sensitive one.

One of the more severe forms of resistance to change in a marriage occurs with the development of symptoms in one or both of the partners. The symptom is then used by the couple, as a disturbed child is used in a family, to avoid defining their relationship and so avoid dealing with the marital distress. Typically the couple will say they would be perfectly happy if it were not for the husband's headaches or if it were not for the wife's anxiety attacks. However, as the symptom is alleviated, they do not evidence this happiness; in fact, their conflict might increase to the point where the disappearance of the symptom may mean separation or divorce. Psychotherapists who see only individuals are likely to miss discovering how a relationship with an intimate family member profoundly affects the patient's rate of improvement.

Typically, symptoms not only protect the individual as an intrapsychic defense, they also protect the marital partner and the marriage itself. A woman with a variety of hysterical symptoms was treated by joint interviews with her husband. The husband was reluctant to enter therapy because he insisted the problems resided in his wife, not in himself or the marriage. The wife, too, indicated that she could not see the relevance of her husband to the physical distress she was experiencing. As her symptoms improved, the couple began to fight more openly. The wife's dissatisfactions became more easily expressed. In the process of treatment, the woman revealed almost accidentally that for many years she had also suffered from claustrophobia. Since she could not ride in an elevator, the couple could not go for a drink at a popular bar on the top of a tall building. As the woman was encouraged in the interview toward planning a drink at the top of that building, both she and her husband became rather anxious. The woman said her symptom was not at all an inconvenience and she would prefer to retain it. Further inquiry revealed the husband suffered from a fear of heights. However, no issue was ever made of this fear because of the "agreement" between the two of them that she had problems and he did not. Should this woman overcome her fear of enclosed places and ride an elevator, she would expose her husband's inability to go with her. Such an admission would require a revision of a basic premise that their marriage was a complementary relationship with the husband the strong one and the wife the one with symptoms and difficulties.

One finds, if he explores this kind of marriage, that characteristically one spouse carries symptoms which are a protective concealment for the symptoms of the other spouse. Improvement in the patient can be a severe threat to a marriage. For example, a wife may appear quite inadequate and helpless because of her emotional problems, but exploration reveals an even more helpless and inadequate husband who is constantly required by his wife's difficulties to maintain the fiction that he is taking care of *her*. Often in such cases, despite the wife's helpless incapacity, one finds that she handles the budget, organizes the family activities, deals with the outside world, and generally manages the home. The credit for strength in the family, however, is handed to the man by mutual agreement.

In this type of marriage the wife will develop her symptoms when the husband is so shaken by something in his life that he is threatened with a breakdown or the development of symptoms. At that moment the wife develops her problems, and the man must pull himself together to help her. Occasionally the wife may develop her symptoms at the time the husband takes a step forward and begins to assert himself with more self-confidence in the marriage. As he makes more demands upon her, the wife may gain control of the relationship by becoming too "ill" to meet the demands. Sometimes these two circumstances may occur simultaneously; the husband experiences some success in his field of endeavor which causes him to assert himself more at home and at the same time shakes him because of his uneasiness about added responsibilities. As he oscillates between breaking down under the threat of greater success and becoming more self-assertive, he offers his wife incompatible definitions of the relationship and she cooperates by developing symptoms which stabilize the situation.

An example of this type of situation is the graduate student who receives his degree and begins his first job. Threatened with a change in his relationship to the world because he must go out and deal with people as an equal adult after years as a student, he, in this time of success, enters a crisis. In the case of a particular student, the wife, who had been supporting him through college, was the one who collapsed. She was suddenly faced with a shift in their relationship as he went to work and started supporting her. He became both more assertive at home and more shaken by his new responsibilities in life. At the moment he was expressing his uncertainty about leaving his new job and going back to school, the wife developed anxiety attacks. She was unable to continue work because of these anxiety attacks, or even to leave the house alone, and so he was required to continue in his new job and support her. When the wife moved in the direction of getting on her feet, the husband indicated he might collapse. Yet when the husband attempted to take more charge of the marriage, which the wife indicated she wished, she would become uncooperative but indicated she "could not help it." Whenever the couple began to deal with their conflicts with each other, the wife would indicate that she would respond to her husband differently if it were not for her anxiety. The husband would indicate that the problem was not between them but centered in her internal anxiety. As long as the couple maintained an emphasis upon the wife's symptoms when threatened with change, the marital relationship could not be worked out in a more satisfying way.

THERAPEUTIC INTERVENTION

The typical marriage therapist brings a couple together and tells them he wants them to talk and correct the misunderstandings which have arisen, to express their feelings, and to gain some insight into their difficulties. However, merely because this procedure for change is outlined to the marriage couple does not necessarily mean that therapeutic change is brought about by self-expression, correcting misunderstandings, or gaining insight into difficulties. The explanation to a patient of what will bring about change need not be confused with what actually brings about a change.

The argument that insight and self-understanding is the primary factor in producing change cannot be sufficiently supported. Some couples will undergo a change from following directives without insight. Other couples will evidence considerable understanding, particularly of the effects of the past on their present behavior, and yet they will continue to behave in distressing ways. More important, understanding and self-expression cannot be separated from the effects of the therapeutic context in which they occur. Shifts in relationship with the therapist can effect a change which appears as a shift in understanding. For example, a wife may "discover" that she is unwilling to let her husband be the authority in the home because of the inadequacies of her father in the past. However, when she makes this discovery in the therapeutic context, she will be presenting the idea to the therapist and so accepting him as the authority on the point she is making. What change occurs may not be brought about by her self-understanding but by her acceptance of the therapist as an authority when she has never allowed anyone to be in that position with her.

The effect of the third person

When a couple comes to a marriage therapist, changes can occur in their relationship because of the mere existence of the therapeutic triangle. The marital partners may have various motivations for entering therapy, including a determination to prove that the other is the villain in the marriage. The ways spouses attempt to use third parties are often what need to be changed about their relationship. Most couples have managed to use in-laws, intimate friends, or children against each other. A marriage therapist, by dealing fairly with each spouse, deals differently with them than others have. By not letting himself be provoked into condemning either marital partner, the therapist disarms a couple and prevents many of their usual maneuvers. (Actually, on the basis of his fee alone the therapist is involved in a different way with a couple than family members can be.)

The mere presence of the therapist, as a fair participant, requires the spouses to deal with each other differently. Each spouse must respond to both therapist and mate instead of merely to mate. For example, a husband who handles his wife by withdrawing into silence will find that he cannot easily continue with this maneuver in the therapy setting. Instead of being inca-pacitated by his silence, the wife can discuss it with the therapist and use it to prove her point. The husband must change his tactics to deal with both people. Many maneuvers a spouse habitually uses to provoke a response in his partner can lose their effectiveness when used against two people at once, particularly if the third party is not easily provoked.

Although it is not possible for a marriage therapist to be "objective" with a couple, since he rapidly becomes a participant in the interaction, it is possible for him to side with one spouse and then with another and so be fair. It is convenient for some therapists to argue that they do not take sides in a marital struggle but merely "reflect" back to the couple what they are expressing. Such an argument requires considerable naiveté. If a therapist listens to a wife's complaints and then turns to her husband and says, "How do you feel about that?" he cannot make this classic statement without his inquiry being in some sense directive. A therapist cannot make a neutral comment; his voice, his expression, the context, or the mere act of choosing a particular statement to inquire about introduces directiveness into the situation. When the therapist is being directive, coalition patterns are being defined and redefined, and a crucial aspect of this type of therapy is continually changing coalition patterns between therapist and each spouse. The wife who drags her husband into marriage therapy soon finds that the therapist does not join her in condemnation of the fellow, and the dragged-in husband discovers with some relief that the focus also shifts to how difficult his wife can be.

A further effect of the presence of the therapist is the change brought about by each spouse when he has the opportunity to observe the other dealing with the therapist. For example, a man who had paid little attention to his wife's protests must sit and observe an authority figure treat her in a symmetrical way by paying careful attention to what she says and encouraging her to say more. Not only do questions of coalition arise in such circumstances, but a model is being set for the spouse. Similarly, a therapist may prevent a wife or husband from dealing with him the way he or she has habitually provoked the marriage partner. For example, by commenting on how he is being handled the therapist may set a model for dealing with such provocations.

The difficulty a couple have in accepting a complementary relationship with each other is profoundly affected by the fact that they place themselves individually and collectively in a complementary relationship with a marriage therapist by asking for his services. When the therapist cooperates in such a relationship by taking charge, as most marriage therapists tend to do, he is accepting this type of relationship. Although such a therapist is not necessarily overtly authoritarian (in fact, that may not be wise or possible except in special circumstances) he is willing to listen and explore the problems. If a couple is to pay attention to him, he must be an authority figure, although not so omnipotent that it is necessary for the couple to topple him. Their acceptance of an authority figure, and therefore the acceptance of a complementary relationship, becomes a part of the process of working out types of relationship with each other.

Defining the rules

Besides intervening in a marriage merely by being present, a marriage therapist will actively intervene by relabeling, or redefining, the activity of the two people with each other. In the early stages of treatment his comments and directives tend to be permissive as he encourages the couple to express themselves in a context where each will have a fair hearing. Accusations and protests are nurtured so that as much as possible is made explicit. One way of encouraging a more free discussion is to define the consultation room as a special place, a "no man's land," where the rules are different from ordinary situations. In this special place it is appropriate to bring up matters which they have on their minds but have avoided discussing. Although this framing of the therapy situation appears a mild directive, couples will often accept the idea that they can protect each other less in that room. Sometimes a therapist may forbid the couple to discuss certain topics between sessions so that only in that special place are they discussed.

As a couple express themselves, the therapist comments upon what they say. His comments tend to be of two sorts: those comments which emphasize the positive side of their interaction together, and those comments which redefine the situation as different from, if not opposite to, the way they are defining it.

An emphasis upon the positive typically occurs when the therapist redefines the couple's motives or goals. For example, if a husband is protesting his wife's constant nagging, the therapist may comment that the wife seems to be trying to reach her husband and achieve more closeness with him. If the wife protests that her husband constantly withdraws from her, the husband may be defined as one who wants to avoid discord and seeks an amiable relationship. Particularly savage maneuvers will not be minimized but may be labeled as responses to disappointment (rather than the behavior of a cad). In general, whenever it can be done, the therapist defines the couple as attempting to bring about an amiable closeness but going about it wrongly, being misunderstood, or being driven by forces beyond their control. The way the couple characterize each other may also be redefined in a positive way. If a husband is objecting to his wife as an irresponsible and disorganized person, the therapist may define these characteristics as feminine. If the husband is passive and inactive, he may be defined as stable and enduring. When the therapist relabels a spouse in a positive way, he is not only providing support, but he is making it difficult for the couple to continue their usual classification. In addition, when the therapist redefines a spouse, he is labeling himself as the one who classifies the couple. By emphasizing the positive, he does his classifying in such a way that they cannot easily oppose him.

The other type of comments by the therapist emphasize the opposite of what the couple is emphasizing. If both husband and wife are protesting that they remain married only because they must, for religious reasons or for the children's sake, the therapist focuses upon the voluntary aspects of their relationship. Emphasizing how they chose each other and have remained together for many years, he minimizes the compulsion in the relationship. When husband and wife are protesting that their relationship is strictly voluntary and they can separate at any time, the therapist indicates that they have remained together so long despite their difficulties and they obviously have a deep unwillingness to end their association.

The therapist also relabels the type of relationship of a couple. If a wife protests that she is the responsible one in the family and must supervise her husband, the therapist not only commiserates with her for depriving herself by cooperating in this arrangement, he also points out the husband's supervision and responsible acts. In addition, he may suggest to the wife that the husband is arranging that she be the responsible one, thereby raising the question who is supervising whom. Similarly, if a husband labels his wife as the helpless one, the therapist points them in the direction of discovering who gets her own way. By focusing upon the opposite, or a different, aspect of a relationship, the therapist undermines the couple's typical ways of labeling the relationship, and they must define it in a different way and so undergo a change.

A further product of encouraging a couple to talk about each other is to make explicit many of the implicit or covert marital rules. When they are explicit, they are more difficult to follow. For example, if an implicit agreement between a couple is that they will visit his in-laws but not hers, the therapist may inquire whether they both prefer this arrangement. If they have not discussed the matter explicitly, an issue is then raised where a decision can be made. Similarly, there may be an implicit agreement that the wife never lets her husband speak. When the therapist points out that the wife seems to be interrupting her husband before he has a chance to say what is on his mind, the wife will be less able to do so, even though the therapist is not suggesting a change but "merely" commenting on what is happening. A comment can also make mutual protection less effective. By suggesting to a husband that his wife seems to be treating him like a sensitive plant, the therapist can provoke a more straightforward discussion. Conflicts about what rules to follow can be resolved by encouraging a couple to discuss their lives together and to work out compromises with a therapist emphasizing the positive. However, conflicts about who is to set the rules require more active direction from a therapist.

Resolving problems of who is to set the rules

Although the major conflicts in a marriage center in the problem of who is to tell whom what to do under what circumstances, the therapist may never discuss this conflict explicitly with the couple. If a husband says that he gets angry because his wife always gets her own way and is constantly supervising him, the therapist will not emphasize the struggle for control but will emphasize the strong feeling in the situation. Explicitly talking about the control problem can solidify it. However, specific directives given by the therapist are most effective when they are designed to resolve the struggle over who is to set the rules for the relationship.

Any comment by a therapist has directive aspects, if only to indicate "pay attention to this," but the marriage therapist often specifically directs a marital couple to behave in certain ways. These directives can be classed for convenience into two types: the suggestion that the couple behave differently, and the suggestion that they continue to behave as they have been.

A marriage therapist will direct a spouse to behave differently only in those cases where the conflict is minor or where it is likely that the spouse will behave that way anyhow and is only looking for an excuse. That is, a husband who never takes his wife out may be advised to take her out to dinner, but usually only if the husband is moving in that direction. Such a suggestion permits a couple an evening out without either spouse having to admit they wish it. Mere advice to a couple to treat each other in more reasonable ways is rarely followed or goes badly if it is followed. A couple, like an individual patient, can only be diverted into more productive directions and cannot be forced to reverse themselves. To tell a husband and wife that they should treat each other more amiably does not provide them with new information or give them an opportunity to follow the directive. More important, if a therapist directs a couple to behave differently, he has often been led into this directive by a couple and so is responding to their directive. A couple in distress have provoked many people to advise them to behave more sensibly; such advice only proves to the couple that the other person does not understand them and they continue in their distress. In general, when a therapist is provoked into giving advice, the advice will be on the terms of the person doing the provoking and therefore will perpetuate the distress. For example, a wife might say to the therapist, "Don't you think my husband should stay home nights instead of going out every night of the week?" If the therapist agrees, he is being led down the garden path. If instead of agreeing and so offering such advice the therapist says, "I think it's important to understand what this is about," the therapist is not only encouraging understanding but making it clear that he offers advice only on his own terms, not when provoked into it. However, this does not mean that the therapist should not offer advice or directives on his own terms. The psychoanalytic approach to couples is largely to listen, and such a procedure avoids being led into directives by the couple. Although there may be theoretical rationales for remaining silent, such as developing deeper layers of the intrapsychic conflicts, the main function of silence is to avoid behaving on the patient's terms. However, a therapist who remains silent also avoids taking those actions which would move a couple in the direction of a more satisfactory relationship. To be silent when provoked by the couple may be necessary; to remain silent when directives which would produce change could be given on the therapist's terms is wasting time.

A couple can be instructed to behave differently if the request is small enough so that the implications of it are not immediately apparent. For example, if a husband says he always gives in and lets his wife have her own way, he may be asked to say "no" to his wife on some issue once during the week. When this is said in the wife's presence, the groundwork is laid for the suggestion to be more easily followed. Further, the suggestion is more likely followed if a rationale is provided, such as saying that any wife should feel free to do what she pleases with confidence that her husband will say "no" to her if she goes too far. Given such a directive, the couple may at first treat the "no" lightly. However, if it is on a major issue, or if the instruction is followed for several weeks, there will be repercussions in their relationship. The more rigid the previous "agreement" that the wife will always have her own way, the greater the response in both of them if he says "no" and thereby defines the relationship differently. The fact that he is doing so under direction, and so still accepting a complementary relationship, will ease the situation. But since the message comes from him, the wife will react. Similarly, an overly responsible wife may be asked to do some small irresponsible act during the week, perhaps buy something she does not need that costs a dollar or two. If the previous agreement was that she was the responsible one and her husband the irresponsible one, a small request of this sort undermines this definition of the relationship. Even though the wife is being irresponsible under therapeutic direction, and so doing her duty by doing what the therapist says, she is still spending money for something she does not need and so behaving irresponsibly. However, in general, when a directive is given for a husband or wife to behave differently, and so break the marital rules they have established, the request must be so small that it appears trivial.

Actually it is extremely difficult to devise a directive which is a request for marital partners to behave differently from their usual ways when their usual ways of behaving are conflictual. That is, a wife who insists that she is the responsible one in the marriage is usually irresponsible at another level. For example, she may be so responsible about the budget that she is irresponsible because she is overemphasizing money at a cost to her husband and children. To ask her to do something irresponsible is not necessarily to ask something new of her. Similarly, a husband who never says "no" to his wife directly, is usually a man who is constantly saying "no" by passive resistance. To tell him to say "no" is only partly asking for different behavior. Even if one should suggest that a husband who is treating his wife coldly be more considerate of his wife, this may not be a request for a change in behavior because treating her coldly may be considerate of this type of woman. In fact if her husband treated her more amiably she might feel great demands were being put upon her or become so overwhelmed with guilt that sudden amiable behavior on his part would actually be inconsiderate.

Often a directive may appear as a request for different behavior when actually it is not. For example, a husband had spent some years crusading to have his wife enjoy a sexual orgasm. He had made such an issue of the matter, and become so angry and exasperated with her, that the issue had become a grim one between husband and wife. The wife was told, in the husband's presence, that one of these days she might enjoy some sexual pleasure and when she did she was to tell her husband that she did not enjoy it. If her husband insisted on her saying whether she had *really* not enjoyed it or was just following this directive, she should say she had really not enjoyed it. This directive had various purposes, including the purpose of introducing uncertainty into the situation and freeing the man from his overconcern about his wife's pleasure (he suffered from ejaculatio praecox). However, from what had been said, there was some indication that the wife was enjoying sex while denying it and so the directive actually was an encouragement of her usual behavior.

Encouraging a couple to behave in their usual way is, paradoxically, one of the most rapid ways to bring about such a change. Such a directive may be calculated or it may occur as a natural result of encouraging a couple to express themselves. A wife may say that her husband should stop being so ineffectual, and the therapist may respond that perhaps he needs to behave in that way at times and they should try to understand his reasons for it. When the therapist makes such a statement, he is permitting—if not encouraging—the husband to continue to be ineffectual. Most procedures which ostensibly emphasize bringing about understanding can be seen as subtle encouragement of usual behavior. Note that this procedure is quite different from the way the spouse typically handles the problem: a spouse usually tells the other to stop certain behavior, and the result is a continuation of it. When the therapist permits and encourages usual behavior, the person tends to discontinue it.

When a therapist "accepts" the way a couple is behaving he begins to gain some control of that behavior. He is placed immediately in the center of their problem: who is to lay down the rules for the relationship. Although a couple cannot easily oppose the sort of relationship the therapist is prescribing if they are already interacting that way, they can still respond to the idea of someone else defining their relationship for them, and this response will produce a shift. For example, if a wife is managing her husband by being self-sacrificing and labeling all her behavior as for the good of others, the husband cannot easily oppose her, even though he may not wish to be in a secondary position in a complementary relationship with her. Such a woman will tend to handle the therapist in a similar way. However, if the therapist encourages her to be self-sacrificing, the woman is placed in a difficult position. She cannot manage him by this method when it is at his request. If she continues to behave that way, she is conceding that she is managed by the therapist. If she does not, then she must shift to a different type of relationship. If the therapist goes further and encourages the wife to be self-sacrificing and the husband to attempt to oppose her and fail, then the couple must shift their relationship with each other to deal with being managed by the therapist.

As an example of a typical problem, a couple may be continually fighting, and if the therapist directs them to go home and keep the peace this will doubtfully happen. However, if he directs the couple to go home and have a fight, the fight will be a different sort when it happens. This difference may reside only in the fact that they are now fighting at the direction of someone else, or the therapist may have relabeled their fighting in such a way that it is a different sort. For example, a husband may say that they fight continually because his wife constantly nags. The wife may say they fight because the husband does not understand her and never does what she asks. The therapist may relabel, or redefine, their fighting in a variety of ways: he may suggest that they are not fighting effectively because they are not expressing what is really on their minds; he may suggest that their fighting is a way of gaining an emotional response from each other and they both need that response; he may say that when they begin to feel closer to each other they panic and have a fight; or he may suggest they fight because inside themselves is the feeling that they do not deserve a happy marriage. With a new label upon their fighting, and directed to go home and have a fight, the couple will find their conflict redefined in such a way that it is difficult for them to continue in their usual pattern. They are particularly tempted toward more peace at home if the therapist says they *must* fight and that they must for certain reasons which they do not like. The couple can only disprove him by fighting less.

As a marriage therapist encourages a couple to behave in their usual ways he gains some control of their behavior because what occurs is being defined as occurring under his direction. At this point he may shift his direction to bring about a change. The change he brings about may be an expansion of the limits of the type of relationship of a couple, or a shift to a different type of relationship.

An example of extending the limits of a type of relationship is a classic case reported by Milton Erickson. A woman came to him and said that she and her husband were finally going to purchase a home, as they had hoped to all their married life; however, her husband was a tyrant and would not permit her any part in the choice of home or in the choice of furnishings for it. Her husband insisted that everything connected with the new house would be entirely his choice and she would have no voice in the matter. The woman was quite unhappy because of this extreme version of a complementary relationship. Erickson told the woman that he wished to see her husband. When the old gentleman came in, Erickson emphasized the fact that a husband should be absolute boss in the home. The husband fully agreed with him. Both of them also enjoyed a full agreement that the man of the house should have complete say in the choice of a house to buy and the choice of furnishings for it. After a period of discussion, Erickson shifted to talking about the type of man who was *really* the boss in the house. When the old gentleman expressed a curiosity about what sort of man was really the boss, Erickson indicated that the real boss was the type of man who was so fully in charge that he could allow his underlings a say in minor matters. Such a boss kept full control of everything, but he could *permit* certain decisions to be made by those beneath him. Using this line of approach. Erickson persuaded the tyrannical old gentleman to lay out 20 plans of houses and 20 plans of house furnishings. Then the husband permitted his wife to choose among *his* plans. She chose a house she liked and the furnishings she liked. In this way the husband was still fully in charge of all aspects of the house purchase, but the wife could choose what she wanted. The limits of a complementary relationship were extended to satisfy both partners' needs.

Accepting what a couple offers, or encouraging them to behave in their usual ways and later suggesting a change can also provoke a shift in the type of relationship. For example, a wife was protesting that her husband avoided her, that he would often leave the dinner table when the family was eating to sit in the living room alone and later make himself some dinner. Although the husband at first indicated he did not know why he behaved this way, he also indicated that his wife spent the time at the dinner table nagging the kids and nagging at him. At the first suggestion that she was behaving in this way at the table, the wife said that she had to correct the children at the table because he never did. The husband said that when he attempted to, she interrupted, and it was not worth a battle.

The wife was instructed to correct the children at the table during the coming week, and to observe the effect of this upon her husband. Her husband was instructed to observe the way his wife dealt with the children, and if he strongly disagreed with it he was to get up and leave the table. Actually the instruction was merely to continue to behave as they had been. However, when they were instructed to do so, the couple found it difficult to behave in their usual ways because the behavior became both deliberate and occurred under duress. After a week of this procedure, the couple was instructed to shift their behavior: for a week the wife was to be relieved of all responsibility for discipline at the table and could just enjoy her meal, and the husband was to fully take charge at the dinner table. The wife was not even to point at one of the children to indicate that her husband should take some action. Since their behavior was defined as occurring at the instigation of the therapist, rather than originating with each other, the couple could tolerate this shift in their relationship at the table with a consequent carry-over into other aspects of their lives together.

Similar encouragement of typical behavior occurs if the therapist instructs a distant couple to maintain a certain distance from each other and not risk becoming too close for a period of time, if he instructs a non-fighting couple to avoid a fight but to rehearse in their minds what they would like to say to each other, if he instructs a spouse who always gives in to give in for a period of time, and so on. This procedure not only gives the therapist some control of what the couple is doing and lays the groundwork for a later shift, but it also utilizes whatever rebellious forces are latent within the couple.

Often an instruction to one spouse in the presence of the other has its effects on them both. For example, a couple who are constantly fighting, with the wife flaunting her extramarital affairs before her husband, will see their struggle from a particular point of view. They will usually see what they do to each other in terms of revenge. If the therapist, from his vantage point of an expert, advises the wife that she is protecting her husband by her dalliances with other men because he is uneasy about sex, the wife is faced with a different point of view. To label her behavior as protective, when she sees it as vengeful, makes it more difficult for her to continue it, particularly if the therapist suggests that it may be necessary for her to continue to help her husband in this way. When such a comment is made in the husband's presence, he is almost obligated to prove that he does not need such protection by attempting a closer relationship with his wife. Naturally the couple will disagree with such a comment, but the idea will continue to work upon them. If there is sufficient disagreement, the therapist may suggest they should experiment; if they manage a closer relationship, they will find that they panic. To disprove this, they must manage a closer relationship. If they become upset as they become closer, they are accepting the therapist's conception of the situation and so accepting him as someone who can arrange a change. If they do not become upset, they have a closer relationship which is the therapist's goal.

When a therapist provides a framework which is to bring about a change, and within that framework he encourages a couple to continue in their usual ways, the couple is faced with a situation which is difficult to deal with without undergoing change. If, in addition, the therapist makes it an ordeal for them to continue in their usual ways, the problem is compounded for the couple. Labeling in a different way what they do often makes it more of an ordeal for the couple to continue their usual patterns. This "different way" may be a relabeling of negative behavior as something positive; it may also be the reverse. The therapist may suggest that certain behavior by one of the spouses which they consider positive is really negative. For example, the therapist may define protectiveness as really selfishness because of the protecting person's needs being satisfied. Another procedure is to raise the question with the marital partners of how they usually punish each other. Typically they say they do not, but when the punishment is defined as that behavior which the other spouse feels as punishing, they become more loquacious. Couples will then discuss such behavior as withdrawing, complaining, arguing, refusing to do what the other asks, and so on. Such a discussion makes explicit many of the maneuvers a couple use against each other, and also leads to a relabeling of those maneuvers. It is possible to lead up to the idea of symptomatic behavior as punishing. Since symptoms in one spouse are always hard on the other, one can suggest that a symptom is a way of punishing the other. A spouse with an obesity problem, headaches, hysterical symptoms, or compulsions usually prefers to define the symptom as something occurring independent of the spouse. To call such a symptom a way of punishing makes it more difficult to exist. At times a spouse may be asked to inquire of the other, "Why are you punishing me?" when the other complains of a symptom. Such an inquiry provokes a denial but also provokes an inhibition of the symptomatic experience. This procedure is similar to other relabeling of symptoms so that they are characterized differently and thus a change is induced. For example, one may ask a spouse, in the presence of the other spouse, to choose a time when the symptom is better that week and announce that it is worse. Such an instruction increases the uncertainty of the severity of the symptom and lays the groundwork for change.

The idea of a therapist encouraging a couple to behave in their usual ways can be varied by a therapist directing a spouse to encourage the other spouse to exhibit symptomatic behavior. Typically the mate of a spouse with symptoms opposes the symptomatic behavior but also encourages it. If a marriage therapist directs a mate only to encourage symptomatic behavior in the spouse, there is often a rather drastic response. For example, a wife became anxious whenever she tried to leave the house alone. When she attempted to go out, she suffered anxiety feelings and a terrible pain in the eyes. She had suffered this problem for years, and her husband was constantly assuring her that she should go out alone and that it was perfectly safe. However, he was also fully cooperating in her staying at home by doing all the shopping, escorting her where she needed to go, and indicating some uneasiness whenever she started to go out alone. After several sessions of marriage therapy, the husband was asked, in the presence of the wife, to do something he might think was silly. He was asked to tell the wife each day as he left for work that she was to stay home that day and not go out alone. He could say this seriously, or as a joke, or however he pleased. The husband agreed to follow this procedure. On the third day that he told her to stay at home the wife went out to the store alone for the first time in eight years. However, the next interview was devoted to the husband's expressions of concern about what his wife might do if she went out alone, where she might go, whom she might meet, and would she even get a job and become so independent that she would leave him.

This directive to the husband to tell his wife to stay at home was actually a double encouragement of usual behavior: the husband was directed to encourage his wife to stay at home, as he had been covertly doing, and the wife was being encouraged by the husband to stay at home, as she had been doing. The product of such a directive is a shift in type of relationship. Although the wife had been behaving like the helpless one, *she was in charge* of being the helpless one by insisting on staying home. When her husband directed her to stay at home, the question of *who* was laying down the rules for their relationship was called in question. The wife responded by a symmetrical move, leaving the house, which was her only way of taking charge in this situation. Although it seems a mild directive when a therapist directs a spouse to encourage the other spouse to behave as usual, there is inevitably a marital upheaval because such a directive centers on the crucial problem of a marriage: who is to define what sort of relationship the two people will have.

Changing the stability of a system: Summary
A marital couple in difficulty tend to perpetuate their distress by attempting to resolve conflict in such a way that it continues. The goal of a marriage therapist is not only to shift, or to expand, the types of relationship of a couple,

but also to provoke a change in the ways the couple keep the marital system stable. Such a change requires influencing the corrective variables in the system so the system itself may undergo a change.

An appearance at the door of a marriage therapist is essentially an attempt by a couple to find a more satisfying means of perpetuating their relationship. The therapist provides an opportunity for change in a variety of ways: he encourages discussion to resolve conflict rather than previous methods, such as withdrawal and silence, he provides a reasonably impartial advisor and judge, he encourages a couple to examine motivations which they might have outside awareness, he makes many maneuvers explicit and therefore more difficult to follow, and he engenders habits of dealing with sensitive topics. Granting that discussion, encouragement of understanding, and new points of view are offered in the marriage therapy context, there is another source of change which has been emphasized in this paper—the paradoxical position a couple is placed in if they continue distressing behavior when undergoing marriage therapy.

For the purposes of this paper a paradoxical position is defined as the position a person is in when he is faced with messages which conflict with one another at different levels. For example, when faced with a marriage therapist a couple is faced with someone offering benevolent help for their difficulties. Yet at the same time the benevolent helper is requiring the couple to go through an ordeal which they can feel as punishing. It is not easy for a couple to expose their problems and petty conflicts, and the situations which couples are most sensitive about are often those most explored so that the therapy can be a process of exacerbating old and new wounds. Insofar as the couple is faced with a benevolent therapist who is helping them to feel better by putting them through an ordeal, they are faced with a paradoxical situation. Still another dimension of paradox occurs when the therapist encourages them to continue in their distress while communicating to them at another level that he is helping them over that distress. Still another paradox is involved when the therapist assumes the posture of an expert who can help the couple and then declines to instruct or direct them as an expert would.

The question of why paradoxical situations are evident in therapy is related to the question of how change is brought about and how difficult it is for a couple to bring about a change in their relationship without assistance. It would seem reasonable that if a couple who are obviously compounding their difficulties by their behavior were advised to behave in more sensible ways they would do so and their conflicts would be resolved. However, such advice is not usually offered in marriage therapy, and if offered, it is not usually accepted. It is possible to postulate deeply rooted psychodynamic causes to explain why change in a marital relationship is so difficult, but it is also possible to approach the problem from a relationship rather than an individual point of view.

People in relationship to each other tend to govern each other's behavior so that their relationship remains stable, and it is in the nature of governors that they act so as to diminish change. Implicit in this way of looking at relationships is a premise which might be called the first law of human relations: *when one individual indicates a change in relation to another, the other will respond in such a way as to diminish that change.* Granting the operation of this law in relationships, it would follow that each attempt by a spouse to change the marital relationship would provoke a response to diminish that change. A distressing relationship would be perpetuated by the act of attempting to change it. As it is sometimes said, if a wife wishes her husband to remain unchanged, she should set out to reform him.

Assuming that people follow such a law in their relationships, family relations would tend to be stable and difficult to change, and it would follow that psychotherapy of any sort would be faced with the problem that each attempt to change a patient could provoke a response to diminish that change. This would not mean that psychotherapy was impossible, but it would mean that tactics of psychotherapy would have to take this law into account. Therefore therapists would not say "I'm going to change you" to a patient. Instead, they would avoid indicating that a change was to be brought about by emphasizing other factors in the interchange, such as self-understanding. They would decline the position of one who is explicitly attempting to bring about change by saying to a patient, "I'm only trying to help you understand yourself," or "The best therapist for you is you and I can only try to help you help yourself." The therapist would be assuming the posture of the expert who can help bring about change, but he could not merely offer advice because that would be an indication for change which the couple would need to diminish. The various tactics of a therapist to avoid indicating a change would make paradoxes evident in the therapeutic setting, since he must bring about change without asking for it to occur.

It would also follow, granted this law, that an obvious way to bring about change in a symptom would be to encourage a change toward an increase in symptomatic behavior; the couple could only diminish that change by a lessening of symptomatic behavior. Again, a paradox becomes resolved if one assumes that people act to diminish those changes which are indicated by others.

Although a marriage therapist typically emphasizes to a couple the need for self-understanding, there is little evidence that achieving understanding causes a change in a marital relationship. More apparently, marriage therapy offers a context where a couple can learn alternative ways of behaving while being forced to abandon those past procedures which induced distress. By advice, counsel, and example the therapist offers other ways of resolving conflict. By imposing paradoxical situations, the therapist both forces and frees the couple to develop new ways of relating to one another.

Family Systems and Approaches to Family Therapy

Virginia Satir

I would like to put together some things and some ideas that have proved very interesting and exciting to me, and, I think, to others in this country and elsewhere. I am connected with working people and their problems by working through the medium of the family unit. Because I believe we are living in a very magnificent time as far as human beings are concerned, I would like to trace for you what I think are the origins of both their growth and change. Many new things are coming up—social psychiatry, community psychiatry, the influences of existentialism and of self-actualization. There is a spirit of experimentation around, which is always exciting. Let me develop some of the ideas that I think lead to the family unit, which I see as a step in evolvement more than any particular form of therapy, as opposed, for instance, to working with an individual, or a group.

I want to cover hundreds of years of history very quickly. The origins of any of the therapeutic entities we deal with at present, it seems to me, come from the witch, the pauper, the idiot, the sick person, and the criminal. Our present areas of interest have evolved from these five kinds of people. We got psychiatry from the witch, criminology from the criminal, medicine from the sick person, social work from the pauper, and psychology from the idiot. It is not exactly one to one, but all of these entities were, at one point, perceived as deviations. With the first deviation, the source and the cause were looked upon as unknown. From these, however, came the first diagnostic categories. And then, as in all diagnostic categories, there were series of causations, and for each of the diagnostic categories there were also series of therapies. Starting from the labeling and the causation of deviations and their treatment, we look back and see that the first theories of causation about deviation were unknown, but the treatment was death, death by indirection or by direction.

I am going back many years to try to develop these three lines: the labeling, the causation, and the treatment within this framework and see what I can do

Reprinted from the *Journal of the Fort Logan Mental Health Center*, Vol. 4, 1967, pp. 81–93. Reproduced by permission.

to make some sense out of where we are today. People were not content to look upon deviation and the fact that its causes were unknown. Human beings are a curious lot, and they try to figure out things. As they began to look at these deviations, one of their first ideas about causation was some kind of unknown infiltration from without, some kind of magic. When the cause is thought to be infiltration from the outside, you treat this with whatever is in keeping with the knowledge about magic at that particular point. We have in some cultures today certain religious beliefs which would be used for this. As the years progressed, it was thought that perhaps it was not all magic; maybe it had something to do with what you were like when you were born—your genetic heritage. If it was something that you were born with, there was not much you could do about it; you had to be content to endure it. You might try to segregate the genetically unwhole people and place them somewhere else.

We had by this time, then, three theories about causation: unknown, infiltration from outside, and genetic. Treatment could be death, or it could be separation of some sort. As the years went on, it looked as if a person's behavior had something to do with his will; that is, he was an "ornery cuss," and that was his trouble. As the idea developed that man was just an "ornery cuss," it seemed that if this were the cause of his behavior, one way of taking care of it was to punish him. Now we had another form of treatment. It looks like man explored a little bit more and got the idea that perhaps where a person lived had something to do with how he behaved. The natural and logical conclusion to that was to move him to a place with different surroundings; thus custodial care came into being, and we have many residuals of that.

Later, it looked as though behavior had something to do with some part of man or woman that motivated him but was out of sight of his awareness. This was, of course, the unconscious. The treatment for that was to discover the unconscious and try to help man by putting him more in charge of himself. Psychoanalysis was one of the main tools for that particular form of treatment. Then it seemed as though the way one person behaved had something to do with the person with whom he was interacting, and the theory of interpersonal behavior was born. Therefore, it seemed sensible to treat the interpersonal relationship and the milieu.

In a brief way I have covered the general kinds of theories of causation and treatment, and these were all one-to-one things. As different ideas came into being, such as the interpersonal theory which Sullivan wrote about in the 1920's, and we saw the rise of something called group therapy in the 1920's with Moreno, Slavson and some of the others, there was born a new idea about how to treat an individual. That is, the additional idea of treating an individual with his peers who were in the same spot. This group treatment, or treatment within a peer group, was based upon one principle, that changes in behavior of an individual were brought about through interpersonal operation. Before World War II, these two ways of treating were invoked—the individual and the group.

At the beginning of the century there developed something called child guidance clinics, which provided the first form of treatment based on an interpersonal relationship. These used the unit of the mother and the child on the premise that the child's behavior was influenced by what the mother did. Fathers were discovered later. We had two uses of the interpersonal relationship, that is, that which was perceived in self, child guidance, and that which was worked out in group therapy. After World War II came another kind of treatment, known as marital counseling, for the husband and wife pair. For the most part, marital counseling was not brought into the profession by psychiatrists, social workers, and such, but rather by clergymen, sociologists, and other people outside of the usual (forgive the expression) "mental ill health" disciplines. I use that term because all of us in the psychiatry, social work, or psychology professions are mental ill health specialists. We had another form of the mental treatment unit then, the husband and wife. So, at this point we have the picture of how to treat an individual, how to treat groups of individuals, the mother-child unit, and the husband-wife unit. If you look at this in terms of a family, you will see that there are only two other units present in the family, but still left out, the father-child unit and the sibling unit. So if we add the sibling unit and the father-child unit to the mother-child unit and the husband and wife unit, we have all the units in a family.

We had the beginnings, if we put them all together, of what would go into a family. To take a little further look, along came the idea that children were there to help, in an indirect way, a husband and wife to get along together. Also, running through all of this was an idea that people could be taught how to take on marital and parental responsibilities. So much, then, for the evolvement up to the time of World War II.

There was a psychiatric entity called schizophrenia, which has been around for a long time and which happens to be a label that in years past usually meant that nothing much could be done for people to whom it was applied. Occasionally, there were scattered reports of improvement or recovery but, by and large, in the treatment of that entity called schizophrenia, the prognosis was not very good. After the last war, some curious people began to think about how a person who was labelled a schizophrenic might look to his own family. Gregory Bateson, an anthropologist who was associated with us at the Mental Research Institute, was one of the people who became curious as to what the whole family looked like if it contained someone with this label. He began his studies in 1954, and around the same time, Murray Bowen, who was at the National Institute of Mental Health, hospitalized whole families just to look at this situation. Some interesting things emerged in the studies of the schizophrenic and his family—when I say "schizophrenic," I mean somebody who has that label. There seemed to be a repetitious and predictable pattern, a direct link between what the labelled person was presenting and the family of which he was a part. This excited people because, again, theories of behavior ranged all the way from the unknown and genetics to the other things I have mentioned. The idea developed that maybe we had something new that would shed some light on the behavior of a person—in this instance, the behavior of a schizophrenic. It was not a very long step then to looking at all other kinds of behavior to see if the behavior of any individual could be linked to the system of which he was a part.

In the earlier days we did not talk much about systems. We just knew that we were seeing a series of patterns that certainly seemed to be a type of link. Now it appears that every group of essential ingredients that must belong together in order to emerge with a single outcome forms a system. The parts have to work together in some kind of organized, orderly, sequential form which begins to develop a rhythm and a balance in order to obtain the outcome that the particular ingredients are designed to do. It began to look as though each family developed a system from its ingredients, a system that somehow kept the whole family in balance. This was a crude beginning, that is, the observation that families were systems which worked like cars. In biology you were well acquainted with systems; it seemed that a similar thing went on in families. At the Mental Research Institute we have done a great deal of work trying to find out about family systems, trying to see how they work, and trying to see what kinds of intervention one needs to change a system that is not functioning toward growth to one that is. This brought a new idea into focus, because when we tried to determine whether or not the behavior of an individual was healthy, we used a whole set of criteria. But when we looked at behavior in relation to a system, these criteria did not fit and we had to look at something else. The words which would describe a functioning person would not necessarily describe a functional system. We had no words to talk about human systems, and we had to devise a new language. I am not satisfied with the language we have worked out for talking about systems, but I think we will learn more about it.

The Mental Research Institute was founded in 1959 to study the relationship of individual behavior to the system of which it was a part. When we started to explore this, we had to review certain things that we knew about the development of a person. And then the "system" idea became even more sensible. All of you probably know, when you think about it, that you arrived where you are right now and became the person you are at this moment in time because of a three-person learning system—a male and a female forbear and yourself. If you did not actually have one of these persons on the premises, their images were on the premises. So we knew that every individual becomes the product of a three-person learning system, a male adult and a female adult, who were his parents, and himself. We also knew, when we reminded ourselves, that every child comes into this world only with ingredients to grow and not a blueprint already developed. There are no cases on record where there was a little bag of directions about how to grow and develop. The important thing we all recognized was that this blueprint had to be drawn as the child went along. Obviously, the blueprint depended upon the way in which the male and the female adult handed down, or over, to their child the directions for how he was to grow. On the face of it that sounds easy—a couple of adults put their heads together and work out, or write out, a blueprint for the kids. It does not seem to work that easily in practice. When two adults get together, even though they are the parents of a child, they are not always in agreement about what makes for the best kind of blueprinting. They are not always able to communicate their messages to the child, or to each other, so there is no particular guarantee that a child will get a clear message from his parents about how he should grow and develop. However, as we looked at how adults pass on to the child their ideas for the child's development, we came onto this very important thing, communication.

Communication has been known about for a long time; in mass communication everybody is connected, that is, knows something about it. But we defined this a little bit further; we said that communication was a two-way street and that it took place between a sender and a receiver, and that whether or not the communication came across depended both upon the sender and upon the receiver. Every child has two senders, the male adult and the female adult. I don't know whether he is lucky or unlucky, but he may have also some other sender around, like grandparents, or aunts. There are at least two senders, but the child is only one receiver. We therefore concocted this idea: Suppose that you were a radio receiver and you were being sent signals from two different stations, neither of which knew that the other one was sending, and they had to come in on the same wave length. You know what happens with that; you get static. You also have a commitment on the receiving end, regardless of what is going on or what the reality is, to make sense of the signals and to use them as though they fit. This is especially true if there is a rule that the sender and receiver cannot comment for one another, or that the receiver cannot send anything back, or that he cannot even comment on the fact that what he was sent does not fit. In a rather homely analysis, it looked to us as if every child was involved in such a situation and dependent upon it for the development of his self-concepts. All of us who have any knowledge from working with individuals knew that the picture a self had of himself, and the feeling of worth that a self had of himself, was going to be very important in determining how that self would behave, how that self would grow, how that self would feel, and how that self would act. It seemed then that it would be worthwhile to scrutinize more carefully the operation between the male adult and the female adult in the interests of their child.

One of the things that we discovered, contrary to what had been thought originally, was that everything the child got from the parent, the parent intended to give. We went through a period when it was quite clear that all the bad things of the world were related to mothers, and bad mothers that did all the harm, and we had techniques that dealt with that, too. But we found that there was not much relationship between what the parent intended and what the child received. Neither was there much relationship between what one parent sent out and what the other sent out, particularly if the two were not aware that they could send out different messages. We learned that the knowledge of the child, in contrast to the intentions of the parent toward the child, would not necessarily be refused by the child. For the first time, someone could look at assistance outside the "blame" frame. There is a difference between seeing how things work and finding blame or credit for the way things work. And I would say at this point in time that all over the world and in all groups that I work with, when people are trying to explain causes, they still get into the "blame" frame. It is very difficult not to do this without raising defenses, without making people feel badly, without making people fight, and fight in a purposeless kind of way.

If it were true that the messages of adults were not necessarily communicated to the child and received by him as intended, then we needed to look at this more carefully. In doing so, we came upon some very simple things. I am quite convinced that it is the simple things in the world that we overlook most often, and, if I am an expert in anything, I would consider myself an expert in the obvious which most likely gets overlooked. We discovered that it is quite possible for us, in sending messages, to give the receiver clues that we are not aware of giving. There is a very simple explanation: When we are preoccupied with our inner selves we do not recognize what we are presenting outside. But the children do! We discovered that parents had the delusion that their children only heard what their parents intended them to hear and only saw what they intended them to see. We discovered also that parents gave out what is known as "double-level messages."

This was one of the contributions that Gregory Bateson made, and I want to tell you about a "double-level," because we're double-leveling all the time. Double-leveling in itself is not pathological. These messages gave us clues that the parents' intent was not received by the child. Let me give you the definition of a double-level message. Suppose that I announce, with a big grin on my face, that the building is burning down. There is something here that does not quite fit. Now, if you are in my presence when I have a big grin on my face and I say to you, "The place is burning down," you are in a dilemma. If you take your message from my smile there is something funny about this; you are not supposed to have joy and pleasure when the place is burning down. If you listen to my words about the place burning down, then what are you going to do with my smile? This is a double-level. Or, suppose I get a bad pain while I am with a friend. I do not want my friend to know that I am in pain because we have other things to do, but she observes that my facial muscles get stiff and taut, and says, "How are you feeling?" If I reply, "Fine," I am really saying, "You don't have to look at my pain, we can go on with what we are doing." But, seeing my face, my friend may very well conclude that I am an idiot, that I am lying to her, or that I do not consider her enough of a friend that I can level with her and other things of this sort. These are double levels again.

Double-levels come about without people knowing it, and, in my opinion, there is nothing pathological about that. It is pathological when double-levels are not commented upon or acknowledged in some way by those to whom they are directed. This can give a chance, at least, for an explanation of what does not fit. Many times in talking to groups, people want to make the point that it is bad if you give out double-levels. I do not think you can live without them. I believe that our whole physical system is made up of so many parts with which we are not in connection that we are unaware of a great many of our clues.

As persons, each of us relates more to what is inside than what is outside; others are more aware of what is presented on our outsides and take their clues from what they see and hear. If they cannot comment on the clues, they must determine for themselves the reasons for the discrepancies. Now, if you happen to be a person with low self-esteem, you probably are going to interpret a discrepancy in some impulsive way. You may conclude that it is a lie, or some form of sick, bad, stupid, or crazy behavior. Unless you can check it out, you are likely to retain a false interpretation of the discrepancy.

Children come into the world unequipped to give any kind of specific feedback. They usually do not learn to talk until the age of twelve months or beyond, and that means that for those twelve months of the child's life he has had to interpret on his own whatever discrepancies he has envisaged or experienced with his parents. By the time the child is talking, he already has a wealth of clues defined; he has a set of expectations to which he will give words later on, much to the surprise of the adults. We were interested in looking at what we thought would help us with the mystery of how a person with good intentions, who is right and loving, could give out faulty messages to a child. I am sure that you have noticed that there is not much relationship between love, niceness, and hard work among the people who have problems in your family. So how could it be that a person who was well intentioned, loving and bright still managed to have children who were not growing properly? I think the answer is not knowing that adults are capable of giving double-levels and that the child has to make some kind of sense out of them. I sometimes wonder how any child, especially if he is around many adults in his first year of life, manages some kind of integration with himself.

One of the things that has been very interesting at the Mental Health Institute is the use of video tapes. I felt that it was most important to acquaint families with the fact that the way they thought they looked and sounded was not the way they really looked and sounded. What somebody else got from them was not necessarily what they thought was there. Another myth was that one should always be one hundred percent in control of the way he manages himself. It was easy to dispel that kind of expectation with television, but you cannot run around with your tape recorder all the time. We looked for other ways in which a person could find out that he did not always look and sound as he thought he did. If you do not believe me, go home tonight, walk in the door and tell the first person you see to look at you, and then you tell him what you think he saw. Describe fully your eyes and your nose, what your ears are doing, and what the muscles in your neck are doing, and whether you are red or not. Then compare the picture with his view. This is a descriptive exercise. Nobody is telling you that anything is wrong with you; you are just comparing pictures.

There is another thing that you can do. Very few of us have ever seen ourselves as we really look. Go to your mirror and put on a name tag. Look in the mirror. You will see that your name tag is backwards. Now if your tag is backwards, your face also will be backwards. If you have never seen yourself on a video tape or in moving pictures, you have been running around all your life with a delusion of what you look like. You have been comparing the feedback to you with a delusion instead of with reality. Similarly, the first time you hear your voice on a tape recorder, you say to yourself, "That is not me, my voice is lower than that, or, it is higher than that." But everybody says that is exactly the way you sound. A very simple physics principle governs that little discrepancy: sound which originates in the same orifice is heard differently than the sound that comes from outside of that orifice. Again, we have the possibility for a delusion, and I use delusion in a nice sense because I am not afraid of them. I used to be, but I am not any more. People run around with some mistaken ideas that they know what they look like, what they intend to say, and what they sound like. There is a fourth part to that; whatever they tend to look like and sound like, they do look like and sound like.

Much of what we have developed in the way of treatment intervention has been based upon these kinds of things, the ways in which the child receives his messages initially on how to develop his blueprints. There are many ways of doing it, and you can see now how many traps there would be for a child in getting messages from his mother and from his father within the expectations that I have described. If this is accompanied by the rule against commenting upon what the child sees and hears when he cannot talk, you can see how the child could continue his early misconceptions of what was intended without his parents being aware of them. Maybe this is so until the child goes to school when suddenly there comes some demand on his growth which he cannot see, and then the whole story comes out. One other point in looking at the development of the child, we were all children once. It sounds a little facetious when I say it, but many adults forget this—that they were once children, and that their origins were as children. Because we were all children, we all have ideas about how children should be different. All adults have in their minds a picture of the ideal child. And from where do they get that ideal child? Where did you get your ideas of what your ideal child is like? You got them from what you were not, from what your parents did not do properly, and from how they told you you ought to be. Everybody wants things to fit their ideals, so each adult applies these same things to his child when he comes along, and we think this is one of the ways that social heredity takes place. It seems that because of the ways in which rules about commenting are made in the family, people develop rules about themselves—whether or not they can comment, whether they can ask questions, whether they can challenge, whether they can criticize, or whether they can make loving comments. And the less the ability and freedom to comment, the more likely are going to be the distortions, inhibitions, and prohibitions about what people can comment on later.

People can grow to adulthood with rules which permit them to comment only on certain things, and the rest of it may be just imagined or believed, even though it may not even be in reality. Then people get married. Their marriage relationship may be founded upon their ideals of what should be, which can be filled in easily if you do not ask for reality to be validated. It is very easy for a woman to believe that a man must always be the leader, because her father was not the leader and her mother said that he should be. Her idea then is that the man tells her what to do; but his telling her what to do in the courtship period means that he always has an idea about where the two can go. Later on, the same things happen except it feels different. What at one point in time felt like a strong man taking care of her later feels like a bully trying to squash her. Where would she get such delusion? Not only from inside herself, but also when he once said, "Let's go to the movies," and she said, "No." He said, "Yes," and she felt that he was a strong man. So this is her fantasy, and she begins relating herself to him in terms of the fantasy. As long as you do not comment upon it, you do not have to break up your fantasy; you can continue.

However, at some time reality presents itself, and it is no longer possible to continue life with a fantasy. We think that a symptom breaks out when the reality can no longer sustain the fantasy. We have quite a bit of evidence to get us on this track, and I think this is a very fruitful way of beginning. Human beings, we find, do not give up easily. Even when the woman should decide her husband is trying to squash her, she will still try to make it out some way, even with her symptom because people do not give up easily. There begin to be such things developing as, "I'm unlovable, now here is the evidence." Then she withdraws more, and of course he sees that he is being withdrawn from, so there must be something wrong with him. Then we get back to the magical thinking—born that way, lived with the wrong people, got a little man in his head telling him what to do. These begin to be some of the explanations that take place. Isn't it interesting that the explanations these people make at this point in time are so similar to what we did, over the ages to the present, to explain deviations?

We are at a very exciting time in looking at these relationships. First of all, there is evolvement of the self-concept within the family system, and the kinds of communication patterns that go into it. Right now we are working on some ideas about child rearing, by having adults know more. It is much easier to know about communication than it is to know about your self-concepts, and apparently it is not so defense-producing. We are working on ways to make it possible for young parents to do a different kind of job regarding what they pay attention to in rearing their children. We are working also on the "well family service," which we think will develop into a preventive device. We see now that every family has a predictable system of operations and a set of expectations and predictions. These expectations and predictions are part of the evolvement of self-concepts of each person involved. They will be expressed through behavior and through communication. If we put all these together we can begin to know something about helping with behavior that is on the road to some kind of destruction. We hope that many people will help us with this; but it is exciting for me, I think that it is for others, and I hope that it is for you, too.

Family Therapy

Gerald H. Zuk

Family therapy studies of the past dozen years, as a recent review establishes,[1] have predominantly reflected the psychoanalytic viewpoint, even though striking departures from psychoanalytic theory and technique have been made by family therapists. For the most part, writers on technique[2-7] have essentially adhered to the view that to promote beneficial change in patients the therapist must formulate and communicate insights and work through unconscious resistances. Even such departures from psychoanalytic technique as those described by Satir[8] and Minuchin[9] recently seem to this writer fundamentally insight-centered.

Among major contributors to family therapy theory and practice today, only Haley[10] has offered a clear alternative to the "insight-centered model," although he is joined to an extent by Jackson[11] and Brodey,[12] using somewhat different approaches. Haley maintains that the therapist secures beneficial change when he enforces a dominant *position* vis-à-vis patient; that is, to the extent he controls the relationship, decides what its goals shall be, and parries the patient's attempts to undermine his control. The therapist is skillful at setting up paradoxical situations in which the patient thinks he can "win" against the therapist, but loses. In the losing, the patient comes to accept the therapist's control and direction and changes accordingly.

As a result of experience in family therapy over the past five years, I am convinced that beneficial change, as Haley suggests, is a creative outcome of a struggle for control between the therapist and family members, but I believe that the skillful setting-up of paradoxical situations is not sufficient as an explanation of change in family therapy, although it does provide a useful basis to consider what does bring about change. This paper will describe a technique which uses sources of therapeutic leverage believed unique to family therapy, although applications are possible in marital and, to a lesser extent, in group therapy. The technique arises specifically from the fact that family therapy is the transaction of a therapist with at least two or more persons who have had an extensive history of relating to one another.

Reprinted from *Archives of General Psychiatry*, Vol. 16, 1967, pp. 71–79. Reproduced by permission.

Preliminary descriptions of technique and theoretical framework have been given elsewhere.[13,14] A cornerstone of the technique is a definition of family therapy as follows: *it is the technique that explores and attempts to shift the balance of pathogenic relating among family members so that new forms of relating become possible.* This definition presumes Jackson's notion[15] that the family is a homeostatic system in which change in one part is likely to effect changes in other parts.

Another cornerstone of the technique that will be described in this paper is the fact that the expression of conflict in family therapy is like that in no other form of therapy, and that conflict generates the energy required to shift fixed patterns of relating among family members. The therapist must be an expert in searching out the main issues in the family, in keeping these issues in focus, and in exploring the sources and intensity of disagreement. Only in family therapy do patients come with an established history of conflict and with well-developed means for expressing or disguising it.

In the more comprehensive of the preliminary papers,[14] I described go-between process in family therapy in four variations rather commonly encountered. In two of the variations the initiative in conducting go-between process rests with the therapist. In the other two variations the initiative resides with the family members; that is, they conducted go-between process "against" the therapist as a means to forestall his attempts to control and direct the treatment. In this paper I hope to take up in much greater detail the steps in the go-between process and describe the theoretical structure in which the process is grounded.

GO-BETWEEN PROCESS: ITS TERMS AND SOME DIMENSIONS

In the sections to follow, terms and some dimensions of go-between process will be elaborated: (1) from the point of view of the therapist vis-à-vis family; (2) in the context of the family's defensive tactics; and (3) in the context of "phases" of treatment, specifically onset and termination.

From the viewpoint of therapist vis-à-vis family

The therapist conducts go-between process when: *Term 1.*—(a) He probes issues in the family, establishes the existence of conflict by eliciting expressions of disagreement, and encourages the open expression of disagreement. (b) He exposes and otherwise resists the family's efforts to deny or disguise disagreement. (c) He encourages the expression of recent or current disagreement rather than rehashes of old. (d) He encourages expression of conflict between members who are *present* rather than absent from the treatment session.

Term 1 sets conditions for the therapist's encouragement of expression of conflict. Families differ greatly in the extent to which they will express it: some appear only too eager to do so; others are most reluctant. The therapist must be as wary of the first type of these families as the second, for the first type often generates a lot of superficial "noisy" disagreement, and frequently deeper sources are disguised. In these families, members will engage in a great deal of mutual recrimination—bitterness, anger, and hostility are openly expressed. But the process might be labeled a "pseudohostility." Wynne[16] has used this term and means by it a shared defense against recognizing feelings of tenderness, affection, or sexual attraction, but I use it here to mean the expression of hostility as a mask for a more pervasive, deeper-lying hostility. A "pseudohostility" may be directed by one family member against another toward whom the first does not really feel the greatest animosity, but who is a convenient scapegoat.

A second, contrasting group of families will deny disagreements and even develop elaborate means for disguising them. Some of these families will appear genuinely puzzled when the therapist calls attention to sources of conflict. Family members appear confused, pained, even deeply hurt if the therapist persists in pointing out conflict. The members pride themselves on their rational approach to the solution of family problems, on their ability to find answers acceptable to all. Even from themselves they skillfully hide the fact that they simply have failed to deal with major problem areas—have swept them under the rug, as it were.

Because memory for detail is likely to be still fresh and emotions running high, the therapist conducting go-between process encourages families to talk about recent conflict as opposed to old. Sometimes therapists will encounter families whose members prefer to talk about their past problems, but this may be a skillful gambit to introduce doubt and uncertainty into the treatment situation—i.e., members have difficulty recalling precisely what was said, who was present, and so on. The therapist will have to judge how much of this "recollection" to allow, and in general will tend to discourage its expression.

Therapists will also encounter family members who prefer to talk about their conflict with a family member, relative, or friend who is not present in the treatment session. Since this process also tends to introduce doubt and uncertainty, the therapist conducting go-between process will in general tend to discourage its expression. Too much control is left in the hands of the member who presents his side of the disagreement. There will be times, to be sure, when the therapist will allow this expression, but only if he thinks it will "open up" sources of conflict between family members who are present.

The therapist conducts go-between process when: *Term 2.* —*(a)* He selects specific disagreements as especially worthy of discussion, rejects others as unworthy, and resists the family's expected efforts to establish its own rules of priority. *(b)* This selection is part of his move into the role of the go-between. He then seeks to establish his authority in the role and resists the family's expected efforts to displace him.

In a previous paper[14] on the topic it was stated that

> In family therapy the go-between may be very active, intrusive and confronting or inactive and passive. He may move into the role of go-between by the device of attacking two parties he hopes to make into principals; or he may move into the role by calmly pointing out a difference between two parties. On the other hand, he may become a go-between by refusing to take sides in a dispute that has erupted; or he may become one by presenting a new point of view in a dispute [p. 165].

The point here is that in the role of go-between the therapist is constantly structuring, and directing, the treatment situation.

A case will be presented to illustrate the terms of go-between process, but Term 2 in particular. A family was referred for therapy on the basis that a young daughter's poor school performance seemed to have origins in disturbed family living. The family was composed of the daughter, 9 years old, her brother, 13 years old, her 40-year-old mother, and 56-year-old father. The family was of Catholic, Irish-German, and upper-lower religious, ethnic, and social status origins. The mother had completed high school, but the father only the fourth grade, and the difference in educational level was a serious source of conflict between them. The father was a steady job holder who was married previously and had been involved in sexual misconduct with other women in his marriages. He considered his main problem to be his explosive temper and the fact that he could not get his children to be respectful to him. The mother began drinking heavily in her late teens, and referred to herself as an alcoholic up until five years ago, when she gave up drinking and joined Alcoholics Anonymous. There was also evidence of some sexual promiscuity on her part before her marriage to her husband 14 years ago, but none since.

The mother reported that at times she believed she was losing her mind. She expressed bitterness toward her husband, who she said deserted her for another woman about the time she was pregnant with her now 13-year-old son. She believed the marriage started to deteriorate since that time. She expressed fear of her husband's quick temper, as did the children. Her son openly expressed bitter resentment of his father and hoped that his mother would separate.

A special source of resentment of the father was that his wife had taken their son into their bedroom, avowedly to attend to him more effectively during an illness, and had not moved him out in several months. She asked her husband to sleep in another room and he complied. Another source of the father's resentment was the chaotic condition of the home, although as it turned out he contributed to the chaos by bringing and storing in the house all sorts of odd, useless objects.

The therapist had little difficulty getting family members to verbalize conflict. (This was one of the "noisy" type families referred to earlier which seem only too eager to express their feelings.) But the conflict did not seem to go anywhere for the first few sessions: each member expressed opposition to another in such a way as to put the other in a bad light, and each seemed to know the means to put the other on the defensive. However, in the fourth session there was a "break" which the therapist was quick to take advantage of, and which will illustrate how the therapist conducting go-between process selects certain types of disagreements as especially worthy of discussion and rejects other types.

A week or so prior to the fourth session the father brought home a bicycle that was given to him by a friend. He told his daughter the bike was hers, that he had bought it from his friend for $10 and that he had had it repaired at an additional cost. His daughter accepted the bike and rode it, but it soon broke down. She took the bike for repair but it broke down again, and again she returned the bike for repair, threatening the repairman that if he did not fix it properly this time or if he refused to fix it she would start screaming at the top of her voice right there in his shop. The man fixed the bike. But later it broke down again and the girl decided to give it to her brother. Her brother repaired the bike and rode it for awhile before it again broke down and was put away in storage. In the meantime, the daughter got her mother to promise to buy her a new bike as a Christmas present.

As this incident was related mainly by the daughter to the therapist, it was apparent that it met the criteria of Term 1 of go-between process in that disagreement was expressed about how the bike was purchased and who was to use it, all members involved were present and capable of telling their versions, and the incident had occurred recently and was still fresh in the memory. Because these criteria were met and because the incident seemed to epitomize so well the way conflict was handled (or rather mishandled) in the family, the therapist selected it for special attention. (A not insignificant factor influencing his decision was that the incident was one about which the father could talk with some show of control, that is, without such excitement or emotion that he would frighten other family members into quiet submission.)

The therapist specifically moved into the role of go-between by stating that he was puzzled by what actually happened in the bike incident and that in order to clear up the confusion he would ask each member to tell his version of the story. The therapist then acted to establish his *authority* as the go-between by indicating that he would not allow interference in the telling of stories. He was thus introducing an unusual structure for the family: they were not used to letting each talk without frequent interruption, for one thing, and without efforts at intimidation, for another.

First, the fuller details of the daughter's story were elicited. When she came to the point at which she threatened the bike repairman with screaming if he did not agree to fix the bike again, the therapist said he thought she was using one of her father's favorite tactics of intimidation. Then the son was directed to relate his story. (He counter-suggested that his father should speak next, but this was disallowed since it was believed by the therapist that it would have helped to subtly undermine the type of procedure he had established.) The son voiced his resentment that the bike was not given to him originally. He said he knew he would get it eventually because it was bound to break down, his sister would come to him to fix it, and then he would be able to claim at least part ownership. He complained that his father never gave him anything— giving the bike to his sister was just another example of the father's stinginess toward him.

In telling his story, the father stressed his good intentions and expressed resentment that they were doubted. He told how he had bargained skillfully with the original owner of the bike to get it for the lowest price, and, if possible, for nothing. He told how he had taken the bike for renovation to a place he knew would do it for little money. He said he fully supported his daughter when she insisted the bike should be repaired properly by the repairman.

When it came the mother's turn to tell her story, she ruefully stated it was incidents such as this one that sometimes made her doubt her sanity. She said she actually felt relieved and reassured that the therapist had also expressed doubt and uncertainty about what really happened. In the following excerpt from the fourth session, the mother relates how her husband and children frequently befuddle her.

> *Therapist:* You've said that two or three times—that you were losing your sanity. What do you mean by that?

Mother: I told you when I first came here I had questions about my own sanity. When you live under these conditions and you hear it morning, noon and night, after a while you do question your own sanity. Am I hearing this, or am I imagining it?

Therapist: What's the worst part of the whole thing? A lot is going on. A lot of it looks to be kind of harmless.

Daughter: (referring to her brother) He teases me—with the cat.

Therapist: Teasing is teasing. I'm asking your mother.

Mother: You mean of this bickering back and forth?

Therapist: Whatever it is that drives you crazy.

Mother: Well, they'll tell me one thing and then there's a twist to the story. You saw it yourself. Each one told a slightly different version. After a while you just can't follow it. All these thoughts get in my head and I think, oh my God, am I imagining this or is this so? I find that the three of them—my husband, the children—are very much alike in this bit. Like even the interruption! I don't think you could say I interrupted here today, but they do and it's constant. Nobody shows each other courtesy enough to hear each other out. . . . They all have to get heard and they all consider their own feelings more important than anybody else's.

This excerpt and the description of the bike incident should show that the therapist as go-between provides the family with a new context in which to express and examine their conflicts. As go-between he acts as the "broker" in the context—for example, he insures that all parties understand his rules for examining the conflict, and he insures that all parties are fairly dealt with. He aims to fashion a context that is different from the established pathogenic patterns of relating among family members. Temporarily freed by the therapist's action from a vicious repetitive pattern, the family may experience the good feeling of more positive and productive relating and explore the possibility of new means to relate in the future.

In his excellent paper on marriage therapy, Haley[17] notes that the therapist is unavoidably a go-between or "broker." He states that the mere presence of the therapist as a third party requires that the spouses deal differently with each other than they have in the past—particularly because the therapist is a third party who is a presumed expert in unraveling the meaning of human interaction. He points out that the marriage therapist may relabel or redefine the activities of the spouses with each other, and he may label the treatment situation as unique in other respects—e.g., as having rules which would not hold in ordinary situations.

The therapist conducts go-between process when: *Term 3.*—*(a)* He sides, either by implications or intentionally, with one family member against another in a particular disagreement. (*Siding is unavoidable*, for even if the therapist thinks he is maintaining a strictly neutral or objective position, the family still judges him to be partial. The problem of the therapist is to decide when and with whom to side *intentionally*—i.e., as a therapeutic tactic—and to decide with whom the family *believes* him to be siding.) *(b)* He may side with or against the entire family unit in a disagreement, as well as with or against single family members.

Haley, in his paper on marriage therapy, notes that a therapist cannot make a neutral statement:

. . . his voice, his expression, the context, or the mere act of choosing a particular statement to inquire about introduces a directiveness into the situation (p. 225). (Haley continues) When the therapist is being directive, coalition patterns are being defined and redefined, and a crucial aspect of this type of therapy is continually changing coalition patterns between therapist and each spouse.

This statement is equally true of family therapy: the therapist's most innocuous-sounding comment will be judged by family members as clear evidence that he favors the "position" of one member against another. Family members will *act* toward the therapist as if he were siding, and even *interpret* him as siding, however he may choose to deny that such was his intention. (It is also true, to be sure, that therapists are rarely fully aware of all the ways in which they *actually may be siding* with one member against another, and may become defensive when this is *fairly* brought to their attention.)

In my opinion, not only is siding unavoidable in family therapy, it is a legitimate tactic of therapeutic value in shifting the balance of pathogenic relating among family members. *By judicious siding, the therapist can tip the balance in favor of more productive relating, or at least disrupt a chronic pattern of pathogenic relating.* By siding with one family member in a disagreement with another, the therapist throws weight to the position of the former. The effect of the therapist siding *against* all members often is for the members to minimize the extent of the disagreement, but it also moves them to examine more carefully the bases of the disagreement. The effect of the therapist siding *with* all members is often subtly disorganizing, for then they become confused as to what their own position should be vis-à-vis the therapist—in other words, it tends to undermine any stubbornly shared family resistance to the therapist's interventions.

It is probably unwise for the therapist to give the message that he consistently sides with one member against others. It is advantageous for him to keep the family guessing as to *whether* he will engage in siding and *what* the tactics of his siding will be. The therapist must retain flexibility in the face of strenuous efforts by the family to get him to side predictably with one member or another with the result that he becomes, in my opinion, a less effective therapeutic agent.

In the fourth treatment session with the family that has been described here, there were several instances of intentional siding by the therapist. For instance, he engaged in siding when enforcing his rule that family members could not interrupt each other in telling the story of the bike incident, for he did not enforce the rule *with equal vigor* for all members. For example, the therapist tended to halt the attempted interruptions of the father with considerably more vigor than such attempts of other family members, particularly when his attempts were directed against his son. In this the therapist showed an inclination to side against the father. One reason for this type of siding was that it seemed necessary to the therapist to guard against the danger that the father would undermine the therapist's rules of procedure by means of an outburst of temper. A correlated reason was to encourage other family members to speak their feelings more freely, especially the son, who was furious at his father for being continually browbeaten by him. In brief, the therapist was intentionally siding *against* the father and *with* other family members in enforcing his rules of procedure for the exposition of the bike incident.

In the fifth treatment session with the family there was a good example of the therapist siding first with one member and then another in a disagreement as a therapeutic tactic to tip the balance of pathogenic relating. The father had accused his wife, in a typically inferential manner, of sexual misconduct with other men in the course of her work in Alcoholics Anonymous. The therapist encouraged the father to talk about his feelings of anger and jealousy which he, again characteristically, strenuously denied having. Turning then to the wife, the therapist asked her to respond to her husband's feelings of anger and jealousy based on suspicion. In confirming the husband's *feelings*, despite his lack of confirmation of actual promiscuity by the wife, the therapist was implicitly siding with the husband against his wife. He was suggesting, in effect, that the husband's feelings were genuine and valid, and that the wife was bound to consider and respond to them. The following excerpt from the fifth session is relevant.

Therapist: The question is—your husband is showing jealousy.

Mother: Right. I've said this from the beginning.

Therapist: And you are responding in a funny kind of way. I don't know whether you're encouraging it or discouraging it.

Mother: You would have to understand AA. I don't know if you do. But each and every one of us help each other out in maintaining sobriety.

Father: But a man don't help no woman, and the woman don't help no man! A man helps a man and a woman helps a woman!

Therapist: Yes. Your husband is raising the question of men in particular; jealousy of the men. And you are not responding to that. You're putting it in terms of humanity. . . .

Mother: I've given in to every whim about jealousy. I've stopped kissing my kids and stopped hugging them.

Therapist: But you're still sleeping with your son.

Mother: He's in my bedroom, yes. . . .

Therapist: Maybe you've stopped kissing him, but you haven't stopped sleeping with him.

Father: Her son is not sleeping with her; he's sleeping in a twin bed.

Therapist: Are you defending her too now? (Laughs) Whose side are you on? I'm not implying anything. . . . This has been something that you brought up here today.

Father: That's right.

Therapist: You're angry about it.

Father: I'm not angry about it.

Therapist: You say you're not and I say you are.

Shortly after this exchange in which, by encouraging the husband to express his jealousy and by confronting the wife with her evasiveness, the therapist appears to side with the husband, the therapist then turns the tables: he now confronts the husband in such a way as to appear to side with the wife.

Therapist: . . . Is that what you're saying to him: "I need companionship. I need somebody"?

Mother: I certainly do need somebody. . . .

Therapist: "I need my son close to me because I get something from him that I don't get from somebody else." This I think is what your wife seems to me to say. She says, "I need something too. And whether you're jealous about it—well, that's just too bad. I need those things." That's what she's saying. . . .

Father: Well, I understand that and I want to try my best to give her what she wants!

By siding alternatively with father and then mother, the therapist believed he "shook up" their relationship and facilitated open expression of a bitter conflict between them that had been raging for some time, but in a rather devious form. In the case of the father, the therapist insisted that he acknowledge his anger and jealousy in the presence of his family. In the case of the mother, the therapist insisted she express her yearning for warmth and emotional closeness. The therapist made it difficult for the parents to employ their usual techniques to avoid confronting each other with their actual feelings and attitudes. He promoted a more direct confrontation than was typical for them in their relationship, i.e., forced them to put aside the usual means both had developed to keep each other at a distance, and opened up the possibility of relating in a new way.

This discussion of siding and the illustrations given should make it quite evident how complex an issue it is in family therapy. Certainly related to it, for example, are the issues of transference and countertransference, although siding is not simply to be explained by either or both of these concepts because as conceived here, it means an *intentional* alignment of the therapist with the position of one family member against another for the purpose of tipping the balance of the relationship between them.

The family's defensive tactics vis-à-vis therapist

Families exhibit a marvelous array of tactics which serve to forestall the therapist in his conduct of go-between process. The therapist must be alert to these tactics and act to circumvent them. Three major defensive tactics may be listed. In the first, family members seek to lead the therapist astray by subtle denials or evasions of his allegations of conflict. For example, the therapist may call attention to an issue between two members on which there seems latent conflict. The members deny the allegation; they say they have never disagreed on the issue. (Technically, they may be telling the truth in the sense that they may never have actually *openly* disagreed on the issue.) The therapist is called on to either hit on some device to "split the team," or give up the issue he introduced—an often not insignificant loss of face. As a face-saving device, I sometimes return to the issue introduced when it seems less anxiety-provoking. This is a kind of therapeutic oneupmanship in that it defines the fact that the members have formed a coalition against the therapist, informs them of his awareness of the fact, and implies a sympathetic understanding of the needs that caused them to join forces against him.

A second defensive tactic of the family vis-à-vis therapist is encountered when a member assumes the role of spokesman and consistently comments on or explains the meaning of the family to the therapist. This role seems most often assumed in families by the mother, but sometimes it is assumed by the father, and infrequently by one of the children. In effect, the family spokesman is in the role of a go-between and as long as he occupies a go-between role, the therapist's capacity to assume it is impaired. Sometimes the therapist will decide early in treatment to prohibit a member from taking the role of family spokesman; sometimes, however, he will temporize and permit the member to be the spokesman in the hope of learning more about the key dynamics of the family. In either case, it is necessary for the therapist to identify the family spokesman early and restrain or check him at some time in the course of treatment.

A third defensive tactic is encountered when family members act toward the therapist as if he was a particular type of go-between, or when they act toward him as if he were constantly siding with a particular member against others. As an example of this type of tactic, the father in the family whose case has been presented would accuse his wife of some misconduct, then turn to the therapist and ask, "Am I right or am I wrong?" He addressed the therapist as he might a judge who would decide a case, somewhat rigging his question to get the answer he wanted, which was to be in effect, "Yes, Mr.———, you are perfectly right."

My practice, as therapist, was to respond to the father in one of three ways: (1) state that I was not a judge and that the purpose of family therapy was not to decide who in the family was right and who was wrong; (2) ignore the father's question and change the subject; or (3) not answer the question directly, but turn to the wife and ask her to comment on the husband's accusation. By means of these responses the therapist takes steps to turn aside the father's attempt to cast the therapist in the role of the family judge, a particularly inflexible type of go-between in family therapy. In the third response, in which the therapist asked the wife to comment on her husband's accusation, there was an implicit message given, to the effect: "There may be something to your husband's accusation and I would like you to defend yourself." The message could be interpreted as evidence that the therapist was mildly siding with the husband against the wife, but evidence not nearly so strong as that initially desired by the husband in his aim to cast the therapist as the family judge.

Change at onset and termination of family therapy

Go-between process constitutes, in the writer's opinion, an alternative to the psychoanalytical insight-centered model to explain the beneficial changes that may occur in family therapy. Onset and termination are key phases in relation to the issue of change. At onset two points at issue between the family and therapist are the questions "Is there something wrong with us?" and "If there is something wrong, how will you treat us as a family?" The family and therapist may be viewed as opponents on these questions. The therapist begins to conduct go-between process when he explores them with the family for areas of expected disagreement.

Some families, in their eagerness to convince the therapist at the onset that there is nothing wrong with them as units, will actually bring about some improvement. The change need not be perceived as the result of insight, but as a function of the "bargaining" transaction between family and therapist on the question, "Is there something wrong with us?" The family changes *in order to achieve a change* in the therapist's expected position. The change is calculated to be the least necessary to secure a change in the expected position of the therapist. By means of judicious siding, by taking the role of go-between, or by shifting between these two positions, the therapist hopes to control the "bargaining" transaction in accordance with his therapeutic goals.

By the tenth therapy session in the case of the family described in this paper, beneficial symptomatic changes had already begun to occur. In the tenth session the mother reported she had begun to clean up the mess in her house and had requested the cooperation of her husband and children in doing so. The mother also reported that she had moved her son back into his own bedroom and that her husband was once again occupying the bed that adjoined hers. It also became evident that her husband had been less verbally abusive to her and her children during the preceding couple of weeks.

I suggest that these beneficial changes in the onset phase constituted moves to try to move the therapist from a position the family members believed he was occupying, and that the mother considered the therapy a means to punish her husband for his past misdeeds, and a means to persuade the therapist of the righteousness of her "cause" vis-à-vis her husband. When in the early sessions it became apparent that the therapist was not easily being sold on her viewpoint, she was compelled to introduce a more subtle means of persuasion. She would show the therapist that *she* could change but her husband could not, and thus the lack of a true foundation for the marriage would become even more apparent. It did not quite enter into her calculations that her husband *would* change in relation to (or as a result of) her own change, and that his change would also be of a positive nature.

It has been my experience that sometimes dramatic improvement may follow upon *the therapist's notice of intention to terminate treatment because there has been no significant progress*. When the therapist puts the family on such notice, he is using go-between process in the sense that he is siding against the family as a whole. He employs this powerful confrontation because he is convinced that only by means of it can he undercut a powerful family resistance to change.

I have had the privilege of seeing, both in cases of my own and of colleagues, dramatic improvement—even including the cleaning-up of bizarre symptoms in schizophrenics—following the therapist's notice of intention to terminate. It may be speculated here also that *what has produced the change is actually the family's strenuous effort to prevent change;* that is, a strenuous effort by the family to frustrate the therapist's avowed intention to withdraw from treatment. In confronting the family with his intention to terminate, the therapist conducts go-between process in accordance with Term 3 stated in this paper; i.e., siding against the whole family as a means to shake up the system.

SUMMARY

Family therapy is defined in this paper as the treatment that examines and attempts to shift the balance of pathogenic relating among family members so that new forms of relating become possible. Go-between process is described as a technique that may be employed in family therapy to promote the shift of pathogenic relating. This process is grounded in the fact that the unique aspect of family therapy is that the so-called patients have had an extensive history of relating to one another.

The three terms of go-between process as conducted by the therapist are: (1) his definition of issues on which the family is in serious conflict and the expression of that conflict; (2) his taking the role of go-between or "broker" in conflicts; (3) his siding with or against the family members in conflicts. As the therapist moves from one step to the next and back again, he exerts a critical leverage on the fixed patterns of relating among family members.

Families display a number of tactics which seem aimed at forestalling the therapist in his conduct of go-between process—in effect, they are a kind of counter go-between process conducted by the family. Three such tactics are: (1) the family denies or is evasive about the therapist's allegations of conflict; (2) with the complicity of other family members, one becomes the family spokesman and thus a kind of go-between who blocks the therapist's access to this critical role; and (3) the family attempts to trap the therapist into becoming an over-rigid type of go-between, such as the family judge, or accuses him of siding unfairly with one family member against others.

It is a main hypothesis of this paper that families change in order to forestall the therapist's expected demands for much greater change, or in order to foil his other attempts to control the relationship. Illustrations of such change are given in which the *phase* of treatment seemed also a critical factor; that is, whether treatment was at the onset phase or termination. The notion of change entertained here is believed consonant with Haley's,[10,17] which was designed to contrast with the insight-centered psychoanalytic model.

REFERENCES

1. Zuk, G. H., and Rubinstein, D.: "A Review of Concepts in the Study and Treatment of Families of Schizophrenics," in Boszormenyi-Nagy, I., and Framo, J. L. (eds.): *Intensive Family Therapy*, New York: Paul B. Hoeber Inc., Medical Division of Harper & Row, 1965, pp. 1–31.
2. Ackerman, J. W.: "Family-Focused Therapy of Schizophrenia," in Scher, S. C., and Davis, H. R. (eds.): *Out-Patient Treatment of Schizophrenia*, New York: Grune & Stratton Inc., 1960, pp. 156–173.
3. Bell, J. E.: *Family Group Therapy*, Washington, D. C.: Public Health Monograph No. 64, Department of Health, Education, and Welfare, 1961.
4. Bowen, M.: Family Psychotherapy, *Amer. J. Orthopsychiat.* **31**: 42–60, 1961.
5. Jackson, D. D., and Weakland, J. H.: Conjoint Family Therapy: Some Considerations on Theory, Technique and Results, *Psychiatry* **24**: 30–45, 1961.
6. Whitaker, C. A., Felder, R. E., and Warkentin, J.: "Countertransference in the Family Treatment of Schizophrenia," in Boszormenyi-Nagy, I., and Framo, J. L. (eds.): *Intensive Family Therapy*, New York: Paul B. Hoeber Inc., Medical Division of Harper & Row, 1965, pp. 323–341.
7. Wynne, L. C.: "Some Indications and Contraindications for Exploratory Family Therapy," in Boszormenyi-Nagy, I., and Framo, J. L. (eds.): *Intensive Family Therapy*, New York: Paul B. Hoeber Inc., Medical Division of Harper & Row, 1965, pp. 289–322.
8. Satir, V.: *Conjoint Family Therapy*, Palo Alto, Calif.: Science and Behavior Books, Inc., 1964.
9. Minuchin, S.: Conflict-Resolution Family Therapy, *Psychiatry* **28**: 278–286, 1965.
10. Haley, J.: *Strategies of Psychotherapy*, New York: Grune & Stratton Inc., 1963.
11. Jackson, D. D.: "Aspects of Conjoint Family Therapy," in Zuk, G. H., and Boszormenyi-Nagy, I. (eds.): *Family Therapy and Disturbed Families*, Palo Alto, Calif.: Science and Behavior Books, Inc., to be published.
12. Brodey, W. M.: "A Cybernetic Approach to Family Therapy," in Zuk, G. H., and Boszormenyi-Nagy, I. (eds.): *Family Therapy and Disturbed Families*, Palo Alto, Calif.: Science and Behavior Books, Inc., to be published.
13. Zuk, G. H.: "Preliminary Study of the Go-Between Process in Family Therapy," in *Proceedings of the 73rd Annual Convention of the American Psychological Association*, Washington, D. C.: American Psychological Association, 1965, pp. 291–292.
14. Zuk, G. H.: The Go-Between Process in Family Therapy, *Family Process*, **5**: 162–178, 1966.
15. Jackson, D. D.: The Question of Family Homeostasis, *Psychiat. Quart.* **31**: suppl. 79–90, 1957.
16. Wynne, L. C.: "The Study of Intrafamilial Alignments and Splits and Exploratory Family Therapy," in Ackerman, N. W., Beatman, F., and Sherman, S. N. (eds.): *Exploring the Base for Family Therapy*, New York: Family Service Association of America, 1961, pp. 95–115.
17. Haley, J.: Marriage Therapy, *Arch. Gen. Psychiat.* **8**: 213–234, 1963.

Behavioral Approaches to Family and Couple Therapy

Robert Liberman

The current splurge of couple and family therapies is not simply an accident or passing fad. These increasingly used modes of treatment for psychiatric problems are anchored in a sound foundation and are not likely to blow away. The foundation of these newer therapies lies in the opportunity they offer to induce significant behavioral change in the participants by a major restructuring of their interpersonal environments.

Couple and family therapy can be particularly potent means of behavior modification because the interpersonal milieu that undergoes change is that of the day-to-day, face-to-face encounter an individual experiences with the most important people in his life—his spouse or members of his immediate family. When these therapies are successful it is because the therapist is able to guide the members of the couple or family into changing their modes of dealing with each other. In behavioral or learning terms, we can translate "ways of dealing with each other" into consequences of behavior or *contingencies of reinforcement*. Instead of rewarding maladaptive behavior with attention and concern, the family members learn to give each other recognition and approval for desired behavior.

Since the family is a system of interlocking, reciprocal behaviors (including affective behavior), family therapy proceeds best when each of the members learns how to change his or her responsiveness to the others. Family therapy should be a learning experience for all the members involved. For simplification, however, this paper will analyze family pathology and therapy from the point of view of the family responding to a single member.

Typically, families that come for treatment have coped with the maladaptive or deviant behavior of one member by responding to it over the years with anger, nagging, babying, conciliation, irritation, or sympathy. These responses, however punishing they might seem on the surface, have the effect of reinforcing the deviance, that is, increasing the frequency or intensity of the deviant

Reprinted from *American Journal of Orthopsychiatry*, Vol. 40, No. 1, January 1970, pp. 106–118. Copyright © 1970 the American Orthopsychiatric Association, Inc. Reproduced by permission.

behavior in the future. Reinforcement occurs because the attention offered is viewed and felt by the deviant member as positive concern and interest. In many families with a deviant member, there is little social interaction and the individuals tend to lead lives relatively isolated from each other. Because of this overall lack of interaction, when interaction does occur in response to a member's "abnormal" behavior, such behavior is powerfully reinforced.[14]

Verbal and nonverbal means of giving attention and recognition can be termed *social reinforcement* (as contrasted with food or sex, which are termed *primary reinforcement*). Social reinforcement represents the most important source of motivation for human behavior.[6,19] Often massive amounts of such "concern" or social reinforcement are communicated to the deviant member, focused and contingent upon the member's maladaptive behavior. The deviant member gets the message: "So long as you continue to produce this undesirable behavior (symptoms), we will be interested and concerned in you." Learning the lesson of such messages leads to the development and maintenance of symptomatic or deviant behavior and to characterological patterns of activity and identity. Sometimes, the message of concern and interest is within the awareness of the "sick" member. Individuals with a conscious awareness of these contingencies are frequently termed "manipulative" by mental health professionals since they are adept at generating social reinforcement for their maladaptive behavior. But learning can occur without an individual's awareness or insight, in which case we view the maladaptive behavior as being unconsciously motivated.

Massive amounts of contingent social reinforcement are not necessary to maintain deviant behavior. Especially after the behavior has developed, occasional or *intermittent reinforcement* will promote very durable continuation of the behavior. Laboratory studies have shown that intermittent reinforcement produces behavior that is most resistant to extinction.[6]

Many family therapists[7,8,21] have demonstrated that the interest and concern family members show in the deviance of one member can be in the service of their own psychological economy. Maintaining a "sick" person in the family can be gratifying (reinforcing) to others, albeit at some cost in comfort and equanimity. Patterson[15] describes how this reciprocal reinforcement can maintain deviant behavior by using the example of a child who demands an ice cream cone while shopping with his mother in a supermarket. The reinforcer for this "demand behavior" is compliance by the mother, but if she ignores the demand, the effect is to increase the rate or loudness of the demand. Loud demands or shrieks by a child in a supermarket are aversive to the mother; that is, her noncompliance is punished. When the mother finally buys the ice cream cone, the aversive tantrum ends. The reinforcer for the child's tantrum is the ice cream cone. The reinforcing contingency for the mother was the termination of the "scene" in the supermarket. In this reciprocal fashion, the tantrum behavior is maintained. I shall return to this important aspect of family psychopathology—the mutually reinforcing or symbiotic nature of deviance—in the case studies below. Indeed, the balance between the aversive and gratifying consequences of maladaptive behavior in a member on the other family members is the crucial determinant of motivation for and response to treatment.

Changing the contingencies by which the patient gets acknowledgment and concern from other members of his family is the basic principle of learning that underlies the potency of family or couple therapy. Social reinforcement is made contingent on desired, adaptive behavior instead of maladaptive and symptomatic behavior. It is the task of the therapist in collaboration with the family or couple to (1) specify the maladaptive behavior, (2) choose reasonable goals which are alternative, adaptive behaviors, (3) direct and guide the family to change the contingencies of their social reinforcement patterns from maladaptive to adaptive target behaviors.

Another principle of learning involved in the process of successful family therapy is modeling, also called imitation or identification. The model, sometimes the therapist but also other members of the family, exhibits desired, adaptive behavior which then is imitated by the patient. Imitation or identification occurs when the model is an esteemed person (therapist, admired family member) and when the model receives positive reinforcement (approval) for his behavior from others.[3] The amount of observational learning will be governed by the degree to which a family member pays attention to the modeling cues, has the capacity to process and rehearse the cues, and possesses the necessary components in his behavioral experience which can be combined to reproduce the more complex, currently modeled behavior.

Imitative learning enables an individual to short-circuit the tedious and lengthy process of trial-and-error (or reward) learning while incorporating complex chains of behavior into his repertoire. Much of the behaviors which reflect the enduring part of our culture are to a large extent transmitted by repeated observation of behavior displayed by social models, particularly familial models. If performed frequently enough and rewarded in turn with approval by others, the imitated behavior will become incorporated into the patient's behavioral repertoire. The principles of imitative learning have been exploited with clinical success by researchers working with autistic children,[12] phobic youngsters,[4] and mute, chronic psychotics.[18] How modeling can be used in family therapy will be illustrated in the cases cited below.

I will limit the scope of the case examples to couples and families; however, the same principles of learning apply to group therapy[11,17] and with some modification to individual psychotherapy.[9] Although learning theory has been associated in clinical psychiatry with its systematic and explicit application in the new behavior therapies, it should be emphasized that learning theory offers a generic and unitary explanation of the processes mediating change in all psychotherapies, including psychoanalytic ones.[1,13]

TECHNIQUE

Before getting to the case material, I would like to outline the main features of an application of behavior theory to family therapy. The three major areas of technical concern for the therapist are: (1) *creating and maintaining a positive therapeutic alliance;* (2) *making a behavioral analysis of the problems(s);* and (3) *implementing the behavioral principles of reinforcement and modeling in the context of ongoing interpersonal interactions.*

Without the positive therapeutic alliance between the therapist and those he is helping, there can be little or no successful intervention. The working alliance is the lever which stimulates change. In learning terms, the positive relationship between therapist and patient(s) permits the therapist to serve as a social reinforcer and model; in other words, to build up adaptive behaviors and allow maladaptive behaviors to extinguish. The therapist is an effective reinforcer and model for the patients to the extent that the patients value him and hold him in high regard and warm esteem.

Clinicians have described the ingredients that go into this positive therapist-patient relationship in many different ways. Terminology varies with the "school" of psychotherapy to which the clinician adheres. Psychoanalysts have contributed notions such as "positive transference" and an alliance between the therapist and the patient's "observing ego." Reality therapists call for a trusting involvement with the patient. Some clinicians have termed it a "supportive relationship" implying sympathy, respect, and concern on the part of the therapist. Recent research has labeled the critical aspects of the therapist-client relationship: nonpossessive warmth, accurate empathy, and genuine concern.[20] Truax and his colleagues[20] have been able to successfully operationalize these concepts and to teach them to selected individuals. They have further shown that therapists high on these attributes are more successful in psychotherapy than those who are not. Whatever the labels, a necessary if not sufficient condition for therapeutic change in patients is a doctor-patient relationship that is infused with mutual respect, warmth, trust, and affection.

In my experience, these qualities of the therapeutic alliance can be developed through a period of initial evaluation of the patient or family. The early therapist-family contacts, proceeding during the first few interviews, offer an opportunity to the therapist to show unconditional warmth, acceptance, and concern for the clients and their problems.

Also during the first few sessions, while the therapeutic relationship is being established, the therapist must do his "diagnostic." In a learning approach to family therapy, the diagnostic consists of a *behavioral* or *functional analysis* of the problems. In making his behavioral analysis, the therapist, in collaboration with the family, asks two major questions:

1. What behavior is maladaptive or problematic—what behavior in the designated patient should be increased or decreased? Each person, in turn, is asked (1) what changes would you like to see in others in the family, and (2) how would you like to be different from the way you are now? Answering these questions forces the therapist to choose carefully *specific behavioral goals.*

2. What environmental and interpersonal contingencies currently support the problematic behavior—that is, what is maintaining undesirable behavior or reducing the likelihood of more adaptive responses? This is called a "functional analysis of behavior," and also can include an analysis of the development of symptomatic or maladaptive behavior, the "conditioning history" of the patient. The mutual patterns of social reinforcement in the family deserve special scrutiny in this analysis since their deciphering and clarification become central to an understanding of the case and to the formulation of therapeutic strategy.

It should be noted that the behavioral analysis of the problem doesn't end after the initial sessions, but by necessity continues throughout the course of therapy. As the problem behaviors change during treatment, so must the analysis of what maintains these behaviors. New sources of reinforcement for the patient and family members must be assessed. In this sense, the behavioral approach to family therapy is dynamic.

The third aspect of behavioral technique is the actual choice and implementation of therapeutic strategy and tactics. Which interpersonal transactions between the therapist and family members and among the family members can serve to alter the problem behavior in a more adaptive direction? The therapist acts as an educator, using his value as a social reinforcer to instruct the family or couple in changing their ways of dealing with each other. Some of the possible tactics are described in the case studies below.

A helpful way to conceptualize these tactics is to view them as "behavioral change experiments" where the therapist and family together re-program the contingencies of reinforcement operating in the family system. The behavioral change experiments consist of family members responding to each other in various ways, with the responses contingent on more desired reciprocal ways of relating. Ballentine[2] views the behavioral change experiments, starting with small but well-defined successes, as leading to (1) a shift toward more optimistic and hopeful expectations; (2) an emphasis on doing things differently while giving the responsibility for change to each family member; (3) "encouragement of an observational outlook which forces family members to look closely at themselves and their relationships with one another, rather than looking 'inside' themselves with incessant why's and wherefores"; and (4) "the generation of empirical data which can be instrumental to further change, since they often expose sequences of family action and reaction in particularly graphic and unambiguous fashion."

The therapist also uses his importance as a model to illustrate desired modes of responding differentially to behavior that at times is maladaptive and at other times approaches more desirable form. The operant conditioning principle of "shaping" is used, whereby gradual approximations to the desired end behavior are reinforced with approval and spontaneous and genuine interest by the therapist. Through his instructions and example, the therapist teaches shaping to the members of the couple or family. Role playing or behavioral rehearsal are among the useful tactics employed in generating improved patterns of interaction among the family members.

The therapist using a behavioral model does not act like a teaching machine, devoid of emotional expression. Just as therapists using other theoretical schemas, he is most effective in his role as an educator when he expresses himself with affect in a comfortable, human style developed during his clinical training and in his life as a whole. Since intermittent reinforcement produces more durable behavior, the therapist may employ trial terminations, tapering off the frequency of sessions prior to termination and "booster" sessions.[1] The strategy and tactics of this behavioral approach to couples and families will be more clearly delineated in the case studies that follow. A more systematic and detailed outline of the behavior modification approach is presented in Table 1. The specification and implications of the items in this outline can be found in the manual by Reese.[16]

CASE #1

Mrs. D is a 35-year-old housewife and mother of three children who had a 15-year history of severe, migrainous headaches. She had had frequent medical hospitalizations for her headaches (without any organic problems being found), and also a 1½-year period of intensive, psychodynamically oriented, individual psychotherapy. She found relief from her headaches only after retreating to her bed for periods of days to a week with the use of narcotics.

TABLE 1. A Behavioral Model for Learning

1. Specify the final performance (therapeutic goals):
   Identify the behavior.
   Determine how it is to be measured.
2. Determine the current baseline rate of the desired behavior.
3. Structure a favorable situation for eliciting the desired behavior by providing cues for the appropriate behavior and removing cues for incompatible, inappropriate behavior.
4. Establish motivation by locating reinforcers, depriving the individual of reinforcers (if necessary), and withholding reinforcers for inappropriate behavior.
5. Enable the individual to become comfortable in the therapeutic setting and to become familiar with the reinforcers.
6. Shape the desired behavior:
   Reinforce successive approximations of the therapeutic goals.
   Raise the criterion for reinforcement gradually.
   Present reinforcement immediately, contingent upon the behavior.
7. Fade out the specific cues in the therapeutic setting to promote generalization of acquired behavior.
8. Reinforce intermittantly to facilitate durability of the gains.
9. Keep continuous, objective records.

Adapted from E. P. Reese, *The Analysis of Human Operant Behavior.* Copyright © 1966 by William C. Brown Company and reprinted by permission.

After a brief period of evaluation by me, she again developed intractable headaches and was hospitalized. A full neurological workup revealed no neuropathology. At this time I recommended that I continue with the patient and her husband in couple therapy. It had previously become clear to me that the patient's headaches were serving an important purpose in the economy of her marital relationship: headaches and the resultant debilitation were the sure way the patient could elicit and maintain her husband's concern and interest in her. On his part, her husband was an active, action-oriented man who found it difficult to sit down and engage in conversation. He came home from work, read the newspaper, tinkered with his car, made repairs on the house, or watched TV. Mrs. D got her husband's clear-cut attention only when she developed headaches, stopped functioning as mother and wife, and took to her bed. At these times Mr. D. was very solicitous and caring. He gave her medication, stayed home to take care of the children, and called the doctor.

My analysis of the situation led me to the strategy of redirecting Mr. D's attention to the adaptive strivings and the maternal and wifely behavior of his wife. During ten 45-minute sessions, I shared my analysis of the problem with Mr. and Mrs. D and encouraged them to reciprocally restructure their marital relationship. Once involved in a trusting and confident relationship with me, Mr. D worked hard to give his wife attention and approval for her day-to-day efforts as a mother and housewife. When he came home from work, instead of burying himself in the newspaper he inquired about the day at home and discussed with his wife problems concerning the children. He occasionally rewarded his wife's homemaking efforts by taking her out to a movie or to dinner (something they had not done for years). While watching TV he had his wife sit close to him or on his lap. In return, Mrs. D was taught to reward her husband's new efforts at intimacy with affection and appreciation. She let him know how much she liked to talk with him about the day's events. She prepared special dishes for him and kissed him warmly when he took initiative in expressing affection toward her. On the other hand, Mr. D was instructed to pay minimal attention to his wife's headaches. He was reassured that in so doing, he would be helping her decrease their frequency and severity. He was no longer to give her medication, cater to her when she was ill, or call the doctor for her. If she got a headache, she was to help herself and he was to carry on with his regular routine insofar as possible. I emphasized that *he should not, overall, decrease his attentiveness to his wife, but rather change the timing and direction of his attentiveness.* Thus the behavioral contingencies of Mr. D's attention changed from headaches to housework, from invalidism to active coping and functioning as mother and wife.

Within ten sessions, both were seriously immersed in this new approach toward each other. Their marriage was different and more satisfying to both. Their sex life improved. Their children were better behaved, as they quickly learned to apply the same reinforcement principles in reacting to the children and to reach a consensus in responding to their children's limit-testing. Mrs. D got a job as a department store clerk (a job she enjoyed and which provided her with further reinforcement—money and attention from people for "healthy" behavior). She was given recognition by her husband for her efforts to collaborate in improving the family's financial condition. She still had headaches, but they were mild and short-lived and she took care of them herself. Everyone was happier including Mrs. D's internist who no longer was receiving emergency calls from her husband.

A followup call to Mr. and Mrs. D one year later found them maintaining their progress. She has occasional headaches but has not had to retreat to bed or enter a hospital.

CASE #2

Mrs. S is a 34-year-old mother of five who herself came from a family of ten siblings. She wanted very badly to equal her mother's output of children and also wanted to prove to her husband that he was potent and fertile. He had a congenital hypospadius and had been told by a physician prior to their marriage that he probably could not have children. Unfortunately Mrs. S was Rh negative and her husband Rh positive. After their fifth child she had a series of spontaneous abortions because of the Rh incompatibility. Each was followed by a severe depression. Soon the depressions ran into each other and she was given a course of 150 EST's. The EST's had the effect of making her confused and unable to function at home while not significantly lifting the depressions. She had some successful short-term supportive psychotherapy but again plunged into a depression after a hysterectomy.

Her husband, like Mr. D in the previous case, found it hard to tolerate his wife's conversation, especially since it was taken up mostly by complaints and tearfulness. He escaped from the unhappy home situation by plunging himself into his work, holding two jobs simultaneously. When he was home, he was too tired for any conversation or meaningful interaction with his wife. Their sexual interaction was nil. Although Mrs. S tried hard to maintain her household and raise her children and even hold a part-time job, she received little acknowledgment for her efforts from her husband who became more distant and peripheral as the years went by.

My behavioral analysis pointed to a lack of reinforcement from Mrs. S's husband for her adaptive strivings. Consequently her depressions, with their large hypochondriacal components, represented her desperate attempt to elicit her husband's attention and concern. Although her somatic complaints and self-depreciating accusations were aversive for her husband, the only way he knew how to "turn them off" was to offer sympathy, reassure her of his devotion to her, and occasionally stay home from work. Naturally, his nurturing her in this manner had the effect of reinforcing the very behavior he was trying to terminate.

During five half-hour couple sessions I focused primarily on Mr. S, who was the mediating agent of reinforcement for his wife and hence the person who could potentially modify her behavior. I actively redirected his attention from his wife "the unhappy, depressed woman" to his wife "the coping woman." I forthrightly recommended to him that he drop his extra job, at least for the time being, in order to be at home in the evening to converse with his wife about the day's events, especially her approximations at successful homemaking. I showed by my own example (modeling) how to support his wife in her efforts to assert herself reasonably with her intrusive mother-in-law and an obnoxious neighbor.

A turning point came after the second session, when I received a desperate phone call from Mr. S one evening. He told me that his wife had called from her job and tearfully complained that she could not go on and that he must come and bring her home. He asked me what he should do. I indicated that this was a crucial moment, that he should call her back and briefly acknowledge her distress but at the same time emphasize the importance of her finishing the evening's work. I further suggested that he meet her as usual after work and take her out for an ice cream soda. This would get across to her his abiding interest and recognition for her positive efforts in a genuine and spontaneous way. With this support from me, he followed my suggestions and within two weeks Mrs. S's depression had completely lifted.

She was shortly thereafter given a job promotion, which served as an extrinsic reinforcement for her improved work performance and was the occasion for additional reinforcement from me and her husband during the next therapy session. We terminated after the fifth session, a time limit we had initially agreed on.

Eight months later at followup they reported being "happier together than ever before."

CASE #3

Edward is a 23-year-old young man who had received much psychotherapy, special schooling, and occupational counseling and training during the past 17 years. He was diagnosed at different times as a childhood schizophrenic and as mentally subnormal. At age 6 he was evaluated by a child psychiatry clinic and given three years of psychodynamic therapy by a psychoanalyst. He had started many remedial programs and finished almost none of them. He, in fact, was a chronic failure—in schools as well as in jobs. His parents viewed him as slightly retarded despite his low normal intelligence on IQ tests. He was infantilized by his mother, who was domineering and aggressive, as an ally against the weak and passive father. When I began seeing them in a family evaluation, Edward was in the process of failing in the most recent rehabilitation effort—an evening, adult high school.

The initial goals of the family treatment, then, were (1) to disengage Edward from the clasp of his protective mother, (2) to get his father to offer himself as a model and as a source of encouragement (reinforcement) for Edward's desires and efforts towards independence, (3) to structure Edward's life with occupational and social opportunities that he could initiate on his own. Fortunately the Jewish Vocational Service in Boston offers an excellent rehabilitation program based on the same basic principles of learning that have been elucidated in this article. I referred Edward to it and at the same time introduced him to a social club for ex-mental patients which has a constant whirl of activities daily and on weekends.

During our weekly family sessions, I used modeling and role-playing to help

Edward's parents positively reinforce his beginning efforts at the J. V. S. and the social club. After three months at the J. V. S., Edward secured a job and now after another seven months has a job tenure and membership in the union. He has been an active member of the social club and has gone on weekend trips with groups there—something he had never done before. He is now "graduating" to another social club, a singles' group in a church, and has started action on getting his driver's license.

The family sessions were not easy or without occasional storms, usually generated by Edward's mother as she from time to time felt "left out." She needed my support and interest (reinforcement) in her problems as a hard-working and unappreciated mother at these times. Because of the positive therapeutic relationship cemented over a period of nine months, Edward's parents slowly began to be able to substitute positive reinforcement for his gradually improving efforts at work and play instead of the previous blanket criticism (also, paradoxically, a kind of social reinforcement) he had received from them for his failures. I encouraged the father to share openly with Edward his own experiences as a young man reaching for independence, thereby serving as a model for his son.

The parents needed constant reinforcement (approval) from me for trying out new ways of responding to Edward's behavior; for example, to eliminate the usual nagging of him to do his chores around the house (which only served to increase the lethargic slothful behavior which accrues from the attention) and to indicate instead pleasure when he mows the lawn even if he forgets to rake the grass and trim the hedge. They learned to give Edward approval when he takes the garbage out even if he doesn't do it "their" way. And they learned how to spend time listening to Edward pour out his enthusiasm for his job even if they feel he is a bit too exuberant.

Our family sessions were tapered to twice monthly and then to once a month. Termination went smoothly after one year of treatment.

CASE #4

Mr. and Mrs. F have a long history of marital strife. There was a year-long separation early in their marriage and several attempts at marriage counseling lasting three years. Mr. F has paranoid trends which are reflected in his extreme sensitivity to any lack of affection or commitment toward him by his wife. He is very jealous of her close-knit relationship with her parents. Mrs. F is a disheveled and unorganized woman who has been unable to meet her husband's expectations for an orderly and accomplished homemaker or competent manager of their five children. Their marriage has been marked by frequent mutual accusations and depreciation, angry withdrawal and sullenness.

My strategy with this couple, whom I saw for 15 sessions, was to teach them to stop reinforcing each other with attention and emotionality for undesired behavior and to begin eliciting desired behavior in each other using the principle of *shaping*. Tactically, I structured the therapy sessions with an important "ground-rule": No criticism or harping were allowed and they were to spend the time telling each other what the other had done during the past week that approached the desired behaviors. As they gave positive feedback to each other for approximations to the behavior each valued in the other, I served as an auxiliary source of positive acknowledgment, reinforcing the reinforcer.

We began by clearly delineating what specific behaviors were desired by each of them in the other and by my giving them homework assignments in making gradual efforts to approximate the behavioral goals. For instance, Mr. F incessantly complained about his wife's lack of care in handling the evening meal—the disarray of the table setting, lack of tablecloth, disorderly clearing of the dishes. Mrs. F grudgingly agreed that there was room for improvement and I instructed her to make a start by using a tablecloth nightly. Mr. F in turn was told the importance of his giving her positive and consistent attention for her effort, since this was important to him. After one week they reported that they had been able to fulfill the assignment and that the evening meal was more enjoyable. Mrs. F had increased her performance to the complete satisfaction of her husband, who meanwhile had continued to give her positive support for her progress.

A similar process occurred in another problem area. Mr. F felt that his wife should do more sewing (mending clothes, putting on missing buttons) and should iron his shirts (which he had always done himself). Mrs. F was fed up with the home they lived in, which was much too small for their expanded family. Mr. F resolutely refused to consider moving to larger quarters because he felt it would not affect the quality of his wife's homemaking performance. I instructed Mrs. F to begin to do more sewing and ironing and Mr. F to reinforce this by starting to consider moving to a new home. He was to concretize this by spending part of each Sunday reviewing the real estate section of the newspaper with his wife and to make visits to homes that were advertised for sale. He was to make clear to her that his interest in a new home was *contingent* upon her improvements as a homemaker.

Between the third and sixth sessions, Mrs. F's father—who was ill with terminal lung cancer—was admitted to the hospital and died. During this period, we emphasized the importance of Mr. F giving his wife solace and support. I positively reinforced Mr. F's efforts in this direction. He was able to help his wife over her period of sadness and mourning despite his long-standing antagonism toward her father. Mrs. F, in turn, with my encouragement, responded to her husband's sympathetic behavior with affection and appreciation. Although far from having an idyllic marriage, Mr. and Mrs. F have made tangible gains in moving closer toward each other.

DISCUSSION

There is too much confusion in the rationales and techniques underlying current practices in family therapy. Although attempts to convey the method of family therapy always suffer when done through the written word, I do not share the belief that "the vital communications in all forms of psychotherapy are intuitive, felt, unspoken, and unconscious."[7] Although this article is not meant as a "how to do it" treatise for family therapists, I do intend it as a preliminary attempt to apply a few of the basic principles of imitative learning and operant conditioning to couple and family therapy.

Although the rationalized conceptualization of family therapy practiced by psychoanalytically oriented therapists differs from the learning and behavioral approach described here, closer examination of the actual techniques used reveals marked similarity. For example, Framo,[7] in explaining the theory behind his family therapy, writes: "The overriding goal of the intensive middle phases consists in understanding and working through, often through transference to each other and to the therapists, the introjects of the parents so that the parents can see and experience how those difficulties manifested in the present family system have emerged from their unconscious attempts to perpetrate or master old conflict arising from their families of origin. . . . The essence of the true work of family therapy is in the tracing of the vicissitudes of early object-relationships, and ... the exceedingly intricate transformations which occur as a function of the intrapsychic and transactional blending of the old and new family systems of the parents. ..."

Despite the use of psychoanalytic constructs, Framo describes the actual process of family therapy in ways that are very compatible within a learning framework. He writes: "Those techniques which prompt family interaction are the most productive in the long run. ... It is especially useful to concentrate on here-and-now feelings; this method usually penetrated much deeper than dealing with feelings described in retrospect. ... As we gained experience in working with families we became less hesitant about taking more forceful, active positions in order to help the family become unshackled from their rigid patterns."

Framo goes on to give illustrations of his work with families in which differential reinforcement for behavior considered more desirable and appropriate is given by the therapists. In dealing with angry and aggressive mothers, "we learned to avoid noticing what they did (e.g. emotional infighting) and pay attention to what they missed in life." Trying to activate passive fathers, "the therapists make every conscious effort to build him up during the sessions. ... A number of techniques have been tried: forcing more interaction between the husband and wife; assigning tasks; having a female therapist give encouragement in a flattering way; occasional individual sessions with the father." Zuk[23] describes his technique of family therapy in ways that fit into a reinforcement framework. He views the cornerstone of the technique the exploration and attempt "to shift the balance of pathogenic relating among family members so that new forms of relating become possible." Zuk further delineates the therapist's tactics as a "go-between" in which he uses his leverage to "constantly structure and direct the treatment situation."

It should be emphasized that the behavioral approach does not simplistically reduce the family system and family interaction to individualistic or dyadic mechanisms of reinforcement. The richness and complexity of family interaction is appreciated by the family therapist working within a behavioral framework. For instance, Ballentine[2] states: "... behavior within a system cannot be so easily modified by focusing on the behavioral contingencies existing within any two-person subsystem, since one person's behavior in relation to a second's is often determined by behaviors of others within the system ... the behavioral contingencies within a family system are manifold and constitute a matrix of multiple behavioral contingencies."

The complexity of family contingencies is exemplified by a transient problem which arose in Case #3. As Edward developed more independence from his parents and spent less and less time at home, his parents began to argue more angrily. Edward had served as a buffer between them—taking sides, being used as a scapegoat for their hostility, and serving as a "problem child" who required joint parental action and solidarity. With their buffer gone, the husband-wife relationship intensified and friction developed. Since the therapeutic goals were limited to Edward's emancipation from his parents and since it seemed that the parents were sufficiently symbiotic to contain a temporary eruption of hostility, the therapist's major efforts at this point were aimed at protecting Edward from backsliding in response to guilt or family pressure. The strategy worked, and within a few weeks the parents had reached a new modus vivendi with each other while Edward continued to consolidate and extend his gains.

A behavioral and learning approach to family therapy differs from a more psychoanalytic one. The therapist defines his role as an educator in collaboration with the family; therefore, the assigning of "sickness" labels to members, with its potential for moral blame, does not occur as it does under the medical model embodied in the psychoanalytic concept of underlying conflict or disease. There is no need for family members to acknowledge publicly their "weaknesses" or irrationality since insight per se is not considered vital.

The behavioral approach, with its more systematic and specific guidelines, makes it less likely that a therapist will adventitiously reinforce or model contradictory behavior patterns. The behavioral approach, consistently applied, is potentially more effective and faster. When patients do not respond to behavioral techniques, the therapist can use his more empirical attitude to ask why and perhaps to try another technique. The orientation is more experimental and "the patient is always right," with the burden on the therapist to devise effective interventions. In the psychoanalytic approach, the tendency has been for the therapist to decide that their failures are caused by patients who were inappropriate for the technique rather than viewing the technique as needing modification for the particular patient.

The work of behaviorally oriented family therapists is not restricted to the here-and-now of the therapy sessions. As the cases described reveal, much of the effort involves collaboration and involvement with adjunctive agencies such as schools, rehabilitation services, medication, and work settings. Family therapists are moving toward this total systems approach.

The advantages of behavioral approaches to family therapy sketched in this paper remain to be proven by systematic research. Such research is now proceeding.[5,10,15,22] Much work will go into demonstrating that family processes are "essentially behavioral sequences which can be sorted out, specified and measured with a fair degree of accuracy and precision."[2] Hopefully, further clinical and research progress made by behaviorally oriented therapists will challenge all family therapists, regardless of theoretical leanings, to specify more clearly their interventions, their goals, and their empirical results. If these challenges are accepted seriously, the field of family therapy will likely improve and gain stature as a scientifically grounded modality.

REFERENCES

1. Alexander, F. 1965. The dynamics of psychotherapy in the light of learning theory. Internat. J. Psychiat. 1: 189–207.
2. Ballentine, R. 1968. The family therapist as a behavioral systems engineer . . . and a responsible one. Paper read at Georgetown Univ. Symp. on Fam. Psychother. Washington.
3. Bandura, A., and Walters, R. 1963. Social Learning and Personality Development. Holt, Rinehart and Winston, New York.
4. Bandura, A., Grusec, J., and Menlove, F. 1967. Vicarious extinction of avoidance behavior. Personality and Soc. Psychol. 5: 16–23.
5. Dunham, R. 1966. Ex post facto reconstruction of conditioning schedules in family interaction. In Family Structure, Dynamics and Therapy, Irvin M. Cohen, ed.: 107–114. Psychiatric Research No. 20, Amer. Psychiat. Assn., Washington.
6. Ferster, C. 1963. Essentials of a science of behavior. In An Introduction to the Science of

Human Behavior, J. I. Nurnberger, C. B. Ferster, and J. P. Brady, eds. Appleton-Century-Crofts, New York.

7. Framo, J. 1965. Rationale and techniques of intensive family therapy. *In* Intensive Family Therapy, I. Boszormenyi-Nagy and J. L. Framo, eds. Hoeber Medical Division, New York.

8. Handel, G. (ed.). 1967. The Psychosocial Interior of the Family. Aldine, Chicago.

9. Krasner, L. 1962. The therapist as a social reinforcement machine. *In* Research in Psychotherapy, H. Strupp and L. Luborsky, eds. Amer. Psychol. Assn., Washington.

10. Lewinsohn, P., Weinstein, M., and Shaw, D. 1969. Depression: a clinical research approach. *In* Proceedings, 1968 Conference, Assn. Advan. Behav. Ther., San Francisco. In press.

11. Liberman, R. 1970. A behavioral approach to group dynamics. Behav. Ther. In press.

12. Lovaas, O., et al. 1966. Acquisition of imitative speech by schizophrenic children. Science, 151: 705–707.

13. Marmor, J. 1966. Theories of learning and psychotherapeutic process. Brit. J. Psychiat. 112: 363–366.

14. Patterson, G., et al. 1967. Reprogramming the social environment. Child Psychol. and Psychiat. 8: 181–195.

15. Patterson, G., and Reid, J. 1967. Reciprocity and coercion: two facets of social systems. Paper read at 9th Ann. Inst. for Res. in Clin. Psychol., Univ. of Kansas.

16. Reese, E. 1966. The Analysis of Human Operant Behavior. Wm. C. Brown, Dubuque, Iowa.

17. Shapiro, D., and Birk, L. 1967. Group therapy in experimental perspectives. Internat. J. Group Psychother. 17: 211–224.

18. Sherman, J. 1965. Use of reinforcement and imitation to reinstate verbal behavior in mute psychotics. J. Abnorm. Psychol. 70: 155–164.

19. Skinner, B. 1953. Science and Human Behavior. Macmillan, New York.

20. Truax, C., and Carkhuff, R. 1967. Toward Effective Counseling and Psychotherapy: Training and Practice. Aldine, Chicago.

21. Vogel, E., and Bell, N. 1960. The emotionally disturbed child as the family scapegoat. *In* A Modern Introduction to the Family, N. W. Bell and E. F. Vogel, eds. Free Press, New York.

22. Zeilberger, J., Sampen, S., and Sloane, H. 1968. Modification of a child's problem behaviors in the home with the mother as therapist. J. Appl. Behav. Anal. 1: 47–53.

23. Zuk, G. 1967. Family therapy. Arch. Gen. Psychiat. 16: 71–79.

Family Psychotherapy—
Theory and Practice

Nathan W. Ackerman

Within the past 15 years, family therapy has emerged as a new dimension in the art and science of mental healing. It bids fair to become the very core of a newly developing pattern of community mental health services.

In the evolution of family treatment, several distinct, though overlapping, emphases have appeared: (1) Reeducation of the family through guidance; (2) Reorganization through a change in the patterns of family communication; (3) Resolution of pathogenic conflict and induction of change and growth by means of a dynamic, depth-approach to the affective currents of family life. It is the last of these that will be considered here.

Family psychotherapy is defined as a special method of treatment of emotional disorders, based on dynamically oriented interviews with the whole family. It is the therapy of a natural living unit, embracing all these persons who share the identity of family and whose behavior is influenced by a circular interchange of emotion. Grandparents, extended kin, or other individuals who are significant participants in the stream of family life may be included. The family is viewed as a behavioral system with emergent properties different from a mere summation of the characteristics of its members. The behavior of any one member may be interpreted in four ways: as a symptom of the psychopathology of the family unit; as a stabilizer of the family; as healer of family disorder; and as the epitome of the growth potential of the group. Treatment focuses on the relations between the psychosocial functioning of the family group and the emotional functioning of its members.

The ideal of family therapy is not merely to remove symptoms but to nourish a new way of life. Its goals are to remove emotional distress and disablement and promote the level of health and growth, both in the family group and its members by relieving pathogenic conflict and anxiety; by raising the level of complementation of emotional needs; by strengthening the immunity of the family against critical upsets; by enhancing the harmony and balance of family

Reprinted from *American Journal of Psychotherapy*, Vol. 20, 1966, pp. 405–414. Reproduced by permission.

functions; by strengthening the individual member against destructive forces, both within him and surrounding him in the family environment; and by influencing the orientation of family identity and values toward health and growth.

Historically viewed, perspectives of psychotherapy have moved from the symptoms and conflicts of the individual to the total functioning of personality, to the relations of personality and role adaptation, and finally to the human relations patterns of family and community. Thus, the clinician is irresistibly drawn, as if by a magnet, from a limited concern with the separate individual to the live, dynamic properties of the network of family and community.

The family approach to therapy is propelled into being by a number of confluent forces: (1) The radical transformation of family life induced by social change; (2) The recognition of the principle of contagion of emotional disturbance, the intimate connections between social and mental disorder; the recognition that the family phenomenon is not peripheral but of the very essence of psychiatric illness; (3) The greater appreciation of the limitations of conventional procedures of diagnosis and treatment that are limited to the individual patient; (4) New developments in the behavioral sciences, in ego psychology, small group dynamics, social psychology, anthropology, and communication; with these, changes in the theory of behavior and of causation of emotional illness; (5) The changed role of the psychotherapist in the modern community.

Family psychotherapy, as a distinct method, needs to be seen in historical perspective in relation to psychoanalysis, group therapy, and child therapy. In its classic model, psychoanalytic therapy depends on an environmental condition characterized by a modicum of stability, dependability, and predictability. It is within such a life situation that analyst and patient can, in effect, treat the environment as a constant, bypass it and concentrate on the task of analyzing transference manifestations of childhood conflicts. When, by contrast, the group environment becomes characterized by eruptive, unforeseeable change, and is realistically threatening, then the optimal condition required for the pursuit of the therapeutic progress is no longer present. There can be then only two choices: to reject the environment and to substitute a hopefully better one, or to change the environment by including it in an expanded system of therapeutic intervention.

The issue is clear. The group environment of our time, family and community, is changing at an unprecedented rate of speed; it is unstable, difficult to know and predict. It provides inadequate and erratic support for the emotional needs and growth of the individual. Only too often the individual is captive to his environment. He is the emotional prisoner of the disordered patterns of his group. He can neither leave his environment nor substitute a better one.

Under conditions of radical social change and realistic danger, the psychoanalyst's special task becomes increasingly handicapped. When the environment becomes unstable, the individual armors himself to carry the fight to the environment. He externalizes his conflict and his way of coping with it. In this setting there is often a selective reinforcement of such defenses as projection, denial, and substitution of aggression for anxiety, magic thinking and the omnipotent urge to reshape the world to suit the self. All too frequently, the individual unable to contain his conflict acts it out irrationally in a shared way with other members of his group. From these considerations, we come to an inescapable conclusion. The sphere of psychic healing must be expanded to embrace the sources of pathogenic influence within the group environment as well as within the individual.

The evolution of group psychotherapy did three things: (1) It focused attention on fundamental interdependence of the individual and the group, and on the phenomena of social role adaptation; (2) It sharpened our understanding of specific deficiencies in existing theories of personality, and broadened our conception of the causation of disordered behavior; (3) It modified our view of the responsibility of the psychotherapist in the modern community.

From still another point of view, the advancing borders of knowledge of child psychiatry, child development, and child psychotherapy, challenged by the concepts of social science, acted as a catalytic force in stirring reevaluation of the principles and practices of psychiatry. Disorders of the marital and parental partnership likewise hindered progress of the child. In child guidance, there was an established tradition of separate treatment of the child by a psychiatrist, the mother by a social worker. The tail seemed to wag the dog. The family was turned upside down. The family was viewed as extension of the child rather than the child as extension of the family. The mother felt accused and guilty; a wave of witch-hunting for rejecting mothers pervaded the climate of child guidance. Therapists took the side of the child against mother and family; therapists were missionaries dedicated to the rescue of hurt children. In a semi-jocular vein, child therapists were labeled "mother-killers." All that was human and good was attributed to the child, the source of evil was the mother. The value distortion is now clear: to save the child, we must also save parents and family. Separate treatment of family members seemed frequently to have the effect of drawing the members apart rather than bringing them closer together. It is by no means rare that one encounters troubled families in which three or four or even all members of the group are undergoing treatment with several therapists. This brings critical complications in the regulation of the emotional life of the family unit.

The artificiality and complications of the custom of separate treatment started a new chain of thought and action, the diagnosis and psychotherapy of the whole family.

In this historical setting, family study and treatment, though relatively new, offers considerable promise. It gives us expanded understanding of the relation between inner and outer experience, past and present, individual and group in the precipitation, course, and outcome of illness. Family therapy lends explicit emphasis to the principle of emotional contagion in family relationships, to the transmission of pathogenic conflict and coping from one generation to the next. It provides a framework for the correlation of the events of family and individual development at each stage of the life cycle. It opens a path to the conceptualization of the relations between family group defense of its continuity, identity and functions and individual defense against anxiety. It clarifies, within the context of family interaction, the meaning of the secondary gain of illness. It illuminates the phenomenon of multiple interacting disturbances among the members of the same family group. It sheds further light on the homeodynamics of family growth and behavior, and on the learning and growth processes of personality within the matrix of family development.

The tasks of diagnosis and treatment are interwoven, interdependent, parallel activities. Diagnosis qualifies the choice of therapeutic goals and the specificity of the techniques of family psychotherapy. Yet, at the same time, the dynamically oriented exploratory interview with the whole family is the pathway to diagnosis.

Regardless of which family member is labeled the "sick one," the whole family is invited to come in and talk it over. Therapeutic interviews with the family group may be conducted both in the office and at home. Home visits are of great value but insufficiently used.

At the outset, the family is troubled, perplexed, frightened. The members know something is deeply wrong, but they do not know how or why nor do they know what to do about it. By tradition, the family pushes one member forward as the sick, disabled one. Yet, in actuality, several, and sometimes all, members are disturbed although in different ways and at different depths. What the psychiatrist faces is a cluster of interrelated illness processes, not a "single patient."

In many families, regardless of the symptom picture, there is no urge for psychiatric referral as long as family role relationships are held in tolerable balance. The timing of the demand for professional help strongly coincides with the immediate dramatic impact of decompensation of the previous state of balance, which then brings in its wake a distressing family conflict. Critical upsets of the emotional equilibrium of the family group thus become a significant health phenomenon.

In the family interview, what one parent conceals, the other reveals. What the parents together hide, the child blurts out. What one member expresses in a twisted, prejudiced way is corrected by another. When certain anxiety filled material is touched upon, the family may engage in a silent pact to avoid such areas. Sooner or later, such denials are broken through. Family life, by its very nature, is inimical to the guarding of secrets. Such secrets exist but they are difficult to preserve. Sooner or later, "the cat comes out of the bag." It is the clinician's responsibility to distinguish valid secrets from false pathogenic ones. He respects the former while supporting the family in dissolving the latter.

Family therapy may begin on the surface, it need not stay there; a competent therapist can achieve access to any emotional depth he may require in meeting the problems of a particular family. The challenge of reaching, as and when needed, selected components of the depth experience of the family, rests, in the ultimate, on therapeutic talent, clarity, know-how, appropriateness of goals, and confidence in action.

A family has a body, a mind, and a spirit; it has a heart; it throbs with the pulse of life; it has both depth and surface; it has an inner face and an outer face. It builds a facade, a mask. If we strip the mask we can glimpse the inner being; we enter the conflict experience of the family in depth. Family therapy begins promptly with the first face-to-face contact. The therapist makes instantaneous observations of the personalities of family members, their adaptation to family roles. How do they enter? Who sits next to whom? Who away from whom? Who speaks? Who listens? Who smiles? Who frowns? At a typical session, the family arrives in a state of pent-up pain, fright, thwarted need, and anger. The therapist gets a quick sense of the emotional climate. He observes the quality of appeal that the members project to one another and to himself.

Are they coercive? Do they simply give up, and in a mood of resigned apathy cease to ask and expect anything? He notes the existing confusion, mistrust, and hostile fragmentation of family bonds.

It is the therapist's responsibility to stir interaction among members; to catalyze and enhance a live and meaningful emotional interchange. He must establish a useful atmosphere of rapport, a touching quality of contact. As the family members come in touch with the therapist, they come into better touch with themselves.

The clinician integrates his knowledge and use of self in a special way. He is participant-observer. He is active, open, fluid, forthright. He moves directly into the stream of family conflict to energize and influence the interactional processes; he withdraws to objectify his experience, to survey and assess significant events, and then moves back in again. Weighing and balancing the sick and healthy emotional forces, he supports health and counteracts sickness by shifting his function at various stages of the family process.

His responsibilities are multiple and complex. They require a flexible, open, and undefensive use of self. Depending on the shifting foci of conflict and anxiety, one or another member joins with and separates from particular elements of the therapist's identity. These partial joinings and separations reflect elements of both transference and countertransference, and reality must be differently conceptualized in the matrix of family interaction. They may be interpreted as a fluid, changing balance between clinging to the old, and receptivity to the new in family experience. The potentials of effective reality testing in this special setting are much enhanced.

In the over-all picture, the therapist feels his way toward the idiosyncratic language of the family—how the members talk, what they choose to talk about, most importantly what they tacitly avoid. He makes rapid note of what is felt and communicated below the level of words in body stance, facial expressions, inarticulate gestures, and postural mask. He perceives and assesses the deeper currents of emotion that parents fear and inhibit; the fright, the suspicion, the despair, the urge for vengeance. He identifies these sources of anxiety which freeze the reaching out of the members, the asking for closeness and understanding, one with the other, and with the therapist. He defines for himself the level of coping struggle that characterizes the particular family. He assays the interplay between preferred defense operations of the family group and individual defenses against anxiety.

In a continual process of communion with self, he brings to his awareness the emotions stirred in him by the deep streams of feeling moving among the family members and toward himself. He uses his disciplined insights into his personal emotions as a diagnostic yardstick for what is being experienced by the family. In so doing, he develops a series of clinical hunches which he progressively tests as he builds his diagnostic image of the family group. This embraces the balance of family functioning, the patterns of complementarity, conflict, and coping, the interplay of the family and individual defense and, finally, the struggle with conflicting representations of family identity, values, and patterns of action. In a selective manner, sequence by sequence, the therapist penetrates the family facade, the patterns of complicity, denials, and disguise of deeper currents of feelings and conflict and fear.

Acting as a catalyst, the therapist provokes increasingly candid disclosures of dormant interpersonal conflicts; he lifts intrapersonal conflict to the level of interpersonal process. In due course, he can trace significant connections between family disorder and the intrapsychic anxiety of individual members. Often one part of the family armors itself, prejudicially attacks and sacrifices another part. When needed, the therapist intervenes to neutralize these patterns of attack. By counteracting scapegoating as a specific defense against anxiety, the therapist retransposes the underlying conflict to its place of origin in the family group; that is, the conflict may be moved back to its primary source. In this phase of therapy, it has become possible to identify a cluster of interrelated roles, that of persecutor, victim, peace-maker, or healer of family conflict.

In intervening on the interplay between family group defense and individual defenses, the therapist makes free use of the device of confrontation. By a variety of interventions, he penetrates and undermines the pathogenic patterns of coping and defense. He calls attention to the inefficiency, inappropriateness, and harmfulness of certain sickness-inducing defenses, and fosters the substitution of healthier ones. This has special relevance for the task of cutting into the vicious cycle of blame and punishment which represents nothing less than an unconscious collusion to prevent change.

To stir movement, the therapist pierces pathogenic operations by a device I call "tickling the defenses." This is a tactic of catching the family members by surprise, exposing dramatic discrepancies between their self-justifying rationalizations and their subverbal attitudes. He challenges empty clichés and static or pat formulae for the problems of family living. He halts fruitless bickering over routine, superficial, or unimportant matters.

Watchful for each clue, he reaches out for more honest and meaningful means of communication. In the service of this effort, he may make effective use of "body talk." He confronts the members forthrightly with the meaning of certain nonverbal forms of communication as revealed in mood, expression, posture, gesture, and movement. To counteract the tendency to substitute empty verbalisms for genuine emotional interchange, he catalyzes in the members the urge to explore the dramatic contradictions between these verbal utterances and body expressions.

Through his calm, firm presence, he functions as a controller of interpersonal danger, steering between the extremes of intolerable closeness and the risk of eruptions of explosive rage, which might lead to panic and disorganization. He executes other functions: he offers security, emotional support, acceptance, understanding, affirmation of worth, and direct satisfaction of valid emotional needs. He catalyzes the interchange among family members toward cooperation in the quest for solutions to conflict or toward finding more appropriate compromise. Along this path, he activates a shift in the allegiances of family members toward improved complementarity of needs.

As a real parent figure, the therapist offers emotional support on a selective basis, now to one part of the family, now to another; so he may, in all honesty, and with considerable effectiveness, support a weaker member of a group against the attack of a stronger. In the long view, the genuineness of the therapist's concern, his fairness, and the manner in which he continually shifts from one part of the family to another, minimizes any destructive rivalry.

At still another level, the family therapist provides support through a kind of substitute gratification, that is, by supplying the family with elements of emotional imagery of self and others in which the family has before been lacking. In this sense, reality testing, fortified by the therapist's activity, begins at the outset. In the spontaneous give and take among the family members, each has an opportunity to experience the self and other with a lessened sense of danger. Each takes a second look at every other, and at the therapist, and readapts toward a more realistic image of family relationships.

Then there is the question of the clash of competing indentities and values. This is expressed in an ongoing contest of needs, identity, and value representations between parental partners which, in turn, can be traced to the links of identity and values of each parent with his family of origin. In this clash, the offspring are forced to take sides and thus the family is split into contesting factions. In such family warfare, each faction competes with every other to push change toward what they want the family to be and do for its members. In this struggle, the family therapist serves as educator to the problems of family living. He epitomizes in his own being a range of models of family health. He shakes up pre-existing alignments and splits and opens ways to new designs of family living. He stirs the family members to find constructive solutions or compromises of conflict, to discover new ways of intimacy, sharing, and identification, to support differences as well as union. Crucial to this, he energizes and enriches the processes of critical reassessment of family identity, goals, and values, especially those that pertain to the maintenance of indispensable family functions.

By the merging of these many functions, as activator or common challenger, common supporter, interpreter, reintegrator, the therapist shakes up pre-existing pathogenic relationship alignments and equilibria, and opens the way to discovery of healthier family bonds.

Summary

The therapist's functions may be itemized as follows:

1. The therapist establishes a useful rapport, empathy, and communication among the family members and between them and himself.

2. He uses this rapport to catalyze the expression of major conflicts and ways of coping. He clarifies conflict by dissolving barriers, defensive disguises, confusions, and misunderstandings. By stages, he attempts to bring to the members a clearer and more accurate understanding as to what is really wrong.

3. He counteracts inappropriate denials, displacements and rationalizations of conflict.

4. He transforms dormant, concealed interpersonal conflicts into open, interactional expression.

5. He lifts intrapersonal conflict to the level of interpersonal exchange.

6. He neutralizes processes of prejudicial scapegoating that fortify one part of the family while victimizing another part.

7. He fulfills, in part, the role of a great parent figure, a controller of danger, a source of emotional support, and a supplier of elements which the family needs but lacks. His emotional nurturing of the family is a kind of substitutive therapy.

8. He penetrates and undermines resistance, and reduces the intensity of

shared conflict, guilt, and fear, using both confrontation and interpretation, but relying mainly on the former.

9. He serves as a personal instrument of reality testing for the family.

10. He serves as the educator and personifier of useful models of family health.

The future of family psychotherapy is hinted at in its unique potentials and revolutionary implications. It has a fascination uniquely its own. The therapist hits home, both literally and figuratively. Family therapy may not only unfold as a method in its own right, but may also serve to correct and improve some of the older methods. That this is so is borne out by the conviction of many psychotherapists who have had training in family therapy. "Once a therapist engages in family therapy, he ain't never the same again." Not only does he discover the value of family therapy; he also becomes a more effective psychoanalytic therapist.

Family therapy is a therapy in vivo, not in vitro. It is a natural, not an artifical level of entry into human distress. It encompasses the interdependent, inter-penetrating relations of individual and group. It does not pit individual against family or family against individual. It does not heal one part of the family at the expense of another; it supports both. It offers a new and different image of mental illness. It is a profoundly honest way of intervening in human prob-lems. It highlights the importance of contagion of anxiety in family inter-change. It provides a natural setting for the continual clash between dream and reality; it offers an effective channel for the living-out of the pain and disillusionment deriving from this clash. It deals with disparities of depth and surface; inner and outer being; the interplay of intra- and interpersonal conflict, and the relations, mutually supporting or oppositional, between fam-ily group defense and individual defense. It confronts the interplay of multiple disturbances among family members. It offers an effective means for penetrat-ing the vicious cycle of blame and punishment for things past. It provides an emotional matrix for enhancing mutual understanding, respect, and esteem.

Contrary to Freud's view of therapy, it does not merely take something away, a pathogenic feeling or idea, it adds something new and better to take the place of sick experience. It illuminates the homeodynamic principle of adapta-tion to change; the matrix for learning and growth in the family. It fosters healthy rather than pathologic healing of family disorders. It does not merely patch-up a damaged individual; it makes room for improved relationship patterns, a new way of life. It relates a valid ethic to the goals of family living.

For the interested therapist, family psychotherapy, however unstan-dardized it is in its presently evolving form, nevertheless is full of challenge, full of surprises, and highly rewarding. A science of family behavior, a system of family diagnosis and psychotherapy, hold the promise of becoming a useful and significant addition to our armamentarium of mental health practices.

Experiential Psychotherapy with Families

Walter Kempler

Upon these two commandments hang all the laws upon which experiential psychotherapy within families stands: attention to the current interaction as the pivotal point for all awareness and interventions; involvement of the total therapist-person bringing overtly and richly his full personal impact on the families with whom he works (not merely a bag of tricks called therapeutic skills). While many therapists espouse such fundamentals, in actual practice there is a tendency to hedge on this bi-principled commitment. This paper is offered as a hedge-clipper.

The extant interaction—the current encounter—demands constant vigil. It means attention to the here and now, not to the exclusion of past and future but to the extent that any pertinent deviation from the here and now be considered a transient, though necessary diversion, and that each detour be succinct and promptly returned and integrated into the current interaction.

A mother, father and their 8 year old daughter are embroiled in a discussion about daughter's behavior. Father, clearly and firmly, contends that daughter is quite able to express herself while mother contends that she never speaks up in her own behalf and needs help on this matter. The therapist, believing direct confrontation is preferable whenever possible, urges mother to explore her concern with daughter rather than gossip with father about her.

M (to dau): "I wish you could speak freely with us about anything you want" (with obvious condescension) "it's so important for you to be able to do that."

D (readily): "I say what I want."

M: "Oh no you don't. You should be able to say anything you wish."

D (again, easily): "I do."

M (ignoring her comment): "I wish you did."

Th (to M): "You ignore her remarks."

M (to Th): "I do because I know I'm right."

Th (attempting to assist them to bridge their distance and negotiate anew): "Can you give her an example?"

Reprinted from *Family Process*, Vol. 7, #1, March 1968, pp. 88-99. Reproduced by permission.

M: "I don't think she's saying here what she wants to."

Th (persevering): "For instance . . ." (The therapist doesn't perceive or share mother's concern but wishes to give her the opportunity to explore further.)

M: "That she thinks we are bad parents. For instance, we don't let her speak about what she doesn't like about us . . . like my husband's yelling and maybe my crying bothers her."

Th (now that mother is more specific): "Check those out with her."

Mother inquires and daughter answers quite lucidly and openly, "I don't like Daddy's yelling but it doesn't bother me too much except when it's to me. I've told him." And then in response to mother's inquiry about her crying, "It doesn't bother me to see you cry. It used to but you do so much of it I don't pay attention to it any more."

To this mother shakes her head sadly as if to say "I know you're suffering, poor child—if I could only help you know how you are suffering."

The therapist, the father and the daughter are now all convinced that daughter isn't suffering—at least not in this area. The therapist offers this to mother and urges her to consider this information. She ponders awhile and finally says, "I know what it's like to be constantly shut up. It's terrible."

She has left the here and now and returned to her own childhood. She is in the "there and now" so to speak, i.e., her current awareness has gone to another time. She is encouraged to stay there by the therapist with "Could you be the little girl now?" She already is. The therapist is merely permitting her to openly acknowledge it. "Close your eyes and speak to your parents about what it's like to be constantly shut up."

Mother closes her eyes and begins crying.

Th: "Talk to them."

M (after sobbing a while she speaks with her eyes closed): "Oh Mother, if you only knew. I don't think you even knew (cries more heavily). I could never tell you anything. And it wasn't even all bad. I just wanted you to listen to me—just once—just let me say what's on my mind." She then went on speaking to her mother in fantasy (her reality of the moment) citing an instance that was particularly painful to her.

When she seemed finished the therapist suggested she respond as though she were now her mother. This was a novel idea to her. As she began to explore she found herself at first apologizing by pleading ignorance and as she continued, now as her own mother, she began defending her right not to listen; then, in tears, explained how inadequate she felt as a mother and dared not listen.

With this awareness she at once became the child again, sobbing heavily, exclaiming "I never knew. That never occurred to me. I never knew. I thought you didn't like me. That's what was so terrible. I never thought it was you, that you *couldn't* listen. I just thought you weren't interested. Oh, how horrible it must have been for you. I feel that way too so much of the time (now she is becoming the parent-mother of today and the crying stops). That's why I keep telling Cathy (her daughter) to speak up. She does, you know, better than I could."

During this work, this mother reunited parts of her own psyche that had become estranged during her own growing up. When she finished she looked pensive and fell silent, staring at an empty chair. A meditative-like stance often follows important cognitions as though the psychic apparatus needs to be allowed time for reorganization.

After several minutes of comfortable silence had passed, mother began to move and look about. The therapist, wanting the experience integrated into her current world, urged her to speak to her daughter.

M (smiling): "I'm not as bad a mother as you may think—I guess it's more accurate to say 'as I thought I was.' You know, you do speak up much better than I ever did."

Daughter smiles. Their encounter seems completed.

Father is invited to respond. To the therapist he begins, "I knew I was right but I never thought . . ."

The therapist, interrupting, suggests that he speak to his wife.

Father turns to her and continues, "I never thought about what was going on. It just made me angry to see the way you nagged at her. That feeling is all gone now. If you start nagging again it will probably come back but I sure feel different about you right now."

Mother replies, "I feel so relieved about all this. I'm sorry I've been such a pill."

Father, doing some work for himself, ignores her apology and says, "Well maybe I can be more helpful to you in the future if you should get upset again about Cathy."

They fall silent. The therapist feels completed with father and daughter. To finish his business of the moment with mother, he adds, "I didn't like your apology. You needn't be the perfect wife, either."

History-taking, ruminating about genetic derivatives to current behavior, discussion about the "why" of the behavior are all antithetical to this approach. Attention to the subject matter of any encounter is considered necessary for launching our encounter, to be jettisoned however, as quickly as possible, to an experience that exposes to our awareness what we do to each other and how we do it. Briefly, what and how of behavior displaces why; experiences displace discussion.

When a family arrives the therapist observes how this family appears, how they impinge on him. Does anxiety prevail in one or more of them? What are they doing? How do they come in? Does father usher his family in or is he one of the ducklings? What is their mood? Does the therapist like the looks of them? Are they friendly with each other?

The therapist's potential awareness about what he sees is infinite and of course colored by his own needs of the moment. The therapist may greet the family much as a good host, smiling and offering his hand. The therapist may begin by introducing himself if a family member has not already done so. Whatever the awareness, hopefully the therapist approaches the family, curious about what they want from him, interested in how they go about seeking what they need and ready to engage them with his feelings of the moment.

Some family member may begin. If not, the therapist is obliged to initiate the verbal exchange. Opening statements (as interventions in general) are considered best when they are an "I" statement which identifies the therapist in the here and now; perhaps an observation about himself. "I'm almost ready for you people. I'm still thinking about the previous session which was quite moving." And if that is not sufficient to complete his departure from the prior hour, a further comment of his current residual would be considered appropriate. The therapist is obliged, not merely urged, to clear himself so that he might be in the present more completely.

Being a good experiential therapist he is likely to have finished his destiny with the previous hour and be more available now. His awareness may go to someone's restlessness, an unusual hairstyle or to an attractive article of clothing. An opening comment acknowledging such awareness is preferred to a studied silence or a trite question that is not self-disclosing such as "And how are you today?" or "What can I do to help you?"

Trivial as this may seem, a self-disclosing atmosphere is best created by example and the opening statement is an excellent place to begin.

In the initial moments of therapy the therapist serves primarily as a catalyst striving to encourage negotiations amongst family members. Later the therapist becomes, at times, a principal in the fray.

"I'd like you to meet my family," a mother begins, introducing her two sons, Daryl 15 and Steve 12, and then her husband who trails in, unsmilingly offers his hand, grunts courteously and heads for a chair, obviously a reluctant dragged-in dragon.

Everyone is seated and during the initial moments of silent settling mother, smiling, visually checks out each member of her family and then looks at the therapist as if to say "I'm ready." The children watch the therapist or look about the office. Father visually alternates between therapist and wife, finally settling on his wife. In the brief silence mother speaks to the therapist. "Where would you like us to begin?"

Th: "Since you seem most ready to engage, I would suggest you begin by telling each member of your family what you do not like about living with them."

The therapist could have intensified the encounter at the outset by directing attention to the dissimilarity of mother and father; in each one's readiness to lead and engage. Preferring a softer opening, the therapist accepts her readiness to engage and moves to create an engagement within the family. Avoiding a question such as "Where would *you* like to begin?" the therapist sets another good example. He says what he wants.

M (to father): "Do you want to start?"

She's done it again. Ignoring the therapist's suggestion for the moment she now tosses a question to father inviting his leadership. Leading with a question is generally not engagement but rather an attempt to remain obscure hoping someone else will respond to the question and initiate the interaction. By turning to her husband after the therapist's instruction she confirms that, at least in part, this was her intention. The therapist now suspects she knows very well where she would like to begin.

F: "You've started. Go ahead."

The therapist notes that an excuse is given ("you've started") and is rather a feeble one at that, a fact which both ignore, as mother, now with his assertion and the therapist's direction, readily begins.

M (to Th): "Our trouble has been mostly with Steve . . ."

Th (interrupting): "Tell him what you don't like about his behavior."

M (to Th): "He knows very well what I don't like. It doesn't help to tell him."

Th: "Then I suggest you consult your husband. That's what husbands and wives are for."

M: "I know. I've talked to him but he's not interested."

Th: "Then I suggest you discuss *that* with your husband."

M: "I have but when I do he either ignores me or just gets mad at the kids and spanks them. And I don't think that's the way to handle it."

Th: "Tell him."

M: "I do. He won't listen to me."

Th: "Then discuss that with him."

Her mood suddenly changes from casual and conversational to sadness. She stares at the floor saying "It's no use," and falls silent.

Mother has withdrawn from the encounter. Her casual conversational posture was acceptable to share with us but to her, obviously, her sadness was not. Since feelings are the cushions of encountering that keep us from crashing into others and breaking, by curbing her feelings of the moment mother has converted this most valuable coping equipment into a wall which inhibits rather than enhances further negotiation. Bringing her nonverbal behavior into the verbal arena can restore the encounter.

Th: "I would like to know how you feel right now."

M (without looking up): "Sad and hopeless."

Th (attending the obstacle rather than the sadness, since this is her observable behavior): "Sharing your sadness and hopelessness with us seems difficult for you."

The invitation is accepted and she begins crying softly.

Th: "Now let's hear the words that go with the tears."

Mother shakes her head evidencing a clear "No." The therapist decides not to push further at this time. Even though reluctant to continue, she is, in this moment, more negotiable than father. The therapist's attention turns to him.

Th (to F): "You sit silently. I'd like to know where you are now."

F (ignoring mother's sadness and criticism of him, he responds on his safest ground): "I tell the kids to listen to her."

M (angrily to F through her tearfulness): "But you're not effective. They don't listen to you either and then you blow up at them. That's not the way to treat kids. You can't be hitting them all the time."

F (whining): "You always stop me. They'd listen to me but they know you'll come in and stop me."

Th (now we begin to see their interaction): "You're whining at your wife."

F: "What else can I do? She stops me at every turn."

Until now the therapist has been a catalyst. However, he may be getting annoyed with the husband, who transiently engages with his wife and then retreats to the posture of a whimpering child. He may also be annoyed with the wife, who double binds her husband by asking him to be the father, and at the same time, by telling him how to be the father, is treating him as a child. The attention, however, goes to the encounter. The wife is ready to engage but her husband is not. The therapist's attention then must go to him in order to bring him to a negotiating posture.

To do this the therapist now must engage more vigorously and become a principal. There are several ways he can do this.

Should he sense that father is fragile and truly needs a good mother, the therapist is likely to become one by remaining at a content level and suggesting, for instance, that father stop whimpering, take his rightful place as leader in his family and demand from his wife the behavior he requires to enjoy his home. This backing may extend from specific suggestions such as advising him to demand from his wife that she settle her problems with the children instead of saving them up for him, or by the therapist himself vigorously confronting the wife by way of example.

Whenever possible the patient should do his own work.

Should the therapist, however, conclude that the person (in this instance, the husband) is capable of an oppositional engagement—as indeed was assumed by the therapist partly from the report of this father's angrily spanking his children on occasion—then this opportunity for him to experience his power with adults should not be denied him. It is the therapist's task to bring this available power into the husband's relationship with his wife. The therapist can best do this by directing his own angry frustration into a vigorous attack on this man's whimpering posture.

Before going further, a word is needed about the transition from catalyst or interloper to a more active participant. This transition is largely related to the therapist's needs, having to do with the therapist's frustration and how he directs his frustration.

In an additional model the therapist does not suffer from a need for "objectivity." He knows this concept of the immaculate perception is a myth and that at every moment he is subjective. In an existential model, therapeutic interventions are most appropriate when they are the richest possible distillation of the therapist's presence. It is not necessary to justify or explain one's behavior in terms of an existing theory so that it may be labeled scientific. In a therapeutic encounter the existence of the therapist-person is more pertinent than the existence of supportive theory.

For such behavior by a therapist the word "spontaneous" may be applied. However, it is incumbent upon any therapist, existential or not, to clearly distinguish within himself the difference between spontaneous and impulsive behavior. Impulsive behavior is not a thorough representation of a person but rather a fractional escape of behavior in a constricted individual.

For the therapist, frustration leads to action and to further engagement with people. For each therapist the intensity and direction will vary. Those who become passive in the face of their frustration are not likely to become Experiential Family Psychotherapists. They are not likely to become family therapists at all. *Family therapy requires active participation if the therapist is to survive.*

The husband in the case above has now whimpered at his wife and, when confronted by the therapist, whimpers at him also, helplessly asking "What can I do? She stops me at every turn."

Th (sarcastically to provoke him): "You poor thing, overpowered by that terrible lady over there."

F (ducking): "She means well."

Th: "You're whimpering at me and I can't stand to see a grown man whimpering."

F (firmer): "I tell you I don't know what to do."

Th: "Like hell you don't" (offering and at the same time pushing). "You know as well as I that if you want her off your back you just have to tell her to get the hell off your back and mean it. That's one thing you could do instead of that mealy-mouthed apology, 'She means well.'"

F (looks quizzical; obviously he is not sure if he wants to chance it with either of us but is reluctant to retreat to the whimpering child posture again): "I'm not used to talking that way to people."

Th: "Then you'd better get used to it. You're going to have to shape up this family into a group that's worth living with, instead of a menagerie where your job is to come in periodically and crack the whip on the little wild animals."

F: "You sure paint a bad picture."

Th: "If I'm wrong, be man enough to disagree with me and don't wait to get outside of here to whimper to your wife about how you didn't know what to say here."

F (visibly bristling and speaking more forcefully): "I don't know that you're wrong about what you're saying."

Th: "But how do you like what I'm saying?"

F: "I don't. Nor do I like the way you're going about it."

Th: "I don't like the way you're going about things either."

F: "There must be a more friendly way than this."

Th: "Sure, you know, whimper."

F (with deliberate softness): "You're really a pusher, aren't you?"

Th: "How do you like me?"

F: "I don't."

Th: "You keep forgetting to say that part of your message. I can see it all over you but you never say it."

F (finally in anger): "I'll say what I damn please. You're not going to tell me how to talk . . . and how do you like that?" He socks his hand.

Th: "I like it a helluva lot better than your whimpering. What is your hand saying?"

F: "I'd like to punch you right in the nose, I suppose."

Th: "You suppose?"

F (firmly): "Enough. Get off my back and stay off."

Th (delighted to see his assertion): "Great. Now, about the rest of them (waving to his family) I'd like you to see if there's anything you'd like to say to them."

F (looks at each of them then settles on his wife): "He's right. I take an awful lot of nonsense from you and I hate it," still socking his hand. "I don't intend to take any more. I'll settle with the kids my way. If you don't like it that's too bad."

His wife says nothing. The children look pleased. The therapist wonders if he will be too harsh on the children and thinks that if he has the power with her, less will spill over on the children. He is no longer socking his hand. He sits up straight for the first time and sits back in the chair looking over his family.

Th (to the children for feedback): "What do you kids think about all this?"

Steve: "Okay." He looks comfortable.

Th: "Do you want to come back?"

Steve: "It's okay with me."

Th: "Daryl?"

Daryl: "I think it's helpful." He looks proudly at his father without saying anything but is obviously pleased.

The therapist, also pleased with what he sees, tell the father, "I like you better when you are being the man I know you are. I had the fleeting thought that maybe you will become a tyrant, but I know you won't. I'm not afraid of your power. I saw you taste it here and use it very justly with us."

He doesn't answer. When the therapist inquires about further visits the father answers without consulting his wife. "We'd better have a couple more."

On the few subsequent visits this man ushered his family in.

In this approach the therapist becomes a family member during the interviews, participating as fully as he is able, hopefully available for appreciation and criticism as well as he is able to dispense it. He laughs, cries and rages. He feels and shares his embarrassments, confusions and helplessness. He shares his fears of revealing himself when these feelings are a part of his current total person. He sometimes cannot share himself and hopefully he is able to say at least that much.

One simple, practical consequence of such negotiating with families, then, is the therapist's lack of concern with "taking sides." On the contrary, it is more suspicious when he is never on a side. A feeling therapist often has a side and is comfortable with it. Hopefully, he is sensitive to his own needs. If he is, he will find himself changing sides often enough to be inspiring to everyone. If not, his family will let him know, provided he has clearly established an atmosphere conducive to free exchange.

A mother, father and 21 year old daughter are seen for the first time. The daughter has just been released from a psychiatric hospital where she was briefly hospitalized with the label of an acute psychotic reaction. At present she is at home, heavily tranquilized, spending most of her time in bed.

Mother begins (as seems remarkably usual) with the aforementioned story. She not only begins but she never ends. Her excited, charm-laden loquaciousness is occasionally interspersed with remarks to her husband such as "Isn't that so, dear?" or "What do you think?" She never waits for an answer but babbles on. The therapist is the only one apparently annoyed enough to object. "Oh I do talk a lot I know. Why don't one of you (turning to husband and daughter) say something?" Before they could, she was off and running again.

This time the therapist tells her to be quiet and invites father to comment on the babbling. "Oh she's like that all the time," he replies. "I'm used to it." Then he offers the observation, "All our daughter needs is a good job. I tell her that all the time but she won't listen." Mother picks up on this and verbally runs nowhere with it. Father permits it.

After several more futile attempts to invite each of them including daughter (who remained silent) to look at their behavior and consider altering each of their encounter-diminishing behaviors, the therapist with great exasperation turns on both parents, telling them in no uncertain terms of their destructive behavior; mother's incessant babbling, father's absurd tolerance of it and, further, the absence of any constructive working with each other: mother, satisfied with her monologue to impress the therapist; and father, meager and repetitive, offering employment as the salvation to all his daughter's ills (and the world's as well) ignoring the fact that daughter had obviously never listened to him, any more than he listened to his wife.

At the end of the therapist's harangue, daughter smilingly speaks for the first time. "We should have had you when I was 10 years old." With some residual grouchiness the therapist retorts, "But you're not 10 now so get started changing times for yourself."

Mother and father both cheered. Therapy had begun. The therapist had sided twice already. Within two months this daughter was working. At three months therapy had terminated by consensus and a year later the therapist was invited by the parents to attend the wedding of their daughter.

There is no obscuring of the therapist behind a title. The therapist brings his personality and life experiences to the family encounter. It is his uniqueness in this family (he is not likely to be caught up in the painful interlocking behavior patterns in this family—at least not initially) and his willingness to fully engage with others that are his most valuable therapeutic "techniques." In other words, in experiential psychotherapy within families there are no "techniques," only people. At every turn the therapist is obliged to struggle for his right to be seen as he perceives himself, and not to permit distortions such as, for instance, an implication that he is all knowing or all powerful. By such example, the family members are likewise encouraged to struggle for what they perceive as their identity. It is during the vigorous clarification of who we are to each other that therapy occurs.

The illustrative samples are admittedly unidimensional. This seems necessary for clarity of exposition. However, this should not deter the reader from translating the basic principles to more complex moments in therapy when many needs seem to arise at once or when chaos seems to temporarily prevail. At such moments it behooves the experientially oriented family therapist to turn to his own needs first. Perhaps he will demand a moment's moratorium from bedlam in order to see in which direction he would arbitrarily wish to proceed. Possibly, he will request some assistance from the working family in this matter. His own transient uncertainty is a welcome expression in a good experientially oriented therapeutic family encounter.

During the course of such encounters personal growth and family integration for each family member become excitingly possible. Even therapists grow in such an atmosphere.

The degree to which the therapist is capable of encountering in the here and now is the degree to which Experiential Family Therapy is propelled on its way.

Multi-Family Group Therapy: A Multidimensional Approach

Elsa Leichter
Gerda L. Schulman

The procedures, dynamics, and process of multi-family group therapy are presented with case examples from the authors' practice.

Multi-family group therapy began to emerge as a new and important treatment modality approximately ten years ago. A number of factors played a part in its development, but the initial impetus came from the first experiments with multi-family group therapy that were carried on within a mental hospital (Creedmore) under the leadership of Dr. Peter Laqueur. The mental health community and more specifically mental hospitals had been aware for a long time that their patients, in spite of some improvement during hospitalization, frequently regressed upon their return home; some did not benefit sufficiently while they were hospitalized. This led to increasing recognition that the families of the identified patients were implicated in the etiology of the schizophrenic illness and that therapeutic work with the families could help the patients improve more reliably during and after hospitalization. The emergence of multi-family group therapy was a natural development, since many families paid regular visits to their hospitalized sons and daughters and often formed spontaneous groups, which gradually were turned into therapeutic groups. Subsequently, many hospitals and out-patient clinics all over the country followed the original model and began to conduct multi-family therapy groups. Due to practical considerations, these groups were mostly open-ended; the individual family attended the group for a relatively short period, yet the group itself tended to go on for a long, often undefined, time. Although these groups were considered to be multi-family groups, in actuality, only triads, namely the parents and the identified patients, attended, and treatment was to a large extent focused on the patient.

Simultaneous with the above development, a few family agencies began to experiment with multi-family group therapy in which family and group therapy were combined and integrated. Preceding this, married couples group therapy had been practiced for a long time and in fact had been the first "break" with the classical model in which participants in a therapy group were total strangers to each other. In a way, one might say that the first multi-family therapy group, which included parents and the identified patient, carried the idea of couples groups (parents groups) still another step further in that the identified patient was added as a group member to the dyadic subsystem of the parents.

The authors, as a co-therapeutic team, were the first practitioners at the Jewish Family Service of New York to develop multi-family group therapy. In line with the agency's concept of family therapy, multi-family group therapy was viewed from the beginning as needing to include the entire nuclear family. Underlying this concept was the belief that all parts of the family are interdependent, affect each other in a most powerful way, and participate in the perpetuation of their system.

As the authors have become both familiar and more experienced with multi-family group therapy, they have at times expanded the nuclear family by including the extended kinship: e.g., grandparents or divorced spouses may be part of the multi-family therapy group where and whenever they play a significant role in the family transactions. As a rule, three or four families compose the multi-family therapy group.

SELECTION OF FAMILIES FOR GROUP

As in all therapy groups, the families are selected for multi-family group therapy by a screening process. The family and the therapists come to a mutual decision as to whether the family is interested and able to become part of the multi-family therapy group. Usually the families are seen several times as a unit. This process reflects the authors' orientation that the understanding and the engagement of the whole has to take priority over involvement with parts of the family. To put it differently, the first goal is to obtain a beginning grasp of the family system rather than attempt to come to an understanding of the whole through its parts. The authors prefer to tell the family almost immediately that the purpose of the first meeting is to determine jointly whether a multi-family therapy group would be the best method of treatment for them. While this remains as an underlying, open question, the process then concentrates on what the family is all about.

Can they be engaged as a family group? If this question is answered affirmatively, those families are selected for multi-family group therapy for whom this seems to be the treatment of choice. Naturally, there are many families who can benefit from either individual family therapy or multi-family group therapy and the happenstance that a multi-family therapy group is being formed may very well be the determining factor.

There are some families for whom multi-family group therapy is clearly preferable: among these are the isolated family or the family whose system is circulatory and rigidified, especially the symbiotic family. For the latter, particularly, exposure to different systems may be the only way to shake up their own.

Another type of family for whom multi-family group therapy can be very helpful is the family with a missing parent—usually the father—since the group provides parental substitutes.

There are families, however, for whom individual family therapy is clearly preferable to multi-family group therapy, beyond of course, those families who staunchly refuse to enter a group. Multi-family group therapy seems to be counterindicated with certain chaotic families in which the children, out of their deep anxiety, tend to drown out any meaningful discussion and transaction. The authors do not usually consider families with very young children (under the age of six) because of their inability to grasp and tolerate the group process. However, families that additionally have older children are, of course, considered. The young child may be invited to an occasional session so that the group can see the total family in action. Also unsuitable for multi-family group therapy are families in which an important, pertinent fact is kept as a secret from other family members and the keepers of the secret insist on maintaining their controls. The following example will make this point more explicit.

> The authors screened the T. family, which consisted of parents and their only son, ten years old. The family wanted help regarding the child's difficulties in school (lack of concentration, restlessness) and with peers (lack of friends). In the course of the initial interview, the T.'s alluded to a secret which they could not discuss in front of their son. Thus, in the second interview, the parents were seen alone and revealed that the child was adopted, but did not know about it. It was obvious to the therapists that a good part of the child's difficulties (pervasive anxiety and isolation) was related to the secrecy around his origin. The parents first fought this connection but after a couple of interviews seemed more ready to accept it. Yet they pleaded strongly that they were unable to overcome their deep fear of sharing the secret with their child.

The therapists felt that the T. family, therefore, would not be suitable for the projected short-term group, as the couple's need to maintain so powerful a secret would not really allow the group to deal helpfully with the family system. This does not mean that a flexible, individual family treatment approach might not eventually enable them to overcome their resistance, and, indeed, they were referred for family therapy. Of course, as in all treatment modalities, secrets emerge in the course of the treatment process as a result of increasing trust, but this does not represent a bind.

The complexity and the size of multi-family therapy groups has led most practitioners to conduct them as co-therapeutic teams. The authors also do their screening jointly, thus giving the family a sense of the therapists as a unit, just as they expect the whole family to get involved with them from the first contact.

As in any other group, the composition of the multi-family therapy group is important. In most of these groups, the families come originally because of a problem concerning a child. While this in itself represents a certain commonality, the authors see value in heterogeneity along other dimensions. Their groups encompass a wide age range (even, occasionally, a three-generational span), complete as well as incomplete families, and a variety of family types. As the group becomes more cohesive, identifications take place on the basis of universality of human emotions and needs, rather than on the basis of external similarities.

LONG-TERM AND SHORT-TERM GROUPS

Like other groups, multi-family therapy groups can be set up for long-term or short-term treatment; the groups can be closed or open-ended.

Short-term groups seem to be particularly helpful in the beginning and ending phases of the overall treatment process. With families that have just started treatment, clarification of the family system and its major pathogenic features can be particularly well accomplished within such a framework. After termination of the group, there may be a mutual agreement that some shift of the pathogenic system has taken place so that the family can operate more effectively on its own. Other families may decide to continue therapy in a more differentiated way with a variety of treatment modalities. Some multi-family groups provide the ending phase of the overall treatment. The family may have had individual family therapy, or there may have been prior treatment of some of the subsystems (couples, mother/child, etc.). Multi-family group therapy lends itself exceptionally well to an integrative process in which the group serves as a bridge to the world at large.

For some families, longer term multi-family group therapy is the treatment of choice—usually, families whose systems are particularly difficult to modify, yet who are motivated to work further on their problem.

The authors, who have experimented with both short- and long-term groups, have found that in spite of the more limited goal, short-term groups demand of the therapists more sharply focused and directive interventions. In a group of longer duration, the group itself can carry more of the treatment process, and the therapists' interventions are less pronounced.

DYNAMICS AND PROCESS PHENOMENA

Reality testing

Nevertheless, in all types of multi-family therapy groups, the initial goal is to enable the group to achieve some cohesiveness, so that it can become an optimal working instrument for therapeutic purposes. While this is true for all therapy groups, there is a dynamic difference between a therapy group composed of strangers and a group in which some members belong to the same family. In the multi-family therapy group, each family represents a subsystem with a shared history and a shared, current life situation. This makes for an enriching and complex process, as each subsystem interacts with other subsystems at the same time that each individual responds to other individuals, whether members of his family or strangers. The multi-family therapy group serves both as an arena for cross transferences—based on each person's introject—and as a reality tester. Of course, reality testing is considerably more pronounced in multi-family therapy groups than in other therapy groups, because distortions within a family are frequently readily apparent to the other group members.

A family perceived and treated a child as "dumb," an image that was largely internalized by the child. The group was not bound by the family's label, nor by the child's self-image. It had the opportunity to observe the transactions within the family that had led to the child's assumption of the role of the "dumb one" and was, therefore, free to view and treat the child differently. The parents, on the other hand, were witness to the group relating to the "dumb" child as a person who at times had something valuable to offer and who also, in response to the group's different treatment, gradually became more of a person. This whole process was to a large extent played out rather than articulated, and, therefore, evoked less defensiveness.

Transferential reactions occur, of course, not only within one family, but across family lines. These transferential reactions are dealt with in multi-family therapy groups as they are in other therapy groups. However, in multi-family therapy groups, the reality function of the group comes into special focus, since the member of the family with whom the transferred reaction really belongs very often is present, be it a marital partner, a parent, or a child. Based on its experience with this member, the group can often see where the overreaction originated and deal with it.

A man who throughout his long marriage had been a non-participatory husband reacted strongly in a most censuring, straight-laced manner to the use of gut language by an adolescent girl of another family. This led to a lot of angry interplay between the man and the girl, including threats to leave the group. The group, however, had frequently experienced the vulgar, almost violent cursing of the man's wife, who was taken on by others but not by the husband. Thus, the group could confront the man with his overreaction to the girl, enabling him eventually to reveal his distaste for his wife's violence.

The authors have been greatly interested in the developing adult-child relationships across family boundaries within the multi-family therapy group. Being troubled about the increasing alienation between adults and young people, one of their goals in starting such groups was to achieve a better mutual understanding and empathy between the generations. This has, indeed, occurred in most of the groups with which the authors have had direct or supervisory contact. While it is very difficult for children and parents to change the image they have of each other, in the multi-family therapy group, adults and young people have a chance to experience the universality of human needs and emotions across family boundaries. The investment of the children in having a "perfect" and "always available" parent is as great as the parents' investment in the "perfect" child, who is an extension of unfulfilled parental hopes and ambitions.

When adults or children who are outside of one's own family reveal vulnerable feelings, the group responds and demonstrates, in general, a greater tolerance than does the individual family. In the freer atmosphere of the group, identifications between adults and children can take place with the accompanying recognition of their mutual humanity. This can have a profound effect on the way in which adults and children perceive each other within their own families.

In multi-family group therapy, adults can use themselves as parent substitutes to children other than their own, even though the adult may be quite defective in his own role as a parent.

Lena, the mother of Florence, an eleven-year-old girl, and the maternal grandparents had imposed a taboo with regard to even mentioning the child's father from whom Lena had been divorced. After some time, in the course of group treatment, the child was freed to bring out her anguish both about the secrecy surrounding the parental separation, and her profound sense of deprivation. Florence, who attended a religious school, sobbingly described the torture she experienced when during the daily morning prayers, she had to "honor thy father" when there was no one to honor! Her anguish about this painful moment was so great that sometimes she could not get herself to school. This child had been brought for help because of an incipient school phobia, among other symptoms.

As Florence cried out her pain, Lena sat stiffly in her seat. The group appealed to her to respond to her daughter. Actually it was already considerable progress that Florence had been able to express feelings that at first she had totally denied and that her mother, just a little earlier in the process, would have censored angrily. Lena helplessly and unhappily cried out that she did not know what to say, nor what to do. At that point, another woman in the group volunteered to show her. She moved toward Florence and took her in her arms, letting her cry on her shoulder. While the child momentarily seemed comforted, after a while she whis- pered, "I want my Mommy," and the woman transmitted this message to Lena. The latter now "knew" what to do; mother and child held each other firmly, and both cried. Following this episode, there was increasing closeness between Florence and her mother, who seemed to have gained a better acceptance of, and feeling for, her maternal role.

The "other mother" who ordinarily was not too perceptive about her own daughter's needs (this child was about Florence's age) seemed to sense her child's momentary aloneness. She moved toward her and held her hand for the rest of the session.

A reversal of roles can also be quite productive, meaning that a child can role-play the parent and a grownup can act as the child.

Donald, an adolescent boy, played hookie from the group session. He had not come home from school, and the family did not know where he was. Donald's father, Sam, threatened angrily that he would punish the boy at home.

Ken, an adolescent from another family, who was himself involved in an angry battle with his mother, felt strongly that punishment was not useful. He took on the role of Donald's father, and the latter played Donald. Ken used himself as a model father who tried hard to make emotional contact with Donald.

Sam played his defiant son using body gestures almost exclusively and could not be reached. Ken then spoke of his rising anger and perhaps for the first time had a glimmer of what can happen to a parent when a child remains impenetrable in his defiance.

Substitute roles can also be performed by a man and a woman, since members of the group frequently can be more nurturing to another person's husband or wife. This happens in married couples groups as well, but it is particularly useful for children to see, as it helps them begin to appreciate their parents' deprivation instead of just witnessing the mutual blame.

Peer confrontation

The multi-family therapy group offers to both adults and children the advantage of at least a partial peer group. Children can be especially suppor- tive to each other, yet can hold each other responsible and at times even challenge each other quite strongly and more effectively than can be done by adults. The fact that the parents witness this confrontation not only relieves them of an unpleasant task, but enables them to trust the young people's judgment. It decreases the parents' fantasy that children always condone, and even stimulate, each other's wrongdoings. Following is an example of peer confrontation:

... An adolescent girl challenged a younger girl for angrily cursing the girl's grandmother. This grandmother, who often acted like a witch, was not liked by the group and, therefore, did not get any group support. The only one responding to the old woman as a human being who had feelings was the adolescent girl, who had a tender relationship with her own grandmother.

Thus, children relate to each other both as peers and as substitute parents. In the latter role, they often take the "scolding parent" part with each other. If a multi-family therapy group has children of different ages, the younger children tend to relate to the older children as "ego-ideals" whom they would like to emulate.

The "well" sibling

Thus far, no differentiation has been made between the "problem child" and the so-called "well" sibling. This polarization occurs more often in families in which one child is treated as a scapegoat. The families that have an investment in making one child the carrier of the family pathology have an equal investment in having another child "well" and "problem free." These children are usually expected to be not only perfect, but "towers of strength" as well. Many of them are perfectionistic, moralistic, and constricted, often displaying obsessional ideations. Frequently, they are achievers, liked by adults, but often shunned by their peers as goodie-goodies, teachers' pets, and sissies. Others have a somewhat flattened affect, which makes them appear superficial and shallow. The girls often seem prematurely ladylike, and the boys tend to have considerable difficulty with their masculine identity. These characteristics are not only accepted but needed and approved in their families.

In considerable contrast to single family therapy, the multi-family therapy group, which has no particular investment in the maintenance of a given family system, notices rather quickly "the unrealness" of the good children and the price they pay for their position in the family. The children, in turn, respond rather well to questions and comments, especially when they are put out lightly and humorously. For example, "Gee, you sound even stricter than your parents," or "Do you ever have any fun?" "Now you sound again like the little old lady." In the accepting atmosphere of the group, which values highly the expression of genuine feelings, the "well" children gradually change from a pattern of denial and blandness (superficiality) to an increasing ability to express emotions. These may be feelings of pain and anger, as well as yearnings for personal acceptance and dependency.

Some children, those who come from families in which self-assertion and the expression of normal impulse drives are perceived as bad and dangerous, learn to repress these feelings and drives. They put their energies into pleasing their parents by doing well in school and by being well-behaved, yet they feel intensely jealous of their "problem" siblings who get a lot of attention, albeit negatively, from their parents. In the course of group treatment, some of these "good" children begin to act out more, much to the dismay of their parents, who become frightened and fight this development. It goes without saying that the goal of multi-family group therapy is not to make "a bad child" out of a "good child"; it is rather to establish a healthier balance in which "good" and "bad" are not polarized and the group and the family can learn eventually to differentiate between acting-out and playfulness.

The way in which the group relates to the "well" children cannot help but affect the "problem" children in the sense that it represents a challenge of the total family system. The indirect approach to the "problem" child is diametrically opposed to his usual treatment in his family and, often, also in the community, as well as in other treatment situations.

Differentiation of families in the group

In the early phase, it is very hard for almost every family to see and to understand itself in terms of its own system, especially to understand those features that are pathogenic and growth-stunting, since they are "family egosyntonic," which means that each member in the family has an investment in maintaining the system.

In the group, it is relatively easy for one family to perceive another family's malfunctioning. If the therapists keep the focus on the most prominent features in each family system, the group gradually learns to think in family terms. As time goes on, individuals apply their new thinking to their own family, even though they rarely become as clear about themselves as a family as they are about others.

Initially, the group tends to use clichés, and generalizations; families, as well as individuals, tend to merge with each other. Gradually, however, the group begins to differentiate between each family's needs and realizes that what is good for one may not be good for another family.

In Florence's family, discussed above, the nonmentionable father needed to become "present," whereas in another family, where a separated husband continued to be in and out of the house and thus created confusion for his children, a more final separation was desirable. It was first hard for Florence to perceive this difference since her need to have her father present was overriding. As the pathology of the other family unfolded, however, Florence was able to distinguish between her own situation and the other family's symbiotic stickiness.

Resistance

Any threat to the equilibrium of the family tends to bring out resistance. The threats may be to the structure (good-bad child axis, marital and other dyadic relationships), as well as to existing family pacts and family myths. The major form of resistance, as in all therapy, is staying away from sessions. This can be acted out by an individual, a pair, or by the whole family. Absence of the whole family cannot help but be intensely experienced by the therapists and the group as a threat to its survival. While the absence of a whole family signifies the existence of a pact, fortunately, some individuals in the family may feel more positively about the group and be able to help the rest of the family return. Since all families in multi-family group therapy go through resistance phases one way or another, they are in a particularly good position to recognize and deal with resistance in an empathetic way.

On occasion, a family leaves the multi-family therapy group for good, in which case a distinction needs to be made between a family that consciously and responsibly faces the fact that the modality of multi-family group therapy is too much for them and between the family who takes flight.

Withdrawal of some family members from the group

An interesting phenomenon in multi-family group therapy occurs when some members of a family want to stay in the group and others do not. Some therapists insist on the participation of the whole family as a basic condition for group treatment. The authors use this approach only if the partial withdrawal from the group takes place very early in the process, since this usually means the family fights the concept of wholeness. However, when the family has reached a more differentiated level of operation, the therapists tend to be more permissive and to allow those members of the family who are more motivated to stay in the group. In further treatment, the knowledge of the family system enables the group to deal more productively with the remaining members.

The following examples demonstrate circumstances under which some members of a family may leave the group, while others stay on.

The father, as well as his adolescent son who had been brought for treatment because of his delinquency (stealing), withdrew from the group at a point at which the boy's stealing was seen as linked to the father's clearly emerging, delinquent tendencies. By then, a shift in the family system had occurred. The mother, who had been seductively involved with her son against the father, had begun to extricate herself from the collusive relationship. This allowed the son to turn to his father for greater closeness, but their alliance was at least partially unhealthy. The father, a very brittle man, left the group in some anger because he could not maintain the denial that his delinquent activities, in which he involved his son, had anything to do directly with the boy's stealing. The son followed suit in order to stay in his father's good graces.

The mother, who had a history of many abortive treatment attempts, was highly motivated to see group treatment through for herself, and she continued productively until the group ended. Subsequent contacts showed that the boy was able to achieve actual, as well as emotional, separation from both parents and was functioning well at an out-of-town college.

In another family, a very disturbed but rigidly defended adolescent boy gained sufficient strength in the group to begin to expose his underlying depression and occasional psychotic ideations. As his pathology emerged, he no longer could tolerate the group but was able to move into and utilize individual treatment.

Max, a fifteen-year-old boy who had taken hashish and had been involved in drinking for about a year, was accepted in a multi-family therapy group together with his parents and younger sister. He had staunchly refused individual treatment but agreed to try the group and was a rather willing participant. Initially, the major focus was on the family's severe dysfunctioning and not at all on his problems. As Max's parents began to take increasing responsibility for their own difficulties, Max, who had been very guarded about himself, became more anxious and began to reveal depressed and suicidal feelings. Even though the group was most accepting of the boy, as his defenses decreased, he could no longer tolerate the many stimuli impinging upon him in the sessions. By this time, however, he was no longer denying his problems and was much more in touch with his real anguish. Therefore, he was ready to move into individual treatment, which was essential for him in terms of his need and level of operation. The rest of the family remained in the group, since they no longer needed to hide behind Max's problem and continued to work profitably on their difficulties.

Spontaneous insights

Naturally, not all growth is accompanied by resistance. As a matter of fact, multi-family group therapy provides a particularly fertile ground for the emergence of spontaneous and unexpected attitudes and insights, which occur almost as a byproduct to the consciously pursued goal. This, of course, is a known phenomenon in all therapy groups, but the very structure of the multi-family therapy group and the process flowing from it can have a very strong impact on its members. These spontaneous changes always have an especially exciting quality.

This actually happened within the B. family, which had a mentally sick son and a young daughter. The latter began to show rebellious behavior toward both parents after her brother's placement. It was quite obvious that there was a serious marital disturbance, However, a variety of earlier treatment efforts had not brought about change, and in their own evaluation, the therapists felt pessimistic about the possibility of change in the marriage. Their plan was to attempt to break into the unholy alliance between mother and daughter against the father, so that the daughter would not need to carry her mother's anger.

The presence in another family of a pair of grandparents whose pathological effect on the next two generations was amply played out in the group led Mr. B. to exclaim suddenly and quite spontaneously that he had just "dethroned" his parents for the first time in his forty-odd years. He spoke about their exploitation of him and of his determination to change his pattern of always needing to give in to their demands. His wife, who had been complaining all along about her husband's overinvolvement with his parents, which she felt affected adversely the marital relationship, seemed astounded at her husband's different view. Subsequently, there was a marked rapprochement in the marital relationship, which was reinforced in the group. In the last group session, Mrs. B. described joyfully the emergence of her husband's "new me."

The above example demonstrated how the structure of the group—namely the presence of grandparents in another family—contributed to an emotional separation between an adult group member and his heretofore idealized parents. On the other hand, the structure of the multi-family therapy group, with its emphasis on the nurturing of children, often brings out secret longings for mothering on the part of the adults.

This occurred quite dramatically with the family in which the three generations were present. The therapists did not particularly aim at improving the relationship between the adult, Lena, and her mother, who seemed quite inaccessible to change. For a long time, Lena acted as if she had accepted the reality of her mother's stark inability to give, but she continued to be quite depressed. Efforts to reach her depression were unsuccessful.

As the end of the group came nearer, Lena's despair seemed to increase. Finally, she revealed with a lot of emotion that in view of the fact that the group was about to end, she realized that she had harbored a secret hope that her relationship with her mother would improve, and now this would never come true. From this point on, Lena became more reachable; she began to deal with her unfulfilled dependency needs and to give up her secret fantasy. As this occurred, her depression lifted.

Ending phase of the group

It is significant that Lena's recognition of her secret longings for her mother's love occurred only under the impact of the approaching end of the group. This is not unusual, since the ending phase brings about a critical sense of urgency for the whole group. Each family and each member of the group, including the therapists, have to come to terms with what is and what might have been, but has not come to pass. This, in fact, is the major theme of the ending phase in which families are quite helpful to each other in drawing a sharp differentiation between fantasy and reality. This process, of necessity, evokes deep feelings of pain, disappointment, and some anger, which is often directed against the therapists for not producing the miracles.

The authors are firmly committed to living out in the group all feelings connected with the ending. As this process develops, a new balance gradually occurs. As one family or individual deals with their ending by regression and denial of change, another family is able to acknowledge growth in themselves and questions the degree of denial in the others, often pointing out significant changes. Gradually, most families are able to view themselves more realistically and are, therefore, better prepared to plan their future direction.

As part of the ending phase, the authors have been using one-day Marathon sessions to give the group an opportunity to deepen the on-going process. During the period of preparation for the Marathon, the group shows anxiety, as well as a good deal of curiosity and even enthusiasm. It may well be that the idea of the Marathon arouses hope that at least for one day, family life will be more satisfying in that there will be meaningful and intimate communication in which nobody looks for the usual escapes. This hope is, indeed, realistic, since in the actual Marathon session—which is usually very well attended—father does not withdraw to the TV, mother does not hang on the telephone, and the children are not a nuisance. In fact, the children are especially enthusiastic and committed to serious participation. Their staying power is amazing, and not infrequently they take the leadership in the session. The Marathon experience usually has a profound impact on the continuing process; it serves especially to sharpen the focus and to enhance integration in the ending phase.

CONCLUSION

While there are many aspects of multi-family group therapy that are similar to both individual family therapy and to group therapy, there are some features that are distinctly unique to it. It is quite unusual in the ordinary life situation, as well as in the therapeutic world, that families expose themselves to one another and try to have a significant effect on each other's way of life.

It is equally unusual that adults expose themselves to children as people, rather than in their customary roles; that children let their guard down in front of adults; that they engage with each other in meaningful encounters that are quite different from the customary intrusiveness and stereotyped perception commonly existing between the generations. The experience that multi-family group therapy offers helps to decrease alienation and isolation between the generations, as they come to see each other in more human and humane terms.

REFERENCES

1. Curry, A. E., "Management of Multiple Family Groups," *Int. J. Group Psychother.*, 15: 90–96, 1965.
2. Daniels, N., "Participation of Relatives in a Group-Centered Program," *Int. J. Group Psychother.*, 17: 336–342, 1967.
3. Davies, I. J., Ellenson, G., and Young, R., "Therapy with a Group of Families in a Psychiatric Day Center," *Am. J. Orthopsychiat.*, 36: 134–146, 1966.
4. Donner, J. and Gamson, A., "Experience with Multi-Family, Time-Limited, Outpatient Groups at a Community Psychiatric Clinic," *Psychiatry*, 31: 126–137, 1968.
5. Leichter, E. and Schulman, G. L., "Emerging Phenomena in Multi-Family Group Treatment," *Inter. J. Group Psychother.*, 18: 59–69, 1968.
6. Leichter, E. and Schulman, G. L., "Interplay of Group and Family Treatment, Techniques in Multi-Family Group Therapy," *Inter. J. Group Psychother.*, 22: 167–176, 1972.
7. Laqueur, H. P., "General Systems Theory and Multiple Family Therapy," in: J. H. Masserman (Ed.), *Current Psychiatric Therapies, Volume VIII*, New York, Grune & Stratton, 1968.
8. Paul, N. L., and Broom, J. D., "Multiple-Family Therapy: Secrets and Scapegoating in Family Crisis," *Inter. J. Group Psychother.*, 20: 37–47, 1970.

3

Specific Areas of Practice

Much of the early literature on family therapy related to the intact, middle-class elementary or nuclear family containing a schizophrenic. Zuk (1979) has characterized this narrow focus as one of the major hurdles that family therapy had to surmount in order to grow as a *general* orientation to practice. Clearly, the life experience of a large and steadily increasing proportion of the population included living in a broken or dissolving elementary family; or living within a merged family; or living with poverty, alcoholism, racism or other forms of oppression, and ties with agencies of social control. Thus, family practitioners gradually were forced to address themselves to the myriad difficulties that constitute social problems in our society: mental illness, crime, family breakdown, alcoholism, and poverty, among others. Social change as reflected in family structure, composition, and lifestyles has rarely been taken into account in the family therapy literature.

The papers included in this section are directed primarily toward describing forms of practice applicable to defined population groups. Validation of practice is only finally possible when the incidence and prevalence of the specific disorders in the population are monitored. Further, family community-based services and programs should be directed at populations of families that share important defining characteristics.

Murray Bowen, a pioneer family therapist and still a central figure in family therapy, views the phenomena of alcoholism through the prism of his conception of systems theory and family practice.

As Kenneth Kressel and Morton Deutsch point out in their paper, there are now at least one million divorces per year in the United States and some nine million minor children who have experienced the breakdown of their parents' marriages. Single-parent families, splitting elementary families, and merging families are all part of the practice of all family therapists. This was not true when the pioneer family therapists were formulating hypotheses and developing the initial methodologies of family treatment. A small but growing number of practitioners now are specializing in divorce therapy. "Divorce Therapy: An In-Depth Survey of Therapists' Views" provides the first complete description linking divorce as a process to therapeutic intervention.

Another major area of social change in the 1970s was the changing status of women in the home and in the workplace. Although the feminist movement grew in influence during the decade, the impact on family therapy was seldom described. Rachel Hare-Mustin, in "A Feminist Approach to Family Therapy," provides a model and prepares the way for further work.

Harry Aponte has for some years been identified with a structural form of family therapy, developed largely by the staff of the Philadelphia Child Guidance Clinic, of which he is the Director. In "Psychotherapy for the Poor: An Eco-Structural Approach to Treatment," he details an approach to economically poor and disorganized families. This paper is followed by Ben Orcutt's contribution on the "Family Treatment of Poverty Level Families." Orcutt outlines four interlocking propositions designed to bring services to poverty-level families: an active outreach approach, a focus on multi-generational interactional processes, an emphasis on four foci of practice (individual, nuclear family, extended kin, and formal caregivers and their organizations), and a strategy of active follow-up. Orcutt's paper is one of a number (see Part V) contained in this text in which the theme is sounded that working exclusively within the boundaries of the elementary family may be *necessary* but often *not sufficient* to succeed in family practice. All of the papers in "Specific Areas of Practice" focus on the subject of the social context of familial problems.

REFERENCE

Zuk, G. H. The three crises in family therapy. *International Journal of Family Therapy*, 1979, *1*, 3–8.

Alcoholism as Viewed through Family Systems Theory and Family Psychotherapy

Murray Bowen

Family systems theory is relatively new as applied to emotional problems. This paper will outline some overall principles of family systems theory, the ways that alcoholism can be conceptualized as a symptom of the larger family or social unit, and ways in which family or systems therapy can be used to alleviate the problem.

Systems theory assumes that all important people in the family unit play a part in the way family members function in relation to each other and in the way the symptom finally erupts. The part that each person plays comes about by each "being himself." The symptom of excessive drinking occurs when family anxiety is high. The appearance of the symptom stirs even higher anxiety in those dependent on the one who drinks. The higher the anxiety, the more other family members react by anxiously doing more of what they are already doing. The process of drinking to relieve anxiety, and increased family anxiety in response to drinking, can spiral into a functional collapse or the process can become a chronic pattern.

Before going into systems theory, some explanation of terminology is in order. Family therapy is well known, but it is far from being a standardized method. There are a few well developed methods, but a majority of family therapists use the term to indicate that multiple family members attend the sessions, without regard for method or technique. About ten years ago the term "system" was introduced from family research, after it became clear that the same patterns that exist in families are present also in social and work relationships, and that relationship patterns have the quality of "systems." Now the term "system" is used loosely, and it is often associated with general systems theory, which has not been clearly defined for relationships. In this paper I will describe my family systems theory, which was developed from family research, and a method of family systems therapy, which is based on the theory. The terms systems theory and systems therapy are really more accurate, especially in referring to relationships outside the family.

The family *is* a system in that a change in the functioning of one family member is automatically followed by a compensatory change in another family member. Systems theory focused on the *functioning* of a system and its component parts. Almost any natural or man-made "system" can be used to illustrate systems concepts, but I have chosen a biological system, the human body, to illustrate the ideas. The total organism is made up of numerous different organ systems. An intricate set of automatic mechanisms controls the smooth reciprocal operation of vital functions such as heart rate, temperature, respiration, digestion, reflexes, and locomotion. Systems function at all levels of efficiency, from robust health to total failure. There are healthy compensated functioning states in which an organ can increase its functioning to handle an increased work load. There are decompensated states in which the organ loses the capacity to increase functioning. These are situations in which one organ increases its function to compensate for the poor functioning of another organ. There are states of dysfunction that range from the short-term dysfunctions of acute illness, through the long-term dysfunctions of chronic illness, to permanent dysfunction in an organ system. An organ that functions for another for long periods of time does not return to normal so easily. There are situations of decompensated over-functioning in which a failing organ works faster and faster in a futile effort to overcome a work overload. An example is the racing of a worn-out heart as it approaches total failure. The same patterns of function, overfunction, and dysfunction are present in the way people relate to each other in families and small social systems. For instance, the underfunctioning of a family member who is temporarily ill will be automatically compensated by other family members who overfunction until the sick one recovers. If the sick member becomes chronically or permanently disabled, the overfunctioning of the others becomes a long-term imbalance in the family. Certainly the overfunctioning of some family members will result in underfunctioning in others. In the case of an anxious mother and a small child, the underfunctioning of the child can become a permanent functional impairment. Another functional imbalance in family systems can occur when family members pretend disability.

Family systems theory was developed during the course of family research for emotional problems. Part of the effort was directed at extracting *facts* from the morass of subjectivity, discrepant explanations, and verbal dialogue that is common in psychiatric research. Eventually the research included the approach that is described here.

Systems theory attempts to focus on the functional *facts* of relationships. It focuses on what happened, how it happened, and when and where it happened, insofar as these observations are based on fact. It carefully avoids man's automatic preoccupation with why it happened. This is one of the main differences between conventional and systems theory. Conventional theory places much emphasis on the *why* of human behavior. All members of the mental health professions are familiar with *why* explanations. *Why* thinking has also been a part of cause-and-effect thinking because ever since man first became a thinking being he began to look around for causes to explain events that affected him. In reviewing the thinking of primitive man, we are amused at the various evil forces he blamed for his misfortunes, or the benevolent forces he credited for his good fortunes. We can chuckle at the causality that man in later centuries assigned to illness before he knew about germs and microorganisms. We can smugly assure ourselves that scientific knowledge and logical reasoning have now enabled man to go beyond the erroneous assumptions and false deductions of past centuries and that we now assign accurate causes for most of man's problems. However, an assumption behind systems theory is that man's cause-and-effect thinking is still a major *problem* in explaining his dysfunctions and behavior. A major effort in systems theory is to get beyond cause-and-effect thinking and to concentrate on facts, which are the basis for systems thinking. There were practical reasons for this disciplined effort. Part of man's cause-and-effect thinking is to blame his fellow man for his own problems. Blaming others for one's own failures is present in all of us to some degree. The greater the degree of anxiety in a family, the greater the tendency for even the most reasonable person to resort to blaming others for his own problems. Further, there is the predictable discrepancy between what man does and what he *says* he does. So, systems research moved into trying to isolate observable facts about man and his relationships, and to carefully avoid verbal dialogue and *why* explanations. The approach also requires the researcher to lay aside his own *why* assumptions. Efforts have been made to discover formulas for converting subjective observations into objective and measurable facts. For example, when applied to dreams, the formula says, "That man dreams is a scientific fact, but what he dreams is not necessarily a fact." The same formula can be applied to a whole range of subjective concepts, such as, "That man feels (or thinks or talks) is a scientific fact, but what he feels (or thinks or says) is not necessarily a fact." The entire spectrum of subjective states, even of the intensity of love and hate, can similarly be stated as functional facts.

Why bother to try to convert human relationship concepts into the functional facts of systems theory? One primary reason was to facilitate research. Focusing on one small aspect of relationship eliminated a complex mass of uncontrolled research data. The theory that evolved from the research resulted in a different kind of therapy. Then it was discovered that a system of therapy based on systems theory and functional facts was far superior to conventional therapy. However, a shift from conventional to systems theory is difficult and the superior results are not possible until the therapist is able to get reasonably beyond his "second nature" cause-and-effect thinking. A "little systems theory" mixed with conventional theory is not enough. Even the most experienced and disciplined systems thinker will automatically revert to cause-and-effect thinking when anxiety is high. The main thesis presented here is that systems theory and systems therapy provide a different approach to emotional problems. Therapists with the motivation and discipline to work towards systems thinking can reasonably expect a different order to therapeutic results as they are more successful in shifting to systems thinking.

How does alcoholism fit into systems concepts? From a systems viewpoint, alcoholism is one of the common human dysfunctions. As a dysfunction, it exists in the context of an imbalance in functioning in the total family system.

From a theoretical viewpoint, every important family member plays a part in the dysfunction of the dysfunctional member. The theory provides a way for conceptualizing the part that each member plays. From a systems therapy viewpoint, the therapy is directed at helping the family to modify its patterns of functioning. The therapy is directed at the family member, or members, with the most resourcefulness, who have the most potential for modifying his or her own functioning. When it is possible to modify the family relationship system, the alcoholic dysfunction is alleviated, even though the dysfunctional one may not have been part of the therapy.

THEORETICAL CONCEPTS

Family systems theory is made up of several different theoretical concepts. Some of the central concepts will be summarized briefly to convey a notion of how drinking dysfunctions fit into the total theory. An important theoretical concept is the degree of "differentiation of self" of the person. It is the degree to which the person has a "solid self" or solidly held principles by which he lives his life. This is in contrast to a "pseudo-self" made up of inconsistent life principles that can be corrupted by coercion for the gain of the moment. The differentiation of self is roughly equivalent to the concept of emotional maturity. The level of differentiation of a person is determined by the level of differentiation of one's parents, by the type of relationship the child has with the parents, and the way one's unresolved emotional attachment to his parents is handled in young adulthood. People marry spouses who have equal basic levels of differentiation of self. These various factors predict the degree of undifferentiation or immaturity to be absorbed in the new nuclear family (this includes father, mother, and children). It is common for young people to get into marriage blaming their parents for past unhappiness, and expecting to find perfect harmony in the marriage. The two pseudo-selfs "fuse" into the emotional "we-ness" of marriage, which has a high potential for impairing the functioning of one spouse. The discomfort of fusion is handled in one of several ways. Almost universal is some degree of emotional distance in the marriage, which helps each to be a more definite self than would otherwise be possible. Then there is the conflictual marriage in which neither "give in" to the other. The conflict provides good reason for them to keep the emotional distance, and the "make-up" between conflicts provides intervals of intense closeness. The most frequent pattern for handling emotional fusion is one in which one spouse becomes the dominant one, and the other the adaptive one, who is "programmed" to support the more dominant decision-making spouse. The adaptive spouse becomes a functional "no self." If this pattern is continued long enough, the adaptive one is vulnerable to some kind of chronic dysfunction, which can be physical illness, emotional illness, or a social dysfunction such as drinking, the use of drugs, or irresponsible behavior. The other pattern is one in which parents project their immaturity to one or more of their children. There are some parents who use one pattern predominantly. Most use a combination of all three patterns.

There is a range of adaptive patterns available in the nuclear family. In periods of calm, the adaptive patterns can function without symptoms arising in any family member. As anxiety and tension increase, the adaptive patterns lose flexibility and symptoms erupt. The family does not have conscious choice about the selection of adaptive patterns. These were "programmed" into the spouses in their own parental families. In general, there is more adaptability in families with a spectrum of patterns than in a family with fewer patterns. Another most important variable has to do with the quality and the degree of emotional contact each spouse has with their families of origin. Here again, there is a spectrum of ways that people handle the relationships to their parental families. Some can distance themselves emotionally while living close by; others maintain emotional closeness while living far apart. Emotional closeness or distance to parental families is determined by a combination of physical distance and quality of relationship. A common pattern in our society is the emotionally distant relationship with parental families, with brief, formal, superficial "duty" visits. In general, the more a nuclear family is emotionally cut off from parental families, the higher its incidence of problems and symptoms. Details about the theory have been presented in other papers.[1,2]

CLINICAL PATTERNS

In general, the person who later becomes an alcoholic is one who handles the emotional attachment to his parents, and especially to his mother, by denial of the attachment and by a super-independent posture which says, "I do not need you. I can do it myself." The level of emotional attachment is fairly intense, but it is no greater than exists in a fair spectrum of all people. It is the way the attachment is handled rather than the intensity that is important. There are a variety of outcomes to his life posture. At one extreme is the person who can make this pseudo-independent attitude work for long periods. He might be a dynamo in his profession or business and appear to be doing well with his immediate family. Such a person usually has an exaggerated sense of responsibility for others. He tries hard to live up to this responsibility, but since it is ultimately unattainable, the outcome is irresponsibility and broken promises. This person has the same "I can do it myself" posture to wife and children, who participate in his over-responsible posture by expecting him to always function at this level. This person's life is burdened by his high self-expectations and unrealistic sense of responsibility. His Achilles heel is the denial of his need for others, and his super-independent posture, which is in turn reinforced by his spouse and children. The harder he works, the more he becomes emotionally isolated. When he feels most burdened and the isolation is most intense, he often finds relief from alcohol, thus initiating a well known drinking pattern.

At the other extreme is the person who is so attached to his parents, and especially his mother, that he is never able to manage a productive life. He was "de-selfed" in the emotional fusion with his poorly differentiated mother. The mechanism of denial permits him to keep his distance from the realization of his need for his mother and from all subsequent such relationships in which need would have to be acknowledged. He collapses into drinking early in life, while loudly affirming his independence and his continuing, "I can do it myself" posture. These are the people who become social outcasts: those whose need for emotional closeness is so great, yet who have to go to such extremes to deny it. From a systems theory viewpoint, they are dysfunctional refugees from the family relationship system. Most of the people with drinking problems fall somewhere between the two extremes presented here. A high percentage of adult alcoholism is in people who are married, and who have the same kind of emotional attachment in marraige that they had in their parental families. They are emotionally isolated from their spouses, who play the reciprocal role in the drinking dysfunction.

People marry spouses with equal levels of differentiation of self, although they usually appear to have opposite ways of dealing with stress. They commonly have a combination of the three patterns for dealing with the marital fusion. They have some degree of marital disharmony, some degree of the adaptive spouse being "de-selfed" in the marital fusion, and some degree of projection of the problem to their children. The pattern of one spouse adapting or giving in to the other spouse is the important pattern in drinking problems. The adaptive-spouse pattern is rarely a simple issue. Each spouse sees him- or herself as giving in to the other. It is the one who gives in the most who later becomes "de-selfed," and then becomes vulnerable to development of a drinking problem. The following is a clinical example of one common pattern. The wife was a productive professional woman before marriage. She was also an adaptive person, dedicated to the notion of agreeableness, emotional togetherness, and marital harmony. She voluntarily devoted herself to supporting the career of her husband, who was a striving business man. She prided herself in having the perfect marriage in which she and the husband thought alike on all important issues. She gradually became "de-selfed" by her husband, who gained functional strength at her expense. As he made more and more decisions for the two of them, she gradually became less capable of making decisions. This is the familiar pattern of the dominant spouse overfunctioning, and the adaptive spouse going into an equal degree of dysfunction. It became harder for her to find energy for the home and children. She began taking drinks during the day to help her through the chores, taking the usual precautions to hide the drinking from her husband, and to be ready for the ideal togetherness when he returned from work. Although he was an integral part of the problem, the husband had the usual degree of "blindness" to his wife's increasing dysfunction. He even overlooked the situation when he brought business associates home for dinner and found the wife "passed out" on the living room couch with no dinner prepared. He took the associates out for dinner and never mentioned the incident. The alcoholism was "discovered" later in another incident in which his wife passed out and was hospitalized for a "surgical emergency." There was fairly prompt relief from the drinking symptom during the course of family therapy for the husband and wife together since the therapy sessions reduced the emotional isolation between them. In the recovery process, as she regained more of her functioning self, they went through a period of fairly intense marital conflict. She discovered that their "thinking alike" had been her failure to think for herself.

The following is an example of another common pattern with an opposite manifestation of symptoms. The wife was a "no-self" adaptive person and the husband a super-functioner. He gained in emotional functioning from the wife's dysfunction, which she was able to maintain at a marginal level through an emotional overinvolvement with their children. The husband assumed overfunctioning responsibility for the full range of decisions for the emotional cocoon of the nuclear family. Both spouses were cut off from meaningful emotional contact with their parental families, and both were isolated from each other. As the husband became more and more burdened by his responsibility at work and by his responsibility for the wife and children, he began to increase and to extend his "social" drinking by excessive drinking in the evening and over weekends. There are thousands, and perhaps millions, of such families in which the family system continues to function on a marginal level, in which the husband's regular consumption of alcohol at home is excessive, and in which he is able to manage a reasonable level of functioning at work. Such a family is motivated for professional help when there is a breakdown in adaptive patterns and symptoms erupt. The family in this example was motivated to seek professional help when there was a breakdown in the emotional cocoon of mother and children. A child developed behavior problems, the wife collapsed into dysfunction in relation to the child's problem, and the husband was then motivated to be part of the therapy effort.

FAMILY AND SYSTEMS THERAPY

Alcoholism has always been one of the most difficult of all emotional dysfunctions to modify regardless of the therapeutic method. Family systems therapy offers no magic solution for the total problem, but the theory does provide a different way to conceptualize the problem, and the therapy provides a number of approaches to the problem that are not available with conventional theory and therapy. The therapeutic principles are derived directly from the theory. The following is a brief summary of the way the various principles are applied.

I have found it helpful to think of the degree of impairment in the person who develops drinking problems. The basic strength or level of differentiation of self, rather than the intensity of the alcoholism, is a rather good predictor of the outcome of any effort at therapy. In the *Clinical Patterns* section I mentioned two profiles at each extreme of the spectrum. The closer a person is to the upper end of the spectrum, even though alcohol consumption may be high and consistent, the greater the basic strength and the more likely a favorable clinical result. The closer a person is to the "social outcast" end of the spectrum, even though alcohol consumption is lower, the less likely there will be any change with any therapy effort.

First, attention is given to the overall level of anxiety. Those family members who are most dependent on the drinking person are more overtly anxious than is the one who drinks. This says much about the nature of the problem. The more the family is threatened, the more anxious they get, the more they become critical, the greater the emotional isolation, the more the alcoholic drinks, the higher the anxiety, the greater the criticism and emotional distance, the more the drinking, et cetera, in an emotional escalation that makes the problem worse and both sides more rigidly self-righteous. Anything that can interrupt the spiraling anxiety will be helpful. Any one significant family member who can "cool" the anxious response, or control one's own anxiety, can make a step toward de-escalation. I have had a number of complete "cures" of serious drinking problems in husbands, in which the husbands steadfastly refused to attend sessions and the total time was spent with the wives. In these situations the time was spent in teaching the wives about the way family systems work, and in helping them to control their reciprocal role in the problem. I have seen two families with alcoholism in a parent, in which neither parent would have anything to do with "therapy." In both cases the total time was spent with a motivated oldest daughter, and the outcome was favorable. In one family, it was the father who was alcoholic, and in the other family it was the mother. It is far more usual to have the drinking person attend at least part of the sessions.

Knowledge of the "I'll do it myself" posture as well as of the emotional isolation from the parental family in the past generation and from the spouse in the present generation provides a number of clues to helpful techniques in therapy. The alcoholic person operates on a narrow margin between too much closeness and too much emotional isolation. When he is drinking, he is emotionally isolated. Frequently, it takes only a slight decrease in the emotional isolation to stop the drinking and get the therapy on a more constructive level. Frequently it is possible to "coach" the family to re-establish more meaningful emotional contact with a parental family. The immediate results can be striking in situations in which the relationships with parents can improve only slightly.

There is one basic principle that applies in any family in which one significant family member is in a marked overfunctioning position, and the other in a marked dysfunctioning position: It is far easier to help the overfunctioning person to tone down the overfunctioning than it is to help the dysfunctional one to increase the functioning. In any situation in which there is an either-or choice on where to put the focus in therapy sessions, it is with the overfunctioning family member. There are numerous reasons for this, which are too detailed for this presentation.

Finally, there are the situations in which one spouse is an alcoholic and both spouses are willing and eager to attend the sessions. In general, these are the families that do best. Most of the time can be devoted to defining the emotional interdependence from the beginning. Results are less favorable when one spouse is reluctant to attend. In these families, I now tend to look for one member who is motivated to work on the total problem alone, until both are willing to be involved together. Family therapy with two spouses is one of the high roads to successful family therapy.

SUMMARY

Family systems theory provides a different framework for conceptualizing alcoholism, and family systems therapy provides a spectrum of effective ways for modification of the family relationship patterns.

REFERENCES

1. Bowen, M. 1966. The use of family theory in clinical practice. Compr. Psychiat. **7**: 345.
2. Bowen, M. 1971. Family therapy and family group therapy. *In* Comprehensive Group Psychotherapy. H. Kaplan & B. Sadock, Eds. Williams & Wilkins. Baltimore, Md.

Divorce Therapy: An In-Depth Survey of Therapists' Views

Kenneth Kressel
Morton Deutsch

In-depth interviews were conducted with 21 highly experienced therapists on the criteria of a constructive divorce, the obstacles to achieving such a divorce, and the strategies and tactics of divorce therapy. The primary criterion of a constructive divorce was the successful completion of the process of psychic separation and the protection of the welfare of minor children. Therapy may focus on the decision to get divorced and/or the negotiation of the terms of a divorce settlement.

Three types of therapeutic strategies were identified: reflexive interventions by which the therapist orients himself to the marital problems and attempts to gain the trust and confidence of the partners; contextual interventions by which he tries to promote a climate conducive to decision-making; and substantive interventions intended to produce resolution on terms the therapist has come to believe are inevitable or necessary.

The nascent state of divorce therapy as an area of therapeutic specialization is noted. The problem of diagnostic criteria for divorce, the relationship between therapists and lawyers, the nature and consequence of therapist impartiality, and the degree to which therapists should mediate the terms of divorce are considered central issues meriting further study.

The rapid rise in the incidence of marital dissolution is well documented. In 1975 there were more than one million divorces in the United States, double the number that occurred a scant ten years earlier (10). It has been conservatively estimated that if the divorce rate continues at the levels that were obtained in 1965 or 1971 (to pick two recent years of high growth), between thirty and forty per cent of all marriages now being formed will end in divorce. If the divorce rate exceeds these previous levels, a marriage may be more likely to end in divorce than not (14, pp. 11-12). Approximately nine million minor children (or one in seven) have experienced at least one parental divorce (1, p.462).

That divorce can be a wrenching, bitter, and even devastating experience for parents and their children needs no documentation. In spite of the magnitude and seriousness of the phenomenon, however, relatively little systematic research has been conducted on the process of divorce and its consequences.[1]

Research on the role of the psychotherapist in divorce is the most underrepresented area of all. It is clear that psychotherapeutic assistance to divorcing couples occurs, and, that along with the rate of marital dissolution, it is increasing. How frequent the assistance is and what it consists of, however, are virtually undocumented. The only data of which we are aware are those reported by Goode, more than twenty-five years ago, who found that of his 425 divorced female respondents only 14 per cent had had any contact with an individual they considered a marriage counselor (6, p.155). Clinical accounts of divorce therapy are only now beginning to appear (3, 5). Systematic investigations are, to our knowledge, non-existent.

The present investigation reports the views of an expert group of therapists on the divorcing process and the nature of therapeutic assistance to those divorcing. It is part of a larger project on the role of third-party assistance in divorce. Papers on the role of lawyers and clergy are currently in preparation.

We began with a straightforward query: Given that two people have agreed to end their marriage (even if only one of them really wants to), what can be done to ensure that they will do so in a constructive and cooperative manner, rather than destructively with lingering hostility? That is to say, our focus was on the process set in motion when a marriage is being terminated, rather than on the causes of the divorce or efforts to prevent its occurrence. We wished, in particular, to answer three major questions:

1. What are the criteria that distinguish a "constructive" divorce from a "destructive" one?

2. What obstacles in the marriage, in the milieu surrounding the marriage, or in the spouses themselves, stand in the way of achieving a constructive divorce and make difficult the task of a therapist wishing to help produce such an outcome?

3. What strategies and tactics of therapeutic intervention are most useful and how can they be classified?

---

[1]Much of the literature on divorce that does exist takes the form of popularly written advice by lawyers, therapists, and the previously divorced to those currently divorcing. It varies widely in quality. Of the empirical investigations, demographic-descriptive studies are the most numerous and reliable (9, 10). On the divorcing process itself, the classic sociological study is Goode's *Women in Divorce* (6), a survey of 425 Detroit-area divorced women done in the late 1940's. More recently, Weiss (14), in a clinical-impressionistic account, has reported on the process of marital dissolution in middle-class couples. Only two first-rate studies, nearly thirty years apart, seems a small number in proportion to the magnitude of the phenomenon.

The effect of parental divorce on minor children has been reported on more frequently, but again the literature appears uneven and, in terms of well-conducted studies, scant. More empirical work on this long neglected topic has begun to appear, of which that of Wallerstein and Kelly (13) is perhaps the best example. For a bibliographic introduction to the literature on divorce, see Brown (3); Israel (7); Kessler (8); the National Council for Family Relations Task Force on Divorce and Divorce Reform (12); and Weiss (14). No systematic, critical review of the literature exists. One is clearly needed.

METHOD

The investigation took the form of a series of in-depth, semi-structured interviews. An effort to locate highly expert practitioners was made through professional organizations, personal contacts, and the referral of one respondent by another. The interviews lasted nearly two hours. They were tape recorded for later transcription.

The interview was in two parts. The first involved a general discussion of the topics enumerated above. In the second, respondents were asked to discuss in detail (but without revealing information that would permit identification of the clients) a case in which they felt they had been particularly successful.[2]

The average age of the respondents was 53 years; they practiced mainly in and around New York and Boston. Most characterized themselves as specialists in marital and/or family therapy, and all had more than five years' experience in which divorce work was at least part of their practice. On the average, approximately 20 per cent of their professional time is spent specifically on divorce cases. They serve a predominantly middle-class, college-educated clientele with a median income of $30,000, and an average length of marriage of twelve to fifteen years. Approximately 50 per cent of the divorcing couples with whom they work are Jewish, 30 per cent Protestant, and 20 per cent Catholic. Fifty per cent of the couples have dependent children.

The respondents' views are presented under three major headings: criteria of a constructive divorce; obstacles to a constructive divorce; and strategies and tactics of intervention. It may be useful to begin, however, with a discussion of the practical and psychological context in which divorce therapy typically occurs.

THE CONTEXT OF INTERVENTION

Practical aspects

Several important practical characteristics of divorce therapy may be noted. First, well-defined training programs for specializing in divorce work do not exist. Recruitment to the field can occur by numerous routes, of which training in individual or marital therapy, child psychiatry, and counseling are among the more common. One does not as yet, however, set out to be a divorce counselor.

Second, therapeutic help in divorce is largely arranged privately. Apart from the opportunities for litigation, there are no highly visible, well-structured public agencies or procedures for the resolution of conflicts arising out of the termination of the marriage contract. Family or Conciliation Courts established by various states have come the closest to playing such a role. However, they have generally sought to reconcile marriages rather than to provide assistance for those wishing to end them (3).

Reflecting perhaps the absence of institutionalized support, as well as the idiosyncratic nature of divorce itself, the external details of therapist involve-

[2]A copy of the interview schedule may be obtained by writing: Divorce Project, Social Psychology Laboratory, Teachers College, Columbia University, New York, New York 10027.

ment are likely to be extremely varied. Table 1 summarizes the respondents' characterization of the specific case discussed during the interview. While these cases are not necessarily representative, they do convey something of the flavor of therapeutic practice.

TABLE 1. Respondents' Characterization of the Divorce Case Discussed during Interview

	Number of Respondents[1]
Initiator of First Contact	
Husband or wife equally likely to initiate	3
Wives more likely to initiate	10
Husband more likely to initiate	0
Duration of Contact	
3 months to 1 year	5
1½ years to 2½ years	6
4 years to 9 years	5
Hours of Contact (per month)	
3 or less	3
Approximately 4	5
More than 6	6
Identity of Client(s)	
Both spouses from start to finish	8
Both initially, then only one	3
One initially, then both	4
Only one and children	1
Types of Contacts during Case[2]	
Client(s) only	1
Clients and:	
Children	10
Relatives	7
Friends (or other nonrelatives)	6
Other professionals (lawyers, therapists, etc.)	9

[1]Completed or nearly completed questionnaires were available for 16 of the 21 respondents.
[2]The total is more than 16 because most respondents had contact with more than one type of "Other."

The modal case was relatively long (median of two years), involved sessions of approximately one hour per week, included both spouses, and, at one time or another, some form of contact with a variety of other individuals (most often children and lawyers or other therapists). There were, however, numerous variations on this modal theme. Thus, therapist contact with a case varied from three months to nine years; sessions occurred less than once a week or more than twice a week; in half the cases only one spouse was involved for at least part of the therapy (and this was equally likely to precede as to follow the use of joint sessions); virtually any permutation or combination of joint or separate meetings, couples' groups, and sessions with extended family was possible; therapist involvement began at any point from marital stress through post-divorce readjustment and ended at any time along this continuum.

Finally, there was no commonly used term to describe what it is that our respondents do for those in the process of divorce. Although several respondents used the term divorce therapy (or divorce counseling), this rubric was not always accepted. On several occasions it was criticized as too narrow to describe what was considered to be either a general practice in marital therapy or a concern with individual growth through any therapeutic channels that seem indicated. For convenience, the term divorce therapy will be used in this report.

The process of psychic divorce

Talking about divorce, I think, really misses the point. Because you're not talking about divorce, we're talking about needs—needs not to be alone, and needs to be related; needs to be attached and needs to avoid anxiety.[3]

The work of the divorce therapist occurs in an often treacherous psychological climate, a climate that owes many of its most distinctive characteristics to the phenomenon of psychic divorce.

Numerous terms were used to allude to psychic divorce: "decourting," "individuation," "differentiation of self," "emotional divorce." Whatever nuances of meaning may differentiate these phrases, all rest on a distinction between what may be called "parallel" versus "passionate" marriages. Parallel marriages are those in which the partners have not had any intense psychological involvement with each other. Most often these are relatively brief marriages involving young people who have no children. They may have been marriages of "convenience" (e.g., a means of escaping the parental home) or may reflect an underlying problem in both mates in forming intimate attachments. In any case, as divorces they produce relatively few fireworks and are accomplished with relative ease.

Passionate marriages are another matter entirely. The vast majority of couples seeking divorce therapy have had marriages of the passionate type. Generally, these are marriages of relatively long duration out of which children have been born and in which there has been an intense, deeply emotional attachment between the partners. In the view of the respondents, the rupture of such attachments, although it may be desirable, and even wished for, can only be accomplished with pain and difficulty. As one respondent noted, "In our culture most people marry for romantic-passion reasons, and the divorces are passionate affairs as well."[4] Psychic divorce is the term that describes the more or less predictable course this "passion" takes.

[3]Quoted comments have generally been chosen as those best summarizing the views of the respondents as a group. The identity of the speakers has been omitted to focus attention on substantive matters and to emphasize our desire to sketch the range of therapeutic views rather than the profile of individual therapists.

[4]As divorces, the most problematic of the passionate marriages are those that owe their intensity to a deeply neurotic component in the original marital attraction, specifically to an unrecognized expectation in one or both partners that the marriage would heal a deep childhood wound.

When a person has looked to marriage to supply and make up for early infantile deprivations—where they really see the spouse as a substitute parent, I think those are very often unrealistic and unsuccessful marriages. Unless people grow in the process of ending the marriage, it leads to very acrimonious divorces with feelings of once again being done in by an ungiving parent.

The concept of psychic divorce, while it is a fundamental one, was rarely articulated in all its complexity by any one respondent. We have, therefore, constructed a composite account of the process. While it is unlikely that this composite would be assented to in every detail by each of the respondents, it will serve to convey the dimensions of the phenomenon and the challenge it poses to the work of the divorce therapist.

The process of psychic divorce has these general characteristics:

1. Within broad limits it is unavoidable and unmodifiable (although self-awareness and/or professional intervention can mitigate its more extreme manifestations).

2. The feelings that mark the process are in addition to, although they may not be easily distinguishable from, whatever other feelings may also be occurring. From the perspective of the emotions, the process of psychic divorce adds insult to what may or may not already be emotional injury (e.g., the sense of hurt at being rejected for another).

3. Throughout the process, decision-making and rational planning are impaired, at certain points markedly so.

4. The process occurs in discriminable stages. These stages embody powerful swings in mood and in quality of marital relating. On balance, the more painful moods and types of relating predominate.

5. Although for marriages of the passionate type the process of psychic divorce is inevitable, the successful completion of the process is not. Thus, legal divorce may, and frequently does, occur in the absence of psychic divorce. The worst examples of post-divorce legal battles, bitterness, and general mayhem may be most often ascribed to a failure of psychic divorce.

Stages of psychic divorce

The stages of psychic divorce include the predivorce decision period; the decision period proper; the period of mourning; and the period of re-equilibration.

The pre-divorce decision period. Strictly speaking, this is not part of the process of psychic divorce. It is, however, the preliminary skirmish, from which the parties may emerge onto the field of divorce already badly shaken.

1. A stage of increasing marital dissatisfaction and tension on the part of both spouses but often felt more acutely by one than the other.

2. Attempts at reconciliation. These may include frantic efforts to recapture a sense of mutual caring and the seeking of advice from friends or relatives. Psychotherapeutic help may be sought here or at any subsequent stage.

3. A clear decline in marital intimacy. One or both spouses may take a lover as psychological "insurance" for the impending separation.

4. A break in the facade of marital solidarity. It is now public knowledge that the marriage is in serious trouble; there is open fighting. Lawyers may be contacted. Physical separation may occur at this or at any subsequent stage, or it may never occur (even, in extreme cases, after the divorce!).

Stages 1 through 4 may last for weeks, months, or years. In some cases the process neither moves to the next stage nor attains resolution in the form of a return to marital harmony.

The decision period.

5. The decision to divorce is firmly made by at least 1 partner; a sense of relief, perhaps exhilaration: a difficult, but liberating, step has been taken.

6. Anxiety and panic at the prospect of separation. "Can I survive alone?"

7. A stage of renewed marital intimacy. In reality, a mutually dependent clinging and unwillingness to face that underlying rupture because of separation anxiety.

8. Renewed outbreaks of marital fighting revealing the true nature of the immediately preceding stages.

Stages 7 and 8 may be repeated several times. The entire decision-to-divorce stage may also be marked by what one respondent labeled the "marital flip-flop," as the partners take turns alternately pushing for and opposing the divorce.

9. Final acceptance of the inevitability of divorce. Renewed anger, now expressed in conflict over the terms of settlement. ("I promised you that I was going to give you half the money in the bank; well, I changed my mind.")

The period of mourning.   This is a complex and critical period. It is during this period that the terms of settlement may be agreed upon.

10. Feelings of guilt and self-reproach for having caused the breakup. An acute sense of failure and diminished self-worth; loneliness and depression are typical. Several respondents noted that mourning a spouse lost through divorce is in some respects more difficult than mourning a dead spouse, since the partner in divorce is alive and there may be a strong temptation to reestablish ties.

11. Anger at the spouse. This signals a return to equilibrium and an upswing in self-regard.

12. Acceptance of the positive as well as the negative side of the marriage. Realistic sadness.

Period of reequilibration.   This is a period of heightened self-growth and diminished dwelling on the marriage. If the mourning process has been successfully completed, this stage will increasingly take on the characteristics discussed below under Criteria of a Constructive Divorce.

In short, through much of the process of psychic divorce, both partners are viewed as being buffeted by strong emotional forces over which they have little control; their behavior, whether loving or hostile, may belie their actual feelings and is, in any case, an uncertain guide to their deepest intentions. The partners are unpredictable, and their ability to plan constructively for their own needs and those of their children is reduced.

It is perhaps because of the vagaries of psychic divorce that every once in a while there surfaces in the respondents' remarks a certain bemusement about their chosen work.

> They came to me for what seemed to be a marital problem, and about the third or fourth session I learned that they were divorced. As a matter of fact, they didn't go on a honeymoon when they got married; they went on a sort of honeymoon when they got divorced. They celebrated by going away together. See, people do strange things—and how the therapist is supposed to follow and understand all those strange things, I don't know.

CRITERIA OF A CONSTRUCTIVE DIVORCE

What distinguishes a successful divorce from an unsuccessful one? If therapeutic assistance in terminating a marriage is sought, what should it accomplish? In the broadest sense, a constructive divorce is one in which the process of psychic divorce has been successfully completed. There was consensus that psychic divorce has occurred when certain conditions prevail with regard to the attitudes and behavior of the former spouses toward one another, the welfare of children, and the level of functioning of each of the ex-mates as a newly single person.

The attitudes and behavior of the former spouses toward one another

A good divorce, like a good marriage, is a mutual enterprise. Both partners must wish to end their relationship just as they once wished to start it.

> One member may be sadder than the other about the disruption of the marriage or feel more distressed, but I think a constructive divorce is when both people realize it is the best solution for the two of them—not necessarily the most wanted solution, but the best solution—the only possible solution.

> Where one member of the divorcing couple still feels that it could have worked or that, "if only,"—some other kind of magic could have kept it going—I think there's bound to be bitterness.

Mutual acceptance of the need to divorce should find concrete expression in active negotiation over the terms of settlement, particularly in cases involving dependent children and the division of accrued material assets. Such negotiation should be undertaken both with a healthy sense of one's own needs and in a spirit of equity and fair play. Failure of one or both partners to take an active negotiating stance suggests psychological nonacceptance of the divorce or guilt about it. The consequences of such passivity are that realistic needs are not met and the post-divorce readjustment is made more difficult. Active participation of both partners also acts to promote a sense of "ownership" of the settlement, thereby increasing the likelihood that whatever agreements are reached will be honored.

It is important and interesting to note, however, that the respondents as a group were relatively indifferent to assisting in negotiations over practical matters. (Only two, for example, mentioned an equitable financial settlement as an important criteria of a constructive divorce.) The paucity of interest about the practical side of divorce reflects, in part, the belief of many of the respondents that difficulties in arranging practical issues are only symptoms of more profound—and "real"—conflicts.

> I think that the issues are emotional and that they get played out in terms of money; they get played out in terms of visitation; they get played out in terms of a lot of things. In a good divorce, those things just don't come up as issues.

We shall return to this important matter in our consideration of strategies of intervention.

The successful divorce should also leave each partner with a balanced view of the other and of the marriage and with a sense of psychological closure.

> The good outcome to me is one in which the individual, without either self-blame or blaming the other, has been able to look at the marriage and retrospec-

tively say, "Here were the good things, which were nice, and they are part of me; here are the things that went wrong, for these and these reasons . . ."

In the post-divorce period it is desirable that the former partners be able to work together cooperatively when the situation requires it—whatever their feelings toward each other may be. The need for such cooperation is greatest for couples with minor children.

> It's worked out in such a way that he will not welch on payments, and they conduct themselves very civilly. She doesn't like him; she says he's a real bastard, but they do meet occasionally to discuss business matters and things regarding the children, and they're very civil about it.

While post-divorce civility is an asset, few respondents were in favor of continued post-divorce involvements between ex-spouses beyond those necessitated by coparenting. Seemingly pleasurable post-divorce interactions were seen as suggesting an unconscious wish to "hang on" to the marriage.

> There are many couples who are divorced and still maintain all kinds of contacts—even without children—of telephone calls or of problems with alimony or in terms of friends, of sharing friends, of keeping them involved in the process. So that there are divorces that are not divorces; and I think those are the most destructive.

A minority viewpoint, expressed by two therapists, was that friendship between ex-mates was desirable when it could be achieved. Said one:

> Sometimes they can become friends for the first time in their lives. It's a strange thing; I mean, I've heard people say, "You know, we have never been so open with each other . . ." because, what more is there to lose; and they can sometimes say truths to each other they haven't said before. It may simply be that there is a kind of recognition: "We really aren't going to make it with each other. You're going one way and I'm going another. But that doesn't mean I have to hate you for it or you have to hate me for it. We can hold each other's hands."

One unambiguous sign that psychological divorce has not occurred is continued court battles.

> They get divorced legally, but the fight continues. I think that's really where I came into divorce counseling—when after the legal divorce, the emotional divorce doesn't truly occur, and the anger is so great that they proceed to use each other. They fornicate in court instead of fornicating in bed. . . . So often they get the satisfaction of battle—they get their orgasms by going to court.[5]

The children

> Kids are always hurt when their parents break up; there's no such thing as, "better have a divorce for the sake of the children." No, the kids are always hurt. We try to hurt them as little as possible.

Whether or not each of our respondents would agree that children are *always* hurt in a divorce, this comment captures the prevailing view of the

---

[5]Although legal divorce was generally viewed as secondary to attaining psychic divorce, marital attachments being as intense as they often are, obtaining a divorce may represent a considerable achievement. One respondent cited the case of a man who threatened to kill his wife at her mere mention of the word "divorce." The respondent congratulated himself on helping the couple achieve a divorce without anybody—including the therapist—getting killed.

sample that children of divorce, particularly very young children, are at considerable psychic risk. The idea of children's vulnerability rests on two major
notions: (a) For optimal psychological growth, children need two parents, one
of each sex, (b) Because they are cognitively and emotionally immature, and
perhaps also, for biological reasons (2), children are poorly equipped to handle
any significant estrangement in their relations with parents. For the child
under the age of six or seven such an event signals, in fact, a major life trauma.

The risks to children are heightened by the temporary but often considerable impairment in the care-taking ability of the parents, who are undergoing
one of the great stressful periods of their own lives.

> Even people who are absolutely determined that they're not going to use their
> kids will do so in some form. For example, the father picks them up on Sunday.
> He's run out of places to take the kids. You know, after a while he does. And then
> the kids are crying, if they're little: they don't have their toys with them, and they
> don't have their playmates. And he's kind of uncomfortable with them at times.
> And then he takes the kids home, and the mother says to the kids: "What'd your
> father give you today? Another hamburger? Another hot dog? He didn't give you a
> full course meal? Who's he dating now?" Even people who are determined not to
> do it are going to do it in some form. Then the kids become message carriers. Even
> if the parents don't use the words, the kids can pick up the feelings.

More devastating to children can be the emotional and legal guerilla warfare
between the parents in which the children become primary weapons. It is
psychologically easier and publicly more acceptable to give vent to feelings of
anger, humiliation, and diminished self-worth by attacking the spouse in one's
parental role, than in the unflattering capacity of rejected husband or wife.

> The fighting goes on for years, after the real part is over; the wife brings the
> husband to court again for additional alimony, for additional child support, and
> eventually even to start some sort of counter-action . . . and the kids pay a terrible
> price for that. That is the main criterion for a bad outcome. The adults get bruised
> in the process. I think they can usually handle it. But the kids are pretty helpless
> and if they get destroyed, I think that's really the worst sort of outcome that
> can happen.

The constructive divorce then, is one in which psychic injury to children is
minimized, principally through the maintenance of a good coparenting relationship between the former spouses. In particular, children should be free of
the apprehension that loving either parent will jeopardize their place in the
affections of the other.

> These kids should feel that they can love one without having to feel antagonism
> to the other, that it's not an act of disloyalty to love both; and those kids should feel
> that in an emergency they've still got a mother and father and they can count
> on them.

The children's relationship with the noncustodial parent was mentioned by
several respondents as having special importance. One therapist, for example,
felt that the success of her assistance consisted, in part, in the working out of
post-divorce living arrangements that took into account the children's need for
both parents.

> One issue was who was going to move; that was a major issue. The other was
> what was going to happen to kids and how that was going to happen. It was dealt
> with by deciding that the kids went with her, to her apartment, but they would be

close enough to walk over and visit their father whenever they chose to. And they spent a lot of time with him. And she feels free to let them do that and not interfere with the relationship. I mean, that's a very big thing with me. I work very hard at working this through for the children, exacting that they should be allowed to have a separate relationship with each parent.

A constructive divorce is also one in which children have mastered the painful experience they have been through, and, if possible, grown in the process. Absence of the fantasy that they were the cause of the divorce was seen as evidence that the worst of the children's difficulties have been resolved.

> I believe that every person who has divorced parents has the secret fantasy that he's going to bring them together again. Even when they're grown up. Analysts of older adults frequently hear the fantasy, "I can bring my mother and father together, who were divorced thirty years ago." I even knew one person who made sure that his divorced parents were buried together.

The self

The minimal criterion for a constructive divorce is the absence of strong, unrelenting feelings of failure and self-disparagement. The truly successful divorce, in addition, entails increased self-understanding, the ability to form satisfying new intimate relationships, and a heightened sense of personal competence. In a word, "growth." This was the single most reiterated theme in the interviews.

Most often, an increase in self-knowledge referred to what one respondent termed a "victory over a neurotic choice of a mate." The primary purpose of such a victory was to avoid a subsequent identical marital choice—the "same-mistake-twice" (or thrice) syndrome. (Although the ability to form new intimate relationships was considered important, few respondents went so far as to suggest that the *sine qua non* of healthy post-divorce adjustment was remarriage.)

> You can't really tell whether the divorce, or the therapy associated with it, was successful until you've seen what kind of relationship the divorced person forms. If they get themselves into the exact kind of neurotic binds, then the divorce hasn't solved anything. But if they are able to form healthy relationships, it has.

The specific components of self-understanding that innoculate against the same-mistake-twice syndrome are insight into one's unconscious conflicts and distortions and an appreciation of one's contribution to the dysfunctional behavior patterns in the old marriage. It is an important therapeutic strategy to elucidate these matters over the course of treatment (see Contextual Interventions below). A one-sided view of the marital breakdown was taken as *prima facie* evidence that something far short of an optimal divorce had been achieved.

> Another kind of destructive divorce is when there is so much animosity between two people that both of them cling to the view of the other as the evil one; and there really is no recognition that each has played a part in—has made a contribution to—the situation.

Increased feelings of personal competence may be a direct result of terminating a psychologically abusive marriage.

The man was very dependent on his wife—she had an income from stocks and bonds—and unquestionably this was one of her attractions for him. But she had little respect for him, tended to side with his children against him, and was mildly paranoid. He was really selling his soul to the devil for money, and his extracting himself was a healthy sign.

In other cases, the growth in self-mastery comes from an active process of coping with the demands of the divorcing process or the postdivorce period.

He was one of the people with whom I've worked who found lawyers at the University who were concerned with the rights of children; he became knowledgeable in finding these people for himself. This was a man who in many other areas of life was a very competent man, but in terms of his personal life there'd been a lot of dependence and helplessness. So that being able to do some of this was part of his growth—to fight for the custody of his children, to face that.

OBSTACLES TO A CONSTRUCTIVE DIVORCE

The major obstacle to a constructive divorce is, as we have noted, the turmoil of psychic divorce. That is not the only obstacle that may exist, however. Additional complications may arise because of certain characteristics of the marital relationship and from the involvement of third parties, particularly the involvement of lawyers.

Characteristics of the marriage

The single most frequently cited predictor of a difficult divorce was one spouse's eagerness to end the marriage coupled with reluctance to do so on the part of the other. The interviews leave the impression that in the clinical practice of the respondents such cases are very common.

Typically, unequal motivation to divorce was linked not only to a changing balance of affection but to a realistic imbalance in postdivorce prospects. A divorced man of thirty-eight or forty, for example, may be just reaching the peak of his professional and financial attainments. Such a man may have reason to believe that, in the event of divorce, his social and sexual horizons can, with some minor time-out for readjustment, be easily and gratifyingly extended. Not so for his homemaker wife with custody of their two minor children. She may have cause to suspect that her postdivorce social and financial situation will be far less easy to arrange and far less satisfying. When, in addition to differing levels in postdivorce "marketability," the less marketable spouse has been rejected for a new lover, the barriers to a constructive divorce can be formidable.[6]

---

[6]Most often the husband was pictured as the spouse wishing to end the marriage because of a new lover, although the rising rate of women who have found new partners was noted by several therapists. A wife's desire to end a marriage, however, was more often linked not to a new man, but to a new consciousness—the wish for a career and/or a greater degree of autonomy and fulfillment than that provided by a traditional marriage.

Low marketability was viewed primarily as a problem for women, most acutely so for the older woman who has been a traditional homemaker and the younger woman with custody of minor children.

Reluctance to divorce on the part of husbands was viewed more as a function of psychological overdependence on their wives and the painful prospect of diminished contact with their children, than of a poor postdivorce social or financial outlook.

The precise effects of an unequal desire to divorce may be difficult to predict, but certain reoccurring patterns were noted.

Frequently, the partner who wishes to end the marriage feels guilt at abandoning the spouse. A frank discussion of the desire for divorce is therefore made more difficult. A series of escalating but misplaced marital conflicts may then occur. Several respondents also noted that much of what is ostensibly conjoint therapy designed to save a marriage is actually a covert form of divorce therapy, resulting from the deserting spouse's desire to assuage his guilt ("I tried my best to save it") and, perhaps unconsciously, to provide the mate with a "lover" in the person of the therapist.

Once the initiator finally broaches the topic of divorce, continued guilt, combined with the equally strong desire to leave, may produce a virulent form of the "settlement at any cost" mentality. At the same time, the settlement terms demanded by the spouse who wishes to keep the marriage may escalate. Such escalating, and often unreasonable demands, may be motivated by feelings of humiliation combined with anxiety at the prospects of a bleak and unchosen future. They may also be a means to prolong the marriage and ultimately prevent the marital breakup.

An opposite pattern was also noted: Guilt in one spouse at leaving the marriage may be expressed as anger directed at the other. In the reluctant partner, diminished feelings of self-worth may inhibit the ability to bargain constructively and effectively, or worse, produce an abject acceptance of almost any terms dictated by the other. Under such circumstances, a settlement may be quickly arrived at. Its inequitable and ultimately unworkable nature, however, may not become apparent until several years and several court fights later.

Chances for a constructive divorce are also much reduced for couples in which one or both partners have a heavy investment in casting blame or in bringing up long past grievances; for "Virginia Woolf" couples who experience gratification in wounding one another and are thus committed to a pathological fighting process; and for couples in which one partner plays a dominating, aggressive role in marital disputes, while the other adopts a passive, submissive stance.

There was also wide consensus that for divorcing couples with minor children the potential for a destructive divorce is greatly increased. First, there must be planning for the children's welfare—their immediate needs as well as those ten or fifteen years in the future. Such planning is complex and difficult even under the best of circumstances. The emotional circumstances during a divorce are not, of course, the best. For many parents there are also extensive feelings of guilt at the damage they feel the divorce will do to the children's emotional development. Guilt may result in defensive anger at the mate, or uncritical acceptance of any childcare proposals, however ill-conceived. As has been noted, children also provide a psychologically inviting opportunity for both spouses to embellish their feelings of anger and bitterness toward one another in a socially acceptable manner. It may be difficult to de-escalate a conflict of this kind since its true roots are unacknowledged.

The effect of wealth or its absence on the divorcing process was one aspect of the marriage on which there was no consensus. Two positions were articulated: One view was that either poverty or wealth can produce complications.

If there is very little money the partners may have great difficulty in negotiating a settlement because the small economic pie makes it difficult to arrange trade-offs and the clear reduction in circumstances that looms ahead produces anxiety and a corresponding increase in self-protectiveness. If there is much money, the high financial stakes may ruin the climate in which negotiations take place.

> In one couple I treated, the guy was a millionaire; he was following his wife while they were separated and having infrared pictures taken of her with men, so the flash wouldn't come out. This is the kind of thing I was trying to avoid, but he said to me, "Look, Buster, there's a half a million dollars at stake, if I don't protect myself with this information."

Large sums of money may also provide increased opportunities for the expression of revenge-seeking and the desire to punish.

The second view was that in and of itself money has no predictable effect on the divorcing process. When money does become an issue, it is because "something deeper" is involved.

> I think money is very often used in our society and in marriages as a way of expressing needs, controls, expectations, wishes—and it continues in the divorce process. And it sometimes is used as a way of punishing or exacting payment for pain. I think where people have had no conflicts around money prior to the divorce . . . the kinds of quarrels that go on around money have nothing to do with the realities of money and how much there is to be shared or distributed. It has to do with the feelings people have about money.

Third-party involvement

The ability of relatives and friends to hinder the divorcing process was a minor theme in the interviews. Several respondents discussed situations in which outside parties made things worse—the boyfriend who eggs on the unhappy wife, the mother who fuels her daughter's resentment against a husband—and there were some who felt that relatives or friends, however well meaning, could rarely be objective. There was also agreement that of all outside parties, the client's own parents loomed largest as complicating factors in the divorce. However, it was not the actual meddlesomeness of parents that was the cause of difficulty but the internalized anticipations of how the parents would react to the divorce.

The place of preeminence as enemy of a constructive divorce was reserved, in the respondents' view, for the divorce lawyer. Although the respondents' attitudes toward the lawyer's role in divorce can best be described as ambivalent—positive relationships between therapists and lawyers do develop—the great majority of the therapists expressed a wary, critical view of the legal profession.

Three major criticisms of lawyers reappeared continually: (a) Under the present legal system lawyers are part of an adversary process and thus under a professional obligation to defend their clients' interests and attack those of the spouse. From the therapists' perspective as agents of a constructive divorce, this is the least desirable posture imaginable; (b) Lawyers are untrained in psychology, and in family and marital dynamics in particular. Consequently, they may easily become unwitting pawns in the escalation of marital conflict;

(c) The lawyer's objectivity may be compromised by financial considerations, since his fee is contingent on the amount of time and energy required to produce a final settlement.

Two of the respondents also mentioned cases in which they had been subpoenaed by one spouse's lawyer to testify against the other spouse. Such legal action not only violates in a direct manner the therapist's jealously guarded impartiality but also raises the unresolved and highly problematic issue of confidentiality between therapist and client in divorce counseling.

> I once got caught in my early years in a custody case. That was, first of all, a lousy position to be in, and, second, it seems to me that, really, nobody knows very clearly what the role of the therapist should be in relation to two people as opposed to one person. There's confidentiality, and that's pretty clear when you're talking with one person, but when you're talking with two people, what is the confidentiality? And particularly if you're in a situation where people are separating, you begin to get mixed up. What was said when you were alone with them, and together with them?

To what degree are the obstacles to divorce perceived by our respondents in their clinical practices characteristic of the over one million divorces that occurred in the United States in 1975? In particular, is the process of psychic divorce inevitable, or is it an extreme, pathological reaction of the few who seek psychotherapy when divorce impends? In the absence of any epidemiological studies of divorce (akin, say, to *Mental Health in the Metropolis* for individual psychopathology), it is not possible to answer these questions. Nor, by the same token, can we say how frequently the criteria of a constructive divorce are met by the divorcing population at large. Research on the effects and effectiveness of divorce therapy—no such studies have yet been done—would benefit immeasurably from such information, as, indeed, would any efforts to modify social and legal policy on divorce. The respondents' views on the goals of, and obstacles to, constructive divorce provide, however, an important backdrop against which to understand the strategies and tactics of the intervention they employ.

STRATEGIES AND TACTICS

Divorce therapy, as reflected in these interviews, has two distinct foci: helping clients decide whether or not to divorce and assisting in the negotiation of a final divorce (or separation) agreement. The tactics by which these two goals are pursued are extremely varied, but all of them may be subsumed under the heading of either *reflexive, contextual,* or *substantive* strategies.

Reflexive strategies are those behaviors by which the therapist attempts to orient himself to the marital conflict and to establish the groundwork upon which his later activities will be built. As the term implies, reflexive strategies are designed primarily to affect the therapist rather than the parties: to make the therapist the most effective instrument of intervention possible under the circumstances.

Contextual and substantive strategies, on the other hand, are aimed specifically at the conflict and the parties to it. In a concrete sense they are what the divorce therapist "does" to help resolve a marital impasse.

Contextual interventions refer to attempts by the therapist to affect the climate surrounding the dispute and, in particular, the foci and ground rules of interaction. The purpose is to create conditions that will allow the couple to do their own decision-making and negotiating. If one thinks of the therapist as an instrument for assisting at the "birth" of a settlement, then one might describe contextual strategies as a "mid-wifery" kind of divorce therapy.

In contrast, *substantive* interventions refer to strategies by which the therapist takes an active and direct hand in promoting specific agreements on matters of substance or attempts to pressure or manipulate the parties directly into resolving their differences on substantive issues. Substantive interventions imply that the therapist has a point of view about the conflict and what should be done to resolve it. Pursuing the obstetric analogy, one might think of substantive interventions as the "Caesarean" approach to divorce therapy.

It is important to note that the distinction among these three strategies hinges on the therapist's purpose in making a given intervention, rather than the extent to which he gives advice or directly manipulates the clients to behave in a particular way. A therapist may be quite "substantive" in the sense of telling the client what to do—to consult a lawyer, for example—but the intervention would be classified as contextual if the therapist's purpose was to reduce the level of emotional tension (by referral to the "right" kind of lawyer), rather than to convince a reluctant client that divorce is necessary and inevitable.

Reflexive interventions [7]

1. Building trust and confidence. A pervasive theme in the therapists' conceptualization of their role was the importance of developing in the clients a sense of trust and confidence. A concern with this issue continues throughout therapy but is likely to be central to the therapist's behavior in the initial stages when therapist and clients are new to each other. In a sense, this is the most subtle of therapist strategies, conveyed as much by the therapist's tone and general bearing as by his concrete actions. Among the specific tactics by which a sense of trust and confidence may be fostered are included explicit statements of reassurance and support, the judicious use of self-disclosure, and the maintenance of confidentiality. While there was a general distaste for becoming the repository of marital secrets, respondents accept and even encourage confidences but at the same time attempt to provide constraints and rules for "secret"-telling.

> I tend to see them alone for two sessions and then bring them back together. When I'm seeing them alone I make it very explicit that they are free to tell me things they want kept confidential, and I will respect that. The advantage is to get them to open up and begin to look at themselves, because if they're constantly worried that their spouse is going to learn this, then they aren't going to open up. I make two explicit exceptions. First, I want the freedom to tell the partner that the things he is telling me could be discussed right now by all three of us sitting here together, and I make it very plain that I'm clued in to what is sensitive and what is

---

[7]Since the modal case involves both spouses, either in conjoint or concurrent sessions, we have employed the plural, "clients," throughout. It is clear, however, that many interventions are employed when only one spouse is in treatment.

free. Second, if there is some sensitive material that I think the other person needs to know, I might urge him to tell the partner. I won't do it myself, but I might urge him to.

2. Diagnosing the marital situation. Before he can intervene effectively, or, indeed, know what interventions are needed, the therapist must educate himself about the nature of the situation confronting him. The key issue on which information is needed is whether or not the marriage is headed for divorce.

Three aspects of divorce and divorce therapy make the task of accurate diagnosis particularly problematic.

(a) *The prevalence of client misdiagnosis.* In a large number of cases, the clients' initial self-diagnosis is incorrect or grossly misleading. Perhaps most common is the request to "save" a marriage that is actually an implicit request (at least on one spouse's part) to help end it. Less frequently, the initial request is for help in divorcing. Here too the probability of client misdiagnosis is high.

> What we have to tune into in working with people is: what do they mean at this time when they hurl the word "divorce" at each other? Is it done like a threat, is it done as some straw to hold onto and get an escape route, or is it really a calmly thought-through decision, so that this is really the logical route to follow?

Partly because the clients are such unreliable guides and because the diagnostic issue is such a complex one, when respondents were asked at what stage of a potential divorce case they prefer to become involved, the overwhelming response was, "as early as possible"—generally meaning before the issue of divorce has been seriously raised, but in any event, well before lawyers have been called in.

(b) *The nascent status of divorce therapy.* That few couples initiate treatment by explicitly asking for help in ending their marriage was often explained as a reflection that the true psychological problem is whether or not to seek a divorce. If that difficult decision has been made, people were said to contact lawyers rather than therapists.

Another explanation, however, has to do with the professional status of divorce therapy itself. A review of the literature conducted in conjunction with this study found only a handful of publications on strategies of intervention in divorce. In comparison, the literature on marital therapy is extensive. We have already noted the lack of agreement among the respondents on whether such a thing as divorce therapy, as distinct from marital or family therapy, exists. Moreover, although all respondents are highly expert, on the average only 20 percent of their time is spent on divorce work. We were unable to locate any practitioners for whom divorce therapy is the preponderant or exclusive area of practice. These, we believe, are all signs that we are dealing with a specialty that has not yet achieved full and independent status. To some degree, then, the diagnostic issue looms large because couples who have made a firm decision to divorce, and who therefore represent no diagnostic problem, do not present themselves for help in dealing with the practical and psychological problems of separating. Quite simply, they are unaware that such help is available.

(c) *The ambiguity of criteria for divorce.* How does the therapist know that, regardless of the couple's presenting complaint, they are or should be headed for divorce? The interviews provide only sketchy answers. To some degree this may reflect our initial naiveté. Had we known at the outset that determining the status of the case is one of the central conundrums of the respondents' work we would have asked more specific questions about the criteria that alert them to the probability that divorce therapy, rather than marital therapy, is required.

Nonetheless, some of the respondents did touch on the diagnostic issue. From these remarks we may infer that the paucity of criteria for divorce is due to a true lack of consensus: who should get divorced and who should stay married is, after all, a highly complex and idiosyncratic matter. In addition, most respondents hold the view that for practical, ethical, and psychological reasons only the clients can make the decision to get divorced. The respondents' motivation to formulate such criteria is therefore low.

Having said this, we may briefly note some of the criteria that were mentioned as evidence to the therapist that he is, or will soon be, dealing with a divorce, whatever the couple's avowed view of the situation may be. These criteria are admittedly sketchy. This is clearly an area in which more clinical and empirical work is needed.

1. Repeated unilateral or mutual sabotaging of therapist efforts to reduce the level of marital distress. This is evidence that one or both parties no longer has a genuine interest in remaining in the marriage.
2. A destructively high level of marital conflict threatening the physical or psychological integrity of one or both spouses.
3. A marriage based on a deeply neurotic wish that is either self-destructive or at fundamental odds with reality.

Of the tactics for diagnosing the state of the marriage, the preferred one is simply observing the marital interaction at first hand. In the early stages of treatment the therapist may be content to do so passively.

> In the beginning, I listen to the story. As a matter of fact, I never make any interventions the first couple of sessions. I don't want to affect the process—let it come out spontaneously. I listen to him, and then I ask her how she reacts to what he is saying. And then I listen to her.

In other cases the therapist may structure the interaction so as to maximize information.

> They can talk about it, but now you want to see it in operation. And I will sometimes do that by actually physically moving the people closer together in the room, to see if they can do it. I'll pay a lot of attention to what they pile up in between them here and in talking about it. But it's the things they do in front of me that are more important.[8]

Friends, parents, and other relatives may also be consulted to expand the therapist's understanding.

[8]An extreme example of a highly structured approach to diagnosis is the use by two of the respondents of the Ravich Train Game Test. The pattern of interaction that results from the couples' "play" is said to be a diagnostic aid and in some cases highly predictive that divorce will occur (11). The game is itself an adaptation of an experimental procedure developed by the second author of the present study (4).

3. Maintaining impartiality. Of all the strategies of intervention, maintaining impartiality was the one on which there was the greatest agreement. A therapist who has lost his impartiality was reviewed as having made the most serious of professional blunders. The therapist must maintain impartiality both toward the spouses as individuals and toward the prospects of their divorce or continued marriage.

> You've got to remain totally open, objective, and unbiased; as soon as you start taking sides and getting into an adversary situation with one party against the other, you're gone. Forget about any constructive work at that point—unless you can recognize what's happening and go back and correct it. . . .

> If someone comes in and says, "Listen, I'm finished and I don't want to work on it; I want a divorce," then, if they want my help at that point, I will help them to make some kind of a resolution. But I don't say, "Listen, I think this marriage stinks, and you really better get out." That's a value judgment I don't bring into a session.

Impartiality is not synonymous, however, with an absence of a point of view. The therapist's commitment is to his own conception of reality and the best interests of all concerned. In defense of this commitment the therapist may be obliged at times to differ very sharply with one or the other spouse.

> You know what I have written here of my four o'clock patient? "Document the wife's errors. She doesn't know where she went wrong." When I met with her I said: "Tell me, did you make any errors?" She couldn't see any: "He's a bastard. I have been the model wife. You name an error for me."
> And I said, "I'm going to ask your husband when I see him on Friday to tell me the errors he sees, and when I meet with you we will discuss what he sees as your errors." They're in the stage of her being bitter, bewildered, angry, blaming; and that's why I'm trying to show her, "Look, you're not a saint, and he's not a bastard."

The stress on impartiality is clearly related to strategic considerations; i.e., the task of producing meaningful alterations in a relationship cannot be accomplished if either party perceives the therapist as biased. There are other characteristics of divorce work, however, that appear to accentuate the respondents' concern with impartiality, even to the extent, at times, of leading them to deny that they have goals of what should be done when, in fact, they may have them.

The emotional strain and upheaval of couples in the process of getting a divorce is one such factor. In the view of the respondents, such couples are particularly likely to want a decision as to who is "right" and who is "wrong" and cues as to whether to end the marriage.

> I think that the original goal of every couple who is on the verge of divorce and comes to a therapist is to lay blame on the other. So they come originally for you to act as a judge and tell the other guy that he was wrong and all the terrible things she's doing to me. That's their original goal—to be proven right.

The emphasis on therapist impartiality may also be a function of the respondents' highly developed awareness that they operate in an area of interpersonal conflict that, by its very nature, is apt to touch uncomfortably upon their own unresolved childhood and family conflicts.

> One of the major pitfalls in working with a couple or family is that you begin to form such strong countertransferences that you become identified with one

member of the family or one partner of the couple. Therefore, part of my function, part of the job I do on myself, is to think very carefully about what I am doing and what kind of contract has been set up—about my own unconscious role; it becomes very important to deal with it and to think about it and to be aware of how I'm responding.

Finally, the prominence of the theme of therapist impartiality also appears related to the highly active role to which nearly every respondent subscribed.

I am a very active therapist; I don't sit passively; I can't imagine doing family therapy passively—nondirectively.

A therapist with a highly activist stance is more likely to be impressed with the importance of "impartiality" for the simple reason that his role conception puts him at a higher risk of losing or appearing to lose it.

The therapists' tactics for guarding their impartiality toward the mates as individuals may involve explicit statements of therapeutic evenhandedness.

I've often had husbands come around and say, "Would you sign an affidavit to the effect that my wife is really unstable and I deserve to have the children?" And I point out that's not where I come in—"I'm the family agent—I'm not going to do something that's going to screw her up. You have to convince me that this is to everybody's advantage. Go to your lawyer. He'll sign affidavits. I'm not a lawyer, I'm a psychologist. I'm an agent of the family." That's the kind of thing you stress again and again.

The therapist may also safeguard his impartiality by inviting clients to openly criticize or question him. One respondent's amplification of his reasons for inviting the parties to evaluate his behavior illustrates well the close relationship between an intense concern with impartiality on the one hand and a highly activist conception of the therapist's role on the other.

There is an occupational disease that we all suffer from—it's called omniscience. And another occupational disease is called omnipotence. And in a case like this, when you're manipulating, where you're dealing with realities and angry people and all kinds of things like that, there is the danger that you may feel you know all the answers. And that what you say ought to be done is the thing that must be done. And if they won't do it, then you whack them, spank them, kick them out, or something. I think these are very great dangers. The one is handled by careful analysis of one's own countertransference to both parties. The second can be handled, I believe, by a great flexibility in letting the parties give in to your proposals. In other words, I would say, "it seems to me the only thing to do is thus-and-so. And I think that's what you ought to do." I rarely say that. I usually say, "Well, putting A and B and C together, it seems to me as though the path to be followed is thus-and-so. What do you think?" And I state at the outset that the people sitting before me always have the right to challenge any statement that I make and ask me why I make it. And I have to present what thought process led me to that conclusion. If it's an error, as it sometimes is, they can correct it, if I allow this kind of openness. That is a counterploy to the omnipotence fantasy we're apt to have.

The therapist's impartiality may by protected not only behaviorally—that is, by what he says during therapy—but also structurally—by his decisions about who should participate in counseling sessions. The strong preference for seeing both spouses, and the common use of cotherapy and marital groups are all, at least in part, justified on the grounds that doing so helps keep the therapist "honest."

> I try at the beginning to see people together. And I don't engage, for example, while I'm doing that, in individual sessions—unless it's by agreement by all of us. And usually, if that occurs, I will balance it off with the other one, too. I will also not get drawn into telephone communication with one person, which I think is an alliance-seeking tactic that is often used.

A respondent who works frequently in cotherapy with her husband explained her rationale:

> Working together as therapists, each of us can make sure that somebody gets supported. It's very important. My husband reacts very badly to hostile, aggressive women, and he's going to find himself giving it to her. I, on the other hand, can soften that; I can say: "Hey, wait a minute, Fred," because I don't react that way to that kind of woman. I say, "Mary was just attempting to get across to John the strength of her feeling on this; it really is very important to her."

The therapist's impartiality toward the issue of the couple's divorce or continued marriage is protected by making two things clear: (a) the decision-making responsibility is the clients', not the therapist's, and (b) the aim of treatment is the growth and well-being of each spouse as an individual.

> "I can't take your burdens on my shoulders. These are your problems, not mine. I can give you a new way of looking at things, new ideas, or new suggestions about how you interact with each other, but you have to do it."

> I do not allow people to say, "We feel," and "we think," because the "we" hides differences. And I insist that each person is responsible for himself. His first obligation is to himself; then to the mate; then to the children; then to the family of origin; and, last of all, to society and the world.

Contextual interventions

While reflexive strategies were most often discussed in connection with the decision to get divorced, contextual and substantive strategies were discussed in both phases of divorce therapy. Accordingly, contextual and substantive interventions have been divided into those occurring in the decision-making phase and those occurring during the settlement phase.

The decision-making phase.   Several respondents took exception to our use of terms like "constructive," "amicable," or "civilized" divorce. To the respondents, such phrases suggest that the breaking of once deep emotional ties can be a relatively simple matter, a proposition that, as the concept of psychic divorce illustrates, contradicts clinical experience.

> A husband and wife who've had sexual intercourse and children together and smelled each other and had a lot of shared experiences—they can only separate violently and savagely. I think, in a sense, anger is a necessary part of the process. It's unrealistic when it's not. I think a friendly divorce is a little bit phony.

The therapeutic task is not to deny or circumvent anger but to reduce the level of hostility to more manageable levels.

> I consider the first task of a therapist to lessen the emotional intensity, because unless you do that, you're not going to get anywhere. And I consider divorce

therapy to be an extremely difficult, very tenuous kind of therapy that is always on the edge of termination. The couple, for example, can have an argument right before a session, and if one thinks that the other wants the therapy, "I'm not going back to that doctor." The need to get back at the partner is more important than working things out in therapy. It is very tricky. I can never tell from one session to the next whether it's going to be the last one.

Respondents' tactics for attempting to reduce the emotional pitch were of two kinds: tactics involving direct interventions during sessions—what we have referred to previously as *behavioral* tactics—and activities involving the manipulation of the context and environment in which the couple interacts— what we have called *structural* tactics.

1. *Reducing the level of emotional tension: Behavioral tactics.* A major source of tension and escalating hostility is the tendency of one or both partners to feel victimized by the other. A variety of tactics may help defuse the situation when this occurs.

(a) *Clarifying the real source of the anger.* The educative function of the divorce therapist is an important one. Since a certain amount of the anger the spouses direct at each other is either a mask for more painful feelings (such as lowered self-esteem, grief, or anxiety) or an over-reaction to the spouse based on an unconscious distortion of the present situation, if the therapist can help clarify these matters, the heat of the marital battle may be significantly reduced.

(b) *Shifting the focus from other to self.*

The average couple will be talking about the other: "What he did to me"—"What she did to me." And you've got to try as much as possible to refocus the individuals' attitudes and feelings: "What am I doing? What am I contributing to this relationship? How am I acting? When this happens, what do I do?" We know what they do—what do *I* do in the situation?

(c) *Relabeling an accusation.*

I try to de-label the behavior as much as possible. For instance, a guy tells me that his wife never leaves him alone, that she's constantly ready to go, and she's driving him out of his mind. I'll say something like, "What did you do to deserve such a lively lady?" I de-label the sting of the epithet—the sense that this is a terrible way to be, that she's demanding.

(d) *Encouraging positive interaction.*

When one partner reaches out, let's say, in a kindly, concerned way toward the other, and then the other sees that as an attack, I'm in there trying to clarify the way I saw it. What was there that made the other person see it in his way, when it's clear that if you look at it in terms of what was happening at the time, it was really an attempt to do something in a very positive kind of way. So I try to emphasize the healthy and respond very positively to that kind of thing—sort of watch for that.

(e) *Focusing on substantive issues.* The resolution of practical matters seemingly remote from the "real issues" may have an immediate calming impact on the marital dialogue.

When you eliminate many of the practical problems, it defuses a lot of the emotional response. I always try to eliminate the obstacles in the practical area before we get into any of the deeper dynamic aspects, because those can only be handled when you don't get interference and static from the practical problems.

(f) *Reducing anxiety through behavioral techniques.* One respondent described the use of cognitive desensitization with a man whose virulent opposition to his wife's request for a divorce was based on his jealousy of her new lover.

> The idea of the other guy produced very high anxiety; so I used a simple desensitization process: just sitting with him and getting him to picture very vividly the wife and some other guy in various acts of intimacy; having him simply relax and at the same time cognitively say, "This takes nothing away from me," until he was able to picture this with equanimity. And then he proceeded apace; he was then quite keen to go through with the divorce.

2. *Reducing the level of emotional tension: Structural tactics.* Among the contextual modifications the therapist may introduce to reduce the destructive levels of hostility are modifications in the format of therapy sessions, physical separation of the parties, and regulation of the clients' contact with lawyers.

(a) *Modifying the format of therapy: Couples groups.* Approximately half the respondents discussed employing this procedure during some part of their work with a couple. A couples' group may inhibit destructive fighting by "embarrassing" the partners into more socially restrained behavior and make them less accusatory of one another by giving them perspective on the common stresses of marriage.

(b) *Modifying the format of therapy: Cotherapy.* The value of cotherapy for protecting therapist impartiality has been noted. Impartiality is, of course, itself a means of lowering the emotional temperature. Cotherapy may also contribute to a hospitable emotional climate by making treatment less "psychiatric," thereby reducing the defensive tendency to seek judgments against the spouse. It may also provide a useful model of constructive methods for resolving differences.

> For us, the whole business of modeling is a very important aspect—that my husband and I can disagree with each other, that one of us can back down gracefully; if we disagree with each other, we don't have to get into a great big fight. We don't have to because we allow each other to have different opinions on matters. And couples will sometimes pick this up. Also, we listen to each other.

(c) *Enforcing physical separation.* In cases of physical assault or where verbal hostility has become so extreme that constructive problem-solving is blocked, a physical separation, either in terms of the therapy sessions, the living arrangements, or both, may be suggested or even required. Respondents spoke of ordering violent husbands out of the home as a condition for continued therapy and suggesting that a couple heavily invested in blaming each other begin by negotiating a "structured separation"—Will dating others be permitted? How often will they see each other? Will extra-marital sex be permitted?—so that "they no longer can play the game 'if it weren't for you.'"

(d) *Regulating contact with lawyers.* Although the respondents generally viewed lawyers as a major source of destructive conflict in divorce, the implications for therapeutic intervention drawn from this belief differed widely. One conclusion was that no constructive therapeutic work can occur if lawyers are involved. The task of the therapist is to prevent such involvement.

> I try to help them see that their lawyers are doing them a terrible disservice. On the one hand, they use their lawyers as weapons; on the other hand, the lawyers

foment more conflict and hostility. I might say that I do not counsel people who have already gone to the point of getting lawyers. You can't do meaningful counseling at that point because they are no longer interested in resolving problems. The lawyers say, "Listen, don't mention this, because it'll compromise your case," and once you have that kind of contamination you don't have treatment. And it's a farce to think that you can conduct any meaningful counseling when you have that kind of external contamination.

Ruling lawyers out, however, was a decidedly minority preference. Several respondents prompt clients to have an initial legal consultation as an aid to decision-making about the fate of the marriage. Legal consultation may also serve to reduce the level of tension and conflict by removing anxieties due to ignorance; by introducing a lawyer who is committed to a constructive, equitable divorce; and by serving as a corrective to fantasies of revenge and destruction.

Occasionally people come in to the treatment situation with fantastic ideas about what they're going to get if the opposing spouse doesn't give in and do what they say. I don't give legal advice—so sometimes it's necessary for them to get an individual lawyer in order to determine realistically what can be done in the specific situation. This frequently will help the total situation, because when the individual is brought back to reality and confronted with the facts—"No, you're not going to be able to do this, and no, you're not going to get that, and you just can't hit him over the head for fifteen years because he didn't do what you wanted him to"—this sometimes makes it easier to work.

(e) *Getting payment in advance.* One respondent noted that a very effective aid in producing a workable emotional climate may be to insist on cash in advance.

In many cases I sense right away that I'm going to have trouble with one or the other of the partners. You know what I do? The second they come in and want my services—they put a check on the table buying a certain amount of my time—and my time is expensive. This guarantees continuity of their participation in the work we do.

3. Clarifying the sources of marital dysfunction.

A couple comes in and they say: "We've been thinking about divorce, but we don't know . . ." So I say, "Look, let's have a period of exploration before either of you decides to leave. When you understand yourselves better and the situation better, then you're in a better position to make a decision about the fate of your marriage."

The educative function is focused on two areas: (a) promoting understanding about *current* patterns of marital interaction and, particularly, each spouse's own role in destructive marital interchanges, and (b) explicating the historical roots of the marital difficulties in terms of each spouse's own psychological development.

(a) *Promoting understanding of current patterns of marital interaction.* Understanding current dysfunctional patterns is facilitated by structural arrangements such as conjoint sessions, marital groups, and the use of audio or video playback. The goal is to keep the couples' interactions "on display" as much as possible to encourage the development of "observing egos." For example, in a couples' group the therapist may focus attention on one couple for half an hour and then invite the others to comment on what they have seen.

Video or audio playback may be used to point out particularly dysfunctional marital interactions. The couple may even be given the tape for at-home training in self-observation. Another respondent discussed arranging sessions between one spouse and the new lover in order to help the client see, in a concrete and compelling fashion, that identical patterns of interaction are occurring in the supposedly idyllic and "totally different" relationship with the new partner.

(b) *Explicating the historical roots of the marital conflict.*

It's important to find out just exactly who they're getting divorced from. Often, it has to do with things still being worked out in the family of origin. For example, if a woman has a brutal, tyrannical father, she's absolutely determined that no man is ever going to push her around again. So she marries a nice, sweet, passive guy; but then when they come in for therapy later on, she can't stand his weakness and passivity. Unless she does something about her relationship with her father, she's not going to be able to make either a rational choice about this divorce or about selecting another mate.

He's the kind of guy who came in saying, "Oh, I never had any problems with my parents; I loved them all the time; they're the greatest people that ever lived." When gradually we began to scratch underneath this very hard facade, we found the fear of his parents not loving him, anger toward them, or their inability to give him what he wanted. Since he was a little boy, he has been asking for the same things that his wife was asking from him. If he never got it from his parents, he wouldn't have much of a capacity to give it.

The historical roots of marital dysfunction may be clarified by client-therapist discussions and the "lesson" taught directly via therapist interpretations:

It's rather common for me to say something like this during the course of the divorce counseling session, "Look, the problem with you"—turning to one or the other spouse—"is that you've been raised with this desire to be treated like a prince or princess, as the case may be. And you've had this incredible need to be served; and your whole trip really seems to be that of being served. And you equate that with love; you haven't quite sorted out the difference between being loved and being served.

A minority of the respondents discussed therapy sessions with the client's family of origin as a more ambitious method for disentangling the past from the present. One respondent, in particular, placed heavy emphasis on this approach.

I do it toward the end of therapy when I feel that people have changed and they're ready to start dealing with their family. And I do a great deal of rehearsal before they bring their family in. "What do you want to take up with your family?" And some people say, "Well, I don't have any issues with my family; that was too many years ago; I get along okay with them." "Alright, let's go over the history again." And then, of course, people have thousands of issues with their family. And then they're prepared, and I turn the session, by the way, over to them. I'm sort of a traffic manager. They may start out, "You know, Dad, I never really felt close to you," that kind of thing. I find it especially important to do this in divorce therapy, but remember I said that a lot of people terminate prematurely. The family-of-origin work, I think, is the most important aspect of the work that I do.

The settlement phase. While the distinction between the decision-making phase and the settlement phase of divorce therapy is useful for descriptive purposes, it raises a critical issue on which there was sharp disagreement. Should the therapist, in fact, play any significant role in arranging the terms of settlement?

Five of the respondents ruled out such a function as inconsistent with their training and the primary goal of divorce therapy—to help clients make the difficult decision to end or maintain the marriage. These respondents become involved with negotiating issues of settlement only to the extent that unacknowledged emotional conflicts in the client are viewed as blocking effective problem-solving. In these instances, therapeutic efforts are needed to explore and resolve the emotional problem. In the absence of such emotional conflicts, substantive differences between the spouses were viewed as solvable without third-party assistance, except for the technical advice of lawyers. The flavor of opinion in this group may best be conveyed by some typical comments:

> People who can already decide to differentiate and separate really need very little help; I'm not a lawyer, and I can't help decide how to separate an estate or make legal commitments for the children.

> I absolutely don't want to get involved in the financial settlements; that really doesn't concern me unless it gets into the dynamics of the case.

Eleven of the remaining respondents, while stressing the psychodynamic aspect of their role, acknowledged that there was a place in their activities for helping couples negotiate terms of settlement. In the interviews, however, they did not detail the nature of this assistance to any great degree. To what extent this is attributable to the failure of interviewers to probe sufficiently is difficult to estimate, but our impression is that, for the most part, the mediation of concrete issues is considered to be of peripheral concern to the resolution of psychological and relationship dynamics.

Three respondents stand apart in their explicit, detailed concern with working to arrange the terms of divorce. Strategies discussed under the settlement phase, whether contextual or substantive, rely heavily on their comments.

1. *Establishing a favorable climate for negotiations.* Reducing the level of emotional tension is a fundamental strategy that underlies therapeutic intervention from beginning to end. Once direct negotiation has begun, the level of tension may rise again, stimulated by the complexities of working out an agreement, as well as by the anxieties produced at the intensified prospects of psychological separation that the agreement so concretely represents. Hence, controlling the emotional climate may take on renewed salience as a therapeutic task. Many of the earlier tactics for so doing may be repeated, but this time with an eye to facilitating negotiations. Two tactics with particular relevance to the negotiating phase of therapy may be noted:

(a) *Stating norms of equity, reasonableness, and cooperation.*

> When they decide to get a divorce, then they get involved with lawyers for whom it is an out-and-out battle to do the best for their clients under a set of rules that have nothing to do with the couple's rules. That can become very bitter and nasty. I think I can help the couple to maintain a perspective on their continued relationship in the future and that there are reasons to cooperate as well as compete. I

take a position: "Look, this doesn't have to be the kind of fight that ends in bitterness. It can end fairly and equitably and more or less to everybody's satisfaction."

(b) *Discouraging vengeance and revenge-seeking.*

I try to help people appreciate the futility of vengeance, of "I won't let him get away with this." It's often more prudent to let the other person get away with it—to see that the price you're going to pay for fighting back will be greater than any price of victory, that the victories of vengeance and a victory of retribution is often empty. So, for instance, a wife will say, "I'm not going to let him get away with paying so little. I'll fight him in court and everywhere else." "But the years of tension and litigation," I try to point out, "aren't worth what you're ultimately going to get. And even if it's granted, there's still no assurance that your husband's going to continue to pay, and they generally don't put people in jail for not paying. So know a lost cause when you see it. And stop batting your brains up against a stone wall. Just admit defeat in certain situations. It's the healthiest thing to do."

2. *Structuring negotiations.* The therapist may increase the flow and ease of negotiations by giving the couple a framework in which to conduct joint bargaining sessions. One respondent has evolved a highly structured format for this purpose. He was unique among his colleagues in this regard. The couple is provided with a detailed memorandum entitled "Factors to Be Considered in Working Out Separation Agreements," which serves as a checklist of issues to be settled. The respondent described his approach in the following way:

This procedure that I outline here is a way that I use to get them to go down the line of all the things that might be sources of contention—like considerations of property and of support and maintenance, both for the spouse who is to be left and for the children that are going to be left with this spouse. The third consideration has to do with visitation, which often is a big hurdle, a big problem. And I try to suggest different topics for them to discuss and to reach an agreement on. And then a last group of considerations concerns relinquishment of the premises— who does the leaving and when does he or she go? Also the costs: the legal fees, psychiatric fees, traveling, living expenses. These are things that cause trouble later on after the divorce has been accomplished. I try to discuss all those things and reach agreements.

I see both spouses, and they sit here and battle everything out so that when it's all finished, when they have reached agreement on all of these points—the topics alone covering two pages of my outline—when it's all finished, I sit down at my little typewriter and I draw up a memorandum of separation, embodying all the points of agreement. And I leave room at the bottom for the husband to sign, and for the wife to sign. Now I sign it as a witness.

3. *Mediating between lawyer and client.* Several respondents discussed their role in helping clients choose a lawyer once a decision to get a divorce has been made. Three kinds of lawyers may be recommended, depending on the circumstances: experts—lawyers who specialize in matrimonial law; conciliators—lawyers who will try to arrange a settlement in the best interest of all parties and who will do their best to avoid high-pressure tactics and protracted litigation; and "tigers"—lawyers who are able and willing to protect their clients' interests if efforts at constructive, equitable negotiations break

down. A legal "tiger" may also be required if, for reasons of guilt or low self-esteem, the client has ceased to protect his or her own interests.[9]

Once the client has established a relationship with a lawyer the therapist may act as a useful go-between. The therapist may help the lawyer by building up the self-esteem and psychological resources of a client so that the client is better able to participate in and withstand the rigors of divorce negotiations or by giving the client some understanding of the lawyer's role.

The therapist may also interpret the client to the lawyer:

> Frequently I'm able to give a lawyer an insight into what's happening with a couple—where they're at, how he could perhaps support the process—because frequently they're tremendously unsophisticated and do not know what goes on between people.
>
> To make up an example: Say I get into the whole question of money with a woman who has gone to a lawyer and wants a divorce, and it turns out that her whole family background is one of being frightened and abandoned; they were poor and the father walked out on them and this is evoking the abandonment fears she had before. So when she tries to grab on to the husband's money, the more the lawyer knows about where this came from the better he can help work it through with her.

Overall, however, collaboration between lawyer and therapist was mentioned infrequently. While this is undoubtedly a reflection of the pessimistic attitudes toward lawyers that the respondents held, four or five of the therapists mentioned that they were lacking in information as to which lawyers shared their views about the divorcing process but would find such information useful.

Substantive interventions

The decision-making phase: Orchestrating the motivation to divorce.

> The more successful divorce—I mean, the least painful divorce—is one in which the two people are at equal points or readiness to split. I think for both partners, when one is more ready than the other, it is much more difficult. For the one there's going to be guilt for deserting the other who doesn't want to be left; for the other there's the pain of being left. Arriving at equal readiness is one of our tasks as marital therapists—to help people time a separation in such a way that they both move to a more or less balanced point of readiness and acceptance of where they're going. So that neither one of them feels too awfully abandoned.

Orchestrating the motivation for divorce emerged in these interviews as the most distinguishing characteristic of therapeutic work with divorcing couples. Once the therapist embarks upon this form of intervention he has most clearly ceased doing marital therapy and has begun divorce therapy proper.

Orchestrating the motivation for divorce is a strategy that rests upon three major and related conceptions of the divorcing process:

---

[9]Recommending a tiger might well be classified as a substantive intervention since, in so doing, the therapist, either explicitly or implicitly, is likely to be attempting to increase the possibility of attaining ends that *he* feels are desirable, e.g., that the wife should get a larger share of the marital property than the husband is willing to give.

1. For most couples the motivation for divorce is a highly ambivalent one. The sources of this ambivalence may include the social stigma attached to divorce; fear of offending and disappointing one's parents; a sense of personal failure at a prescribed cultural task; guilt about possible damage to children and/or to a spouse who still wants the marriage; fear of living alone and functioning autonomously; and the inevitable emotional turmoil of the psychic separation process.

2. In spite of mutual ambivalence, in most divorce cases seen in clinical practice one spouse wants out of the marriage much more than the other.

3. A constructive divorce is unlikely if the motivation to end the marriage is not approximately equal in both partners.

Once the basic need for, or probability of, divorce becomes apparent, the task of the therapist becomes one of shoring up the motivation for divorce wherever it is weakest and strengthening it whenever it begins to flag too markedly under the stress of separating. Six major tactics by which these goals are accomplished can be identified: weakening attitudinal impediments to divorce; disputing negative assertions about self; enforcing physical separation of the spouses; increasing marketability; and enlisting the support of family and friends.

1. *Weakening attitudinal impediments to the divorce.* Various fears, realistic and unrealistic, may keep a couple from broaching the issue of divorce or from pursuing it steadily once it has been raised. Therapists may smooth the divorcing process by addressing these fears directly.

> There's often a lot of shame related to mothers and fathers and relatives and friends. And dependent upon what we know about the parental situation, we help them see that there are ways of getting support from their parents. If they can't get it because of the hangups of that other person, then that's the way it has to be. That doesn't change anything—"you don't die from it," is a favorite statement that I'll make. "It hurts, but you don't die from it."

One respondent discussed a sequence of steps by which he gradually shifted marital therapy to divorce therapy by attacking the underlying fears that, for different reasons, the idea of divorce aroused in each partner. (A schematic account of the kind that follows may make matters appear simpler than is the actual case. We wish primarily to focus attention on the "orchestrating" quality of the therapist's role in producing a mutual readiness to divorce.)

(a) Repeated efforts were made during joint sessions to solve marital problems and enhance the marriage. All such efforts were sabotaged by one or the other spouse.

(b) A separate meeting with the wife was held, during which the therapist asked directly whether she had considered divorce.

> Yes, in fact she had, and he had threatened to kill her and had actually come after her with a gun, and she was just terrified. Therefore, she put divorce out of her mind, and she felt imprisoned.

(c) The therapist raised the possibility that he might be able to reduce the husband's rage at the idea of divorce and aim the therapy in that direction in a constructive, protected manner. Would the wife be interested? Her response, "Definitely."

(d) Separate sessions were held with the husband to uncover the source of his deep-seated rage.

Why is he sticking around? Why is he putting up with it? And all this kind of thing. Not saying she wanted a divorce but saying, how come *he's* never thought of divorce. Never. And it was becoming very clear to me that he would see himself deprived of the children. That was the main thing.

(e) Attempts were made to reassure the husband about his parental role.

The intervention that was really concrete and specific was my saying to him, "Look, even though the two of you may get divorced, I want you to remember one thing: you will always be the biological father of those children. No other man can possibly take your place as the father"—giving him some kind of identity, some separation, because his feeling clearly was that the divorce spelled the end of everything.

(f) A return to joint sessions during which the possibility of divorce was discussed and the prospects of a continuing post-divorce alliance was used to control the husband's anxiety.

"I see the divorce is over, and you people have been able to do what few people can do, which is to have an amicable relationship as friends. And you go over; you know she's married or has another guy, and it doesn't bother you. Of course that man is not the father of those children, and you're really going over there primarily to be with your kids, to pick them up, and to see her as a friend. And whatever she has going with that guy is immaterial."

(g) Continued strengthening of the parental alliance by emphasizing to the husband the wife's importance as mother to their children.

Then he got into another of these death fantasies—that she would die, and he would have the children, and his mother would look after the children, and she'd raise them properly. And then we got into, "What would that really be like?" And he began to see very clearly that his mother didn't do a very good job on him and wouldn't do a very good job on his own kids—and that his wife was doing a pretty good job. That was a very important breakthrough there.

(h) A return to separate sessions with the husband to dissipate another emotional roadblock to divorce—his intense jealousy of the idea of his wife with another man. This was accomplished through the desensitization procedure described earlier.

2. *Arguing in favor of divorce.* While attacking the fears that are holding up the divorcing process, the therapist may also become a subtle or not-so-subtle advocate of divorce. The most commonly described tactic for advocating divorce was an appeal to self-interest combined with an articulation of the drawbacks of the marriage.

The task was to help her get angry enough—instead of pleading—"I need you"— to recognize: "I deserve something better. Why shouldn't I be genuinely loved by a man, instead of having you, who's really wanting to be with somebody else. . . ." The task so often in marital therapy is helping people to build sufficient self-esteem so that when they're making the decision or the choice, they make it really with a greater sense of what's in their own best interests—and not out of fear. The therapeutic goal was for her to recognize that, even though she at first cried bitterly and understandably about feeling so abandoned, she could come around to the view that there was plenty wrong with him; she had idealized this man to the point that he was quite unreal. Because he was not giving her all that many good things. And so her view changed from the feeling that "I'm being betrayed and abandoned" to "I don't really need you any more than you need me."

3. Disputing negative assertions about self.

I, as a professional, know this is what is going to get in your way: You're going to say, "I failed"; What can we do to combat it?

Although many respondents spoke of the importance of being supportive and caring of clients in the throes of a divorce crisis, the nature of this therapeutic assistance was most often reflected in comments about the importance of contradicting negative self-assertions rather than in direct praise or encouragement. Depending on the source of self-doubt, the therapist may directly challenge the notion that the failure of the marriage was due exclusively to one spouse's shortcomings (the other spouse also played an important role); that one spouse's decision to leave the marriage is a reflection of the other's undesirability (both spouses had their own problems, distortions, or needs); or that ending a marriage is an admission of failure (it may be a sign of, and opportunity for, growth).

4. Enforcing physical separation.
Physically separating the parties may be used as a tool for assisting in the decision to dissolve the marriage.

Maybe the people are hanging on to each other, and yet they are obviously on the way toward divorce—or I believe that they're going toward divorce. I will suggest some movement apart that will allow them to draw back from each other—figuring that drawing back will allow them to decide either that they want to come back together or that they really want out. . . . Instead of talking about one person leaving the house, I'm suggesting the space; a change in the space between them—sometimes what happens is, instead of doing that, they'll move into different rooms, for example.

Several respondents felt that once a decision for divorce has been made, joint sessions are no longer indicated, since such sessions may foster unrealistic fantasies of reconciliation. Given the notion of psychic divorce as an inherently ambivalent and unstable process, such a concrete representation of the new reality was viewed as particularly desirable. (The disinclination to see the couple jointly after the divorce decision is also, of course, correlated with the view that the therapist has no role to play in the mediation of divorce settlements. For respondents who do see such a role for themselves, joint sessions in the postdecision phase are viewed as desirable and even necessary.)

5. Increasing "marketability."
A client cannot be expected to work constructively on divorce if to do so implies the attainment of a condition of poverty and social isolation. An important therapeutic task, therefore, is to assist in the development of needed work or social skills. The development of such skills can also facilitate withdrawal from psychological dependency on the spouse.

I make very specific suggestions: "Who are your friends? Do you have friends who give parties? How about a political club? How about going to church?" I'm very specific about pushing them out into the world, because if they don't get out into the world they're going to continue to feel the loss and abandonment and resentment of their spouse; and when they bump against their own real world outside, the separation and loss of the spouse ceases.

Couples' groups can also provide useful positive social feedback for a client with an unrealistically low sense of his appeal to the opposite sex.

It may be necessary for the therapist, supportively but firmly, to put the client in touch with the apprehensions that have motivated avoidance of constructive problem-solving:

A technique that's been quite useful is a future-projection technique in which I get people imagining they are divorced—time is passing—and what they anticipate. And very often if they get into it, they get in touch with the loneliness, the aloneness, and so on. And then it's a matter of my saying, "What could you do to offset that? What kinds of reinforcements could you look for—and how do you go about doing it?" And then you get a kind of modus operandi: "Well—would I advertise in a 'Singles' newspaper? Would I go to a singles bar?" And then we begin to explore the various options.

Role-playing techniques may also be used.

I'm a great believer in all kinds of therapy, of having fire drills—we do a lot of rehearsals; we'll role-play party scenes and small-talk.

In some instances a more blunt approach may be needed:

At one point I said to her when she was talking about whether she should get a job—she'd always delay—"You've been agreeing to get a job, talking about it, doing nothing; don't come back until you get a job." She said that she was indignant. She said, "I've never heard of anything like that; that's terrible." It was that sort of high-pressure tactic I was using.

6. *Enlisting the support of family and friends.* Ambivalence about the decision to get a divorce may also be weakened if the client's closest associates can be enlisted as allies.

Where a husband has left a rather dependent wife, partially as a means of controlling her, partially as a threat—if she doesn't do as he says, he's going to stay away—sometimes I utilize friends to help provide support, immediate emergency support for the wife, in order not to give in to the husband's threats, in order for the wife to maintain some kind of stability, so that the husband is not able, then, to come back, find the wife shattered psychologically and then be able to take over and be twice as bad as he was before.

The settlement phase.

1. *Making the parties face "reality."* Because they are undergoing an emotionally trying experience and because there are many complex matters to decide, a divorcing couple may need help in planning the terms of their divorce in a realistic manner. While permitting the husband to visit the children whenever he likes may have the appearance of a generous concession on the part of the wife, wouldn't a clearly defined visitation schedule allow her the necessary freedom to begin dating again? A man may wish to contest the financial demands of his wife, but how do the anticipated gains compare with the predictable costs?

Fights over money, in particular, may lend themselves to the forceful presentation of reality:

I had one couple come in here, and they were going to get a divorce, there's no question about it. And the wife said, "Look, I need twelve hundred dollars a month and he won't give it to me." And the husband said, "But the most I can give her is six hundred dollars; that's all I can afford." "Why twelve hundred? Why six hundred?" And I pulled out paper, and I said, "Do you think that what you're going to offer and what you're going to get bears no relationship to reality? What is your rent? Let's put it down. What is your telephone bill? Let's put it down. How much do you use for groceries and for the butcher and the baker and so forth?"

Introducing a needed time perspective is another reality function the therapist may perform.

Very often people fight like hell with lawyers about the agreement when it deals with visitation. They fight over that so hard, when actually the needs of the children at this age level will not be so important five years from now. They will have their own lives; they are going to say "no" to you on occasion. I point this out—that this is for now, that she needs this structure, that life will change, other things will happen, she may get married. There are certain things that seem important now—and they are important—but they will change; it is temporary.

The therapist may also make the partners see the psychological facts of life with regard to their spouse:

Well, he's a very funny fellow, and he was willing to be very generous if she would agree not to have a lawyer make the terms. He's willing to be a very generous man if he is in control. He's afraid of loss of control. So it was quite possible to help her to see that she could leave him that sense of control without being too scared that he was not going to take care of her properly; he'd take care of it for her. And he is more generous and loyal than I have been able to get him to be at any time.

However important making the parties face reality may be, the ambiguous quality of therapeutic claims of impartiality is nowhere better indicated than in a consideration of the reality-orienting function. This function, it would appear, is a fairly common method—and perhaps the principal method—by which therapists may encourage substantive agreements that seem desirable to them and, at the same time, avoid the appearance of partiality. Not bias, but an accurate perception of matters as they are is the ostensible motive behind such interventions. Pointing to the "reality" involved in a complex divorce settlement, however, is not the same kind of reality as pointing to a chair sitting in the middle of the room. It is apparent that at times the definition of "reality" that the therapist chooses may represent an implicit but nonetheless firm value position. That therapists stress the impartial role and gloss over their more substantive interventions is ascribable, we believe, not to any generalized tendency toward deviousness or Machiavellianism, but to the considerable tactical and subjective pressures to appear impartial, sketched earlier. Blindness to one's own agenda would seem to be an occupational hazard.

2. *Making suggestions for compromise.* Although this is an obvious third-party function, and one that was alluded to, there is little in the interviews detailing the role of the therapist in this regard. A more common strategy for arranging compromises was trying to work through the emotional barriers to accepting reasonable proposals or dealing with self-critical feelings that are blocking the pursuit of a viable solution.

3. *Protecting the welfare of children.* The one area in which respondents

were not reluctant to acknowledge having goals for settlement other than those chosen by the marital partners had to do with the interests of children. One explanation for their lack of reticence may be that the risks of appearing biased are much lower here than in other areas where therapists might take a substantive position. Presumably, both parents love their children and want to do the best for them. The therapist can scarcely be accused of partiality by either partner if he shares this concern with them, even if he does not share their concept of what should be done.

The therapists' interventions on behalf of minor children fall into four categories: preventing the worst; mediating terms of custody and visitation; handling emotions; and promoting constructive post-divorce arrangements.

(a) *Preventing the worst.* Several respondents took a very firm stance with regard to preventing children from becoming pawns in a parental battle. The list of abuses that can occur in such a case is extensive but may include violent fighting in front of the children; demeaning of the other spouse to the children; angry and sullen handling of visitation arrangements; and the use of custody fights purely as a bargaining ploy ("I'll give up the custody battle if she'll ask for less money"). "Laying down the law" was the preferred tactic for handling such excesses.

> There's a lot of talk now about child abuse, but there are a lot of other ways of abusing children without beating them—and these kids were taking a beating, in a real sense, psychologically. And so I laid down the law as far as I saw it—that they didn't have a right to do this to their children, that we should get on with a discussion of how to do it so that the kids aren't caught in between.

(b) *Mediating terms.* Preventing the worst represents minimal standards for protecting child welfare. Most respondents who discussed their role vis-à-vis children attempt to do more. Fostering cooperative negotiation of custody was one. One therapist advises that this important decision be deferred until the emotional climate between the spouses has cooled down. Two respondents mentioned inviting children to therapy sessions so that their wishes with regard to custody and frequency of visitation can be taken into account.

During negotiations, the therapist may also assume the role of advocate of the present and future financial needs of the children. The therapist may suggest close post-divorce physical proximity of the parents to make it easier for children to see the noncustodial parent and may give advice on how the moment of the physical separation of the parents can best be handled to involve minimal emotional turmoil for the children.

(c) *Handling emotions.* Three respondents discussed conducting therapy sessions with parents and children together for purposes of dispelling in children notions of guilt about the parental break and the fantasy that the parents can be reunited through some behavior of the child's. Joint sessions of this kind may also serve to de-escalate the parental battle by making vivid the turmoil and pain being inflicted on the children.

(d) *Promoting constructive post-divorce arrangements.* Tactics designed to foster the post-divorce welfare of the children include such things as encouraging regular visitation, advising against the simultaneous presence of both parents during visits (to prevent fantasies of reconciliation in the child), and suggesting dating patterns that will do the least damage to the child's sensibilities.[10]

CONCLUSION

Divorce therapy, as it is revealed in these interviews, can mean very different things to different practitioners. It seems likely that we are in a transitional stage in the emergence of this therapeutic specialty. It is our belief that there is considerable need at present for extended discussion among marital and family therapists of the kind of training that will best equip the therapist for effective intervention once the decision for divorce has been made. It remains to be seen what the final amalgam will be—in what proportions will be represented traditional therapeutic training and training in the applied skills of the negotiator, the lawyer, and the accountant.

REFERENCES

1. Anthony, E. J.,"Children at Risk from Divorce: A Review." In E. J. Anthony and C. Koupernik (eds.), *The Child in His Family: Children at Psychiatric Risk*, vol. 3, New York, John Wiley & Sons, 1974.
2. Bowlby, J., *Attachment and Loss: Attachment*, vol. 1, New York, Basic Books, 1969.
3. Brown, E., "Divorce Counseling." In D. H. Olson (ed.), *Treating Relationships*, Lake Mills, Iowa, Graphic Publishing, 1976.
4. Deutsch, M. and Krauss, R. M. "The Effect of Threat on Interpersonal Bargaining," *J. Abn. Soc. Psych.* 61: 181–189, 1960.
5. Fischer, E. O. *Divorce: The New Freedom*, New York, Harper & Row, 1974.
6. Goode, W. J., *Women in Divorce*, New York, Free Press, 1956.
7. Israel, S., *A Bibliography on Divorce*, New York, Bloch Publishers, 1974.
8. Kessler, S., *The American Way of Divorce*, Chicago, Nelson Hall, 1975.
9. Levinger, G. L., "A Social Psychological Perspective on Marital Dissolution," *J. Social Issues*, 32: 21–47, 1976.
10. Norton, A. J. and Glick, P. C., "Marital Instability: Past, Present, and Future," *J. Soc. Issues*, 32: 5–20, 1976.
11. Ravich, R. A. "The Marriage/Divorce Paradox." In C. J. Sager & H. S. Kaplan (eds.), *Progress in Group and Family Therapy*, New York, Brunner-Mazel, 1972.
12. Task Force on Divorce and Divorce Reform, Minneapolis, National Council on Family Relations, 1973.
13. Wallerstein, J. S. and Kelly, J. B., "The Effects of Parental Divorce: The Adolescent Experience." In E. J. Anthony & C. Koupernik (eds.), *The Child in His Family: Children at Psychiatric Risk*, vol. 3, New York, John Wiley & Sons, 1974.
14. Weiss, R. S., *Marital Separation*, New York, Basic Books, 1975.

[10] Since the focus of this study was on the therapeutic role during the divorcing process, little information was gathered about post-divorce interventions. It is apparent, however, that such help, usually in individual sessions with only one partner to the former marriage, is common. Post-divorce therapy may concern itself with the rebuilding of self-esteem, the working through of unconscious factors in new romantic attachments in order to permit a sound remarriage, and assistance in dealing with postdivorce adjustment in work, child-rearing, and social life.

There is also a type of post-divorce therapy in which divorced husband and wife jointly seek therapy for a problem child. The cause of the child's difficulty in these cases was conceptualized as the parents' uncompleted psychic divorce. The child's problem becomes the means by which marital involvement of an intense kind can be continued with neither partner admitting, or aware of, the true motivation for seeking therapy. In such instances one respondent spoke of the necessity of "remarrying the spouses in order to divorce them," i.e., of reviving the matrimonial fantasies for the purpose of successfully laying them to rest.

A Feminist Approach to Family Therapy

Rachel T. Hare-Mustin

Although family therapy recognizes the importance of the social context as a determiner of behavior, family therapists have not examined the consequences of traditional socialization practices that primarily disadvantage women. The unquestioned reinforcement of stereotyped sex roles takes place in much of family therapy. A feminist therapy orientation that considers the consequences of stereotyped sex roles and the statuses prescribed by society for females and males should be part of family therapy practice. This paper describes the ways in which family therapists who are aware of their own biases and those of the family can change sexist patterns through applying feminist principles to such areas as the contract, shifting tasks in the family, communication, generational boundaries, relabeling deviance, modeling, and therapeutic alliances.

One might well ask what family therapy has to do with feminist therapy. Have not the family and the institutions that support it been the primary cause of maintaining women in their stereotyped sex roles? As feminists can readily point out, "The family has been the principal arena for the exploitation of women, and however deeply rooted in social structure that exploitation may be, it is through family structure that it makes its daily presence felt" (10, p. 19). Chase's question, "What does feminism demand of therapy?" (10, p. 3) is the question I would like to examine in the form, "What does feminism demand of family therapy?"

In discussing family therapy from a feminist point of view, I will first briefly consider the principles of feminist therapy and review the structure of the family as we know it today. I will then discuss how family therapy has evolved. Some of the ways in which family therapy differs from the feminist approach will be examined. Finally, I will present in greater detail the ways feminist values can be translated into techniques for working with families.

FEMINIST THERAPY

Feminist therapy grew out of the theory and philosophy of consciousness raising. Central to feminist therapy is the recognition that (a) the traditional intrapsychic model of human behavior fails to recognize the importance of the social context as a determiner of behavior, and (b) the sex roles and statuses prescribed by society for females and males disadvantage women (29, 30, 42, 45).

Feminism sees as the ideal for the individual the ability to respond to changing situations with whatever behavior seems appropriate, regardless of the stereotyped expectations for either sex. This idea of the androgynous personality reflects a recent shift away from dualistic notions of masculine-feminine personality types (21). In helping women develop in line with an androgynous model, feminist therapy has encouraged women not only to become aware of the oppressiveness of traditional roles but also to gain experiences that enhance their self-esteem as they try new behaviors as part of gaining self-definition. The feminist therapeutic relationship itself embodies these principles in its emphasis on greater equality between the therapist and the client. By differentiating what is personal from what is external, feminist therapy may be distinguished from nonsexist therapy or humanistic therapy. These approaches may encourage individual development free of gender-prescribed behaviors, but they do not (a) examine and (b) seek to change the conditions in society that contribute to the maintenance of such behaviors.

THE FAMILY

The American family as we know it from research and clinical practice is one in which the husband bears the main responsibility for the economic mainte-nance of the family and the wife bears primary responsibility for domestic work and child care. The nature of the family today is a consequence of the dramatic changes that took place during the nineteenth century, chief among which was the separation of work from the home (41). Where productivity was rewarded by money, those who did not earn money, such as women, children, and old people who were left at home had an ambiguous position in the occupational world (22). The instrumental role for males and the expressive role for females that evolved were held up as normative by Parsons and Bales (40) and even necessary for the well-being of individuals, the family, and society.

The employment of women outside the home has not released women from the assigned expressive role that accompanies homemaking responsibility. Employed wives labor longer than either employed men or full-time house-wives, and the fact that child care is not available for working women in the United States reinforces the idea that women are not about to be released from their primary responsibility in the home merely because they work outside (6). Recent work patterns for women are actually not innovative but regressive in terms of the decreasing proportion of women in any but low-paying jobs (44). Being female is regarded as uniquely qualifying a woman for domestic work, no matter what her interests, aptitudes, or intelligence (5). Equalitarian ar-rangements by which both parents share equally in domestic areas or by which contributions to the family are based on personal preferences and individual capabilities are rare when these preferences diverge from traditional role expectations.

In marriage, the power of the male in the family is guaranteed by society's expectation that he will be older, bigger, have more education, and come from a higher social class than his wife. This tends to assure that he has the strength, credentials, experience, special knowledge, and training on which power in part is based. Marriages in which this is not the case are regarded as deviant. The power in the female role that derives from the woman's responsibility in organizing the household, the children, and the husband has depended on being married and having children (22). With the decline in the importance of the family, such power has been reduced. Women's lack of power is obscured and attributed to women's being more emotional and less able to "handle power" than men. As in other unequal relationships, the dominant group defines the "acceptable" roles for the less powerful, which are those activities like domestic work that the dominant group does not choose to do. There is research demonstrating that loss of power or chronic powerlessness are frequent precursors of psychological disorder (31).

Marriage typically demands that women give up their activities or place of residence to adjust to the needs of men. It has been observed that the partner who sacrifices or gives up the most for the marriage must of necessity be the one most committed to it (37). The woman, who may have given up her occupation, family closeness, or residence for marriage must rely more on the marriage to fulfill her needs. The expectation that women will adjust to men's patterns leads to an often unrecognized difference in the number of stressful life events impacting on men and women. Dohrenwend (11) has found that women are exposed to a relatively higher rate of change or instability in their lives compared with men, which can be seen as contributing to frequent psychosomatic symptoms and mood disorders.

The inequality in the traditional family is rarely recognized by individual or family therapists. It has been observed that power aspects of sex roles are largely disregarded or denied, except when women have power (35). The formulation of dominant-mother/ineffectual-father as the cause of practically every serious psychological difficulty is made without regard for the underlying inequality that leads to such a situation. Few therapists recognize that the stress on family members and particularly on women from required sex roles that assign them an inferior position has led to the family becoming the arena of conflicts that arise from the inequity sanctioned by the larger society (34).

FAMILY THERAPY

In the late 1940s and 1950s, researchers such as Wynne, Lidz, and others, focusing on the schizophrenic patient, identified the overinvolved mother as the source of pathology. In terms of the social events of the time, women who had been more fully involved in activities outside the home during World War II were now being encouraged to return to their natural feminine occupations as wives and mothers and to apply themselves to these responsibilities. The profound impact on the field of Parsons and Bales' (40) idea of fixed sex roles, with males having the instrumental role and females the expressive, has been pointed out (24). Observations of these stereotyped sex roles in the American family were then used by researchers and therapists as the basis for the argument that these were the necessary conditions for normal family life and successful child rearing. Advances in the 1960s saw the application of principles of general systems theory to the understanding of the family. The most notable change in family therapy in the 1970s, and one that has implications for women, is the growing acceptance of the family developmental point of view that follows from the work of Hill and other sociologists (19).

The family developmental orientation is analogous to the individual life cycle perspective in its focus on the stages in family development over the family life span—from the initial courtship phase to the death of the last member of the couple. Stages are defined in terms of the dominant developmental tasks faced by individual members of the family and the family as a system at that point. "Normal" crises in family development are usually identified as those that occur around the addition or loss of a member, whether actually by birth or death, or symbolically by change in activity or residence. The importance of this model is that it can provide an orientation toward prevention rather than pathology by identifying predictable crisis points in advance. Therapeutic interventions are directed at preparing the family for such stress points as well as helping the system move on from crises to resume its characteristic functioning.

If the systems approach to family therapy has adopted a prevention model of mental health and has shifted from a focus on the individual to recognizing social systems as determinants of behavior, one might ask why has it not been discovered and acclaimed by feminists as sex-fair therapy? In point of fact, while espousing a theory that might seem to assure equality for family members, family therapists in practice share the same biases and prejudices as others in the society and often have not freed themselves from their past training in a traditional orientation that views the mental health of males as akin to adulthood and that of females as not (9). For example, Bowen's Differentiation of Self Scale (8) can readily be identified as a sex-stereotyped masculinity-femininity scale with femininity at the devalued end. Bowen's approach is akin to the Ego Strength Scale based on the Minnesota Multiphasic Personality Inventory (MMPI), which is biased in favor of males by including more masculine than feminine scored items (32). Bowen ignores the fact that women's socialization encourages them to be emotional and intuitive rather than rational.

To restore the family to healthy functioning, family therapists often intentionally or unwittingly reinforce stereotypic role assignments for man, the doer, and woman, the nurturer, assuming that the traditional roles are the basis for healthy functioning. That some people are more comfortable in these roles for which they were trained cannot be denied, but, as suggested earlier, they may pay a price in psychological functioning. The fact that married women have a higher incidence of mental illness than men but single women do not (15) should lead family therapists to question the structure of the traditional family as it affects women. Representative of family therapists who support sex-stereotyped roles as important for healthy development are Boszormenyi-Nagy and Spark (7). They point out that "A heterosexual (therapy) team permits each individual to function more comfortably in his or her life-long assigned biological-emotional role. ... Mutual respect is needed to confirm the differences between masculinity and femininity" (p. 204). They criticize women who live vicariously through their husbands and children, thus avoiding facing their own lack of identity; however, they also criticize women who seek identity elsewhere, as in the following example.

A young married woman who received superior ratings as a school teacher refused to cook or shop for food since she considered this beneath her. . . . She seemed to expect the therapist as well as her family to be completely accepting of her passive, dependent attitude that it was beneath her dignity to fulfill this aspect of a woman's role. [7, p. 203]

Minuchin (37) sees himself as modeling the male executive functions, forming alliances, most typically with the father, and through competition, rule-setting, and direction, demanding that the father resume control of the family and exert leadership as Minuchin leads and controls the session. In a comparable manner, Forrest (12) describes the female therapist as using her feminine warmth, wisdom, and interest in men to appeal to their masculine instincts.

These illustrations reveal how the unquestioned acceptance and reinforcement of stereotypic sex roles takes place in much of family therapy, despite the possibilities inherent for change in the systems point of view. As Klapper and Kaplan (24) point out in their survey of sex-role stereotyping in family therapy literature, current writing has been minimally affected by the emerging consciousness. "Someone being trained as a family therapist would have to maintain stern vigilance in order not to be caught up in the oftentimes subtle reinforcement of behavior patterns which are so debasing and humiliating to women" (p. 28).

TECHNIQUES FOR FAMILY THERAPY

Despite the fact that a feminist approach to family therapy has not developed, I would contend that such an approach is possible. The obstacles can be summed up as (a) the socially reinforced sex roles that exist in the family; (b) the therapist's own family and clinical experience that renders her or him unaware of and insensitive to alternatives to stereotyped sex roles; and (c) the family's concerns, which are rarely identified as related to traditional sex-role assignments. My purpose in what follows is not to analyze family therapy techniques, per se, but rather to consider certain areas of intervention in which a feminist orientation is important. These areas are: the contract, shifting tasks in the family, communication, generational boundaries, relabeling deviance, modeling, ownership and privacy, and the therapeutic alliance with different family members.

The contract

Feminists stress the equality in the relationship between the therapist and the client as a departure from the paternalistic medical model in which the doctor is presumed to always know best. Recognizing that the capacity to influence people comes in part from their expectations (the placebo effect), feminists are contending that an equal relationship with mutual respect can still raise expectations that are beneficial in achieving goals (13). One method of attaining equality is by use of a contract.

Many family therapists use an informal or unwritten contract with families that come for help that facilitates agreement on arrangements for treatment and goals (18). As has been pointed out by the Nader group, a contract that is written assures the protection of client rights to an even greater extent (1). The contract is probably not intended to be legally binding, but it does establish a mutual accountability between the therapist and family. Furthermore, the negotiation of the contract can be an important part of the therapeutic process itself. The contract can include arrangements for treatment, the amounts and kinds of responsibility to be assumed by the therapist and by the family, issues of confidentiality, the goals of therapy and measurement of their accomplishment, and provisions for renegotiation of the contract.

One of the problems in contracting with families is the need to involve all family members, some of whom are more reluctant to participate than others. Hines and Hare-Mustin (20) have pointed out the ethical problems in requiring reluctant children and adolescents to participate in family therapy. Most families come because the mother is distressed about something in the family. The father, from his less involved position, feels that there is nothing to worry about, while the children have little choice. Too strong initial support by the therapist of any one member's point of view is likely to alienate the other members and lead to sabotaging or early termination of treatment. The therapist must reach some shared agreement with all family members.

To the extent that the father is paying for the sessions, he controls the sessions. It is hard to complain about the person paying the bills, as women and children are well aware. Part of the therapeutic process that relates to the contract and the setting of fees is the shifting of the conventional idea that the one who contributes money to the family is the only meaningful contributor. Unpaid services of other family members, primarily the mother, must be viewed as contributing to and subsidizing the person who is bringing in the money. Another aspect of the money economy is the inflexibility of most job schedules that can be pointed out to the family in connection with scheduling appointment times that the father can attend. In like manner, when babysitting arrangements are necessary, the value of the mother's unpaid work should be focused on, rather than merely her traditional responsibility for locating babysitters.

Beginning with the contract helps the family learn about negotiation and makes explicit the "rules" for the therapy. From the negotiations about the contract, the family can begin to understand how rules regulate the behavior of family members. Many family conflicts center about what the rules are and who makes them, which is basically the issue of power. In family conflicts, Zuk (49) has pointed out that the weak person traditionally espouses values such as justice, compassion, and relatedness, while the powerful person advocates control, rationality, law, and discipline. In husband-wife conflicts, wives usually espouse values concerned with caring, while husbands espouse rationality. In parent-child conflicts, children espouse the relatedness values, while their parents stress control and discipline. The family therapist can help the family recognize the value differences that accompany the shifts in power among participants in family conflicts.

Shifting of tasks in the family

Family therapists recognize that it is impossible to change the role of one family member without changing the role of another. However, the division of labor and functions in the family is often looked at in very limited perspective. The therapists who ask about the sharing of chores in the family may not recognize that the division of labor in the home is in part a result of the separation of paid work from the home and the consequent devaluing of domestic work. Traditional therapists who see some women having a greater share of responsibility and power within the home than men overlook the fact that men typically have power and status elsewhere. Family therapists should not rush to "restore" the power in the family to the father, thus further reducing the mother's self-esteem and limited authority. As noted earlier, the observation that fathers typically have the instrumental role and mothers the expressive role in families has led family and child care experts to assume that these role assignments are necessary for normal functioning, an assumption for which the evidence is at best equivocal.

Many couples share responsibilities without regard for traditional stereo-types until the birth of the first child (43). The arrival of a child precipitates a change in power and relationship status between the partners. Resentment can build up at this point in the person who has to shift to the major child care responsibilities—resentment that can lead to the breakdown of the bonds of affection established in the previous period. At the same time, the woman with authority is too often seen as a monster by her family and by therapists because for a woman to have authority deviates from the stereotype. In point of fact, the limited power that women have to make decisions and guide the lives of family members has declined as the family has declined in importance.

Often, women would like others to share more of the decision-making in the family (36). Mothers are burdened with many small decisions, but the fact that fathers do not participate signals to the mother as well as to the children that the decisions are about matters that are not really important. The family therapist needs to help family members examine how decisions are made and who shares in the process.

The practice of the mother's thanking other family members for household chores also needs to be examined. As long as the mother thanks others and they expect to be thanked, the implication is that they are doing her work, rather than family work, and they are doing it as a favor to her. In addition, children are not going to participate willingly in chores that the father signifies by his nonparticipation are demeaning.

What should take precedence, the job or the family? The feminist therapist needs to be aware of the complexities of this question. The intense pressure on the person working with technology in the money economy often results in a choice having been made in favor of the job. Because men bring in the money, it is expected that women and children will adjust to their needs. Yet, when a woman works, the family still demands primary allegiance (6). Women who work are expected to be interrupted by and respond to the demands of the family. I had a case in which an unemployed father and the teen-age daughter waited for the working mother to come home and cook supper. Not all therapists would have questioned this practice.

Family therapists need to be aware of the options for women as well as men and not oversell work for women outside the home when the jobs available are frequently repetitious, demeaning, and underpaid. In addition, there are women whose socialization is such that they are genuinely happy with the "professionalization" of housework in their current lives. The encouragement of women to go out to work without a reduction of their work load at home may be but a thinly disguised punitive act. The economic realities are also such that if both individuals work part-time or if the woman works full-time instead of her husband, there will be a loss in family income owing to the differentials in earning power of men and women and the loss of fringe benefits for part-time work. Despite these limitations, outside work can be an enhancing experience. Therapists need to help the family recognize not only the positive aspects but also the enormous societal barriers operating against meaningful change in the family and not advocate facile solutions that may have slight chance of success. On the other hand, counseling women to remain in traditional roles can have repercussions for their families in terms of anger, frustration, and a smothering overinvolvement with their children (47).

The mother, as well as other family members, needs to give up the view that she should be totally available to respond to every demand family members make upon her. If she is to give up some of the power associated with being central in the family, she must be connected with areas outside the home where she can have autonomy, respect, earning power, and opportunities to develop her capabilities. Women's ambivalence and resistance to giving up responsibility in the family is often a defense against the guilt they feel about not fulfilling their traditional sex roles and the anxiety they experience when departing from the familiar patterns of wife and mother. Some of the specific directions the therapist can take with the family are drawing up and trying out new schedules of household chores, involving the father in home tasks, child care, and decision-making, assigning age-appropriate responsibilities to the children, and helping the family develop network supports that will be encouraging of the anticipated changes. More appropriate assertive behaviors can be developed by the mother at the same time she is learning to set more realistic goals for herself. One of the first things that signals change may be a reduction in the mother's behavior as a critic, which is an often unacknowledged consequence of her inferior position. All family members can benefit from consciousness-raising as a part of family therapy. Understanding of different roles develops as parents and children are asked to examine what they like and do not like about being male or female.

Communication

Many family therapists focus on communication, but few have analyzed the relation of communication styles to male and female roles. Women are typically not listened to as having something important to say because the woman in the family or marital relationship is viewed as an adjunct. ("Hello, Mrs. Smith. What does your husband do?") Like children, women are not taken seriously, or when they talk about serious things, are accused of imitating a man (4). Research on nonverbal communication consistently shows that women are treated and behave as inferiors (33). There are several consequences of this lack of confirmation experienced by women that therapists should be aware of: women are regarded as nags because they talk constantly in seeking to be attended to or as devious or vague because they express themselves indirectly and tentatively in order to avoid disapproval.

The transactional nature of family therapy reveals habitual family communication patterns as no other approach has been able to do. For example, the nagging person can be viewed not only in terms of the withdrawn or disinterested partner that provokes the nagging behavior, but also in terms of the third person in the triangle who is being given a lesson, drawn in, distanced, supported, alienated, or the like. Changing communication patterns in the family is regarded by some family theorists as the single most important technique for changing behaviors and attitudes (16, 48). The family can practice new ways of communicating, shifting roles through role play, critique, and practice in order to learn new ways of interacting and to understand the confining aspects of one's own or another's traditional role.

Rules for communication have been developed by women's consciousness-raising groups to help women express themselves and be heard. Some of these are similar to those used by family therapists, such as not interrupting, relating the particular experience to the universal (generalizing), becoming specific ("What does that mean to you?"), and attaching significance to feelings, not just to facts. The latter leads to less disqualifying of women's experiences or style of expression than the rational mode to which men have been socialized. The therapist can also reinforce a greater range of genuine emotional expression and sensitivity to emotions in men who have avoided or disparaged emotional expression.

Generational boundaries

Clear generational boundaries are often seen as congruent with healthy family functioning (37). The breakdown in boundaries can occur when one of the parents is more closely allied with a child than with the spouse. The therapist who is not sensitive to the power differences in family roles may not understand the alliance of the powerless mother and child against the powerful father or the father and child against the demanding mother. Sometimes there seem to be no generational boundaries but an amorphous unit consisting of parents and children in which the parents avoid the burden of decisions and responsibility by a spurious equality. Children may find themselves parenting the parent with exaggerated dependency needs. The low status accorded to older people in our society and particularly to older women needs to be kept in mind by the therapist who sees a mother trying to be an age mate to her daughter. The therapist should work to restore the alliance between the parents without the exaggerated status differences that have evolved between adults and children in modern times.

It has been pointed out that children have a deteriorating effect on the marital relationship in terms of a decline in understanding, love, and general satisfaction (19). This could well be a consequence of the mother's dissatisfaction with the burden of her assigned role and the lack of genuine sharing and interest in child care by the father. The availability of the mother to the children leads to close alliances as well as the perpetuation of stereotyped sex roles. Mothers tend to use their daughters (or sons) as confidants because their isolation in the home from other adults confines them to housewife and mothering functions. In this way, women pass on their sense of worthlessness and denigration to both daughters and sons. The unavailability of fathers affects sons and daughters as well as mothers, sons because the unavailable father does not provide a model for learning, daughters because the father's unavailability leads them to develop an image of the male as a romantic stranger, an unrealistic ideal that cannot be satisfied when they reach adult life.

During adolescence, daughters are particularly torn between identification with the mother and with the father. This is the time when it becomes increasingly apparent to young women that career paths may be closed to them. The daughter who has a close relationship with her mother but is interested in a life different from her mother's may see herself as betraying and competing with her mother. If she aspires to a career path and identifies with her father, this can interfere with her relationship with her mother as well as with the development of feminine aspects of her identity (38). The therapist who is sensitive to the confusion of young women during this period can provide support to the girl as a facilitative model who values both career and family.

Siblings can sometimes develop a strong subsystem independent of the parents. Freedom from assigned sex roles among siblings can be supported by the therapist and the parents. It is frequently not recognized how much siblings contribute to one another's development through socialization, control, and rescuing operations.

Younger children are often coopted by one or both of the parents in terms of their own needs. Therapists need to be aware of the extent to which children bring zest and life to a family and misbehave to keep the family system functioning. A range of behaviors should be equally allowed both girls and boys. Children's disturbing behavior may be subtly encouraged by the parents who can be united only when dealing with a child's misbehavior. School refusal and other disruptive behaviors may actually be supportive of a depressed parent, usually the mother. To the extent the family therapist can help the mother develop independence and self-esteem, as well as gain the positive regard of the father, the therapist frees the children from the need to rescue the mother by "bad" behavior.

Relabeling deviance

Diagnostic labels are not useful in a family systems approach because they carry intrapsychic and causal connotations that do not fit into a systems model. Like the feminist therapist, the family therapist can avoid labels implying that the attribute belongs to the individual rather than the situation. Diagnostic labels, by focusing on the individual, serve to mask the prevalence of particular conditions in society that stress individuals. That behavior has become habitual as a result of socialization patterns of reinforcement does not mean that the therapist should shift to the intrapsychic model. For example, it should be recognized that the unhappiness of women in families is too widespread to be viewed as an individual weakness or defect. As Halleck (17) has emphasized, treatment that does not encourage the patient to examine and confront her environment merely strengthens the status quo.

The use of language is important because in this way sex differences can be exaggerated, often with disparaging connotations (14). Some of the pejorative labels used are imposed by the male-dominated culture such as pretty, sexy, ugly, blonde, dumpy, and the like (23). Others clearly reflect the double standard of terminology for men and women. The use of the generic masculine pronoun denies women's experiences. Consider also, for example, "father absence" and "maternal deprivation." Or the fact that a family is called traditional when the man is breadwinner but matriarchal when the woman is the breadwinner (35). "Weak" is a label applied to women and pejoratively to men, but like "strong," its meaning can only be understood in transactional terms. All too often, the weak person in the family, by appearing incompetent, is shoring up the strong one in order to prevent the latter's true frailty from becoming apparent. In this way, the inadequate housekeeper or the fearful woman is making her partner as well as other family members appear strong, and so in reality, she is protecting them.

An example of a pejorative and overused label in contemporary society is "passive-aggressive." What the therapist needs to do is examine the conditions that make individuals use covert and indirect means rather than direct means for gaining their ends. Some behaviors, such as phobic behaviors, can be understood as exaggerations of the dependency and timidity that women are taught or as a consequence of women's inexperience and the taboos against women successfully coping with and overcoming obstacles in a "man's world." Too often therapists, like others, blame women for the dependency in which they have been trained.

There are a number of ways by which therapists who are sensitive to the misuse of labels can bring about change. They can help both women and men free themselves from stereotypic expectations that lead them to try to hide attributes in themselves they have been taught are unacceptable. In addition, therapists can often perceive attributes of family members that are not usually noticed and by drawing attention to them can shift family members' ways of perceiving and interacting. Labels of "good" and "bad" illustrate how labels deny the complexity of persons. In the case of an older "bad" sister who was always in trouble, I was able to shift some of the "good" from the younger "good" child to the "bad" one by drawing the family's attention to the contribution that older children make to younger ones by testing the limits and the rules in the family. This emphasized the similarities between the children rather than their differences.

Modeling

Feminists recognize that one of the important aspects of consciousness-raising groups is the opportunity for women to model for each other. There are a variety of successful male models available in public life, business, the professions, and the media, but women have lacked female models because of the relatively few women in positions of prominence. Women have also been isolated from others in their daily lives in their homes. The female therapist can model a successful woman for clients. I have found that it is hard for even the most liberal male to acknowledge that a female therapist could provide something that he could not. Some male therapists claim that they are better therapists for female clients because they can provide a different kind of male model than the client is accustomed to (26). What goes unrecognized is that the male therapist, in providing a different male model, is reinforcing traditional stereotypes by assuming that the female client needs a special male who will treat her differently than other males have done. What a woman needs to learn is not that some men are different but how she can become a different woman.

By modeling different behaviors, the female therapist can help women free themselves from minority group traits that they have developed because of lack of power and secondary status, traits such as dislike of one's own sex, a negative self-image, "shuffling," insecurity, low aspirations, and appeasing behaviors (23). Another quality that female therapists can model for all the family is competency in a woman. However, in family therapy, the therapist needs to be careful not to render family members incompetent by being a better parent, a better mother, or a better partner—more wise, just, and all-seeing. Traditional therapy has too often fostered the woman's view of herself as incompetent. The therapist who can acknowledge a lack of knowledge in some areas is a better model for parents and family members than one who is either a superwoman or a superman.

Ownership and privacy

Just as Gestalt therapists have sought to develop ownership of an individual's feelings and attitudes by "I" statements, so family therapists can encourage ownership. Women typically have not been sure of their share in family resources that relate to the money world. Therapists may need to help women negotiate with other family members to gain ownership of many aspects of their lives. Women often lack ownership of the means of privacy, such as personal space, their space being that associated with their household job, like kitchen or sewing room (28). They also do not own personal time without feelings of guilt or the use of money without accountability. A sensitive therapist can also encourage a woman to own and develop her talents and hobbies, as well as her thoughts and feelings. By encouraging ownership in other areas, the therapist may be able to help women assert ownership of their own bodies. Experiences like menstruation, menopause, hot flashes, tension around menstrual periods, impregnation, lactation, and childbirth can be crisis situations that women never discuss with male therapists.

Is family solidarity incompatible with individual ownership in the family? The therapist needs to point out that personhood for the mother as well as other family members is important, that the family need not be either a fortress or a prison. Since women have been raised to believe that their self-worth and identity is inextricably bound to finding the right husband and caring for a family, they may use therapy to talk about relationships with men rather than about their own identity (3). The family therapist deemphasizes "talking about" in favor of interaction and can be influential in reinforcing assertive steps toward a sense of self that does not result solely from identification with family goals, family service, and family responsibility.

Therapeutic alliances

An issue raised in modeling and in the interventions and alliances of the family therapist is the therapist's own gender. Does the therapist interact differently with men and women? Can a male be a feminist therapist? Certainly a nonsexist male therapist is better than a sexist female one. The power differential between males and females is still an enormous obstacle. Furthermore, because the stereotyped male role requires men always to appear competent, it may be that men find it harder than women to recognize and acknowledge sex biases in themselves. These therapist blind spots lead to reinforcing traditional patterns, whether the male therapist is allying with a woman to "protect" her, which is really a competitive move against her husband, or allying in a male bond with the husband, against the wife.

An essential aspect of family therapy is that the therapist must be committed to each person in the family (20). This means the therapist must frequently shift alliances congruent with therapeutic goals. An alliance does not necessarily mean an "agreement" with. The experienced family therapist can ally with one family member in terms of feelings, attention, or emphasis on syntonic aspects of therapist and client personalities, while supporting the views and attitudes of another family member. For example, an initial alliance of one kind may need to be made with the typically reluctant father in order to assure his attendance and participation in the beginning stages of therapy.

The female therapist will frequently be viewed as allied with the mother because of their common gender just as the male therapist will be perceived as allied with the male when sometimes this is not the case. The husband and the therapist as the two reasonable (powerful) persons are often assumed to have a natural alliance. Rawlings and Carter (42) report a family therapy session with two therapists, a psychiatrist and social worker, both males, where the mother felt like a rabbit being attacked by a wolf pack. Women may need the support of a female therapist to oppose traditional alliances and to be able to release pent-up rage, helplessness, and envy of men (25).

Many married couples who do cotherapy assume that they provide a model of a normal or a liberated couple, as the case may be. I would agree with Sager (46) that "the therapy couple's use of themselves as role models is a dubious procedure based on the treating couple's idealization of their own self-image" (p. 188). Marriage per se of a cotherapy team is no guarantee of therapeutic effectiveness (27). If there are differences in experience, training, and status of the cotherapy pair, there is a basis for inequality that is not lost on family members, no matter what roles the cotherapists imagine they are playing in the therapy sessions. Male-female cotherapy teams have been found to reinforce patterns of behavior that are oppressive to women (2). The cotherapy team in which the female rather than the male therapist is the senior member is virtually unheard of. Some therapists prefer a cotherapist because they recognize that family therapy can take on aspects of an adversary proceeding in which each spouse is seeking an ally for a scolding match (42).

The family therapist needs to be aware of the alliance-seeking behaviors of some family members who draw the therapist into a triangle at the expense of other family members. Therapists who expect and assume that female behaviors toward males are basically envious or seductive are themselves locked into stereotyped thinking that will interfere with their capacity to be helpful. Nor can one disregard the enormous emotional significance of men qua men in our society. Orlinsky and Howard (39) have pointed out that the client's emotional reactivity solely to the sex of the therapist may override the experience, talent, and warmth that the therapist brings to bear. A problem for the male therapist may be to deal with the woman's anger as she recognizes the irrelevance and goallessness of the activities that are her daily lot. A problem for the female therapist is the lack of respect and questions of therapeutic competence that are leveled at the female professional. As the husband and children learn to deal with the competent female therapist, they will learn to deal with the wife and mother in the family in a new way.

CONCLUSION

Family therapy provides opportunities for social change unavailable in other therapeutic approaches. The therapist is addressing problems in the family that reflect the traditional norms and expectations the parents bring from their own families of origin and attempt to maintain in their current family. The systems approach to family therapy is congruent with feminist therapy in examining behavior in terms of its economic and social determinants rather than using an individual-centered approach. A feminist-oriented family therapist can intervene in many ways to change the oppressive consequences of stereotyped roles and expectations in the family. As consciousness-raising takes place in families, family members come to recognize the sociocultural pressures that perpetuate traditional sex roles and seek ways to free themselves from these pressures. A review of family techniques from a feminist perspective indicates that family therapy is indeed possible without encouraging stereotyped sex roles.

REFERENCES

1. Adams, S. and Orgel, M., *Through the Mental Health Maze*, Washington, Public Citizen's Health Research Group, 1975.
2. American Psychological Association, *Report of the Task Force on Sex Bias and Sex Role Stereotyping in Therapeutic Practice*, Washington, Author, 1975.
3. Barrett, C. J.; Berg, P. I.; Eaton, E. M.; and Pomeroy, E. L., "Implications of Women's Liberation and the Future of Psychotherapy," *Psychother.: Theo. Res. Pract.* 11: 11–15, 1974.
4. Beauvoir, S. de, *The Second Sex*, New York, Bantam Books, 1970.
5. Bem, S. L. and Bem, D. J., "We're All Nonconscious Sexists," *Psychol. Today*, November 1970, p. 22.
6. Bernard, J., *The Future of Motherhood*, New York, Dial Press, 1974.
7. Boszormenyi-Nagy, I. and Spark, G. M., *Invisible Loyalties: Reciprocity in Intergenerational Family Therapy*, New York, Harper & Row, 1973.
8. Bowen, M., "The Use of Family Theory in Clinical Practice," *Compr. Psychiat.* 7: 345–374, 1966.
9. Broverman, I. K.; Broverman, D. M.; Clarkson, F. E.; Rosenkrantz, P. S.; and Vogel, S. R., "Sex Role Stereotypes and Clinical Judgments of Mental Health," *J. Consult. Clin. Psychol.*, 34: 1–7, 1970.
10. Chase, K., "Seeing Sexism: A Look at Feminist Therapy," *State and Mind*, March-April 1977, pp. 19-22.
11. Dohrenwend, B. S., "Social Status and Stressful Life Events," *J. Pers. Soc. Psychol.* 28: 225–235, 1973.
12. Forrest, T., "Treatment of the Father in Family Therapy," *Fam. Proc.* 8: 106–117, 1969.
13. Frank, J. D., *Persuasion and Healing*, Baltimore, Johns Hopkins University Press, 1973.
14. Gingras-Baker, S., "Sex Role Stereotyping and Marriage Counseling," *J. Marr. Fam. Couns.*, 2: 355–366, 1976.
15. Gove, W. R., "The Relationship between Sex Roles, Marital Status, and Mental Illness," in A. G. Kaplan and J. P. Bean (Eds.), *Beyond Sex-Role Stereotypes: Readings toward a Psychology of Androgyny*, Boston, Little, Brown, 1976.
16. Haley, J. (Ed.) *Changing Families*, New York, Grune & Stratton, 1971.
17. Halleck, S. L., *Politics of Therapy*, New York, Science House, 1971.
18. Hare-Mustin, R. T.; Marecek, J.; Kaplan, A.; and Liss-Levinson, N., "Rights of Clients, Responsibilities of Therapists: A Training Module," Unpublished manuscript, 1977.
19. Hill, R. and Rodgers, R. H., "The Developmental Approach," in H. T. Christensen (Ed.), *Handbook of Marriage and the Family*, Chicago, Rand McNally, 1964.
20. Hines, P. and Hare-Mustin, R. T., "Ethical Concerns in Family Therapy," *Profess. Psychol.*, 9: 165–171, 1978.

21. Kaplan, A. G., "Clarifying the Concept of Androgyny: Implications for Therapy," Paper presented in Symposium on Applications of Androgyny to the Theory and Practice of Psychotherapy at the meeting of the American Psychological Association, Washington, September 1976.

22. Keller, S., "The Female Role: Constants and Change," in V. Franks and V. Burtle (Eds.), *Women in Therapy*, New York, Brunner/Mazel, 1974.

23. Kirsh, B., "Consciousness-Raising Groups as Therapy for Women," in V. Franks and V. Burtle (Eds.), *Women in Therapy*, New York, Brunner/Mazel, 1974.

24. Klapper, L. and Kaplan, A. G., "The Emerging Consciousness of Sex-role Stereotyping in the Family Therapy Literature," Unpublished manuscript, 1977.

25. Kronsky, B. J., "Feminism and Psychotherapy," *J. Contemp. Psychother.*, 3: 89–98, 1971.

26. Lazarus, A. A., "Women in Behavior Therapy," in V. Franks and V. Burtle (Eds.), *Women in Therapy*, New York, Brunner/Mazel, 1974.

27. Lazarus, L. W., "Family Therapy by a Husband-Wife Team," *J. Marr. Fam. Couns.*, 2: 225–235, 1976.

28. Lennard, S. H. C., and Lennard, H. L., "Architecture: Effect of Territory, Boundary, and Orientation on Family Functioning," *Fam. Proc.*, 16: 49–66, 1977.

29. Lerman, H., "What Happens in Feminist Therapy," Paper presented in Symposium on Feminist Therapy in Search of a Theory at the meeting of the American Psychological Association, New Orleans, 1974.

30. Marecek, J., "Dimensions of Feminist Therapy," Paper presented in Symposium on Liberating Psychotherapy: Changing Perspectives and Roles among Women, at the meeting of the American Psychological Association, Montreal, September, 1973.

31. Marecek, J., "Powerlessness and Women's Psychological Disorders," *Voices: J. Am. Acad. Psychotherapists* 12: 50–54, 1976.

32. McAllister, A. and Fernhoff, D., "Test on the Bias: An Experiential Assessment of Sex Bias in the Psychological Battery," *Division 35 Newsletter*, American Psychological Association, 3 (4): 10–12, 1976.

33. Mehrabian, A., *Nonverbal Communication*, Chicago, Aldine-Atherton, 1972.

34. Miller, J. B. and Mothner, I., "Psychological Consequences of Sexual Inequality," *Am. J. Orthopsychiat.*, 41: 767–775, 1971.

35. Millman, M., "Observations on Sex Role Research," *J. Marr. Fam.*, 33: 772–775, 1971.

36. Minturn, L. and Lambert, W. W., *Mothers of Six Cultures, Antecedents of Child Rearing*, New York, Wiley, 1964.

37. Minuchin, S., *Families and Family Therapy*, Cambridge, Mass., Harvard University Press, 1974.

38. Nadelson, C. M., "Adjustment: New Approaches to Women's Mental Health," in M. L. McBee and K. A. Blake (Eds.), *The American Woman: Who Will She Be?*, Beverly Hills, Glencoe Press, 1974.

39. Orlinsky, D. E. and Howard, K. I., "The Effects of Sex of Therapist on the Therapeutic Experiences of Women," *Psychother.: Theo. Res. Pract.* 13: 82–88, 1976.

40. Parsons, T. and Bales, R. F., *Family, Socialization, and Interaction Process*, Glencoe, Ill., Free Press, 1955.

41. Peal, E., "'Normal' Sex Roles: An Historical Analysis," *Fam. Proc.*, 14: 389–409, 1975.

42. Rawlings, E. I. and Carter, D. K., *Psychotherapy for Women*, Springfield, Ill., Thomas, 1977.

43. Rice, D. G. and Rice, J. K., "Non-Sexist 'Marital' Therapy," *J. Marr. Fam. Couns.*, 3: 3–10, 1977.

44. Rosenthal, E. R., *Structural Patterns of Women's Occupational Choice*, Ph. D. dissertation, Cornell University, 1974.

45. Sachnoff, E., "Toward a Definition of Feminist Therapy," *AWP Newsletter*, Fall 1975, pp. 4–5.

46. Sager, C. J., *Marriage Contracts and Couple Therapy*, New York, Brunner/Mazel, 1976.

47. Smith, J. A., "For God's Sake, What Do Those Women Want?" *Personnel and Guidance J.*, 51: 133–136, 1972.

48. Watzlawick, P., Weakland, J. H. and Fisch, R., *Change*, New York, Norton, 1974.

49. Zuk, G. R., "Family Therapy: Clinical Hodgepodge or Clinical Science?" *J. Marr. Fam. Couns.*, 2: 229–304, 1972.

Psychotherapy for the Poor: An Eco-Structural Approach to Treatment

Harry J. Aponte

The treatment of psychiatric problems among the poor continues to be a disheartening experience for many clinicians who attempt it. But just as public health concepts revolutionized the attack on physical illness, an ecological view of mental illness offers a key to the understanding and treatment of the emotional problems of the poor.

Who are the poor? Those with little money? What about the monks and the young people who choose to be without? Then is it those who are involuntarily without money? Are these the poor most of us are worried about? What about the formerly middle class mother who now a widow supplements her social security check with a welfare check so that she can care for her children and whose family is otherwise functioning happily and is well established within the community? Is she poor?

Consider for a moment. Whom do you think of when you think of the poor? Do you think of a Black mother with four kids, living on welfare in a ghetto? Do you think of an Appalachian white family, father unemployed, a mother and six kids living on welfare? Do you think of a Puerto Rican mother with five kids living with her common law husband whose income is a sometime thing? Whom do you think of?

What about that family with a good income? But they live in a ghetto. Father has a highly paid skill and works regularly, but he is never home. He has a girl friend that everyone knows about. Mother as often as not is drinking at the bar. Neither parent knows where the older kids are, and the younger ones are somehow taking care of themselves at home. They have money, but might they be considered poor? Did you picture them as white? Whom do you really picture as the poor?

When you think about organizing your services for the poor, whom are you thinking about? Let me tell you whom I'm thinking about. I am thinking of those whom Oscar Lewis described as living in the "culture of poverty."* He spoke of their local community as having a "minimum of organization beyond the level of the nuclear and extended family."[1] Minuchin and Montalvo have described the families themselves as disorganized, lacking clear generational boundaries and differentiated communication patterns.[2] Lewis talks of the individuals in this culture as suffering from feelings of "marginality" and "helplessness."[3] Others have described in detail the sense of worthlessness with which the children from this culture can become imbued.

The poor to whom I refer are suffering from a poverty of structure and organization, on a personal level, a family level, and a community level. Let me quote Auerswald at some length: "Most intricate of all is the process in the growing child of differentiating, labeling, and identifying the many diverse ingredients of human interaction necessary if he is to function efficiently in a large variety of roles demanded by different life situations. . . . only then will he be able to define his own identity boundaries in that situation and tie his own internal feelings to the external, or internalized referents that will allow him to identify them. . . . Belonging to a group is not enough; he must have a clear picture of the structure and operations of the group to which he belongs, and within the context of this knowledge he must see quite clearly and in detail the nature of his usefulness, his function, and his tasks within the group."[4]

The poor I am concerned about are those whose childhood lacks or lacked this experience of personal and contextual differentiation. Take this description of the developing child, lacking structure in his life context, and clarity about his relationship with that context, and relate it to Minuchin and Montalvo's description of the disorganized family. "The stereotyped interaction in our families can be expressed as a result of paucity and rigidity of interpersonal transactional patterns and also on a higher level of abstraction, as frozen development of the family as a total system. The system is 'at rest' as a relatively simple social 'organism' with a concomitant lack of specialization and differentiation in the component functions of its members."[5]

Add to that Lewis' statements about the relative lack of organization within the ghetto community, and you have a striking picture of poverty of organization at various levels from the individual to the community and the effects of this kind of poverty on the children living in this context.

Psychoanalytic theory about the neurotic personality assumed an average, expectable environment. As such, this theory could focus on conflict between certain distinct parts of the personality structure, the superego against the id, for example. Psychoanalytic treatment of these personality problems did not have to address itself to changing the family or community. These were assumed to function within a certain expectable range. Change was to come from within the identified patient. But what when there is not the average, expectable structure in a person's ecological context? The individual child

*The author employs Lewis' phrase "culture of poverty" because of the usefulness of the concepts about disorganization that the term covers. However, the author does not subscribe to Lewis' suggestion that the life style of the poor is a cultural heritage. The devastating effects of a life of poverty are not rooted in a cultural inheritance, but in a lack of cultural, economic, and political options.

cannot develop a well differentiated personality structure if his immediate family is not organized with clearly designated generational boundaries. The family cannot organize itself if the societal structure of its socio-political context does not support it in doing so. The poor about whom I refer here are those poor who are poor in structural organization at every level of their ecology, including their own personalities.

How then to help these poor? With individual psychotherapy? I don't think you would expect me to make that suggestion. Help the disorganized poor through family therapy? Not if it is the family therapy that is still basically rooted in traditional insight therapy—where the object is still to get the members of the family to understand their own and each other's problems. This form of family therapy uses the family members to help one another achieve insight which hopefully will motivate each individual in the family to feel and behave differently.

THE JOHNSON FAMILY

This is not the therapy that will help the Johnson family. Mrs. Johnson is Black and 38. She's been raising her four kids alone for the past five years. Her boyfriend left her while she was still pregnant with her last child. She comes to the clinic about her ten-year-old son, but what you see is a depressed woman with such severe psychogenic stomach pains that she is living in the twilight of heavy doses of prescribed drugs. Her two oldest are taking care of her and the other children and are no longer living like children themselves. Mother spends her day in bed, and what the two youngest are getting from the older ones is not enough for them to develop on.

Mrs. Johnson's situation needs to be understood from an ecological standpoint. Auerswald says that the ecological approach "...begins with an analysis of the structure of the field, using the common structural and operational properties of systems as criteria for identifying the systems and subsystems...."[6]

Mrs. Johnson brought in her ten-year-old son as the identified patient. He was having trouble in school. He was not doing his work and not getting along with the other children. That ten-year-old lives not only within his own skin, but he also lives within his sibling subgroup, part of which has turned into a pseudo parent. He lives also within his family group, where his mother functions partly as a parent and partly as his sibling. Furthermore his contextual systems take in his maternal grandmother, who has a special dislike for him and never had any closeness with her daughter, the boy's mother. His contextual systems likewise include his community with its subsystems: the school, the inner city neighborhood, and the context in which his racial group exists in relation to the majority group.

I am sure the therapists could have talked with Mrs. Johnson about many things, but what they did was go home with Mrs. Johnson, have the family plan a menu under her direction, go shopping with the family, join Mrs. Johnson in preparing the meal, as her assistants, and give all the children distinctly children-type duties to perform for their mother. The therapists helped Mrs. Johnson assume an executive role around the preparation of the meal that evening and actively supported her taking charge of the household thereafter.

Mrs. Johnson was out of her depression and stopped living off pain-killers within a couple of weeks. Symptom removal was the beginning of the work with the Johnson family. Thereafter, the two therapists intervened at many levels of this family's ecology, at times together, at times separately, at times with the entire family, on occasion with one member alone, at other times with the school, and in some instances with other members of the community. What were the therapists doing? They were bringing structural and ecological order into the disarray of this family and its community context. They were helping Mrs. Johnson become a competent mother within her family. They later went further, helping her become a competent adult who dated and involved herself in community activities where she could be an active citizen who could exert influence. They were making the two oldest kids children again, which created a crisis for the oldest, a boy, who had long since given up his friends to become mother's companion. The second oldest, a girl, also became a child again, and lo, it was discovered she had been having serious trouble too, but it had gone unnoticed while she was functioning as the cook and house cleaner at home. Yes, the ten-year-old had been having problems, but he now had his mother back, as did the youngest, and mother with her two new adult assistants could begin learning with her children about the distribution of functions at home and new patterns of communication and problem solving. Much organizing and patterning also had to take place for the family members in relation to the other systems to which they were related.

THE ECO-STRUCTURAL APPROACH IN THERAPY

Still, what is the eco-structural approach in therapy, and what is its relationship to other therapies? The ecological view of human behavior is based on a systems conceptualization. Quoting Peter Laqueur: "But GST (General Systems Theory) provides a conceptual framework that makes sense of the very complex systems that we deal with in multiple family therapy ... GST sees the individual as a subsystem of a higher system ... and again as part of the next higher system, the family, kinship, community."[7]

The structural aspect of the eco-structural approach to people and their problems involves the relationship of the parts of a system to the functional operations of the system.

The eco-structural approach helps us perceive human behavior from a perspective broader than the individual. Through it we see the actions of the individual as rooted not only in his personality, but as sprouting from relationships between himself, other individuals, and other groups. We therefore do not see the dysfunctional person through the disease model, containing within himself the germ of a psychiatric illness which disrupts his personality and may infect others. In the eco-structural view we recognize the internal structural organization and ecological balance of the many psychological and biological systems within the individual, but we also look beyond to the interaction and structural relationship of these systems with the other systems in the individual's life context. To view them as systems we must not only see parts or sub-systems impinging, relating, and depending on one another, but we must also view these interactions as time-related. The ecological context for an action is not only as broad as a historical trend, but also as narrow as a reflexive reaction triggered by another's sudden, unexpected gesture. The ecological view does not negate any phenomena. It organizes them all in systematic, dynamic relationships. Quoting from Auerswald again: "Concepts from cybernetics, the study and treatment of the family as a system, small group processes, theory of perception and cognition, communications, and so forth, all become usable in an integrated way."[8]

I would add to that that our knowledge of individual psychology, biology, and other sciences also contributes to our ecological understanding. Moreover, they also contribute to our techniques. I propose that what we have learned from the various methods that have been used for psychological treatment continues to be useful, but more useful when employed within the broader perspective of the eco-structural model. I believe that what methods we cannot now integrate, are more in conflict because of our lack of knowledge about their ecological relationships than because of intrinsic contradictions. Note that I refer here to *methods* of treatment, not *theories* of treatment, which indeed can be dogmatic and incompatible.

Behavior modification is a useful technique, but if the oldest boy in the Johnson family, one of the parental children, had tried to help his younger brother improve his school performance through a system of rewards, he probably would have failed, even with the most carefully planned behavior modification program. He would have failed because the conditioning technique was not allowing for the organizational structure of the ecological systems of the family and school. The younger boy was in competition with his older brother and needed to receive the rewards from his mother whose approval he craved. But the school and the mother needed also to cooperate in ways that supported the mother's efforts to positively reinforce her younger son's school efforts.

The oldest boy in the Johnson family had also begun himself to devalue his manhood and his Blackness. He could well profit from a series of individual sessions. He was a young adolescent and needed to begin considering certain personal life issues away from his family. Some form of individual counseling or therapy could be useful, but certainly a white, female therapist would not be my first choice for the youngster. His maleness and his Blackness identify him with specific ecological groups. But also the functional organization of his family would need to be considered. He would need to know from his mother that she does not need him to be the compliant, attached son who both performs some of her duties at home and acts as a companion to her. As long as his mother is suffering from a serious depression and is further incapacitated by pain, no therapist in individual sessions will move this boy to assume any other posture than the one he has adopted.

While the eco-structural viewpoint helps to integrate other methodologies, it also brings with it its own methods and skills. The therapist must be able to conceptualize what he or she sees in terms of systems and their structural bases. The therapist must also be able to talk and behave in such a way that the members of the family system and other systems will themselves be able to experience the relevant issues as phenomena founded on the interactions between people and organizations. The therapist must be able to use himself or herself to promote changes in authoritative hierarchies, communication lines, interpersonal alliances, and other organizational structures which will change the functioning of systems. The therapist needs to know how to communicate, pair himself or herself, and in other ways interact with others so that they will change the ways their particular systems are operating. Along with this, the therapist will need to know ways of assisting others to bring about organizational changes within the ecological systems to which they are related. There are a knowledge and skill here that are not the property of any single profession. This brings us to the next issue, the delivery of these services.

NEW PROFESSIONAL ROLES

Remember, I am not just talking about the economically poor, but of those who are poor in structure and organization. The ecological approach is specific to their problems. However, the use of this approach in a mental health center does not just involve the adoption of some new methods. These methods have implications that will affect in essential ways the structure and organization of the clinic itself.

Jay Haley has written a paper entitled "Why a Mental Health Clinic Should Avoid Family Therapy."[9] It may sound strange that one of the most prominent proponents of family therapy should write such a paper. He does so with tongue in cheek to make a serious point that the adoption by a traditional psychiatric clinic of an ecological systems approach to treatment will create conflict and stress within the clinic that should not be underestimated. If you change to an ecological conceptualization of mental illness, what will happen to your diagnostic categories, listing affective and thought disorders? Who will you designate as the patient? Who will be responsible for diagnosis and treatment?

Since the ecological and family approaches to treatment are not the property of any one discipline, anyone can learn the theory and methods. What then happens to the distinctions between professional roles? The psychiatrist can no longer have the exclusive right to diagnose and oversee treatment. The psychologist's skills as a tester for individual psycho-dynamics will be underutilized. The social worker who has been accustomed to depend on others to assume responsibility for patients will have to face the need to take this responsibility, himself or herself. When it comes to diagnosing and treating, there will be a leveling effect as all begin to exercise the same skills. This will create tension within the organization as the functions which dictated the structure of the clinic change radically.

Within the staff members themselves there will be struggles as individuals begin to appreciate the far-reaching implications of their learning new skills and taking on new roles vis-a-vis other professionals. Most clinicians will retain an identity with their professional disciplines and because of it will have a variety of distinctive skills to offer the clinic team. What this will be for each professional will depend on the special interests he or she has developed in his or her profession, and on the way his or her profession has shaped the person's professional identity. But, the issue of professional identity will not be facilely resolved for most clinicians adopting the structural and ecological systems model.

Let us take this issue of professionalism a step further. In working with the poor, issues related to style of life and communication loom large. Certainly many clinical failures with the poor are due to the therapist's inability to identify enough with the poor and to work with sufficient understanding of the poor. If you yourself are not and have never been a member of the "culture of poverty," how do you navigate within the framework of priorities and realities of the poor and the communication, affective, and other cultural styles of the ethnic and social minorities who have sizeable representation among the poor? Because you must, you know, if you wish to be effective. I cannot tell you how, except to suggest you somehow live with the poor and find some way to genuinely see inside of and feel with their reality. To deal with the poor of an ethnic or racial group to which you are an alien will demand a further effort to recognize sameness where it exists and recognize and respect difference where it is discovered.

If your staff has difficulty bridging the gap, should you not look to hire professionals who come out of poverty themselves? They are scarce and in demand. How hard will you try to find them? But remember that belonging to a particular ethnic group does not ipso facto qualify a person as a member of the "culture of poverty." Being Puerto Rican does not make you a ghetto citizen. Black is not a synonym for poverty.

You can also seek to hire so-called paraprofessionals. Mental health aides who can identify with the life of poverty can go a long way in bridging communication gaps. By adapting an ecological model you have already begun to reshuffle the professional hierarchy in your clinic, however; and if the so-called paraprofessional becomes skillful, you will have another contender for status in your clinic. This situation will be aggravated if you have persons coming out of poverty who do not have the traditional professional mental health backgrounds but who are fully trained to work in the ecological model. There are programs for persons with barely a high school degree which are training competent, autonomous family therapists.

DELIVERY OF SERVICES

Aside from a change in professional roles within the eco-structural model, there will be a change in your work style, particularly if you are working with the poor. The "culture of poverty" implies a lack of organizational structure that is endemic. The therapist who offers help is offering to assist in the creation of a structure where structure is lacking, not just to restore structure where it has been temporarily upset or to reorganize a dysfunctional structure. In some families organization is so lacking that the only way a therapist can begin to intervene usefully is by putting in long hours of personal commitment to help organize family members around the most basic functions of family life. The therapist may be able to find others in the family's ecology to offer this help, such as other relatives, friends, or other agencies, but this kind of help is not easily come by.

I was recently asked by a staff member of a pediatric clinic to see a child who frequently went into apparent trances, staring into space. She had been thoroughly examined physically and all tests proved negative. She had a younger sister and no father at home. Her young mother was a former heroin addict who lived now on methadone. The mother spent most of her days out of her own apartment and in the home of the woman who raised her, who is not a relative. This step-mother of the patient's mother has six other children still at home, and her home is itself a picture of depressed and despairing people. The young mother had never had the stimulation and nurturence a growing child needs and was herself quite unable to cope with the demands of life, and certainly unable to provide her child with the interest and attention the child requires. The child was staring into space because her mother stares into space. There was a lack of stimuli from within the family, and the child could do little else. I suggested to the worker from the pediatric service to begin with an hourly visit a day supervising the mother who agreed to number paint with her daughter for fifteen minutes a day. The worker was to help the mother attend to every detail of her daughter's painting, praising, and correcting as warranted. Another block of that daily hour was to be used to help the mother toilet train her younger child, who was now five. The training methods would be meticulous and involve a carefully detailed plan of positive reinforcement. And these daily visits would take place in the mother's own apartment, where she was away from the crowded stepmother's home and where she was at least nominally in charge. This will be a long-term commitment for the worker whose work with the mother and children will need to begin at a most rudimentary level of structured mother-child interaction and will only later evolve into other areas of functioning of this family.

Some work with these families can be long and tedious. Other interventions can be brief where sectors of the ecological structure can be organized to do the work with other sectors. In one situation the school complained about a young girl's high absenteeism. When she called the clinic at the school's behest, the mother said she had no problems with the girl at home. Only the school was complaining. We, therefore, asked that the first appointment be held at the school with the mother and all her children, the child's teachers, counselor, and the principal. We learned in a multistaged interview, engaging various combinations of the paticipants in the interview, that the girl had performed well in school the semester before with a teacher to whom she had become closely attached. Her absences had begun this semester with a change of teacher. Also, the mother was using the girl as a babysitter for her younger children when she had to be out of the house during the day. The school principal agreed to send the girl back to her former teacher, who could help her with her current assignment, and the school counselor accepted the responsibility to help the mother find other babysitting arrangements. The school as a part of the girl's ecology altered how its teaching and counseling staff were related to this girl and her family. No other interventions by the clinic were necessary.

Because time is also part of ecology, one must consider the timing of a request for help as a matter of paramount importance. A request for help from a disorganized family is prompted by some change in the structural organization and ecological balance of their lives that requires your intervention *now*. A clinic that cannot see a family within two weeks of a request for help is not organized to work with the poor. And here I am not referring to emergencies that require instant response. The ecological shift may pressure a family to ask for help, but if help is delayed, the poor family may absorb the change into its disorganization and see no reason to come for help.

THE CLINIC AND THE COMMUNITY

There are many other issues that should be dealt with in discussing mental health services to the poor. But I will make reference to only one more, the relationship of the clinic to the community. With the advent of social psychiatry and particularly with the social consciousness of the last decade, mental health centers have begun not only to hire community people, but also to be active in community organization. This community activity has at times preempted efforts that the community itself needed to carry out. A community perhaps may well profit from an activity and discussion group for its gang-involved adolescents, a tutoring program for poorly motivated youngsters, or a parents group for adults concerned about neighborhood issues involving their children. However, a community may be better off not having some activities if they cannot be run by the local citizens themselves. A clinic would do well to seek out neighborhood folk who are trying to organize such activities and support their efforts to obtain funds and to run a successful program of their own. Since few clinics have boards that have a large proportion or majority of persons who represent the poor whom the clinic serves, the clinic is not responsible to the community. Community organizing by a clinic with a board of outsiders may only further serve to take control of the community out of the hands of the poor. From an ecological point of view the organization and functioning of the community are very much related to the mental health of the families within the community. If a clinic wishes to contribute to this aspect of the lives of those it serves, it can invite more community members to its board, and it can support the effort of the community groups to organize their own programs.

SUMMARY

I have talked here of the poor whose personal, family, and community lives lack the structure to make these systems do what they are supposed to do. The task of providing services to the poor is a difficult one since it means helping with basic structural issues for which most of us have not been trained by our professions. But the service can be given through an eco-structural approach to treatment and through a commitment to relate the clinic as an organization to the community it wishes to serve.

REFERENCES

1. Lewis O: La Vida, Vintage Books, New York, 1968, p XLVI.
2. Minuchin S and Montalvo B: Techniques for working with disorganized low socioeconomic families, Amer J Orthopsychiatry, Vol XXXVII, No. 5, October 1967.
3. Lewis O: La Vida, Vintage Books, New York, 1968, p XLVII.
4. Auerswald E: Cognitive development and psychopathology in the urban environment, in Graubard (ed) Children Against School: Education of the Delinquent, Disturbed, Disrupted, Jollett, Chicago, Fall 1968, pp 3-5.
5. Minuchin S, Montalvo B, et al: Families of the Slums, Basic Books, New York, 1967, chapter 8, p 368.
6. Auerswald E: Interdisciplinary versus ecological approach, Family Process, Vol 7, No. 2, Sept 1968, p 204.

7. Laquer H P: Multiple Family Therapy and General Systems Theory, ed by Ackerman, Family therapy in transition, Int Psychiatry Clinics, Vol 7, No. 4., Little, Brown and Co., Boston, 1970, p 100.

8. Auerswald E H: The Noncare of the Underprivileged: Some Ecological Observations, ed by Belasso, Psychiatric care of the underprivileged, Int Psychiatry Clinics, Vol 8, No. 2, Little, Brown and Co., Boston, 1971, p 54.

9. Haley J: Why A Mental Health Clinic Should Avoid Family Therapy, to be published.

Family Treatment of Poverty Level Families

Ben A. Orcutt

Changes in family functioning are complex, especially when there is a parental life pattern of self-defeating behavior with few nurturant and stimulating resources.

Poverty is both an objective and subjective phenomenon. Objectively, there is too little income to provide adequately for basic needs. Subjectively, the inability to meet needs and expectations is shrouded with emotion and may be felt differentially, depending on lifestyle and exposure to affluence. The increase in modern technology, wide availability of goods, and powerful advertising serve to stimulate the desires and expectations of people; however, those who are chronically poor may be so enmeshed in a struggle for survival that hope and expectations become blunted.

Poverty is currently measured by a poverty index centered around the economy food plan developed by the United States Department of Agriculture, and reflected in changes in costs of living. The Bureau of the Census,[1] in 1975, identified as poverty level: an income of $5,038 or less for a family of four for the year 1974. Regardless of how poverty is measured, however, it has a depressing and erosive effect on individuals and families.

It is reported that 25.5 million Americans are living on submarginal incomes.[2] Of those persons sixty-five years old and over, about 4.3 million (22 percent) were below the low income level. In addition, statistics reveal that 12.6 million persons below the poverty level were living in families headed by a male and there were 5.5 million related children under eighteen years of age in these families. Further, 7.8 million persons were living below the poverty level in families with a female head, in which there were 4.8 million related children

[1] U.S. Bureau of the Census, *Statistical Abstract of the United States*, 96th (Washington, D.C.: U.S. Government Printing Office, 1975), p. 399.

[2] U.S. Bureau of the Census, Characteristics of the Low Income Population, 1971, *Current Population Reports*, no. 86 (Washington, D.C.: U.S. Government Printing Office, 1972), pp. 4–30.

under eighteen years of age. It is clear from these statistics that a great number of submarginal families have a male head, which suggests relatively intact, but struggling families.

This article describes the poor family with multiple deficits in relational processes in which socioenvironmental conditions are so impoverished that interaction at the marketplace is limited. It is important to emphasize that all poor people do not have social, psychological, or relationship problems, but being poor greatly increases one's vulnerability. Florence Hollis warns of the fallacy of lumping together the so-called multiproblem, hard-to-reach, and impoverished families.[3] Although there may be overlapping problems, many low-income families are not multiproblem or hard to reach. It seems advantageous to identify poor families who may be poorly functioning in many areas of their lives as those with multiple deficits. It is this author's intent to underscore the need for social work concern with these families, who experience multiple concomitant deficits; problems of poor and crowded housing, health problems, relationship difficulties, family breakdowns, delinquency, addictions, and so forth. All of these problems mean pain and frustration for the individual, the family, and the larger society.

Helen Harris Perlman writes dramatically of experience with poor people in the Washington Heights and the Harlem areas of New York City, where she learned the lesson

> that a long repeated experience of being deadpoor, disadvantaged, stigmatized, closed off from the common good, a chronic experience of deficits of means, resources, opportunities or social recognition, will cut down the human spirit, constrict its capacities, dwarf or debilitate its drives. I became agonizingly aware of how details of everyday living may add up to a massive, overwhelming sense of defeat, frustration, and anger, and of how, then, to maintain social relationships and carry daily tasks, all the energies of the ego must be used chiefly to cover over, hold back, defend, protect. Yet even in this squalid jungle there were here and there those persons, young or old, whose thrust and ability and determination to beat the devil—to study, to help the kids look forward to a better day, to hold on to a job and "make it"—leaped forth as affirmations of life and hope.[4]

Perlman is cautioning that the conscious strivings and energies of the ego must be reached for in the human being. It is imperative that the family and the environmental strengths be supported for change.

In the multiple deficit families, structural organization may be characteristically loose, inefficient or conflictual, and dependency generationally perpetuated. The parent as the primary agent of socialization may have never learned cognitively or affectively what he needs to teach or to be a parent to children. Inadequate learning and self-image tend to be generationally perpetuated. Ivan Boszormenyi-Nagy and Geraldine Spark emphasize that children can be used as an arena to rebalance the parent's own unfair exploitation; underlying abusive behavior toward their children may be unresolved individual and marital conflicts, which derive from negative loyalty ties to the family of

[3]Florence Hollis, Casework and Social Class, in *Differential Diagnosis and Treatment in Social Work*, rev. ed., Francis J. Turner, ed. (New York: The Free Press, 1976), pp. 552–64.

[4]Helen Harris Perlman, *Perspectives in Social Casework* (Philadelphia: Temple University Press, 1971), p. xviii.

origin.[5] Shirley Jenkins' research also notes the pain and despondency of the neglectful parent when his child needs to be placed.[6] Evidence is mounting that direct intervention must be multifaceted in order to serve families undergoing multiple stresses.

All foci of the social work practice system—social policy, planning, organization, and the direct services to individuals, families, and groups—must be utilized to alter poor environmental conditions and to foster the growth potential of these families. This article is focused, however, on four major propositions important to the task of mobilizing direct social services efficiently to aid this target population. First, a major effort must be made by social agency systems to reach the multiple deficit, dysfunctional family in need. Second, intervention must address the transmission of generationally perpetuated problems. Third, intervention strategies must be carried out in combinations to include four foci: the individual, the nuclear family, the family of origin, and the representatives of the interlocking community agencies. This step requires individual and conjoint sessions with a coordinated plan of action identified and participated in by the clients and the interlocking agencies with which they are linked. The final suggestion involves planned followup of treatment with accountability for service located with a central agency to provide an open door in the event of future insurmountable stress.

Danuta Mostwin's model of short-term multidimensional family intervention covers many of these aspects in its unique approach to dealing with the stress and magnitude of family difficulties in individual and family sessions that may include the additional participation of other agency workers.[7] This idea can be further expanded through agency commitment, organization of service patterns, a combination of individual and family group strategies, and maintenance of a followup and open-door policy.

OUTREACH TO FAMILIES

In regard to proposition one, a concerted, organized pattern of identifying and reaching vulnerable families that enables and stimulates their mutual participation in a change process will be acceptable to them and is required for any substantial change. The unit of attention must be the family as it transacts with the systems of its environmental space.

Families who are alienated from the larger community and have become locked in to a lifestyle fraught with poor tolerance of frustration, weak controls of rage or sexuality, self-defeating relationships, who have parents functioning as siblings, and who are prone to acute crises in their lives, pose special problems for growing children. The White House Conference of 1970 reported that in 1968, approximately 10 percent of the fifty million school age children had moderate to severe emotional problems.[8] This statistic does not imply that

[5]Ivan Boszormenyi-Nagy and Geraldine Spark, *Invisible Loyalties* (New York: Harper & Row, 1973), p. 300.

[6]Shirley Jenkins, *Filial Deprivation and Foster Care* (New York: Columbia University Press, 1972).

[7]Danuta Mostwin, Social Work Interventions with Families in Crisis of Change, *Social Thought*, 2:81–99 (Winter 1976), and Mostwin, Multidimensional Model of Working with the Family, *Social Casework*, 55:209–15 (April 1974).

[8]James K. Whittaker, Causes of Childhood Disorders: New Findings, *Social Work*, 21:91-96 (March 1976).

all of these children came primarily from families of lower socio-economic status, but the magnitude of the problem deserves attention. The family must be viewed systematically, with its transaction to all linking systems assessed, for interventions to enhance the restorative exchanges with the environment for the individual and family.

Virginia Satir points out that it may well be that the family system is the primary means by which individual internal dynamics are developed. From Satir's observations of families where there are symptoms of problems, the rules of the family system do not totally fit the growth needs of its members in relation to survival, intimacy, productivity, and making sense and order, for all of the family members who are parts of the system.[9] Salvador Minuchin and Lynn Hoffman, as well as others, graphically describe the structure dysfunctioning in the family, which may or may not be multiple deficit, of cross-generation coalitions that tend to maintain, detour, or perpetuate marital conflicts, or that prevent normal growth and separation.[10] The emphasis in family intervention is on restructuring boundaries, shifting and delineating role tasks, and dealing with the dynamics of the relationship system that lock in the scapegoated or problem member. Actions are stimulated that will maximize family competence and self-confidence with the expectation that structural and relationship changes, supported by environmental changes, will indeed move the family to a new and more functional equilibrium.

Changes in family functioning are complex, especially when there is a parental life pattern of self-defeating behavior with few positive environmental resources, nurturance, and stimulation. Motivation and hope can be difficult to achieve. Intervention must be massive to unleash family adaptive forces for change. Although social work must serve families from all segments of society, the social worker must emphasize innovative direct services to help the impoverished who suffer multiple deficits, especially in their environment and in their interpersonal relationships. Advocacy and negotiation of environmental resources and services to reduce the frustration and deprivation must be as high on the helping scale as the intrafamilial, interpersonal relationship dimension. The social worker must reach out to link the family with every possible systemic input that can transmit new energy, knowledge, information, and emotional relatedness into the family system.

Attuned to the impact of environmental transactions, Ross V. Speck and Carolyn Attneave, through social network intervention, use the massive, relational environment for nurturing, growth, and healing.[11] They report network intervention in which as many as fifty friends and relatives of a patient may be assembled for intensive sessions of discussion, interaction, and psychodynamic exploration. In these sessions the difficulties experienced by the patient and his family are discussed and dramatized within the larger network, which itself goes through several distinct stages and where successful changes may occur.

[9]Virginia Satir, Symptomatology: A Family Production, in *Theory and Practice of Family Psychiatry*, ed. John G. Howells (New York: Brunner/Mazel, 1971) pp. 663–64.

[10]Salvador Minuchin, *Family and Family Therapy* (Cambridge: Harvard University Press, 1974); and Lynn Hoffman, Enmeshment and the Too Richly Cross-Joined System, *Family Process*, 14:457–68 (December 1975).

[11]Ross V. Speck and Carolyn Attneave, *Family Networks* (New York: Pantheon Press, 1973).

SECOND-GENERATION PROBLEMS

The second proposition concerns the finding that dysfunctional families tend to reflect transmission of problematic behavior and adaptive patterns originating in their families of origin. The relationships over three generations must be assessed and the intervention processes must include the three generations.

Murray Bowen asserts that a certain amount of immaturity can be absorbed by the family system and that large quantities may be bound by serious dysfunction in one family member. The family projection process focuses on a certain child or children and may leave others relatively uninvolved. Bowen notes, however, that there are other families where the quantity of immaturity is so great, that there is maximum marital conflict, severe dysfunction in one spouse, maximum involvement of children, conflict with families of origin, and still free-floating immaturity. The mechanisms that operate outside the nuclear family ego mass are important in determining the course and intensity of the process within the nuclear family. When there is a significant degree of ego fusion, there is also a borrowing and sharing of ego strength between the nuclear family and the family of origin.[12]

Boszormenyi-Nagy and Spark postulate that the major connecting tie between the generations is that of loyalty based on indebtedness and reciprocity.[13] Loyalty ties and the forms of expression may be a functional or a dysfunctional force connecting the generations. The person remains deeply committed to the repayment of benefits received; the struggle for all adults is to balance the old relationships with the new and to continuously integrate the relationships with one's early significant figures with the involvement and commitment to current family relationships.

Of the voluminous literature describing multiple deficit, loosely organized, low-income families, none is so poignant with regard to generational immaturities as the descriptions of Louise Bandler on the North Point Family Project in Boston.[14] The parents' immaturity and inability to exercise even minimal skills in maintenance of daily routines in the home, in care and discipline of children, and in interaction with the outside community were striking. It was common for one-parent mothers to parentify the older child, assume a sibling position, and reflect the deep unmet dependency needs that stemmed from their own parental deprivation. Bandler speaks of the mothers' relationship to and nurturing of their children as being so affected by their own pressing needs that they could not distinguish them from the needs of their children, even when their children's needs were urgent. When the parent's own affective development and learning has been greatly impaired by a depriving social environment and parental failure of dependable, consistent, nurturing objects, it is predictable that immaturity will abound with deep dependency needs, feelings of resentment, anger, inadequacy, and low self-esteem. The needs and loyalties in the conflictual family relationships diminish family strengths for coping and must be addressed.

[12]Murray Bowen, The Use of Family Theory in Clinical Practice, in *Changing Families*, ed. Jay Haley (New York: Grune & Stratton, 1971), pp. 177–78.

[13]Boszormenyi-Nagy and Spark, *Invisible Loyalties* (New York: Harper & Row, 1973), pp. 216–24.

[14]Louise Bandler, Family Functioning: A Psychosocial Perspective, in *The Drifters*, ed. Eleanor Pavenstedt (Boston: Little, Brown and Co., 1967), pp. 225–53.

COMBINATION OF INTERVENTION STRATEGIES

The third proposition, to repeat, states that intervention targeted to the family unit must be a combination of sessions with the individual, conjoint nuclear family and family of origin, and community agencies. These four foci must be balanced in regard to the use of a modality that can address itself to: (1) the parent's and child's individual need for nurturance and growth; (2) the family system's communication, structural, and role deficits and the scape- goating mechanisms that have become patterned or supportive of myths and collusions within the family; (3) the inclusion of the family of origin to deal with destructive patterns or loyalties that are transmitted and to strengthen what- ever positives that can be enlisted for growth; and (4) the conjoint meeting of the linking agencies and family to weave a massive, coordinated effort toward new goals and change. The coordinated agency sessions with the family are of the highest importance, for the family system then becomes more thoroughly integrated in a positive way with linking services and social resource systems. Hypothetically, if the individual and family sessions are agreed upon to be carried primarily by the social worker in the residential treatment center where the child is placed, the child welfare, probation, or related agencies involved would also plan together in family sessions a course of action that supports the major goals. When the child can be returned from residential treatment to the home, new plans for continuation and followup should emerge, depending on the case situation. In this example, the responsibility and accountability would be carried by one agency—the residential treatment center—for the major treatment role with the collaboration and additional service input of linking agencies. As growth and change occur, the collaborat- ing agencies should continue with the family to locate the central responsibil- ity of the helping service.

NEED FOR FOLLOWUP

High risk families require followup at intervals and a central resource for help when stresses become insurmountable. Too often their ties to the agency have not been strong enough to stimulate their reapplying for help in times of stress and they lose the gains they had made. The four steps outlined above should substantially improve the families' social functioning and their capacity to anticipate and deal with stress, reducing the self-generated crises that bring the families to agencies at the time of stress and that allow a dropping out when the crisis subsides.

It has been observed that seriously impaired families do not always use a crisis approach effectively. For example, Naomi Golan suggests that:

> While they manifest the overt symptoms of urgency, disordered affect, disorga-
> nized behavior, and ineffectual coping, closer examination shows that under-
> neath the superficial appearance, the basic character structure reveals severe and
> chronic ego depletion and damage. The crisis appearance involved is not a
> reaction to the original hazardous event, but a maladaptive attempt to ward off
> underlying personality disturbance or even psychosis. While such persons, often
> classified as borderline personalities or character disorders, may need help in
> emergencies, they do not seem to be able to engage in the crisis resolution work

involved in learning from earlier experiences and in developing more adaptive patterns.[15]

With coordinated and massive input, learning can occur that will make possible some shifts in the social functioning of immature families.

In such families, a family service agency might well be the central agency among the collaborating agencies which maintains the open door for help and periodic followup, especially when there are growing children. Margaret B. Bailey's findings in the Alcoholism Inter-Agency Training Project conducted by the staff of the Alcoholism Programs of the Community Council of Greater New York reported that regardless of whether the alcoholic was referred to a special agency such as an alcoholism clinic, to a mental health clinic, or to another service, it was imperative for the family agency making the referral to retain the locus of treatment.[16] Otherwise, the sensitive alcoholic tends to fall through the cracks between the services. This situation is quite analogous to the multiple deficit family or a severely impaired family.

With the overburdened staff of social service agencies, including the correctional, mental health and medical facilities, is there sufficient time for the suggested followup, collaboration, and location of central responsibility? In the long run, it would be more economical for resources to be used massively and in a coordinated way during periods of stress. Depending on the needs of the family, substantial improvement in the family system equilibrium could be predicted with this kind of consistent help and strengthening of their coping powers to handle their predicament when threatened.

It has been more than twenty years since the Report of the Family Centered Project of St. Paul, Minnesota.[17] It reported that 6 percent of the city families accounted for 77 percent of its public assistance, 51 percent of its health services, and 56 percent of its adjustment services in mental health, corrections, and casework. The striking fact was that many of these families were known to a range of agencies during chronic periods of crisis, but coordination in agency services and resources was not sufficiently integrated to insure improvement in the family system's equilibrium. Today, families are still divided among agencies without sufficient attention to the transactional processes within the family, the agencies, and the social environment that could be coordinated for a change.

ILLUSTRATION OF NEED FOR INTERVENTION

The following case illustration highlights the need for the strategies indicated—focus on a family unit with a growth-inducing individual relationship, conjoint sessions of the nuclear family with the family of origin, and the agency service network. Formed groups could also be used as appropriate. Exemplified in the following is the fact that coordinated efforts with clients

[15]Naomi Golan, Crisis Theory, in *Social Work Treatment*, ed. Francis J. Turner (New York: The Free Press, 1974), p. 442.

[16]Margaret B. Bailey, *Alcoholism and Family Casework* (New York: New York City Affiliate, National Council on Alcoholism, 1974), p. 189.

[17]Alice Overton, Katherine H. Tinker and Associates, *Casework Notebook Family Centered Project* (St. Paul, Minn.: Greater St. Paul Community Chest and Councils, 1957).

can bring change in a family in which there is severe psychological damage and where overt rage and child abuse are generationally perpetuated.[18]

James, an eight-year-old, white, Catholic boy of lower socioeconomic advantage was referred for residential placement because his mother was considered emotionally disturbed and unable to handle him.[18] James ran away from home taking his younger brother, Jerry, aged five, with him. James frequently set fires in the home and in the community. He was also enuretic and his school attendance was poor.

Mrs. A, James's mother, was a twenty-eight-year-old divorcée who received an Aid to Families with Dependent Children grant. She resided with her younger son, Jerry, in a five-room apartment in the central city. James was born out of wedlock when Mrs. A was seventeen. His father disappeared before birth and his whereabouts were unknown. Mrs. A's mother would not permit her to keep the child so that she was forced to relinquish James to a foster placement, where he spent the first twenty-one months of his life. She later married and while pregnant with her second son, Jerry, she was able to regain possession of James. She was separated from her husband soon after the birth of Jerry and eventually divorced him, because he was serving a sentence in the penitentiary. Since her divorce, she had dated several men and just prior to James's placement in residential care she was jilted in an affair of several months' duration.

James was placed in residential treatment to provide him with a consistent environment of warmth, acceptance, and discipline. Initially, he had great difficulty adjusting to the environment: disrupting his class by manipulating fights between others and running away from school, his cottage, and the treatment center. When his mother and brother visited him, he would go into wild temper tantrums when it was time for them to leave, and the early visits precipitated his running away.

Initially, it was extremely difficult to engage James in regular treatment sessions; he was hostile, resentful, and frightened. His home environment included inconsistent, abusive, and seductive mothering coupled with neglect. His punishment for misbehavior was severe and cruel. For example, following a fire-setting episode, Mrs. A would punish him—first by holding an extinguished match against his hand; second, by burning him with a lighted match, and third, by holding his hands over a lighted stove. One time he was badly injured.

Mrs. A readily admitted that she had tormented James with a knife, urging him to stab himself to prove that he was a man. When he had failed to do so, she dressed him in girls' clothing to make fun of him. This act was a frequent punishment which she had used when James argued or disagreed with her. When questioned, she seemed unable to grasp the potential danger of her act, with its psychological implications.

On another occasion, it was reported that because James forgot to remind her to turn off the gas when cooking and the food burned, she knocked him unconscious. When he came to, she did allow him to lie down and rest for several hours. Mrs. A admitted to beating him severely and said that at times she thought she might kill him.

In contrast to her loss of control when enraged, Mrs. A spoke in loving terms of her children and openly demonstrated affection for James on her visits to the treatment center. She said she missed him very much, that he would often sleep with her, and that they were a great comfort to one another. She brought him gifts and books, showed pride in his reading ability, and encouraged his education. She also brought construction toys, which he liked.

[18]The author is grateful to Thomas J. Ciallello, student at Columbia University School of Social Work, New York, New York, for the case illustration.

The disturbed mother-child relations described here bear close relationship to the mother-grandmother relationship and to the larger family constellation in which Mrs. A was reared and continued to be actively involved. Mrs. E, Mrs. A's mother, also lived in the central city with her fourth husband and two teen-age sons. One of these sons was Mrs. A's natural brother and the one person in the family for whom she felt some closeness. He was a narcotics addict.

Mrs. E's treatment of Mrs. A as a young girl bore similarity to Mrs. A's treatment of James. For example, Mrs. E had disciplined Mrs. A for wearing a short skirt to school by forcing her to strip naked and sit on the steps in the hall outside their tenement apartment for other tenants to observe. In relating this incident, Mrs. A said, "No wonder I started to act like a whore; she made me feel like one."

Mrs. A spoke of having tried suicide several times. She had seen several psychiatrists and was once hospitalized. She had also been seen intermittently at an outpatient psychiatric clinic in the city. Its records indicated that she had been placed in a parochial children's home at age six after stabbing her father and attempting to kill her mother. She had also received psychiatric treatment at age nine, age fifteen through seventeen, and again as a young adult in the city hospital. Mrs. A related details of attacking her husband with a knife for intimating that she behaved like her mother.

Mrs. A and her family of origin have a history of impulsive violent outbursts and fights. However, their ambivalence and distorted loyalties compel them to seek out one another repeatedly. At the time of one of these violent episodes, a family life space session was held on the spot to evaluate the situation. During the session, which was full of arguing and shouting, a pattern emerged of the belittling and scapegoating of Mrs. A by her own family.

From the above material, it can be observed that three generations of disturbed family relationships are characterized by inadequate nurturance and weak control of rage. As communication with Mrs. A's own family was characterized by harsh violence, inconsistency, and ambivalence, so she related to her own children. In the early sessions she appeared to be a rebellious adolescent and at the same time was in strong competition with her mother for possession and control of her own children. Her relationships with men were marked by abandonment, disappointment, and failure. Her role as healthy mother-father for her two children has been distorted and generational boundaries crossed as she alternately seduced and aggressively rejected her son James. However, because she had been the scapegoat in her family of origin, James, who was split off from the family in infancy and represented her bad self, came to serve the same role within the nuclear family.

Over the years, attempts were made by various agencies to help Mrs. A but no consistent change was noted. She reached out by attending a few individual therapy sessions at a local mental health clinic, but then would discontinue. A homemaker was once sent by the bureau of child welfare to assist with care of the home and children, to teach her more consistent methods in child rearing, and to free her to utilize her skills as keypunch operator. She was unable to follow through. The evidence was clear that while the grandmother openly encouraged these interventions on her daughter's behalf, she also undermined their success with interference and criticism. There was no purposeful plan to work with the family of origin. In addition, Mrs. A's caseworker at the bureau of child welfare reported being so overloaded with cases that she could not adequately support and assist her in her efforts.

The worker described Mrs. A clinically as having a severe borderline disorder. Individual interventive sessions, where Jerry was generally present, attempted to strengthen her grasp of reality situations and anticipation of consequences and to increase impulse control through learning and identification in a dependable relationship and through active tasks and limits so as to experience achievement and to relieve stress. It was hoped that order and routine in the home could be accomplished. These sessions were laborious and trying in the beginning as Mrs. A lashed into tirades blaming her mother and step-father for interference in her life and in the care of her children. She condemned the bureau of child welfare worker for failing to maintain contact with her or to assist her with care of Jerry or job placement; she blamed the residential treatment center for giving her double messages and keeping James away from her. At the same time, Jerry would run wildly about the house grabbing food from the table, smashing toys, and hitting at the worker. Mrs. A would attempt to reprimand him verbally, but when this procedure failed she would hit him and threaten him with punishment "by you know what!" without clarifying what she meant. She would seem to restrain herself from harsh discipline during the interview as the worker utilized the situation to discuss dealing with Jerry and his multiple health problems. Mrs. A talked of taking him to the hospital but criticized the doctors for incompetence and lack of action. She blamed the bureau of child welfare worker for not helping her follow through with the out-patient clinic appointments for him. In due course, however, her anger and projections began to subside as she worked in individual sessions with the young male social worker. Gradually she began to accept some responsibility for her own actions.

As the work progressed and the worker checked the validity of her claims against the bureau of child welfare and the mental health clinic, he arranged with Mrs. A to have an interagency meeting for the purpose of clarifying their assistance on her behalf and for Jerry. Problem-solving also included the issue of home visits for James.

The worker helped Mrs. A to expand her understanding of James's needs as they toured together the campus of the center and visited James's teachers, childcare staff, religious instructor, and other involved personnel so that she, as a parent, could get first-hand reports on his adjustment and progress.

On one such occasion, she returned to her individual session and began to speak of her current personal problems with her family of origin. She became very emotional and tearful and began to consider why James had had to be placed; however, in the beginning she was not able to connect the consequences to her own behavior. She could only see James as the problem (running away and setting fires) and being interfered with by her mother.

Confrontation to help her begin to see her own responsibility brought further tears, evasion, and an attack on the worker and the institution for giving her a run-around and keeping her from her son. However, her worker moved to a more supportive approach; he communicated his belief that she sincerely loved James, that James had expressed love for her, but that James was very frightened of her.

She responded thoughtfully that she believed James feared her because at times, when she was in a bad mood or was extremely nervous, she had punished him too severely for not obeying her. She quickly added that she had recently changed her method of punishment from physical beatings to having him kneel on the floor with his arms outstretched, as she had been punished by a teacher in her youth. This discussion was the first time that she could consider alternate methods of punishment and consequences and could begin to use concrete suggestions. Later, she brought out that she thought James's fearfulness was also connected with his witnessing much physical violence between herself and her mother and her ex-husband.

Once Mrs. A had made the above disclosures and shared these insights, she was helped to draw further connections between her severe treatment as a child and her present handling of her own children. Family treatment sessions with Mrs. A, her children, and her family of origin were not held. However, the destructive intergenerational ties, modeling, and scapegoating can be seen. Conjoint sessions could increase their ability to detach and reduce the destructive hostile-dependent indebtedness. Any strengths and family supports could then be more easily mobilized.

Individual sessions were equally important with James. The worker tried to meet James at his emotional level by using play in the treatment sessions and to interact with him at his cottage setting. In play James was initially cautious in inviting the worker to join in his games and creative activities. He enjoyed immersing his hands in globs of brown paint and smearing them over paper. He seemed to look for disapproval. When his paintings began to take form, the worker noticed that he chose bright red, black, and gray. He was intense and aggressive in his painting. Verbalization of such feelings as anger and fear by the worker brought responses associated with blood, monsters, and fires.

Often he enjoyed punching a toy clown in a very aggressive way. He asked whether the clown inside the toy was being hurt when he hit him. He questioned whether a person would be hurt if a picture of someone he disliked were pasted on the toy clown's face and he hit it. He stated he did not really want to hurt anyone, even if he did dislike them. To alleviate this confusion between reality and fantasied thoughts, the worker began to help him separate his fantasies and feelings from actions. In the course of one session when punching the toy clown, James said that he wished that it were his mother and little brother.

This discussion occurred at the time of a heightened controversy over his home visits. He spoke of a recurrent dream which he had had at home and which had reappeared. The dream involved the stabbing and killing of his mother and brother. Observing his fear and disturbance, the worker explained that many people have similar dreams or nightmares and that they usually follow feelings of anger at being punished unjustly that cannot be expressed to people they love or depend upon. He seemed somewhat relieved by the explanation, and it marked the beginning of their talks to straighten out his disturbing fears and feelings. It served to connect these with his experiences at home.

The interagency meetings inspired Mrs. A to obtain further help at the mental health center. She later began to work part time to supplement her Aid to Families with Dependent Children check and took the initiative to arrange for an appropriate sitter and health care for Jerry. She was helped to be more active in age-appropriate activities and to achieve some skill and success toward enhancing her strengths and the ability to regulate and control herself.

Social work practice that is family system oriented and coordinates the treatment among the significant interlocking systems with followup and centralization of responsibility will vastly improve the outcome with the high-risk and vulnerable poor family that has been locked in to a generationally perpetuated destructive lifestyle.

4

A Variety of Techniques

Family therapy techniques are rooted in particular theoretical orientations and are designed to promote the engagement of the practitioner with the family and family change. Because we recognize that a cataloging of techniques would not be especially useful, we have attempted to select for inclusion in Part IV conceptualizations and descriptions of techniques that illustrate the range and depth of the field.

One of the more recent and fruitful directions in family therapy is the application and testing of *action techniques*. Action techniques, broadly speaking, are requests or demands by the therapist for specific behaviors from family members. These requests or demands are made either in the therapy session or in the period intervening between sessions. These requests, for example, may be in the form of the therapist's asking the family to map out actual sets of relationships through double-binding directives, or they may take the form of specific tasks that the family is directed to carry out.

Action techniques can be thought of as having three distinct dimensions: the pragmatic, the diagnostic, and the therapeutic. Pragmatically, the employment of action techniques promotes the involvement of the therapist and the family and enables the therapist to enter the life space of the family in new ways (either during the session or at the family's home as they struggle with the directive between sessions). These techniques also promote the continuation of the family in treatment, since portions of the therapy at least are seen as enjoyable activities. The diagnostic dimension of action techniques refers to the fact that family members' responses to the techniques provide the therapist with useful information about family relationships and give prognostic signs as to the likely outcome of treatment. The therapeutic dimension of action techniques implies that such techniques may be employed to help families achieve their goals. Any action technique can be evaluated along these dimensions without regard to the particular theoretical orientation in which the technique is based.

"Dimensions of Family Therapy," by Cloë Madanes and Jay Haley, typifies this section of the book, in that a wide number of therapeutic techniques are contained in that paper. In his article "Psychotherapy of the Absurd," Carl Whitaker connects recent developments in 20th-century avant-garde theater with concurrent trends in therapy. Carl Whitaker's name has long been associated with a humanistic-experiential approach to family therapy, and he is widely considered to be a master clinician.

A primary area of family assessment is the acquisition of knowledge concerning the actual set of family relationships (as opposed to purely verbal reports about those relationships). Larry Constantine provides a comprehensive procedure designed to promote the accurate mapping of an entire set of family relationships through the techniques of "sculpting." Thus, although the diagnostic dimension of techniques is emphasized, a strong initial focus on therapeutic activity is permitted.

Marvin and Netta Kaplan, in their contribution, provide a method orientation to technique in family therapy. Originally associated with individual psychotherapy, the principles of individual change contained in the Gestalt method are applied by the Kaplans to family growth.

Neil Jacobson and Barclay Martin review the literature on behavioral approaches to marriage therapy in their paper. It includes discussions of intervention strategies and contingency management procedures, along with a thorough review of theories that deal with marital disturbance.

The concept of the "double bind" was originally formulated by Gregory Bateson and his colleagues in 1956. "Varieties of Double Bind" by Milton Erickson and Ernest Rossi both describes the use of the double bind as a therapeutic technique and at the same time provides a theoretical analysis of the double bind operation. In doing this a differentiation between Bateson's and Erickson's notions of the double bind is made.

Mara Selvini Palazzoli and her co-workers of the "Milano School" have vigorously pushed forward the theoretical framework for practice initially developed by Bateson, Haley, and their colleagues during the 1950s in Palo Alto. The two case examples contained in the paper "The Treatment of Children through Brief Therapy of Their Parents" offer striking instances of complex action techniques designed with clear therapeutic intent. In addition, they describe a general method utilizing two cotherapists and two observers, problem formulation within a system's framework (including a restatement of perhaps the earliest finding of family therapists—the necessity of making positive interpretations), and carefully thought-out "prescriptions for action."

The prescriptive element of task giving to family members

(see introduction to Part I) troubles some family practitioners. The boundary between authoritarian and authoritative practice is at times difficult to define. Because various action techniques are found in all the ascendant "schools" of practice (for example, structural-Bowen/systems-problem solving), we believe that learners in the field require some rough guidelines as to their usage. We suggest that, if the following criteria are met, the odds are increased in the family's favor:

1. that the task/prescription for action is related to a goal or objective of the family;
2. that the task can be easily accomplished;
3. that the task contains no blame;
4. that the task asks for an acceleration of behavior (a "doing" versus a "not-doing"); and
5. that the task contains pragmatic, diagnostic, and therapeutic value.

Dimensions of Family Therapy

Cloë Madanes
Jay Haley

*This article is a description of different approaches to therapy with a family orienta-
tion. There are general categories of family therapy which had their origins in
individual therapy, such as the approaches based upon psychodynamic theory, those
derived from experiential procedures, and the behavioral approaches. There are
also family therapies which have not developed from individual therapy, such as the
extended family system approach and the communication school of family therapy.*

    *The different therapy approaches are described within a set of dimensions which
characterize most therapy. Such dimensions include whether the past or present is
emphasized, whether the therapist uses interpretation or directives, whether the
approach is in terms of growth or specific problems, whether hierarchy is a
concern, and whether the unit is an individual, two people, three people, or a wider
network.*

    *Illustrations of the different family therapy approaches are given in terms of the
kinds of information that would interest the therapist of each school and the kinds of
actions he or she would take to bring about change.*

Twenty years have passed since therapists took the revolutionary step of
bringing whole families under direct observation in therapy interviews and the
dimensions of the different schools of family therapy are becoming more
evident. Until recently the issues between different family therapies were less
clear than those between a family orientation and an individual one. Now it is
evident that "individual" therapy is one way to intervene into a family—by
seeing one person in the family and not the others. It is also becoming more
clear that therapy works best if a person is contained in his natural situation.
Therapy appears less successful if the person is lifted out of his situation and
treated in isolation from the community of intimates with whom he lives. With
these new premises have come new explanations of psychological problems
and new innovations in therapy.

"Dimensions of Family Therapy," by C. Madanes and J. Haley. In *The Journal of Nervous and
Mental Disease*, 1977, Vol. 165, No. 2, pp. 88–98. Copyright 1977 by The Williams and Wilkins
Company. Reprinted by permission.

    Readers interested in pursuing this topic further may wish to consult *Strategic Family Therapy*,
by Cloë Madanes. Copyright 1981 by Jossey-Bass, Inc., Publishers, 433 California Street, San
Francisco, California 94104.

Even though there is more agreement that the social situation rather than the person is the problem for therapy, still there is no agreement on how to approach the problem. Some therapists oriented to the family continue with a medical model of an individual patient, while others have dropped that framework entirely. Some will use an approach based on learning theory, while others do not. Many family therapists offer interpretations while others primarily offer directives. A hypothetical example might illustrate the issues. Let us say that a woman presents to a therapist the problem that she becomes overwhelmed with anxiety when she tries to go for an interview for a job. She wishes to work, but her anxiety attacks prevent her from doing so. Therapists of different "schools" would conceptualize this problem in different ways and so would approach therapy differently. Some would say that the woman has an inner anxiety that is based on her past experiences with authority figures, and that is why she cannot go for a job interview. Others would say that the crucial issue is whether there would be consequences with her husband or other intimates if she should get a job. Such contrasting views represent the differences in view between a person as a problem or a situation as a problem.

What will be presented here are dimensions on which therapists differ, and various approaches to family therapy based on them. The comparison will focus less on the nature of problems and more on the dimensions of therapy relevant to a theory of change.

DIMENSIONS

Past versus present

One of the major dimensions on which therapists differ is whether the emphasis should be on the past or on the present. There has been a transition in the psychodynamic theory from the idea that a specific trauma caused a present symptom to a more complex theory that involves internal objects and processes of projection and introjection. The behavior therapists have gone through a similar transition. From believing that a specific traumatic event caused a present behavior problem, they have shifted to assuming that reinforcements in the present are important to the continuation of that behavior. If one accepts the idea that the current situation is causal to the problem, past causes become less necessary as an explanation relevant to theory. The extreme position on this dimension is that the present situation causes the problem and the past is irrelevant, as is argued by some family therapists.

Interpretation versus action

Whatever the cause of a problem, the therapeutic issue is what to do about it. Those therapists who must emphasize a past cause also tend to assume that exploration and interpretation of the past will cause change. For example, if a person recalls and understands his past relationship with his father, he will behave differently toward his current employer. Those therapists who emphasize a cause in the present while also believing that self-awareness causes change will interpret to the person how he is behaving in the present. For example, they will point out to him how he is provoking his employer and so causing difficulties. Other therapists who believe that the present situation is the cause of the problem do not assume that understanding that situation will cause change and so do not make interpretations. The experiential therapists will provide a new experience, such as having the person rehearse in a group how to deal with an employer. More directive therapists, such as certain behaviorists and strategic family therapists, will suggest ways in which the person is to behave with his actual employer rather than with a simulated one. Experiential therapists tend to provide new experiences within a family interview, while directive therapists tend to require new behavior outside the interview in the real life of the person.

Growth versus presenting problem

Another dimension on which therapists differ is in relation to the goals of therapy. Some believe that therapy should solve the problem which the client offers and think that therapy has failed if this problem is not solved, no matter what other changes have taken place. Others, although they are pleased if the presenting problem is solved, do not have this as their basic goal but instead emphasize the growth and development of the person. Family therapists are divided on this issue, with some focusing upon the presenting problem and some emphasizing the growth and development of the whole family. The psychodynamic and experiential therapists tend to emphasize growth while the behavior therapists emphasize the presenting problems.

Method versus specific plan for each problem

When a therapy solidifies into a school, it tends to create a formal method of working. The same set of procedures and techniques is applied to every case no matter what the problem. For example, the psychodynamic therapies provide interpretations and the experiential therapies provide specific exercises for individuals or for groups. Other therapists do not use a standard method but design a specific procedure for each person and each problem. They work on the assumption that everyone does not face the same situation and that people cannot be classified into different types with a specific method used for each type. For example, if an adolescent steals, a method-oriented therapist will apply a "method." He may always discuss the problem individually with the adolescent, or he may always see him in a group, or he may always meet with him and his family. A problem-oriented therapist faced with an adolescent who steals might see him with his whole family, or with his siblings, or sometimes alone, or he might intervene in school. The method-oriented therapists tend to continue using the same method whether it fails or not, while the problem-oriented therapists tend to change what they do if it is not succeeding.

Unit of one, two, or three people

What tends to differentiate the individual from the family therapist is the concept of the unit with the problem: whether it is one person, two people, or three people or more. By definition, psychodynamic therapy has a unit of one, since it is the therapy of the individual psyche. When one person is the focus, the therapy tends to center on that person's feelings, ideas, perceptions, and behavior. In family therapy with a one-person focus, the therapist tends to emphasize the feelings of the family members about each other and each one's awareness of how he deals with others.

With a unit of two or more, the emphasis shifts to the relationship between the people. A psychiatric problem is understood in terms of a contract between at least two people. For example, if a woman is afraid to leave her house alone, the therapist with a unit of one person will try to understand her and help her in terms of her fears, perceptions, and behaviors. The therapist with a unit of two will assume that her not leaving the house is related to her husband. His unit will be husband and wife, since he will assume that the problem is part of a marital contract.

Some therapists think in units of three or more instead of just one or two. With a unit of three, it is possible to think in terms of coalitions and in terms of a hierarchical structure of an organization. For example, a wife who is afraid to leave the house alone might be thought of in terms of a coalition with mother and husband against her.

The issue here is not how many people are actually involved in a problem or how many people are actually seen in the interviews, but how many people are involved in the therapist's way of thinking about the problem. A family of eight can be thought of as eight individuals or four dyads or as a variety of triangles.

Equality versus hierarchy

When the emphasis is on the individual and on groups of unrelated people, the participants are considered of equal status. When dealing with a family or other natural group, there is inevitably an issue of hierarchy because the participants are not all equal. They have status differences in terms of age, control funds, community-vested authority and responsibility, etc. Therapists who think in a unit of one person tend to treat a family as a group of individuals of equal status. Children and parents are allowed to criticize each other equally and all family members have the right to make rules. Therapists who think in terms of a unit of three tend to be concerned with status and power in the family. They respect generation lines by not giving equal rights or responsibilities to children, parents, and grandparents.

Analogical versus digital

It is possible to describe human behavior as "bits" of behavior; that is, one can describe it as events or acts which are countable. For example, the headaches of a man can be described as an event that can be counted as so many per day. This is a digital type of description which breaks down behavior into bits like a computer program.

Another way to describe human behavior is to say that any act has a meaning in a context of other acts. In that sense, any behavior is an analogy to other behavior. For example, when a woman is talking about her headaches to a therapist, she is talking about more than one kind of pain. That is, behavior is always a communication on many levels. The message "I have a headache" is a report on an internal state, but it may also be a way of declining sexual relations or of getting the husband to help with the children.

The behaviorists who classify a sympton as a "bit" that can be counted as present or absent are thinking differently from therapists who consider a symptom to be a communication about a person's life situation and therefore an analogy about something else.

SCHOOLS OF THERAPY

A therapist who places a patient on a couch and has him free associate does not seem to have much in common with a therapist who brings in a whole family and has them mourn for a dead grandfather. A therapist who requires his client to visit distant relatives does not seem to be similar to a therapist who has parents give candy to a child every time he performs a certain act. How similar or different they are depends on the dimensions by which you compare them. One can have quite different therapeutic approaches and yet have the individual be the unit, just as one can have various ways of dealing with past situations and yet they are past and not present ones. A difference thought to distinguish family therapists from individual therapists is the number of people in the room, because family therapists tend to see intimate groups of people together. However, the same therapeutic assumptions may guide therapy with a family as with a single individual.

What follows will be a comparison of different approaches to therapy according to the dimensions previously described. The reader is referred to Table 1 for a presentation of this description.

Psychodynamic therapy

A therapy based upon psychodynamics has an individual focus whether a person is seen alone or in a family group. The therapist is concerned with each family member's memories of the past, feelings about relevant people, motivation, and so on.

More specifically, the dimensions of therapy characteristic of this school are the following. There is an emphasis on the past both for the cause of a symptom and the means to change it. It is assumed that a person has symptoms because of a past set of experiences that are programmed within him. These experiences are repressed outside awareness. The therapist focuses upon the past and bringing these ideas and experiences into awareness. The method of therapy is largely interpretive, whether interviews are with one person or a whole family, and the therapist's comments are aimed at helping the person become aware of both past and present behaviors and the connections between them. As one therapist described the psychodynamic family approach, it is "typified by an emphasis on explanation or interpretation and reference to nonverbal expression in the family" (42, p. 228). Directives are not given, and the therapist does not take responsibility for what happens outside the session. The emphasis tends to be on a long-term process with the goal of helping a person grow and develop rather than just getting over the presenting problem. Usually the emphasis is upon method with each family treated in a similar way no matter what the problem. Typically the whole family is seen once a week for 1-hour sessions and there are two therapists. The theory focuses upon a unit of one, with families usually described as a set of discrete individuals with repressed ideation and emotions. Hierarchy is not emphasized. The therapy is largely analogical insofar as the therapist is interested in metaphors and statements about the meaning of experiences rather than with "bits" of behavior (1, 8, 13, 15, 29, 39).

This approach to family therapy is most congenial for a therapist who has worked with individuals in traditional psychodynamic therapy. The therapist need change little of his theory since he can continue with the idea of repression and with interpretations and educative comments. The goal is to bring about insight and understanding and to express emotions.

TABLE 1. Comparison of Different Approaches to Family Therapy according to Various Dimensions

Dimensions	Psychodynamic	Experiential	Extended Family	Behavioral	Communication	
					Structural	Strategic
Past	X	X				
Unit 1 person	X	X		X		
Interpret (past)	X	X				
Interpret (present)	X	X	X		X	
Method	X	X	X			
Growth	X	X	X		X	
Analogical	X	X	X		X	X
Present		X	X	X	X	X
New experience		X		X	X	X
Directives			X	X	X	X
Plan for therapy				X	X	X
Unit 2 people			X	X	X	X
Unit 3 People			X		X	X
Hierarchy			X		X	X
Presenting problem				X		X
Digital				X		X

In the hypothetical case of a woman who becomes anxious about job interviews, this approach would assume that the anxiety is based on past experiences with authority figures. If seen individually, the therapist would help the woman transfer her anxiety from the original authority figures to the relationship with the therapist and would help her understand its causes. If seen in family therapy, she would be helped to understand how she transfers her anxiety about original authority figures not only to the therapist but also to her husband and other relatives.

The experiential school

The basic contribution of this school, which differentiates it from the psychodynamic approach, is its greater emphasis on the present and the introduction of new experiences in the session as a therapeutic tool. While there seems to be an emphasis upon the unit of one because of the focus on expressing emotions, the emphasis on new experiences in the present may involve other people.

A woman with anxiety attacks about job interviews would be thought of not only as repressing rage against authority, but as being angry at a particular person, like her husband. Experiential therapists with an individual orientation would put this woman in an artificial group to help her break out of her inhibitions by expressing her feelings about the members of the group. Those with a family orientation would see the woman together with her husband to help her express her feelings to him and would teach the couple to fight constructively. Rather than interpret about past causes, family experiential therapists tend to enlighten their clients about their feelings and about the ways they deal with one another. This is the school that most emphasizes the value of honesty in expressing views and feelings and the importance of clear communication to solve interactional difficulties.

Like the psychodynamicists, experiential therapists tend to use interpretations (sometimes in the form of confrontations). They emphasize growth rather than the presenting problem, and they are not concerned with hierarchy. They are focused on method insofar as they put people through a standard set of procedures. They are analogical since they are concerned with meanings of experience rather than bits of behavior. The school differs from other family therapies in the willingness to do group therapy with unrelated groups of strangers as well as with natural groups. There is wide variety ranging from the more conservative to the most extreme in the kinds of experiences asked of clients (14, 16, 25, 41).

The behavioral school

The behavioral school differs from the previous ones because the theory and practice come from learning theory rather than Freudian psychology. The only dimension in common is the unit of one person. With the experiential school it also shares the emphasis on the present and on new experiences; but whereas the experiential therapists emphasize new experiences in terms of expressing emotions, behaviorists do so in terms of modifying specific behavior. In the case of a woman with anxiety attacks about job interviews, an experiential therapist might have her act out the situation to express her emotions. A behaviorist might have her act out a job interview to learn how to go through such an interview correctly so she would have confidence. What is unique about this school in comparison with the two previous ones is the sharp focus on the presenting problem. The emphasis is on the change desired by the client rather than upon the client's growth and development.

Instead of using a standard method, many behavior therapists will design a procedure for each presenting problem. They do not offer interpretations but give directives for behavior both in the interview and outside of it. The concern is largely with digital acts rather than with the analogical meaning of those acts. Hierarchy is not a relevant issue for this school.

Behavior therapists are a minority among family therapists (22, 37, 38, 44). Rather than the three-person orientation of many family therapists, the family behavior therapists tend to focus on a unit of two persons. For example, in the case of a woman with anxiety about a job interview, the behaviorist might have the husband give her positive reinforcements for each step toward a job interview. If the patient's mother seemed involved, the therapist might have the mother reinforce her instead of the husband. However, the behaviorist does not think in terms of three persons and so would not think of the situation as one where a woman is caught between a husband who wants her to go to work and a mother who does not, and so consequent anxiety.

Extended family systems

In the previously described schools of family therapy, the family therapy developed out of a previous individual therapy. There are other family therapies where this does not seem to be the case. These schools took ideas from different individual therapies and also contributed novel developments so that it is not possible to describe them as coming from one particular school of individual therapy. One such group constitutes what can be referred to as the extended family therapists.

The main characteristic of this group is an emphasis on the wider kinship structure (6). They might conceptualize the situation in terms of a unit of one, two, or three, but they involve many relatives in the therapy. There is a tendency for the form of the therapy to take one of two foci: either the therapist brings together all of the significant people in the client's life in one large group, or he sends the client to visit all of the significant people in his life.

The large group, or family network, is often similar to experiential therapy in its focus on growth and development of family members and sometimes on a confrontation experience. The focus is on a general method that is applied to all cases and not a specific plan for each problem. It is an analogical therapy and is focused on the present and not on the past (3, 43).

In the approach requiring a client to contact significant people in his life, relationships are thought to be analogical in the sense that changing one set of relationships in a network will change another set. For example, if a woman presents the problem of anxiety attacks about job interviews, she would be expected to change if she activated her wider kin network and dealt differently with her parents and grandparents. According to this school, family issues in one generation are replicated in the next. This repetition can be avoided if the therapist coaches or directs the patient to differentiate himself by behaving in new ways with the extended family.

Like the psychoanalytic and experiential schools, this approach emphasizes growth and method. Unlike these schools it emphasizes directives, intergenerational processes and hierarchy. In contrast to the experiential school where families are encouraged to express emotions in the sessions, this approach attempts to avoid emotional interchanges and focus on rational processes.

Despite the fact that a great deal of the literature of this school (2, 9–12) frequently uses individual terminology (undifferentiated "ego" mass, differentiation of "self" scale, "emotional" system), the focus is on a unit of three. It is a theory of the instability of a dyad in the sense that when two people are involved in an emotionally intense relationship they will triangulate a third person. The therapist's task when talking to a couple is to not be emotionally triangulated.

One of the groups of family therapies not dealt with here since their theories are the same as those of other schools, is that group in which different families are brought together into one large group (26). This is called "multiple family therapy" and the emphasis is upon group process. The extended family systems school also has groups of married couples—not whole families—brought together, but unlike several of the multiple family therapy approaches this particular school allows no group process among the couples. The therapist works with one couple while the others observe, and then with the next couple.

Communication

The communication approach was the first family therapy which did not have its origins in a form of individual therapy. It was also an approach that did not so much become a school in itself as a body of theory adapted by other schools.

Instead of developing from previous therapy, this approach stemmed from the biological and social sciences. Unlike psychodynamic theory, which had roots early in the century, communication theory did not develop until the mid-century. In 1948, Norbert Wiener published *Cybernetics*, and through the next decade all of the sciences began to emphasize homeostatic systems with feedback processes that caused the system to be self-corrective. This theory appeared in the field of therapy in the 1950s as part of the development of family theory. Although the ideas became evident in a number of therapies, the communication approach became most well known through Gregory Bateson's research project on communication which existed from 1952 to 1962 (4, 18, 20, 23, 24, 46). The idea of the double bind was published in 1956 (5) and influenced many therapists to begin to think from a communication point of view. The approach suggested that the interchange of messages between people defined relationships, and these relationships were stabilized by homeostatic processes in the form of actions of family members within the family. The minimum unit was two people since there was a sender and a receiver of messages. The therapy developing out of this view emphasized changing a family system by arranging that family members behave, or communicate, differently with one another. It was not a therapy related to lifting repression or bringing about self-understanding, nor was it based upon a theory of conditioning. The past was dropped as a central issue because it was how people were communicating at the moment that was the focus of attention. Over the decade of the 1950s the unit shifted from two people to three or more people as the family began to be conceived of as having an organization and structure. The unit became more and more a child in relationship to two adults, or an adult in relation to another adult and grandparent, and so on. The emphasis was upon analogies in one part of a system for another part, so analogical communication was emphasized more than digital (although these terms themselves were emphasized by Bateson as a way of classifying any communication).

In the early family therapy with this approach, awareness was still thought to bring about change and so interpretations were used because other therapy techniques had not developed to fit the new ways of thinking. By the 1960s a therapist using the communication approach was finding it necessary to defend himself for using interpretations and was not educating the family. It was assumed that new experience, in the sense of new behavior that provoked changes in the family system, brought about change. Directives were used in the interview to change communication pathways, such as requiring people to talk together who had habitually not done so. There were also directives used outside the interview, particularly with the influence of Milton Erickson's directive therapy on the communication therapists (17, 21). The tendency in the early days was to be growth oriented because of a concern with encouraging a wider range of communicative behavior in the family system. Some adherents, influenced by Milton Erickson, focused more on the presenting problem, but even then it was a way of increasing complexity in the system. However, the presenting problem was never dismissed as "only a symptom" because symptomatic behavior was considered a necessary and appropriate response to the communicative behavior that provoked it. There was little emphasis upon hierarchy in the early stages; family members were encouraged to communicate as equals. The emphasis was upon clarifying communication in some approaches (40). Later there was a developing concern with status in the family organization. Don Jackson, one of the foremost innovators in the communication approach, was emphasizing the structural aspects of parental authority when young people were defined as psychotic. Parents and young people were not interviewed as peers as they would be in a therapy based on free association or individual self-expression.

The communication approach tended to become part of other approaches. Virginia Satir developed a more "experiential" communication approach after participating in Esalen experiential groups (41). The extended family system theories were influenced by communication ideas. However, there were basically two branches of therapy developing out of the communication approach; one was structural, emphasizing the hierarchical organization in the family and describing different communication structures. The other was strategic, also emphasizing organizational structure but focusing more on the repeating sequences on which structures are based.

Communication: Structural. The structural family therapy school adopted many communication ideas when attempting therapy with lower-class families where traditional therapy was not helpful (32, 33). In this approach there is a focus on hierarchy with parents expected to be in charge of children and a family not considered an organization of equals. Families are conceived of as being composed of subsystems such as husband-wife, mother-child, and siblings. "Subsystems can be formed by generation, by sex, by interest or by function" (30, p. 52). Pathology is considered to occur in families that are too enmeshed (there is little or no subsystem differentiation) or too disengaged (each person constitutes an independent subsystem). The emphasis is on the present, not the past, and the unit tends to be the triad. A transactional pattern in a family may be the following: the mother encourages the daughter to disobey the father, who attacks the daughter when he is angry at the mother. The conflict between the parents is said to detour through the daughter.

A main focus of the therapy is on differentiating subsystems. For example, parents are encouraged to talk to each other without interruptions from the children, or when siblings are talking with each other the parents are prevented from interrupting. In disengaged families, the therapist increases the flow among subsystems so that family members will be more engaged and supportive of each other.

In the hypothetical case of a woman who is afraid of job interviews, this approach would assume that fear is related to others in the family and all members would be brought together. If both the husband and the mother were involved, the therapist would focus on differentiating the couple subsystem so that the wife would feel more secure in their relationship and would therefore be able to leave it temporarily to be involved in outside activities such as a job.

Within the sessions, the main therapeutic technique is to change the ways people relate by arranging who talks to whom about what and in what way. The rationale is that changes in communication pathways lead to important structural changes in the family. These changes are continued outside the sessions through tasks. For example, a father may be asked to spend a certain amount of time every day talking to his son about a specific subject.

In this therapy, educational interpretations are made in a special way. Ordinarily interpretations are made with the belief that if people understand the ways they deal with each other, they will change. In this approach, the therapist uses interpretations to create a situation that may not be an accurate portrait of what is happening but that is one the therapist can change. For example, the therapist may bring a couple together by pointing out that the daughter rules and divides them. Although this "interpretation" may be only partially true, the parents will dislike being thought of in this way and will pull together to take charge of the daughter.

In this school, the emphasis is more on structural problems in the family than on the presenting problem, except with life-threatening situations where the emphasis is on the presenting problem as in anorexia and diabetic coma (27, 31). Since the emphasis is usually not on resolving symptoms, the therapy tends to be growth oriented. This school does not have a set method but varies what is done with the family structure, with the exception of certain problems such as anorexia where there is a set of procedures and stages that are routinely followed in the therapy (7, 28).

Communication: Strategic therapy.   The main characteristic of this therapy is that the therapist plans a strategy for solving the client's problems (17, 19, 20, 34, 36, 45, 47). The goals are clearly set and always coincide with solving the presenting problem. The therapy is planned in steps, or stages, to achieve the goals. Every problem is defined as involving at least two and usually three people. The therapist must first decide who is involved in the presenting problem and in what way. Next, he must decide on an intervention which will shift the family organization so that the presenting problem is not necessary. This intervention usually takes the form of a directive about something that the family is to do both in and out of the interview. Directives may be straightforward or paradoxical, simple and involving one or two people, or complex and involving the whole family. These directives have the purpose of changing the ways people relate to each other and to the therapist.

The approach is digital in its focus on the presenting problem, like the behavior therapies, but analogical in the way it conceptualizes the problem. It is assumed that a problem in a child or a symptom in an adult is a way that one person communicates with another. In the case of a woman who becomes anxious at job interviews, it would be assumed that this is the way the woman and her husband (and/or her mother, father, etc.) communicate about some specific issues, such as whether the husband approves of the wife working and being that independent, or whether the wife should do what her husband or her mother wishes, and so on. In the case of another couple who become unstable over the same presenting problem, a child might develop a problem which will keep the wife at home to take care of him and deal with the job issue that way. It is assumed that a symptom analogically, or metaphorically, expresses a problem and is also a solution, although usually an unsatisfactory one for the people involved.

There are no interpretations in this therapy but the focus is upon change by directives. In this hypothetical case, the therapist might ask the husband to teach the wife how to go through a job interview. Ostensibly this would be to relieve her anxiety, but in actuality the therapist would be changing the relationship between husband and wife, for example by helping the husband tolerate the wife going to work and achieving that independence, or by making the task a joint endeavor between husband and wife from which other people, such as the wife's mother, are excluded.

Since this therapy focuses on solving the presenting problem, it is not growth oriented or concerned with the past. The emphasis is on communication in the present. Families go through new experiences as they follow the therapist's directives, but the experience is not a goal in itself; nor is there an emphasis on working through something or being aware of how communication takes place; if the family can get over the problem without knowing how or why, that is satisfactory, since so much necessarily is outside awareness (35). The goals of the therapy are primarily to prevent the repetition of sequences and to introduce more complexity and alternatives. For example, a typical sequence is one where the child develops problems when the parents threaten to separate, the parents stay together to deal with their problem child, and as the child behaves more normally the parents threaten separation again which leads to the child developing problems. The task of the therapist is to change this sequence so that improvement of the child is unrelated to whether the parents separate or not.

There is a concern with hierarchy in this approach. Parents are expected to be in charge of their children, and cross-generation coalitions, such as one parent siding with a child against another parent, are blocked. There is also a cautious concern about where the therapist is in the hierarchy so that he does not inadvertently form coalitions with members low in the hierarchy against those who are higher. It is assumed that therapy must occur in stages and the presenting problem cannot be solved in one step (19). Similar presenting problems can require different therapeutic plans which must be designed for each particular one.

CONCLUSION

The developing field of family-oriented therapy includes several major trends. There is an increasing realization that the individual therapies are based upon a set of premises about psychology and about change differing from those developing out of a communication perspective. The new ideas place less emphasis on the past and more on the present situation; there is a shift from bringing about awareness with interpretations to bringing about new behavior with directives. In practice, more responsibility is put on the therapist since therapy is not defined as a spontaneous happening but a planned and organized procedure. The social unit defined as the problem has shifted from one person to two or three and even to a unit of extended kin and the social community. The trend is away from thinking of people as autonomous individuals and toward recognizing that autonomy is defined in relation to other people and that everyone is a member of hierarchical organizations. "System" means the repeating pattern, and the structure of an organization is the repeated sequences which crystallize into a structural form. As for therapy, there is an increasing understanding of human dilemmas and a recognition of the need to design a specific approach for each problem rather than to attempt to follow a method that all problems must fit.

REFERENCES

1. Ackerman, N. *Treating the Troubled Family*. Basic Books, New York, 1966.
2. Anonymous. Towards the differentiation of a self in one's own family. In Framo, J., Ed., *Family Interaction: A Dialogue Between Family Researchers and Family Therapists*. Springer, New York, 1972.
3. Attneave, C. L. Therapy in tribal settings and urban network intervention. *Fam. Proc., 8:* 175–193, 1962.
4. Bateson, G. *Steps to an Ecology of Mind*. Ballantine Books, New York, 1972.
5. Bateson, G., Jackson, D. D., Haley, J., and Weakland, J. Towards a theory of schizophrenia. *Behav. Sci., 1:* 251–264, 1956.
6. Bell, N. W. Extended family relations of disturbed and well families. *Fam. Proc., 1:* 175–193, 1962.
7. Berger, H. G. Somatic pain and school avoidance. *Clin. Pediatr., 13:* 819–826, 1974.
8. Boszormenyi-Nagy, I., and Spark, G. *Invisible Loyalties*. Harper & Row, New York, 1973.
9. Bowen, M. Family therapy after twenty years. In Arieti, S., Ed., *American Handbook of Psychiatry*, Vol. IV, pp. 367–392. Basic Books, New York, 1975.
10. Bowen, M. Principles and techniques of multiple family therapy. In Bradt, J., and Moynihan, C., Eds., *Systems Therapy*. Authors, Washington, D.C., 1972.
11. Bowen, M. The use of family theory in clinical practice. In Haley, J., Ed., *Changing Families*. Grune & Stratton, New York, 1971.
12. Bradt, J., and Moynihan, C., Eds. *Systems Therapy*. Authors, Washington, D. C., 1972.
13. Dicks, H. *Marital Tensions*. Basic Books, New York, 1967.
14. Duhl, F., Kantor, D., and Duhl, B. Learning, space and action in family therapy: A primer of sculpture. In Bloch, D., Ed., *Techniques of Family Therapy: A Primer*. Grune & Stratton, New York, 1973.
15. Framo, J. Symptoms from a family transaction viewpoint. In Ackerman, N., Lieb, J., and Pearce, J., Eds., *Family Therapy in Transition*. Little, Brown and Co., Boston, 1970.
16. Gehrke, S., and Kirschenbaum, M. Survival patterns in family conjoint therapy. *Fam. Proc., 6:* 67–80, 1967.
17. Haley, J., Ed. *Advanced Techniques of Hypnosis and Therapy: The Selected Papers of Milton H. Erickson*. Grune & Stratton, New York, 1971.
18. Haley, J. The development of a theory: A history of a research project. In Sluzki, C., and Ranson, D. C., Eds., *Double Bind*. Grune & Stratton, New York, 1976.
19. Haley, J. *Problem Solving Therapy*. Jossey-Bass, San Francisco, 1976.
20. Haley, J. *Strategies of Psychotherapy*. Grune & Stratton, New York, 1963.
21. Haley, J. *Uncommon Therapy: The Psychiatric Techniques of Milton H. Erickson*. W. W. Norton, New York, 1973.
22. Hawkins, R. P., Peterson, R. F., Schwied, E., and Bijou, S. Behavior therapy in the home: Amelioration of problem parent-child relations with the parent in a therapeutic role. In Haley, J., Ed., *Changing Families*. Grune & Stratton, New York, 1971.
23. Jackson, D. D., Ed. *Therapy, Communication and Change*. Science and Behavior Books. Palo Alto, 1968.
24. Jackson, D. D., and Weakland, J. Conjoint family therapy: Some considerations on theory, technique and results. *Psychiatry, 24:* 30–45, 1961.
25. Kempler, W. *Principles of Gestalt Family Therapy*. A. S. J. Nordahls Trykkeri, Oslo, 1973.
26. Lacquer, H. P., Laburt, H. A., and Morong, E. Multiple family therapy: Further developments. In Masserman, J. H., Ed., *Current Psychiatric Therapies*, IV. Grune & Stratton, New York, 1964.
27. Liebman, R. R., Minuchin, S., and Baker, L. An integrated treatment program for anorexia nervosa. *Am. J. Psychiatry, 131:* 432–436, 1974.
28. Liebman, R., Minuchin, S., and Baker, L. The use of structural family therapy in the treatment of intractable asthma. *Am. J. Psychiatry, 131:* 535–540, 1974.
29. MacGregor, R., Ritchie, A. M., Serrano, A. C., et al. *Multiple Impact Therapy with Families*. McGraw-Hill, New York, 1964.
30. Minuchin, S. *Families and Family Therapy*. Harvard University Press, Cambridge, 1974.
31. Minuchin, M., Baker, L., Rosman, B., et al. A conceptual model of psychosomatic illness in children. *Arch. Gen. Psychiatry, 32:* 1031–1038, 1975.
32. Minuchin, S., and Montalvo, B. Techniques for working with disorganized low socio-economic families. *Am. J. Orthopsychiatry, 37:* 880–887, 1967.

33. Minuchin, S., Montalvo, B., Guerney, B., *et al.* *Families of the Slums*. Basic Books, New York, 1967.
34. Montalvo, B. Aspects of live supervision. *Fam. Proc.*, *12:* 343–359, 1973.
35. Montalvo, B. Observations on two natural amnesias. *Fam. Proc.*, *15:* 333–342, 1976.
36. Montalvo, B., and Haley, J. In defense of child therapy. *Fam. Proc.*, *12:* 227–244, 1973.
37. Patterson, G. R. *Families: Applications of Social Learning to Family Life*. Research Press, Champaign, Ill., 1971.
38. Patterson, G. R., Ray, R., and Shaw, D. *Direct Intervention in Families of Deviant Children*. Oregon Research Institute, Eugene, 1969.
39. Rubinstein, D. Family therapy. *Intern. Psychiatr. Clin.*, *1:* 431–442, 1964.
40. Satir, V. *Conjoint Family Therapy*. Science and Behavior Books, Palo Alto, 1964.
41. Satir, V. *Peoplemaking*. Science and Behavior Books, Palo Alto, 1972.
42. Sigal, J. J., Barrs, C. B., and Doubilet, A. L. Problems in measuring the success of family therapy in a common clinical setting: Impasse and solutions. *Fam. Proc.*, *15:* 225–233, 1976.
43. Speck, R., and Attneave, C. *Family Networks*. Pantheon Books, New York, 1973.
44. Stuart, R. B. Operant interpersonal treatment for marital discord. *J. Consult. Clin. Psychol.*, *33:* 675–682, 1969.
45. Watzlawick, P., Weakland, J., and Fisch, R. *Change*. W. W. Norton, New York, 1974.
46. Weakland, J. Family therapy as a research arena. *Fam. Proc.*, *1:* 63–68, 1962.
47. Zuk, G. *Family Therapy: A Triadic Based Approach*. Behavioral Publications, New York, 1971.

Psychotherapy of the Absurd:
With a Special Emphasis
on the Psychotherapy of Aggression

Carl A. Whitaker

TYPES OF PSYCHOTHERAPY

Any discussion of psychotherapy must begin by defining the character of psychotherapy one intends to present. Are we talking about *reparative psychotherapy?* Are we talking about the *relief of symptoms?* Are we talking about *character restructuring?* Are we talking about a *growth-accelerating experience?* Qualitatively, the character of psychotherapy patterns may take many forms. A classification could include:

(a) Interpersonal feedback as in group psychotherapy, some sensitivity training experiences, and communication training.
(b) The development of self-induced feedback—a kind of recycling experience with content and affect rediscovered or re-experienced, as in the psychoanalytic pattern.
(c) Psychological education, as in rational psychotherapy and the late phase in the usual transference kind of treatment. This psychotherapeutic process is very much like the parent-child conference with a late adolescent offspring.
(d) A here-and-now experience with a professional who can share in activating and accelerating the feedback to the patient by his own non-rational participation and by his here-and-now growth process.

This later mode, which includes family therapy, has elements of the play that makes child therapy different from insight therapy. It requires control by power in the early part of treatment and makes broad use of the symbolic aspects of the total relationship, including body language, now sometimes labeled Gestalt techniques or non-verbal communication. There is also a freedom to see therapy include a manipulative process, as with children and psychotics. This facilitates the ability of the therapist to shift from a peer give-and-take to an authoritative position of making decisions like sending the psychotic back to his bedroom or interrupting the child's play to end the hour. This model assumes the therapist will also push to experience his own craziness, his own LSD kind of turn-on, and a non-rational exposure of himself. (A rational pattern in the therapist's function doesn't help the patient break his own prison of reason.) It also assumes the use of deliberate paradox, a kind of chess-playing with the patient—a sense that therapy is not just being sincere and honest and open and even crazy with the patient, but is also the freedom to shift back and forth between being intimate and crazy-like to being deliberately manipulative and managerial.

The author and T. Malone (9) have previously presented the concept of individual therapy as a forced, regressive process or as induced regression. This approach assumed that the psychotic is himself also playing at being an adult and therapy is an effort to force him into becoming fully crazy, fully infantile, regressing to the year-and-a-half or two-year-old point at which he began distorting his growth process.

Psychotherapy structure, of course, is not a variant of social relating. "Love is not enough"—unless the patient has sufficient maturity and integration to carry most of the initiative for the process. Dr. Barbara Betz says the quality of all psychotherapy is profoundly dependent upon the therapist as a person: his inherent freedom to share and his inherent capacity and freedom to care. A noncaring therapist may be useful to a patient who is fairly well along in his growth process but is probably not of much use to the more immature patient.

The process of family psychotherapy is generally characterized by a transference phase in which there is established a symbolic generation gap and a supra-system in which the family becomes part of an extended family including the therapeutic team. With this structuring, there develops an *induced regression* of the component parts of the subsystem, that is, the individuals, the dyads, the triangles, and the two generations. The therapeutic process then begins to establish the integrity of the individual components of the system. Given this integrity, the individual components of the family system develop a specific autonomy and become capable of functioning without the need for the supra-system—its control and its integrative power. There emerges because of this regression a gradual restructuring of the family system itself with greater mobility and greater flexibility.

The second phase of the process of this psychotherapy I label the existential phase. This develops later, although it of course overlaps the transference phase, and consists of the establishment of a peer-like balance between the patient group and the therapist group with the autonomy of the components. It has an adult-to-adult character with contributions from each side to the other and from each unit to the whole system.

THE FAMILY HOSTILITY SYSTEM

As defined by Partridge (6), aggression really arises out of two components, assertiveness and hostility. Assertiveness relates to words meaning to get fed, to get together with, to walk toward, whereas hostility has two aspects, one to assail and one to destroy.

Culturally, aggression wins hands down in the competition with sex for what is *most unacceptable* in our interpersonal living pattern. Thus, assault and battery is taken much more seriously by the authorities than rape or incest. Furthermore, most crimes of violence take place within the family rather than on the sidewalk. Such aggression is usually an effort to be a personal savior to a Significant Other and best defined by a famous schizophrenic, not a patient of mine, who said in defining his therapeutic effort to save us all, "I come not to bring peace but a sword," translated as "You've got to fight to get to heaven." Furthermore, Dr. Winnicott, a London child analyst, in an exceptional paper called "Hate in the Counter-Transference" (10) said, "If you haven't been hated by your analyst, you've been cheated," and at another time, "The psychotic patient can't tolerate his own hatred unless the analyst hates him." Even the Old Testament participates, saying, "He that hideth with smiling lips is a fool."

THE THERAPIST'S MADNESS

Constructive aggression by the therapist is one way of defining his integrity as a person. It's a modeling process and, not so secondarily, is also a way to destroy the myth of the omnipotent parent. Although our overt aggression early in therapy may be clinically inappropriate, aggression once it does develop may be hidden by the doctor's famous bedside manner or by that poker face that hints indifference or a fear of involvement. We may even repress our anger until the patient in his transference loyalty acts it out for the therapist like a child stealing cars for his pre-delinquent father's sake. Sometimes a therapist dare not admit his simple ambivalence lest his aggression explode. Thereby, we also conceal our free associations, mis-hearing, slips of tongue, and even creative fantasies. Such suppression of self will hide our own night dreams and anger at our real world, as well as any love for, and identification with, the family.

How does the modern therapist express this therapeutic anger? The four simple ways are pigmy versions of the patterns that are detailed in the standard American Psychiatric classification of "madness": First, the *sneer* or *snarl* that they label in its extreme form paranoid psychosis. It's the open style and at least an interpersonal turn-on. More powerful is the *poker face freeze* that, carried to an extreme, they call catatonia. Still more serious is that contentless *inner boredom* called by Baudelaire (1) the worst crime. If carried to its extreme, they label it simple psychosis. Finally, and most destructive, that *derisive laughter* that, carried to its ultimate, is the hebephrenic system for withdrawing from the interpersonal world. If the patient (family) is personal enough, these withdrawal models may fail and the therapist is forced to come alive. Then his madness explodes into the family.

THE PATIENT'S MADNESS

The patient's madness may become growth-accelerating and creatively re-channeled when aided by the therapist, either through direct intervention or by indirect means. Those who have practiced psychotherapy for long usually become exponents of indirect methods. I should like to list several that seem definable within the usual ongoing treatment process:

(a) Handling aggression by forgiveness—the typical mother support pattern that may result in an induced regression and a return to child-like directness and openness.

(b) The second type I call counter-attack. It's a kind of *judo* approach to aggression that tends to neutralize the anger or the bitterness or the physical assault. It's an interpersonal retraining in which, because of superior strength and superior confidence, the therapist is able to shunt the aggression out of its escalation or render it impotent without seriously threatening the aggressor, whether an individual or the family as a whole. For example, a curt command to "Sit down" can prevent a physical attack.

(c) A third method is to one-up the situation rather than the person. One-upmanship is like *aikido*—a method of *judo*-like character except that it does not involve any aggressive response to the attacker but rather prevents him from doing damage with his aggression. It renders the aggression futile—for example, the therapist who doesn't notice a murderous look.

(d) A fourth method is to justify the aggression, to go with it, thus reducing the guilt and producing a loss of the aggressive affect. One day, in an initial interview with an adult veteran, I became terrified lest he kill me there and then. I excused myself, went across the hall and got Dr. John Warkentin and brought him back into the interview; I told him and the patient of my fear. He said to the patient with a perfectly straight face and in a serious tone, "I don't blame you a bit; I've often wanted to kill Whitaker myself." This confused me, but it made the patient's anger much more controllable and we went on with a comfortable interview.

(e) Still another way of handling aggression is to defuse or redirect it. For example, one can help the patient project anger at his father onto the therapist or redirect hatred against his wife back into the residual hatred for mother or father or big sister.

(f) It is also possible to handle aggression by direct attack. Thus, the therapist can dominate the patient psychologically, making him suppress his anger. This is similar to *karate*—the therapist can defeat the patient and thus render his anger something he dare not use.

PSYCHOTHERAPY OF THE ABSURD

Finally, I should like to talk at some length about a method that I seem to have developed in spite of myself. It's a method of augmenting the unreasonable quality of the patient's symptom or situation to the point of absurdity (8). It includes a kind of tongue-in-cheek attitude—a kind of put-on by the therapist but is surprisingly useful if it's a natural component of the ongoing relationship. The therapist may so augment or escalate the incongruity of a symptom or bit of the patient's behavior that the absurdity is easily apparent to the patient and he enjoys the implications, as one does after a slip of the tongue. Success with this maneuver demands that it be lovingly done, and this caring is the anesthesia for the amputation of pride that takes place. A most elementary example would be responding to a child's angry scream by pseudo-screaming back at him. With enough of these imitation screams that echo his screaming, he feels impotent and stops because nothing is happening the way he expected it to, or he joins the therapist and the two of them laugh at what's happening.

When working with a grossly aggressive patient or family, bits of absurdity may serve as a quantum jump from rational psychotherapy to an effective tactic that reduces aggression and establishes a creative craziness in the therapeutic group. The therapist may expose his own absurd behavior or respond to his own boredom by a flight into absurdity via minute, incongruous bits of behavior—e.g. (a) give the top of old coffee percolator to college sophomore schizoid without comment when she leaves interview: (b) identified patient is accused by parents of having poor ego boundaries—therapist offers blank sheet of paper with large X to "use as ego boundary as needed," (c) unannounced exit from office and return five minutes later without excuse and with inane reason—"My foot itched'" (d) write a letter during hour to your co-therapist entitled "Why this family won't make it"—offer it to family if anyone questions the behavior.

The use of the absurd may be a fragment, as described, or it may become an ongoing process. When it is such, it resembles the leaning tower of Pisa. The patient comes in offering an absurdity, and the therapist accepts the absurdity, builds upon it, escalates it until the tower has become so high and so tilted that it crashes to the ground. The steps in this seem fairly clear:

Step 1. The patient or the family presents an absurdity—for example, "I can't stand my husband." The therapist agrees, "Men are pretty difficult."

Step 2. He then extends the inference "Why haven't you divorced him?" or "Why not try an interim boyfriend?"

Step 3. The therapist then expands the absurdity by escalating the patient's feedback to the original interaction. She says, "But, I love him." The therapist says, "Of course, that's why you'd have an affair—to prove your love and to stimulate his love 'till it equals yours.'" The patient says, "But I love my kids," and the therapist says, "Well, if you do, then you should make a sacrifice by leaving them so they'll learn that father also loves them." "But he'll neglect them." "Then you can prove your love of them by suing him for child neglect."

Step 4. The patient or the family attempts to break this escalation, to take off the top floors of the Tower as it were. The patient says, "This is silly." Therapist: "No, it's very logical and loving and human, and I'm only trying to help you. I believed you when you said you couldn't stand him, and I was trying to help you find and figure out ways of making things work out right." Although this pattern may seem ridiculous when it's looked at in this verbal and logical framework, it may develop quite naturally and become an extremely powerful force. This raises the question of what happens when it goes on for most of the hour or for week after week?

Step 5. It seems as though the fifth step emerges when the patient's attempt to break the escalation does not pay off. There is then a break in the patient's integration and his imprinted thought pattern. This resembles a Zen enlightenment experience. The tower of absurdity comes crashing down. This may happen in three different ways: (a) By sudden development of a profound dependency so that the patient reports, "We've had a very good week, and I don't understand it"; (b) The crash may be experienced as a flare of rebellion. The patient says to the co-therapist or to her partner, "Let's get out of here; I can't stand this screwball and the way he talks"; (c) The break and crash may come by transcendence. The patient says, "Carl, you're crazy, but I think I see what you're talking about. I really couldn't stand my husband, the rat. I would have left him long ago, but there must be something about him that makes me go on loving him."

Step 6. The sixth step, of course, is the therapist's acceptance of the patient's flight into health or enlightenment experience. I call this the benediction and just say, "Have fun."

Let me give another example. The patient presents with a fear of sex. The therapist says, "Yes, I understand sex is a very frightening experience." Thus accepting the absurdity, he begins to escalate it to step three. "Do you find sometimes that you also have difficulty eating, that after eating you get the feeling of being very full and maybe you shouldn't eat more or that maybe it would be better if you didn't eat at all and then you wouldn't feel so full? There is also the possibility of choking or of getting some food that has glass in it. I read recently of a boy who ate something and was so badly poisoned he almost died." In the fourth step, the patient attempts to break the sense of absurdity. "I have started eating less. The other day I had to throw away a whole T.V. meal because it didn't look right." Or he says one day, "We really had a great orgasm last night," or in a transcending way, "I'm feeling all sexed up this week."

Let me give still another example. This is a real family story: There is father, mother, 13-year-old daughter, and 6-year-old son. Wife insists husband is unfaithful and that, anyway, he lies all the time. Husband says the affair is over and that, anyway, she shouldn't complain because he is working two jobs and giving her all the money. The therapist suggests that if he's not careful and she stays suspicious she may hold back his allowance. He says, "Well, she has already held back some of it." The therapist notes that the wife looks very happy and asks *her* if she has expressed appreciation to her husband for stimulating their relationship by this affair. The wife is quite indignant but a little confused. Therapist explains that it's his belief that when these things happen the two of them have done a long-range planning project with great care and that the result is a concealed decision that he should have an affair. It obviously worked out well since she looks very pretty and both had agreed she has been a better wife since the affair. The therapist then asks if mother's mother believes the affair should be tolerated, or should the wife get a divorce. The wife explains that her mother thinks she shouldn't split from her husband. The therapist then suggests to the husband that since the wife is so happy maybe he should be careful not to go back to his wife. Had he thought about having several girls—then he could get an allowance from each of them. If he should decide to do this, he should add on one at a time because girls are very apt to get jealous of each other. A man must learn how to handle a team of girls when each of them is paying him an allowance from her earnings. At this point father attempts to break the escalation of the tower by getting sarcastic with the six-year-old son who is gently restless. Father also backs off after he explodes, so the boy does not modify the behavior. Finally, the father snarls, "Fool," at the son with great bitterness. The son is as unimpressed by this apparent viciousness as father is unimpressed by mother's verbal attack. Son, like father, keeps a poker face. As the entire absurd episode explodes the wife's organized coping process, she begins to cry and yet wonders why she's crying.

The success of the break is further signaled by the wife's willingness to return for another appointment and the husband's agreeing to come back and to bring the only surviving grandparents, his father and her mother, for the next interview.

Gus Napier suggests a different explanation for the above episode. The couple is deliberately mystified by the therapist who then escalates the confusion by his seeming serious attitude. He denies the couple's effort to demystify by repeated affirmation of good faith ("I'm just trying to help you."). As he does this, he encourages rebellion against previous mystification. Furthermore, as the process escalates, the therapist, in contrast with the spouse or mother, encourages rebellion by the couple and thereby joins them in a low-profile game of teasing each other.

A marital counselor and his wife came as patients to two co-therapists with whom they had had previous interviews. They requested help for their marital relationship. It seemed that each had developed an affair with the full awareness of the other partner. The affairs were doing well on each side, but they had decided to spend six months trying to clarify their marital relationship before they decided about divorce. The therapists requested a 24-hour delay while they considered a possible plan. Next day they suggested that there were two ways to go on with treatment. One, the co-therapists would begin couple psychotherapy with a contract specifying no sexual relationships during the therapy so as to potentiate the affective relationships with the two therapists. The couple must also contract to have no sexual experiences with their two affair-partners. An alternate plan specified that the husband and wife bring in their girl friend and boy friend and the spouses of those two so that the co-therapists could work with all six. Both offers were declined, but a letter six weeks later indicated that the couple were doing much better and appreciated the help we had given them.

This multiple triangle was presented to the co-therapists with a request that was itself absurd—mystifying?—double-binding? The therapists took the absurd task and escalated the absurdity—mystification?—double bind?—paradoxical intention? They further encouraged the rebellion by offering an alternative escalation of the original absurdity: multiple triangles. The couple did rebel and indicated the success of the process in a letter.

POSSIBLE MECHANISM

Why does the theatre of the absurd have such a popular hold on audiences? Esslin (3) talks about this question, as do Bogard and Oliver (2). Oliver believes this attraction derives from its relation to our general problem in living—our world is absurd, our culture is absurd, my life is absurd, my reason is absurd. Is psychotherapy, like this drama, a microcosm of the process of our living?

The drama critics state that man's thinking is absurd to his senses, and his senses are absurd to reasoned thought. Paradoxically, we attain power at the sacrifice of reason. When we try to act reasonably, we deny our personhood. Furthermore, as we struggle to "be" who we are, it is impossible to stop acting. These are the self-defeating paradoxes of our lives. They portray our power and our impotence but also our knowledge and ignorance, our attunement and alienation. In essence, we are both tragic and farcical. This Janus mask is thus our absurdity. Absurdity is both metaphilosophical and the existential summation of man. Our absurdity is ironic and a fragment of our craziness. The drama of the absurd says, "This is not life I express, this is a work of art about life." The logic of the drama of the absurd is never directly stated but indirectly and symbolically expressed. The use of deliberate obscurantism makes it necessary for the audience not only to *recognize* a body of thought but also to *learn* it. In contrast, direct presentation many times leads to recognition but results in a failure to learn. Obscurity is one method to activate learning and models the absurdity we find in life. In contrast, realism in drama and, I think, in psychotherapy reduces the actor or the patient or the therapist to a puppet, and furthermore, one then lives in a perpetual distrust of language.

Many times the process of relating to patients consists of moving in for an experience of belonging and then asserting the freedom to move out. *Most therapists develop empathy. They learn to move in, but they stumble as they try to move out, i.e. to individuate without leaving the patient rejected.* One possible method is to utilize this process of activating the absurd. For example, a therapist makes some derogatory remark about the patient's appearance and then says as the patient is about to counter, "Isn't it silly of me since I'm not your husband," or, "I was only kidding." The therapist may also move in with a note of affection such as, "You look pretty," or, "I'm sorry you had this scheduling problem," and then moves to a note of absurdity. "I'm glad I don't look pretty," or, "I slept in the office last night so getting here was no problem for me." The therapist thus establishes a bond—a "we"—with the patient (or couple or family) and then breaks it. Since he identifies with the patient, he does so with a roguish touch that seems enjoyable and not rejecting. There is even the maternal voice tone—"Just you wait, I'll be right back."

By this microcosmic experience, the patient evolves a kind of immunity to the strange assault of the absurdity in our living process and some experience in how to zig and zag with the absurdity of his life. Hopefully, the patient also gets a kind of objective distance by participating in the therapist's distancing. Subsequently, he expands his capacity to tolerate the anxiety and the stress and even chaos of his ongoing life.

There is, of course, a similarity between this process and Don Jackson's prescribing the symptom or his forcing the development of a "runaway" within the family, thereby reducing to absurdity the escalating process of the family struggle. There is also a similarity to advising the family to augment the confusion of psychotherapy and try *not* to understand psychotherapy as a process but allow themselves to experience it more fully by not objectifying it or talking about it even among themselves outside the interview.

If psychotherapy is indeed a pilot plant to try out patterns of living different from those we are imprinted with in our childhood, then psychotherapy of the absurd can be a deliberate effort to break the old patterns of thought and behavior. At one point, we called this tactic the creation of *process koans*. It's a constant, exaggerated extension of the patient's self-concept, a constructed elaboration, an effort to help the patient develop a caricature of the implicit stance he has been assuming or the life style that he has presented by his symptoms or by his effort to explain himself. It is as though the therapist stretches the inferences the patient makes by manipulating the transference until the therapist's credibility is at the breaking point and the patient must either develop a new *gestalt* that excludes the therapist or regress to keep the transference *gestalt* alive—that is, to keep the therapist magic, keep him the God of their joint reality from which the "therapist-as-a-person" has now withdrawn. The therapist then develops a deviant quality or fantasy that excludes reason and impugns, or at least threatens, the rational aspects of the patient's daily life. The therapist may even escalate the absurdity to the ultimate of credibility and then beyond it. It's as though an individual patient comes with a leaning tower of Pisa and the therapist, instead of trying to straighten the tower, builds it higher and higher until, when it falls, the entire building falls rather than just the construct that the therapist has helped with.

Why then would we want to use the family as a whole for this kind of process? William Taylor (7) notes that the single deviant produces an emotional income for each member of the family—that is, each member of the family looking at the deviant feels so much better about each of the other members and so much better about the group as a whole, excluding the deviant, that it makes a very sensible way of handling family stress. Just so, if in family psychotherapy everyone is present, the emotional income for each person, because of his investment of affect in the family treatment effort, produces a large total investment by the family. The family therapy makes a sizable down payment toward changing the entire system with an increased flexibility or induced chaos of the total ecosystem—that is, the increased chaos, the increased craziness makes it possible for the deviant to re-enter the family and for the whole system to develop, thereby increasing flexibility.

This brings us to a conclusion in contrast to the older, direct therapy in which the effort was to reconstruct in a rational way. This psychotherapy of the absurd, or what Schwartz and Wolfe (11) years ago called irrational psychotherapy and which Malone and I acknowledged as non-rational therapy (5), *is a way of saying that the therapeutic problem is to increase the complexity of the situation rather than restore order.* Following the second law of cybernetics as defined by Lynn Hoffman (4), we are trying to induce chaos and craziness rather than restore order. May I stretch your patience to include three more examples of this kind of psychotherapeutic approach.

Mary F. arrived at the inpatient service after a very serious suicidal attempt. After being on the ward for several days, her family was invited for a family conference. With the seven of them there and with a general history of the family's way of living and some effort to establish for them a sense of whole so that it was clear we were dealing with a systems problem, I asked her who in the family wanted her dead. She was not able to answer this, but a younger brother got around to saying that he felt Dad would be happier if sister were out of the way. We moved from there to a discussion that activated her fantasy about what would have happened if she had been successful in her suicide attempt. How big a funeral, how expensive a casket, how many flowers, how long would Dad mourn, how long would Mother cry, what would happen to her belongings, her room, her boyfriend's picture, her old clothes? In each case, the therapist made considerable point of his own fantasy about this, wondering if mother could wear the patient's clothes, wondering if they would throw all her old letters from boy friends into the garbage or burn them, wondering whether boy friends would come to the funeral, whether the family could live in that house, who would sleep in her room, would they have to repaper it, etc.? A byproduct of this strategem is the discovery that when the patient goes through a full-fledged fantasy of this nature, the suicidal threat seems much reduced. The therapist may participate at great length, and what appears on paper like ridiculous expansions are well-tolerated and surprisingly useful. The usual suicidal fantasy—"They'll be sorry when I'm dead and gone," or, "I'll fix the bastards"—is thereby so contaminated that the exquisite pain of isolation is hard to maintain. I wonder if they'll really burn all my clothes? Would Bill go back to making it with Mary Jones? I'll bet Mother would leave Dad within a month.

Jane W., a 50-year-old mother in ongoing family therapy, had been picked up drunk on the street and brought to the hospital. She declared the problem was her younger daughter. She must make this daughter either marry her boy friend or get rid of him. Her efforts to resolve the problem were becoming increasingly painful since daughter and boy friend were sleeping in his car in the driveway and daughter would come in each morning to get breakfast for the boy friend and take it out to the car. Later, mother had to rap on the car window and yell at them to back their car out, so she could get her car out and go to work. The therapist suggested that she was not loving enough. She really should invite them in to sleep in the basement—the car was very cold and such treatment would run down their battery. She did this and came back the next month to report that she went down to the cellar one morning, found the boy friend in his undershorts, and "I ordered the daughter out of the house, but they have just gone on doing the same thing in the car." The therapist then suggested that she might alternate nights with them. She could sleep in the car one night and they in the house, and they could sleep in the car the next night and she in the house. Or she could at least get their breakfast so that the daughter wouldn't have to get out of the warm car and come in to make breakfast for him. Simultaneously, the therapist expressed his admiration for her getting drunk—something she had never done before. He encouraged her to continue that process, since it would undoubtedly help her alcoholic husband whom she had been neglecting for so many years. He might very well have to quit drinking if she got picked up for being drunk like this because he'd have to take care of her and it might even cure her daughter who would begin to worry about mother and the extreme cost of being hospitalized every night for being drunk on the street. This kind of induced confusion and expansion of the absurdity brought about a diminution of anger by an overlay of confusion and chaos. Surprisingly enough, although the retelling of this kind of experience sounds ridiculous, the patient is able to utilize a tremendous amount of absurd initiative from the therapist as the next case will show.

Susie Q., 29, who came from a foreign country, had survived two abortions and one missed abortion. That one was now five years of age and was called "It." Her husband was a square of the first caliber, and the problem as stated was that they wanted to get a divorce shortly and therefore he'd brought her for couples therapy. The therapist suggested that they could also put off getting divorced until they were older and psychotherapy would be one way of delaying it. The secondary problem seemed to be that each time she became pregnant she was convinced that she was so immature she couldn't possibly raise a child and therefore would get an abortion and each time the abortion would leave her so guilty that she would immediately want to get pregnant. The assistant professor husband was passively cooperative in all this, unconcerned about the $250 per abortion or her impulse to get pregnant again. He was glad to help in any way he could. After living through two more of these episodes, the co-therapists had developed a constant pattern of kidding in dead seriousness. They finally suggested the couple really try to have at least three abortions a year and in the twenty years remaining of her childbearing life, she probably could have sixty abortions and establish a world record. This was taken so seriously that three weeks later the husband suggested to the wife that she must get pregnant within the next six weeks or she wouldn't have her third pregnancy for that current year and thus not have her third abortion.

CONCLUSIONS

Clinical observation would indicate that insight psychotherapy may well be even more useless in growth-activating family treatment than in one-to-one therapy. The need for power tactics suggests that many group therapy techniques may be valuable. Responding to aggression in one or more of the family members, the author is increasingly free to use these group-activating tactics and the power politics of his own intervention. An attempt is made to describe a method for activating the tendency to resolve behavior paradoxes through transcendence by elaborating the absurd.

If the therapist is a caring person, he can frequently modulate aggression by cutting diagonally across the affect through use of tongue-in-cheek humor or a non-rational extension of the situation that leaves the aggressor off-balance and often amenable to more open family interaction.

Aggression is an overt and covert component in all family interaction. Family homeostasis is such a powerful component of family therapy that the therapeutic team must be able to manipulate the group dynamics or the *family will not change in spite of intense effort on his part and theirs*. Therefore, power techniques become a central factor in the process of treatment. The paradoxes so characteristic of their now instrumental, now symbolic, interaction can many times be resolved by positive feedback to the point of absurdity. The saber-tooth tiger starved to death when mother nature overdid the blessing of that absurd tooth.

Craziness is the only real solution to boredom, as with the chimpanzees who generate territorial wars to amuse themselves.

REFERENCES

1. Baudelaire, Charles, "Au Lecteur" from *Les Fleurs du Mal* in Robert Lowell, *The Voyage and Other Versions of Poems* by Charles Baudelaire, New York, Farrar, Strauss Giroux. 1968.
2. Bogard, T. and Oliver, W., *Modern Drama*, New York and Oxford, Oxford University Press, 1965.
3. Esslin, M. *The Theatre of the Absurd (Revised)*, Garden City, N.Y., Anchor Books, 1969.
4. Hoffman, L., "Deviation-Amplifying Processes in Natural Groups" in Jay Haley (Ed.), *Changing Families*, New York, Grune & Stratton, 1971.
5. Malone, T. P., Whitaker, C. A., Warkentin, J., and Felder, R. E., "Rational and Non-Rational Psychotherapy," *Am. J. Psychother.* 15: 212–220, 1961.
6. Partridge, E., *Origins*, New York, Macmillan Co., 1959.

7. Taylor, W., "Research on Family Interaction," *Fam. Proc.*, 9: 221–232, 1970.
8. Webster, Definition of "Absurd": incongruous, ridiculous, self-contradictory, contrary to reason.
9. Whitaker, C. and Malone, T., *The Roots of Psychotherapy*, London, Blakiston Publishers, 1953.
10. Winnicott, D. W., "Hate in the Counter-Transference," *Int. J. Psychoanal.*, 30: 69–74, 1949.
11. Wolf, A. and Schwartz, E. K., Irrational Psychotherapy I, II, III. *Amer. J. Psychother.* 12: 300–314, 508–521, 744–759, 1958.

Family Sculpture and Relationship Mapping Techniques

Larry L. Constantine

An overview is constructed of a substantial array of space and action techniques of broad utility in marriage and family therapy. Family sculpture and a variety of closely related techniques have gained wide acceptance by counselors, therapists, and educators. The roots of these techniques and their basic concepts are traced. A heuristic typology is presented which highlights the essential interrelatedness of diverse methods and lays the foundation for further open-ended innovation by working professionals to develop customized variations especially fitted to their personal style and to the needs of their clients.

Family sculpture comprises a body of powerful evaluation and intervention techniques already in wide use by marriage and family counselors and therapists, and increasingly by educators, consultants, and organizational development specialists. Through the symbolic and metaphorical use of real space a person can be helped to "sculpt" a living tableau of people embodying essential features of their interrelationships. Externalized as an active spatial metaphor, these insights become available to both client and change agent.

Family sculpture is related both historically and in method to psychodrama (Moreno, 1946) and to experiential exercises widely used in human relations training. Its principal departure from psychodrama is in its portrayal of symbolic processes and events through spatial analogies; relatively infrequently are events reenacted literally as in psychodrama. The difference is more than a mere matter of technique or emphasis. Psychodramatic reenactment tends to promote recall of both expressed and unexpressed affectual components of the experience. Often a strong emotional reexperiencing and catharsis are primary aims of such a technique, toward the end of freeing the individual from blocked emotions in order to make new contemporary behavioral choices. By contrast, sculpture aims toward *distancing* the client from the emotional experience and, through this disengagement, enabling new insight into complex relational determinants of past and present situations. Where psychodrama may be thought of as putting the client more centrally into experiences, sculpture seeks to "decentrate" the client, promoting increased objectivity and insight into personal participation in ongoing interpersonal patterns.

Sculpture was developed into its present forms by a number of professionals, working both independently and with some interactions. The mainstream of family sculpture was originated by David Kantor with important early contributions and elaborations by Bunny Duhl, Fred Duhl, and their colleagues at Boston State Hospital and the Boston Family Institute. According to the Duhls, the earliest experiments utilized the placement of objects rather than people. The development was catalyzed by a visit from Virginia Satir, who demonstrated the use of people to metaphorically represent specific abstract types of family configurations. The basic reference work on the subject is Duhl, Kantor, and Duhl (1973). It has been popularized by Virginia Satir (see e.g., Satir, 1972) and others (Papp and Silverstein, 1972). Its emphasis on space as a key dimension of human process has its roots in the work of Hall (1959; 1969), as elaborated in family theory by Kantor and Lehr (1975).

Evidence from various fields of investigation strongly suggests that people sort out, map, and store understanding of the complex interpersonal systems in which they are imbedded in the form of compressed spatial metaphors. These visual, spatial, metaphorical representations (probably associated with the right or subdominant hemisphere of the brain) summarize a vast amount of information in a compact and efficient manner. They constitute maps of the world (Bandler and Grinder, 1975), working theories on which everybody manages their moves through the complicated interpersonal landscape. Hartmann's comprehensive review (1973) and synthesis of the findings on the function of dreaming sleep can be interpreted as supporting this contention on the neurophysiological level. Dreaming is the active process by which these metaphorical maps are constructed, reworked, and resolved (Swonger and Constantine, 1976). Kantor's pioneering study of families in their day-to-day affairs suggests that distance regulation is the core mechanism by which families may be understood to operate. Distance regulation is both a process in physical space and a metaphorical operation. The everyday use of spatial metaphor forms a rich vocabulary in common use. We speak, for example, of emotional distance. "If you can grasp that." "I hope that I am bridging the gap between us."

Sculpture (also known as space sculpture, family sculpture, relationship sculpture, spatialization) is a body of techniques which enables people to tap into their metaphorical maps, to make these internal realities external, visible, and accessible to study and change.

BASIC CONCEPTS AND ISSUES

Sculptures and other spatializations may be conducted with almost any meaningful unit—with an individual, with couples, with a co-therapy or other work team, with a parent and child subsystem, with the sibling subsystem, with a whole family, with a family kinship network, or even with an entire corporation, although the staging and format will differ with the unit of choice. It has been used not only in family counseling and therapy, but in training (Constantine, 1976) and organizational development. The context may include only the sculptor and the therapist or other "monitor," or it may include all members of the system being sculpted. It may even incorporate an "audience" as in a training group or multiple family therapy group.

Sculpture is useful as both an evaluative and interventive measure. Though its most obvious function is exploratory or revelatory, the exposure or previously hidden or unarticulated dynamics have an impact on the system being sculpted. It can be a powerful antidote to blockage and dragging in therapy.

Sculpture is not a difficult technique to learn. In a very real sense, sculpture is based on a spatio-temporal, physical "vocabulary." The most important thing for the user to do is become at ease with and conversant in this spatial "language," that is, to read and speak freely in spatial metaphors and analogies. The possibility of a universal vocabulary within this spatial language has been suggested by recent work on kinesics and body language (Scheflen, 1972; Spiegel and Machotka, 1974).

Once certain fundamentals are acquired through a little practice, the therapist, counselor, or educator should become able to develop customized spatial techniques and procedures to fit contexts not anticipated by already developed "standard" forms. The most common abuse of spatial techniques is to use them only as mechanical procedures. "Sculpture is an organic part of an on-going process. It is not a mere gimmick or exercise thrown willy-nilly into an interactional heap" (Kantor, 1975). While some therapists might find only occasional uses for sculpture, there are some who can effectively make it the primary method for almost all their assessments and interventions.

Correctly done, all such sculpture involves three stages:
(1) Establishing the mapping between physical and metaphorical space.
(2) Constructing the sculpture.
(3) Processing the sculpture, or debriefing.
In some uses, the first and last stages are abbreviated, but they cannot be omitted altogether without losing much of the value. In some forms, notably the complete family sculptures discussed below, each stage may involve several distinct steps.

Establishing the map

To make the fullest metaphorical use of space and objects and to access an individual's internal maps, it is necessary to build a bridge from external, real space to internal, metaphorical space. A bridge can be crossed in either direction. Once a mapping of physical space into metaphorical space has been established, it is easier for the sculptor (the client) to project internal reality onto external reality. This process sets the stage for the sculpture by defining the mapping (a correspondence) between one space and another. For example, the mapping might be between distance in physical space and emotional distance. The bridge might be built by having participants explore the real physical space, then inviting them to get in touch with their feelings for each other as they move about in this space, then to begin to sense their subtle feelings of comfort and discomfort as they move closer and farther away from each other.

Sculpting

A feature common to all forms of sculpture is that the sculptor uses himself, bodily, to construct the sculpture. By actually moving about in the physical-metaphorical space that has been established, touching and physically molding elements of the sculpture, the sculptor taps into information stored or accessible as kinesic, musculomotor memories. Talking about or thinking about a sculpture is inadequate. Even sculptures that have been carefully "rehearsed" often emerge as something quite different when actually carried out. The sculpting process facilitates access to memories and processes in the non-verbal right (subdominant) hemisphere (Ornstein, 1972).

Processing

Closure on the sculpting process is reached by crossing the bridge again, back into the real, here-and-now space. The sculpture is explored from multiple points of view and thoroughly discussed for its meaning, impact, implications, and ramifications. Each participant in the process, including members of the audience, has had a different emotional-cognitive experience of the sculpture and therefore has unique perspectives and insights to offer. On rare occasions, a sculpture which is simply constructed but not processed may be of value, but without a thorough debriefing, the full richness of the lode cannot be mined.

Sculptures may be classified into three groups: (1) simple spatializations, (2) boundary sculptures, (3) family (or other system) sculptures. Each of these groups has subcategories. The three stages discussed above may proceed differently in the three main groups. The main grouping is purely heuristic with little fundamental significance.

SIMPLE SPATIALIZATIONS

Spatialization is a direct use of physical space to map a simple or limited personal or interpersonal construct. It is akin to constructing a graph or plot on a room-size scale with people as the markers. In a group, spatialization can rapidly reveal a large amount of information about a particular subject in a way which makes it possible for group members to assimilate the information.

The examples below are only suggestive of the range of possibilities. Spatializations can be designed to deal with almost any construct or set of constructs to fit some special need in a workshop or in therapy with a family. For example, in working with one family, a polar sculpture around an object representing "head of household" proved very productive. The children were able thus to express their awareness of their mother's ambivalent desire to be "head of the house" yet to leave responsibility with her husband. He in turn was adamant in occupying the center, however ineffectively. All were able to relate this pattern to the same struggle between the parents and to use this awareness to explore alternative strategies for themselves.

Linear sculpture

In a linear sculpture, the simplest form of spatialization, people place themselves along a line representing a unipolar (one way) dimension (such as "powerfulness," "frequency of jealousy," or "risk-taking") or a bipolar dimension such as "head-oriented vs. gut-oriented," or "open vs. closed"). An especially useful form of linear sculpture is the "Power Line" wherein family or group members sculpt themselves in terms of perceived powerfulness.

Linear sculptures work best when careful attention is paid to the following steps:

(1) *Define the space*—Carefully explain the dimension on which to sculpt, giving special attention to what each of the poles (end points) represents. Delineate the physical area by walking along the line as its meaning is explained, standing at the appropriate pole when describing it. It is helpful to have signs at each pole which vividly describe the character of the pole, such as "all the time" and "never" or "heady, rational, intellectual, thoughtful" and "gutsy, emotional, empathic, feeling."

(2) Invite people to walk slowly back and forth along the entire length of the line. This must be done non-verbally. "As you walk along this line, try to get in touch with what you're feeling, especially how comfortable you are at each point. Continue to move along this line until you find a place that feels like the right spot for you." In this way preverbal, unarticulated self-perceptions are accessed.

(3) *Process in place*—Process (debrief, discuss) the experience while people remain in position on the line; this heightens the experience, promotes "owning" one's position, and makes it easier for people to relate what others have said to where they said it from. Examples of questions: How did you end up where you are? Were you surprised? What did you feel (think) while doing this? Were you conscious of where other people were placing themselves? Who? Why? How did this influence your placement? The perceptions of people at the extremes and those in clusters generally warrant special exploration.

(4) The sculpture may be repeated on the same dimension with a different "set" to explore: ideal self vs. real self, or future desired vs. future expected vs. present.

Matrix sculpture

The matrix spatialization developed by the author is a straight-forward extension of the linear sculpture into two dimensions. This is an exceptionally efficient way to explore the relationship between two variables in a manner that gives everyone in a group a rich picture. After the first dimension is sculpted and processed in place, each person is asked to turn sideways to the original line and imagine themselves on a new line of their own which runs at right angles to the original. It is also on this new line that each is to move and place themselves. The matrix technique has been used, for example, in workshops on jealousy to sculpt simultaneously on "frequency of jealousy" and "seriousness of jealousy as a problem."

Polar sculpture

In a polar spatialization, people place themselves at some distance from a single reference point which may be a person, an object, or an abstract concept. A more elaborate variation has people also place themselves in relation to each other. The following specific examples serve to indicate the range of possibilities.

(1) An object is placed in the center of the room to represent "the 'center' or heart of this family, not a physical place but an abstract, the very core of this family as family." Family members are invited to "walk around it, think about it, move closer, then further away" until each finds that place which feels right for themselves, that is, represents how close or distant they feel they are from the "center of the family." The sculpture may be elaborated by next asking them to move in relation to each other until those distances feel like they really are. This often results in a continuous shifting of positions as members seek to accommodate varying perceptions.

(2) A *value sculpture* spatializes degree of comfort-discomfort or attraction-repulsion in relation to a value-laden or affect-laden statement. For example, on the chalk board there is a statement: "In the near future, *most* couples will permit and even value open sexual relations with other people." Then: "How do you feel about that? Move around, closer, farther from that statement. Try to get in touch with the feelings you are having. Keep moving until you find some place that feels right to you."

(3) Two chairs (or some other objects) are placed in the center of the room to represent "the family you grew up in." The sculpture is in relation to "how much like or unlike that family you would *like* your family living situation as an adult to be." Right next to center represents identical, farther and farther away represents increasing degrees of difference. After processing in place, this can be repeated around "how much like or unlike that old family you *expect* your new family living situation will be." A date, say ten years in the future, may be specified.

BOUNDARY SCULPTURES

The purpose of boundary sculpture is to explore the way in which a person (or persons) defines and experiences personal boundaries. In one sense, the boundaries as explored are perceptions of real physical distance and individual experiences of closeness, distance, intrusion, or exclusion in real physical space. In this sense, boundary sculpture is an exploration of personal kinesics and proxemics. At the same time, however, the boundary sculpture explores the metaphorical boundaries of personality, the limits of self, the means of ingress and egress across the boundaries of the self. The degree to which practical proxemics or personality structure are revealed in the boundary sculpture can be influenced by the approach of the monitor.

Individual boundary sculpture

Boundary sculpture as a variation of family sculpture was first conceived by Bunny Duhl (Duhl, Kantor and Duhl, 1973). Typically, the monitor begins by inviting the sculptor to explore the actual physical surroundings and, as he does, to begin to get in touch with his sense of "the space you carry with you. The edge of that area which feels as if it was you or yours, where your space leaves off and the rest of the world begins." When the sculptor indicates he has a sense of this boundary, the monitor begins to probe and investigate the nature of the boundary with the sculptor.

(1) One type of exploration involves the physical parameters of this personal space such as size, shape, variability.

(2) Personal boundaries can also be explored metaphorically in terms of color, texture, thickness, firmness, transparency, and penetrability. It is frequently helpful to have the sculptor close his eyes and imagine his boundary is actually made of some substance and to report on what material that might be or what it is like. The monitor should ask about inhomogeneities, the existence of openings, and changes with time.

(3) Dynamic exploration involves specific probes of the boundary with various manners of approach using subjects of various ages and both sexes, strangers, acquaintances, or intimates. The sculptor may have to be asked to assume that a certain person is, say, an elder stranger. Fast, slow, aggressive, submissive, seductive, and stealthy approaches might be tried from various directions to determine the sculptor's response, where the boundary is, and how clearly defined and how strongly defended it is. Since the number of possible probes is limitless, the monitor must rely on intuition and therapeutic knowledge in exploring significant features.

When the second type of exploration is emphasized, there usually emerges a complex but unified idiosyncratic image of the personal boundaries which models or accounts for much interpersonal behavior. To the extent that the first and third methods of investigation are emphasized by the monitor, more straightforward and less dramatic features of the normal social boundaries emerge.

Relationship sculpture

This form of sculpture, also known as "Negotiating the Space," could be considered to be a variation of either boundary sculpture or family sculpture. It is a brief, efficient way to explore a limited relationship. In its most common application the work relationship of two or more people is explored. A space of arbitrary size and shape (usually a rectangle of about 50–80 square feet) is defined as representing the work relationship of the pair (or other group); outside of that space is all the rest of their life experience. A time limit is set (10 minutes works well) and the sculptors are directed to use that time to explore and negotiate that relationship space nonverbally. It should be made clear that the full time is to be taken even if they feel finished after a shorter period. Frequently completely new aspects of the relationship will emerge late in the process, after everyone thinks all is done. This is an especially valuable exercise for a newly formed co-therapy team and has been used in training to facilitate student team formation (Constantine, 1976).

SYSTEM SCULPTURE

In the system sculpture, the sculptor is assisted by the monitor in utilizing a number of other people or objects to spatialize personal perceptions of an entire family or other system. System sculptures may be relatively general in scope or specifically focused. Among possible foci are: a specific problem or knot; a critical time period or event; a single dimension of family relationships, such as power. Generally, it is at least desirable to pin the sculpture down to a particular time period.

In the "full" or most complete form of family sculpture, the sculpture builds in stepwise fashion and may take up to an hour or more. The steps are:

(1) Exploring the physical space.

(2) Getting in touch with the feel of the metaphorical family space to be represented.

(3) Defining and describing the boundaries of the family space. Here the parameters can be as rich and varied as with personal boundary sculpture.

(4) Peopling the sculpture, adding one person at a time and thoroughly exploring that person's interactions with the sculptor and previously added members.

(5) Assembling the action of each sculpted person into a composite "strategic sequence" representative of the family's operation.

(6) Ritualizing the sequence by repeating it in its entirety at least three times. The repetition, though often skipped by therapists and sometimes thought of as silly, frequently leads to important additional discoveries and insights as to how a family system operates.

(7) Debriefing, beginning with the experiences of the players in the sculpture, then the contributions of the audience, and ending with the sculptor. It can often be useful to modify a sculpture by asking the sculptor to show how he would improve things.

Mini-sculptures

Two common errors therapists make in using sculpture are rushing the sculpture and pushing for premature closure. A deliberate mini-sculpture is better than an intentionally hurried full sculpture. Most commonly demonstrated sculptures are mini-sculptures. Mini-sculptures abbreviate the process, primarily by leaving out certain steps, for example, step (1); steps (1), (2), and (3) and/or step (6). In briefest form, the sculptor may simply be directed to position other members in ways that represent how he sees them in the family in relation to himself and to each other. The entire sculpture, including debriefing, might last only a few minutes. Often brevity is achieved by limiting or constraining the sculpture in some way, commonly by permitting only static tableaux. Abbreviated system sculptures have their applications in rapid assessment of a situation or of a specialized and limited context or aspect of a system.

Dimensionalized mini-sculpture

Kantor has recently introduced a powerful but simple variant of mini-sculpture that uses a limited but very natural spatial vocabulary. The sculptor is told to represent emotional involvement by physical closeness or distance, to represent differences in power by vertical displacements, higher being more powerful, and to show the general nature of the relationship between members by facial expression, gesture, and body orientation. In this way, the dimensions of family process—affect, power, and meaning (Kantor and Lehr, 1975; Constantine, 1974)—are all captured. This form of sculpture approaches the richness of a "full" sculpture in a fraction of the time.

Typological sculpture

Another variation on mini-sculpture depends on limiting the sculpture to a fixed set of individual or collective options. For example, the therapist might describe several basic types of family and how to represent them spatially, asking the sculptor to choose one of these basic forms to build from. Satir (1972), for example, describes basic stances for individuals based on their preferred defended communication style which may be assumed by participants in a sculpture, as well as what she sees to be certain prototypical family configurations.

In the absence of more solid theory and better sociological data on family types, this approach may risk too much imposition of the therapist's assumptions on the client.

Current family

Sculpture of the current family with family members playing themselves, that is, without stand-ins, is undoubtedly the most commonly used form. This can be somewhat less effective than other forms in helping the sculptor to gain needed distance and perspective on the sculpture. Playing oneself minimizes this "analogic distance," the players inside the sculpture have difficulty seeing the whole, and the sculpturing process itself involves and can become stuck in the same dynamics as disable the family otherwise. For example, it can sometimes be impossible for family members to be directed by the sculptor. Actors might continually offer suggestions and corrections, thus invalidating the sculptor's perceptions or a major control struggle can prevent the parents from participating in each other's sculpture.

Unfortunately, stand-ins are only available in multiple family groups and in workshops. Unless the therapist is specifically interested in eliciting and exploring transference, the therapist does not usually serve as a stand-in. When this is done, it is essential that there be a co-therapist as monitor. In some cases it might be appropriate to direct that current family members be chosen by the sculptor to stand-in for each other, say in establishing the map between father and son's behavior. This functions much as role reversals do.

Under circumstances where the sculptor experiences difficulty in gaining distance and objectivity on his own sculpture, he can be asked to appoint a stand-in and to step aside to watch with the therapist.

Family of origin

Sculpting the families of origin of adult family members can be tremendously productive, yielding much insight into origins of contemporary stuck behavior patterns and the ways members of the present family are induced into playing the parts of members of previous generations. Stand-ins for the absent members of the family of origin can be members of an ad-hoc group, such as a training seminar, or members of the current family. The latter is especially useful in revealing the mappings from the last to the present generation. Seeing their parents' families can be an especially freeing experience for children.

Multiple sculpture

In a multiple sculpture (sometimes called consensus or composite sculpture [Duhl, Duhl, and Watanabe, 1975]), all family members simultaneously attempt to place themselves in relation to others. Usually this would be around a single dimension or simple construct, such as emotional distance. Each member tries to place himself in correct relation to all other members. Differences in needs for distance, and perceptions of relationships emerge rapidly and dramatically. If Dad sees himself as closer to Susie than she does to him, he might end up pursuing her around a pole.

A more elaborate form (introduced by the author) focuses on the self in family relationships and dramatizes individual roles in maintaining stuck patterns and in working out relationships. Each member is asked to use some gestures, movement, expression, or stance to represent how he feels in relation to each other family member, taking on these in sequence with each member one at a time. This is repeated continuously until a complicated dance is thus choreographed which could show either great order or an inability to match rhythms and actions. At some intermediate stage, the therapist might ask the family to continue their nonverbal interaction but with each member doing something slightly different to break up the pattern or attempt to work out a "fit" with the rest of the family that "feels right."

This type of sculpture might be started by having all family members standing around the space and thinking for a minute or two about what they would do in relation to each other before all begin simultaneously. If the family has difficulty doing it in this way, it can be built sequentially by adding one member at a time to the marital dyad.

Sculpture using objects

If family members or live stand-ins are not available, objects may be substituted. At the point where it becomes appropriate to "bring in" a family member, the sculptor can be invited to select any object in the field to substitute and to place this appropriately. It is usually productive to explore the basis of choice: "What about this reminds you of your brother? How is he like this?" The new imagery that is tapped into can more than compensate for the fact that gestures, movement, or expression are impossible. The therapist could also temporarily take the part of the missing player to elicit such nuances.

In ritualizing the strategic element of a sculpture using objects as stand-ins, the therapist may describe or talk-through the actions that have been given to the inanimate players or move them around for the sculptor.

Within one family seen by the author, although everyone had great difficulty engaging in non-verbal tasks of this sort, there was a shared love of board games. A successful family sculpture was conducted, completely on a chess board using chess pieces as objects, in this way effectively using the family's own imagery. The task revealed a consensus that the father and his alienated son had moved closer together and that the family viewed the therapists as less integral to their continued functioning. As a result, a decision was reached to proceed with terminating therapy.

SPECIAL TYPES OF SCULPTURE AND SPATIALIZATION

Space can be used in an endless variety of ways to metaphorize many things of interest in therapy, counseling, and education. The following are just a few of the ways in which spatialization has been employed to facilitate access to complex personal and relationship information.

Developmental sculpture

A succession of circles or otherwise arbitrarily shaped spaces are defined on the floor, each space representing a significant period or stage in the sculptor's life, for example, living at home with parents, as a single adult, as a newlywed couple, or family with infant child. The sculptor enters each space and describes its quality, talking about significant features, and important people in the space. The nature and circumstances of the transition to the next space, and the changes in feelings are also explored.

Life line

A line is marked the length of the room to represent the sculptor's life from birth to the present. The sculptor is directed to traverse the line and, as he does, to describe whatever occurs to him in terms of events, people, relationships, and feelings. The technique works best when a fixed time is set for completing the traversal. This keeps the sculptor from either rushing and skipping over things or filling with insignificant information. A clock should be clearly visible.

Life space

The sculptor is told to consider the room or an arbitrary space within it to represent his current life and to identify and "place" within it anything—like a person, experience, event, or object—which he considers is significant to his current life situation. A fixed time limit is desirable.

Sculpture as feedback

The therapist can use sculpture as a mechanism for communicating to clients, as well as gaining information. The monitor might, for example, suggest modifications to a completed sculpture to share his insights about the family, not as better or correct information but as an alternative perspective the clients are invited to consider. Or the sculptor (or other participants) could be instructed to experiment with different positions or movements the therapist thinks might reveal new information or offer new relational options.

On occasion the therapist might choose to be the sculptor. Working with one family that had an especially difficult time getting perspective on their situation, the author and his co-therapist sculpted using objects and family members to present their evaluation of the family system. When the family members saw the entire picture they were able to recognize their roles in the current crisis and to offer more insight and further modifications to the sculpture. Later sessions confirmed that required changes implied by the therapists' sculpting had begun to take effect.

APPLICATION AND CONCLUSIONS

The purpose of this paper is not an exhaustive cataloging of sculpture techniques but a mere heuristic organization. Any attempt to index all sculpture techniques *should* be doomed at the outset. The purpose of presenting a range of techniques is not to fix the armamentarium but to spur the creativity of the therapist, counselor, consultant, or educator. By displaying themes and variations it is hoped that each professional will be freed to innovate new variations custom-fitted to the situation at hand.

Real comfort and creativity with sculpture techniques come only from trying them out, from liberal experimentation. Experimentation can take place in almost any setting. One of the delights of sculpture is that it so seldom fails to liberate and to supply fresh inputs to almost any process. It can be used whenever

the therapist, or client—feeling inducted, bored, trapped, or at impasse—may wish to: free up blocked, denied or ambiguous feelings and communication; help a system resolve a conflict or reach a consensus; discover a new emphasis or direction in the therapy; explore a previously identified "gray area"; condense a great deal of information into a spatialized image; evolve a complete system map or elaborate some substructure in it; or explore the system's responses to alternate outcomes.

These specific clinical hunches, goals and strategies affect the types of sculpture used. (Kantor, 1975)

For example, within one family with a history of overt incest were certain members who had early made clear their refusal to reconsider these painful past events, denying any current relevance, while another family member attributed every negative in their lives to those same transgressions. The therapists became effective change agents simply by leaving the sexual issues alone and concentrating on the contemporary relationship dynamics for several months. When the index patient's girlfriend—who had been responsible for exposing the incest—was to join the family for a session, the therapists planned a "power line" sculpture to enable the family to deal with current effects of the incest. Although the announced purpose of the sculpture was to explore power relationships, the daughter who had been involved with her father became physically ill in anticipation. All family members saw themselves as comparatively powerless. The girlfriend was seen as the most powerful and the index patient as least. The awkwardness of this position became painfully evident, and it was quickly discovered by the family that attributions of power were associated with an individual's ability to use knowledge, especially of the incest, as a threat. The sculpture proved to be a breakthrough, legitimizing re-examination of the incest and its present impact while spotlighting the real arena in which the family was disabled.

Even the professional's own family is a fertile and productive context in which to try out these techniques. The rewards are manifold, as when the author recently "negotiated the space" (a relationship sculpture) with his eight year old daughter. The sculpture clarified a pattern in which close contact could only be initiated by the daughter, but the author also learned that by sitting still he could signal his receptiveness, leaving the initiative to her. Both found they have since been better able to obtain the intimacy each wanted by respecting the other's style of contact.

The imagination is the only limit to new variations and applications.

REFERENCES

Bandler, R. & Grinder, J. *The structure of magic: A book about language and therapy.* Palo Alto, California: Science & Behavior, 1975.

Constantine, L. L. Dimensions of family process. Unpublished monograph, Center for Training in Family Therapy, Boston State Hospital, IRR Building, 591 Morton Street, Boston, MA 02124, 1974.

Constantine, L. L. Designed experience: A multiple goal-directed training program in family therapy. *Family Process*, 1976, *15* (4).

Duhl, B., Duhl, F. & Watanable, S. Types of sculpture. Unpublished notes, The Boston Family Institute, 1170 Commonwealth Avenue, Boston, MA 02134, 1975.

Duhl, F., Kantor, D. & Duhl, B. Learning space and action in family therapy. Block, D. (ed.) *Techniques of family psychotherapy: A primer.* New York: Grune & Stratton, 1973.

Hall, E. T. *The silent language.* Garden City, New York: Doubleday, 1959.

Hall, E. T. *The hidden dimension.* Garden City, New York: Anchor Books, 1969.

Hartmann, E. L. *The functions of sleep.* New Haven: Yale University Press, 1973.

Kantor, D. Introduction to family sculpture. Unpublished notes, The Family Institute of Cambridge, 256 Concord Avenue, Cambridge, MA 02138, 1975.

Kantor, D. & Lehr, W. *Inside the family: Toward a theory of family process.* San Francisco: Jossey-Bass, 1975.

Moreno, J. L. *Psychodrama.* New York: Beacon, 1946.

Ornstein, R. E. *The psychology of consciousness.* San Francisco: Freeman, 1972.

Papp, P., Silverstein, O. & Carter, E. Family sculpting in preventive work with "well families." *Family Process*, 1973, *12* (2).

Satir, V. *Peoplemaking.* Palo Alto: Science and Behavior, 1972.

Scheflen, A. E. *Body language and social order.* Englewood Cliffs, New Jersey: Prentice-Hall, 1972.

Spiegel, V. P. & Machotka, P. *Messages of the body.* New York: Free Press, 1974.

Swonger, A. and Constantine, L. L. *Drugs and therapy: The psychotherapist's handbook of psychotropic drugs.* Boston: Little, Brown, 1976.

Individual and Family Growth: A Gestalt Approach

Marvin L. Kaplan
Netta R. Kaplan

Gestalt therapy is described as a comprehensive framework of theory and techniques for experiential family therapy. Like other experientially oriented therapies, it is systems-oriented, immediate-experience-oriented, and affect-oriented. Unlike others, this method regards the client system's emergent processes as the central focus, and it emphasizes that growth occurs as the family and its members are helped to greater self-awareness and responsibility for their own functioning.

In recent years, a number of family therapists have explored and developed experiential approaches in their work with families. This trend has come about partly in recognition of the power of self-maintenance functions of the family as a system. There is acknowledgment that something experiential has to take place in order to disrupt entrenched family patterns and to help the family members reintegrate relationships around altered experiences of self and of one another. Generally, these therapies proceed with an informal diagnostic phase in which the therapist locates major difficulties, determines how they are perpetuated, and maps out at least a general strategy for moving the family toward alternative kinds of experiences. The therapist seeks techniques that either circumvent or take advantage of anticipated systems reactions. Satir's approach (9) can be seen as an example of circumvention as she uses a finely tuned method of making use of what family members express but continually *reframes* their verbal content to lead them to a greater congruence of experience and expression. Haley (1), on the other hand, creates conditions under which the family, in pursuit of recognized goals, accomplishes unrecognized "piggy-back" changes. He uses strategically the family's expected systems reactions to serve therapeutic goals.

These very brief references to goal-oriented strategies serve as contrast to our view of Gestalt therapy. While there is an overlapping focus on working experientially, in Gestalt therapy the approach is that of helping clients achieve greater self-awareness, greater clarity of experience, a greater range of functioning potential, and greater self-direction. The goal of this work is not primarily "problem-solving" but "growth" that opens the way for people to do their own problem-solving. In Gestalt therapy, the role of the therapist is closer to that of a facilitator than that of a strategist, and although the therapist uses "techniques," she/he respects the client's emergent awareness as a guide for therapeutic focus.

While enjoying some popularity as a method for individual and group therapies, the Gestalt framework appears to have been neglected or incompletely developed, at least in a "pure" form, for family therapy. The facts that families have a common history and an entrenched pattern of relationships are perhaps some reasons that a "growth" orientation has been seen as less applicable. However, the family can be seen as a system having potential for supporting growth as well as for supporting entrenchment. By working with the family at its own current level of taking responsibility, the therapist can facilitate awareness of its holding onto entrenched behavior as well as helping it to explore its own emergent potential for choice and alternatives.

The framework is developed first in terms of the organismic or individual-system view. From this focus the more adequate and encompassing system of a person in his social context, the family, is presented. The issues of using here-and-now experience, therapist role, and systems considerations are developed.

THE SYSTEM IN INDIVIDUAL THERAPY

Therapeutic efforts in Gestalt are not aimed at discovering how a difficulty or symptom came about or its original purpose. Rather the focus is on how such behavior is now experienced, how it fits into a person's current schemata, and how it is linked to her/his total organization. The experience of a client is seen as unified. Her/his behaviors and self-perceptions are seen as parts of a self-system that carries his/her experience: "This is I; I am the person who is (impaired, helpless, capable, etc.)." The behavior a person emits demonstrates to her/him who and what s/he is; responses from others are interpreted to reinforce these perceptions. We note that this is a circular system and it can be self-limiting and self-maintaining.

This system is integrated as a mesh or matrix of self-views and self-understandings that forms a unified perceptual network and provides a stable identity. At the same time, there is a continuum of self-limitation or rigidity. Individuals functioning at the more rigid end expend a preponderance of their energy on self-protective and avoidant maneuvers. The rigid system functions automatically and mechanically rather than through awareness and choice. Such self-systems produce experiences of things happening to one and of being acted upon and being victimized, with concomitant experiences of frustration, helplessness, and confusion. The distressed person clings to the familiarity of this dominant self-system, and alternatives are blocked from awareness or dismissed as unreal or hopeless. Where there are parts of one's self that are occasionally experienced as discrepant—subsystems involving feelings of strength or potential for alternatives—such parts are fragmented, isolated, and locked away from integration into the dominant self-maintaining system (3).

Therapeutic strategy follows the Gestalt principle that the person is helped to work toward self-awareness and self-responsibility—steps in blocking the cycle of automatic, enmeshed behaviors. As a person explores her/his experience and becomes more self-aware, s/he moves from experiencing confusion and helplessness to a position of recognizing choice and responsibility for behavior. This movement provides a basis for allowing the person to regain control and thus to reexperience and reintegrate aspects of self that had been isolated or lost to awareness and to self-responsibility.

Therapy in this context begins with the therapist facilitating the person's attention to what he or she is currently experiencing in its most concrete and direct expression: to bodily experience, to muscular actions, to emotional experiences. This process leads to clarification of needs in the "here-and-now" of the therapy situation. The therapist avoids explanations or "why" and "what for" questions, but helps the person maintain attention to the "what" of immediate experience. The focus is frequently on concrete and minute aspects of experience, thus facilitating the process by which a person becomes more aware of how s/he functions, how s/he blocks awareness of self, of her/his needs, or her/his experience, and of alternatives (8). Therapy provides opportunities for circumscribed, exploratory risk-taking as stepping stones in preparation for change and experimentation outside of therapy sessions.

THE SYSTEM REACHES BEYOND THE INDIVIDUAL

While it seems helpful to understand how a person carries her/his own structure of enmeshed feelings, attitudes, and behaviors, the individual's "system" is viewed most clearly and validly in terms of integration within a social context. An individual experiences her/his self-percept and her/his anxieties at the interface of self and environment. Her/his mode of self-perception, her/his communication, and her/his physical stance are all seen as an interlocking of action and reaction (feedback) patterns; the system is actively operative and maintained at the interactional level. From the individual's perspective, the roles played and the patterns followed form a structure for perception, a locus of familiar experience, and a stable place in the social schema; from this perspective, each member in the larger system serves a function in the homeostasis of the group, organization, or family. In an interactive system, the responsibility for behavior does not lie solely with the individual or with the environment. Rather, the system, of individual in context, operates interdependently in a self-maintaining manner.

The Gestalt emphasis on polarities

In a family, the interactive patterns can be stabilized or "locked in" as a function of the restricted awareness of the members of a family. In "locking-in," individual family members may experience and be aware of only one "pole" of a polar dimension of self-experience. In the Gestalt approach any aspect of a person's experience implies the existence of its antithesis or polar opposite, even though the latter may be outside of awareness (8). One's toughness is experienced against an experiential sense of what nontoughness (i.e., softness, tenderness) can be. When the self quality is affect-laden, a more sharply differentiated experience comes about through disowning the opposite and/or projecting it onto others (7). The mechanism complementary to projection is introjection, which involves incorporating into the self characteristics perceived in others or acquiescing to attributions to self made by others. Thus, a characteristic is assumed by "swallowing it whole" rather than absorbing or integrating it through experience and choice. Projection and introjection function in a given family to produce rigidified relationships among members that tend to fall along specific polar dimensions affectively charged in that family.

Members perceive themselves and respond to one another in ways that reinforce and lock in the polar attributions and acquiescences. In one family, a member's need to block or hide dependency may require his being controlling while other members respond either by dependent yielding or by resisting along this dimension. In another family, a member's disowning of her/his sensual and loving feelings may be enmeshed with other members so that some of the others act in a very sensual manner while others acquiesce to "morality." The overall system has the effect of maintaining its components in positions that complement and lock in poles or reciprocals. Thus, it is not surprising to discover that various members take divergent or complementary roles—carrying one another's disowned, projected, and introjected parts. In a rigidified family, the system carries its members (or most of them) in charged relationships that are activated as tensions rise and require the members to assume their complementary positions and to block and disown parts of self that are discrepant with the system.

Confluence and contact

The ongoing, patterned interactions create a system that is "confluent," the Gestalt term indicating that rigidified interaction is a ritual playing-out of roles rather than a "contact" between humans. Under these conditions, family members perceive one another in "boxes" and relate to such preconceptions. The husband does not "see" that which contradicts his preset image of his wife; he does not "hear" her effort at reaching out to him or he mishears it as ungenuine. Such dyadic interaction is confluent.

The inverse of confluence is contact, the experience of reaching out to recognize and discover, or rediscover, the human in one's presence. Low contact occurs when mates "plug" one another into boxes or "know" each other because they have lived together for years rather than because they learn or discover something of each other in the present. Contact may involve simply noticing an expression or affective tone; it is an experience of the person as he or she exists at the moment rather than a perception of a role: e.g., "I see sadness in your eyes," or "I feel distant from you." Contact frequently involves noticing change—change in tone or stance or attitude or feeling. And contact frequently has an implication of crisis or mini-crisis in the sense that the outcome of the contact episode is unpredictable; it can lead to discovery of discomfort, pain, closeness, or affection.

Family enmeshment

In this model of family interaction, the behavioral-communication system traps the family members in restricted communication and restricted awareness of what they are together and what each one can be. The system maintains itself in a process of mechanical entrenchment. Thus, roles and relationships flow from preconceptions and expectations, and the system is reinforced by its interactions. It is maintained by its members' loss of awareness of how they are locked in and doubly maintained by their experiences of frustration, confusion, and helplessness. The term "myth" is used for the restricted role categorization forced on and acquiesced to by members. If Dad is perceived as the harsh, angry disciplinarian, the tentative approach and hopeful anticipation of a smile fails to be perceived; Dad is thus written off. Just as within an individual, awareness of "nonsystem" parts is lost, so in the family context nonsystem data that do not fit role ascriptions or myths are lost to perception and communication. The father anticipates from son defensive, avoidant behavior and prepares himself for this by a posture that withholds his more positive and warm responses.

But what of the breaks in the pattern? What of the memories of Dad's being fun and his occasionally extending himself? Here the system in families is subtle and complex, and in its entrenchment, it accounts for all data. Each family member is accorded a *range* within which he or she is seen as functioning: "Sure, Mom has her good days, but she'll come back with her bitchiness, and it's even more frustrating because I know that she does have good days." Family members, in effect, develop more complex myths to accommodate certain limits of variation. In fact, it is the expectancy of variation (role-deviance limits) that helps lock the system more rigidly into a homeostatic balance (2). Instead of mother breaking out of the confluent system, absence of bitchiness is part of a wider pattern contained within expectations: "She has her good side, and I'd like to see more of it, but I can't rely on it, and I don't know what it is in her that makes her one way one time and another later on." Rather than undermining the system, variation helps maintain it against possibly contravening perceptions.

ENTERING THE SYSTEM

Growth is the process of venturing into new experiences, and in a family therapy context, this involves breaking confluence, disrupting system expectancies, unblocking awareness, and permitting members to move toward individuation. This process is seen as a gradual expansion of awareness of self, of others, and the discovery of excitement, fear, and gratification that can come with exploration of potential in oneself and in other family members. The process is not problem-oriented but is geared to the family's current level of awareness and responsibility. Similarly, as the process basically is a response to where the family experiences itself, the therapist's role is that of facilitator rather than manipulator.

Individuation and support

In speaking of the family's "level of awareness" or of how the family "experiences" itself, we recognize the system/enmeshment phenomena of entrenched families. Functioning as an interactive network that elicits, supports, and maintains behavior, we can view the restricted family as an entity that carries its members in relational positions. With polarized "locking-in" and restricted awareness, family members can be described as functioning in a relatively undifferentiated manner. Individuation in a family therapy context is moving beyond one's family systems role and claiming (or reclaiming) a wider range of who one can be. In the family system, this growth requires support for exploration and for taking responsibility for self. Family members in therapy begin with a basic, mutually shared, defensive position: "I must be this way because you (and others) are the way you are; I can change only if you will be different." Yet a wife who discovers that she can complain and that her husband, instead of reacting defensively, can "hear" her complaint has opened herself to an individuating experience. The husband in hearing her and allowing himself to express compassion has likewise opened himself to an individuating experience. Individuation in one family member breeds it in others because it is a manifestation of trust as well as a disruption in expectancies (5). Breaking out of role behavior is acknowledgment of feelings previously hidden, disguised, or expressed as blaming.

Enmeshed as family members are, support and trust are called for to help such venturesome efforts. In Gestalt therapy, support is basic; it is the anchorage for helping a person locate his current focus of self-experience as a starting point for expanding awareness. The person who explores is always the decision maker; s/he decides what s/he will express of her/himself, and when, and s/he is free to balk. The therapist assumes a guiding role much like the teacher in the passenger seat helping a person learn to drive; the learner is at the controls. When the learner feels panic or chooses not to go further at some point, the "teacher" helps her/him return to her/his areas of competence in which experience is firm and comforting. Thus, a person and a family work at the borderlines of their own supportive experience. In facilitating a supportive framework for risk-taking, the Gestalt therapist aids in helping the family to locate and use three bases of support: (a) support that comes from the contact of the therapist entering the system as a "human"; (b) support that comes from a basic "grounding" of location of self in current experience; (c) support that comes from shared appreciation among family members of the common experiences of risking and of discovery.

The initial focus is on awareness of immediate experience. This may be around fantasies of what is expected, what is about to happen, who the therapist is, etc. The therapist far from being free of such experiences may be aware of them and relate her/his own awareness. S/he may say, "I notice that I feel my heart fluttering as I sit down. I don't know you people yet. I'd like a few minutes to look at you and to begin to get to know you." S/he acts on her/his needs and stays with her/his experience until s/he feels more ease. S/he "reaches out" and makes individual contact with each person: e.g., "Sarah, I see that you have a beautiful dress—I like it." S/he invites responses and invites people to say what they can about what is of importance or concern to them now: e.g., "Would you like to say something to me about what you would like or how you feel?" To a father who says, "I guess we all feel pretty nervous," s/he replies, "I'd like to know how it is for *you* as you sit here with your family." Thus, father can relate to the therapist, expressing his own awareness as an individual rather than as a spokesman for others.

Focusing on the here-and-now

The therapist allows whatever unfolds to proceed and assumes that nothing occurs but the family experience. S/he does not await the end of pleasantries to "get down to business." Any such conception presupposes that the family is to bypass current experience rather than to get in touch with it. Some Gestalt therapists find that a helpful beginning structure is provided by asking each member for a statement of "wants" from therapy. "I'd like each of you to tell me what you want for yourself in what we will do here. And notice that I ask that you put it in terms of 'for yourself.'" Perhaps the most important aspect is that what ensues gives each person a beginning opportunity to individuate at the onset, to express something personal for her/himself, as well as to make contact with the therapist. Mother may say, "Well what I want is to have everyone be happier, especially Johnny, who seems so unhappy now." The therapist can ask "How would that help you with what you want for yourself?" and the mother can reply, "Then I can relax and not feel pressured to step in and make peace." A further reply here might recognize the feelings mother has partly communicated: "I hear that you feel under strain and long for relief." In this exchange, mother moves toward a clearer expression of her experience and a clearer sense of her goals. She moves toward individuation in the sense of telling others where she is, what her wants are, and in assuming responsibility for personal goals. At the same time, the family witnesses a contact episode: one person recognizes the experience of another not as a role but in terms of perceiving communicated feelings and wants.

Gestalt family therapists generally prefer to avoid any format designed to elicit data for the therapist's use in how to proceed. Such procedures are seen as manipulation. The preference is to work strictly with what emerges. This can extend to avoidance of any announced rules of what to do or not do. For example, a rule used by some Gestalt therapists is "no-gossip," meaning "Here we talk about ourselves and how we feel about one another but not about outside people or outside situations." This rule can be useful but also may be seen as unnecessary. When a family moves toward recitation of past events or discussing people not present, the therapist applies the same guidelines as at other times: s/he helps the focus of attention move toward current experience perhaps even calling attention to the avoidance involved, since avoidance may be the family's *current* experience.

A father says, "My beef is that nothing is ever done around the house; it's a mess. I come home, and everyone is yelling, the kids' clothes are scattered, newspapers all over. Some firmness is needed. I have talked and talked, and she [mother] says she agrees and nothing happens." Rather than clarify what his specific complaint is (which may come at another time), the therapist draws attention to the here-and-now phenomena; perhaps this man's experience is that of not being heard with its resultant feelings of frustration. S/he focuses on her experience of him and says, "I hear exasperation in your voice; can you say what you are experiencing?" Or s/he can ask him to speak directly to his wife about his concerns so that they can both become clearer about their experience in the here-and-now: "Tell your wife your complaint and your wishes and see what she does." Here, we note the content is used as a vehicle to help this couple become aware of their processing, that is, what they experience as they struggle to make (or avoid) direct contact.

The husband may say, "Well you know what bothers me, yet you do nothing about it," and the wife can reply, "I try. I feel you don't pay any attention to my efforts." Since husband initiated the interchange and shows appropriate affect, it might be assumed that he is more energized or tuned to his wants and feelings. He could be asked, "How was her reply for you? Can you tell her?" He might say, "I've heard it before, I just don't see the effort. You act helpless." Seeing mother's reaction, therapist turns to her and says, "I see your chin quiver, Mary, and I see your eyes moisten. Can you tell Jim what you are feeling?" Holding back sobs, she says, "You always criticize me." "But what are you feeling now?" persists the therapist. Mary stops fighting her tears, cries, and then says, "I feel I'm a failure as a wife and as a mother. I do feel helpless and ashamed, and I feel I have all this to do alone." In "owning" her experience, this mother breaks out of her system entrenchment and opens the way for her husband to let go of his confluent reaction and find support for his own self-awareness and owning.

At some later time, when the couple is clearer regarding how they feel about themselves and about one another and what they want from each other, they will be in a better position to move toward clarification of how to implement some new agreements to deal with back home issues, or they can even work on this at home. What is needed now, and where the therapist directs attention, is a clearer awareness of what each experiences with the other and how they can express this awareness directly. As they are helped to explore, they gain clarity; the entrenched system is in some small measure disrupted, and a way is open to see how they can be with each other through choice rather than through automatic reactions.

In Gestalt therapy, unblocking and exploration come about through expanding awareness of what people do with themselves and with one another. The Gestalt therapist uses the medium of the emergent here-and-now experience to help the family (a) locate current awareness; (b) explore how awareness is blocked; (c) facilitate discovery and expression of hidden (or lost) experiences; and (d) experiment with individuation in the family context.

Locus of energy and affect/figure-ground

In individual work, the therapist focuses on what s/he considers to be the boundary of awareness. In the family context, the issue is not only on what to focus but where: on the whole, or a subcluster of the family, or on one person. In principle, the choice is easy; just as in individual work attention is directed to the borders of awareness, in the family attention is directed to the locus of readiness for exploration of awareness. Thus, the question is to determine who or what members are "energized." This does not always mean the people who speak up or declare readiness but instead refers to a therapeutic judgment based on observations of tension or pain, concern, or other signs of activation. Note that the guide to where and how to intervene is based on what the therapist judges to be the family's current experience and not on some underlying strategy about where they ought to work or what the next step should be.

While a family is understood to be in a system equilibrium and members are in interrelated roles, the members are not in the same experiential position. At any point, some members indeed have greater discomfort or pain, some are more highly motivated to seek change, some are more tightly locked into roles, some have much more at stake in avoiding disruption, and some are more peripheral to system forces and less entrenched. The therapist observes interactions so as to gain a sense of where energy for movement is to be found. In a sense s/he makes use of a Gestalt psychology concept, that of "figure-ground," with the term referring here to the pattern of current energy in the family. In the family's entrenched pattern, the members lock in to interactions in confused and helpless behavior. Their "experiential field" is one of hectic cluttering; figure and ground are not clearly differentiated. The family members are focused on a limited awareness of their immediate experience, an experience caught up in confusing family events.

The figure in a family is what is *going on* rather than what is being *talked about*; the figure is the dominant *process*. In one family, the parents appear to discuss important issues, but the figure is the dispassionate way in which they do this; there is energy in their avoidance. A child may be discussed but not addressed; it is as if s/he is not there, and this phenomenon may be the figure. Parents may work on an issue of concern but quickly shift to their concern with a "problem" child as tension mounts; the avoidance (or scapegoating) is the figure. Frequently, a sudden shift in focus signals avoidance as the unattended figure in the system. Similarly, the style of members' communication may be scanned for the unattended figure as well as for what may be observed about events that the family seems to ignore.

In drawing the family's attention to its figural perspective, as s/he notes it, the therapist may draw reactions of chagrin, embarrassment, surprise, amazement, further deflection, or relief. Generally the figure appears phenomenologically loud and clear once it is recognized and brought into focus. While some family therapy models prefer to refer to such phenomena as themes, issues, or conflicts, our preference in using the term figure is in line with the goal of seeking to heighten and focus members' awareness of their experiences. Where figural patterns are operative but lost to shared awareness, the family functions as if it were out of focus and feels appropriately strained and confused.

THERAPIST USE OF SELF

Since the therapist's awareness is not locked into the "reality"-determining system of the family, s/he has some freedom to discern what goes on beyond the overt content of what is discussed. But the therapist, too, is vulnerable, especially as s/he shuns an "objective" and nonreactive role. Sometimes it is difficult to avoid being caught up in the family's perspective. This frequently occurs when the therapist feels concern about how the family sees her/him, e.g., as fair, confused, capricious, or malicious. Thus, a therapist is always to some degree in the system, and the danger of being swallowed up in the family's reality can mount (4). S/he comes with her/his own needs: s/he wants to help, to be appreciated, to enjoy human companionship, to empathize with pain, to show understanding, and to appreciate the beauty of love and growth. As s/he experiences both gratification and frustration, s/he uses her/his awareness of these affective reactions as invaluable instruments in registering what may frequently escape the intellect.

In this paradigm, we discover another similarity between an individual and a family system. Just as an individual finds corroborative data in environmental feedback, the family discovers that whatever happens fits its system expectancies and requirements. Moreover, because a family system functions as many people colluding to define reality, there is greater seductive danger for the therapist. The family members present themselves, react to, and interpret what comes from the therapist in terms of their fixed notions about who they are and how they will be dealt with. The therapist works with this potential not by cold objectivity but by allowing her/himself to enter and experience what goes on. Her/his resource is to allow her/himself to tune to her/his affective experience to save her/himself as well as to react therapeutically. Her/his therapeutic stance is to react with awareness and seek contact and experience with family members to express her/his aroused feelings and needs. In this s/he not only presents a model for taking risks and seeking contacts but, by interacting as a person, helps the family achieve awareness of their experience (6).

FUNCTIONS OF THE THERAPIST

The therapist primarily allows the family system to emerge but guides attention to that which surfaces. The therapist takes a step beyond allowing and guiding by facilitating action that permits the family and its members to integrate newly discovered parts. Thus, the three basic therapist functions are: allowing, termed *observing;* guiding, classed as *focusing;* and *facilitating,* used for work on reintegrating new awareness. These functions operate within the overall structure laid out previously: working within a supportive framework and attending to the figural processes. In what follows we delineate these three functions and clarify the shifting of attention from individuals to dyads and to the whole family in a systematic manner.

The therapist observes

We see *observing* as an active process calling for the therapist's sharp attention and energy. Observing connotes tuning into or trying to be in touch with the members and the family. The therapist notes expressions, tones, interruptions, gestures, postures. S/he observes how some members appear to function "automatically," without awareness, and notes how interactions take place, or fail to take place, and how deflections occur. The therapist tries to imagine what it is like to be each person in this family, how each experiences the present situation and the other members. The therapist says to her/himself, "If I were in this person's shoes, what would I experience now? Does s/he seem aware of any such experience? Are there any clues that tell me s/he is closer or farther from awareness of what s/he might be experiencing? Could s/he tune into this experience? Is s/he energized or motivated to do this? If I intervene now, will that open an awareness that will facilitate this person, or will it distract from the movement going on? Am I clear that what I am attending to is that which is the figural aspect of family experience or have I missed something? If I enter to focus, is it to be with father's anger and sharpness of tone or with mother's quiet, subdued sullenness? Is either one figural or does the circularity of the interaction constitute the figural unit? And what of Johnny's agitation and interruptions? Can that be "bracketed" while mother and father work, or are they "using" the distraction? And what of my own emotional reactions? What is my current experience? Am I feeling pressure to *do* something? Where is this coming from? Am I being pressured to enter and divert attention or to take on responsibility? Am I feeling helpless or ignored? And what is this about?"

Observing, then, has a passive quality of permitting the family experience to emerge. It also has an active quality in that the therapist is involved in energetically "seeing" and "hearing" the family experience.

The therapist focuses

Merely by being a group of people assembled and interacting together, the family has a locus of communication—who is speaking and what s/he attends to—even if there is distraction or confusion or what appears to be lack of continuity. Sometimes the family is partially aware of what is going on, and such awareness may vary among members; sometimes there appears to be a gross lack of congruence between what may be going on and what people are aware of. When the therapist observes discrepancies or blocks or deflections, s/he enters to help *focus* so that awareness can be gained and broadened. S/he enters to pick up at the point where the members' awareness appears to be disrupted or blocked. The first goal of a focusing effort is to bring attention more clearly to the here-and-now experience of the members. The focusing is directed to that member or those members who are most figural at the moment—those who are most active or energized.

The therapist is like a lighting director of a stage play: s/he can focus a sharp beam in one place or a pair of lights on a dyad, or a soft light that spreads out over a wider range. S/he focuses the lighting on the aspect that appears most amenable to broadening of awareness and, as awareness grows, opens up the beam to foster a wider range of awareness. S/he may notice that a husband and wife are not making counter-accusations so the "beam" focuses on either one or both depending on how the therapist senses their awareness or energy. S/he may say to one who seems more frustrated or anguished, "What are you experiencing now?" or to both "I hear you going over the same things. Can each of you be aware of how this is for you now and tell one another?" The therapist may notice that a son in talking with his mother keeps looking toward his father and she asks, "I see you look over at Dad when you ask Mom a question. What is that about?" Or s/he may notice that, in speaking, Dad uses "we." "Would you tell Mary what your personal concern is; say 'I' and notice how that is for you." When the conversation shifts from encounter between mother and father to concern with a son's problem, s/he says "I noticed that you moved away from talking about yourselves. Can you say what happened to you there?" Or s/he may notice constant interruptions and say, "Everyone seems to have something to say and you all keep jumping in. This is confusing to me. Is it confusing to others as well?" The focusing comments are brief and where possible give the therapist's observations so that the family member(s) can more easily tune into what struck the therapist. S/he encourages a person to attend to her/his awareness and to pursue it to the level at which it captures the greatest affect and clarity.

The focusing comments aim at helping one or more members clarify what they are experiencing at the moment, which they may be expressing but not be aware of, even though their outward behavior suggests that they are in the midst of an energized, affective experience. Focusing generally has a two-part goal: (a) clarifying the experience of one or more persons, and (b) redirecting the person(s) back to a communicative interaction with their new awareness. Starting with one person, focusing may move toward bringing awareness back into the communication stream of two or more members. When an inter-change between two members reaches some completion, the therapist ob-serves how this has affected others and is ready to focus anew to help the reverberation in others come to awareness. "I'd like to know how others feel about what just went on here," or "Johnny, I noticed that you were watching and listening closely as Jane and Mom were talking. What was that like for you?"

Focusing can involve greater activity than that implied by our metaphor of a stage-lighting director. The therapist can also at times be compared to a stage manager using more directive techniques to heighten awareness, perhaps by suggesting exaggeration of members' experiences. For example, with one couple, the therapist says, "I notice that you hardly look at each other. Can you move your chairs so that you face away—now talk to each other. Now face back and look directly at each other as you talk and tell each other how that feels."

The therapist as facilitator

Facilitation is the term for the next degree of therapist activity, that of helping family members integrate their new awareness by suggesting trial actions in a guided structure. Generally, facilitation follows the step of family members reaching a level of awareness that taps greatest energy, clarity, and responsibility for self. As a father says, "I see that we are going in circles and I don't know what to do about it," the therapist asks, "How do you feel now?" "I feel like bursting," says the father. "And how is that for you?" asks the therapist. "I just feel that I am pushed and pulled. I feel lost, I don't know what to do. I feel helpless." "Do you feel that you can get any help anywhere in your family?" asks the therapist. Thus, with some greater awareness of his current experi-ence, this father is prepared to move toward responsible individuating action with respect to his wants.

Facilitation can be described in this usage as the channeling of new aware-ness and released energy toward constructive reintegration. While oppor-tunities are afforded merely by the family being together in an atmosphere that supports risking and exploring interactions, the therapist also makes use of structural "experiments." An experiment is a structured, guided "situation" designed to help the family, or part of it, focus its attention in a circumscribed way, on a specific issue. The experiment is collaborative in that the whole family supports the structure even if not everyone is directly involved, and it is permission-giving in that there is a guiding support to "try out" and to "get reactions." An experiment can be as simple as asking a father and son to turn their chairs toward one another and to explore the experience of facing and looking at one another, or it can be complex, include several members, use physical contact, or role reversal, etc. Actually experiments can be used at any point in therapy but are used most frequently to help family members explore choice and responsibility that accompany new awareness.

CONCLUSION

Although Gestalt therapy overlaps with other experientially oriented ap-proaches to working with families, there are distinct differences. The overlap is in attention to current experience, to affective experience, and to the totality of the family as an interactive, self-maintaining system. However, Gestalt therapy pursues a course of working with the family's current awareness of its emergent experience so that family members are in a collaborative relationship with the therapist and work on how they restrict themselves and how they can expand their awareness and discover their resources. As such, the family moves toward developing its own support for its primary goal of risking and growing.

REFERENCES

1. Haley, J., *Problem-Solving Therapy*, San Francisco, Jossey-Bass, Inc., 1976.
2. Hoffman, L., "Deviation-Amplifying Processes in Natural Groups," in J. Haley (Ed.), *Changing Families: A Family Therapy Reader*, New York, Grune & Stratton, 1971.
3. Kaplan, N. R. and Kaplan, M. L., "A Gestalt Therapy Approach to Stuttering," *J. Communic. Disorders*, 11: 1–9, 1978.
4. Kaplan, M. L. and McDermott, W. V., "Systems Theory and the Client-Professional-Agency Complex," in R. W. Manderscheid and F. E. Manderscheid (Eds.), *Systems Science and the Future of Health*, Washington, D. C., Groome Center, 1976.
5. Karpel, M., "Individuation: From Fusion to Dialogue," *Fam. Proc.* 15: 65–82, 1976.
6. Kempler, W., *Principles of Gestalt Family Therapy*, A. S. J. Nordahls Trykkeri, Oslo, 1973.
7. Perls, F., *Gestalt Therapy Verbatim*, Moab, Utah, Real People Press, 1969.
8. Polster, E. and Polster, M., *Gestalt Therapy Integrated*, New York, Brunner/Mazel, 1973.
9. Satir, V., "Family Systems and Approaches to Family Therapy," in G. D. Erickson and T. P. Hogan, *Family Therapy: An Introduction to Theory & Technique*, 1972. (Reprinted from *J. Fort Logan Mental Health Center*, 4: 81–93, 1967.)

Behavioral Marriage Therapy: Current Status

Neil S. Jacobson
Barclay Martin

The literature on behavioral approaches to marriage therapy is reviewed. First, theories regarding the nature, etiology, and maintenance of marital problems are presented; second, behavioral approaches to treatment are described; and third, attempts to assess the efficacy of these treatments are evaluated. Although there is some highly suggestive evidence that behavioral interventions are effective, conclusive demonstrations have not been forthcoming. A series of suggestions are offered regarding future research.

Until 1969, the contribution of behavior therapists to the treatment of marital discord was sparse. Although reports of behavioral strategies applied to couples occasionally appeared in the literature before this time (e.g., Goldiamond, 1965; Lazarus, 1968), recently there has been a proliferation of such reports. Strategies have varied from relatively pure operant approaches (e.g., Goldstein, 1971) to those which borrow heavily from theoretical perspectives generally considered nonbehavioral (e.g., Stuart, 1975). While empirical validation of behavior change strategies is still in the initial stages, sufficient evidence has accumulated to warrant a review of the progress to date.

The purpose of this paper is to summarize and discuss the recent developments in behavioral marriage therapy: first, to examine behavioral formulations regarding the etiology and maintenance of undesirable marital interaction; second, to discuss intervention strategies which have evolved from these formulations; third, to evaluate the attempts on the part of researchers to assess the efficacy of these intervention strategies; and fourth, to derive from the existing research implications and directions for future research. The discussion has been restricted to the literature specifically concerned with marital discord; strategies for dealing with specific sexual dysfunctions have been omitted (e.g., Masters & Johnson, 1970), as have reports of couples being

Behavioral Marriage Therapy," by N. S. Jacobson and B. Martin. In *Psychological Bulletin*, 1976, Vol. 83, No. 4, pp. 540-556. Copyright 1976 by the American Psychological Association. Reprinted by permission.

treated in the service of individual behavior problems, such as depression (e.g., Lewinsohn, 1974).

THEORETICAL FORMULATIONS OF MARITAL DISTURBANCE

Exchange and reciprocity

In attempting to elucidate the development and maintenance of maladaptive marital interaction, some social learning theorists have borrowed the concepts of social psychological exchange theories; Thibaut and Kelley's *Social Psychology of Groups* (1959) has been particularly influential. Central to Thibaut and Kelley's formulation is the interdependence of social behavior among individuals engaged in dyadic interaction. In any relationship involving two people, according to Thibaut and Kelley, individuals are mutually striving to maximize "rewards," that is, "pleasures, satisfactions, and gratifications the person enjoys," while concurrently minimizing "costs," that is, "factors which operate to inhibit or deter the performance of a sequence of behavior" (p. 12). Social behavior in a given dyadic relationship is maintained by a high level of rewards relative to costs; continuation of the relationship is also affected by the participants' perceptions of alternative relationships and their comparative rewards and costs.

According to Thibaut and Kelley's formulation, over time the interaction of a particular dyad becomes governed by a set of norms reflecting a balance between rewards and costs. In the event that these norms are violated, for example, by one member of the dyad withholding rewards, the other member will attempt to reestablish the equilibrium by, for example, coercing the other by punishment. At the point where rewards and costs are again balanced, equilibrium is reestablished.

An exchange formulation which is even more operant in its conception is that of Homans (1961), who explicitly postulated frequency of social interaction to be a function of the number of mutual rewards exchanged in the relationship. According to Homans, the extent to which rewards are exchanged in a relationship determines not only the frequency of interaction but also the degree of favorable "sentiment" felt by each member of the dyad toward the relationship (Homans, 1950, p. 135).

In a direct application of the exchange model to the interactional difficulties evidenced in troubled marriages, Stuart (1969a) described marital discord as a function of the low rate of positive reinforcers exchanged by spouses; the outcome of this low rate of positive reinforcement is that each spouse becomes less "attracted" to the other, and the relationship is experienced as less attractive (Stuart, 1969a, p. 675). Consistent with the normative conception of dyadic interaction described by Thibaut and Kelley (1959), Stuart assumed that patterns of interaction between married couples are never accidental, that such patterns represent the most rewarding alternative available at a given time—that is, the pattern reflects a balance between maximizing rewards from the other while minimizing the costs of emitted behavior. Similarly, Patterson, Weiss, and their associates (Weiss, Hops, &. Patterson, 1973) have argued that marital conflict results from faulty behavior change operations implemented by spouses. Rather than relying on positive control as the primary strategy for ensuring rewards, cooperation, and compliance from the partner, spouses in distressed marriages make excessive use of aversive control tactics. Whether aversive control strategies initiated by one spouse lead to the reciprocal use of aversive tactics by the other, as proposed by Patterson and Hops (1972), or withdrawal from contact by the other, as proposed by Stuart (1969a), the end result is a low rate of positively reinforcing interaction.

In support of these notions, Birchler, Weiss, and Vincent (1975) compared distressed and nondistressed couples on average rates of rewarding and punishing behaviors. For both directly observed problem-solving behavior in the laboratory and spouse-recorded data in the home, distressed couples had lower rates of rewarding or pleasing behaviors and higher rates of punishing or displeasing behaviors. Moreover, couples were *able* to make rewarding responses in excess of the frequency directed toward their spouses; all the couples in the sample, whether distressed or nondistressed, directed more rewards and fewer aversive responses toward opposite-sex strangers than toward their spouses.

In another elaboration of exchange theory into social learning terminology, Patterson and Reid (1970) applied the concepts of *reciprocity* and *coercion* to family interaction. Following Thibaut and Kelley, these authors proposed that, for nondistressed families and over an extended period of time, rates of rewards would be reciprocated on an equitable basis by any pair of family members. *Coercion* refers to an inequitable exchange whereby one member's behavior is controlled by positive reinforcement, while the other member's behavior is controlled by negative reinforcement; for example, A delivers a punishing stimulus such as a verbal command to B, and B positively reinforces A by complying with the command, which in turn eventuates in a removal of the aversive stimulus by A (cessation of command), thereby negatively reinforcing B's response. It was proposed that coercive patterns would exist to a greater degree in distressed families.

Some empirical support exists for the above notions. Wills, Weiss, and Patterson (1974) had seven couples count (with a wrist counter) frequencies of pleasing and displeasing affectional responses directed at them by their spouses over a period of 14 days. A perfect rank order correlation (rho = 1) was obtained for average levels of pleasing behaviors and a rank order correlation of .61 (not significant) was obtained for displeasing reactions. Birchler (1973) obtained similar data on 12 nondistressed and 12 distressed couples over a 5-day period and found Pearson correlations, respectively, of .97 ($p < .01$) and .74 ($p < .01$) for average rates of pleasing affectional responses between spouses. For displeasing affectional responses, the correlations were .26 (not significant) and .54 ($p < .05$) for the nondistressed and distressed couples, respectively. For pleasing affectional reactions there is clearly some evidence for reciprocity; for displeasing responses reciprocity appears less strong. The authors did not make a direct statistical comparison of the difference in magnitude between the correlations of pleasing and displeasing reactions, but by our own computation the difference between the correlation of .97 and the correlation of .26 in Birchler's nondistressed group is significant ($p < .001$). It may also be of interest that, in both of the above studies, husbands received higher rates of aversive responses and lower rates of positive responses than did wives.

The picture becomes more complex when we look at data in these two studies that reflect more immediate fluctuations in social interchange. Wills et al. (1974) found greater reciprocity for displeasing affectional responses than for pleasing responses when correlations were computed separately for each couple over the 14 days of data collection (a within-couples analysis). And Birchler (Note 1) found similar trends when rates of pleasing and displeasing responses were obtained from a brief sample of directly observed laboratory interaction. There is no necessary contradiction in the results of these two types of analyses—correlations based on averages over a long time period versus a within-couples analysis that partials out differences in mean levels or a more fine-grained measure based on direct observation of brief problem-solving interaction.

Both sets of findings need further confirmation before elaborate theories are spun, but the findings of greater reciprocity in pleasing than in displeasing responses for the average level data seem more substantial at this time, and do suggest that some inequity in aversive control may be more characteristic of marriages than inequities in levels of positive affection. There is, in fact, an interesting trend in the Wills et al. (1974) data suggesting greater imbalances (lower reciprocity) in aversive control ($r = .26$) in nondistressed couples than in distressed couples ($r = .54$). Perhaps some "nondistressed" marriages are characterized by one-sided coercive relationships that are nevertheless stable and in which the spouses deny any dissatisfaction or distress. As Patterson, Hops, and Weiss (Note 2) have pointed out, if one spouse acquires skills at coercing the other, contingencies maintaining the behavior of both members can be quite powerful. Distress is more likely to become overt and admitted to when the coerced partner rebels and begins to reciprocate aversive control. Imbalances of this kind are not necessarily inconsistent with Thibaut and Kelley's exchange theory in that the coerced spouse may still perceive the relatively unsatisfying marriage as better than any other alternative.

To summarize, empirical findings support the notions of exchange theory (Thibaut & Kelley, 1959) and reciprocity (Patterson & Reid, 1970) with respect to equity in the interchange of rewarding actions by married couples over an extended period of time. There is apparently less reciprocity in the exchange of aversive responses over extended time periods and some tentative evidence that with general level held constant, daily variations in these characteristics are more likely to be reciprocal for aversive responses than for rewarding responses. And there is some evidence that distressed marriages are characterized by higher levels of aversive behaviors and lower levels of rewarding behaviors than are nondistressed marriages.

Communication theories

A related description of marital discord has emphasized the ambiguous, vague, and inconsistent nature of communication between spouses. This description has taken many forms in the literature, and as Stuart (1975) has pointed out, the theoretical speculations of "systems theorists" (e.g., Lederer & Jackson, 1968; Watzlawick, Beavin & Jackson, 1967) have contributed generously to this perspective. Friedman (1972) emphasized the role of inconsistent and ambiguous communication in disturbed family interactions (e.g., verbal messages which contradict non-verbal messages), with the result that each spouse's behavior becomes unpredictable to the other, a condition that eventuates in mistrust (p. 127). Knox (1971) cited the lack of honest and direct communication among distressed couples. Honest communication was defined as a statement by A to which B could respond candidly without any anticipated penalty; direct communication describes an inquiry by A in which he/she states his/her wishes explicitly and precisely, rather than concealing an underlying malevolent intention in an ostensibly benign request for information. Others have emphasized the inability of distressed couples to express both positive and negative feelings (Eisler & Hersen, 1973; Fensterheim, 1972). These accounts of disturbed communication have not been subjected to systematic research, and a demonstration that distressed and nondistressed couples can be differentiated along such communication dimensions is needed.

INTERVENTION STRATEGIES

Modification of couple interaction in the clinical setting
If it is believed that disturbed marital interaction is a function of a low rate of positive reinforcement exchanged by the couple along with an excessively high rate of punishment, one obvious goal of therapy would be to increase the rate of rewarding interaction while decreasing the rate of aversive interaction. The primary means for achieving these changes has been to focus on the couple's interaction in the clinical or laboratory setting, directing spouses to alter their interactional responses toward each other in desirable ways (Carter & Thomas, 1973b; Eisler & Hersen, 1973; Eisler, Hersen, & Agras, 1973a; Friedman, 1972; Knox, 1971; Patterson & Hops, 1972; Thomas, Walter, & O'Flaherty, 1974; Weiss et al., 1973). A concomitant goal has been to improve communication in such a way as to facilitate problem solving, that is, the resolution of specific areas of conflict in the relationship (e.g., Weiss et al., 1973). Broadly speaking, focusing on couples' interaction in the clinical setting has served a dual function according to its advocates: First, couples learn more effective strategies for solving specific problems; second, in the process of becoming efficient problem solvers, couples generally begin to increase the rate of rewarding interactional responses, while at the same time lowering the rate of aversive responses.

Altering interactional responses and training in problem-solving skills comprise the initial focus of a treatment program developed at the Oregon Research Institute and the University of Oregon (Patterson & Hops, 1972; Weiss et al., 1973; Patterson et al., Note 2). Initially, couples are taught to communicate their desires and dissatisfactions specifically and operationally. "Pinpointing" or "discrimination training" involves reversing the predilection of distressed couples for stating their complaints in "global, intention ascribing" terms (Weiss et al., 1973, p. 326). By translating abstract statements of intention (e.g., You're always trying to hurt me) into operational statements (e.g., Yesterday you criticized my driving in front of Lois and Fred), it is believed that expectations and dissatisfactions are clarified; furthermore, Stuart (1975) has pointed out that "terminal," unchangeable complaints become changeable when operationalized.

The next segment of the treatment program concentrates on teaching couples how to communicate in less destructive and more rewarding ways. Explicit training in communication skills consists of demonstrating to couples what their self-defeating, destructive patterns of interaction are—that is, presenting them with feedback, suggesting alternative methods (either by instructions or modeling), and monitoring their attempts to practice techniques suggested or modeled by the therapist (behavior rehearsal).

This sequence of feedback, instructions with modeling, and behavior rehearsal has been used by many behavioral marriage therapists in their efforts to modify the interaction patterns of unhappy couples (Eisler & Hersen, 1973; Friedman, 1972; Knox, 1971; Liberman, 1970; Rappaport & Harrell, 1972). Feedback has been provided by verbal comments from the therapist (e.g., Friedman, 1972), role playing by the therapists (e.g., Eisler & Hersen, 1973), written instructions from the therapists (e.g., Carter & Thomas, 1973b), and videotapes (e.g., Patterson & Hops, 1972). Modeling, as Eisler and Hersen (1973) pointed out, is thought to be a useful procedure in this context for a number of reasons: First, the necessity of discovering effective responses through the laborious process of trial and error is obviated; second, both verbal and nonverbal aspects of new responses can be demonstrated; third, by observing the spouse's reaction to the modeled response, the other spouse can appreciate the potential benefits of adopting it; fourth, resistance to change is minimized by defining change as emulation of respected authority (the therapist). Through behavior rehearsal, couples practice new responses while being monitored and corrected by the therapists; by practicing the skills learned in therapy both in the clinical setting and at home (Patterson, 1971), dependence upon the therapist is gradually reduced, and it is believed that generalization is fostered.

Another communication dimension focused upon in the clinical setting has been the verbalization of both positive and negative affect. Eisler and Hersen (1973) viewed such training as an important aspect of a short-term intervention approach for families in crisis. Others have suggested that the inability to express feelings honestly and directly is a fundamental problem in many disturbed marriages (Fensterheim, 1972). The treatment advocated by these writers for facilitating the direct expression of affect has been *assertiveness training* (Eisler, Miller, Hersen, & Alford, 1974).

Contingency management procedures

Thus far, the focus has been on the direct modification of couples' interactional responses in the clinical setting. Another prominent element of the behavioral approach to marital discord has been direct training in contingency management procedures for use in the home. By far the most ubiquitous strategy used with married couples for this purpose has been *contracting* (Weiss, Birchler, & Vincent, 1974). As applied to marriage therapy, *contracting* refers to the negotiation of written agreements between spouses; it is a systematic procedure for setting forth behavior change agreements" (Weiss et al., 1973, p. 328). The purpose of contracting is to reverse the process of aversive control for desired change. Explicitly emphasized in the training is the notion that spouses must be willing to "give to get more out of the relationship" (Rappaport & Harrell, 1972, p. 203). It is contended that since distressed couples relying upon aversive control tactics enter therapy mistrusting each other, it is critical that any behavior change efforts initiated by either spouse are immediately reinforced (Eisler & Hersen, 1973). Other advantages of written contracts were enumerated by Rappaport and Harrell (1972): First, they act as references, obviating the necessity for relying on memory in the recollection of a prior agreement; second, written agreements can easily be modified; third, written agreements act as cues (discriminative stimuli), reminding forgetful spouses of their agreement and symbolizing their commitment to therapy.

The most common contractual form used in behavioral marriage therapy has been the "quid pro quo" agreement (Knox, 1971; Rappaport &. Harrell, 1972; Stuart, 1969a, 1969b), a form first suggested by Lederer and Jackson (1968). A quid pro quo agreement ensues when each spouse agrees to make a specified change in his and her behavior, but the change of one member is made contingent upon prior change exhibited by the other. If X signifies the change agreed to by the husband and Y signifies the change agreed to by the wife, the form of the quid pro quo is as follows: If X, then Y; if not X, then not Y.

This model of contracting illustrates precise contingency control over each agreed-upon change. Furthermore, since desired behavior changes are used as reinforcers, the troublesome task of discovering separate reinforcers for each agreed-upon change is obviated. However, Weiss et al. (1974) have criticized the quid pro quo form, contending that the contingent relationship between agreed-upon changes makes it necessary that one partner change *first;* it is argued that in a relationship lacking in trust, requesting that one partner change unilaterally is untenable (Weiss et al., 1974; Weiss et al., 1973). Moreover, under the quid pro quo arrangement, if one member fails to fulfill his/her contractual obligations, the other is sanctioned to abdicate his/her own contractual responsibilities.

Weiss et al. (1973) have recommended an alternative form, referred to as the "good faith" contract (p. 328), in which each spouse independently agrees to implement behavior changes desired by the other. In this type of agreement, each partner independently commits himself/herself to behavior change, and each change is independently reinforced; the changes contracted for by each spouse are not contingent upon the other's behavior change. Thus, the positive consequences provided upon compliance with agreed-upon changes are not the other's target behaviors; rather, reinforcers are derived from "menus" consisting of stimuli formerly deemed desirable by spouses. Reinforcers may be provided by the spouse (e.g., back rub), by the environment (e.g., one night out per week), or by the therapist (e.g., reduced fee). Failures to comply with a contract are followed either by a simple withholding of the specified reinforcer or by additional aversive consequences.

Several rules have been specified for optimal contracting (Weiss et al., 1974). One that has been most emphasized states that responses targeted for change should be those for which the desired outcome is "acceleration" rather then "deceleration." Weiss et al. (1974) argued that adherence to this rule is sound contingency management, since reinforcing the occurrence of a response is considerably easier than reinforcing its nonoccurrence. If the target behavior is a highly aversive response occurring at an excessively high rate, the authors suggested attempting to accelerate a response incompatible with that target behavior. Stuart (1969a) has similarly cautioned against contracting for additional aversive control in relationships in which such control is already pervasive. Since the strategies used for decelerating behaviors are usually aversive control strategies, deceleration seems to run counter to the more general goal of treatment, that is, establishing a predominance of mutually rewarding behavior maintained by positive reinforcement. Whether or not focusing on acceleration only is more effective than a combination accelerations-decelerations is an empirical question. The assumption made by the acceleration-only advocates is that as desired behaviors become more prevalent, frequently occurring noxious spouse behaviors will automatically decrease. There is some evidence that, at least with normal couples, this is an invalid assumption. A study conducted by Wills et al. (1974) indicated that the dimensions of "pleasing spouse behaviors" and "displeasing spouse behaviors" are relatively independent and that increases as well as decreases in one dimension do not in themselves affect the frequency of the other.

Various procedures have been used to buttress contracting procedures. Stuart (1969a, 1969b) has instituted token economy programs in the homes of distressed couples. Tokens redeemable for backup reinforcers help compensate for the delay between performance of the desired behavior and the concrete reinforcer; moreover, according to Stuart, "(a) they can be redeemed for the specific consequences which the recipient deems desirable at that point in time, (b) they are concrete and unambiguous, and (c) the giving and receiving of tokens is customarily associated with positive social interchange . . ." (Stuart, 1969a, p. 676). Others (e.g., Azrin, Naster, & Jones, 1973) have used informal contracts in which spouses exchange lists of activities and desired behavior changes. Although no contingencies are specified in these exchanges, they actually constitute implicit quid pro quo agreements.

There is no empirical evidence to recommend the good faith strategy. Because of the greater efficiency of the quid pro quo form, its use would be indicated were it found that there were no differences in effectiveness between it and the good faith form. Multiple exchanges, in which both spouses agree to change an entire series of behaviors without specifying explicit contingencies, would be equally efficient. The cumbersome, time-consuming process of separately reinforcing each agreed-upon change is justified only if such a strategy proves to be significantly more effective than these alternative procedures.

Some have directly instructed couples in the selective use of positive reinforcement without relying on negotiations or contractual exchanges (Goldstein, 1971; Liberman, 1970). Liberman (1970) described a rather informal approach in which spouses are taught to use their own behavior in modifying their spouse's behavior by selectively ignoring that which they are desirous of decelerating and reinforcing highly valued spouse behavior. Essentially the same message was conveyed by Goldstein (1971), although his approach was more strictly operant in its extensive utilization of objective, behavioral data collected in the home by spouses. Indeed, charting and recording were believed to be an extremely important part of the intervention procedure, viewed as change-inducing agents in their own right (Goldstein, 1976).

Stuart's (1975) five categories of intervention summarize the major areas of emphasis in a behavioral approach to the treatment of marital discord. First, new behavioral vocabularies are shaped in which vague, intentionality-attributing statements are replaced by hypotheses in the form of functional descriptions. Second, new techniques of influence are taught, that is, couples are taught to use positive rather than aversive means in modifying the other's behavior. Third, communication is altered in desirable ways. Fourth, decision-making norms are altered; the assumption behind this endeavor is that distressed couples tend to form ambiguous or ineffective distributions of decision-making authority, as a result of which power (hence coercion) determines who in the marriage is to make particular decisions. Fifth, techniques for maintaining changes occurring in therapy are introduced, that is, strategies for solving future problems are taught.

A number of behavioral intervention strategies for altering couples' behavior have been discussed; techniques involving feedback, modeling, and behavior rehearsal, and assertive training have received much attention as ways of improving couples' interaction in the clinical setting. Contingency management techniques designed to alter spouse behavior in the home have also been elaborated. The ultimate goal of such procedures has been to facilitate behavior change efforts based upon positive control. Contracting has been the most extensively used strategy in this regard. In the next section, empirical findings are discussed.

RESEARCH ON BEHAVIORAL MARRIAGE THERAPY

Most of the research devoted to the question Does behavioral marriage therapy work? has consisted of uncontrolled case studies (Azrin et al., 1973; Goldstein, 1971; Hickok & Komechak, 1974; Stuart, 1969a, 1969b; Weiss et al., 1973; Patterson et al., Note 2). For the most part, the existing evidence for the effectiveness of various behavioral strategies is suggestive rather than experimentally demonstrated. In evaluating the outcome research conducted to date, certain questions need to be addressed. First, Are the dependent measures suitable? Weiss et al. (1973) have articulated the need for both specific outcome criteria and a "multidimensional approach to the assessment of marital functions" (p. 339). The global indexes of marital satisfaction traditionally used to evaluate behavior change procedures (Gurman, 1973; Olson, 1970) belie the diversity of difficulties manifested by couples seeking assistance; moreover, the susceptibility of such measures to social desirability variables (Welch & Goldstein, Note 3) and demand characteristics renders them problematic as criterion measures in outcome research. Second, Do the studies contain sufficient controls to demonstrate the effectiveness of the techniques used in the studies? Third, Assuming that change has been demonstrated, can the techniques or components of the treatment program which elicited the changes be pinpointed? Fourth, Do the studies provide evidence suggesting the persistence of positive changes occurring in therapy? Finally, Are the conditions under which the treatment's effectiveness is maximized known (i.e., Are two therapists superior to one? Are good faith contracts more effective than quid pro quo contracts? etc.)?

Evaluation of clinical treatment packages
The first published investigation of the effectiveness of a behavioral approach to marital discord was Stuart's (1969a, 1969b) application of contingency contracting procedures to the treatment of four distressed couples. All four of the wives complained of a lack of conversation with their husbands. Quid pro quo contracts were formed in each case in which husbands received

tokens in exchange for accelerating their time spent engaged in conversation with their wives. These tokens could be cashed in for physical contact with their wives (e.g., 3 tokens for kissing, 15 tokens for sexual intercourse, etc.). Each couple recorded daily rates of conversation and sexual activity prior to, during, and for 24–48 weeks following the end of treatment, which lasted an average of 7 hours per couple spread over a 10-week period. In all four cases, the rates of conversation and sexual activity increased in the desired direction; the increases were substantial, and follow-up data indicated that these changes were maintained. Furthermore, an inventory designed to measure marital satisfaction was administered prior to, at the conclusion of, and either 24 or 48 weeks following the termination of treatment. For all couples, increased satisfaction was reported at the conclusion of treatment.

Stuart documented a promising technique for treating married couples, but the lack of a control group, total reliance on self-report data, and considerable variability in the spouse-recorded data leave many of the above listed questions unanswered.

A research program conducted at the Oregon Research Institute and the University of Oregon by Weiss, Patterson, and their associates (Patterson & Hops, 1972; Weiss et al., 1973; Patterson et al., Note 2) has followed a format for investigating therapeutic effectiveness advocated by Bergin and Strupp (1972). Rather than evaluating behavior change procedures in the context of one or more group studies, the Oregon group developed a "treatment package" which was applied to various couples in a series of replicated case studies; following these applications, the techniques were refined and subsequently reapplied to new cases.

The treatment package involves training couples in communication skills (restructuring interaction so that problem solving is more efficient and so that there is a greater proportion of positively reinforcing interaction relative to aversive interaction), as well as negotiation training (instruction and practice in behavioral contracting). In order to adequately assess their treatment program, the Oregon group developed a set of assessment procedures involving both observational and self-report instruments. Two self-report indexes which they used to supplement the traditional Locke-Wallace Marital Adjustment Scale (MAS) (Locke & Wallace, 1959) were found to significantly differentiate distressed from nondistressed couples (Weiss et al., 1973). A third quasi-observational procedure, the Spouse Observation Checklist (SOC) was designed to measure the rate at which reinforcers are exchanged between spouses in vivo. Spouses were asked to record, from a comprehensive checklist of potential spouse behaviors, daily frequencies along with judgments of whether each spouse action was experienced as pleasing or displeasing. Validity studies indicated a significant relationship between recorded pleasurable events, recorded displeasurable events, and overall ratings of marital satisfaction (Wills et al., 1974).

The Marital Interaction Coding System (MICS) (Hops, Wills, Patterson, & Weiss, Note 4) was developed as a means of systematically evaluating the quality of marital interaction in the laboratory along two dimensions: a rewardingness dimension (i.e., the extent to which spouses emit rewarding as opposed to punishing interactions toward one another); and a problem-solving dimension, designed to measure the efficiency of marital communications in terms of solving problems in their relationship. Both the verbal and nonverbal responses of the spouses were videotaped and reliably coded under 1 of 30 categories, each defined operationally.

In one report by Patterson et al. (Note 2), 10 couples described as moderately severe in regard to their marital problems were treated by one of the three authors. The results on the observational measure indicated significant changes in the direction of improvement on only 3 of the 29 categories for husbands (more agreements, fewer denials of responsibility, and fewer problem descriptions), and 3 of the categories for wives (fewer complaints, fewer excuses, and fewer problem descriptions). Many of the other categories changed in the expected direction, although the changes were not significant. The authors interpreted these results as indicating "a general improvement in negotiation skills" (p. 16). On the self-report measure (SOC), significant increases in number of recorded *pleasures* were reported for both husbands and wives from baseline to posttest; while husbands also reported a significant decrease in number of *displeasures*, the wives reported a nonsignificant decrease.

Similar equivocal results were found in the first of two studies reported by Weiss et al. (1973). Here too, only some behavioral categories changed significantly in the desirable direction (compromise, problem description, putdown). In fact, there were some significant changes which seemed in the opposite direction to that which might have been predicted or considered desirable beforehand (e.g., *accept responsibility* decreased in frequency, *criticism* increased in frequency for husbands). In both of the above studies, the statistical methods used are somewhat questionable. By using each separate category of the MICS as a measure of therapeutic effectiveness, and thereby conducting 29 separate t tests, the researchers may have been capitalizing on chance; the minority of individual t tests which were significant are difficult to interpret since an overall multivariate test was not conducted.

The results of a second study reported by Weiss et al. (1973) were more clear-cut. Five couples were seen from 56–91 days at the rate of once a week. In addition to the MICS and SOC, three self-report measures were used as evaluative criteria. Further, the 29 MICS categories were collapsed into 6 overall categories. The results indicated significant changes in the direction of improvement in all 6 observational categories, and similarly on all but 1 of the self-report measures. Looking at the couples individually, three of the five seemed to improve substantially, whereas for the other two, at least one member was still reporting considerable dissatisfaction with the relationship at the conclusion of treatment.

Weiss and Patterson have engaged in what is to date the most thorough investigation of the effectiveness of behavioral strategies for alleviating marital distress. Especially in the last study described above, their data indicated that couples undergoing treatment experienced substantial gains; these gains were manifested both in the clinical setting and, according to data collected by spouses, in the home. Further, most of the posttest data was solicited 3–6 months following the end of treatment, so that there was reason to believe that the changes were persistent. Nevertheless, conclusions regarding the effectiveness of the Oregon treatment package remain tentative due to the absence of control groups. Moreover, since the treatment was multifaceted and included many individual components, further research is necessary to ferret out the components responsible for treatment efficacy, given a controlled demonstration of effectiveness.

Jacobson (Note 5) recently completed a study which tested the effectiveness of a treatment program derived from that of Weiss and Patterson and included a minimal treatment, waiting-list control group. A methodological innovation in Jacobson's study was the inclusion of a series of replicated single-subject experiments within the context of a between-groups design. After defining a set of target behaviors for each couple, spouses observed and charted each other in the home, tracking two target behaviors simultaneously. Appropriate accelerations or decelerations were evaluated for each couple individually using multiple baselines. Thus, in addition to the general dependent measures forming the basis for group comparisons, specific data on the relevant behavior problems for each couple were collected and evaluated.

Jacobson's results indicated that for both observational (MICS) and self-report (MAS) measures, the group receiving the treatment package developed by Weiss and Patterson improved significantly more than the minimal treatment, waiting-list control group, which exhibited negligible changes. Furthermore, each of the five couples comprising the treatment group showed appropriate changes in target behaviors, changes which were attributable to treatment manipulations. Treatment couples exhibited substantially fewer negative behaviors in their laboratory problem-solving interactions, substantially more positive behaviors, reported a significantly greater degree of marital satisfaction, and manifested many of the behavioral changes deemed desirable by complaining spouses. This is the only clinical study to date in evaluation of behavior change procedures for married couples which has employed a control group. Moreover, the inclusion of data which are couple-specific along with the more general evaluative criteria obviates one of the difficulties in evaluating behavior change procedures with couples: Couples are quite idiosyncratic in their presenting complaints, and such individual differences are often submerged in general, cross-couples measures of effectiveness. Unfortunately, as in the studies reported thus far, Jacobson did not examine the relative contribution of the various components of the treatment package, nor did he control for nonspecific effects.

In an attempt to control for nonspecific attention-placebo effects, Azrin et al. (1973) gave couples 3 weeks of a placebo procedure ("catharsis counseling") prior to a 4-week treatment program ("reciprocity counseling"). Based on the notion that marital problems result from a lack of reciprocal reinforcement in the relationship, the treatment program focused upon training couples to behave in a more rewarding manner toward each other. Through homework assignments and various structured tasks, couples were taught to pinpoint specifically which behaviors were pleasing to the other, which were not, and what specific changes might be implemented to render each spouse's behavior more pleasing to the other. An attempt was made to instruct couples in the art of compromising, and informal contracts (i.e., contracts without specified contingencies) were utilized as a way of facilitating behavior change. The therapists avoided technical language and minimized didacticism. No record keeping or data collection was required of the couples.

Each evening from initial contact until termination and then at 1-month intervals following termination, couples completed a Marital Happiness Scale (MHS); this scale, serving as the sole dependent measure for the study, required spouses to rate their degree of happiness on a 10-point scale in regard to each of 9 problem areas in marriage as well as a 10th category referring to general happiness for a particular day. Of the 12 couples who served as subjects, all but 1 individual reported significantly more happiness during the last week of reciprocity counseling than at the end of the 3-week placebo procedure; at the 1-month follow-up, 88% of the spouses reported significantly more happiness than was indicated on the last day of the treatment program. No significant change in average ratings occurred during the placebo procedure, although considerable variability existed in the couples' responses to nonspecific counseling. Furthermore, there was some evidence of generalization from positive changes in areas directly dealt with in therapy to increased happiness in other areas not directly focused upon. Besides indications of increased marital satisfaction at the 1-month follow-up, 11 of the 12 couples continued to live together for at least the duration of the follow-up inquiries.

Azrin and his associates provided a treatment program which was considerably more informal in its use of behavioral technology than the programs discussed thus far. Their results suggest that a relatively exclusive focus on structured practice in reciprocity outside the clinical setting may be beneficial, even without the additional emphasis on the direct training of communication skills. However, some cautions militate against the conclusion of Azrin et al. (1973) that their study was the first to experimentally validate a behavioral approach to marital discord. Since each couple received 3 weeks of a placebo treatment prior to the 4-week behavioral regime, it is possible that the effects which began to manifest themselves only during the reciprocity counseling period were generated in part by the previously given procedures. More importantly, the researchers have not demonstrated internal validity; they have really provided a series of replicated AB designs (Birnbrauer, Peterson, & Solnick, 1974).

A careful reading of the researchers' description of their placebo procedure raises some question as to its credibility, and no data have been presented to support the implicit claim that couples perceived themselves as receiving therapy during the catharsis counseling period. The reciprocity counseling regime included a number of nonspecific tactics which might have induced improvement in and of themselves and yet were not incorporated into the placebo procedures. As an example, although the couples initiated the completing of the MHS at the beginning of the placebo procedure, it was only during reciprocity counseling that they were instructed to exchange their forms each evening subsequent to rating their degree of happiness for that day. It is conceivable that simply exchanging their rating sheets each night significantly altered the ratings; since these ratings constituted the criterion measure of marital happiness, it would have been desirable to rule out this extraneous source of change by instructing the couples to exchange their rating sheets during the placebo treatment.

A final shortcoming of the Azrin et al. (1973) study is its reliance on the MHS as the sole criterion for change. In addition to the difficulties inherent in the exclusive reliance on a self-report index such as this one, there was no reported pilot work completed on this instrument prior to the study.

The studies reviewed thus far cumulatively yield highly suggestive evidence of the efficacy of the behavioral approach and its emphasis on the programming of positive control into the marital relationship. In all studies, the treatment package consisted of a great number of component techniques. Substantial change seems to have occurred in all of the studies, but although Jacobson (Note 5) demonstrated that one particular behavioral approach was effective relative to minimal treatment, more controls are needed to experimentally validate the efficacy of specific behavior change procedures.

Analog studies

An alternative to the evaluation of treatment packages is the isolation and examination of specific behavior change procedures in quasi-therapeutic or analog settings. Despite the caution which must be exercised in generalizing from the analog setting to the clinical situation, this approach can serve as an expeditious means of investigating specific questions outside the context of the complex clinical milieu. The research reported by Goldstein and his colleagues (Goldstein, 1971, 1976) is most appropriately categorized as analog research, since (a) he has worked primarily with couples recruited from the general population who were not necessarily distressed, and (b) his intervention strategies have focused on the modification of one isolated target behavior rather than attempting to increase the overall level of satisfaction in the relationship.

In a series of replicated case studies (Goldstein, 1971), Goldstein collaborated separately with 10 wives to modify specific complaints which took the form of behavioral deficits or excesses in their husbands. With each wife, one husband behavior was selected for modification utilizing strategies of positive control. In each case, the husbands were unaware of the novel contingencies to which they were subjected. Stimuli made contingent upon accelerations of desired behavior were decided by the wife and the therapist and were applied subsequent to a base rate taken by each wife. All data were recorded by the wives in the home. An average of three sessions with the therapist produced substantial changes in the desirable direction for 80% of the husbands. Nonparametric statistical analyses revealed that the rate changes were statistically significant. Informal follow-ups indicated that, although systematic charting and contingency management were officially discontinued, the wives estimated that the changes were maintained. The relatively short-term, selective application of positive reinforcement seems to be a successful strategy for altering the rate of spouse target behaviors in the desired direction.

More recently, Welch and Goldstein (Note 3) attempted to demonstrate the therapeutic value of charting and recording events that took place between spouses in the home, without the explicit implementation of reinforcement principles. The subjects for this study were relatively satisfied, normal couples. The researchers hypothesized that the recording of pleasing and displeasing spouse behavior in the home would result in a greater degree of reported marital satisfaction, reflecting the belief that the direct feedback provided by spouses to one another regarding the consequences of the other's responses toward them would result in an increase in mutual rewards and therefore increased satisfaction. A group presented with charting instructions in addition to a didactic lecture on the use of reinforcement principles was compared to a group receiving only the lecture. Another factor investigated by the researchers was the effect of positive feedback on spouse ratings of marital satisfaction. Some couples, after participation in a laboratory task requiring mutual cooperation, received praise in regard to their performance. Thus, there were four groups: (a) a group receiving positive feedback and a lecture; (b) a group receiving positive feedback, a lecture, and charting instructions; (c) a group receiving a lecture without charting or positive feedback; and (d) a group receiving charting instructions and a lecture but no positive feedback. Both prior to and at the termination of experimental procedures, the couples completed the Locke-Wallace Marital Adjustment Scale (MAS), which served as the dependent measure in the study. The results indicated that the group receiving charting instructions, positive feedback, and the lecture reported a significantly greater improvement in marital satisfaction than did any of the other groups, which did not differ from one another. In general, the couples who charted reported greater change in the direction of satisfaction than did noncharting couples, although the differences did not reach statistical significance.

The authors interpreted their data as supporting the change-inducing power of recording reinforcing events, suggesting that even without specifying desired behavioral changes, such a procedure may be at least as effective as "a laboratory manipulation" (p. 14). In speculating on possible reasons for the effectiveness of charting, Welch and Goldstein pointed to the attention paid to positive spouse behaviors necessitated by the selective recording of pleasing events, claiming that this biased scanning aided the couples in becoming aware of the positive elements in the relationship. Moreover, it was argued that once the spouses became aware of their responses which pleased the other, they would be better able to accelerate the frequency of such responses. Contracting and related exchange strategies emphasizing reciprocity were criticized by the authors as being unrealistic in a distressed marriage characterized by mistrust and suspiciousness.

It must be pointed out that the investigators, as they themselves acknowledged, worked with well-adjusted couples in a setting only vaguely similar to a clinical setting. At this stage there is little reason to believe that disturbed couples would benefit substantially from a therapeutic regime focusing exclusively on the charting of the spouse's behavior. Further, the laboratory manipulation included in the Welch and Goldstein study bears little resemblance to the interventions employed in the clinical setting by the researchers already discussed; therefore, it is not particularly surprising that the positive feedback administered to couples on a cooperative task had little effect on the couples' reports of marital satisfaction. It does not follow that a more clinically salient laboratory manipulation would have been less powerful than charting in producing positive changes in couples' reported marital satisfaction, at least on a short-term basis.

The modification of verbal communication between married couples has been of primary interest to Thomas and his associates at the University of Michigan (Carter & Thomas, 1973a, 1973b; Thomas, Carter, & Gambrill, 1970, 1971; Thomas et al., 1974). Through retrospective analyses of tapes of couples engaged in conversation, the researchers have been able to modify specific problem areas of verbal communication through brief, direct instructional feedback and specific suggestions (Carter & Thomas, 1973a, 1973b). The investigators have also developed a promising procedure for the assessment of specific problem areas of marital communication, involving the in vivo rating of conversations for the presence or absence of 49 categories of problem communication (Thomas et al., 1974). Rather than counting the frequency of specific categories of verbal responses, the raters simply placed each member of the dyad somewhere on a 4-point scale indicating to what extent interactions of a particular type were manifested.

A primary goal of the investigations conducted by Thomas and his associates has been the transformation of complex verbal communication into simpler, more specific response units. In the interests of objectivity and simplicity, they developed an electromechanical signaling system (Thomas et al., 1970). The system consists of boxes on which the clients can communicate to each other by pressing buttons, client light boxes on which the clients can receive signals from each other, and therapist control boxes on which he may both monitor client communications and signal to the client. The signaling system has been used for the assessment of marital communication; further, the signal system has been used to facilitate the modification of a couple's verbal behavior in a laboratory setting (Carter & Thomas, 1973a, 1973b).

Although the researchers have yet to demonstrate the clinical utility of their signaling system, their technology for the assessment and modification of verbal communication appears promising. One advantage of their approach is its emphasis on data generated by the couples through direct interaction in the laboratory; problem areas were identified by the researchers through an analysis of the couples' exhibited verbal behavior, and assessment as well as treatment intervention was based upon this analysis. This research is still in the analog stage, although the technology has been used in clinical contexts with some reported success (Carter & Thomas, 1973a, 1973b).

Eisler and his associates have also investigated the assessment and modification of marital interaction in an analog setting (Eisler & Hersen, 1973; Eisler, Hersen, & Agras, 1973a, 1973b; Eisler et al., 1974). One element of their investigation has been an examination of the effects of assertiveness training procedures on a couple's interaction in a laboratory setting (Eisler et al., 1974). In three uncontrolled case studies, the training of passive husbands to behave more assertively produced desirable changes in couple interaction; changes were measured by quantifying and categorizing responses occurring during videotaped conversations both before and after assertiveness training. Substantial changes from pretest to posttest occurred in two of the three couples treated. Although this study was uncontrolled and included no indexes reflecting either the permanence of these changes or the extent to which such changes generalized beyond the laboratory setting, assertiveness training seems to be a promising strategy for improving marital interaction when problems include an unassertive spouse. The results would have been more convincing if the experimenters had collected multiple baseline data rather than simply measuring each target behavior before and after intervention.

Of particular interest are this group's investigations of videotaped feedback as a therapeutic technique (Eisler et al., 1973a). Many behavioral marriage therapists and researchers have recommended the use of videotaped feedback as an intervention strategy, and some of the research discussed above has used such feedback as a component of its treatment package (e.g., Patterson & Hops, 1972). Although the research conducted by Eisler and his associates supported the usefulness of videotape as an assessment device (Eisler et al., 1973b), one study cast doubt on its value as a behavior change procedure (Eisler et al., 1973a). In attempting to modify specific couples' nonverbal interactions (smiling and eye contact), the authors discovered that videotaped feedback in addition to verbal instructions was no more effective than instructions alone in increasing couples' "looking" behavior. These results have received indirect corroboration in an investigation which found that videotaped feedback could result in deleterious effects for the couples receiving it (Alkire & Brunse, 1974).

To summarize, studies investigating behavioral marriage therapy, although not conclusive, strongly suggest the efficacy of a treatment approach combining contingency contracting with direct training of communication skills in the clinical setting (Weiss et al., 1973; Jacobson, Note 5). Furthermore, there is suggestive evidence that either of the two main components of this approach can be of some benefit when used alone; the efficacy of contracting procedures used alone receives support from clinical research (Stuart, 1969a, 1969b); the effectiveness of training in communication skills derives some support from analog research (Carter & Thomas, 1973a, 1973b; Eisler, Hersen, & Agras, 1973b; Eisler et al., 1974). Finally, research has tended to support the notion that couples can be trained to use positive control in modifying selected problem behaviors in their spouses (Goldstein, 1971; Jacobson, Note 5).

CONCLUSION: SUGGESTIONS FOR FUTURE RESEARCH

We conclude that behavioral marriage therapy holds great promise in the elimination of suffering experienced by married couples in distress. On the basis of the literature, a number of suggestions for future research seem warranted.

First, as in any area of behavior change research, controlled studies are needed, whether they include control groups in between-groups designs or within-subjects controls in single-subjects designs. Also, investigations focusing on the identification of components contributing maximally to change must be conducted. Variables which must be evaluated within the context of a comprehensive treatment program include not only specific therapeutic techniques (e.g., contracting, role playing, modeling) but also nonspecific variables (expectancies, demand characteristics, etc.). Currently, placebo effects cannot be ruled out as primary change-inducing factors in any of the studies reported in the literature thus far. In order to evaluate conclusively the contribution of such nonspecific effects, carefully constructed placebo control groups are needed, control groups which are both credible to the clients and procedurally similar to the actual treatment groups.

Second, in the interests of procedural refinement, investigations should focus on comparisons of various ways to implement specific procedures. As one example, research should determine which of the two predominant contracting models is more effective—the quid pro quo model or the good faith model (Weiss et al., 1974). The quid pro quo procedure is clinically more efficient; therefore, if the two forms are equally effective in bringing about desired behavior changes, the quid pro quo form would be preferred. Perhaps, as Weiss et al. (1974) have suggested, the more aversive the marital relationship has become to both spouses, the greater the need for the good faith model, in which case the quid pro quo model would be introduced to extremely disturbed couples subsequent to a certain amount of progress resulting from use of the good faith model. These are empirical questions. Other procedural issues which warrant investigation include the following: a comparison of different methods for identifying appropriate reinforcers to be used in written contracts; evaluating the effects of adding extinction and punishment procedures to the couples' contingency management repertoire; the importance of including a specified consequence in the written contract; the relative merits of treating couples individually versus treating them in groups; and the effect of implementing token economy programs in the homes of disturbed couples.

Third, procedures designed to measure the effects of behavioral interventions need further development. Self-report inventories are insufficient, but to the extent that they are used to corroborate other assessment techniques, both their reliability and validity must be confirmed. Criteria involving the direct observation of behavior in the clinical setting or at home is essential; the Marital Interaction Coding System (MICS) developed by Weiss et al. (1973) is a laudable achievement in this regard. However, the MICS was designed primarily to evaluate couples engaged in problem-solving discussions; as such its validity may be limited to this specific type of marital interaction. Moreover, interaction between spouses in the clinical setting may not be representative of their in vivo behavior, so that ways of assessing the latter should be developed. Patterson and Hops (1972) experimented with home observations; of course, this method presents its own validity problems, which up until now have contraindicated its widespread use (Lipinski & Nelson, 1974).

Fourth, investigations of behavioral approaches to marital discord must strike a balance between developing standardized treatment procedures and allowing sufficient flexibility to cope with the considerable variability in complaints exhibited by couples in distress. We are in agreement with those who view behavior therapy essentially as a method for investigating individual cases, rather than simply a set of techniques (Yates, 1970). It follows from this view that behavior change procedures should never be applied without a thorough analysis of each individual case. However, it is also believed that nomothetic research can provide estimates, parameters, and "best guess" statements which serve to facilitate the focus of this idiographic approach in the direction suggested by group averages. Striking a balance is particularly crucial in developing a technology to aid married couples; dissatisfied spouses are no more a monolithic group than are dissatisfied individuals, and outcome research, particularly with a clinical population, must combine group evaluative criteria with criteria specific to the problems manifested by each individual couple. Jacobson's approach is offered as one strategy for achieving this balance (Jacobson, Note 5).

Fifth, progress in the development of effective behavior change procedures for couples has been retarded by the relative independence of various projects; an increased emphasis on the exchange of techniques as well as assessment instruments would be facilitative. For example, it is exceedingly difficult to compare results from various studies when the methods used to assess treatment outcomes are discrepant with one another. Progress is not served by the development of new self-report indexes to measure marital satisfaction when a surfeit of such instruments already exists. Nor are new behavioral rating systems needed while those already created are in the process of being evaluated.

Finally, married couples are not the only category of adult dyadic relationships in need of assistance. Behavior change procedures should be expanded and applied to other types of dyads, including heterosexual and homosexual couples cohabitating in an unmarried state. Similarly, Stuart (1975) has pointed out that the goal of dyadic therapy is not always to "save" the relationship. A technology needs to be developed for assisting couples desirous of separation.

Behavioral marriage therapy is a relatively recent development, and as such any set of clinical procedures currently advocated should be viewed skeptically and used cautiously. Until recently, marriage counseling has been viewed by professionals and experienced by clients as relatively dissatisfying and insubstantial (Bergin, 1971); no traditional therapeutic approach to marriage counseling has received direct empirical support in the literature (Gurman, 1973; Olson, 1970). The growth and application of social learning principles to marriage counseling may signal an end to this less than illustrious tradition.

REFERENCE NOTES

1. Birchler, G. Personal communication, October 15, 1974.
2. Patterson, G. R., Hops, H., & Weiss, R. *A social learning approach to reducing rates of marital conflict.* Paper presented at the meeting of the Association for the Advancement of Behavior Therapy, New York, October 1972.
3. Welch, J. J., & Goldstein, M. K. *The differential effects of operant-interpersonal intervention.* Manuscript submitted for publication, 1974.
4. Hops, H., Wills, T. A., Patterson, G. R., & Weiss, R. L. *Marital interaction coding system.* Unpublished manuscript, University of Oregon, December 1971.
5. Jacobson, N. S. *Problem-solving and contingency contracting in the treatment of marital discord.* Manuscript submitted for publication, 1975.

REFERENCES

Alkire, A. A., & Brunse, A. J. Impact and possible causality from videotape feedback in marital therapy. *Journal of Consulting and Clinical Psychology,* 1974, *42,* 203–210.
Azrin, N. H., Naster, B. J., & Jones, R. Reciprocity counseling: A rapid learning-based procedure for marital counseling. *Behaviour Research and Therapy,* 1973, *11,* 365–382.
Bergin, A. E. The evaluation of therapeutic outcomes. In A. E. Bergin & S. L. Garfield (Eds.), *Handbook of psychotherapy and behavior change: An empirical analysis.* New York: Wiley, 1971.
Bergin, A. E., & Strupp, H. H. *Changing frontiers in the science of psychotherapy.* Chicago: Aldine, 1972.
Birchler, G. R. Differential patterns of instrumental affiliative behavior as a function of degree of marital distress and level of intimacy. (Doctoral dissertation, University of Oregon, 1972.) *Dissertation Abstracts International,* 1973, *33,* 14499B–4500B. (University Microfilms No. 73–7865, 102)
Birchler, G. R., Weiss, R. L., & Vincent, J. P. A multimethod analysis of social reinforcement exchange between maritally distressed and nondistressed spouse and stranger dyads. *Journal of Personality and Social Psychology,* 1975, *31,* 349–360.
Birnbrauer, J. S., Peterson, C. R., & Solnick, J. V. Design and interpretation of studies of single subjects. *American Journal of Mental Deficiency,* 1974, *19,* 191–203.
Carter, R. D., & Thomas, E. J. A case application of a signaling system (SAM) to the assessment and modification of selected problems of marital communication. *Behavior Therapy,* 1973, *4,* 629–645. (a)

Carter, R. D., & Thomas, E. J. Modification of problematic marital communications using corrective feedback and instruction. *Behavior Therapy*, 1973, *4*, 100–109. (b)

Eisler, R. M., & Hersen, M. Behavior techniques in family-oriented crisis intervention. *Archives of General Psychiatry*, 1973, *28*, 111–116.

Eisler, R. M., Hersen, M., & Agras, W. S. Effects of videotape and instructional feedback on nonverbal marital interaction: An analogue study. *Behavior Therapy*, 1973, *4*, 551–558. (a)

Eisler, R. M., Hersen, M., & Agras, W. S. Videotape: A method for the controlled observation of nonverbal interpersonal behavior. *Behavior Therapy*, 1973, *4*, 420–425. (b)

Eisler, R. M., Miller, P. M., Hersen, M., & Alford, H. Effects of assertive training on marital interaction. *Archives of General Psychiatry*, 1974, *30*, 643–649.

Fensterheim, H. Assertive methods and marital problems. In R. D. Rubin, H. Fensterheim, J. Henderson, & L. P. Ullmann (Eds.), *Advances in behavior therapy*. New York: Academic Press, 1972.

Friedman, P. M. Personalistic family and marital therapy. In A. A. Lazarus (Ed.), *Clinical behavior therapy*. New York: Academic Press, 1972.

Goldiamond, I. Self-control procedures in personal behavior problems. *Psychological Reports*, 1965, *17*, 851–868.

Goldstein, M. K. Behavior rate change in marriages: Training wives to modify husbands' behavior. (Doctoral dissertation, Cornell University, 1971). *Dissertation Abstracts International*, 1971, *32*, 548B. (University Microfilms No. 71–17, 094)

Goldstein, M. K. Increasing positive behaviors in married couples. In J. D. Krumboltz & C. E. Thoresen (Eds.), *Counseling methods*. New York: Holt, 1976.

Gurman, A. S. The effects and effectiveness of marital therapy: A review of outcome research. *Family Process*, 1973, *12*, 145–170.

Hickok, J. E., & Komechak, M. G. Behavior modification in marital conflict: A case report. *Family Process*, 1974, *13*, 111–119.

Homans, G. C. *The human group*. New York: Harcourt Brace, 1950.

Homans, G. C. *Social behavior: Its elementary forms*. New York: Harcourt Brace, 1961.

Knox, D. *Marriage happiness: A behavioral approach to counseling*. Champaign, Ill.: Research Press, 1971.

Lazarus, A. A. Behavior therapy and group marriage counseling. *Journal of the American Society of Psychosomatic Medicine and Dentistry*, 1968, *15*, 49–56.

Lederer, W. J., & Jackson, D. D. *The mirages of marriage*. New York: Norton, 1968.

Lewinsohn, P. M. A behavioral approach to depression. In R. J. Friedman & M. M. Katz (Eds.), *The psychology of depression: Contemporary theory and research*. New York: Halsted Press, 1974.

Liberman, R. Behavioral approaches to family and couple therapy. *American Journal of Orthopsychiatry*, 1970, *40*, 106–118.

Lipinski, D., & Nelson, R. Problems in the use of naturalistic observation as a means of behavioral assessment. *Behavior Therapy*, 1974, *5*, 341–351.

Locke, H. J., & Wallace, K. M. Short-term marital adjustment and prediction tests: Their reliability and validity. *Journal of Marriage and Family Living*, 1959, *21*, 251–255.

Masters, W. H., & Johnson, V. E. *Human sexual inadequacy*. Boston: Little Brown, 1970.

Olson, D. H. Marital and family therapy: Integrative review and critique. *Journal of Marriage and the Family*, 1970, *32*, 501–538.

Patterson, G. R. *Families: Applications of social learning to family life*. Champaign, Ill.: Research Press, 1971.

Patterson, G. R., & Hops, H. Coercion, a game for two: Intervention techniques for marital conflict. In R. E. Ulrich & P. Mounjoy (Eds.), *The experimental analysis of social behavior*. New York: Appleton, 1972.

Patterson, G. R., & Reid, J. B. Reciprocity and coercion: Two facets of social systems. In C. Neuringer & J. L. Michael (Eds.), *Behavior modification in clinical psychology*. New York: Appleton, 1970.

Rappaport, A. F., & Harrell, J. A behavioral-exchange model for marital counseling. *Family Coordinator*, 1972, *21*, 203–213.

Stuart, R. B. Operant-interpersonal treatment for marital discord. *Journal of Consulting and Clinical Psychology*, 1969, *33*, 675–682. (a)

Stuart, R. B. Token reinforcement in marital treatment. In R. D. Rubin & C. M. Franks (Eds.), *Advances in behavior therapy*. New York: Academic Press, 1969. (b)

Stuart, R. B. Behavioral remedies for marital ills: A guide to the use of operant-interpersonal techniques. In T. Thompson & W. Docken (Eds.), *International symposium on behavior modification*. New York: Appleton, 1975.

Thibaut, J. W., & Kelley, H. H. *The social psychology of groups*. New York: Wiley, 1959.

Thomas, E. J., Carter, R. C., & Gambrill, E. D. A signal system for the assessment and modification of behavior (SAM). *Behavior Therapy*, 1970, *1*, 252–259.

Thomas, E. J., Carter, R. C., & Gambrill, E. D. Some possibilities of behavior modification of marital problems using 'SAM'. In R. D. Rubin, H. Fensterheim, A. A. Lazarus, & C. M. Franks (Eds.), *Advances in behavior therapy*. New York: Academic Press, 1971.

Thomas, E. J., Walter, C. L., & O'Flaherty, K. A verbal problem checklist for use in assessing family verbal behavior. *Behavior Therapy*, 1974, *5*, 235–246.

Watzlawick, P., Beavin, J. H., & Jackson, D. D. *Pragmatics of human communication—A study of interactional patterns, pathologies, and paradoxes*. New York: Norton, 1967.

Weiss, R. L., Birchler, G. R., & Vincent, J. P. Contractual models for negotiation training in marital dyads. *Journal of Marriage and the Family*, 1974, *36*, 321–331.

Weiss, R. L., Hops, H., & Patterson, G. R. A framework for conceptualizing marital conflict, a technology for altering it, some data for evaluating it. In L. A. Hamerlynck, L. C. Handy, & E. J. Mash (Eds.), *Behavior change: Methodology, concepts, and practice*. Champaign, Ill.: Research Press, 1973.

Wills, T. A., Weiss, R. L., & Patterson, G. R. A behavioral analysis of the determinants of marital satisfaction. *Journal of Consulting and Clinical Psychology*, 1974, *42*, 802–811.

Yates, A. J. *Behavior therapy*. New York: Wiley, 1970.

Varieties of Double Bind

Milton H. Erickson
Ernest L. Rossi

This paper begins with an autobiographical account by Erickson of the experiences from childhood that led to his use of the double bind in hypnosis and psychotherapy. Erickson presents a number of examples of the use of the double bind in everyday life and a few case studies of its use in psychotherapy. In the second half of this paper, Rossi summarizes the characteristics of Erickson's clinical approach to the double bind. He outlines several varieties of the double bind and offers an exploratory analysis of the operation of the double bind in terms of Russell's Theory of Logical Types. A clear differentiation is drawn between Erickson's therapeutic double bind and Bateson's schizogenic double bind. The ethics and limitations in the use of the double bind in psychotherapy are proposed together with suggestions for further research.

When I was a boy on the farm, it was not uncommon for my father to say to me, "Do you want to feed the chickens first or the hogs, and then do you want to fill the woodbox or pump the water for the cows first?"

What I realized then was that my father had given me a choice; I as a person had the *primary* privilege of deciding which task I was to do first. I did not realize at the time that this primary privilege rested entirely upon my *secondary* acceptance of all the tasks mentioned. I was unwittingly committed to the performance of the tasks which had to be done by being given the primary privilege of determining their order. I did not recognize that I was accepting the position of being placed in a double bind. The tasks had to be done; there was no escaping the fact that the kitchen range burned wood to cook my breakfast and that the cows did need to drink. These were items of fact against which I could not rebel. But I did have the profoundly important privilege as an individual of deciding in which order I should and would do them. The conception of what a double bind was escaped me though I often wondered why I was seemingly willing to "pick off" potato bugs or hoe potatoes rather than playing.

"Varieties of Double Bind," by M. H. Erickson and E. L. Rossi. In *The American Journal of Clinical Hypnosis*, January 1975, Vol. 17, No. 3, pp. 143–157. Copyright 1975 by The American Journal of Clinical Hypnosis. Reprinted by permission.

My first well-remembered intentional use of the double bind occurred in early boyhood. One winter day with the weather below zero, my father led a calf out of the barn to the water trough. After the calf had satisfied its thirst, they turned back to the barn but at the doorway the calf stubbornly braced its feet and, despite my father's desperate pulling on the halter, he could not budge the animal. I was outside playing in the snow and, observing the impasse, began laughing heartily. My father challenged me to pull the calf into the barn. Recognizing the situation as one of unreasoning stubborn resistance on the part of the calf, I decided to let the calf have full opportunity to resist since that was what it apparently wished to do. Accordingly I presented the calf with a double bind by seizing it by the tail and pulling it away from the barn while my father continued to pull it inward. The calf promptly chose to resist the weaker of the two forces and dragged me into the barn.

As I grew older I began employing my father's alternate choice double bind on my unsuspecting siblings to secure their aid in the performance of farm chores. In high school I used the same approach by carefully arranging the order in which I did my homework. I put myself in a double bind by doing the bookkeeping which I disliked first and then the geometry which I liked as a reward. I gave myself a reward but the double bind was arranged so that all the homework was done.

In college I became more and more interested in the "double bind" as a motivational force for the self and others. I began experimenting by suggesting to college mates the performance of two tasks, both of which I knew they would reject if presented singly. They would, however, execute one or the other if I made the refusal of one contingent upon the acceptance of the other.

I then began reading autobiographies extensively and discovered that this way of managing behavior was age-old. It was an item of psychological knowledge that properly belonged to the public domain and no one person could lay claim to it. Coincident with the development of my interest in hypnosis I began to realize that the "double bind" could be used in a variety of ways. In hypnosis the double bind could be direct, indirect, obvious, obscure, or even unrecognizable.

I found the double bind to be a remarkable force, but dangerously double edged. In negative, enforced and competitive situations the double bind yields unfortunate outcomes. As a child, for example, I knew where all the best berry picking patches were. I'd offer to show them to my companions if I could keep all I picked plus half of what they picked. They would accept the deal eagerly but later they would greatly resent it when they actually saw how much I got. In college I was interested in debating, but when I tried to employ the double bind I always lost. The judges invariably sought me out after the debate to tell me that I had actually won but that I had so aroused their antagonism that they could not help voting me down. The result was that I never made the college debating team even though I was frequently proposed. I noted in these debating contests that double bind arguments lead to unfavorable reactions when those double binds were in favor of myself against an opponent. I learned that the competent debator was the one who presented a double bind argument in favor of his opponent and then demolished the advantage he had given his opponent.

It took me a long time to realize that when the double bind was used for personal advantage it led to bad results. When the double bind was employed for the other person's benefit, however, there could be lasting benefit. I therefore practiced it extensively in favor of my roommates, classmates and professors with the knowledge that I would eventually use it to help patients.

When I entered psychiatry and began hypnotic experimentation at the clinical level (the experimental level had been previously explored extensively), the double bind became an approach of extensive interest for eliciting hypnotic phenomena and therapeutic responses.

In essence, the double bind provides an illusory freedom of choice between two possibilities, neither of which is really desired by the patient but are actually necessary for his welfare. Perhaps the simplest example is provided by children's reluctance about going to bed. Instructed that they must go to bed at 8:00 P.M., they have the feeling of being coerced. If, however, those same children are asked, "Do you want to go to bed at a quarter of eight or at eight o'clock?" the vast majority respond by selecting by their own "free will" the latter (which was actually the intended time). Regardless of which specified time the child selects, he commits himself to the task of going to bed. Of course the child can say that he does not want to go to bed at all, whereupon another double bind can be employed, "Do you wish to take a bath before going to bed or would you rather put your pajamas on in the bathroom?" This latter example illustrates the use of a non sequitur in a double bind. The lesser of the two evils is usually accepted. Either choice, however, confirms the matter of going to bed which long experience has taught the child is inevitable. He has a sense of free choice about it, but his behavior has been determined.

Psychiatric patients are often resistant and withhold vital information indefinitely. When I observe this I emphatically admonish them that they are not to reveal that information this week; in fact, I am insistent that they withhold it until the latter part of next week. In the intensity of their subjective desire to resist, they fail to evaluate adequately my admonition; they do not recognize it as a *double bind requiring them both to resist and to yield.* If the intensity of their subjective resistance is sufficiently great they may take advantage of the double bind to disclose the resistant material without further delay. They thereby achieve their purpose of both communication and resistance. Patients rarely recognize the double bind when used on them, but they often comment on the ease they find in communicating and handling their feelings of resistance. In the cases that follow the critical reader may question the effectiveness of double binds because he is actually on a secondary level when he reads *about* them. The patient, who comes to therapy with many emotional needs, however, is on a primary level when he is exposed to the double bind; he is usually unable to analyze them intellectually and his behavior is thereby structured by them. The uses of the double bind are greatly facilitated by hypnosis and it adds greatly to the multitude of ways in which it can be used.

CASE ONE

A 26-year-old man with an M.A. degree in psychology came reluctantly to the writer for hypnotherapy at his father's dictatorial demand. His problem was fingernail biting, begun at the age of four as a measure of escaping four hours daily practice at the piano. He had bitten his fingernails to the quick until they bled, but his mother was unmoved by the bloodstains on the keys. He continued the piano and the fingernail biting until the latter had become an uncontrollable habit. He resented greatly being sent for hypnotherapy and freely stated so.

I began by assuring him that he was justified in his resentment, but I was amused that he had allowed himself to participate in self-frustration for 22 long years. He looked at me in a puzzled way so the explanation was given, "To get out of playing the piano you bit your fingernails to the quick until it became an unbreakable habit despite the fact you have wanted long fingernails. In other words, for 22 years you have literally deprived yourself of the privilege of biting off a good sized piece of fingernail, one that you could really set your teeth on satisfyingly."

The young man laughed and said, "I see exactly what you are doing to me. You are putting me in the position of growing fingernails long enough to give me some genuine satisfaction in biting them off and making the futile nibbling I'm doing even more frustrating." After further semi-humorous discussion he acknowledged that he was not sure he really wanted to experience a formal hypnosis. I accepted this by adamantly refusing to make any formal effort. This constituted a reverse set double bind: He asked for something he was not sure he really wanted. It was refused. Therefore, he was bound to want it, since he could now do so safely.

In the ensuing conversation, however, *his interest was maintained at a high pitch and his attention was rigidly fixated*, as he was told earnestly and intently that he could grow one long fingernail. He could take infinite pride in getting it long enough to constitute a satisfying bite. At the same time he could frustrate himself thoroughly by nibbling futilely at the tiny bits of nail on the other nine digits. Although no formal trance was induced, his high response attentiveness indicated he was in what we might call "the common everyday trance" that is brought on by any absorbing activity or conversation.

The light trance suggestion was reinforced by the measure of arousing him with casually irrelevant remarks and then repeating the instructions. What is the purpose of this measure? When you casually repeat suggestions in the awake state right after they heard them in trance the *patient says to himself*, "Oh, yes, I know that already, it's okay." In saying something of this sort to himself the patient is actually taking the first important step toward internalizing and reinforcing the suggestion as an aspect of his own inner world. It is this internalization of the suggestion that makes it an effective agent in behavior change.

Many months later the patient returned to display normal fingernails on each hand. His explanation, while uncertain and groping, is adequately descriptive of the effect of the double bind. He explained, "At first I thought the whole thing hilariously funny, even though you were serious in your attitude. Then I felt myself being pulled two ways. I wanted 10 long fingernails. You said I could have one only and I had to end up by biting it off and getting a 'real mouthful of fingernail.' That displeased me but I felt compelled to do it and to keep gnawing at my other fingernails. That frustrated me painfully. When the one fingernail started growing out I felt pleased and happy. I was more resentful than ever at the thought of biting it off but I knew I had agreed to do so. I eventually got around that by growing a second nail—that left eight fingers to gnaw on and I wouldn't have to bite the second long one off. I won't bore you with the details. Things just got more confusing and frustrating. I just kept on growing more nails and nibbling on fewer fingers, until I just said 'to hell with it!' That compulsion to grow nails and nibble nails and to feel more frustrated all the time was just unbearable. Just what were the motivations you put to work in me and how did it work?"

Now, more than eight years later, he is well-advanced in his profession, he is well-adjusted, a personal friend and he has normal fingernails. He is convinced that the writer used hypnosis on him to some degree because he still remembers a "peculiar feeling as if I couldn't move when you were talking to me."

CASE TWO

A father and mother brought their 12-year-old son in to me and said: "This boy has wet the bed every night of his life since he was an infant. We've rubbed his face in it; we've made him wash his things; we've whipped him; we've made him go without food and water; we've given him every kind of punishment and he is still wetting the bed." I told them, "Now he is my patient. I don't want you interfering with any therapy that I do on your son. You let your son alone and you let me make all my arrangements with your son. Keep your mouths shut and be courteous to my patient." Well, the parents were absolutely desperate so they agreed to that. I told Joe how I had instructed his parents and he felt very pleased about it. Then I said, "You know, Joe, your father is 6'1", he is a great big powerful husky man, you are only a 12-year-old kid. What does your father weigh? Two hundred twenty and he isn't fat in the least. How much do you weigh? One hundred seventy." Joe couldn't quite see what I was driving at. I said, "Do you suppose it is taking a deuce of a lot of energy and strength to build that great big beautiful chassis on a 12-year-old kid? Think of the muscle you've got. Think of the height you've got, the strength you've got. You have been putting an awful lot of energy in building that in 12 short years. What do you think you'll be when you are as old as your father? A shrimpy six foot two weighing only 220 pounds or do you think you will be taller than your father and heavier than your father?" You could see Joe's mind turning handsprings in all directions getting a new body image of himself as a man. Then I said, "As for your bed wetting you have had that habit for a long time and this is Monday. Do you think you can stop wetting the bed, have a permanent dry bed by tomorrow night? I don't think so and you don't think so and nobody with any brains at all will think that sort of thing. Do you think you will have a dry bed permanently by Wednesday? I don't. You don't. Nobody does. In fact, I don't expect you to have a dry bed at all this week. Why should you? You have had a life-long habit and I just simply don't expect you to have a dry bed this week. I expect it to be wet every night this week and you expect it. We're in agreement, but I also expect it to be wet next Monday, too, but you know there is one thing that really puzzles me and I really am absolutely thoroughly puzzled—*will you have a dry bed by accident on Wednesday or will it be on Thursday and you'll have to wait until Friday morning to find out?" Well Joe had been listening to me and he wasn't looking at the walls, the carpet, or the ceiling or the light on my desk or anything else. He was in the common everyday trance listening to all these new ideas.* Things he had never thought of before. Joe didn't know I was putting him in a double bind because the question wasn't, "Will I have a dry bed?" The question really was, *"which night?"* He was in a mental frame of reference to find out *which night* he would have the dry bed. I continued, "You come in next Friday afternoon and tell me whether it was Wednesday or Thursday, because *I don't know; you don't know. Your unconscious mind doesn't know. Your conscious mind doesn't know. The back of your mind doesn't know. Nobody knows. We will have to wait until Friday afternoon."* So "we" both waited until Friday afternoon, and Joe came in beaming and he told me the most delightful thing, "Doctor, you were mistaken, it wasn't Wednesday or Thursday, it was both Wednesday and Thursday." I said, "Just two dry beds in succession doesn't mean that you are going to have a permanent dry bed. By next week half the month of January is gone and certainly in the last half of January you can't learn to have a permanent dry bed and February is a very short month." (Never mind the speciousness of that argument, because February is a short month.) *"I don't know whether your permanent dry bed will begin on March 17, which is St. Patrick's Day, or it will begin on April Fools Day. I don't know. You don't know either, but there is one thing I do want you to know that when it begins it is none of my business. Not ever, ever, ever is it going to be any of my business."*

Now why should it be any of my business when his permanent dry bed began? That was actually a post-hypnotic suggestion that would go with him for the rest of his life. Now that is what you call a double bind. Little Joe couldn't understand what a double bind was. *You use double binds, and triple binds always as a part of the strategy of psychotherapy. You present new ideas and new understandings and you relate them in some indisputable way to the remote future.* It is important to present therapeutic ideas and post-hypnotic suggestions in a way that makes them contingent on something that will happen in the future. Joe would get older and taller. He would go on to high school and college. I never mentioned high school to him. I mentioned college, the remote future and the idea of being a football player. I didn't want him thinking about a wet bed. I wanted him thinking about the remote future and the things he could do instead of thinking: what am I going to do tonight—wet the bed.

CASE THREE

The serious question of what constitutes power and dominance and strength and reality and security had apparently been given considerable thought by Lal, approximately eight years old. At all events, shortly before the evening meal, he approached his father and remarked interrogatively, "Teachers always tell little kids what they have to do?" Another interrogative affirmation was offered. Continuing, Lal said, "And they make their little children do what they say?" A questioning assent was given.

Bracing himself firmly with his feet widely apart, Lal declared through clenched teeth, "Well, you can't make me do a single thing and to show you, I won't eat dinner and you can't make me."

The reply was made that his proposition seemed to offer a reasonable opportunity to determine the facts, but that it could be tested in a manner fully as inadequate if he were to declare that he could not be made to drink an extra large glass of milk. By this test, it was explained, he could enjoy his evening meal, he would not have to go hungry and he could definitely establish his point of whether or not he could be made to drink his milk.

After thinking this over, Lal agreed but declared again that he was willing to abide by his first statement if there were any doubt in the father's mind about the resoluteness of his declaration. He was airily assured that the glass of milk being extra large would be an easily adequate test.

A large glassful of milk was placed in the middle of the table where it would be most noticeably in full view, and dinner was eaten in a leisurely fashion while the father outlined the proposed contest of wills.

This exposition was made carefully and the boy was asked to approve or disapprove each statement made so that there could be no possible misunderstandings. The final agreement was that the issue would be decided by the glass of milk and that he, Lal, affirmed that his father could not make him drink the milk, *that he did not have to do a single thing his father told him to do about the milk*. In turn, the father said that he could make Lal do anything he wanted Lal to do with the milk, and that *there were some things he could make Lal do a number of times.*

When full understanding had been reached and it was agreed that the contest could begin, the father commanded, "Lal, drink your milk." With quiet determination the reply was made, "I don't have to and you can't make me."

This interplay was repeated several times. Then the father said quite simply, "Lal, spill your milk."

He looked startled, and when reminded he had to do whatever he was told to do about his milk he shook his head and declared "I don't have to." This interplay was also repeated several times with the same firm negation given.

Then Lal was told to drop the glass of milk on the floor and thus to break the glass and spill the milk. He refused grimly.

Again he was reminded that he had to do with the milk whatever he was told to do, and this was followed with the stern admonition, "Don't pick up your glass of milk." After a moment's thought, he defiantly lifted the glass. Immediately the order was given, "Don't put your glass down." A series of these two orders was given, eliciting consistently appropriate defiant action.

Stepping over to the wall blackboard the father wrote "Lift your milk" at one end and at the other he wrote, "Put your milk down." He then explained that he would keep tally of each time Lal did something he had been told to do. He was reminded that he had already been told to do both of those things repeatedly, but that tally would now be kept by making a chalk mark each time he did either one of those two things he had been previously instructed to perform.

Lal listened with desperate attention.

The father continued, "Lal, don't pick up your glass," and made a tally mark under "Lift your milk" which Lal did in defiance. Then, "Don't put your milk down" and a tally mark was placed under, "Put your milk down" when this was done. After a few repetitions of this, while Lal watched the increasing size of the score for each task, his father wrote on the blackboard, "Drink your milk" and "Don't drink your milk," explaining that a new score would be kept on these items.

Lal listened attentively but with an expression of beginning hopelessness.

Gently he was told, "Don't drink your milk now." Slowly he put the glass to his lips but before he could sip, he was told, "Drink your milk." Relievedly he put the glass down. Two tally marks were made, one under "Put your milk down," and one under "Don't drink your milk."

After a few rounds of this, Lal was told not to hold his glass of milk over his head but to spill it on the floor. Slowly, carefully he held it at arm's length over his head. He was promptly admonished not to keep it there. Then the father walked into the other room, returned with a book and another glass of milk and remarked, "I think this whole thing is silly. Don't put your milk down."

With a sigh of relief Lal put the glass on the table, looked at the scores on the blackboard, sighed again, and said, "Let's quit, Daddy."

"Certainly, Lal. It's a silly game and not real fun and the next time we get into an argument, let's make it really something important that we can both think about and talk sensibly about."

Lal nodded his head in agreement.

Picking up his book, the father drained the second glass of milk preparatory to leaving the room. Lal watched, silently picked up his glass and drained it.

Reality, security, definition of boundaries and limitations all constitute important considerations in the childhood growth of understandings. There is a desperate need to reach out and to define one's self and others. Lal, with full and good respect for himself as a person and as an intelligent person challenged an opponent whom he considered fully worthy and who, to Lal's gain, demonstrated no fearful sense of insecurity upon being challenged to battle.

The battle was one in defense of a principle considered by one contestant to be of great merit, and his opinion was rigorously respected but regarded as faulty by the other contestant. It was not a petty quarrel for dominance between two petty persons. It was the determination of the worth of a principle. Lines were drawn, understandings reached, and forces were engaged in the struggle for the clarification of an issue finally demonstrated by both contestants to be in error and of no further importance.

More than twenty years have elapsed and Lal has children of his own. He recalls that experience with pleasure and amusement and also with immense personal satisfaction. He defines it as "one time when I felt that I was really learning a lot. I didn't like what I was learning but I was awful glad I was learning it. It just made me feel real good inside the way a little kid likes to feel. I even want to say it like a little child."

CASE FOUR

One day one of my children looked at the spinach on the dinner table and said, "I'm not going to eat any of that stuff!" I agreed with him totally, "Of course not. You are not old enough, you are not big enough, you are not strong enough." This is a double bind that makes his position less tenable and the spinach more desirable. His mother took his side by maintaining that he was big enough and the issue then became an argument between his mother and me. The boy, of course, was on her side. I finally offered the compromise of letting him have a half a teaspoon full. They felt that was an unsatisfactory offer so I had to let him have half a dish. He ate that as fast as he could and loudly demanded more. I was reluctant but his mother agreed with him. Then very grudgingly I admitted "You are bigger and stronger than I thought." That now gave him a new status in his own eyes. I did not directly ask him to revise his self-image, but it occurred *indirectly* by (a) giving him an opportunity, a stage (the two sides of the argument between his mother and I) on which he could view and carefully consider a *revision of his own behavior*, and (b) the implications of this behavior change which *he drew himself* from my grudging admission of his growth. The essence of this indirect approach is that it arranges circumstances that permit the subject to make his own appropriate choices.

ERICKSON'S CLINICAL APPROACH
TO THE DOUBLE BIND

A review of Erickson's charming presentation of his approach to the double bind reveals the following characteristics.

1. The issues the patient is involved in are usually of immediate and deeply involving personal concern. There is *high motivation* that Erickson structures into the form of a double bind that can be used for behavior change. This is evident in all cases from the calf-tail pulling incident of his childhood to the problems of dealing with resistant patients.

2. Erickson always *accepts* the patient's immediate reality and frames of reference. He forms a *strong alliance* with *many different sides and levels* within the patient.

3. The patient has a problem because different response tendencies are in conflict in such a way that behavior change is stalemated. Erickson *facilitates expression of all response tendencies in such a way that the stalemated conflict is broken*. This was particularly evident in the case of the piano playing nail biter who wanted to (a) frustrate his parents, and yet (b) break his nail biting habit, (c) enjoy long fingernails, and yet (d) enjoy biting off a long nail. He wanted to (e) resist his father's demand for hypnosis, and yet (f) have it for his own purpose in his own way.

4. Erickson invariably adds something new to the situation that is related to the patient's central motivations in such a way that the patient is fascinated. The patient is opened with curiosity about the new point of view that Erickson is presenting; he *develops a creative moment* (Rossi, 1972), *or acceptance set for all the suggestions that follow*. The patient listens with such attentiveness that a formal trance induction is often unnecessary. The patient listens with that sort of rapt response attentiveness that Erickson recognizes as the *common everyday trance*.

5. The actual double bind is set by implications which structure the critical choices within the patient's own associative matrix. This was particularly evident in the way the father structured his son, Lal's defiance into an appropriate issue where a reverse set double bind could operate within the son. The father then "exercised" the reverse set to make sure it had "taken hold" before giving the critical suggestion. The importance of structuring and utilizing the patient's own internal responses to facilitate suggestions was emphasized in

the piano playing nail biter when Erickson *casually* repeated important suggestions so the patient would naturally affirm that he had already
had them.

6. *Erickson usually offers a number of double or triple binds.* The double
bind does not work by magic. It only works if it fits an appropriate need or
frame of reference within the patient. The simple case where one double bind
fits so exquisitely as to effect a precise and predictable behavior change all by
itself as in the case of Lal is probably rare. Erickson does not always know
beforehand which double bind or suggestion will be effective. He usually uses
a buckshot approach of giving many suggestions but in such an innocuous
manner (via implications, casualness, etc.) that the patient does not recognize
them. While watching Erickson *offer* a series of double binds and suggestions,
Rossi frequently had the impression of him as a sort of mental locksmith now
gently trying this key and now that. He watches the patient intently and
expectantly always looking for the subtle changes of facial expression and body
movement that provide an indication that the tumblers of the patient's mind
have clicked; he has found a key that works much to his mutual delight with
the patient.

7. Erickson tries to tie the double bind and post-hypnotic suggestions of
behavior change to reasonable future contingencies. *The suggestion is made
contingent on an inevitability.* Erickson thus uses both time and the *patient's
own inevitable behavior as vehicles for the suggestions.* Again we note that the
effectiveness of Erickson's approach is in the way he binds his suggestions to
processes occurring naturally within the patient. The effective suggestion is
one that is tailor made to fit within the patient's own associative matrix.
Erickson is always busy observing and tinkering for the best fit.

THE VARIETIES OF DOUBLE BIND AND
RUSSELL'S THEORY OF LOGICAL TYPES

Erickson's first unrealized exposure to the double binds that bound him to
his humble farm chores reveals a fundamental characteristic of all double
binds: There is free choice on a *primary or object* level that is recognized by
the subject, but behavior is highly structured on a *secondary or metalevel* in a
way that is frequently unrecognized. Other investigators (Bateson, 1972; Haley,
1963; Watzlawick, Beavin & Jackson, 1967; Watzlawick, Weakland & Fisch, 1974)
have related this fundamental characteristic of the double bind to Russell's
Theory of Logical Types in Mathematical Logic (Whitehead & Russell, 1910),
which was developed to resolve many classical and modern problems of
paradox in logic and mathematics. The double bind, from this point of view,
can be understood as a kind of paradox that the subject cannot easily resolve
so he "goes along with it" and allows his behavior to be determined. In this
sense the double bind can be recognized as a fundamental determinant of
behavior on a par with other basic factors such as reflexes, conditioning and
learning.

The free choice on the primary level of deciding whether to feed the chickens or hogs first was actually contained within a wider framework, the secondary or metalevel, of "tasks which had to be done." Little Erickson could

question what he wanted to do first on the primary level and he could feel proud of being permitted choice on that level. What the boy Erickson could not question was the metalevel of "tasks which had to be done." No one could question the metalevel, probably not even his father, because it was a mental framework that was built-in on the meta- or unconscious level as a basic assumption of their way of life. These first examples of the double bind may therefore be described as *free choice of comparable alternatives* on a primary level with the acceptance of one of the alternatives determined on a metalevel.

FREE CHOICE OF
COMPARABLE ALTERNATIVES

For didactic purposes we may now list how a number of double binds of this type can be used to facilitate hypnosis and therapy. The positive metalevel which determines that one of the free choices among comparable alternatives *will be accepted* in the therapeutic situation itself. Because we come to therapy of our own free will, for our own good, *we will accept* at least some of the therapeutic choices that are offered. The "transference" and "rapport" are also binding forces that usually operate at an unconscious or metalevel. In hypnosis we may consider that it is the trance situation itself which is the metalevel determining that some choice will be accepted among the comparable alternatives presented on the primary level by the hypnotherapist. In the following examples free choice is offered on the primary level of the "when" or "how" of trance, but it is determined on a metalevel that *trance will be experienced.*

"Would you like to go into trance now or later?"

"Would you like to go into trance standing up or sitting down?"

"Would you like to experience a light, medium or deep trance?"

"Which of you in this group would like to be first in experiencing a trance?"

"Do you want to have your eyes open or closed when you experience trance?"

It is easily seen from the above that there are an infinite number of such double binds that can be constructed in the form of a simple question offering free choice among comparable alternatives, one of which will be chosen. The skill of the therapist is in recognizing which possible sets of alternatives will be most appealing and reinforcing for the patient to choose from.

The double bind question is uniquely suited for Erickson's experiential approach to trance phenomena. Thus:

"Tell me whether you begin to experience the numbness more in the right or left leg?"

"Will your right hand lift or press down or move to the side first? Or will it be your left? Let's just wait and see which it will be."

"Will your eyelids grow heavy and close or will they remain comfortable and open in that one position?"

"Do you want hypnosis to remove all the pain or do you want to leave a little bit of the pain as an important signal about the condition of your body?"

"Time can be of varying intensity. Will it be condensed? Expanded?"

"What part of your body will be most heavy? Warm? Light? etc?"

THE DOUBLE BIND IN RELATION TO THE
CONSCIOUS AND UNCONSCIOUS

Probably the most fascinating double binds to the depth psychologist are those that somehow deal with the interface between the conscious and unconscious (Erickson, 1964). Many of these are trance inducing such as the following:

"If your unconscious wants you to enter trance your right hand will lift. Otherwise your left will lift."

Whether one gets a yes (right hand) or no (left hand) response to this request, one has in fact begun to induce trance since any truly autonomous response (lifting either hand) requires that a trance state exist. This is a particularly curious situation because in this case the double bind request at the primary conscious level appears to effect a change at the unconscious or metalevel. It is precisely because of this possibility that humans fall prey to paradoxes. Paradoxes, of course, raise problems, but they can also be used to facilitate the first stages of the therapy process where it is sometimes necessary to break up a patient's old and inadequate frames of reference (their metalevels) to facilitate the possibility of creating new and more adequate frameworks (Erickson, 1964; Rossi, 1972, 1973; Watzlawick, Weakland & Fisch, 1974).

Double binds can also be used to facilitate a creative interaction between the conscious and unconscious. When a patient is blocked or limited on the conscious level, the therapist can simply point out that the limitation is on the conscious level only and proceed to facilitate the unconscious somewhat as follows:

> Now it really doesn't matter what your conscious mind does because it is your unconscious that will find new possibilities that your conscious mind is unaware of or may have forgotten. Now you don't know what these new possibilities are, do you? Yet your unconscious can work on them all by itself. And how will they be communicated to your conscious mind? Will they come in a dream or a quiet moment of reflection? Will you recognize them easily at a conscious level or will you be surprised? Will you be eating, shopping or driving a car when they come? You don't know but you will be happy to receive them when they do come.

In this series of double binds consciousness is depotentiated by *not knowing* and the unconscious is facilitated by a number of truisms about the autonomy of the unconscious and the many possible ways it has of communicating with consciousness. The person is in a double bind with a positive metalevel of hopeful expectation for constructive work. But because his conscious cannot deal directly with the unconscious, the limitations of the conscious level are held in check until the unconscious can marshal a solution through some original problem solving.

Weitzenhoffer (1960) has convincingly presented the view that the term "unconscious" in contexts such as we have used here is not the same as Freud's "unconscious." Our use of the term unconscious is similar to its usage with finger signaling and the Chevreul pendulum (Cheek & LeCron, 1968) where Prince's (1929) definition of *subconscious or co-conscious* as any process "of which the personality is unaware" but "which is a factor in the determination of conscious and bodily phenomena" is more appropriate. To adequately conceptualize the double bind and hypnotic phenomena in general, it may well be that in the future the term "metalevel" could usefully replace labels like "unconscious, subconscious or co-conscious," since metalevels can be more precisely defined and thus enable us to apply the tools of symbolic logic, mathematics and systems theory to human problems.

THE TIME DOUBLE BIND

Erickson will frequently use time as a double bind to facilitate a psycho-therapeutic process. Typical examples are as follows:

"Do you want to get over that habit this week or next? That may seem too soon. Perhaps you'd like a longer period of time like three or four weeks."

"Before today's interview is over your unconscious will find a safe and constructive way of communicating something important to your conscious mind. And you really don't know how or when you will tell it. Now or later."

In explaining the use of such therapeutic double binds, Erickson feels they are approaches that enable the patient to cooperate with the therapist. The patient experiences great uncertainty, fright and inner agony in not knowing how to give up a symptom or reveal traumatic material. The therapeutic double bind gives the power of decision to the patient's unconscious and provides the conscious mind with an opportunity to cooperate.

THE REVERSE SET DOUBLE BIND

Erickson gave a number of examples of the reverse set double bind: (a) Reversing the calf's direction by pulling his tail, (b) enabling patients to reveal material by enjoining them not to, (c) utilizing Lal's reverse set to make him drink milk. We will analyze the example of Lal to illustrate how the Theory of Logical Types could handle the reverse set double bind.

1. The father immediately recognizes Lal's defiance from his behavior and verbal challenge about not eating dinner.

2. Recognizing that it is a matter of principle, the father's first move is to shift the battleground from a whole dinner to a mere glass of milk.

3. Father then defines the rules of the game so that the defiance is verbally crystallized into a reverse set: Lal "did not have to do a single thing his father told him to do about the milk." The father recognizes the reverse set but the son does not. The son believes the contest is about drinking milk; he is on the primary or object level in that belief. The son does not recognize the reverse set that is operating within him on a metalevel.

4. The father then gives the son a chance to exercise the reverse set so that its operation becomes firmly established within him. The father is now giving commands to the son on the primary level while also locking the son firmly into his reverse set on the metalevel.

5. The father sets up a tally sheet to clearly demonstrate to the son *that there were some things he would make Lal do a number of times.*" Lal begins to feel "hopelessness" with this repeated demonstration. He knows that he is losing in some way but he does not know why or how since the reverse set is operating on a metalevel that is unconscious.

6. The father finally gives the critical command "Don't drink your milk"

which completes the double bind. Lal raises the glass to drink but the father steps in to save Lal's self esteem just in the nick of time by telling him "to drink" so he does not have to.

7. Lal finally does drink the milk, but only when the name of the game is changed to *we drink milk together*. Lal's original defiance is transformed; the conflict between father and son is finally resolved as a joint behavior of drinking milk together.

THE NON SEQUITUR DOUBLE BIND

Illogic continues to have a field day with Erickson's casual insertions of all sorts of *non sequiturs* and *reductio ad absurdi* in the form of double binds. As was illustrated in Erickson's "going to bed" examples with children, he will often give a series of double binds when one does not suffice. Frequently, the more he gives the more absurd they become except that consciousness does not recognize their absurdity and is eventually structured by them. In the *non sequitur* double bind there is a similarity in the *content* of the alternatives offered even though there is *no logical* connection. Thus Erickson says, "Do you wish to take a *bath* before going to bed, or would you rather put your pajamas on in the *bath*room?" One could get vertigo trying to figure out the sense or illogic of such a proposition. One cannot figure it out so one cannot refute it, so one tends to go along with it.

THE SCHIZOGENIC DOUBLE BIND

The relation between Erickson's use of the double bind and the studies of it by Bateson *et al.* (1956) in the genesis of schizophrenia offers an interesting study of similarities and contrasts. (See Table 1.)

It may be noted in summary that the schizogenic double bind carries negative injunctions that are enforced at the metalevel or abstract level that is outside the victim's control on the primary level. Erickson's therapeutic double binds, by contrast, always emphasize *positive agreement on the metalevel and offer alternatives that can be refused on the primary level.* Erickson has stated that "While I put the patients into a double bind they also sense, unconsciously, that I will never, never hold them to it. They know I will yield anytime. I will then put them in another double bind in some other situation to see if they can put it to constructive use because it meets their needs more adequately." For Erickson, then, the double bind is a useful device that *offers* a patient possibilities for constructive change. If one double bind does not fit he will try another and another until he finds a key that fits.

ETHICS AND LIMITATIONS IN THE USE
OF THE DOUBLE BIND

As Erickson indicated in his early exploration of the double bind, there are significant limitations in its use. When the double bind is used in a therapeutic milieu there is a positive feeling associated with the therapeutic metalevel which determines that some choice will be made. Because of this basically positive context or metalevel the patient will accept one alternative even if he does not care for any. He will accept bitter medicine, if it is good for him.

When a free choice among comparable alternatives is offered without a positive metalevel structuring the situation the subject is free to refuse all choices. If we walk up to a stranger and ask "Will you give me a dime or a dollar?" we will obviously be turned down more often than not because there is no metalevel binding the stranger to accept one of the offered alternatives. If the stranger happens to be charitable, however, this characteristic of charitableness may function as a positive metalevel that will determine that we get at least a dime.

TABLE 1.

The Bateson Schizogenic Double Bind	The Erickson Therapeutic Double Bind
1. *Two or More Persons* The child "victim" is usually ensnared by mother or a combination of parents and siblings.	1. *Two or More Persons* Usually patient and therapist are ensconced in a positive relationship.
2. *Repeated Experience* Double bind is a repeated occurrence rather than one simple traumatic event.	2. *A Single or Series of Experiences* If one is not enough, a series of double binds will be *offered* until one works.
3. *A Primary Negative Injunction* "Do not do so and so or I will punish you."	3. *A Primary Positive Injunction* "I agree that you should continue doing such and such."
4. *A Secondary Injunction Conflicting with the First at a More Abstract (Meta) Level, and Like the First Enforced by Punishments or Signals Which Threaten Survival.*	4. *A Secondary Positive Suggestion at the Metalevel That Facilitates a Creative Interaction Between the Primary (Conscious) and Metalevel (Unconscious).* Responses at both levels are permitted to resolve stalemated conflicts.
5. *A Tertiary Negative Injunction Prohibiting the Victim from Escaping the Field.*	5. *A Tertiary Positive Understanding (Rapport, Transference) That Binds the Patient to His Therapeutic Task but Leaves Him Free to Leave if He Chooses.*
6. Finally, the complete set of ingredients is no longer necessary when the victim has learned to perceive his universe in double bind patterns.	6. The patient leaves therapy when his behavior change frees him from transference and the evoked double binds.

When the relationship or metalevel is *competitive or negative*, however, we can always expect a rejection of all double bind alternatives offered on the primary level. The competitive situation of a debate yields negative results as Erickson found unless the alternatives favor the other side. In the utterly negative situation of war or harm, "Do you want a punch in the nose or a kick in the teeth?" we can expect universal rejection of the alternatives. The therapeutic usefulness of the double bind, then, is limited to situations that are structured by a positive metalevel. The structuring presence of a positive metalevel together with free choice on the primary level also defines the ethical use of the double bind.

RESEARCH ON THE DOUBLE BIND

Since the successful use of the double bind on the clinical level is so highly dependent on the rapport and recognition of the patient's unique individuality, we can anticipate difficulty in securing positive results in experimental work where standard approaches may be used with large groups of subjects with little or no knowledge of their individual differences. Statistics on the amount of success of a single double bind in the standardized laboratory situation would therefore have little applicability to the clinical situation. A standardized testing situation that employs a *series of double binds* all directed to facilitate one or a few closely related behaviors would have a better chance of producing a significant experimental effect than a single double bind, however. A second major difficulty in such research is in the difficulty of defining and recognizing just what is a double bind for a particular individual. Bateson (1974) has commented that "a good deal of rather silly research (has been done) by people who think they can count the number of double binds in a conversation. This cannot be done for the same reason that you cannot count the number of jokes."

To be able to count the number of double binds or possible jokes in a conversation one would theoretically have to have access to a person's entire associative structure. Even with computers this is not practical. It may, however, be possible to write computer programs for double binds that could operate on the finite associative structure built into the computer program. On another level we anticipate that much fascinating research could be done investigating parameters influencing the simple reverse set type of double bind illustrated in the case of Lal. In addition to Bateson's (1972) relating of the double bind to deuterolearning, experimental work with animals and humans on reversal and nonreversal shifts (Kendler and Kendler, 1962) suggests other research paradigms relating the double bind to fundamental problems of learning. The fundamental nature of the double bind in structuring all forms of human behavior indicates that such research should have a high priority.

REFERENCES

Bateson, G., Jackson, D., Haley, J. & Weakland, J. Toward a theory of schizophrenia. *Behavioral Science*, 1956, 1, 251–264.

Bateson, G. *Steps to an ecology of mind*. New York: Ballantine Books, 1972.

Bateson, G. Personal communication letter, 1974.

Cheek, D. & Le Cron, L. *Clinical hypnotherapy*. New York: Grune & Stratton, 1968.

Erickson, M. H. A hypnotic technique for resistant patients: The patient, the technique and its rational and field experiments. *American Journal of Clinical Hypnosis*, 1964, 1, 8–32.

Haley, J. *Strategies of psychotherapy*. New York: Grune & Stratton, 1963.

Kendler, H. & Kendler, T. Vertical and horizontal processes in problem solving. *Psychological Review*, 1962, 69, 1–16.

Prince, M. *The unconscious*. New York: Macmillan, 1929.

Rossi, E. *Dreams and the growth of personality: Expanding awareness in psychotherapy*. New York: Pergamon Press, 1972.

Rossi, E. Psychological shocks and creative moments in psychotherapy. *American Journal of Clinical Hypnosis*, 1973, 16, 9–22.

Watzlawick, P., Beavin, J. & Jackson, D. *Pragmatics of human communication: A study of interactional patterns, pathologies and paradoxes*. New York: W. W. Norton, 1967.

Watzlawick, P., Weakland, J. & Fisch, R. *Change: Principles of problem formation and problem resolution.* New York: W. W. Norton, 1974.

Weitzenhoffer, A. Unconscious or co-conscious? Reflections upon certain recent trends in medical hypnosis. *American Journal of Clinical Hypnosis,* 1960, 2, 177–196.

Whitehead, A. & Russell, B. *Principia mathematica.* Cambridge: Cambridge University Press, 1910.

The Treatment of Children through Brief Therapy of Their Parents

Mara Selvini Palazzoli
Luigi Boscolo
Gian Franco Cecchin
Giuliana Prata

This is a report on the successful resolution of behavior problems (encopresis and anorexia, respectively) in two small children through the brief therapy of their parents. Treatment was based on general systems theory and the cybernetic model and employed interventions designed specifically to bring about rapid change in family interaction. The course of the treatments, as well as the technical problems arising out of such rapid changes, are discussed.

Granted that there does not exist to date a comprehensive theory of family therapy, it seems nevertheless possible to state a common denominator: the trend away from the disturbed individual seen as an artificially isolated monad toward the study and the treatment of dyads, triads, the entire nuclear family and, finally, of the complex network of relationships in which every family is embedded. However, beyond this one point of agreement, workers in our fields are known to hold radically divergent views about questions of epistemology and practice, as described very comprehensively by Beels and Ferber (1). These views range from models based on group dynamics in the psychoanalytic sense to role theory, learning theory, games theory, systems theory, and cybernetics.

After various trials and errors, our research team at the Center for the Study of the Family in Milan began to adopt in 1971 the theoretical model proposed in the late 50's and early 60's by the so-called Palo Alto Group under Gregory Bateson's theoretical leadership and the extensions of this model developed by Jay Haley in Philadelphia and by the Brief Therapy Center of the Mental Research Institute in Palo Alto (5). In terms of this model, the family is considered an interacting error-controlled system.

"The Treatment of Children through Brief Therapy of Their Parents," by M. S. Palazzoli, L. Boscolo, G. F. Cecchin, and G. Prata. In *Family Process*, December 1974, Vol. 13, No. 4, pp. 429–442. Copyright 1974 by Family Process, Inc. Reprinted by permission.

Our method of procedure is to have two co-therapists meet with the entire family (i.e. all members of the nuclear family actually living together) from the first session. The remainder of the team observes the sessions from behind a one-way vision screen and after each session meets with the therapists to devise the interventions for the next session. The families are informed of this arrangement.

As a general principle, all sessions are with the entire family, except when in the course of treatment it seems appropriate to deviate from this rule for the purpose of observing one of its sub-systems or of making a specific intervention. In particular, there is one exception to this rule that we consider especially important. It has to do with those parents who seek therapy for behavioral problems in very young children (two to four years) or in older children who have already been traumatized by numerous medical and psychiatric interventions and are therefore already labeled as "sick"—a label we do not wish to attach to them even more firmly. To this one may object that the convocation of the entire family is in and of itself an implicit communication that the problem is one of the family and not just of the identified patient. It is our experience, however, that the parents often inform their child of the forthcoming first visit with the implied message, "We have to go there because of you." It sometimes also happens that families are referred to us on the strength of some misconception about the Center and contact us in the belief that they should "hand over" their youngster for individual treatment.

Since our first contact with the family is usually by telephone, we have set aside special hours for these calls so that we may talk to them at length and thereby avoid many mistakes and misunderstandings that may otherwise occur due to lack of time. The fact that treatment (and often also its outcome) begins with this first telephone contact can hardly be stressed too much. The member of the team who takes the calls tries to obtain as much information as possible and immediately enters it on a fact sheet. He especially attempts to elicit as accurate a definition of the problem as possible, as well as other information about the family's present situation and their real reasons for seeking help.[1]

If the call comes from the parents of a very young child, whose problem, in our view, is almost always the expression of a marital problem of the parents or from the parents of a child who has already been traumatized by unsuccessful treatments, we usually invite only parents to the first session in order to observe their interaction.[2]

During the first visit the therapists collect the information necessary to decide whether they should continue to work with the parents alone or

[1]This first telephone contact deserves special study. It already enables us to observe, and to note, a number of phenomena: disturbed communication, tone of voice, general attitude, peremptory demands for all kinds of information, immediate attempts at manipulation by requesting a certain date and hour for the interview or by imposing certain conditions, thus attempting a role reversal and making it appear as if it were the therapists who are "looking for" the family. Except for a very few special cases, we have generally found it counterproductive to schedule the family for an emergency session.

[2]An exception are those families whose treatment has been discussed beforehand with a referring colleague who is seeing the child in individual therapy. In these cases the families have already been informed by the referring therapist that he considers it necessary for them to meet together for the purpose of observing them as a family group. This is, for instance, the case with autistic children.

whether the child should participate. In the following two cases, the team decided to continue the therapy with the parents alone. The reasons will become evident.

A CONTRACT FOR A CASE OF STOOL INCONTINENCE[3]

An anxious mother called the Center with regard to problems with her youngest child, Tonino, who was nine years old. Since early childhood Tonino had had a problem with encopresis of moderate degree, which until recently the mother was prepared to tolerate. The reason she now needed help was that in recent months the incontinence had worsened to an intolerable degree (almost daily he "craps in his pants" at school) and the child had developed other "strange" behaviors, in addition, that finally prompted the teacher to call his mother. Tonino not only entertained his school friends by telling them incredible stories in which he always played the role of the hero and which he firmly insisted were true, but he also "lied" in his in-class compositions. For some time these papers had been full of grammatical and spelling mistakes and he had been writing about "things which are neither here nor there."

In the first session the parents brought along two such compositions. In one of them, entitled "An Important Event in My Life," Tonino described with the verve (and the bad grammar) of a sports reporter his overwhelming victory at an imaginary Italian swimming championship for eight-year-old boys, allegedly held in Florence. In the other essay, with the title "How to Help Others," Tonino described at length his ferocious battle with a wolf during a recent Sunday trip into the mountains. He explained how, alerted by the screams of his oldest brother, he rushed into a nearby forest and there, after a wild struggle, managed to strangle this huge wolf that had sunk its teeth into the brother's arm and bitten it off. "That evening," concluded his essay, "I was pleased with my good deed, but somewhat dissatisfied because my brother had lost his arm."

The "mendacious" accounts that had so greatly shocked the elderly teacher thus revealed a Tonino for whom there was no other space or method to assert himself in life. The parents explained that physically Tonino was the least fortunate of their four sons. He was short, puny, cross-eyed, and seemed to have spent a large part of his young life in "repair shops." He underwent an operation for his strabismus at an early age and had since been wearing clumsy prescription glasses (which he frequently lost and which the mother promptly replaced with a new pair despite the considerable expense involved). Every week he was taken to an orthoptic specialist to exercise his eyes. As he also suffered from a knock-kneed condition, he had been made to wear, since age four, heavy orthopedic shoes that were laced all the way up above his ankles. And now, the mother reported, it also turned out that his permanent teeth were growing irregularly and a radical program was under way to have a dentist pull some and straighten out the others. It goes without saying that with all these treatments and other measures Tonino had been largely deprived of the psychophysical freedom necessary for a child's normal develop-

---

[3]These two cases have been published in the journal *Neuropsichiatria Infantile* (46: 539–554, 1973) and we wish to thank the Editor for his permission to include them here.

ment. His brothers, on the other hand, were all handsome, healthy, and strong boys, especially the oldest (the one who had his arm bitten off).

The observations reported by the parents, the description of their relationships with their respective families of origin, and much of what we could intuit about their relationship with Tonino, all seemed highly significant. Upon Tonino there seemed to converge a series of problems that the parents had been unable to resolve in their own lives. The mother, still young and attractive, came from a family in which religious observance was pushed to almost fanatical extremes. When she fell in love and decided to marry her present husband, she followed his example of refusing certain religious practices, whereupon her mother cursed her, saying that God would punish her: never would living children issue from her womb!

The first three years of her marriage were spent in increasing anxiety over this curse since, indeed, she did not become pregnant. After many unsuccessful attempts to receive specialist help, she eventually turned to Padre Pio, a famous wonder healer, and received from him a great consolation: "Go in peace," he told her, and children would soon come, like flowers in spring. The prediction turned out to be only too true: she had three sons, with only ten months between one birth and the next. After that much grace, the spouses agreed (albeit with a great sense of guilt on the wife's part) to use a birth-control method. But not even that worked: there ensued the totally unwanted conception of Tonino. With great embarrassment, the mother confessed that at first she had even felt the temptation to have an abortion. But eventually she resigned herself to her fate and hoped for the arrival of a baby girl. Who did arrive, however, but that ugly gosling, Tonino, the result of "grave sins" that logically demanded heavy "retributions." The father, himself homely, puny, and cross-eyed, stated that he saw in Tonino all those negative aspects that made his own life miserable. He came from a broken family in which he had never received any affection and thus not only grieved for having passed on to Tonino his own physical defects, but stated he felt a great need to protect and help him and to spare him his own suffering. On account of this he always agreed to whatever steps, regardless of cost, his wife would propose to "repair" Tonino.

At this juncture, then, the latest treatment program, orthodontics, was to be followed by yet another and far more dramatic one: psychiatry. It was for this reason that we decided to spare Tonino an additional humiliation and to treat only the parents. Our expectations were quite optimistic since the marital relationship seemed basically good. The parents appeared to respect each other, to be deeply concerned with Tonino's well-being, and sufficiently motivated to follow any prescriptions given them by the therapists. The opportunity for a decisive intervention came about after the third session. A few days before their next session the mother called in a state of great anxiety, informing us that she had taken Tonino to his orthoptic appointment and waited for him outside. After a while the ophthalmologist came out of the exercise room alone and asked her to follow her into another office. She told the mother that she was very worried about Tonino's mental state and that he probably needed psychiatric help. It turned out that Tonino had willingly sat down in front of the viewer into which she had introduced the slides that the child was supposed to describe. What he did see, however, was something totally different, and he insisted that this was what he really saw. Thus, on viewing the last slide, showing a St. Bernard, Tonino looked up at her and stated delightedly, "I see . . . a large flock of colorful birds."

When the parents came to their fourth session, the mother was asked to call the ophthalmologist to find out whether the orthoptic exercises were still indispensable. The answer was no, since the condition had remained unchanged for quite some time and did not seem to be amenable to further improvement. The therapists then decided to have the parents enter into a contract with Tonino which was to be solemnly signed by all three parties. This contract was a kind of barter. The parents were to take Tonino aside and tell him in all frankness that they were fully aware how thoroughly fed up he was with treatments and specialists. They were also aware of the fact that he was now grown up and about to become a man. For this reason they had decided to cancel the appointment with the orthodontist; after all, it was not important for a male to have teeth as regular and perfect as those of the young ladies in toothpaste commercials. They were also willing to replace the special eye glasses with normal ones and to terminate the sessions with the eye doctor. All this, however, was on condition that Tonino would recognize himself that he was now grown up and that he would once and for all agree not to soil himself anymore. If he accepted these conditions, the contract was to be drawn up by the father and signed by all three of them.

We were told that Tonino did not hesitate for a moment; he immediately accepted the conditions and signed the document with his full signature, i.e., his two Christian names *and* his last name. The contract became valid at once and produced the expected results: the encopresis stopped immediately.

In the following session, and in addition to the terms of the contract, it was agreed that the father would initiate a sports program that was within Tonino's physical capabilities and from which his brothers were to be rigorously excluded. It was also considered necessary for the parents to inform the teacher of these decisions and of their purpose, hoping that Tonino would thus gradually also abandon his exhibitions at school.

Treatment was terminated after the seventh session and it was agreed that the parents would call us in three months. This they did punctually, informing us that everything was going well. Tonino was very proud to have joined a group of hikers who were training for a mountain camp. This telephone conversation served as our follow-up. If the parents had told us that things were not going well, we would then have taken the entire family into treatment, as the absence of progress would have indicated that we were indeed faced with a more complex and rigid problem than we had originally assumed.

A FUNERAL RITE FOR AN ANORECTIC GIRL

A young married couple requested help for their daughter, Marella, who was two years and two months old and had been suffering from anorexia for the last six months. The call to us was made by the mother who sounded anxious but controlled. In this very first contact, she already linked Marella's anorexia with the birth of a baby brother whom Marella had not yet seen. The reason for this was that he had remained in the hospital with a septicemia, contracted four days after his birth, which left him severely brain-damaged. Now, seven months later, he was still alive, but there was no hope for his survival. "For

Marella he is only a sort of phantom"; this was how the mother literally described the situation. Her request for help was due to a sudden worsening of Marella's eating problem. For the last two weeks, she had been on a veritable hunger strike, accepting only very small quantities of baby food and even those few spoonfuls only from persons other than her parents.

In the first session with the parents, their relationship pattern soon became evident: they maintained a complementary relationship in which the husband, whom we shall call Edoardo, clearly occupied the superior position. He was thirty years old, good-looking, dressed with casual elegance, and came from a wealthy family of local patricians, a large clan comprising four generations, complexly interrelated and headed by a centenarian grandmother. He worked with great indifference in one of the family's several business enterprises, but otherwise devoted every free moment to electronic music, his exclusive passion. He spent entire days in his music room, recording and composing, neglecting all social relations and talking very little. He came on as the "artist," with his head always in the clouds, thus signaling that he was not available for any request, especially not for a practical one.

The wife, whom we shall call Lucia, was extremely graceful and dressed with refined taste. She was emotional and vivacious and tried very cautiously but unsuccessfully to obtain from her husband some appropriate recognition of, and reaction to, her feelings. She came from a middle-class family, and it appeared that Edoardo married her more or less out of gratitude for having cured him of impotence. It was quite evident that Lucia tried very hard to adapt herself to the style of the husband's "great" family and to be accepted by them as a full member in her own right, but it also seemed that these efforts were rather unsuccessful.

Lucia was an only child and her parents' marriage was marred by a long neurological infirmity of her father. From adolescence on, Lucia seemed to have assumed the role of "somebody who thinks of everybody else and asks nothing for herself," who was efficient and always there when needed. She never failed to help her mother who came to depend heavily on her and demanded that she assume certain functions as head of the family. In keeping with this role, Lucia also obtained a diploma as a Red Cross nurse.

She had continued to perform this role as a member of the husband's large clan. It was she who came running when a need arose, who patiently listened to and cheered up the old melancholy aunts, who kept reins on the servants staffing the family's large country estate where everybody got together during the summer months. All of this was very convenient for everybody, including the husband, but it did not seem to confer upon Lucia any sign of distinction. From some indications that emerged in the first session, it appeared that the noble family referred to her at best as "our dear Lucia." In this system of rigid complementarity, Lucia's increasingly frantic attempts to gain the desired recognition only served to reinforce in the members of the clan that very attitude of seignorial condescension that she wanted to change.

Her husband's relationship to her was not very different from that of the extended family. He was certainly not rude, quite the opposite—but he treated her with that slightly annoyed and condescending or amused mien that a grandseignior would put on when disturbed in his elevated thoughts by the petty preoccupations of his butler.

As a result of this interaction, Lucia had turned all her attention to Marella, employing her usual style of omnipresent helper. The father, on the other hand, respected the little girl as being the mother's exclusive territory. It turned out that Marella had developed the habit of calling him in the shrillest of voices even when he was silently sitting next to her—it seemed that difficult to attract his attention.

The birth of the brain-damaged baby had upset this precarious balance. Marella had been separated from her mother for many days, which were spent at her maternal grandmother's, and after the mother returned, Marella saw her disappear every afternoon to spend several hours at the hospital. What was amazing, but at the same time perfectly in keeping with Lucia's role, was that in order to protect Marella she had decided not to tell her about the baby brother's birth, let alone to let her see him. She therefore explained to Marella that she went to the hospital to look after the child of a poor friend. "Since Matteo will not live," she said, "there is no need to complicate Marella's life." As far as the members of the clan were concerned, they had almost ignored Lucia's misfortune and after a few telephone calls had shown no further interest in it. Edoardo was certainly upset but could not, or did not want to, show his feelings to his wife.

The sudden worsening of Marella's anorexia, which had seriously reduced her weight, coincided with the family's return from a vacation with the clan. There was reason to assume that this visit had left Lucia exasperated, but she did not dare to say so. In the next session she expressed only her suffering in connection with her husband, who left every burden and every decision to her. The girl refused all food from the parents. It became necessary to take her for every meal to the "little restaurant," i.e. the apartment of the maternal grandmother who managed to make her swallow a few spoonfuls of mush.

During the three sessions following the initial interview, the therapists showed little interest in the girl's plight and cautiously tried to focus their attention on the marital relationship. The spouses, however, appeared extremely defensive and very adept at changing the subject as soon as sensitive arguments were touched upon. The decisive moment occurred in the fifth session. The spouses reported that Matteo had died a few days ago and had been buried in the family tomb. The mother, therefore, did not go to the hospital anymore, but Marella, whom the mother had again decided to leave in the dark, was eating even less. This time the father also seemed worried. It was obvious to us that the child, with her unusual sensitivity and intelligence, had understood a great deal from the very beginning. Her determination not to eat was now reinforced by this further conspiracy of silence.

We therefore decided to have the parents tell Marella the truth. But mere words would have obviously been insufficient. What was needed was a dramatization, a rite involving all three family members and designed to convey to Marella, who was only at the beginning of the verbal phase of her development, a clear and unequivocal message. Such a rite, it seemed to us, was also indispensable, in view of the father's emotional distance, for the purpose of involving him in a dramatic, emotional experience consistent with that of his wife and daughter. We therefore prescribed that on the following day the official exequies for the deceased child would take place in the garden of their house: Papa had to explain to Marella in simple terms everything that had taken place. He had to explain the reasons for the pitiful lie, tell her that she had indeed had a little brother by the name of Matteo and that he had been the very ill baby that mama used to help in the hospital. Now her baby brother was dead; he was no longer there but was buried in the family tomb at the cemetery. But it was important to bury also his clothes, because Matteo was dead and did not need them anymore. The parents agreed to carry out this ritual.[4]

They went into the garden, where Papa dug a fairly deep hole into which, one after the other, Mama slowly laid the baby's clothes. Marella herself took a pair of little shoes and gently placed it on top of them. The parents were quite moved, as if it were a real funeral. Finally Papa took the shovel again, filled the hole, and planted a tree on top of it.

That same afternoon Marella was found playing in her room chewing with great appetite a large piece of bread which she had fetched from the kitchen. Since the phantom was not there anymore, there was no longer any need to compete with it by means of eating "mush." On the following day, Marella not only ate normally but showed further signs of great improvement. She stopped being whiny and clinging to her mother's skirts but for many days kept talking almost obsessively about her little brother, as if to reassure herself that it was finally possible to talk about him and to receive an answer. One day she asked her mother why she had never told her that the baby at the hospital was Matteo. When the mother said, "Because he was never here at home and would never have come," Marella exclaimed, "But he *was* here, in that big tummy of yours," leaving the mother speechless.

In spite of the confidence the spouses gained through this rapid success (five sessions), they signaled in various indirect ways that they were not willing, for the time being, to deal with the core problem of their marriage and their relationship with the extended family.

After discussing this in a staff meeting, the team decided to respect their resistance. Our experience has indeed taught us that these joint resistances are insurmountable. Any attempt to meet them head on leads to negative results. One thus has to be modest and content with the successes achieved over the presenting complaint. Moreover, in this particular case, we were convinced that by respecting their reluctance we would strengthen their rapport with the therapists and this, of course, was an indispensable condition for any further course of treatment.

The couple indeed came to see us again six months later. Marella had continued to do very well, and the wall of silence was broken. In this session, it was decided to have the wife meet with one of the co-therapists for some individual sessions to overcome the difficulties of her relationship with her husband's family.

DISCUSSION

The problem of deciding at what point to suspend or terminate treatment is specifically examined by our team in every single case. We have often wondered if it is indeed right and honest to terminate therapy shortly after the

---

[4]Family rituals of this kind are among the most important and effective therapeutic techniques that we devised in the course of our research into rapid and decisive intervention with dysfunctional families. We have presented their rationale in detail in another publication (3).

disappearance of the identified patient's symptom. Have we perhaps worsened the situation? Have we perhaps deprived the family group of the indicator of its dysfunction? At this juncture we can only say that therapeutic
interventions in family therapy do not merely affect one individual, but the
system as a whole: the disappearance of the symptom is always the expression
of a certain change in the family's modes of interaction. It is, of course, possible
that this change may be insufficient to guarantee further improvement. If so, it
is up to the team to take this possibility into account and to make allowance
for it. In the above-mentioned case, we decided to respect the couple's resistance and in doing so to convey to the spouses an implicit message intended to
strengthen their feelings of trust, freedom, and spontaneity toward us. In other
cases, we prefer to have the spouses call us or to come to a session at an
appointed date within a few months. By means of this expedient we maintain
the family "in therapy" and implicitly assure them of our continued interest
and availability.

As far as the technique of our approach is concerned, it should be pointed
out that it is not based on the use of interpretations. While our experience may
permit us to infer the past causes of a family's present behavior, we do not
verbalize this, just as we do not point out to the family members what we see
going on in the interviews or what their patterns of interaction are. We keep
these observations to ourselves and utilize them in the design of our therapeutic interventions. As should be evident from the above-mentioned examples,
our interventions are of an active-prescriptive nature and through them we set
out to change the interaction of the family as a whole. Obviously, they vary
from one family to the next. But how do we go about changing these patterns?

In the course of our research we have discovered a kind of intervention that
offers more than encouraging results, and we have provisionally called this
intervention, to be applied very early in the course of treatment, the *positive
connotation*.[5] It consists of approving all observed behaviors of the identified
patient or the other family members, and especially those behaviors that are
traditionally considered pathological. For instance, in the cases described
above we praised the attitude of the parents as admirable expressions of
affection and concern. From sad experience we have learned that any criticism
directed at the parents (which, incidentally, is "culturally" expected and se-
cretly feared) can have no other effect than to produce indignant and negative
reactions or, worse, depressive maneuvers of the "we-have-completely-failed"
type, which then reduce the therapists to impotence.[6]

We do not consider this *positive connotation* a ploy or a trick. Quite the
contrary, its application is all the more our method of choice since the
acceptance of the systems model has enabled us to go beyond the causal-
moralistic bounds of traditional psychiatry. We therefore consider the observ-

---

[5]We are quite aware that from a systems theoretical point of view this term is incorrect. On the
other hand, conditioned as we are by the linear-linguistic model, "positive" helps to make
ourselves clear to others, at least until we hit upon a better name. In essence, the positive
connotation is nothing but a metacommunication (about the system) that has the property of a
confirmation.

[6]In this connection, we feel that the gist of Braulio Montalvo's and Jay Haley's article, "In Defense
of Child Therapy," (2) relates to this fundamental problem, i.e. how to avoid making the parents feel
that they are being accused.

able behavior of a family in therapy as self-corrective and thus tending to maintain the equilibrium of the system. A family who comes into therapy is usually a family in crisis, frightened by the possible loss of homeostasis and therefore anxious to maintain it at all cost. If we were to tell them explicitly that they must change, it would make them enter into a virtually monolithic coalition in order to ward us off. To be accepted into the family system, it is necessary for us to approve their behavior, no matter what it is, since it is directed at a more than understandable goal: the cohesion of the family. (Let us mention as an aside that none of our dysfunctional families has ever challenged this point of view.)

Through the *positive connotation* we implicitly declare ourselves as allies of the family's striving for homeostasis, and we do this at the moment that the family feels it is most threatened. By thus strengthening the homeostatic tendency, we gain influence over the ability to change that is inherent in every living system.

Homeostatic tendencies and the ability to undergo change are, indeed, essential characteristics of living systems. Neither of these two properties is in and of itself better or worse than the other; rather, the one cannot exist without the other. It is, therefore, not a question of "better or worse," but of "more or less."

Thus, it seems to us that the *positive connotation* is a therapeutic intervention of prime importance to bring about change in a family system. Change does not come about automatically, but rather as a result of a behavior prescription that is accepted and carried out (thereby triggering the desired change) precisely because, paradoxically, the therapists have aligned themselves with the homeostatic tendency. The therapeutic problem presented by each separate case is thus the design of a specific behavior prescription. Invariably, this prescription will be different for every family and will depend on its particular way of conceptualizing its problem.

REFERENCES

1. Beels, C. C., and Ferber, A., "Family Therapy: A View," *Fam. Proc.*, 8: 280–314, 1969.
2. Montalvo, B., and Haley, J., "In Defense of Child Therapy," *Fam. Proc.*, 12: 227–44, 1973.
3. Palazzoli, M. S., *Self-Starvation—From the Intrapsychic to the Transpersonal Approach to Anorexia Nervosa*, London, Chaucer Pub. Co., 1974.
4. Palazzoli, M. S., Boscolo, L., Cecchin, G. F., Prata, G., *Paradosso e Contro-Paradosso. Per un Nuovo Modello Concettuale e Metodologico nella Terapia della Famiglia a Transazione Schizofrenica*, Milano, Feltrinelli, 1975.
5. Watzlawick, P., Weakland, J. H., and Fisch, R., *Change*, New York, W. W. Norton & Co., 1974.

5

Extending the Scope
of Family Therapy

One of the early and still cogent criticisms of individual therapy was that individuals were treated as if they lived in a social vacuum. Disorders were located within the person, and certain deficits, varying with the theory adopted by the clinician, were postulated to account for the pathology. In a similar manner, family therapy has been open to the charge that the family is treated as if it, too, exists in a social vacuum. Although the locale has been shifted to the broader unit of the family, over a period of time this step may prove as artificial as purely individual approaches to pathology and therapy. Thus, we see the primary tasks of family therapy in the 1980s are to move from the family itself into the social context of the family and to develop modes of intervention that relate to individual, elementary family, and context variables.

In the first edition of this book, we described three distinct stages in the development of family therapy. In the first stage, the study of so-called "pathogenic" families was of central importance. That is, before therapeutic procedures could be readily undertaken, it was first necessary to delineate specific types of pathology within families that could be taken as targets for therapy. Many of the studies in the 1950s were centered on the problem of dealing with the family that was maintaining a schizophrenic member. Thus, Theodore Lidz and his group (1957) produced several works on the family environment of the schizophrenic; Murray Bowen's family project examined hospitalized families (1960); and Gregory Bateson and his colleagues (1956) discussed his concept of the double bind as a necessary but not sufficient precondition for schizophrenia. The second stage in the development of the field was devoted to the development of particular diagnostic and therapeutic techniques of working with families. Parts III and IV of this text are largely concerned with current contributions in this area.

We referred in the first edition to the third phase of development as one of consolidation—that is, the addition of family therapy as a mode of treatment to the general armamentarium of mental health professionals and its extensive inclusion in actual practice.

We now posit a fourth phase of development—namely, the extension of the scope of family therapy to the social context and environment in which the elementary family exists. We do not view this movement from analysis and intervention to the social context of the family as being complementary to or competitive with intra-family therapy. Rather, we view this extension of scope as a new and significant period of development.

The movement beyond the boundaries of the elementary family, although not necessarily inevitable, is readily understandable. Several reasons can be offered. First, the rediscovery of the extended family in modern life during the 1950s and 1960s has led to the inclusion of kinship relationships in family therapy. Second, the developing philosophy of community care in mental health services has forced a reexamination of the meaning of "community." Now community very often refers to immediate family, friends, and the extended kin of an identified patient. Third, current notions of the necessity of providing preventive services have stimulated thought and research in defining support systems and informal patterns of caregiving. Finally, the social changes noted in the previous section have left many people in exposed positions, outside the shelter of any but the most slender and tenuous family structures. Thus, we would maintain that a family orientation must include elements of the social context. The state of the art of defining the appropriate "elements" is reflected throughout the section.

We have included in this section two papers that we view as classics in the field: William Bolman's paper on "Preventive Psychiatry for the Family" and Edgar Auerswald's careful description of an ecological approach. Bolman takes a population-based approach, Auerswald a single-case approach. Together they constitute both a description of and an argument for the desirability of conceptualizing families as members of populations affected by particular constellations of social forces and organizational arrangements.

John E. Bell has been identified with family therapy as a leader since his first paper in 1953. His recent contribution on family-context therapy outlines the directions of his thought and practice over three decades. The reader may gauge the degree of depth of the change that has occurred in family practice over the years by comparing and contrasting Bell's first paper (also the first paper in this text) with his most recent work.

Currently, the most adequate and concrete means of analyzing the immediate social environment is through social-network analysis. Gerald Erickson's paper provides an overview of the concept of network and practice, and Diane Pancoast applies a type of network therapy in detailing her method of strengthening the ties that natural caregivers have with the families with whom they interact. Erickson deals with specific clinical applications of the network concept, whereas Pancoast concerns herself with a more comprehensive network approach. In order to explicate this further, it appears that there are two vantage points for perceiving and conceptualizing social networks. The first is to anchor one's observations on an individual (or couple or family) and then move outward to account for the numbers, compositions, and configurations of people in the client's *personal network*. The second is to examine a number of personal networks and then identify those forms of connectedness that emerge from the analysis. Differing forms of intervention follow from each perspective. For example, with respect to the personal network, Erickson mentions a number of practice forms (such as the network as a curative grouping) that are based essentially on a prior identification of a demand for service (a person or family needs help). With a total-network approach, however, a view may be adopted based not on those who need assistance but on those who give assistance (natural helpers).

There seems little doubt that a general social antecedent of the many pathways that lead a patient to social and mental health agencies is the truncated personal network (Ebringer & Christie-Brown, 1980; Erickson, 1976; Hawkes, 1975; Pattison et al., 1975; Tolsdorf, 1976). That is, the client's personal universe contains few, if any, effective members who are both available at a time of crisis and inclined to be helpful. A network perspective helps place the person or family in a larger context that can be measured and described. These measurements and descriptions are often accounts of the complex ways in which families cope with loose, lost, broken, or conflicted ties to others. It remains to be seen during the 1980s how family practitioners will address themselves to the broader social context of family "troubles."

We believe that the variety of methods, techniques, and schools of thought described in this text and elsewhere define the current state of family therapy. As efforts toward outcome evaluation and theoretical validation proceed, some positions will be abandoned and new methodologies will be developed. Yet it is difficult to imagine that family therapy will ever be anything if not a large and growing set of concepts linking person to family to immediate social environment, with prescriptions for contextual change.

REFERENCES

Bateson, G., Jackson, D. D., Haley, J., & Weakland, J. H. Toward a theory of schizophrenia. *Behavioral Science*, 1956, *1*, 251–264.

Bowen, M. A family concept of schizophrenia. In D. D. Jackson (Ed.), *The etiology of schizophrenia*. New York: Basic Books, 1960.

Ebringer, L., & Christie-Brown, J.R.W. Social deprivation amongst short stay psychiatric patients. *British Journal of Psychiatry*, 1980, *136*, 46–82.

Erickson, G. D. *Personal networks and mental illness*. D. Phil. Dissertation (unpublished), University of York (U.K.), 1976.

Hawkes, D. Community care: An analysis of assumptions. *British Journal of Psychiatry*, 1975, *127*, 276–285.

Lidz, T., Cornelison, A., Fleck, S., & Terry, D. The intrafamilial environment of the schizophrenic patient: I. The father. *Psychiatry*, 1957, *20*, 329–342.

Pattison, E., DeFrancisco, D., Wood, P., Frazier, H., & Crowder, J. A psychosocial kinship model for family therapy. *American Journal of Psychiatry*, 1975, *132*, 12, 1246–1250.

Tolsdorf, C. Social networks, support, and coping: An explanatory study. *Family Process*, 1976, *15* (4), 407–417.

Preventive Psychiatry for the Family: Theory, Approaches, and Programs

William M. Bolman

In the planning of preventive psychiatric programs, the family is the most strategic social unit toward which services should be oriented. Although this has long been recognized as a truism, it has been more a platitude than a scientific statement. However, this position is changing rapidly due to the development of useful theory and an expansion of clinical research and therapy which views the family as a basic functional unit.

This paper presents an effort to pull together some of this theory and the derivative family-oriented preventive programs that emerged during the course of my two years' work as staff person for the prevention subcommittee of the State of Wisconsin's Comprehensive Mental Health and Mental Retardation Program Development Committee. The prevention subcommittee was charged with the task of assessing the current status of prevention and developing a concrete, useful framework of preventive programs. Two early results of this work have recently been published, one a general overview (14), and the other an outline of preventive programs oriented toward children (11).

These papers, however, did not connect theory, general programmatic approaches, and specific programs. It is hoped the present paper begins to bridge these gaps. Because of extreme condensation, it is hoped that the references will serve in place of an extended discussion.

THEORETICAL FRAMEWORK

It was apparent early in our work that one of the obstacles to a systematic approach to preventive planning was the lack of a sufficiently comprehensive theory. Our theoretical requirements were twofold; the primary need was for an applied theory, although the need for a basic framework, capable of integrating the multilevel variables (molecular through large population) under consideration, was of nearly equal importance. These two needs were sig-

Reprinted from the *American Journal of Psychiatry*, Vol. 125, pp. 458–472, 1968. Copyright 1968, the American Psychiatric Association. Reproduced by permission.

nificantly helped by combining the public health approach developed by Gerald Caplan and the systems theory of James G. Miller.

Caplan's work provided an extremely useful and comprehensive view of the range of biopsychosocial forces in the community that affect the health of its members, as well as a discussion of techniques for altering these forces. In our planning for family programs, the concepts of crisis intervention, consultation, and community organization were especially important (22). The view of the community as a central unit for analysis, which has proved so fruitful in the development of community mental health programs in general, is central to preventive psychiatric planning. A recent paper on the theoretical and empirical bases of the community mental health approach (13) and a practical outline of the kinds of data useful in community planning (64) proved helpful to the committee.

The underlying theoretical framework that helped to clarify the multiple levels in the community implied by the term "biopsychosocial" has been Miller's analysis of living systems (60, 61, 62). Recent applications of a "systems" approach to psychiatry that we used included the following references: (2, 12, 30).

Finally, because our focus was on the family group, it proved helpful to select a way of viewing the family as a functional unit in its social environment. Because of its fit with the other theories, we found the approach of Hill (45) particularly applicable for preventive planning. Following his lead, we viewed the family unit as subject to a variety of stresses apt to impair its structure and function. These stresses include:

1. Loss of a family member (death, desertion, chronic illness).
2. Acquisition of a defective or stigmatized member (congenital defect, illness, or perhaps even an adoptive member).
3. Acquisition of excess members (number of children exceeding the adaptive resources of the parents).
4. Excessive environmental pressures or handicaps (severe poverty, community disorganization, racial discrimination).
5. Disordered relationships and patterns of communication (pseudo-mutuality, double bind, various types of marital schisms).
6. Severely limited coping or adaptive capacity (insufficient income, schooling, or other social-personality handicaps).
7. Normal developmental stages or crises that surpass a family's adaptive capacity (birth of a child, school entrance, adolescence, climacteric, retirement).

In sum, our theoretical framework views the family as a uniquely flexible, primary social organization, an open system subject to stress or crisis from its environment depending upon the nature of the event, how it is perceived, and the resources available for adaptation or coping versus defense or construction. This environment includes the total range of forces from biologic (e.g., illness) to intrapsychic (e.g., neurosis) to interpersonal (e.g., disorder in intrafamily communication) to sociologic and community levels (e.g., poverty and community disorganization). At the present state of knowledge, each of these levels of description tends to have its own theory, concepts, and approaches according to the discipline. The following sections will draw upon this knowledge where appropriate.

GENERAL PROGRAMMATIC CONSIDERATIONS

Before we could outline specific programs it was necessary to look at some intermediate considerations that applied to program planning in general. We felt it was essential to specify as clearly as possible the who, where, when, and how aspects of programming, even though their application in the community did not always follow such divisions. Therefore, we attempted to specify the class or type of family toward whom the service is directed (the target population), the intended goal of the service, how delivered, by what types of helping persons and patterns of care, and at what point in the family life cycle and the course of disorder preventive intervention is aimed. Toward this end we mostly followed public health terminology.

First, prevention is characterized as primary, secondary, or tertiary, depending upon the point in the course of disorder at which a given program is aimed. Primary prevention attempts to prevent a disorder from occurring, secondary prevention attempts to diagnose and treat at the earliest possible point so as to reduce the length or severity of the disorder, and tertiary prevention attempts to minimize the handicap or chronicity of the disorder. From the standpoint of the community, these distinctions are equivalent to reducing the incidence, prevalence, or extent of disability, respectively.

In family-oriented programs, the distinctions between the three types of preventive intervention will vary depending upon the family member involved. For example, a program in a prenatal clinic which has the goal of identifying and providing services for those mothers who are likely to have trouble with the product of their pregnancy on a variety of medical, psychiatric, or social levels could be categorized as primary prevention for the child and secondary or tertiary prevention for the mother or father. We have set aside the complex issues of health promotion and positive mental health on the basis of both theoretical and practical objections at the present time.

Second, the type of approach used may be classified as community-wide, milestone, or high-risk (10). *Community-wide* approaches, as implied by their name, are those that affect all members of the community. Some are individually oriented and others are mental health analogues of long-established public health approaches. Examples might include swamp drainage in a malarial area (community development in a disorganized slum community) or supervision and control of food and water supplies (attention to the provision of quality police, housing, job, education, health and welfare supplies). In general, this type of approach involves the state of organization or disorganization in a community that affects families both via the quality of the environment and the network of family supportive services.

Milestone approaches are those oriented toward members of the community as they encounter those nodal or focal points of life which are common to most members in the community. Examples include birth, school attendance, marriage, and retirement. From a primary prevention viewpoint, the set of socially institutionalized contacts involved in prenatal, natal, and postnatal care are especially important, while from a secondary prevention standpoint, attendance at school is most salient.

High-risk approaches are those oriented toward families who have been shown by clinical or epidemiologic studies to have a greater likelihood of disorder. The latter type of study has received a great deal of attention in psychiatry in recent years, and the studies in Nova Scotia, midtown Manhattan, New Haven, and other areas have contributed greatly to the identification of high-risk groups.

There are several general program principles that must be mentioned regarding high-risk groups; we found them so important that they require some detail in presentation. These principles stem from the characteristics of the target population, particularly those of income, educational level, place of residence, and other components of social class. We found it to be virtually axiomatic that the social class of the target population not only affects what is needed but also the types of approach. For example, we have not included as a high-risk group those middle-class suburban adolescents suffering from the twin deprivations of affluence and limited opportunities to interact meaningfully with members of other races and social classes (even though these should probably be sources of social concern), because it was not clear that such deprivation predisposed to mental disorder other than degrees of ego restriction or prejudice.

On the other hand, we have included programs that attempt to provide cognitive enrichment for low-income groups because of the very great handicap this lack imposes upon a family's adaptive resources. Occasionally, we have included middle-class oriented programs such as educational discussions on child raising because it looked as though this type of program is wanted and useful and also because it helped clarify the vast differences in programming between these approaches and those for other socioeconomic groups.

An especially important part of the high-risk group is that part of the population which is described by the poverty profile. They are more apt than not to be poor, underemployed, undereducated, under 16 or over 65, of a minority group, and having a different life style. In addition, they are more likely to have come in contact with the community's police and welfare functions and are apt both to view and be viewed by the community in stereotyped ways. The net result is the existence of a sizeable social and communicative distance that requires specific attention when planning high-risk family-oriented programs. The urgency of this need has been called attention to in a number of places. Specifically, Orshansky estimates that as many as 20 percent of all children in the nation live in families in this sector of the population (68). Because of its importance, this group must receive particular attention in planning programs.

A first principle in high-risk programming is that services must conform to the needs and life style of the target group if they are to be effective. A humorous yet excellent example of this principle is one related by George James when he was health commissioner of New York City (47). A program for the early detection of cervical carcinoma (secondary prevention) was set up in a Manhattan hospital and well publicized. The population that responded was the lowest risk group, namely middle-class Jewish women. In order to bring the services closer to the high-risk Negro women, the program was moved to Harlem. As Dr. James relates it, the major effect was that the Jewish women complained of the increased cost in time and carfare!

Due to the obvious lack of congruence, the service was changed so as to conform more closely with the life style of the target population. It was decided that the best way to reach the greatest number of Negro women in Harlem was to link the preventive program to the group of services associated with the milestone events of pregnancy and delivery, i.e., to do a routine check for cervical carcinoma during the course of prenatal care. With this change, the program began to show significant results. This type of thinking has led to a great number of imaginative and effective ways of reaching high-risk groups with both medical and mental health services. Two professional groups that have a great deal of experience and knowledge in this area are the public health educators and public health nurses; psychiatrists involved in planning family-oriented programs will find that much time can be saved and mistakes avoided by seeking out such consultation.

Another principle that is related to the need for congruence or fit just described is best characterized by the term "outreach approaches." Because of the social distance between the target population and mental health professionals, needy groups do not, as a rule, seek services if indeed they even define the need as servable. This quality requires the psychiatrists and others to develop programs that reach out to those individuals and families of greatest risk. One innovation that is especially worthwhile is the use of "bridging persons." These may be residents of the area, members of the same minority groups, people with the same difficulties, etc. An application that has particularly great promise for urban slum areas is the neighborhood service center (63, pp. 89–92; 72; 77). This is usually a store-front operation offering a range of services such as job advice; health, mental health, and legal assistance; and also serving as a catalyst and support for efforts designed to improve the quality of biopsychosocial supplies in the community, i.e., community organization and social action programs.

A final principle in high-risk planning is the easy-to-state but difficult-to-achieve requirement for effective coordination and continuity of care between the multiple groups, agencies, and programs (local, state, and federal) that are attempting to offer service to multiple-problem families. There are forces in every community that act against effective coordination, even with the best administrative structure and interagency relationships. Among other obstacles, it is worthy of special note that those products and services being dispensed by a community (the biopsychosocial network of educational, police, welfare, health services, etc.) do not lend themselves as readily to the type of evaluation that, say, economic services do. As a result, choices and priorities of service inevitably tend toward agency-based goals versus interagency or community goals in the face of the usual limitations of finances and manpower.

Thus, the most commonly desired services are those which are short-range with high visibility, such as clinical and rehabilitative services, versus the longer-range and lower visibility preventive services. In these highly complicated matters, it is probably essential for psychiatric planners to join forces with other professionals struggling with similar problems, for example the groups of public health, sociologic, economic, and other specialists who are working in the field of health care. The community mental health center concept is certainly a needed development, but it too is unable to achieve optimal coordination, and supplementary mechanisms are required.

Although answers are not clear, there are some promising developments for improved coordination, such as the neighborhood service center mentioned earlier, the Ombudsman (35), the expansion of preventive law programs (19), and other mechanisms through which needy individuals and groups are better enabled to receive community services to which they are entitled. In some instances community development or organization approaches are in order, and in others, especially big city slums, social action approaches are necessary. The success and problems of some of the Office of Economic Opportunity patterns of service, such as New Haven's Community Progress, Inc., will be particularly valuable to follow. It has already led to some unique and stimulating developments in psychiatry, as recently discussed by Solnit (82). Similarly, the Model Cities concept being developed by the U. S. Department of Housing and Urban Development should be highly productive.

In summary, there are a number of general principles of approach and strategy relating the theoretical bases and specific preventive programs for families. Those discussed in this section are largely related to public health psychiatric theory, since this paper is slanted toward the applied side of the coin. Regarding approach, preventive programs may be primary, secondary, or tertiary in relation to the disorder, and may be community-wide, milestone, or high-risk in relation to the community.

Regarding strategy, there are three especially important principles: 1) achieving a satisfactory fit between what is needed and what is offered, considering the total range of biopsychosocial needs from food and housing to psychotherapy; 2) outreach approaches utilizing all possible key people and groups, whether professional or nonprofessional; 3) sophisticated attention to the community network of supplies so as to assure equal access for needy groups and adequate coordination and continuity among the service facilities. At all stages community involvement and sanction are essential.

SPECIFIC PROGRAMS

We have divided the specific programs into several groups to illustrate some differing patterns of fitting preventive services into community practices.

Group 1

A logical point to initiate family-oriented prevention is around the milestone events of pregnancy and childbirth. There are three major goals of such programs. The first is to ensure that each child is born with all faculties intact and that the mother is provided usable opportunities to facilitate its achievement. The major vehicle is that of adequate prenatal care and birth in a hospital. Although there is a solid body of knowledge about the medical requirements for such care, unfortunately the variables that now influence adequate care are less those of knowledge than they are those of income, social class, residence and skin color (46). This is, of course, simply one instance of the broad association between poverty, low social class, nonsuburban residence, and nonwhite skin color and a variety of biopsychosocial disorders. However, it does not mean that the only way of changing the patterns of care is massive social change, as some have felt. Such changes are by and large evolutionary and do not lend themselves to inclusion in preventive planning.

Instead, a number of specific manageable approaches are available. These fall into two overlapping categories—those which influence the provision of service and those which influence the population needing service. The former received a powerful stimulus from the 1963 maternal and infant care projects directed by the Children's Bureau, and have resulted in a variety of new or extended services (27). The latter—approaches which influence pregnant women who fail to use available services—have received a great deal of stimulus as a result of the experiences of outreach programs directed toward the so-called "hard-to-reach groups." It seems clear that these groups are more accurately termed "hard-to-serve," in recognition of the fact that they are reachable but their multiple needs are difficult to meet.

A second major family oriented goal that may be achieved in conjunction with the milestones of pregnancy, delivery, and aftercare services is that of family planning. The aim here is simply to enable each family to regulate its own size by preventing the addition of new members beyond its capacity to raise. The stress on a family of having more members than it can care for has been extensively documented, and the development of birth control advice and services is becoming an integral part of obstetrical units, public health nursing care, and social service agencies. Action programs directed toward the low-income groups who have the highest number of unwanted children uniformly find that family planning services are well and responsibly used. However, their development is so recent that at most only one-third of needy families are currently being served. Reports of these trends and the fairly current status of family planning activities are available in three recent publications (29, 56, 73).

The third group of preventive services that can be programmed around the patterns of care for pregnancy and delivery is the detection of qualities or defects in mothers and children which are apt to lead to difficulty without specific support. The most obvious are events such as the birth of a defective child (congenital abnormality, brain damage, mental retardation, etc.), but even prematurity may constitute a crisis for some families (23). In addition, our knowledge of the opportunities presented by the normal developmental tasks of pregnancy has led Bibring (7) and Caplan (21) to programs which offer service to this group. Some of this rich variety of possible programs are summarized in table 1. In this, as in subsequent tables, we have attempted to specify the target population, the intended goals, the basic program characteristics, and some specific examples.

TABLE 1. Approaches to Providing for Family Health Care Needs through Community Facilities

Target Population	Goals	General Approach	Specific Examples
1) Pregnant women in low-income, high-risk groups.	Provision of adequate prenatal care for these mothers, who have a much higher incidence of prematurity, pregnancy wastage, brain-damage.	Primary preventive high-risk approaches for the child, secondary and tertiary for the mother.	Provision of comprehensive care during pregnancy, delivery, and into the inter-conceptional period by local and state health department facilities developed in the target area (58, 59).

TABLE 1. (Continued)

Target Population	Goals	General Approach	Specific Examples
2) Families under stress due to more children than their financial and emotional resources can manage.	Provision of family planning services for all families so as to correct current patterns favoring upper-income groups.	Primary preventive community-wide and high-risk approaches.	A wide variety of voluntary private and public programs under many auspices, either as a separate program or a part of other services (29, 56, 73).
3) Families with a child requiring special care (congenital abnormality, brain damage, retardation, prematurity, physical defect, blindness, etc.).	Provision of comprehensive care for child and education and support for family to assist in coping with the stress of a handicapped member.	Primary preventive for normal members including siblings, tertiary preventive for child. Community-wide approaches.	Family pediatric clinic (55); parent education and guidance by a "family" of therapists (37); teen-age discussion groups of sibs of retarded (79); supportive guidance for parents of premature infant (23).
4) Individuals with familial or inheritable disorders.	Systematic identification of affected families and provision of accurate information and services.	Primary preventive community-wide approaches.	Public health nurses obtain family pedigrees from those in their caseload with congenital or chronic disorders; degree of risk interpreted by a specialist and a report is sent to family physician; genetic counseling provided as desired (48).
5) Pregnant women generally.	Awareness of the normal developmental crisis of pregnancy, and provision of supportive services for those under stress or with indications of later difficulty.	Primary preventive for child, secondary preventive for mother. Milestone and high-risk.	Prenatal clinics and obstetrical services using nurses or mental health specialists in individual or group meetings (7, 21).

Group 2

This group of approaches derives from the view of the family as an open system existing in a relative equilibrium or steady state. Disruptions of this state may arise either from within or without the family and may be characterized as "stress" or "crisis." Stress, together with its relationship to illness and disorder, has been extensively studied and is a valuable concept for viewing a family's patterns of coping and for planning preventive intervention. A good definition is: "A stress may be any influence, whether it arises from the internal environment or the external environment, which interferes with the satisfaction of basic needs or which disturbs or threatens to disturb the stable equilibrium" (32).

The related concept of crisis has a slightly different focus. Caplan defined it as a time-limited period of disequilibrium which is precipitated by a psychological task to which the person is temporarily unable to respond adequately. During this period of tension, the person grapples with the problem and develops novel resources (either constructive or destructive), both by calling upon internal resources and by making use of the help of others. These new resources are then used to handle the precipitating factor, and the person achieves once more a steady state (22). Hence, crisis refers more to that class of stressor which is an acute or novel event whose occurrence cannot be handled by the family's ordinary repertory of coping techniques. In the state of disequilibrium associated with a crisis, it is thought that families or individuals are more apt to be accessible to assistance and change if provided with help. If this proves to be generally so, it will be of enormous value for planning services, allocating resources, and helping otherwise hard-to-serve groups.

Regarding planning, this group of programs cannot as easily be fitted into some type of normal milestone event as those in the first group. Instead, it looks to us as though the major systematic way for these stress and crisis disorders to be identified is their inclusion in the curricula of the relevant professions. This would include the various schools of law, medicine, religion, nursing, social work, clinical psychology, etc. Although this is being done in a rapidly growing number of professional schools, there is still far to go.

An excellent example of one organization's multiprofessional approach to the challenges of recognizing and meeting crises and stresses is a case example from the Mobilization for Youth group in New York City (74). In this case, the initial request for service involved a mother's complaint that the tenement she

TABLE 2. Approaches to Providing for Family Mental Health and Psychosocial Needs through Community Facilities

Target Population	Goals	General Approach	Specific Examples
1) Families in crisis due to the loss of a member (death, desertion, chronic hospitalization).	Provision of flexible support according to the event, how perceived and managed, and the resources and the life style of the surviving family fragment.	Primary and secondary preventive, high-risk and community-wide approaches.	Group meetings in hospital of parents of fatally ill children (40); expanded emergency room coverage (4, 88); neighborhood information centers (49); walk-in clinics for problems of living (83); some mental health clinics (51).
2) Families under stress due to a handicapped parent (mental illness, retardation, alcoholism, or other chronic disorder).	Identification and support as needed for these families as in 1) above.	Primary and secondary preventive, high-risk approaches for children: tertiary preventive, community-wide approaches for parents.	Public health nurse makes regular home visits to family of alcoholic (60); family medical clinics (5, 18); mental hospital based services (42, 57, 78); homemaker services for mentally ill mothers (66).

TABLE 2. (Continued)

Target Population	Goals	General Approach	Specific Examples
3) Families under stress due to internal imbalance or disorder (schism, double bind, skew, pseudo mutuality and other types of marital discord).	Assistance either in correcting the imbalance or in minimizing the impact on the children.	Primary or secondary preventive, high-risk approaches for children; secondary or tertiary preventive, community-wide approaches for parents.	Marital counseling (31, 39, 85); family therapy, parents' groups, individual therapy; legal guardian *ad litem* for children in divorce actions (43); legal aid for low-income families through neighborhood law offices (28, pp. 70–71; 41).
4) Families under stress as a result of vulnerability to normal developmental changes (birth of a child, school entry, puberty, climacterium, retirement).	Sensitivity to the variety of family stresses or crises that may result, leading to earlier recognition and intervention as needed, often via very short-term crisis-oriented therapy.	Primary and secondary preventive, high-risk community-wide, and milestone approaches.	Many of the above programs, especially neighborhood and/or comprehensive health, mental health, and social welfare services. Awareness of the opportunities for stress and crisis assistance is more important than the specific program setting.
5) Families living in areas lacking necessary biopsychosocial supplies (police protection, housing, quality education, etc.), in areas such as urban slums, depressed rural areas, migrant workers' camps, Indian reservations, housing projects, etc.	Provision of these basic necessities through community development approaches.	Primary, secondary, and tertiary preventive, high-risk approaches.	Community development approaches originating through the schools (52, 65), churches (8), social agencies (38, 74), neighborhood service centers (63, pp. 89–92; 72; 77), family life educators (25, 44), mental health centers (42, 53), etc.
6) Families caught in the cycle of intergenerational poverty.	Provision of multiple and flexible opportunities for attaining desired personal, social, and economic goals.	Primary, secondary, tertiary preventive, high-risk approaches.	As in 5; also a variety of anti-poverty programs such as Headstart, Upward Bound, Job Corps, etc., and agencies such as Mobilization for Youth, Community Progress, Inc., etc.
7) Disorganized families characterized by multiple and complex problems (emotional disorder,	Use of a problem-centered versus a discipline-centered approach to diagnose the total range of	Primary, secondary, tertiary preventive, high-risk approaches for adults and children.	All programs in this section may be relevant. Again, the point of view or approach is more

TABLE 2. (Continued)

Target Population	Goals	General Approach	Specific Examples
social dependency, poverty, chronic physical illness, child neglect or abuse, alcoholism and other addictions) and multiple needs (personal, social, medical, economic).	causative factors, identify those most accessible to change, and plan a step-by-step program.		important than the program. Several additional possibilities include 24 hour emergency home-makers (17), and other emergency care for children needing substitute parenting (6).
8) Families with potentially stressful role handicaps (childlessness, adoptive parenthood, foster-parenting, working mothers, and student families such as medical and other graduate students).	Awareness of the potential for stress or crisis so that early recognition and supportive help is available.	Secondary preventive high-risk and community-wide approaches.	Groups for adoptive or foster parents (3), groups for adoptive children (15); reliable day care centers (26).

lived in had been without heat and hot water for several weeks. Instead of referring this request for help with housing to the "appropriate" service, the social worker chose to inquire more closely about the total system. She got in contact with the other families (including a sizeable number of children) attempting to cope with the same stress, and helped to set in motion a much larger effort to provide both immediate and long-range help.

This type of approach is not as strange to psychiatry as it might appear at first glance. Psychiatrists have long recognized that a patient's chief complaint is simply the tip of an iceberg of out-of-awareness disorder. Hence, there is no real change in approach required other than an expansion of focus. To return to the problem of community-wide planning, the change needed, then, is largely one of an expansion in the training and activity of the key persons in the community who are most likely to encounter families in states of stress or crisis. Some have referred to the changed view as being "problem-centered" instead of "discipline-centered."

Group 3

This group of approaches overlaps with those in the preceding section but is mentioned separately because the degree of family stress or crisis is often less prominent and hence this group is socially less visible. Many of these families are operating in a steady state or equilibrium; the difference is that they are presumably functioning at lower capacity than their optimum potential. Although these approaches have elements of the "positive mental health" we eschewed earlier as attainable programmatic goals, the population groups listed in table 3 below should clarify that these programs are largely high-risk in orientation.

A second reason for their separate mention is that they clarify certain features of programming that are not always made specific. The most apparent is the need for different types of programs according to the socioeconomic realities of the groups being served. A comparison of the approaches to acquainting parents in lower-income versus middle-income groups with principles of child-rearing or child development makes this quite obvious. The middle-income groups by and large seek out educational programs, probably because such programs are constructed by professionals who share the same general view of life. These include the many classes and panels in which an expert or specialist functions in a familiar and valued role as the teacher.

On the other hand, lower-income groups generally avoid this type of approach, also probably because programs that reach those groups effectively require adaptations that fit better with their life styles. We have learned from those who work with lower-income groups that there are in fact a variety of groups, emphasizing further the need for fitting services to the particular segment being served.

A family-oriented study by Pavenstedt illustrated this exceptionally well (70). She compared the child-rearing environment of two segments of the low-income group, one which was upper-lower class (working class) and the other

TABLE 3. Approaches to Providing for Family Social and Economic Needs through Community Facilities

Target Population	Goals	General Approach	Specific Examples
1) Low-income families, mainly the mother.	Providing opportunities for enhancing a variety of skills (homemaking and child rearing as well as personal and social). Services with sociocultural congruence may foster community development as well as family development.	Primary preventive, high-risk approaches for children; primary, secondary, and tertiary preventive, high-risk approaches for mothers and (to lesser degree) fathers.	A rich variety of outreach programs, ideally parent-run as much as possible and associated with a pre-school include a swap shop in a housing project, sewing groups, good housekeeping clinics (mandatory for poor housekeepers in some housing projects), coffee-klatsch discussion groups, "go and do" expeditions —to supermarket, department store, zoo, museum, etc. (25, 44, 81).
2) Middle- and upper-income families, mothers and fathers.	Provision of professional information about child-rearing, developmental, and behavior problems.	Primary and secondary preventive, community-wide approaches.	Parent discussion groups with a panel of pediatricians, psychologists, educators (34).

TABLE 3. (Continued)

Target Population	Goals	General Approach	Specific Examples
3) Low-income families, especially the father.	Enhancement of work skills.	Primary, secondary, and tertiary preventive, high-risk approaches for fathers.	Neighborhood employment centers in low-income areas offering a variety of training programs which include work and education. Programs vary to include high school dropouts and long-term unemployed; recruitment via outreach efforts of neighborhood residents (28, pp. 2–17).
4) Low-income families, parents and children.	Provision of a single, family-oriented source for advice and assistance with any type of problem.	Primary, secondary, and tertiary preventive, high-risk and community-wide approaches.	The neighborhood service center (63, pp. 89–92; 72; 77), neighborhood information center (49), the community school (28, pp. 47–54).
5) Low-income families in need of legal assistance.	Provision of preventive and traditional legal services in both civil and criminal law.	Primary preventive, high-risk and community-wide approaches.	Neighborhood-based legal services which provide a range of educational services for legal rights and obligations (e.g., installment-buying, arrest) as well as public defender and "no-bail" programs (28, pp. 70–71; 41).
6) Low-income families, especially the father.	Provision of more equal economic opportunities for men with limited financial and technical resources.	Primary preventive, high-risk and community-wide approaches.	Small businessmen in an urban area are sought out, advised of federally supported opportunities (e.g., the Small Business Development and Opportunity Corp.), and given needed legal, technical, and educational services (63, pp. 77–78).

a "very low lower-class" group. Preventive approaches suggested for the upper-lower-class group were largely those of cultural and intellectual enrichment programs which should not present any serious difficulties in reaching the target population. On the other hand, the very low lower-class group presented chronic, multiple needs that required major outreach efforts. In both cases some type of vehicle that is capable of widespread application is needed. Pavenstedt's suggestion that the school system may be the best vehicle has recently been supported by the work of Kellam and Schiff in Chicago (50) and Rafferty in Baltimore (75). Additional social vehicles that look valuable for reaching very young children in disadvantaged groups are the day care center supported by health services and parent education (20).

A program feature that is consistently neglected in planning family-oriented preventive services is the role of the father. A review of the programs in all the tables will show that they are heavily biased towards the mother and children. The situation is reminiscent of the "discovery" of the role of the father in child guidance clinic practice within the past ten years. There it was found that fathers were not only of crucial importance in therapeutic work with children, but also they were reachable and able to be included in therapeutic efforts if an effort was made and if work responsibilities were treated more as a reality factor than as a resistance.

Unfortunately, preventive planners have to cope with the fact that this is a seriously underdeveloped area. Despite the obvious importance of his relationship with his wife as it affects her mothering role and the importance of his relationship with the children as it affects their identifications, this area has attracted little research in psychiatry. Our work as a committee turned up mostly articles pointing to the neglect of the father and little in the way of specific programs. The reasons for this are not at all clear. One we would like to mention in an optimistic vein is that our professional and disciplinary views have not quite yet come to include much collaborative exploration with the social institutions and professions involved in work, business, and economics. The quality of the work environment on the mental health of the worker has only recently begun to receive systematic attention, and unfortunately the role of psychiatry continues to be largely in providing curative services. Ideas and programs that have preventive usefulness may, however, be found in the works of other behavioral scientists, for example, Argyris (1), Likert (54), Pearl and Riessman (71), Reiff (76), and Tannenbaum (84).

As these approaches become more widely known and used in planning preventive psychiatric services, we should see stimulating theoretical developments in this area, as it involves many of the system levels alluded to in our section on theory. That is, work involves the individual, the group, and the organization and provides an opportunity for studying their interrelationships as they affect a variety of mental health issues. Wolford has written an overview of the relationships between mental health and occupation as they are now understood (86).

For planning purposes, the social structures involved in work also offer a more systematic way of providing services for fathers in hish-risk groups. Although family life educators have found that some low-income fathers can be involved in their programs, this approach depends largely on fortuitous factors that probably miss those most in need. On the other hand, entrance into the work force permits the use of milestone approaches, especially those of screening, early detection, and correction of disorders. Examples include entering the military, college, and large business organizations. This type of approach is used in some of these settings, but its potential promise is largely untapped. Table 3 simply touches upon some of these possibilities.

Group 4

To conclude this selection of preventive psychiatric approaches to families, we have selected for special mention the population group that is and will be creating new family units, namely, adolescents. This is an extraordinarily complicated area because of the many unknowns and the complex social attitudes centered around this group. Consistent with our committee's practice of focusing upon the high-risk groups, the programs mentioned in table 4 are largely conservative.

For example, it probably would be valuable if teen-agers generally received an honest presentation of the available knowledge about biologic sex, its relation to the complex interpersonal states of love and marriage, and the currently available technical information about contraception. However, this

TABLE 4. Approaches to Providing for Special Difficulties of Teen-Agers through Community Facilities

Target Population	Goals	General Approach	Specific Examples
1) Pregnant teen-age girls and their babies.	Opportunity for teen-ager to place or keep child on rational basis, and to continue schooling and get other assistance as needed.	Primary preventive for child; secondary and tertiary preventive, high-risk, and/or milestone for teen-agers.	Comprehensive centered services providing medical, nutritional, and case-work care which includes instruction in child care, sex education, family planning, etc. (36, 87).
2) Married teen-agers and their children.	Provision of support and guidance in the hope of salvaging more of the very young marriages and their offspring.	Primary preventive, high-risk approaches for child; secondary and tertiary preventive, community-wide, milestone, and/or high-risk approaches for parents.	Group and individual counseling services, educational supports including budgeting, family planning, homemaking, schooling, and career planning, etc.
3) Teen-agers in serious school difficulty.	Prevention of school dropout.	Tertiary preventive, community-wide approach.	Provision of special class with a talented teacher whose goal is to salvage these children, usually more by relationship than by formal teaching.
4) School dropouts, whether in an urban slum community or in the suburbs.	Provision of opportunities to find meaningful work as an alternative to failure at school.	Tertiary preventive, community-wide and/or high-risk approaches.	Neighborhood Youth Corps programs (28, pp. 20–22) which provide training and remedial education; Job Corps programs; mental health clinic; school and business collaboration (80).

TABLE 4. (Continued)

Target Population	Goals	General Approach	Specific Examples
5) Teen-agers generally, in urban slums.	Provision of more equal opportunities for support jobs, higher education, and counseling.	Primary, secondary, and tertiary preventive, community-wide and high-risk approaches.	Adolescent service centers in an urban slum (63, pp. 16–18); widely varied, useful vocational training (65, pp. 56–71); higher education programs (63, pp. 48–50), Upward Bound, etc.
6) Delinquent teen-agers.	Reaching and changing these anti-social and alienated boys and girls by a variety of outreach approaches.	Tertiary preventive, high-risk approach.	A variety of approaches for street gangs (9), including use of former gang-leaders (67). Half-way houses for delinquent youth (24); self-governing youth action group (63, pp. 22–24).
7) Teen-age narcotic addicts.	As in 6).	As in 6).	Aggressive case-finding, referral, and follow-up utilizing all available resources for 10–15-year-olds (63, pp. 93–94).
8) Teen-age children of alcoholic parents.	Provision of education and support to foster normal adolescent development.	Primary, secondary, and tertiary preventive, high-risk approaches.	Group meetings of affected teen-agers with largely educative focus (33).
9) Teen-agers referred for counseling or psychotherapy.	Prevention of the high dropout rates, especially of the young teen-ager, by using a peer-group setting as support.	Tertiary preventive, milestone approach.	Linkage of clinical services to some sort of group activity as in above examples or by agency itself (16).

continues to be an area of social planning that is not widely available, as it lies in a no-man's land of opinion and values.

Therefore, the groups selected above are those for which the weight of available knowledge is seen by us as generally overbalancing the variations of community opinion and mores. As a result of this choice, the programs appear to be largely tertiary or salvage operations as far as the teen-ager himself is concerned. We suspect, however, that this view is unduly pessimistic as regards the recuperative capacities of adolescents. Whatever the case, our major goal in this section is to identify and suggest programs that may reduce the incidence of teen-agers contributing to the multiproblem and hard-to-serve families that require so much of the community's social resources a few years later.

REFERENCES

1. Argyris, C.: Interpersonal Competence and Organizational Effectiveness. Homewood, Ill.: Dorsey Press, 1962.
2. Auerswald, E. H.: The "Interdisciplinary" Versus the "Systems" Approach in the Field of Mental Health, read at the 122nd annual meeting of the American Psychiatric Association, Atlantic City, N. J., May 9–13, 1966.
3. Bache-Wiig, B.: Education for Adoption, unpublished paper, 1966.
4. Bellak, L.: Psychiatry in the Medical-Surgical Emergency Clinic, Arch. Gen. Psychiat. 10: 267–269, 1964.
5. Beloff, J. S., and Weinerman, E. R.: Yale Studies in Family Health Care, J. A. M. A. 199: 383–386, 1967.
6. Bernstein, R.: Emergency Care of Children—Necessary Evil or Meaningful Child Welfare Service? Child Welfare 45: 326–333, 1966.
7. Bibring, G. L., Dwyer, T. F., Huntington, D. S., and Valenstein, A. F.: A Study of the Psychological Processes in Pregnancy and of the Earliest Mother-Child Relationship I. Some Propositions and Comments, Psychoanal. Stud. Child 16:9–72, 1961.
8. Biddle, L. J., and Biddle, W. W.: Community Dynamics Processes. New York: United Presbyterian Church, 1962.
9. Blake, M. E.: "Youth Groups in Conflict," in Mental Health and Social Welfare, New York: Columbia University Press, 1962, pp. 54–68.
10. Bloom, B. L.: Evaluation of Primary Prevention Programs, read at the conference on Comprehensive Mental Health: The Challenge of Evaluation, University of Wisconsin, Madison, Wis., June 2, 1966.
11. Bolman, W. M.: An Outline of Preventive Psychiatric Programs for Children, Arch. Gen. Psychiat. 17: 5–8, 1967.
12. Bolman, W. M.: School Phobia: A Systems Approach, read at the 44th annual meeting of the American Orthopsychiatric Association, Washington, D. C., March 27, 1967.
13. Bolman, W. M.: Theoretical and Empirical Bases of Community Mental Health, Amer. J. Psychiat. 124: Oct. Suppl. 8–13, 1967.
14. Bolman, W. M., and Westman, J. C.: Prevention of Mental Disorder: An Overview of Current Programs, Amer. J. Psychiat. 123: 1058–1068, 1967.
15. Boverman, H., and Watson, K.: Anticipatory Treatment for Foster Children: A Collaborative Project Between Agency and Clinic, read at the annual meeting of the American Association of Psychiatric Clinics for Children, San Francisco, Calif., April 13, 1966.
16. Braverman, S.: The Informal Peer Groups as an Adjunct to Treatment of the Adolescent, Social Casework 47: 152–157, 1966.
17. Brodsky, R.: Administrative Aspects of a 24-Hour Homemaker Service, Child Welfare 45: 34–39, 1966.
18. Brown, H. J.: The Gouverneur Ambulatory Care Unit: A New Approach to Ambulatory Care, Amer. J. Public Health 54: 1661–1665, 1964.
19. Cahn, E. S., and Cahn, J. C.: The War on Poverty: A Civilian Perspective, Yale Law Journal 73: 1317–1352, 1964.
20. Caldwell, B. M., and Richmond, J. B.: Programmed Day Care for the Very Young Child — A Preliminary Report, J. Marriage and the Family 26: 481–488, 1964.
21. Caplan, G.: "The Role of the Nurse in Maternal and Child Care," in An Approach to Community Mental Health. New York: Grune & Stratton, 1961.
22. Caplan, G.: Principles of Preventive Psychiatry. New York: Basic Books, 1964.
23. Caplan, G., Mason, E. M., and Kaplan, D. M.: Four Studies of Crisis in Parents of Prematures, Community Mental Health J. 1: 149–161, 1965.
24. Carpenter, K.: Halfway Houses for Delinquent Youth, Children 10: 224–229, 1963.
25. Chilman, C. S., and Kraft, I.: Helping Low-Income Parents I. Through Parent Education Groups, Children 10: 127–132, 1963.
26. Close, K.: Day Care as a Service for All Who Need It, Children 12: 157–160, 1965.
27. Close, K.: Giving Babies a Healthy Start in Life, Children 12: 179–184, 1965.
28. Community Progress, Inc.: The Human Story. New Haven: Community Progress, 1966.
29. Department of Health, Education, and Welfare: Report on Family Planning, 1966.
30. Duhl, F. J.: Intervention, Therapy and Change, read at the 122nd annual meeting of the American Psychiatric Association, Atlantic City, N. J., May 9–13, 1966.

31. Elkin, M.: Short-Contact Counseling in a Conciliation Court, Social Casework 43: 184–190, 1962.
32. Engel, G. L.: "Homeostasis, Behavioral Adjustment and the Concept of Health and Disease," in Grinker, R. R., Sr., ed.: Mid-Century Psychiatry. Springfield, Ill.: Charles C Thomas, 1953, p. 51.
33. Fairchild, D.: Teen Group I: A Pilot Project in Group Therapy with Adolescent Children of Alcoholic Parents, J. Fort Logan Mental Health Center 2: 71–75, 1964.
34. Flemer, A.: Parent Counseling: Description of a Successful Community Program, Clin. Pediat. 5: 524–526, 1966.
35. Gelhorn, W.: Ombudsman and Others: Citizens' Protectors in Nine Countries. Cambridge, Mass.: Harvard University Press, 1966.
36. Goodman, E. M., and Gill, F. M. L.: A Multi-Disciplinary Approach to a School-Centered Rehabilitation Program for Pregnant School-Age Girls in Washington, D. C.: A Summary Report. Washington, D. C., 1966 (processed).
37. Green, M., and Durocher, M. L.: Improving Parent Care of Handicapped Children, Children 12: 185–188, 1965.
38. Grosser, C. F.: Community Development Programs Serving the Urban Poor, Social Work 10: 15–21, 1965.
39. Hallowitz, D., Cutter, A. J., and Pitkin, K.: "Parent Consultation," in Mental Health and Social Welfare. New York: Columbia University Press, 1961, pp. 134–151.
40. Hamovitch, M.: Parent and Fatally Ill Child, Children 12: 85, 1965.
41. Handler, J.: Neighborhood Legal Services: New Dimensions in the Law. Department of Health, Education, and Welfare, 1966.
42. Hansell, N.: Patient Predicament and Clinical Service, Arch. Gen. Psychiat. 17: 204–210, 1967.
43. Hansen, R. W.: Guardians Ad Litem in Divorce and Custody Cases: Protection of the Child's Interest, J. Family Law 4: 181–184, 1964.
44. Hill, M. E.: Helping Low-Income Parents II. Through Homemaking Consultants, Children 10: 132–136, 1963.
45. Hill, R.: "Generic Features of Families Under Stress," in Parad, H. J., ed.: Crisis Intervention: Selected Readings. New York: Family Service Association of America, 1965, pp. 32–52.
46. Hunt, E. P., and Huyck, E. E.: Mortality of White and Non-white Infants in Major U.S. Cities, Health, Education, and Welfare Indicators. Department of Health, Education, and Welfare, 1966.
47. James, G.: The Function of Health Facilities in the Total Medical Care Complex, Public Health Rep. 81: 497–504, 1966.
48. Jolly, E., and Blum, H.: The Role of Public Health in Genetic Counseling, Amer. J. Public Health 56: 186–190, 1966.
49. Kahn, A. J., Grossman, L., Bandler, J., Clark, F., Galking, F., and Greenawalt, K.: Neighborhood Information Centers: A Study and Some Proposals. New York: Columbia University School of Social Work, 1966.
50. Kellam, S. G., and Schiff, S. K.: "Adaptation and Mental Illness in the First-Grade Classrooms of an Urban Community," in Greenblatt, M., Emery, P. E., and Glueck, B. C., Jr., eds.: Poverty and Mental Health. Psychiatric Research Report No. 21. Washington, D. C.: American Psychiatric Association, 1967.
51. Klein, D. C., and Lindemann, E.: "Preventive Intervention in Individual and Family Crisis Situations," in Caplan, G., ed.: Prevention of Mental Disorders in Children. New York: Basic Books, 1961, pp. 283–306.
52. Leighton, A. H.: Poverty and Social Change, Scientific American 212: 21–27, 1965.
53. Libo, L. M., and Griffith, C. R.: Developing Mental Health Programs in Areas Lacking Professional Facilities, Community Mental Health J. 2: 163–169, 1966.
54. Likert, R.: New Patterns of Management. New York: McGraw-Hill, 1961.
55. Markowitz, M., and Gordis, L.: A Family Pediatric Clinic at a Community Hospital, Children 14: 25–29, 1967.
56. Meier, G.: Research and Action Programs in Human Fertility Control: A Review of the Literature, Social Work 11: 40–55, 1966.
57. Meyer, R. E., Schiff, L. F., and Becker, A.: The Home Treatment of Psychotic Patients: An Analysis of 154 Cases, Amer. J. Psychiat. 123: 1430–1438, 1967.
58. Michigan Department of Mental Health: Progress Report: A Plan to Combat Mental Retardation in Michigan. Lansing, Mich., July, 1966.

59. Milio, N.: A Neighborhood Approach to Maternal and Child Health in the Negro Ghetto, Amer. J. Public Health 57: 618–624, 1967.
60. Miller, J. G.: Living Systems: Basic Concepts, Behav. Sci. 10:193-237, 1965.
61. Miller, J. G.: Living Systems: Structure and Process, Behav. Sci. 10: 337–379, 1965.
62. Miller, J. G.: Living Systems: Cross-Level Hypotheses, Behav. Sci. 10: 380–411, 1965.
63. Mobilization for Youth, Inc.: Synopsis of Programs. New York: Mobilization for Youth, 1966.
64. Moore, D. N., Bloom, B. L., Gaylin, S., Pepper, M., Pettus, C., Willis, E. M., and Bahn, A. K.: Data Utilization for Local Mental Health Program Development, Community Mental Health J. 3: 30–32, 1967.
65. Morris, G., and Gosline, E.: Mobilizing a Rural Community for Mental Health. Boonville. N. Y.: Willard Press, 1964.
66. Mother's Big Helper, Amer. J. Orthopsychiat. 36: 936, 1966.
67. News Item, Children 12: 163, 1965.
68. Orshansky, M.: Counting the Poor: Another Look at the Poverty Profile, Social Security Bulletin 28: 3–29, 1965.
69. Pattison, E. M.: Treatment of Alcoholic Families with Nurse Home Visits, Family Process 45: 75–94, 1965.
70. Pavenstedt, E.: A Comparison of the Child-Rearing Environment of the Upper-Lower and Very-Low-Lower Class Families, Amer. J. Orthopsychiat. 35: 89–98, 1965.
71. Pearl, A., and Riessman, F.: New Careers for the Poor. New York: The Free Press, 1965.
72. Peck, H. B., Kaplan, S. R., and Roman, M.: Prevention, Treatment and Social Action: A Strategy of Intervention in a Disadvantaged Urban Area, Amer. J. Orthopsychiat. 36: 57–69, 1966.
73. Polgar, S., and Cowles, W. B., eds.: Public Health Programs in Family Planning, Amer. J. Public Health 56, Jan. Supple., 1966.
74. Purcell F. P., and Specht, H.: The House on Sixth Street, Social Work 10: 69–76, 1965.
75. Rafferty, F. T.: Child Psychiatry Service for a Total Population, J. Amer. Acad. Child Psychiat. 6: 295–308, 1967.
76. Reiff, R.: New Approaches to Mental Health Treatment for Labor and Low Income Groups. New York: National Institute of Labor and Education, 1964.
77. Riessman, F., and Hallowitz, E.: The Neighborhood Service Center; An Innovation in Preventive Psychiatry, Amer. J. Psychiat. 123: 1408–1412, 1967.
78. Rolfe, P.: "The Psychiatric Team Comes to the Home," in Mental Health and Social Welfare. New York: Columbia University Press, 1961, pp. 105–133.
79. Schreiber, M. F., Feeley, M., and O'Neill, J.: Siblings of the Retarded, Children 12: 221–229, 1965.
80. Shore, J. F., and Massimo, J. L.: Mobilization of Community Resources in the Outpatient Treatment of Adolescent Delinquent Boys: A Case Report, Community Mental Health J. 2: 329–332, 1966.
81. Simpson, W. J., and Cosand, M. E.: Homemaking Teachers in Public Health, Amer. J. Public Health 57: 869–877, 1967.
82. Solnit, A. J.: The Psychiatric Counsel: Applied Psychiatry in an Anti-Poverty Program, Amer. J. Orthopsychiat. 37: 495–506, 1967.
83. Strickler, M., Bassin, E. G., Malbin, V., and Jacobson, G. F.: The Community-Based Walk-In Center: A New Resource for Groups Under-Represented in Outpatient Treatment Facilities, Amer. J. Public Health 55: 377–384, 1965.
84. Tannenbaum, R.: "New Approaches to Stresses on the Job," in Ojemann, R. H., ed.: Recent Research on Creative Approaches to Environmental Stress. Iowa City: State University of Iowa, 1963, pp. 121–131.
85. Wanck, L. A.: The Clergy as Marriage Counselors, J. Religion and Health 5: 252–259, 1966.
86. Wolford, J. A.: Mental Health and Occupation, Public Health Rep. 79: 979–984, 1964.
87. Wright, M. K.: Comprehensive Services for Adolescent Unwed Mothers, Children 13: 170–176, 1966.
88. Zusman, J.: The Psychiatrist as a Member of the Emergency Room Team, Amer. J. Psychiat. 123: 1394–1401, 1967.

Interdisciplinary versus Ecological Approach

Edgar H. Auerswald

The explosion of scientific knowledge and technology in the middle third of this century, and the effects of this explosion on the human condition, have posed a number of challenges for the behavioral sciences that most agree are yet to be met. The overriding challenge is, of course, the prevention of nuclear holocaust, but such problems as crime and delinquency, drug addiction, senseless violence, refractive learning problems, destructive prejudice, functional psychosis and the like follow close behind.

Practically all behavioral scientists agree that none of these problems can be solved within the framework of any single discipline. Most espouse a putting together of heads in the so-called "interdisciplinary approach." The notion is not new, of course. The "interdisciplinary team" has been around for some time. Some new notions have emanated from this head-banging, but there have been few startling revelations in the last decade or so.

However, a relatively small but growing group of behavioral scientists, most of whom have spent time in arenas in which the "interdisciplinary approach" is being used, have taken the seemingly radical position that the knowledge of the traditional disciplines as they now exist is relatively useless in the effort to find answers for these particular problems. Most of this group advocate a realignment of current knowledge and re-examination of human behavior within a unifying holistic model, that of ecological phenomenology. The implications of this departure are great. Once the model of ecology becomes the latticework upon which such a realignment of knowledge is hung, it is no longer possible to limit oneself to the behavioral sciences alone. The physical sciences, the biological sciences, in fact, all of science, must be included. Since the people who have been most concerned with constructing a model for a unified science and with the ingredients of the human ecological field have been the general systems theorists, the approach used by behavioral scientists who follow this trend is rapidly acquiring the label of the "systems approach," although a more appropriate label might be the "ecological systems approach."

These terms are currently being used metaphorically to describe a way of thinking and an operational style. They do not describe a well formed theoretical framework as does the term "general systems theory." It is with the former, the way of thinking and the operational style, that I am concerned in this paper.

The two approaches described above differ greatly. Let us examine why the difference is so profound. The ongoing accumulation of knowledge and its application to practice follows a well known sequence. This might be broken down into steps as follows: the collection of information or data, the ordering of that data within a selected framework, analysis of the data, synthesis of the results of analysis into hypotheses, the formulation of strategies and techniques (methodologies) to test the hypotheses, the construction of a delivery plan for use of these strategies and techniques, the implementation of the plan, and the collection of data from the arena of implementation to test its impact, which, of course, repeats the first step, and so on.

The key step in this sequence is the second one, the ordering of data within a selected framework, because it is this step, and this step alone, that gives structure to the rest, all of which are operational. Not only do the nature and outcome of subsequent steps depend on this structuring framework, but so does the prior step, the collection of data. What data among the infinite variety of available natural data are considered important, and are, therefore, collected in any given arena, will depend on the conceptual framework used. It is here that the difference between the two approaches is to be found.

The "interdisciplinary" approach maintains the vantage point of each contributor within his own discipline. While it has expanded the boundaries of the theoretical framework of each discipline to include concepts borrowed from other disciplines, only those concepts which pose no serious challenge or language difficulties are welcomed. More importantly, I think, the interfaces between the conceptual frameworks of different disciplines are ignored, and, as a result, the interfaces between the various arenas of systematic life operation (e.g., biological, psychological, social or individual, family, community) represented by different disciplines are also ignored.

The structural aspects and the clarity of context of the data collected are lost as a result. The precise source, pathway, and integrating functions of messages passing between various operational life arenas in the ecological field cannot be clearly identified. Analysis of such data depends almost entirely on the *content* of these messages, and much distortion can and does take place.

The "systems" approach, on the other hand, changes the vantage point of the data collector. It focuses precisely on the interfaces and communication processes taking place there. It begins with an analysis of the *structure* of the field, using the common structural and operational properties of systems as criteria for identifying the systems and sub-systems within it. And by tracing the communications within and between systems, it insists that the structure, sources, pathways, repository sites and integrative functions of messages become clear in addition to their content. In my opinion, this, plus the holistic nonexclusive nature of the approach, minimizes the dangers of excessive selectivity in the collection of data and allows for much more clarity in the contextual contributions to its analysis. And the steps which follow, including prescription and planning of strategies and techniques, gain in clarity and are more likely to be rooted in concrete realities.

There are some very practical advantages that accrue as a result of the above. At the level of *theory*, for example, the ecological systems model, by clarifying and emphasizing the interfaces between systems, allows for the use of a variety of theoretical models which have to do with interactional processes and information exchange. These models form bridges between the conceptual systems of single disciplines. Information theory, crisis theory, game theory, and general communications theory, for example, represent some of the bodies of research and knowledge which become usable in an integrated way.

Knowledge that has been accumulating from the study of specific ecological systems, such as the family and small groups, the development of which lagged until recently because the systems did not fit neatly into the bailiwick of any one traditional discipline, can also be included without strain. And the developmental model of the life cycle of the individual man and of various larger human systems as they move through time in the ecological field of their environment assumes meaning in a larger context.

In addition, the use of this model in planning has demonstrated its many implications for the design and operational implementation of delivery systems, especially for community programs (e.g., "comprehensive community health" programs). The ecological systems approach insures that the entire process of planning for a community is rooted in the realities and needs of that community. The organized identification of the ecological systems making up a target community allows for the planned inclusion of information collection stations in each key system and at primary interfaces which provide feedback to the planning arena, thus setting up a servo-system which assures that planning will remain closely related to changing need. Over a period of time, as a picture of a target community emerges from such data, it will emerge as an idiosyncratic template of the structural and operational configurations of that community. It will not, as in the "interdisciplinary" approach, emerge as a predetermined template of the theoretical structure of the dominant discipline.

As a result, program designs constructed in this manner are deeply imbedded in the target community. They will develop as another ecological system among the many, thus greatly clarifying the context in which any program can be integrated into the life of the community as a whole. Furthermore, the delivery organization itself becomes viewed as a system with assigned tasks made up of sub-systems performing sub-tasks including intra-organizational tasks. This allows for more clarity in the selection of staffing patterns, in the definitions of staff role functions, in the construction of communication systems and data collection (record-keeping) systems, and of the assignment of tasks within the organizational structure to staff members best equipped to handle them. Of special import to community programs is the fact that with the clarification of specific tasks to be performed comes the increased possibility of identifying those tasks that can be carried out by staff members or volunteers who need relatively little training.

At the *operational* level the strategies of evolution and change can be more clearly designed. More important, perhaps, use of the ecological systems approach allows for the development of a whole new technology in the production of change. Many techniques have, as a matter of fact, already appeared on the scene, largely within organized movements aimed at integration in its broadest sense, such as the Civil Rights Movement and the "War On Poverty." Some community organization and community development programs, techniques using economic and political pressure, and techniques which change the rules of the game such as the non-violence movement, all represent a new technology, and all have their relevance to the broadly-defined health needs of socially isolated individuals, families, and groups.

In service programs working with individual people and families, this new technology is also emerging, more slowly perhaps. Many new ways of coping with familiar situations are being developed. Techniques of treating families as systems, for example, represent one advance. In particular, an emphasis which stresses the organization of events in time and traces the movement of the developing infant-child-adolescent-adult-aged individual's degree of participation versus his isolation in relation to his family and to the flow of surrounding community life—such an emphasis makes it possible to determine with much more clarity in what life arenas the individual, the family, or a group of individuals needs assistance, and thus to more effectively combat the anomie and dehumanization characteristic of our age. The result is that the targets of therapeutic activity are much clearer and therapeutic work is more clearly focused on forces and situations that are truly etiological in a given problem situation. Techniques of producing therapeutic change can be brought to arenas much larger than the therapy room or even the home. I think that a single story will serve to illustrate more concretely what I mean.

In the story I wish to tell, two therapists, one a "systems" thinker, the other a member of an "interdisciplinary" team, became involved in the case of a runaway girl.

To give you some initial background, I should explain that I have been involved in designing and implementing a "Neighborhood Health Services System" for provision of comprehensive biopsychosocial care to a so-called "disadvantaged" community. The main aim in setting up this unit was to find ways to avoid the fragmentation of service delivery which occurs when a person's problem is defined as belonging primarily to himself, and he is sent to a specialist who is trained to deal primarily with that type of problem. The specialist naturally sees the problem not only as an individual matter, but defines it still further according to the professional sector he inhabits. He is not accustomed to looking at the total set of systems surrounding the individual with the symptom or to noticing the ways in which the symptom, the person, the family, and his community interlock, and he is often in the position of a man desperately trying to replace a fuse when it is the entire community power line that has broken down. Furthermore, the specialist's efforts to solve the problem are apt to be confined to arbitrarily chosen segments of time called "appointments." And finally, there is that unfortunate invention, the written referral, a process of buck-passing that sends many a person in trouble from agency to agency till he finally gives up or breaks down. As a beginning we decided that we would have to pilot some cases in order to gain some experience with the different approach we felt was needed.

At this point, a case providentially dramatizing the points we had in mind fell into our hands. (We have since found that almost every case that falls into our hands providentially dramatizes these points.) One of our psychiatrists was wandering about the neighborhood one day in order to become better acquainted with it and to explore what sort of crises and problems our neighborhood program must be prepared to serve beyond those we already anticipated. I should say here that this psychiatrist,[1] by virtue of several years of pioneering work with families, including the experimental use of game theory and games in diagnosing and treating them, was particularly well qualified to handle the situation I will describe. His explorations that day had brought him to the local police station, and while he was talking to the desk sergeant, a Puerto Rican woman arrived to report that her twelve-year-old daughter, Maria, had run away from home. This was apparently not the first time. She described the child to the police, who alerted their patrols to look for her and assigned two men to investigate the neighborhood. Our psychiatrist, whom I will refer to from now on as our "explorer," was intrigued and decided to follow up the situation himself.

He first identified himself to the mother as she left the police station and asked if she would be willing to allow him to help her with her current difficulty. She agreed. He learned that she lived a few blocks away with her now absent daughter and another daughter, aged 14. Her own parents lived nearby, and she had a paramour who also lived in the neighborhood. The father of her two children had long since deserted his family, and she was uncertain as to his whereabouts. The exploring psychiatrist learned also that the runaway girl had been seeing a psychotherapist at the mental health clinic of a local settlement house. In addition, he ascertained the location of her school.

He then decided that his behavior might appear unethical to the child's therapist, so he proceeded to the mental health clinic, a clinic which prided itself on the use of the "interdisciplinary" team approach. The original therapist turned out to be a social worker of considerable accomplishment and experience, who agreed to cooperate with him in his investigation after he explained what he was up to and that he had the mother's permission. He read the child's case record and discussed the girl with the therapist at some length. He learned that at a recent team case conference, the diagnosis which was originally assigned to the girl, that of childhood schizophrenia, was confirmed. The team also decided that in the light of repeated episodes of running away from home, her behavior was creating sufficient danger to indicate that she be placed in a situation where that danger would be alleviated while her therapy continued. For a twelve-year-old Puerto Rican girl in New York City, especially one carrying a label of schizophrenia, this almost always means hospitalization in the children's ward of a state hospital. Accordingly, the arrangement for her admission to the state hospital covering the district had been made and was due to be implemented within a few days.

The next stop for our explorer was the school, where Maria's teacher described her as a slow but steady learner, detached from most other children in the class, vague and strange, but somehow likeable. The guidance counselor reported an incident in which she had been discovered masturbating an older boy under the school auditorium stairs. This behavior had led the school

---

[1]Dr. Robert Ravich. I am indebted to Dr. Ravich for the case material reported.

authorities to contemplate suspending her, but since they knew her to be in treatment they decided to hold off, temporarily at least.

The exploring psychiatrist also learned at the school that Maria was involved in an after-school group program at the settlement house. He returned there and got from the group worker a much more positive impression of the girl than he had previously encountered. She participated with seeming enthusiasm in the projects of the group and got along very well with the other children. The group worker, by way of providing evidence that Maria had much potential, showed the therapist a lovely and poignant poem she had contributed to a newspaper put out by the group. It was never ascertained whether the girl had written or copied the poem. She had, nevertheless, produced it, and there was general agreement that its theme of isolation was one which was expressive of her.

Back at Maria's home, our explorer talked to Maria's sister, who at first grudgingly, but then with some relish, admitted that she knew where the girl had gone during her previous runaway episodes. She was the sometime mascot of a group of teenage boys with whom she occasionally traveled for two or three days at a time. The sister did not know where she went or what she did during the junkets, but she suspected that sex was somehow involved. She also volunteered the information that neither she nor her mother had ever found it easy to communicate with her sister, and that if the therapist really wanted to talk to someone who knew her, he should talk to her grandfather. So off to the grandparents' apartment he went.

The grandmother turned out to be a tight-lipped, highly religious Pentecostalist who was at first unwilling to say much at all about the girl.

The grandfather, however, was a different kettle of fish. Earthy, ebullient, jocular, bright, though uneducated, his love for Maria was immediately apparent. He spoke of her warmly, and bemoaned the lack of understanding that existed in her home. Remembering a passing reference in the case record at the mental health clinic to a suspicion that the grandfather may have engaged in seductive play with the girl, if not open sexual activity, our explorer raised the issue of the girl's emerging adolescent sexuality. This brought an outburst from the hitherto silent grandmother that confirmed the mutually seductive quality of the grandfather's relationship with the girl, followed by a return blast from the grandfather who revealed that his wife had refused to sleep with him for several years. He readily admitted his frustrated sexuality and the fact that he was at times aroused by his budding granddaughter.

I have presented only a sparse picture of the rich amount of information collected by our explorer up to this point. In a continuous five hour effort, without seeing the absent Maria, he was able to construct a picture of her as a child who had grown up in relative isolation in a home where she received little support and guidance. Communication between herself and her mother had become more and more sparse over the years, most likely because of efforts of her older sister to maintain her favored position in the home. She had turned to her grandfather, who, feeling frustrated and himself isolated in his own marriage, brought his sexually-tinged warmth willingly into a relationship of mutual affection with her. Furthermore, it seemed clear that with someone like the group worker who liked her and who, because the group was small, could spend time with her, Maria could respond with warmth and exhibit an intelligence that otherwise remained hidden. But, and this was, of course, speculative, the tools she perceived as useful in her search for a response from others would most likely be limited to infantile techniques of manipulation developed in early years prior to the need for verbal communication or, based on the relationship with the grandfather, some form of seduction where the currency of acceptance was sex. And, at the age of puberty, having been shut out of the female world of her mother and sister, she was using this currency full blast in the world of boys.

The next day our explorer talked again to the mother, who told him that the girl had been found by the police on the street and had been hospitalized at a large city hospital on the adolescent psychiatric ward. Before visiting her, he briefly questioned the mother about her paramour. It turned out that the subject of marriage had come up between the two of them, but because he earned a limited income, both he and the mother had decided against living together or getting married. Either action would result in loss of the support the mother was receiving from the Department of Welfare for herself and her two children.

All that had been predicted the day before was corroborated when our explorer visited the girl in the hospital. Her behavior with him, and, as it turned out, with the resident physician on the ward, alternated between childish manipulation and seductive behavior of a degree which appeared bizarre in a 12-year-old. But she was, at the same time, a lithely attractive girl with a lively wit which blossomed once she felt understood. She was ambivalent about the alternatives of going home or of going to a state hospital, mildly resisting both.

Our exploring psychiatrist then returned to the mental health clinic to discuss what he had observed with the child's therapist and the consulting psychiatrist. He suggested a plan of action as an alternative to hospitalization. By targeting on key issues in various systems surrounding this child, it seemed theoretically plausible that the conditions which held her fixed in a pattern of behavior that had been labeled as sick and crazy might be changed, thus freeing her to accept new coping patterns which she could be helped to learn. An effort to re-establish communication between the child and her mother, who had shown with her other daughter that she could raise a child with relative success, would be one step. It might not be feasible to work with the grandparents' unsatisfactory marriage, but an explanation to the grandfather, who had already tentatively understood his contribution to the girl's dilemma, might be useful. If the Department of Welfare were willing, and if the boyfriend's income could be enhanced by at least a little supplementary public assistance, the mother and her boyfriend might be induced to marry. Teacher and guidance counselor could be helped to understand the girl's behavior more fully and might cooperate on a plan for helping the girl learn new ways of relating in school. The group worker's investment in the girl could be used to a good effect in this joint effort to help her grow. And the original therapist, instead of concerning herself with defense systems and repressed conflict could concentrate on helping the family provide the maximum of support and guidance possible, or, if she wished, could still work with the girl herself. With these suggestions, our exploring psychiatrist bowed out.

A month later, a follow-up visit to the mother revealed that the girl had been sent to state hospital on the recommendation of the resident on the adolescent ward who agreed with the diagnosis and felt that, since she was "a schizophrenic," she should be in a hospital. No one had made any counter-move and contact between all of the helping people except the state hospital doctor and the girl's family had been terminated. This outcome had occurred *despite the fact that the mother and her boyfriend had, after a conversation stimulated by our therapist-explorer, presented themselves at the mental health clinic and expressed their willingness to marry if it seemed wise, their wish to have Maria come home, and their hope that someone at the clinic would help them learn what they must now do for her as parents.*

I have, I realize, presented an unusual situation. Reasonable question could be raised, I suppose, as to how often this sequence could occur. And my own bias is obvious in the manner of my presentation. But I think the case illus-trates the radical difference between the two approaches under discussion. The approach of the therapist from the interdisciplinary clinic and that of our exploring psychiatrist are not merely two points on a continuum of tech-niques. The "ecological systems" approach literally changed the name of the game. By focusing on the nature of the transactions taking place between Maria and the identifiable systems that influenced her growth, it was possible for the "systems" psychiatrist to ascertain what strengths, lacks, and distor-tions existed at each interface. Two things happened when this was done.

The first was that Maria's behavior began to make sense as a healthy adaptation to a set of circumstances that did not allow her to develop more socially acceptable or better differentiated means of seeking a response to her needs as a developing child. Thus, the aura of pathology was immedi-ately left behind.

The second was that the identification of lacks and distortions in the transactional arena of each interface automatically suggested what needed to be added or changed. Thus the tasks of the helping person were automatically defined. Rigidity of technique in accomplishing these tasks could not, under those circumstances, survive. Flexibility, ingenuity, and innovation were demanded.

The implications of what can happen if this approach is used universally are obvious. If proper data are kept, it seems inevitable that new clusters of data will occur to add to our knowledge, and a new technology of prevention and change develop.

The case of Maria has a certain uniqueness that separates it from most similar cases across our country. The uniqueness is not to be found in the "interdisciplinary" approach used, but rather in the quantity of skilled people who were trying to help her. Despite their dedicated efforts, all they managed to accomplish was Maria's removal from the only system that could be consid-ered generic in terms of her growth and socialization—her family—and her removal from the school and community which should provide the additional experience she needed if she were to become a participant in the life of her society. In addition, they succeeded in stamping a label on the official records of her existence, a label which is a battleground of controversy among diag-nosticians, but which means simply to the lay public that she is a nut.

By chance, Maria wound up in a mental hygiene clinic where her behavior was labeled as sick. She might just as easily have joined the many girls showing similar behavior who wind up in court and are labeled delinquent. Either label puts her in a category over which various members of "interdisciplinary" teams are in continued conflict. The needs of the girl, which are not clearly apparent in either arena, become hopelessly obscured. Decisions made by those charged with the task of helping her are likely to be made without cognizance of those needs, since they depend for their outcome too often on the institutionalized procedures and momentary exigencies in the caring organization or person.

As a final point, let me explore the nature of the communications breakdown that occurred between the two therapists.

In his explorations, our "systems" psychiatrist collected a good deal of data that was not known to the "interdisciplinary" therapist and team in order to insure that he understood the operations that had been going on at each interface in which he was interested. This additional data only supplemented the data previously collected and agreed with it in content. Thus the two agreed substantially as long as they confined their communications to content and to inferred construction of the internal psychodynamics of the persons involved, Maria and the individual members of her family. And, as it happened, this was all they discussed until the exploring "systems" psychiatrist returned for a final chat. At that time, having ordered his data in such a way as to clarify the transactions which had been taking place at the interfaces between Maria and the various systems contributing to her growth, his suggestions flowed from a plan designed to affect those interfaces. The "interdisciplinary" team, including the original therapist, had not ordered the data in this way. Since the dominant disciplinary framework used in their arena was psychiatric, they had ordered the data around a nosological scheme for labeling illness. The outcome of their plan of action, therefore, was to apply a label signifying the nature of Maria's illness, and to decide, reasonably enough within this framework, that since treatment of her illness on an outpatient basis had not been successful, the next step was hospitalization, a decision backed by the assumption that her runaways were dangerous.

It was literally impossible, at the final meeting, for the suggestions of our "systems" therapist to have meaning to the "interdisciplinary" team. They fell on ears made deaf by a way of thinking which could not perceive them as meaningful. They came across as a dissonance which had to be screened out. Communication between the two approaches thus broke down completely.

The instance of breakdown is characteristic of efforts of communication between people from the two arenas. Conversations I have had with a variety of people who take the ecological systems view, backed by my own experience, seem to add up to the following:

There seems to be no serious problem of communication between the systems thinker who emphasizes structure and the experimental behavioral scientist who does basic research in his laboratory or even the researcher who is attempting to deal with a wide range of natural data. Such researchers have selected and defined the structure of the theoretical framework in which they wish to work and are the first to admit that the outcome of their research carries the label of validity within that framework alone.

The clinical scientist, whose emphasis is more on the content of his data, is for the most part a different animal. Most clinical theorists, planners, and practitioners, regardless of discipline, seem caught in the highly specialized sequence of their own training and intradisciplinary experience, upon which they seem to depend for the very definition of their personal identity. Generally speaking, a situation seems to exist in which the integration of the cognitive apparatus of the clinician is such as to exclude as a piece of relevant data the notion that his intradisciplinary "truths," which he carries to the interdisciplinary arena, are relative. He most often will hear and understand the notion when it is expressed. But, again speaking generally, he treats it as unimportant to his operations, as peripheral to the body of knowledge he invests with meaning. Why should this be?

I think it is because the clinician is a product of the specialized fragmentation of today's world of science. To him, admission of this fact would mean that he would have to rearrange his cognitive style, his professional way of life, and, all too often, his total life style as well, if he were to maintain a sense of his own integrity. Not only would he have to renounce his idols, but he would have to go through a turbulent period of disintegration and reintegration. He would have to be willing and able to tolerate the fragmentation of identity boundaries such a transition entails. He would have to leave the safety of seeming truths, truths he has used to maintain his sense of being in the right, his self-esteem, his sense of values, and his status in the vertical hierarchies of his society. He would have to give up the games he plays to maintain his hard-won position in his discipline, games such as those which consist of labeling persons from other schools of thought as bright but limited, misguided, or insufficiently analyzed. More often than not, he would rather fight than switch.

I imply, of course, that he should switch. Thus the question must reasonably be asked: Why should he? Why should he attempt such a fundamental change? After all, he can point with pride to the many accomplishments and successes of his discipline and his own work within it.

But to rest on his laurels, in my opinion, is to abdicate responsibility. It is like crowing over the 70% or so of juvenile delinquents who become law-abiding citizens and ignoring the 30% who do not. The major responsibility of today's behavioral scientist is to those who don't or won't make it, not those who do, to Maria, not to Little Hans, whom he already knows how to help.

The least he can do is examine his labels and how he uses them. In the life-space of Maria's world, there is a serious question as to which system deserves the prefix, *schizo*.

Family Context Therapy:
A Model for Family Change*

John Elderkin Bell

Starting where family group therapy fails, this article breaks new territory in family context therapy. Consolidating the past 14 years of his work, Dr. Bell sets forth a conceptual program and methods to meet problems that earlier forms of family therapy could not reach. Here he provides a model drawn from studies, theories, and personal experience of organizational patterns, interrelations, and change among community institutions that provide settings for family functioning. His new methods are designed to modify the family environment so as to solve family problems and promote beneficial family growth—a framework that may bring together a broad variety of existing family development approaches.

Family context therapy attempts to change environmental conditions that cause or accentuate family difficulties and to construct contexts that promote family well-being. It undertakes intentional transformations of the world beyond the family in order to reach therapeutic aims. It is a major extension of family therapy, enabling impact on single families or many families simultaneously. The method seeks to alter contextual physical, economic, and social factors in order to lessen or remove problems that are caused or accentuated by the environment and to assure the external resources needed for family well-being. Its ultimate aim is to heighten family competence for liberating themselves from the past, confronting problems, redirecting family resources and reducing their waste, preparing for the future, improving family efficiency, developing and attaining new goals and adapting to the unchangeable. In extreme cases it may be concerned with restoration of a scattered family or with slowing the pace of family deterioration and family death.

This approach moves the center of family interventions from the arena of the clinical office into the larger society, to helping agencies and institutions, and

*dates of research: 1963–present

many other settings, some alien to therapists, which may become the site for therapeutic effort.

Expressed even more abstractly, the family context therapist is involved with the family environment entity as the primary *functional* unit. The mediating *structural* unit is a component of the environment, normally an institution. The target *structural* unit remains the family. For observational, analytic, and operational purposes, the comprehensive functional unit is segmented into family in relation to particular institutions (basic or helping). Families in this respect may be dealt with as a class—one of many in their relations to and with an institution, and in regard to some common characteristic(s). The family context therapist is an agent (individual, group of individuals, or organization). The therapist seeks to intervene in the institution to affect directly the environment for indirect impact on family functions; he or she observes, analyzes, conceives, and takes advantage of the patterns and processes of institution-family relations to devise particular interventions to accomplish organization changes to the advantage of families.

BACKGROUND

Before describing and illustrating the methodology, let me first set this advance in its historical framework. It is regarded as an advance because problems that could not be solved by family therapy are now remediable through these new developments. After 12 years of doing family group therapy, I became convinced that the method was not working well with hospitalized patients. My concern led to delegation within my overall duties in NIMH to direct a long-range program to reduce the separation of families from patients in psychiatric hospitals, and to devise methods by which staff in such hospitals could improve patient-family relations.

Consistent with my usual inductive approach to the development of techniques and theory, I immersed myself in observation rather than theoretical analysis. Stimulated by the overall idea that there must be solutions to the problems of institutional separation, I observed the family in the hospital here and abroad (Bell, 1970a). This gave me entrance into the scene of family-hospital interactions, and from that, access into the whole field of the family in relation to social institutions (Bell, 1970b).

At the same time, the knowledge that family therapy was not functional for all classes of families was just beginning to become apparent. Family therapists have found that the nature of problems within the family, the family's perception of the amenability of these problems to therapy solutions, and family priorities given to solving them, may predispose against the effectiveness of family therapy. They know the limits of the therapist's own competence, acceptability, and power and understand the intractability of problems that are lodged in the handicaps and disabilities of individuals. They comprehend the immensity of social disorders that family members by themselves cannot solve. Further, they have confronted the practical problems that diminish the accessibility of the therapist, and the will of the family to persist in seeking therapy. In addition, they have met the issues of the separation of the family from individual members—in hospitals, prisons, nursing homes, at distant places of employment, and in political jobs that may be incompatible with family life.

Such problems as the above established the need for methods other than family group therapy for helping the family. Family therapy was and is still showing itself to be effective in redeployment of intrinsic family resources. But disturbing generalizations and false assumptions about the therapy's utility were being promoted, often unwittingly. We still hear persons advocating: If there is a family problem, use family therapy. If an individual presents a problem, it can usually be approached as a family problem, so use family therapy. A period of family therapy can be constructive for family development, restructuring, and renovation, no matter what the presenting problem.

It is increasingly clear that family therapy is not the generic mode of intervention in families. It is specific, even though broadly applicable. Other direct and indirect modes of intervention are easy to identify, though not immediately in the consciousness of all family therapists. Many technologies for affecting families existed long before family therapy. These are observable, particularly in settings that are not congenial to a family therapy model, such as: (a) where established patterns for family change, development, and support have been long-established and function well. Examples include parent education and training, premarital education and counseling, crisis support within extended families and within established community support networks, both informal, such as the rallying of neighbors, and formal, such as services through agencies and businesses; (b) where patterns of relating to individuals are entrenched and generally seen, rightly or wrongly, as incompatible or inconsistent with relations to a family unit. Many industrial personnel counselors hold to such a position; and (c) where patterns of operation are regarded as beyond the family, even though possibly acknowledged as having family impact. Such patterns are observable in many commercial and community enterprises. Consider, for instance, the impact on the family of the housing construction industry, or of city zoning, or of location of industrial plants, or of transportation systems. The functional point of intervention to affect a family under such broad influences would point toward community and institutional change, although help for a single family in crisis because of far-reaching changes in the community is commonly desirable as well.

Earlier I had pointed to the broad scope of the field of the family, and toward an extended range of programs and professional interventions potentially available to family therapists (Bell, 1970b). Since then I have been attempting to formulate specific methodologies for coming to grips with the original problem—psychiatric hospital-family interactions. Moreso, I have been thinking about hospitals in general, and have been able to profit from choosing to work again in a hospital environment with general medical, surgical, and psychiatric patients. There, many of my evolving ideas have been tested in practice. At the same time, the general issues of family relations with all community institutions have been kept in the forefront of my thinking.

In retrospect, I see that my priority on family-hospital interactions prepared me for the emergence of fresh concepts about relations between family and environment and out of those concepts new methodologies are growing. I am indebted to the fields of sociology, social ecology, organization-environment relations, and social change. Through studying these areas I have escaped from the prevalent attention to "family systems," which continues to have formal significance, but has led to only limited progress in the ordering of techniques. In contrast, alternative theories now appear capable of generating an ever-increasing catalogue of interventions.

For the present I am calling the extended methods by the useful term, therapy. This is to provide a bridge to my early work with families, and to invite thought and communication among many now practicing in the still growing field of family therapy. The goals in family group therapy and in family context therapy may be the same. In speaking of changing the family context as therapy, I hope at the same time not to alienate those whose work is similar to mine but outside a medical framework. Together we should seek links among various approaches to helping families, to develop some common theoretical bases on which professional collaboration may be fostered, so later we may replace the term therapy with one that will denote a comprehensive program of interventions on behalf of families.

Therapy used broadly implies a relation between and direct interventions by a therapist with a patient. The route by which a context therapist helps a family may not even involve a direct relationship with them. As a family group therapist, I am concerned essentially with affecting directly the processes within the family. As a family context therapist, as a planner and a coordinator, I have become a strategist, mobilizing the community, its institutions, and their resources to center attention and effort on family change. I am directing the community toward change through providing settings for family problem-solving and attaining of well-being. The modifications in the environment induced by the therapist as change agent may be experienced by the family without direct personal association with the therapist. A team of persons functioning together, an institution, or a community may take the initiative for family change, affect the environment, and provide the requisite environmental resources to achieve therapy aims.

The rationale for using the term therapy also includes recognition that the outcome of environmental interventions may be therapeutic. The first order of outcome is the result of the specific actions in the environment in which a therapist engages on behalf of a family or families. The second and higher order is the consequence of the actions within family life. It seems appropriate to call this therapeutic, if in fact there is an enablement by which a family functions more adequately, and is able to reach family goals which previously were difficult or impossible for them to achieve on their own.

METHODOLOGY

The methodology in process interventions for institutional change is multi-faceted and evolving. Situations are approached in terms of personal and organizational considerations that are complex, organization- or person-centered, fluid, only partially predictable, and subject to sudden change. Interventions may vary in their impact between the extremes of creating virtually no identifiable consequences, to starting a surge to all-embracing change, positive or negative. The results vary when the interventions are designed to change an institution's relations with many small and diverse units such as families.

Taking the above into account, it would not be helpful to present a comprehensive description of the change methods I have used. They are too specific to persons, times, families, policies, problems, readiness for change, management, organization, resources (especially money), and priorities. Rather, I shall describe some of my approaches to conceiving change methods, give brief illustrations to show how some have been applied, and in some instances, show the outcome. Implicit in this approach is knowledge that my methods are often exploratory, to see what happens; whereas others are planned over long periods, set forth in written proposals, tested in pilot efforts, and begun only when the signs for success are propitious.

The first intervention may start within the therapist. Before functioning as a family context therapist, a person must have a developed orientation toward families. This is in a sense a value position, involving a favorable attitude to families, and a commitment to family advocacy. Many who work with families have already adopted such a position, but some who might wish to create methodology must decide for themselves to honor the family.

Through such an imperative, many efforts can be generated, within which innovative action potentials may be envisioned and implemented. I shall cite examples from my hospital work. The hospital is an illustration of a helping institution, as differentiated from basic institutions such as the school or church, which are typically non-problem oriented and engaged in personal and resource development. The hospital, in contrast, is problem-oriented, and the problems are usually identified as belonging to an individual. This results in three basic social relations in the hospital that involve family members: patient-staff, family-staff, and family-patient. The therapist's interventions focus on changing the environment for these relations for the sake of the family.

It is not difficult to recognize that the hospital has a major impact on the families of most patients. Planned admission of a patient may be a sign that the family recognizes their need of the hospital's resources. This is so when the illnesses that bring a patient to the hospital are acute, although emergency admissions often do not involve families. When acute illness turns into a chronic health problem and a hospitalization becomes periodic or prolonged, the impact on the family is not necessarily reduced. Though relations change in form, they continue by thought and action as aspects of the total family life (Maddox, 1975).

The family typically begins from the position that their aims are identical, coordinate, or complementary with those of the institution. Since families are dependent on staff, most intend to support the work of staff, at least initially, and to meet staff expectations. Families pass on information, make private family relations public, learn appropriately, transfer some functions to staff as required, and accept some functional assignments from staff. On balance, families have their own expectations of staff and they make demands in accordance with those expectations. They engage in evaluating the staff. Not infrequently they deal with particular staff members according to stereotypes, especially those based on images of professional roles and functions.

It would be inappropriate to try to characterize all staff relations with families. Staff may range all the way from meeting each family in terms of their individuality, to the other extreme of dealing with all families according to set ideas and patterns of action. Among the activities that staff may engage in with family members are: acknowledge their existence and presence; hold out requirements for them; formulate anticipations for them; accept and support them; lean upon them; train them; evaluate them; dismiss them; reject them totally; pass on or withhold professional information to them; transfer some professional functions to them, or keep them back.

Coordinate with these relations of patients and families with staff are the relations within the hospital between patients and their families. These may be continuous with the past and easy, or virtually discontinuous and difficult. Commonly they are in response to demands that require new ways of thinking and acting. Frequently they express anxieties that are especially difficult to cope with, because fantasy takes over when knowledge is missing, and communication with those who know or may be presumed to know may be difficult. Hopes and goals then become based on what-if fantasies that remain unstable and reduce commitment to present relations. Family communications may be transformed, as when the reduction in speech by a patient demands extraordinary efforts to read body signs and movements. The need to adapt to changes in a patient's status may intrude on the comfortable regularity of family relations. But the relations may be excellent for both the family and the patient. Communication may be opened, adaptive changes may be appropriately mastered, transitions may be made with ease, and the whole experience of hospitalization of a member may enrich family living.

Yet, the family frequently encounters situations where their aims and purposes are in conflict with those of the hospital, and an adversary stance escalates the conflict. Some family-hospital problems are essentially family problems being shown in the hospital; others are problems that emerge in the family's efforts to adapt to the hospital, and its handling of them.

Recognizing that family relations with the hospital are complex and can become tangled, the family context therapist begins to examine hospital programming and its consequences for the continuation and growth of the family, or for the alleviation of their problems. The family context therapist asks, "What resources may be introduced here in this program and environment to facilitate family processes, to ensure or increase the possibilities that the family will meet their goals, and to help sustain or improve family well-being?"

Assessment and modification of family-hospital relations

The first concrete method demonstrates a fundamental approach of the family context therapist. It describes efforts to change the hospital and particularly the hospital staff as a mediating population.

To devise techniques to change staff actions with families and patients, a great deal of knowledge of the hospital setting, the staff and their relations with families is helpful. Sources of such knowledge are usually accessible to someone who is a staff person, but a newcomer to staff may have to take considerable time to build confidence within which sharing of knowledge may become free, especially if it refers to interpersonal behaviors. My responsibilities, assigned in 1973, brought me into association with staff serving approximately 250 patients—four wards, including one for women, in one division of the hospital, and three in the other. In the latter divisions, staff readiness to establish communication about the programs and about the families of patients was measurably present. Within one and a half months of my appointment, a representative staff group of eight to ten persons began to meet weekly to discuss family relations with the patients and the hospital. This committee has been meeting weekly ever since, with nurses functioning as chairpersons.

In the other division, the development of a functioning committee was slow. A group of three persons representing various professions began to meet weekly with me, toward the aim of funding a committee. Over a year this group studied the situation for families in the building, especially concentrating efforts on establishing confidence among the nursing staff, since they did not agree to meet with us. This staff was organized in a hierarchical structure, heading up to a nurse clinical coordinator who was in accord in many ways with our aims, but was unwilling to involve nurses in the committee. The planning group scheduled separate interviews of at least an hour's length with her, each of the four head nurses on the wards, and the physicians and other treatment staffs in the unit. The interviews were completely recorded, with permission, and transcribed. The theme of each was, "What is happening with families here?" This provided a baseline of information, revealed the limited formal investment of ward staff in working with families, and the infrequency of family visiting. It also produced some suggestions, even though securing them was beyond our intent.

It took over a year of such regular and quiet meetings before the nurse coordinator agreed that ward nursing staffs might join the committee. During this year, minutes of the committee's meetings were prepared and circulated to all staff, to build knowledge and involvement. The delay in securing the permission of the nursing staff might be explained in part by the committee's wish to cut across protocol whereby a head nurse represented each ward staff in almost all off-ward meetings. We hoped for appointments from all levels of the staff who have consistent and intensive contacts with family members.

Finally nursing staff joined the committee, and regular and alternative representatives from each ward have since provided the link with the total nursing staff. The committee's work moved into an action phase that has continued to expand especially through the work of the nursing staffs on the wards. Staff education, mostly informal, has been an indirect consequence of ward participation, and the culture for families has been transformed. Ongoing assessment of family participation has been kept active. Now 87 percent of patients receive visits from family members, who come an average of 52 miles to the hospital.

Curiously, the committee has never had a chairperson. This was partly a consequence of my own unwillingness to take such a role, for fear that would identify the committee's work too strongly with me. I did not wish to create circumstances that would reduce the visibility of the other committee members, all of whom have become involved actively. We function as peers, and I have been the minute-taker.

I have gone into detail about the organization of the committee to illustrate that functions of the family context therapist in the hospital may include organization, study, involvement of others and team-building, communication and visibility, training, evaluation, and programmed action.

Delegation of responsibilities to families

The second method illustrates a technique for conceiving changes in the situation for families in the hospital. It begins with the intent to determine aspects of hospitalization that can be delegated to the family and leads, then, to negotiating with staff to organize the hospital as a social and spatial environment within which delegations may be made.

There is no sharp dividing line between functions that families are experienced in performing and many performed by hospital staffs. Obviously there are private aspects of family life in which a hospital cannot function, and conversely many aspects of hospital life that families cannot undertake. However, between these exclusive functions there is an area of overlap wherein performance is appropriate to either institution. Diagrammatically this is portrayed in Figure 1.

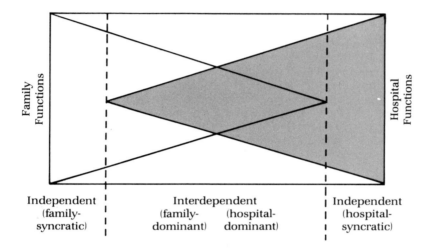

Independent	Interdependent		Independent
(family-	(family-	(hospital-	(hospital-
syncratic)	dominant)	dominant)	syncratic)

Posed at either extreme are the separate functions of the family and those of the institution. In intermediate areas on each side of the center, the family and hospital functions overlap. On the left, the family functions are dominant; those of the hospital overlap somewhat. At the counterpoint area on the right, the hospital functions predominate. In the center, the functions are identical, so may be performed by either—at the risk of competition or relief. The patient's position on the figure has not been indicated because it changes, from the far left while at home to the far right when a medical crisis demands hospital functions almost exclusively. Recovery and convalescence move the patient's position increasingly over to the family side.

Delegation of tasks to the family would be inconceivable if many of the functions assumed by the hospital were not natural continuations of domestic functions. For instance, in hospital literature there is increasing distinction made between medical and "hotel" aspects of service. In hospitals in developing countries, families carry such functions for a patient as feeding, dressing, laundering, bathing, exercising, hairdressing, and keeping the room tidy (Bell, 1970a). By comparison, in our country, hospital delegation of many such functions is prescribed by custom, law, regulations, insurance, professional standards, staffing protocols, and other limiting factors. Nevertheless there remain areas for negotiation and change within present codes, and broad areas for change in the codes themselves. For selected families, carryover of domestic family functions can be an intense way to communicate with a patient to ensure close family relations. To make this possible, the family context therapist brings influence on staff, helping them to work out issues about delegation, training, supervision, space, timing, and support.

Such a program is actively in progress now for a number of long-term severely disabled patients who can no longer feed themselves and have problems in swallowing. Staff who used to do the feeding are relieved that family members will come often for the prolonged feeding process; and family members seem to welcome this chance to supplement speech with activities to demonstrate their continuing affection and concern. Similarly, some are now taking full responsibility for their patients' clothing.

Programs should not be restricted to such practical tasks only. Many families are well able to take part in selected aspects of treatment. Family monitoring of a patient's condition is an especially good illustration, since it happens spontaneously in many hospital rooms. With staff collaboration, the scope of family monitoring may be extended, for the sake of patient welfare and the concentration of staff energies on other activities. A wife, experienced in observing and interpreting her husband's daily condition, may have a better base of knowledge about her husband than a staff person, and thus a broader perspective for making sound judgments about changes and their meanings—and a husband may do the same for his wife. Since physical signs and nonverbal behavior provide primary data in planning and modifying treatments, the family member used as a monitor can be a valuable resource for staff.

The family context therapist becomes an agent to help the hospital utilize families for functions that are direct carryovers from home and becomes valuable in helping families and staff to arrive at clear definitions about where they will set the dividing line between them. This line is usually established somewhere in the area of overlapping functions, not necessarily by reason. Once the line is firmly decided, the tension of competition decreases.

Pertinent but more remote from families is the therapist's participation in securing changes in formal codes that circumscribe family functioning in the hospital. The therapist becomes a speaker for families in forums that pay particular heed to the voices of professionals and officials, sometimes of patients, but often insufficiently of families.

Methods illustrated by the above may be summarized as identification of functions in common between staff and families; broadening staff awareness of the overlap; assisting staff in planning delegation of functions, or families in claiming them; staff training; helping staff to supervise and educate families; facilitating solutions for problems of space and time; trouble-shooting; and speaking for families in official forums.

Courses and outcomes of family involvement

A third way of developing intervention techniques has been through analyses of courses and outcomes of patients' hospitalizations, to encourage different modes of family relations appropriate to various hospital programs.

In a large comprehensive hospital, several basic patterns of hospitalization are common and predictable: (a) outpatient treatment, with continued community living; (b) hospitalization for acute or chronic illnesses, where recovery to prehospital functions and rehabilitation to home are the expected outcomes; (c) hospitalization for acute or chronic illnesses where residual health problems and treatments will involve a patient in transfer to a community facility, temporarily or permanently; (d) hospitalization permanently for chronic illnesses or disabilities, where maintenance of the patient's current condition is the desired and expected outcome; (e) hospitalization where the patient will remain in the institution, the patient's physical or psychological status is deteriorating, and retardation of the pace of deterioration is the aim and anticipated outcome; (f) hospitalization in anticipation of death.

Detailing such a list became the starting point for the question, "What hospital programming on behalf of families would be desirable within each pattern?" This exercise led the family context therapist to insights on the basis of which to plan interventions, design ways to modify hospital services and physical spaces, reduce or remove hospital-created family stresses, and to provide supports for families. Implicit in this programming is early formulation of rehabilitation and placement objectives, and explicit selection of program elements and resources for individual patients and their families.

By providing an overall framework for long-term planning, programming toward distant objectives becomes a complement and sometimes a corrective to responding to immediate needs and demands of patients and families. Such a framework, with its patient and family orientation, reduces the likelihood that a patient's schedule, treatments, activities and experiences will become routinized, and inadvertently general rather than personal.

To illustrate how the family context therapist uses the contingency of anticipated outcome to facilitate staff-patient-family relations and benefits, several examples follow.

(a) If the ultimate goal for the patient is return to home, the program may be organized to maintain all possible links between the patient and home during hospitalization. Representative steps might include the bringing of possessions from home such as a pillow, books, pictures, or an object of sentiment. The person of the patient, according to appearance and behavior characteristic of domestic life, might be sustained by encouraging a patient to dress in his or her own clothing, and continue functions undertaken at home, such as decision-making, financial management, or emotional support for others. Frequent family visits at the hospital, and patient visits home may be scheduled. Family members may be trained for treatment and management activities they will assume on the patient's return home. Specific care may be conducted in such a way as to facilitate adjustment in the home environment; for instance, using a bathtub like that at home rather than a hospital shower, or transferring the patient into a regular bed out of a hospital bed as soon as possible. Patient maintenance tasks—hairdressing, bathing, assistance in eating—may be delegated to family members when possible. Problem-solving conferences for staff, patient and family working together may be set up.

(b) By contrast, where it is openly rather than tacitly agreed that placement in the hospital is terminal, the hospital-family program is then oriented in a markedly different direction. The family context therapist intervenes with staff to assist them in formulating a program where the following elements are offered: the final nature of the placement is openly acknowledged, to provide circumstances to overcome pseudo-optimism, and to lead to an environment where staff, patient, and family may coordinate their efforts toward enriched understanding and communication, realistic expectations and plans, and mutually acceptable ways of integrating activities. Families are given help to prepare for the patient's death, so the pain of bereavement may be anticipated and somewhat reduced by pre-planning and management of the practical steps required in the hospital and elsewhere. Family members are invited to relate to the patient according to the patterns they prefer. Staff support is provided to assume family-like functions that have become inappropriate or onerous for family in light of the illness, staff are prepared emotionally for the expected final outcome through discussions about their experiences with staff colleagues and are assisted in providing treatment, relations, and an enriching environment, in recognition that families may not be able or may not wish to be engaged very actively in assisting the patient.

(c) If a patient is to be sent, following treatment, to a community facility, such as an extended care facility, a domiciliary institution, or a half-way house, a still different programming becomes relevant. Where family members have been involved closely with the patient prior to hospitalization, assistance may be needed from staff to help them make the transition to relations across physical separation. For the family, preparation will vary according to the circumstances. It may include: participation in placement planning; tapering off visits; transfer of family functions to staff; support for the family in dealing with the transition emotionally; and development of alternate relations and activities for the family. For the patient, hospitalization is programmed to orient him or her to some aspects of life in the anticipated placement setting. The transition may be eased by going with the patient to visit the new location, making introductions to staff and residents there, carryover of personal belongings, and communication of information.

Where family members are emotionally distant and where the patient has difficulty in relating to the family, staff may need help to build bridges to the family, so staff will be able, at least, to assure the patient that the family knows where he or she is going and understands that they may visit in the new setting. If the family is completely disengaged, planning for family surrogates may also be of use.

Such illustrations in no way exhaust the variables to be accounted for in relation to the course of treatment. So, also, planning for families in relation to specific illnesses and their consequences becomes a similar mode of intervention. The above examples are set forth to highlight how new insights and programs merge when adequate account is taken of the projected outcomes and the family is considered in relation to those outcomes.

To summarize additional interventive strategies now in use: the family context therapist and hospital colleagues analyze and project the nature of family relations during hospitalization; relate family participation to treatment and placement objectives; organize programs to maintain all possible links with home; arrange for patients' possessions to be available in the hospital; provide opportunities for a patient to continue some family functions in the hospital; facilitate home visits, when possible; train family members for carry-over of treatment and management activities; develop home-like spaces and furnishings; schedule staff-patient-family conferences; acknowledge prognosis for patients, and develop circumstances and environments to promote adaptations; facilitate preparations for death; adjust patient-family interactions in hospital program to family preferences; prepare staff for dealing with families during a patient's dying and death; assist staff to make allowances for non-involvement of families; facilitate patient-family separation; and build bridges to assure patient knowledge of family and family knowledge of the patient and his/her setting.

Derivations from constructs regarding hospital-family relations

The next method for determining interventions grows from study of constructed dimensions of institution-family relations. Inasmuch as little systematic theory about such relations has been formalized and research has been scanty, many of the dimensions that follow are assumptive and abstract. From such abstractions, though, the family context therapist can derive specific approaches and techniques for modification of the relations, and project programs to affect and benefit families. By paying heed to what is happening within an institution regarding any of these constructs, and observing or projecting family impact, the therapist can then use developed methods or devise new ones to ward off injurious results and promote beneficial ones for families.

It is useful to examine briefly a range of constructs to illustrate ways by which the family context therapist might intervene in a hospital.

Construct 1. An institution relates to families over time and relations may be structured in terms of time-spans (stages).

In a hospital, relational time runs from pre-admission contacts, through admission and the course of inpatient treatment, to discharge (or death), and followup. The total time span may be brief or prolonged over years. Modifications in the duration of patient-family associations with the hospital can affect the family in diverse ways (Rosen, 1976). For example, undue delay in admission may accentuate family breakdown and patient problems. Prolonging hospitalization for one patient may promote family well-being, and for another, speed family breakdown. Extension of hospitalization beyond treatment effectiveness may consolidate family arrangements for living separately from the patient and make temporary adjustments permanent. A family context therapist can help the hospital control the length of hospitalization, not just to achieve treatment purposes, but also to facilitate family well-being.

A modest example illustrates such an intervention. A patient with several disorders required three prostheses prior to discharge, new glasses, dentures, and a wheelchair, each of which had to be supplied in a different hospital service. The simplest method, especially because of problems in securing escorts, would have been to complete prosthetic fitting in one service, then move on to another, until done. The family context therapist, sensing an urgency for the patient's return home, undertook to initiate, coordinate, and integrate a schedule to allow coterminous fittings, and to make all secondary arrangements for transportation and escort.

Construct 2. An institution engages in relations with a family that are directional: (a) institution-initiated toward the family, or family-initiated, calling forth institution response; and (b) pro-family or contra-family.

The directional quality of institution-family relations can affect patients and families in harmful or helpful ways. When an institution fails to take needed initiative and waits to respond to family pressure, those families with ability for taking action are likely to accomplish their aims; those who deferentially wait for staff are likely to be overlooked. Fortunately because of the spread of effect, those who are more vigorous or vocal may accomplish directional changes of benefit far beyond themselves.

This translates into interventions for a family context therapist. As an example, a therapist instituted a forum for family members to encourage their input into hospital program planning. The needs as seen by family members are not always realizable, nor would they necessarily be advantageous. Even so, confrontation of issues raised by families often forces staff to rethink and replan programs and procedures. A dramatic illustration of this occurred in an African hospital in response to an English nurse who tried to eliminate families from their customary 24-hour bedside vigil and care. In a mass exodus families took their sick and went elsewhere, forcing the nurse to revise her policies.

Another illustration: on one ward anger and punitive responses between families and staff became so intense that I was invited in to help. I met for an hour with the family visitors to record all that they liked about the hospital staff—with the understanding that I would share what they said with the staff. I had to allow the discharge of some negative feelings, but I did not record these. I then met with the staff, showed them the family session notes, received a similar list from the staff of what they liked about the family members, and then fed that back to the families. The tension deescalated, and this strategy helped to establish a relation wherein some joint planning followed.

Fundamentally, the flow of actions should allow initiative on both the institution's and the family's sides. Operationally this is extremely difficult to accomplish. Each organization (institution and family) is complex, and if the institution had only one family to cope with, problems would probably be worked through effectively. But many families have to be accommodated, and their needs, wishes, expectations, and reactions differ immensely. The aim of the hospital is normally individuation of services for patients and families; imperatives for coordination and organization in implementation of programs make the aim unrealistic. Thus the family context therapist who works in an institution must try to comprehend and relate to each side, not for compromising the effort to benefit families, but for understanding the scope and difficulty of achieving institution change, and for working out necessary steps to aid both families and the institution.

Construct 3. The institution relates to the family within space: (a) the institution's space (where family members visit a patient); (b) the family's space (when a hospital social worker visits the home on behalf of the institution); and (c) neutral space (where a hospital representative meets a family member in a community agency).

Space is expensive to construct; the very act of construction to allow a wide range of activities by staff and patients can only be achieved by negotiation among competing persons and groups, and compromise of priorities. Accordingly, staff develop territorial possessiveness. Changes in space, or in use of space, are often accompanied by intensification of tension, jealousy, resentment, and other negative feelings. In terms of space, families and patients normally have low priority—they are migrants, staff are settlers. Yet patients and relatives also need space.

Families respond to the environment. Depending on the privacy, tone of voices can change, confidences may be shared or withheld; freedom of action or paralysis may follow. Take for example the differences of behavior in a four-bed ward and on a sundeck. In the ward, family may be so frozen as to scarcely shift in their seats, let alone adjust a pillow or stroke a patient's face. On the sundeck, they may laugh, joke, move about, play, whisper secrets—all affected by the change in physical space within a few moments in time.

Institution space or lack of space develops communicative value. It conveys a message about status and worth, the form of relations, functions, and expected outcomes. Hospital buildings, wards, and beds get labeled, and patients and families respond in terms of the labels, as well as on personal terms. The family context therapist must be aware of space and its therapeutic importance, which can be increased by systematic attention.

A project to transform space of a whole ward to create a domestic type environment for long-term patients encouraged consideration of features of home spaces of which patients and relatives are often deprived in a hospital. Habituation to the physical features of a ward, such as a day-room, is natural. Patients claim their "own" chairs, sit facing a TV set to watch, or ignore programs they have not chosen, and respond to every environmental support for withdrawal, inactivity, and non-communication. Meanwhile, they are also being trained to forget the demands of a home-like environment, being deconditioned to the adaptations required in a living-room, kitchen, or bathroom, and dispossessed of the forms of activity and relations possible at home—thus discouraging family visitors from continuing former relations, and accentuating the problems of rehabilitation.

A family context therapist might seek development of a series of increasingly home-like rooms, through which patient transfer could mark progress, and prepare the patient and family for discharge and return to the community. In our hospital one small step toward implementation of such a concept has taken place. One four-bed ward and a neighboring portion of a communal toilet have been remodeled. A bed-sitting room, small kitchen, and private shower and toilet make up the modest apartment that has been created. Its intended uses have been thwarted, however, by protocol, regulations, pressures for beds, restrictions on patient transfer, and a change in the patient population being served. The space continues to serve as a four-bed ward.

A demonstration of the possibilities for domestic space has been in operation for the past seven years, however, in the Family Focus program at the Stanford Medical Center, where physical therapists and I have established a transitional facility (a modular home) to which a newly handicapped patient and family move three days before the patient's discharge (Sasano et al., 1977). Here the family live together again and learn the new functions and skills needed to adjust to the disabled patient. The home environment of the facility produces striking transformations in patient and family behavior, creating an incentive to learn and resume activities, reducing anxiety and depression, energizing temporarily immobilized persons to take initiative, and facilitating adaptive readjustments in family relations.

As staff and families move beyond hospital spaces, their relations change, and new opportunities to intervene become possible. Going beyond a newly-constructed environment to meet with a family in their home allows experience with some of the daily activities of the family, direct observation of individual and interpersonal behaviors, including some with staff not visible in a hospital environment, information about problems and potentials for individual and interpersonal functions not previously seen, and a sense of the resources of the natural physical environment. As a family therapist, the professional can intervene directly in such a setting if the family will find therapy relevant. As a family context therapist, going to the home may give the professional insights to plan future changes in the hospital to assist such families, or to direct mobilization of external resources.

Meeting the patient and family on neutral territory also expands the possibility for new insights and plans. Combining experiences from all three settings can permit comprehensive planning of environmental supports for treatment and rehabilitation.

Construct 4. The institution specifies criteria governing the relations with families. These specifications may be formal or informal; voluntary for the family, or involuntary; applied rigidly or loosely; and, in general, for all families, or specifically, to certain kinds of families.

One illustration is sufficient to show application to context therapy. When I came to the Palo Alto VA Hospital in 1973, family visiting in one service was limited to three hours on Wednesdays, and weekends. This pattern was established by a hospital-wide memorandum setting forth official policy: "Visits by relatives and friends can be of considerable value, but they must be controlled so that they do not conflict with patient care ... patient care should be uninterrupted."

The family committee took as one of its first steps the changing of this policy. The revision that emerged did not include all our recommended language, but transformed the orientation to visiting. Now the policy reads: "Visits by relatives and friends can be of considerable value and, on certain services, participation of relatives and friends in patient care is usually desirable. Such visits are customarily encouraged when they do not interrupt patient treatment." Such a reorientation of policy facilitated a gradual reduction of rigidity about visiting. Family members now visit any weekday, and generally according to their own time preferences.

Not all criteria governing family-patient-staff relations are expressed in formal rules. Traditions develop and have similar potency in determining family interactions with the hospital. The family context therapist becomes a reviewer of policies, and intercedes to adjust policies to increase family-patient involvement.

Construct 5. Over time any institution changes functional processes with families. The institution confronts many external and internal factors that affect functions. Technologies change, goals shift, personnel are hired or leave, and internal and external resources extend or abridge functions and relations. The changes may take place rapidly, or so slowly that they are barely perceptible even in retrospect.

This dimension clarifies definition of the functions of a family context therapist. Initiation of change is not the only task. On behalf of families, efforts may need to be expended to influence the direction of change efforts that are pending or already in motion. Attempting to prevent family-destructive institutional changes can be equally relevant. The family context therapist becomes a monitor of change, evaluating the potential impact on families of anticipated and new developments in programs, personnel, money, political climate, and laws. Out of the evaluations comes knowledge of new opportunities for families, new resources to bring to bear on their problems and support their growth, and new modes to affect the institution on their behalf. Likewise the therapist becomes alert to changes potentially injurious or destructive to family welfare. Some monitoring takes the form of research or collecting statistical data, some is through communications on the grapevine, and some derives from keeping current with journals, newspapers, official memoranda, and other information sources. Another is through projecting possible organizational directions, and watching for signs to confirm or negate such projections.

The place of the family context therapist within the hospital staff and structure is a salient factor. For example, I am assigned to the service in the hospital that formerly had the lowest prestige among all patient services—extended care. My position includes no direct authority over patient programs and carries no administrative status. My job description places me in a "staff" role, as a consultant, planner and teacher, which gives me no direct power to implement programs. These may appear at first to be disadvantages but in practice, they are an immense advantage.

I have to work through other staff and, through them, I am linked to ongoing change. Their input is invaluable; they bring their knowledge of patients, families, and they have considerable freedom within their positions to change their functions and to influence others, particularly at the levels of direct care for patients and of relations with families. Through them I am tied into a broad communication network. Other staff keep me informed of conflicts and problems that can affect the timing of changes and together we are able to pace adaptations to readiness for change and to ongoing change efforts. Thus it becomes apparent that the responsibility and credit for the future benefits of program changes do not belong to any one person but are shared by all who help bring them about.

Construct 6. Any institution is one of a number that relate to and affect a family at any given time, sometimes in complementary or parallel directions, and sometimes in competition and conflict. An institution's awareness of the impact of other institutions may range from full and explicit knowledge to total ignorance.

The impact of many organizations inevitably creates conflicting pressures that accentuate family problems, limit family resources, and structure family goals. The hospital is so monolithic an organization that the worker inside is likely to forget the variety of other organizational impacts on families. The family context therapist, in contrast, may become the agent who keeps bringing to the attention of staff some of the influences of other institutions to account for a patient's behavior and for the ways in which a family acts. It is probably over-idealistic to believe that such information can lead a hospital and other community institutions to engage to any great extent in joint planning and integrated programming, particularly on behalf of individual families. But the stresses of multi-institution involvement do affect patient health, the course of illnesses, the responses to treatments, and the outcomes.

Since occasionally a hospital changes relations with patients and families in response to institutional pressures elsewhere, the family context therapist can help families by serving as a generalist in regard to institutions, as well as a specialist within the institution in which interventions are being engineered. In such a role, the therapist can help to maintain a cross-institutional perspective, and occasionally help the hospital staff to keep the larger picture in mind.

In the foregoing section the basic process has been shown to entail selecting a component of an institution, in its form or processes, as a stimulus to examining its impact on the family, and from that starting point projecting interventions that will modify the institution toward increasing family benefits. However, the above illustrations do not comprise the full scope of the work of the family context therapist. To prevent the misconception that the range of the therapy is narrow, let me mention other stimuli that have prompted moves toward comprehension and definition of the therapy, and toward specification of methods.

Included in the initial stimuli are the following:

(a) When a patient has lost or must lose family functions temporarily or permanently, interventions needed to organize hospital assistance to the patient and family, toward as advantageous adaptations as possible, have been thought out and introduced.

(b) Analysis has been made of sociological, economic, and historical studies of the family, such as those recently brought together (Daedalus, 1977), toward understanding factors that suggest or contraindicate certain interventions in an institution such as the hospital.

(c) The relations and functions of hospitals with patients (and by implication their families) of different ages, with some particular disease entities, various involvements of body systems, and different conditions of severity or chronicity, have been studied for precise determinations of possible family relations and how to improve them.

(d) The resource services in the hospital—administration, finances, supplies, engineering, building management—have been examined to understand their direct and indirect impact on patients and families and to suggest some future interventions.

(e) The developing literature on cross-organization and organization-environment relations, as reported with increasing sophistication in the fields of sociology and business (Hannan & Freeman, 1977; Shortell, 1977; Dornbusch & Scott, 1975; Warren, 1977; Turk, 1977), and to a limited extent in the field of marriage and the family (Burr, 1973; Safilios-Rothschild, 1976; Heintz, Held & Levy, 1975), have shown how infrequently small institutions, such as the family, have been studied as they relate to large organizations, such as the hospital. Two directions for family context therapy have followed: to examine if variables identified in describing large organizations suggest directions for research on family-organization relations; and to test if some of the factors seen as important with large organizations suggest possible change strategies through family context therapy.

(f) Critiques of comprehensive health and mental health programs are becoming more incisive and sophisticated; they are allowing us to project possible family relations with anticipated programs, to compare the relevant advantages of various systems for families, and to think through some of the steps needed to assure that families are benefitted.

(g) Philosophies and strategies of social change (Cooper, 1976; Rothman, 1974; Warren, 1977; Hernes, 1977) have been studied to determine implications for methods of environmental and interpersonal change for families.

(h) Comparative studies of organizations are being reviewed to suggest, develop, and change variables of relevance to the family and the hospital.

Restating the fundamental developmental process: The family context therapist keeps asking the questions, "What implications does this situation or issue within an institution, and/or its relations with the family, have for institution interventions on behalf of the family?" and "What methodology would make it possible to implement such interventions?"

In summary, then, a new and very broad conceptual framework and program for changing families has been set forth. The core of the program is change in the family environment for the welfare of families. In practice this has been begun primarily in community institutions relating to the family. The specific illustrations set forth here are drawn from work in hospitals. The framework expands the role of family therapists and groups their functions with those of change and linking agents such as educators, clergy, managers, and human service professionals. Applications are anticipated in both helping and basic institutions in the community, and potentially in community change itself—all for the benefit of the family.

REFERENCES

Bell, J. E. *The family in the hospital: Lessons from developing countries.* Washington, D.C.: U.S. Government Printing Office, 1970.(a)

Bell, J. E. The future of family therapy. *Family Process,* 1970, 9, 127–141. (b)

Burr, W. R. *Theory construction and the sociology of the family.* New York: John Wiley & Sons, 1973.

Cooper, R. The open field. *Human Relations,* 1976, 29, 999–1017.

Dornbusch, S. M. & Scott, W. R. *Evaluation and exercise of authority: A theory of control applied to diverse organizations.* San Francisco: Jossey-Bass, 1975.

Graubard, S. R. (Ed.), The family. *Daedalus: Proceedings of the American Academy of Arts and Sciences,* 1977, 106(2), 1–242.

Hannan, M. T. & Freeman, J. The population ecology of organizations. *American Journal of Sociology,* 1977, 82, 929–964.

Heintz, P., Held, T. & Levy, R. Family structure and society. *Journal of Marriage and the Family,* 1975, 37, 861–870.

Hernes, G. Structural change in social processes. *American Journal of Sociology,* 1977, 82, 513–546.

Maddox, G. L. Families as context and resource in chronic illness. In S. Sherwood (Ed.), *Long-term care: A handbook for researchers, planners, and providers.* New York: Spectrum Publications, 1975, 317–347.

Rosen, B., Katzoff, A., Carrillo, C. & Klein, D. F. Clinical effectiveness of "short" vs. "long" psychiatric hospitalization: 1. Inpatient results. *Archives of General Psychiatry,* 1976 (Nov.), 33(11), 1316–1322.

Rothman, J. *Planning and organizing for social change: Action principles from social science research.* New York: Columbia University Press, 1974.

Safilios-Rothschild, C. A macro- and micro-examination of family power and love: An exchange model. *Journal of Marriage and the Family,* 1976, 38, 355–362.

Sasano, E. M., Shepard, K. F., Bell, J. E., Davies, N. H., Hansen, E. M. & Sanford, T. L. The family in physical therapy. *Physical Therapy,* 1977, 57, 153–159.

Scottish Home and Health Department. *Suggestions and complaints in hospitals: Report of the working party.* Edinburgh: Her Majesty's Stationery Office, 1969.

Shortell, S. M. The role of the environment in a configurational theory of organizations. *Human Relations,* 1977, 30, 275–302.

Turk, H. *Organizations in modern life.* San Francisco: Jossey-Bass, 1977.

Warren, R. *Truth, love, and social change.* Chicago: Rand, 1977.

The Concept of Personal Network
in Clinical Practice

Gerald D. Erickson

The practice of clinicians in all the helping professions has undergone wide-ranging change in the past two decades. This change has been uneven and halting, but an essential aspect has been a movement toward a wider arena of practice, including a variety of social network practices. The concept of personal network holds high promise for becoming a major unifying framework in clinical practice: as an analytic viewpoint, as a schema for problem location, and as an arena of practice and research. This paper will review the developing strands of network practice, examine some of the forms and characteristics of personal networks, and consider several theoretical and practice issues.

SOCIAL NETWORKS

An initial difficulty with the concept of social networks is the relative lack of a commonly accepted terminology that can be used descriptively and the rather limited set of concepts available for analytic purposes. As an area of research, the study of social networks is only about twenty years old. Barnes (5) apparently first used the concept as a mode of analysis in a study of a small community reported in 1954; Bott (7) developed the idea in her seminal work *Family And Social Network* in 1957; it entered the clinical field a decade later and has since been utilized in several practice forms. Much of the basic research has been conducted by British social anthropologists and sociologists (6) (17) (18) (20), while practice applications seem to be largely a North American product (1) (10) (12) (21) (22) (23) (24). There appears to be only a minimal connection between basic research and interpersonal practice. For example, while Bott's study is frequently cited in the practice literature, references to her central hypothesis relating network connectedness and conjugal relationship are rare.

"The Concept of Personal Network in Clinical Practice," by G. D. Erickson. In *Family Process*, 1975, Volume 14, No. 4, pp. 487–498. Copyright 1975 by Family Process, Inc. Reprinted by permission.

Mitchell's (20, p. 2) definitions of social network as a specific set of linkages among a defined set of persons, with the additional property that the characteristics of these linkages as a whole may be used to interpret the social behavior of the persons involved is quite exact and specific. In practice, and elsewhere, everyone is free to use terminology in whatever way seems helpful. The idea of "network" as used in practice is often little related to the concept as Mitchell defines it. Usually, only something similar to the first clause is provided as a rationale—e.g. the set of kinship or friendship links that exist between an identified patient or client and close others in the environment. Characterizing these links as a whole is of a different order of complexity and may or may not contribute to the efficacy of therapeutic work.

SOME CURRENT USAGES OF SOCIAL NETWORK

While the idea of network has a variety of meanings and uses currently, an attempt at categorization may be useful prior to discussing the concept of personal network. In general, usage related to practice seems to fall into four categories: (a) network as a curative grouping of individuals; (b) as a location of resources; (c) as an interpreter of help-seeking behavior and utilization of services; (d) as a mitigator of the effects of multi-organizational involvement with a family.

These categories are not mutually exclusive, being present in most practice applications, but vary in the degree of emphasis given.

Network as a curative grouping

This represents perhaps the most extensively developed area of practice. Here, network is defined as ". . . all members of the kinship system, all friends and neighbors of the family, and, in fact, everyone who is of significance to the nuclear family that offers the presenting problem" (22, p. 312). The aim of therapy with this grouping has been formulated by Attneave (1, p. 192) as ". . . mobilizing the family, relatives, and friends into a social force that counteracts the depersonalizing trend in contemporary life patterns." In some ways this represents an expansion of family therapy, since the nuclear family is usually taken to be the focal group. The model is a clinical one involving an already identified "patient" and drawing together close others while utilizing action and verbal techniques drawn from group and sensitivity work. The wider network is said to be at least partially pathological—thus the group is assembled not only for the curative effect on the patient, but also to bring about relationship changes in the network. As many as six network sessions are held with a team of therapists. There is a strong belief that network bonds should be tightened and that close-knit networks promote mental health to a greater degree than loose-knit networks.

Network as a resource grouping

The grounding for this facet of network practice lies in the work of Litwak (15), Sussman (25), and others who have emphasized the continuing ties between nuclear families and their extended kinship systems. These links are largely voluntary and tend to be reinforced at times of crisis. The basic theme is that "... nuclear families are active with other units within a kin-related network ... (which) ... is capable of providing for its members economic, emotional, educational, welfare, and other supports complementary or competitive to those furnished by other societal institutions" (25, p. 240). The set of relationships posited are based on theories of social exchange and the concept of reciprocity.

The notion of the network as a storehouse of resources is held in common in some way in all network practice. A possible employer may be in the group, someone may know of a vacant apartment, someone may possess a specific skill, or general positive expectations may be tapped (13). A similar theme is found in viewing individuals in the neighborhood as possible resources — the "natural neighbor" (9). The logic is that since patterns of mutual aid and caregiving exist in family networks, these should be identified and perhaps intensified in practice. Policies of early discharge from mental hospitals (or refusal to hospitalize) stem at least in part from the concept of the family network as a resource center.

An antithetical viewpoint is revealed in concerns about family or network overload (28): that community mental health often means largely the substitution of family care for professional care (26) and that the adaptive capacity of small networks may be exceeded by attempting to extract more resources than can be supplied. Further, families are said to lack means of effective feedback to professionals and program planners about their adaptive capacities. One concrete result of this has been the formation of a new kind of network—one composed of groups of families containing schizophrenics (16). Their central concern is to act as a corrective to planning bodies and institutions who tend, in the group's estimation, to overrepresent the capacity of the family network.

Network as interpreter of help-seeking behavior

Here the emphasis is on interactive processes in the network prior to referral and treatment and on ways in which networks act as constraints to, or as facilitators of, service utilization (18). Studies of at least partial networks have been conducted in the mental health field in relation to hospital admission (14), re-hospitalization (8), and community maintenance (11).

Of some importance here is McKinlay's finding that under-utilizers of health and social services differed from utilizers in network patterns of communication and exchange behavior (17) (18). Yet health and welfare policy makers and program planners tend to act as if family networks were uniform.

One area clearly requiring network analysis involves the frequently made observation that large numbers of clients "drop out" after one or two sessions at mental health treatment agencies. Non-continuance in treatment, while certainly linked to such variables as treatment method, organizational procedures, and disjunctions in values and objectives between client and practitioner, is also clearly related to activities in the clients' social networks (6). Little of precision is known, however, of the nature of these influences.

Network as mitigator of effects of multi-organizational involvement

The difficulty of describing the characteristics of network linkages as a whole has been mentioned. It is this step, though, that differentiates networks from other forms of organizations and makes possible the characterization of networks as having patterns and properties of their own. If this were not so, we could speak of "expanded families" or "individuals and close others" and forego the concept of network.

There is a practice method, however, that does attempt to account for linkages as they exist independently of the focal family. This method was first described by Auerswald as the "inter-systems conference" (4) and refers to the bringing together of whole families and representatives of all their helping or care-giving organizations in an attempt to solve family problems. An essential by-product of convening the family network is the possibility of also bringing about change in the care-giving organizations' rules, policies, and inter-organization communication patterns. Auerswald's description (3, p. 211) of "how several systems inadvertently combine in their day-to-day operations in such a way as to frustrate other's activities . . ." is a statement about the state of a personal network containing multiple care-givers with mutually contra-dictory or mutually canceling goals and expectations. Viewing the family and all of its caregivers as a single unit of intervention is what sets this approach apart from the traditional case conference in social casework (10) (12).

A mention of Bott's findings may clarify the importance of taking into account the set of relationships in networks as they operate independently of the focal person or family. Briefly, Bott found that conjugal role performance varied with the connectedness of the bi-lateral kinship and friendship net-work. That is, couples whose kin, friends, neighbors, and workmates knew one another ("close-knit" networks) tended to have segregated role relationships; couples whose kin, friends, etc., tended not to know one another ("loose-knit" networks) had relatively non-segregated, or joint roles. Thus, a set of relation-ships that existed quite apart from the marriage relationship was found to be significant for the relationship. Specifying such linkages is the *sine qua non* of the network concept.

If the concept of network offers anything for clinicians other than an expan-sion of family therapy (valuable enough in itself), it must be shown that additional assessment and treatment ability can accrue to practitioners by developing and expanding the concept. An analogy with the development of family practice is apt. It was not long ago that the family was perceived as forming a part of the backdrop for individual functioning. It was not until families were seen as "wholes" that a family practice became possible. The analogy breaks down at one major point: Family practice can be thought of as an alternative to individual practice; it seems likely, however, that the network concept as expressed in practice will be complementary, and not competitive, with other forms of practice. Service network intervention combined with continuing family therapy (10) is one example. Network practice as a routine procedure will not be fully possible until a number of typical practice situ-ations can be perceived as network problems and reliably described. This may be a long-term task. Yet, it may be worth the effort.

PERSONAL NETWORKS

Social networks can have as their point of anchorage either a person, a conjugal pair, a nuclear family, or another type of organization. As a rule of thumb, if a point of anchorage is not specified, "network" is being used as a metaphor and not a mode of analysis. In the following discussion, the individual is taken as the focal point. If we take the personal network as the unit for inclusion as a framework in clinical practice, it may be possible to appreciate its current utility and short-range possibilities.

A personal network is a flexibly bounded grouping of individuals comprising at least a focal person, everyone the focal person knows or interacts with, the set of relationships between those individuals and the focal person, and the set of relationships that exists independently of the focal person. A minimal personal network in practice would contain (for a member of an intact nuclear family):

(a) the focal person, a conjugal pair, a nuclear family, a bi-lateral kinship grouping—in short, a kinship sector.
(b) a number of friends, acquaintances, neighbors, workmates—a friendship sector.
(c) a social worker, physician, clergyman, and others who stand in relation to the focal person as socially sanctioned helping persons—a service or caregiving sector.

These three sectors are not static; members may be dropped or added, long dormant connections may be rivived at time of crisis, caregivers connected to other family members may be included. Thinking of interpersonal practice as related to one whole personal network offers several immediate advantages:

(a) A sufficiently large number of relationships is included as context for an understanding of behavior.
(b) A number of intervention points can be envisaged within the network.
(c) A number of compatible relationship theories and intervention strategies can be utilized.
(d) Large areas of social science content can be integrated in the structure of the framework.
(e) The clinicians and other caregivers are included in the network, thereby including one or more organizations, their policies, and their programs as legitimate subjects of interest.

There are an equal number of difficulties. We have already seen that defining network in terms of membership alone is not a sufficient basis for description or analysis. Further, we know much more about some sectors of the network than others, and our knowledge of some linkages is virtually non-existent. For example, we know little about the whole area of service-sector relationships and impact on treatment. That is, does it make any difference to the course of treatment if the several members of the service sector differ about theories of causation; know one another; like one another? The connectedness of the network as a whole in clinical practice is largely a mystery, and we are unable to say how network "A" differs from network "B" in essential features and thus how they will differ in treatment needs.

Practitioners customarily work with a high degree of uncertainty about where any given problem is located. Almost any problem dealt with can be thought of as belonging to the individual, the couple, the family, the social structure, or as an epiphenomenon of societal inequality. The act of attempting to perceive the whole personal network forces us to raise at the practice level new kinds of questions—not only about the adaptive capacity of the kin sector, the curative possibilities of the kinship and friendship sectors, the possible resources located in the network for problem-solving, and the facilitative or hindering activities in the kin and friendship sectors, but, at least as importantly, questions of problem location, questions of linkages within and between sectors, and questions about the mesh of needs, services, and policies. The concept of personal network provides a framework for thinking and analysis, as well as a practice structure.

Practice based on a personal network framework is based then on acts of cognition and perception and not acts of faith. There is then no particular reason to attempt interpersonal work with whole or partial networks unless the characteristics of the network are such that this seems the treatment of choice. The only such configuration so far described has been that of multiple-caregiver involvement with a person or family. We might expect the development of some minimal and tentative criteria for involving a wider unit of intervention than the person, conjugal pair, or nuclear family—for whom there exists extensive treatment methodologies and interventive rationales. It would be expected, however, that a personal network view would tend to alter the content and goals of individual, couple, and family practice.

Network indicators for intervention

A few characteristics of personal networks that provide a basis for wider forms of intervention can be suggested. Since problematic network shapes, connections, and content are largely yet to be identified, the following examples are offered as tentative models indicating possibilities for intervention:

(a) A network is moving from a tight-knit to loose-knit (or vice versa) form. For example, the writer has worked with all the members of a residential religious order in transition from an extremely tight-knit network to a considerably looser shape. The consequences of each member making friends and acquaintances who do not know one another or the other members can have profound effects on the development of, and confusion about, new behavioral norms.

(b) The kinship and friendship sectors of the network are severely truncated and the service sector large and marked by a low degree of connectedness—i.e. when the caregivers do not know one another. It may be hypothesized that truncated kinship and friendship sectors precede the development of an elaborated service sector.

(c) The flow of communications between focal person and the kinship sector is uni-directional—e.g. where the focal person is the recipient of behavioral advice from a number of members without opportunity to reciprocate. Thus it is, for example, that many people do not want their kin to know of their hospitalization for an emotional disorder; it is not that the kin will not want to help, but rather that this help, because it cannot readily be returned, will be experienced by the person as stigmatizing.

Prescriptions for action

It is remarkable that so little is known of specific behavioral recommendations made to individuals with emotional problems from any network sector. But one way kin and others attempt to provide assistance is to offer "prescriptions for action." These range from the conventional ("pull yourself together") and emotionally distant ("one should sleep more") to the idiosyncratic ("see a faith healer") and emotionally involved ("tell me how you feel"). It may be supposed that the quantity and quality of prescriptions, their timing, source, and congruence, influence the identification of problems, the help-seeking process, and the course of treatment. The whole area of "prescriptions for action" may be a fruitful one in network analysis in that it provides a bridging concept between sectors. If we define a "prescription for action" as a behavioral recommendation made by a network member to a focal person, which if carried out is said to offer hope of improving a situation, condition, or state, then we have a means of quantifying and comparing prescriptions for such items as agreement, ambiguity, conflict within and between sectors, and the like.

(d) The network is characterized by a low degree of reachability—i.e. the focal person has difficulty getting in touch with kin, friends, caregivers. Network connections in which "A" reaches "C" and "D" only through person "B" would demonstrate this characteristic. While this certainly occurs in kin sectors, network analysis may also make a contribution here in the study of service availability and the formation of service sectors. In Great Britain, for example, a person believing himself in need of mental health services does not directly link up with a psychiatrist, psychologist, or social worker. Access to the system is controlled by the general practitioner, who may or may not agree with the desired link. There are always at least two professionals (general practitioner and consulting psychiatrist) standing between a person wishing help and, say, a clinical psychologist. The existence of this simple structural characteristic of service sectors has had major consequences for the development of the mental health professions, timing of entry to treatment, and prevailing treatment philosophies. These are matters worthy of detailed study and cannot be developed here.

(e) The network is marked by a low degree of permanence and durability—i.e. caregivers come and go, shifts from rural to urban settings have separated the person or family from the wider network with no compensating growth in a revised network.

CONCLUSIONS

It can be seen that only a beginning has been made in developing a descriptive and conceptual framework for network analysis. But the study of attribution processes in networks (how problems are defined by whom), patterns of mutual aid, the differentiation of problems that can be solved within the kin and friendship sectors from those that require professional care, and the appraisal of network capacity for adaptation, are often matters of everyday concern to all clinical workers.

A note of caution and a degree of humility is indicated. The irony of sociological analysis as described by Mennell (19, p. 168) is also appropriate for the helping professions confronting complex organizations like networks. He writes: "It is a facet of the social distribution of knowledge that the facts of the situation may be incompletely known to any of the actors; even if they each pool their particular knowledge, they may still not possess every piece of the jigsaw puzzle. There may be links in the system, interdependencies unrecognized by anyone, and the system may play tricks on those enmeshed in it."

On the other hand, the importance of coming to grips with networks can be indicated by saying that if Bott was right, a great deal of mutuality-promoting marriage and family therapy has been wrong—or worse yet, rejected by large numbers of people without the service sector knowing why. For if conjugal role performance is linked to network configuration, efforts to help modify some distant marriage relationships without perceiving the wider network (and its behavioral concomitants) will be largely met by failure or non-continuance in treatment.

The current task in relating networks to the field of mental health is to discover how particular configurations, content, and connections vary with respect to a range of phenomena: specific mental health problems, the definition of problems, course of treatment, hospitalization and rehospitalization, corrective activities, and the reduction or amplification of pathology. Of overriding importance is the development of concepts that actually link and bridge the three network sectors: kinship, friendship, and caregiving. One has been suggested here—the prescription for action.

REFERENCES

1. Attneave, Carol, "Therapy in Tribal Settings and Urban Network Intervention," *Fam. Proc.*, 8: 192–216, 1969.
2. Auerswald, E., "Interdisciplinary vs. Ecological Approach," *Fam. Proc.*, 7: 211–238, 1968.
3. Auerswald, E., Introduction to L. Hoffman and L. Long, "A Systems Dilemma," *Fam. Proc.*, 8: 211–234, 1969.
4. Auerswald, E., "Families, Change, and the Ecological Perspective," *Fam. Proc.*, 10: 263–280, 1971.
5. Barnes, J. A., "Class and Committees in a Norwegian Island Community," *Hum. Relat.*, 7: 39–58, 1954.
6. Bloor, M. J., "Current Explanatory Models of Pre-Patient Behavior—A Critique with Some Suggestions on Further Model Development," Unpublished doctoral dissertation, Aberdeen University, 1970.
7. Bott, E., *Family and Social Network*, (2nd Edition) London, Tavistock Publications, 1971.
8. Brown, G. W., Birley, J. L. and Wing, J. K., "Influence of Family Life on the Cause of Schizophrenic Disorders: A Republication," *Brit. J. Psychiat.*, 121: 246–258, 1972.
9. Collins, A., "Natural Delivery Systems: Accessible Sources of Power for Mental Health," *Am. J. Orthopsychiat.*, 43: 46–52, 1973.
10. Erickson, G., Rachlis, R. and Tobin, M., "Combined Family and Service Network Intervention," *Soc. Worker* (Canada), Winter, 1974, 41: 276–283.
11. Freeman, H. and Simmons, O., *The Mental Patient Comes Home*, New York, John Wiley Publishing Co., 1963.
12. Gliva, G. and Lesser, A., "Involving the Family in the Case Conference," *Canada's Mental Health*, 22: 5-7, 1974.
13. Garrison, J., "Network Techniques: Case Studies in the Screening-Linking-Planning Conference Method," *Fam. Proc.*, 13: 337–353, 1974.
14. Hammer, M., "Influence of Small Social Networks as Factors on Mental Hospital Admission," *Hum. Org.*, 22:243–251, 1963–64.
15. Litwak, E., "Geographic Mobility and Extended Family Cohesion," *Am. Sociol. Rev.*, 25: 385–394, 1960.
16. *Living with Schizophrenia—by the Relatives*, published by National Schizophrenia Association, 29 Victoria Road, Surbiton, Surrey.
17. McKinlay, J., "Social Networks, Lay Consultation, and Help Seeking Behavior," *Soc. Forces*, 51: 275–292, 1973.
18. McKinlay, J., "Some Aspects of Lower-Working Class Utilization Behavior," Unpublished doctoral dissertation, Aberdeen University, 1970.
19. Mennell, S., *Sociological Theory: Uses and Unities*, London, Thomas Nelson & Sons, Ltd. 1974.

20. Mitchell, J. C., (Ed.) *Social Networks in Urban Situations*, University of Manchester Press, 1969.
21. Speck, R., and Rueveni, U., "Network Therapy; A Developing Concept," *Fam. Proc.*, 8: 182–191, 1967.
22. Speck, R., and Attneave, C., "Social Network Intervention" in J. Haley (Ed.), *Changing Families*, New York, Grune & Stratton, 1971, pp. 313–332.
23. Speck, R., "Psychotherapy of the Social Network of a Schizophrenic Family," *Fam. Proc.*, 6: 208–214, 1967.
24. Speck, R., and Attneave, C., *Family Networks*, New York, Pantheon, 1973.
25. Sussman, M. B., "Adaptive, Directive, and Integrative Behavior of Today's Family," *Fam. Proc.*, 7: 239–250, 1968.
26. Titmuss, R., *Commitment to Welfare*, London, George Allen & Unwin, Ltd., 1968.
27. Vincent, C. E., "Familia Spongia: The Adaptive Function," *J. Marr. Fam.*, 28: 29–36, 1966.
28. Vincent, C. E., "Mental Health and the Family," *J. Marr. Fam.*, 29: 18–39, 1967.

A Method of Helping Natural Helping Networks

Diane L. Pancoast

Currently there seems to be a good deal of interest in the mobilization of informal community supports as part of a broad strategy of prevention and treatment in community mental health. The recommendations of the President's Commission on Mental Health, which include a heavy emphasis on identifying and strengthening community support systems and natural helping networks, will undoubtedly increase the exposure of mental health professionals and politicians to these ideas. While community support systems should not be viewed as a panacea, and should not be seen as a substitute for professional services, they do have the potential for meeting needs which the formal systems are unable to address.

It seems to me that The Commission Report signals the acceptance of the importance of community supports and that we need no longer be advocates. What is needed now is to pool what we already know about informal community support systems and networks in order to decide on issues which deserve further research and to develop ways of interacting productively with them.

If mental health professionals are to be convinced in any significant numbers that part of their practice should include the understanding and support of informal systems of care, they must be provided with information and skills with which to proceed. Otherwise they are likely either to reject such a change or to intervene in ways which are destructive to the informal systems.

I would like to describe an approach which permits the identification of natural community caregivers who are embedded in networks of mutual caring and service exchange. Whenever we could we have supported their efforts through consultation and, in some cases, the provision of other resources. Our activities have been carried on by professionally trained mental health workers under a variety of auspices. In some cases, the workers were in direct contact with the natural caregivers. In others, the workers guided the project but the actual contact with caregivers was made by neighborhood workers, aides or volunteers. Sometimes we have focused on specific populations at risk such as discharged mental patients, the elderly, and young families in need of day care. Other programs have had a more general neighborhood focus. Our book, *Natural Helping Networks*, (Collins and Pancoast, 1976) describes our theory and approach. Two handbooks recently published by our colleagues (Smith, 1975; Crawford, Smith and Taylor, 1978), present some additional examples as well as simple, straightforward advice about how to develop such a program. These sources present our methods in much greater detail than I can do here. In this paper, I want to give you a general idea of what we do and discuss some of the issues that arise.

First, let me be as precise as I can about the type of helping networks that we have been working with. So far, I have been referring to support systems and helping networks interchangeably. Although there is no standard usage at this time, I tend to think of support systems as a more inclusive term which can include mental health activities by any person or organization in the community that is not specifically designated as a mental health agency. Networks, on the other hand, are linkages and patterns of relationships among individuals which do not have boundaries or collective identities. Social network analysis can be used to study these patterns and supplies concepts with which to describe them (Barnes, 1972; Mitchell, 1974). Our work centers on networks in which people are linked by exchanges of social and emotional support, but people can be linked together in many other ways.

There are many types of social support networks in any community. Some of them are formed around an institutional affiliation such as a church, school or club. Others draw people who have a common problem or interest and interaction is based on their status of fellow sufferers. These networks frequently coalesce into self-help groups which take on a more formal character (Caplan and Killilea, 1976; Katz and Bender, 1976). Other networks are even less visible. The members of these networks, though highly cognizant of their relationships with each other, do not consider themselves to be members of a group and seldom think about the patterns formed by the interrelationships. Such networks can be based on kinship, friendship, residence in a common locality or employment in the same workplace. If these various kinds of networks can be ranged along a continuum based on degree of formal organization and level of awareness of membership, it is the ones at the most informal end of the continuum that have been the focus of our intervention.

There are two ways of looking at networks: from the perspective of individual members and as total entities. Each of us has a personal support system—a network centered on ourselves—consisting of the people we count on when we need help. This network may include professionals and other people we pay for services, such as babysitters, as well as people with whom we have ties of mutual obligation. The size, configuration and membership of these networks obviously varies from person to person. In clinical work, there is much to be gained from understanding the meaning and functioning of an individual client's support network. Some therapists are working out ways of intervening in these networks on behalf of their clients (Speck and Attneave, 1973; Erickson, 1975; Pattison, 1977). Others have developed programs which supply supportive persons to bolster individuals' networks at points of crisis such as the Widow-to-Widow programs (Silverman, 1970).

The other way of looking at networks is to focus on the larger patterns made by the interconnected individual networks. We can identify the actual linkages among a set of individuals who might potentially be linked together, such as the residents of a neighborhood or certain members of the larger community, such as the parents of retarded children or Indochinese refugees. In some of these networks a variety of services are exchanged (Warren and Warren, 1977; Wellman et al., 1971). Others serve more specialized functions such as the provision of family day care (Collins and Watson, 1976) or supportive services among the elderly (Smith, 1975).

In our work, we have adopted the second perspective. Our aim is to strengthen the total network for the benefit of all of its members. This task is not as difficult as it might seem because there are natural helpers in these networks who can be the focus of intervention. We call these natural helpers, central figures or natural neighbors. Our approach is based on finding such individuals in ongoing networks. We do not attempt to create networks or to nominate individuals for the role of central figure. Our central figures are not usually community caregivers such as clergymen, public health nurses or policemen. They are not persons who have a culturally designated role of healer or helper such as medicine men or herbalists. Instead, they are "ordinary people" going about their daily lives; working, raising families, participating in community activities. What makes them a little bit special is that they are seen by others as particularly resourceful and empathetic. In addition to sharing their personal resources, they are also matchmakers linking individual members of their networks who could mutually profit from an exchange. I am sure that most of us can identify central figures in networks of which we are a part. We may even occupy this role ourselves in networks to which we belong.

Since stable patterns of exchange are useful to people (or perhaps, just because we are social animals), in most circumstances people will participate in support networks and help to maintain them. It has been found, for example, that even among severely disabled older adults living in welfare hotels, such patterns of relationships are common (Shapiro, 1971). Also, since individuals are differentially endowed with personal relating skills and access to resources, it is likely that those individuals who are particularly well endowed will occupy central positions in their networks. Most of these central figures can probably continue to function very well without outside assistance. In many cases, it may be enough for a professional who is working with a particular population to be aware that such networks exist and to try to avoid doing anything which might interfere with the operations of the network.

In other cases, however, a professional might want to go beyond "benign neglect" and attempt to strengthen the role of the central figure. A number of circumstances might prompt this more active approach. The professional might identify a particular population which will not make use of formal services but which does rely on natural caregivers. For example, many teenagers will not make use of family planning agencies but would be receptive to contraceptive information from trusted members of their network, whether they be peers or trusted adults.

Another reason for forming an active partnership with natural caregivers is to offer preventive services while avoiding the problems of stigmatizing the recipients or creating dependence on formal services—negative side effects which often accompany formally organized preventive services. Informal caregivers can be assisted in their efforts to strengthen family life and prevent serious instances of child abuse and neglect, for example, without ever labeling the families involved (Garbarino, 1978).

A third reason for forming an alliance is to provide information about formal services to a population which may not be using them because they do not know about them. For example, Leutz describes a program of providing information about hospital-based services for drug abusers to natural caregivers in a Puerto Rican neighborhood who were not able to deal with the needs of this group (Leutz, 1976).

Another purpose of such an alliance would be to extend the service capacity of formal agencies. There will never be enough money to meet all of the needs for day care for children by providing day care centers. Similarly the services which are required to permit the elderly to remain in their homes, though partially disabled—homemaker services, meals, transportation, nursing care, etc.—are expensive and can never be funded well enough to completely meet the need. Even if these and similar services could be provided in sufficient amounts by formal agencies, many people would prefer to rely on personal relationships rather than put themselves in the hands of bureaucracies. A professional who has responsibility for meeting needs for day care, services for the elderly, services for discharged mental patients, etc., can develop relationships with the natural helpers who are providing such services informally as part of a comprehensive approach to the problem.

The key to the development of a mutually profitable partnership between a professional and a natural helper is the cultivation on the part of the professional of a sensitive understanding of the functioning of the network and the role of the natural helper within it. Before deciding on any particular form of intervention, therefore, it is crucial that the professional learn as much as possible about the network. The procedures used by anthropologists and ethnographers are the most appropriate methods to employ and there is no substitute for much patient, unobtrusive observation of the operations of the network.

One device that is commonly used and that mental health professionals may be somewhat more familiar with than observation is the survey or canvass. If it is done well and as a first step, it can be an acceptable way of entering the community and searching for networks. The professional must always keep in mind, however, that the process of conducting the survey is more important, for this purpose, than the quality or quantity of "data" gathered by the survey instrument and will need to be open to the spontaneous events and unanticipated information that will inevitably accompany the survey. One specific data gathering device which doesn't seem to work very well is to ask people whom they turn to for help. The professional will learn much more by asking about patterns of acquaintanceship (e.g. "How many of your neighbors do you know?") and specific instances of interaction than by asking general questions about helping patterns.

Jane Howard, the author of *Families*, gives some very useful suggestions when she describes her techniques for gathering information. "My way is to use my intuition as a compass, go where I feel welcome, stay as long as I can manage to, meet whoever is around, help them do what they are doing if they will let me, and try to remember that she who asks least learns most" (*Time*, July 3, 1978, p. 84).

Such a process takes time and one of the biggest problems that a professional may have in initiating a program of support for natural helpers is convincing administrators or granting agencies that the investment will pay off. Agencies that are already knowledgeable about the population rather than a specific caseload seem to be most receptive to this approach and probably make the best sponsors of such a program.

The single best indicator of central figure status is multiple nomination. During the search process, which can include contacts with agencies and community leaders as well as local residents, certain names will be mentioned again and again. Once the professional has collected a list of such persons, he or she can decide how many of them to contact and proceed to make arrangements to see them. During an informal interview or two on the central figure's home turf, the professional can learn about the role of the central figure in the network and decide whether or not to propose further contacts.

Once the professional understands the workings of the network and has become acquainted with the central figure it should be relatively easy to decide what kinds of intervention would strengthen the functioning of the network. We think that mental health consultation along the lines of the model developed by Gerald Caplan (Caplan, 1970, 1974) offers the best general prescription for intervention which will improve the network without changing it.

The consultation partnership between the professional and the natural helper is based on their mutual interest in the well being of the members of the network. The central figure is free to accept or reject such a relationship although he or she does not initiate the contact as a consultee would in a more conventional consultation setting. The content of the consultation sessions is determined by the central figure consultee. Initially, the consultant may want to suggest some regular meetings in order to learn about the network and build a relationship with the central figure. In addition to helping the central figure solve specific problems the consultant can offer an appreciative understanding of the skillful efforts of the central figure. This can be extremely helpful to natural helpers whose respect for the confidentiality of their relationships with network members precludes the sharing of their triumphs and failures with other people.

Over time, the regular contacts can be spaced out or dropped altogether as the central figure becomes comfortable with contacting the consultant when the need arises. As the number of contacts diminishes, the professional can initiate contacts with other central figures. We think that a full-time consultant can probably sustain approximately 15 consulting relationships at a time.

Other forms of intervention such as training, providing information through newsletters or group meetings, linking unaffiliated persons with natural helpers and facilitating referrals from the helpers to formal services may also be appropriate in some circumstances. The professional may also be an advocate and defender of the natural helping network to the larger community. All of these forms of intervention, however, probably carry more potential for damaging the network than consultation does and therefore should be approached more cautiously.

The ideal staffing pattern for a program of consultation to natural neighbors is probably one that combines professionals who are familiar with consultation techniques and neighborhood workers who are well acquainted with the local networks and cultural patterns. Neighborhood workers will be able to locate central figures much more efficiently than professionals who are unfamiliar with the particular area. They may be less able to see how they might intervene to strengthen the network, however, and in any case, will need encouragement and suggestions from the professional. Some natural neighbors may prefer to have the more distant professional as a consultant because of the prestige of the professional or greater assurance of confidentiality.

We have seen projects succeed with only one half of the team but there are drawbacks. If only professionals are used the process of identifying natural neighbors will take longer and the whole project will consume more expensive professional time. If only neighborhood workers are used, natural neighbors may be quickly located but the workers may fail to develop productive partnerships with them.

One way to reduce the costs of the program might be to hold group meetings of the natural neighbors. We think this is unadvisable for several reasons. In the first place it is too great a disruption of the way natural neighbors usually function. They are not comfortable with sharing their problems with other community members. Secondly, the consultant loses too much information when the natural neighbor is seen outside of the setting in which he or she normally functions. Finally, the content of the meetings will usually be too general to be helpful to the natural neighbor who wants to discuss a particular troublesome situation. Since each natural neighbor affects a number of other people in the network who might otherwise become candidates for formal services, the one-to-one approach of consultant to consultee is not really as uneconomical as it may seem, particularly when the impact of the sessions will be much greater than that of group sessions.

The issue that is raised most frequently when I talk about our methods to professionals is their concern about whether the natural helpers are truly beneficial to the members of their networks. We need to do a great deal more research before we can specify to what extent and under what conditions, the natural helpers actually provide socially useful services. At this point, I can only report that every professional I have talked with who has become involved with natural helpers, even if they were initially skeptical, has become convinced of the worth and importance of the natural helpers' services. If you remain unconvinced, I urge you not to wait for the results of the research to come in, but to go out and see for yourselves.

REFERENCES

Barnes, J. A. "Social Networks." Addison-Wesley Module in Anthropology, 1972, 26, 1–29.
Caplan, G. *The Theory and Practice of Mental Health Consultation.* New York: Basic Books, 1970.
Caplan, G. *Support Systems and Community Mental Health.* New York: Behavioral Publications, 1974.
Caplan, G., & Killilea, M. (Eds.) *Support Systems and Mutual Help: Multidisciplinary Explorations.* New York: Grune and Stratton, 1976.
Collins, A., & Pancoast, D. *Natural Helping Networks.* Washington, D. C.: National Association of Social Workers, 1976.
Collins, A., & Watson, E. *Family Day Care: A Practical Guide for Parents, Caregivers and Professionals.* Boston: Beacon Press, 1976.
Crawford, L., Smith, P., & Taylor, L. *It Makes Good Sense: A Handbook for Working with Natural Helpers.* Salem, Oregon, 1978.

Erickson, G. D. "The Concept of Personal Networks in Clinical Practice." *Family Process,* 1975, Vol. 14, No. 4, 487–498.

Garbarino, J. (Ed.) *Supporting Families and Protecting Children: Building Neighborhood Social Resources to Meet the Problem of Child Maltreatment.* 1978.

Katz, A. H., & Bender, E. I. *The Strength in Us: Self-Help Groups in the Modern World.* New York: New Viewpoints, Franklin Watts, 1976.

Leutz, W. N. "The Informal Community Caregiver: A Link between the Health Care System and Local Residents." *American Journal of Orthopsychiatry,* October 1976, Vol. 46, No. 4, 678–688.

Mitchell, J. C. "Social Networks." *Annual Review of Anthropology,* 1974, Vol. 3, 279–499.

Report of the Task Panel on Community Support Systems. Submitted to The President's Commission on Mental Health, February 15, 1978.

Silverman, P. "The Widow as Caregiver in a Program of Preventive Intervention with Other Widows." *Mental Hygiene,* 1970, Vol. 54, No. 4, 540–545.

Shapiro, J. H. *Communities of the Alone.* New York: Association Press, 1971.

Smith, S. A. *Natural Systems and the Elderly: An Unrecognized Resource.* Portland, Oregon, School of Social Work, Portland State University, 1975.

Speck, R., & Attneave, C. *Family Networks: Retribalization and Healing.* New York: Pantheon, 1973.

Warren, R. B., & Warren, D. I. *The Neighborhood Organizer's Handbook.* Notre Dame, Indiana: University of Notre Dame Press, 1977.

Wellman, B., Craven, P., Whitaker, M., DuToit, S., & Stevens, H. "The Uses of Community: Community Ties and Support Systems." Research Paper No. 47, Centre for Urban and Community Studies, University of Toronto, 1971.

Index